NAME INTO WORD

OTHER MACMILLAN BOOKS BY THE SAME AUTHOR

A DICTIONARY OF THE UNDERWORLD, British and American, 16th–20th Centuries.

SLANG TODAY AND YESTERDAY: A History and a Study.

A DICTIONARY OF SLANG: from the 16th Century to the Present Day.

A DICTIONARY OF CLICHÉS, with introductory essay.

NAME

into

WORD

PROPER NAMES THAT HAVE BECOME
COMMON PROPERTY

A DISCURSIVE DICTIONARY

With a Foreword

by

ERIC PARTRIDGE

THE MACMILLAN COMPANY

NEW YORK

1950

First published in the United States in 1950
by The Macmillan Company
2nd edition, revised and enlarged, 1950

Made and Printed in Great Britain by Butler & Tanner Ltd., Frome and London

For

MY OXONIAN AND ENDURING FRIEND

THE VERY REV. CANON J. W. DUNNE

in affection and respect

CONTENTS

PAGE

FOREWORD ix

DICTIONARY OF PROPER NAMES BECOME COMMON PROPERTY   I

APPENDIX : BORDER-LINERS AND POTENTIAL CANDIDATES . 479

POSTSCRIPT 645

FOREWORD

On a not too busy Sunday in April or May, 1945, several of my companions in ' the Writers' Team ' at the Air Ministry (P.R.3, where I had the privilege and the pleasure of working from mid-January until my release on July the 4th of that year) got into conversation on the never-dying subject of words—and drew me into it. Squadron Leader Vernon Noble deplored the lack of a dictionary such as this and urged me to write one ; Flight Lieutenant Ronald Delderfield suggested a title, *They Came To Stay*. To both of these well-known writers, I wish to express my thanks and my gratitude, for the book has been great fun in the writing : in the reading, it will not, I hope, prove either dull or unuseful.

To my loyal friend ' J. J. Connington ' (Professor A. W. Stewart*) I owe many useful reminders : and many scientific terms of which I had been either absolutely or virtually ignorant. Which reminds me that only occasionally have I included those *-ite* and *-ia* derivatives which are always associated with the elements name-ending in *-ium*, for I disliked the idea of being either pedantically methodical or tediously exhaustive ; besides, the terms omitted can hardly be called ' common property ', belonging, as they do, to the preserves of scientists. Yet how many scientists have more than a nodding acquaintance with the etymologies of the elements and of so many ' properly named ' metals and minerals ? How many realize, for instance, that of the (provisionally) ninety-two elements, some thirty-nine have their origins in Proper Names ? But the scientists will be fully justified when they accuse me of making an arbitrary selection of metals, minerals, processes, ' laws ', instruments, and what-have-you, and all I can pre-defensively say is that I have attempted to include the majority of those scientific terms which the ordinary cultured person and the non-scientific reader of the daily newspapers are likely to meet ; not to list every scientific term that a scientific polymath may know. The same restriction applies to the technicalities of metaphysics, psychology, pathology, psychiatry ; history and economics ; geography and geology ; botany ; etc., etc., etc. But I can at least say this : the dictionary includes most of the terms that are likely to be encountered by the intelligent newspaper-reader, by the voracious fiction-reader, by

* Who died in 1947.

the student and reader of history, biography, the drama, poetry, and by the student of geography, politics, ethics, metaphysics and so forth. I have, in short, been pretty thorough, despite the avoidance of pedantry.

In short, I stand to be shot at ; by every ' expert ', at least. The average person like myself—not that abstraction, ' the economic man '—will, I trust, act more charitably. Though not to the extent of refraining from the indication of reprehensible omissions, nor from the correction of heinous errors. I wish future editions (if any) to prove worthier of the conception and the purpose of this book.

In addition to my obligations to ' Webster ', to *The Oxford English Dictionary*, to Weekley, to Skeat, I owe much to the late Professor Lionel W. Lyde, who graciously and generously allowed me to quote freely from those two fascinating works on Geography, *The Continent of Europe* and *The Continent of Asia*, and to Dr W. W. Tarn, who has done the same in respect of his magistral *Hellenistic Civilisation* ; also a little to many other historians and scholars, whose works I have ' tapped ' and to whom I gladly acknowledge indebtedness.

* * * * *

The justly inquisitive will ask, What formal and specific degree of comprehensiveness is to be expected from this dictionary ?

It contains every term that I deem to be relevant in both *The Concise Oxford English Dictionary* (3rd edition) and Ernest Weekley's *An Etymological Dictionary of Modern English* ; the same holds good for Horwill's *Modern American Usage* and Weekley's *Words and Names*. I have included a number of additional terms from *A Dictionary of American English*, carefully examined ; a further eighty-or-so terms gathered from my tolerably various reading (much of it *ad hoc*) ; and perhaps fifty or sixty more that I have encountered, not all accidentally, in *The Oxford English Dictionary* and Webster's *New International Dictionary*.

Most of the relevant terms current in the everyday speech of those who speak English (whether British or American), not jargon, are here. From the thousands of relevant technical terms in chemistry and physics, botany and mineralogy, I have included only those implied in the preceding sentence, with the addition of a few others that have an interesting story and of a larger number that met me rather than I met them. With these reservations, the main dictionary is perhaps not unsatisfactory ; but the subsidiary glossary, consisting of border-line cases, must, by definition, depend upon my own, not others', opinion of what, among a far larger number of applicants, I believed to be ' the most deserving cases ' ; I have tried to be as little arbitrary as

x

possible and to exclude no manifestly worthy candidate, to be as far as possible guided by two criteria : widespread use ; potential usefulness. Wine-names have given me far more headaches than ever wine has.

But where I have failed, as often I must inevitably fail, to include some term that clearly demands inclusion, I shall be grateful for notice thereof.

*   *   *   *   *

In reading Claude Houghton's unusual novel, *Passport to Paradise* (1944), I came upon this passage concerning the London of the 1890's :

' A West End of tinkling hansoms, lovely ladies with eighteen-inch waists and muffs attached to jewelled chains : a West End which, by night, was frequented by " Johnnies " wearing satin-lined Inverness capes over evening clothes, collapsible top hats, fobs, diamond studs, gardenias and carrying gold-mounted malacca canes ' :

and in that brief glance at a London for ever lost, I noticed six terms that find a rightful place in the ensuing dictionary, whereof the second part consists of terms that have failed to ' make the grade ' or have not yet done so, terms not yet vested with the dignity of a small initial letter, terms that are dying, terms not widely known.

It is true that the main vocabulary contains a few terms written always with a capital initial, but only such as are indisputably common property (*Mrs Grundy*, for instance) or such as represent a character from, or the title of, a book or a play. That this division into two vocabularies will be adversely criticized, I am fully aware, but if it satisfies the criterion implied in ' Is there more to be said for it than against it ? ', then—and only then—am I justified.

There is no need to write at length upon the subject of those Proper Names (persons, places, titles) which have yielded common nouns, adjectives, verbs, for this has already been done by Dr Bruno Migliorini in *Dal Nome Proprio al Nome Comune*, 1927, and by Professor Ernest Weekley in *Words and Names*, 1932 ; to repeat, even to elaborate upon, their excellent books would be both an impertinence and a supererogation. My justification is threefold : that this dictionary contains four or five times as many terms as they, together, mention at all ; that, where we three *have* covered common ground, my etymologies are more detailed and my quotations—they, for the most part, eschew quotations—are fuller, and some of them more apt, more revealing ; and that they have accorded to American terms a quite inadequate attention.

xi

Yet a few brief remarks, though unnecessary, may perhaps be not unwelcome.

The common-property terms from Proper Names can be regarded from at least two angles. Either in themselves, formally, as nouns, adjectives, verbs, or in reference to the originating terms —famous persons, significant places, well-known characters and titles in literature.

Our nouns are more numerous than the adjectives *plus* the verbs. For every *macadamize* there is many a *mentor*, for every *jovial* there are several *jehu*'s. As often as not, the original noun, the generative Proper Name, has lost no more than its initial-grandeur ; *Tantalus* becomes a *tantalus*. And where the form of the word has been changed, it is merely from (say) a Greek to an English shape—*Odusseia* to *odyssey*, *Pegasos* to *Pegasus*, *Phaethon* to *phaeton* ; or, in chemistry, physics, geology, botany, the ending *-ium* or *-ia*, imitative of Latin, is added, as in *forsythia* or *ruthenium* ; mineralogy often prefers *-ite*, as in *samsonite*. Our adjectives have a typically English, not a Greek, Latin, French, German ending : Greek *Platōn* yields *platonic*, Latin *plutonius* becomes *plutonian*, French *rabelaisien* becomes *Rabelaisian*, and German *jüdisch*, *yiddish*. The verbs lose the initial capital and take an English ending or, an equally English trait, no verb-ending at all (*hector*) ; *Macadam* yields *macadamize* as well as the noun (or adjective) *macadam* ; *Tantalus*, *tantalize* ; *Slav*, *enslave*.

But the approach from the angle of the sources is more basic. These are, some ancient and some modern. The former include The Bible (*Noah's ark*, *sheba*, *Solomon*, *David and Goliath*, *Laodicean*), the Scandinavian mythologies (*thorium*) and, by far the most fertile, Classical mythology, history and literature (*copper*, *greek* and *trojan*, *mercurial* and *saturnine*, *peach* and *quince*, *stentorian* and *jovial*). A glance at Migliorini's book or a reading of E. V. Rieu's delightful translation of *The Odyssey* would soon give some slight idea of our debt to Greece and Rome—to their great men and noble architecture and institutions, to their women, to their mythology as well as their history, to their geography, to their dramatic literature as well as to their science and philosophy.

Literature and science, history and geography—these operate no less in the modern than in the ancient sources.

For English, the two greatest literary sources are Shakespeare (*Ariel*, *dogberry*, *Caliban*, and the rest) and Dickens (*gamp*, *Gradgrind*, *micawberish*, etc.), although Milton and Scott at home, Rabelais and Cervantes abroad, have made their contribution, and many a lesser, perhaps unimportant writer has, like that Morton who fathered Mrs Grundy, achieved an immortality of which not even he ever dreamed.

To science we owe a multitude of terms ; to almost every main

xii

branch of science, a number. Chemical elements, mechanical and other processes, flowers (*dahlia, fuchsia*), and minerals, things invented (including weapons), these and others exhibit so many examples of words derived from the names of persons and places that it were invidious to select this, that or the other one ; almost every ensuing page, whether in the main vocabulary or in the lesser glossary, offers an example.

So too with history : battles (Waterloo, Magenta, Balaclava) and religious or political movements, great doers and great sufferers, generals (Wellington, Blucher, Raglan) and statesmen (Napoleon, Peel), navigators, explorers, travellers, all these and others have left an indelible mark upon the language, as upon the life, of the British Commonwealth of Nations and the United States of America.

The navigators and explorers link history with geography. In the field of historical geography—see notably the books by Professor Lionel W. Lyde—we find a very large number of sources. Such men as Marco Polo, Columbus, Magellan, Drake, Raleigh, Cook, Stanley, and with them such geographers as Mercator, such historians as Gibbon, have either coined or been the occasion of others coining many of the most interesting, informative, entertaining of the terms to be found in the following pages or, for those I have omitted, in *The Oxford English Dictionary* and in Webster.

To both geography and history, so often inseparable, we owe the numerous terms derived from the names of places : *silk* and *china* ; *copper* and *magnesia* ; *calico, cambric, muslin, tweed* ; garments (*tuxedo*) and furniture (*ottoman*) and furnishings (*valance*) ; innumerable wines and spirits—mostly from France (*champagne, cognac*), but a few, not the least illuminating, from Spain (*sherry*), Holland (*hollands*), Italy (*chianti*) and the New World (*bourbon*) ; fruits (*peach, quince, bartlett*) ; *tobacco* ; and a host of others, including non-material, non-physical things like *barbarism* and *solecism*.

Such names as these merely serve to prove, to the astounding number of people apparently in need of proof, that language, in addition to being primarily a means, the principal means, of communication between man and mankind, the instrument of science, the brush and the burin of art, the vehicle of that imagery without which religion is almost inconceivable, the medium of history, the *sine qua non* of philosophy,—that, in addition to serving these activities of the mind and the spirit, language is the mirror of society and the index of civilization.   Words are not so much things as transmigrations of persons and events, of ideas and facts, of minds immediately operative and spirits effectually, efficaciously active.

Trace the history of *silk* and you have the impact of China upon Greece, hence upon the world ; work out the implications of *barbarism* and you understand why a Hitler temporarily triumphs, eventually fails ; *tobacco* relates how a small island in the New World has conquered most of the Old World ; *peach* sweetly links Persia with Europe ; *old Newton* causes every man and every woman to watch their step ; *stoicism* sustains a *real christian* and a *true Briton* ; *Attic salt, Gallic wit, British phlegm,* and *American go* counteract *Oriental fatalism* ; *golgotha* passes through at least five languages and as many civilizations to imprint itself upon the conscience of Britain and America.

The history of language is the history of the human race : and in many a word we find an enlightening vignette of history, universal, international, national, social, individual. In the word, the individual speaks to his contemporaries and to posterity. No word is ' a *mere* word '. He who despises the history of words despises the history of mankind : and he who ignores the history of words ignores that one part of himself which can lastingly affect the world outside himself, the sole part that merits a posterity. By the words of others shall we, using intelligence, know them ; by our own words do we, if we strive, know ourselves.

NOTE TO SECOND EDITION

I owe some valuable corrections and additions to Professor Ernest Weekley, Dr D. C. Somervell, and Professor John W. Clark of Minneapolis.

ABBREVIATIONS

adj. : adjective

André Simon : André Simon, *Wine*, 1946 (Section viii of *A Concise Encyclopædia of Gastronomy*)

ca. : circa, 'about' (in dates)

cf. : compare

Chisholm : George G. Chisholm, *The Times Gazetteer of the World*, first issued in 1895

COED : *The Concise Oxford English Dictionary*

DAE : *A Dictionary of American English*

Ency. Brit. : *The Encyclopaedia Britannica*

Harvey : Sir Paul Harvey, *The Oxford Companion to English Literature* or *to Classical Literature*, as the context suggests

Hart : James D. Hart, *The Oxford Companion to American Literature*

Lewis & Short : C. T. Lewis & Charles Short, *A Latin Dictionary*

Liddell & Scott : H. G. Liddell & Robert Scott, *A Greek-English Lexicon*

M : Bruno Migliorini, *Dal Nome Proprio al Nome Comune*, Geneva, 1927

n. : noun

OED : *The Oxford English Dictionary*

PS : Eric Partridge, *A Dictionary of Slang and Unconventional English*

PNTC : Eric Partridge, *Name This Child*

q.v. : which see !

Scholes : Dr Percy Scholes, *The Oxford Companion to Music*

Skeat : W. W. Skeat, *Etymological Dictionary of the English Language*, 4th ed., 1910

v. : verb

W : Ernest Weekley, *An Etymological Dictionary of Modern English*

WWAM : Ernest Weekley, *Words Ancient and Modern*

WWN : Ernest Weekley, *Words and Names*

Webster : *Webster's New International Dictionary*

Webster BD : *Webster's Biographical Dictionary*

+ : plus or and (in blends)

> : become(s), became (in etymologies)

= : equal(s), is (are) equivalent to

DICTIONARY OF PROPER NAMES BECOME COMMON PROPERTY

A

Abelard. See **Eloïsa and Abelard.**

aberdeen. ' He saw a heavy round man in early middle-age, with a distinctive ugly face and impudent eyes beneath brows as fierce and tufted as an Aberdeen's ', Margery Allingham, *Traitor's Purse*, 1941.

As a shortening of *Aberdeen terrier* (shaggy-haired, affectionate, loyal), *aberdeen* is the sensible form. The same applies to the word when it shortens *Aberdeen (fishing-)hook* : anglers use the hook for large-mouthed trout.

abernethy. ' Some places seem to have been particularly favoured, e.g. *Bath*, with its *bun, chair, stone, brick, chap* and *Oliver*, the last being a biscuit named from a well-known Bath doctor, just as the less palatable *abernethy* bears the name of a physician . . . equally famous for his dietary theories and his bad manners,' WWN.

Dr John Abernethy (1764–1831) was, in addition to being a dietician, an English surgeon of some repute, especially for his ' operation for ligation of the external ıliac artery (1797),' Webster BD; his lectures upon anatomy were attended by many students. Socially, a very rough diamond; in bedside manners, something of a boor.

abigail, ' a lady's waiting maid ', comes immediately from Beaumont & Fletcher's comedy, *The Scornful Lady*, 1616 : there, Abigail is the name of a ' waiting gentlewoman'. Those witty dramatists may have got the idea of the name from 1 *Samuel*, xxv, where Abigail, the wife of Nabal and later of David, frequently refers humbly to herself in the phrase ' thine handmaid ', as in verses 23–24, ' When Abigail saw David, . . . she bowed herself to the ground, And fell at his feet and said, Upon me, my lord, upon me let this iniquity be : and let thine handmaid, I pray thee, speak in thine audience, and hear the words of

1

thine handmaid '. More widely, any maidservant, as in Dorothy M. Stuart, *The English Abigail*, 1946.

abruzzese. An Italian song, an Italian dance, so named because it originated and is popular in the Abruzzi district (east of Rome).

Short for *danza abruzzese*.

academy. 'A legally organised association, like Plato's Academy ' (W. W. Tarn, *Hellenistic Civilisation*, 1927) ; hence, **academic.**

The sense ' learned assembly ' (The French Academy, The British Academy) comes from the Italian *accademia* ; that of ' a school of learning, a superior grammar school ' from the French *académie* (compare *lycée* : see **lyceum**). Both the Italian and the French words derive from Latin *academia*, which transliterates Greek *akadēmeia*. The *Akadēmeia* was that gymnasium in a suburb of Athens where Plato lectured, taught and, like Socrates, conversed : his pupils and disciples and successors soon became known as the *Academics* (Latin *Academici*, Greek *Akadēmikoi*) ; the ' merely theoretical ' sense that has attached itself to *academic* reflects popular prejudice against metaphysical discussions and subtleties.

The gymnasium took its name from the grove wherein it was situated (' The olive grove of Academe, Plato's retirement,' as Milton sang) : that grove was sacred to the hero *Akadēmos*.

aceldama or **A—.** With a small initial, i.e. derivatively, it means ' a field of bloodshed ' ; with a capital initial, it denotes ' the scene of the suicide of Judas (*Acts*, i, 19), identified with the " potter's field " of *Matthew*, xxvii, 8, and called the " Field of Blood " because purchased with the thirty pieces of silver which Judas received for betraying Christ ' (Webster).

Aceldama is the Latin form of the Greek *Akeldama*, which transliterates the Syriac *okel damo* and Aramaic *h'qual d'ma*, ' field of blood '.

Achates. See **fidus Achates** in the Appendix.

acherontic, ' gloomy, moribund ', derives from *Acheron*, one of the rivers of Hades, the infernal regions : compare, therefore, **stygian.**

Acheron, Greek *Akherōn*, is traditionally explained as a conflation of *akhea rheōn*, ' river of woe '—literally, ' the distresses flowing ',

2

where *akhea* is cognate object and *rheōn* is a present participle used as a noun (compare *stream*, verb and noun).
'Sad Acheron of sorrow, black and deep', Milton.

acheulian(-ean) or **A—**. 'A Chellean is distinguished from the later Acheulian scraper by having a straight-lined edge, not a double curve,' S. E. Winbolt, *Britain B.C.* (1943). *Acheulean* means 'belonging to, characteristic of, deriving from, resembling that palaeolithic period—the Old Stone Age—which is represented and characterized by archaeological remains, (especially graving tools, small hand-axes, flat oval implements) discovered in France at St *Acheul*, near Amiens, chiefly among the gravel beds there'. The acheulian culture followed the chellean.

adieu, 'good-bye' to a person going on a journey or never to be seen again—or not, at least, for a long time—is a merging of *à Dieu*, 'to God': *Je vous recommande à Dieu*, I commend you to God, God be with you. 'Originally said to the party left, as *farewell* was to the party setting out' (W).
The French *à Dieu* translates the Church Latin *ad Deum*.

admirable Crichton. See **Crichton.**

Adonis; adonize; adonics. An *Adonis*—cf. **Apollo**—is a strikingly handsome (young) man; *adonize* is to ape Adonis, *adonize oneself* is to adorn oneself as a dandy; *adonics,* a term in prosody for a metre consisting of a dactyl ($- \cup \cup$) followed by a spondee ($- -$), devised and first used to chant the death of Adonis.
Of a certain medieval Latin poem, Helen Waddell has remarked that 'the metres are astonishingly varied, glyconics, asclepiads, adonics, iambic dimeter' (*The Wandering Scholars*). Of *adonize* and *Adonis* we may note that their connotations are somewhat derogatory: foppishness, excess of beauty over brains, and so on; *Adonis,* however, when used by a man versed in the Ancient Classics, denotes the superlative of true male beauty, as in 'The dark Adonis of diplomacy' (Lord David Cecil, *The Young Melbourne,* 1939).
Greek *Adōnis* is probably a re-shaping, either of Aramaic *Adonai* or of Semitic *Adon*: both of these words mean 'lord'.

aeolian; Aeolian harp; aeliopyle. In geology, *aeolian* means 'wind-borne'—as in 'A wide distribution of typical desert conditions, with considerable areas of aeolian deposits' (Lyde, *Asia,* 1933); used figuratively in Charles Morgan's description

3

of Verlaine as an ' aeolian genius without parallel in literature '
(*Reflections in a Mirror*, 2nd Series, 1946). The *Aeolian harp* is
' a stringed instrument adapted to produce musical sounds on
exposure to a current of air ' (The OED), and an outmoded
instrument called the *aeolina* or *aeoline* was a kind of rudimentary
concertina. An *aeolipyle* (or *-pile*) is a device to show the force
with which steam or vapour, heat-produced in a closed vessel,
rushes through a narrow opening, like winds released from the
cave of *Aeolus*. According to the Virgilian version of the Greek
legend, Aeolus held the winds imprisoned within a cave
(*Aeneid*, i, 50–59), whereas in the Homeric version he presented
Odysseus with a bag containing the winds likely to impede him
in his voyagings; in the later Greek, as in the ensuing Latin
myth, Aeolus is the god controlling the winds.

Aesculapius; hence, **Aesculapian** or **a—**. Aesculapius is the
Latin form of the Greek *Asklepios* (often latinized as *Asclepius*),
in Greek mythology the son of Apollo, and the god of medicine,
who learned the art from the wise old centaur *Chiron* (excellent
name for a surgeon : ' The Handler '). Homer makes Asklepios
the father of the two surgeons attending the Greek host besieging
Troy. Asklepios came to be revered and worshipped as the
God of Healing, the chief cult-seat being at Epidaurus; the
first Roman temple in his honour was founded as early as
293 B.C., the Romans having been terrified by a devastating
pestilence.

Compare **galenical** and **Hygiea**.

Aesculap (or *a—*) *water* is an aperient mineral water, from a
spring near Budapest; short for *Aesculapian water*, it means no
more than ' health-giving water '.

afghan, (1) a knitted coverlet made of wool. These coverlets
were originally made in Afghanistan; but nowadays most of
them are made elsewhere.

(2) Short for *Afghan dog*, a wise and gentle, gentlemanly
creature, long-headed and thoughtful-eyed; originally a native
of Afghanistan.

' Whether the Afghans and Pathans are " Beni Israel "—
descendants of Afghan, King Saul's grandson—or not, their
racial pride is unlimited ', Lionel W. Lyde, *The Continent of Asia*,
1933.

Agag, walk delicately as—or **like.** ' " I must walk like Agag
—odd's fish, even to think of these ranters makes me speak like
'em—I must walk warily, I say " ',' David Pilgrim, *No Common
Glory*, 1941.

'Then said Samuel, Bring ye hither to me Agag the king of the Amalekites. And Agag came unto him delicately' (1 *Samuel*, xv, 32) : but his soft-footedness saved him not from being hewn to pieces.

agaric, as used in botany, pharmacy, chemistry, derives from Latin *agaricum*, which merely transliterates Greek *agarikon*, ' said to be from *Agaria* in Sarmatia ' (W) or what is now east Poland and south Russia in Europe, the *Sarmatici Montes* forming part of the Carpathians.

agate comes from Latin *achates* (Greek *akhatēs*), via Old French *acate*; Middle English has the variant *achate*. Traditionally named after the river *Achates* in Sicily : W appositely quotes, from Marbod's 12th-Century lapidary (Book of Precious Stones), the words : ' Acate est ceste apelee | Por un eve u el est truvee ' (Agate is thus called for—after—from—a stream where it is found). Compare **fidus Achates** in the subsidiary list.

agave and derivatively **agave cactus.** This plant, belonging to the Amaryllis family, is named directly from Latin, and the Latin word represents Greek *agauë*, the feminine singular of *agauos*, ' noble, famous, illustrious ', or rather from that mythological personage who bore the name of *Agauë*, the mother of Pentheus, a legendary king of Thebes and the grandson of Cadmus (see **Cadmean victory** in the subsidiary list).

agnostic; hence, **agnosticism.** *Agnostic*, noun and adjective, ' (one) professing agnosticism; involving no dogmatic statement ' : coined by T. H. Huxley (1825–95) in 1869. He himself recorded that he invented the title as being ' suggestively antithetic to the " gnostic " of Church history, who professed to know so very much '—although Richard Hutton, theologian and man of letters, said, in a letter of March 13, 1881, that Huxley ' took it from St Paul's mention of the altar to " The Unknown God " ' (The OED).

The point is that the ' gnostic ' mentioned by Huxley himself is properly written ' Gnostic ' and that Huxley conceived it as *a-Gnostic*, ' not subscribing to the tenets of the *Gnostics*— especially, that grace and salvation accrued from *gnosis* or knowledge '.

Greek : *a*, privative prefix + *gnostikos*, ' claiming to know '.

airedale shortens *Airedale terrier*, a breed with wiry hair, black- or blackish-backed and -sided, tan elsewhere; a breed supposedly evolved by poachers, who needed a dog with good scent and fighting abilities and of a colour that, at night, is baffling. The word *Airedale* signifies the *dale* of the *Aire*, a river in Yorkshire. The name was registered by the Kennel Club in 1886 as a substitute for the earlier **Bingley,** where the dogs were first bred.

akeldama. See **aceldama.**

alabaster. In reference to Italy, Professor Lionel W. Lyde, in *The Continent of Europe*, notes that ' the borax comes mainly from the Volterran district of Tuscany, famous also for its alabaster (a sulphate of calcium) '—and, in *Man and His Markets*, that ' The only genuine alabaster is Italian, and comes from Volterra and other outlying districts of Pisa '.

Alabaster is the English form of Old French *alabastre* (modern Fr. *albâtre*), from Latin *alabaster*, itself from Greek *alabastros*, said to derive from *Alabastron*, a town in the Thebais region of Ancient Egypt—the authority being Pliny's *Natural History* (xxxvi, 8; xxxvii, 10). Note, too, that *alabastron* is a narrow-necked jar for perfumes or a box for ungents : such a receptacle was doubtless made often of alabaster.

albert is the natural development from *Albert chain*, a kind of watch-chain worn by Prince Albert of Saxe-Coburg-Gotha (1819–61), whom Queen Victoria married in 1840 and who, a man of charm and insight, has not yet been assessed at his full value. He would have seen the humour and appreciated the deep-lying compliment of the fact that, among the poorer Australian tramps and beggars, *alberts* are the toe-rags worn in lieu of the socks they cannot afford.

alcaics is the name of the metre devised (' invented ' seems too ponderous a word) by *Alcaeus* (Greek *Alkaios*), that lyric poet who lived in the 7th–6th Century B.C. and was a contemporary compatriot of Sappho, to whom he addressed a partly surviving ode. An ardent patriot, he was yet superior in his songs of love, wine, his personal sufferings ; he also hymned various gods. The alcaic metre is perhaps better referred to as the alcaic stanza, often employed by Horace, who also used **sapphics.**

alchemy may come from Greek *khumeia*, ' a pouring ; infusion ', the *al* being caused by the association of ancient chemistry with Arabia, where *al* simply means ' the ' : this is the etymology preferred by The OED, Skeat and Webster. Weekley compromises, but he does at least add that ' It seems clear that

6

the word came from Alexandria via the Arabs into Europe'. It is true that Alexandria, founded by Alexander the Great, contained thousands of Greeks, including scholars and scientists; yet even they may have understood *alchemy* as the art of Egypt and have derived the 'chemy' part of the word (the Arabic *al* is hardly in doubt) from *Al Kkem*, 'Egypt' (Plutarch's *Chymia*): 'the (land of) black earth'; the hiero-glyphic for 'black earth' is, when transliterated, *khmi*, the earth in question being that of the inhabited confines of the Nile and set in opposition to the desert sands of the vast remainder of Egypt.

alderney is an *Alderney bull, cow*, or *ox*; *alderneys* are *Alderney cattle*. Raised in *Alderney*, the alderney is yet, like the **jersey,** common to all the Channel Islands, of which Alderney forms part of the bailiwick of Guernsey (see **guernsey**). The word *Alderney* is an anglicization of the French *Aurigny*, which seems to come from *Riduna*, the old Latin name of the island.

aldine has the small initial only when it denotes a certain style of display type, introduced in 1501 by *Aldus* Manutius, the latinized form of the name of *Aldo* (i.e., Teobaldo) Manucci or Manuzio, who (1450–1515) was a Classical scholar and a famous printer. He settled in 1490 at Venice, where he estab-lished the Aldine Press: whence the *Aldine editions* of the Classics. He was, by the way, the first printer to use **italic.** His son Paolo and grandson Aldus carried on the founder's fine printing and his tradition of scholarship.

alec, smart. See **smart alec.**

alexanders (sometimes, incorrectly, *alexander*) is, in the United States, the meadow parsley; The DAE records it as early as 1637, cites 'golden alexanders' and 'purple alexanders', and notes that the botanical name of one variety is *Smyrnium*. That The DAE essays no etymology matters little, for it has generously supplied the data. The alexanders is golden or purple, therefore royal; it is associated with Smyrna in the Near East: is its name not, therefore, short for *Alexander's flower*, the flower of Alexander the Great, the world's most royal conqueror? Compare:—

alexandrines are iambic verses (or lines) of six feet or twelve syllables. The origin is 'obscure': but not impossibly so. It is a regal measure and, I have little doubt, traceable ulti-mately to **Alexander the Great**—the archetype, and the

7

nonpareil, of successful and enlightened conquerors: Alexander III of Macedon, who, aged but thirty-two, died in 323 B.C. ' Of all the heroes, warriors and statesmen of the ancient world, none, not even Caesar himself, stands out like Alexander; none changed so profoundly the ideas of men whether they thought of the government of states or the government of the universe, of peoples, men, Nature or God; none influenced more strongly the imaginations of those who came after him, whether princes or thinkers, writers or the tellers of legend,' T. R. Glover, *The Ancient World*, 1935; to the Middle Ages he was a demi-god, and in medieval French literature there was an *Alexandrine* poetic cycle, of which at least one piece was written in this measure, as Weekley points out; ' Alexander and Caesar stride colossal across the Elizabethan imagination, imperial prototypes prefiguring Elizabeth ', (G. Wilson Knight, *The Burning Oracle*, 1939). See especially W. W. Tarn, *Alexander the Great*, 1948.

Algernon. See **Algy.**

algorism is the Arabic, i.e. the decimal, system of notation; hence, arithmetic. From the Old French *algorisme*, from Medieval Latin *algorismus*, from Arabic ' *al-Khowarazmi*, i.e. the man of *Khwarazm* (Khiva), famous Arab mathematician (fl. 9 cent.) through whose works the Arabic numerals became known in Europe,' W. Medieval works on arithmetic bore the title *Algorismus*; the mathematician's real name was Jafar Mohammed ibn-Musa.

Algy or **Algernon,** ' a young aristocrat or play-boy ', from the fact that *Algernon* has, since ' 1066 and all that ', been an aristocratic given-name reminiscent of Norman blood. (See especially PNTC.)
  ' Algy met a bear: the bear was bulgy: the bulge was Algy.'

alisonite is an indigo-copper; a variety of **covellite** found in Chile. It is named after a Mr R. E. Alison of that country. *Covellite* (or *covelline*): a copper sulphide, commemorating the Italian mineralogist *Covelli*, who found it in the lava of Vesuvius. Nicola Covelli (1790–1829) was an authority on vulcanology.

alleluia is the Latin form of that Hebrew exclamation which is more closely represented by *Hallelujah*, ' praise Jehovah! ': Hebrew *hallel*, ' praise ' + *Jah*, ' Jahveh, i.e. Jehovah '. The most famous Hallelujah Chorus is Handel's (at the end of
8

Part II of his *Messiah*); but nearly all such choruses bear some reference to *Revelation*, xix, 1 : 'And after these things I heard a great voice of much people in heaven, saying, Alleluia, Salvation, and glory and honour, and power, unto the Lord our God '. (With thanks to Dr Percy Scholes.)

> 'The Easter Alleluias hung
> Their graceful bells and gently sung,'

John Wynn, cited in *Wild Flowers in Literature* (1934), by Vernon Rendall, who adds : 'An old name for the Wood-sorrel '.

allemande; in the 16th and 17th Centuries, often *Alman* or *Almain*, *Almand* or *Almayne*.

(1) A part, traditionally the first, of a musical Suite ; (2) a dance, three beats to a measure and therefore prelusive of the waltz.

Both are regarded as having a German origin, hence the name (French *Allemand*, 'German '), even though (1) was, according to Dr Percy Scholes, probably of Dutch or even of French origin.

almagest, 'a great treatise ; the best book on a scientific subject ', comes from the Arabic title of an astronomical treatise in Greek by Ptolemy (Latin : Claudius Ptolemaeus), that astronomer, mathematician and geographer who flourished at Alexandria in the 2nd Century A.D. His *Megalē Syntaxis tēs Astronomias*, 'great system of astronomy ', became in the Arabic translation *Al Majiste*, 'The Greatest . . .', from Greek *megistē*, 'greatest '.

almandine, ' a dark-red, or a purple, variety of the garnet ', is a corruption of the French *alabandine*, which represents *alabandina*, itself from *Alabanda*, a town in Caria, an ancient district (under Roman rule, it became a province) in the south-west of Asia Minor. Alabanda—now Arab Hissar—was so prosperous a place that it fell into corruption and luxury, including an excessive love and display of precious stones, among them the *gemma alabandina*, 'Alabandine gem ', the almandine.

Alman. See **allemande.**

alp; alpine. Respectively ' a (very) high mountain ' and, derivatively, ' (very) mountainous ', these words came straight from the Latin *Alpes*—Greek *hai Alpeis*—the High Mountains, especially those of Switzerland. Indeed, *Alpes* always referred

9

to the Swiss Alps, except in the poetical *geminae Alpes*, ' the twin Alps ', i.e. the Alps and the Pyrenees. The *Alpes* were so named from their snowy summits, their *white* peaks : the word is cognate with Latin *albus*, ' white '; compare England's poetic name *Albion*, from the white cliffs of Dover. (Lewis & Short.) Certain scholars deride this origin of *Alpes*.

alphonsin, a surgical instrument for the extraction of bullets from wounds, commemorates its deviser, not *Alphonsus* Ferrier, a physician of Naples, as I have seen it stated, but *Alfonso* Ferri (or Ferro), physician to the Popes. He died in 1595, and the instrument was in the 16th–17th Centuries known as the *alphonsinum* ' (the instrument) of *Alphonsus* '—the Latin form of *Alfonso*.

alsatian, or **A—,** is short for *Alsatian wolf dog* (or *hound*), often defined as ' the German shepherd dog '.

 Alsatian is the adjective of *Alsatia*, the latinized form of Old High German *Elisaz* (modern German *Elsass*), French *Alsace* : the marches, or disputed border-region, between France and Germany.

 Compare **pomeranian.**

alsike, a European clover with pinkish flowers—a plant culti-vated for forage, is short for *Alsike clover*, so named from *Alsike* in Sweden. Alsike, near Upsala, is mentioned as a notable— perhaps the original—habitat of this plant.

althea is in North America a species of hibiscus; especially *Hibiscus Syriacus*, the shrubby althea. Also the ' rose of Sharon '. The precise reason why it should have been given a girl's name is unknown : but, in these matters, precision is beside the point : it is a pretty piece of personification, and that is—or should be—enough.

amaryllis, a genus of bulbous plants flowering in the autumn (see especially the delightful account in Vernon Rendall's exquisite, erudite *Wild Flowers in Literature*, 1934), comes from the Greek proper name *Amarillis*, which, in Theocritus and elsewhere, typifies the country girl and which was adopted by the Latin poets. In Greek, the name signifies ' refreshing stream ' and thus it affords a pleasant parallel to the Chinese ' Lady Precious Stream '.

 ' A chattering, giggling swarm of Lalages, Marias, Cerusas, and Amaryllides, from the laundries and the spinning-rooms, stood upon their tiptoes ', Conan Doyle in ' An Iconoclast ' (reprinted in *Tales of Long Ago*).   Richard Jefferies has used the name as that of a type in *Amaryllis at the Fair*, and it recurs, thus, in Charles Morgan's *Reflections in a Mirror*, 1944 : 'They '— the Victorians—' seem to have had the gift, whenever it suited them, of sitting down at the roadside in the shade of a tree, or, better still, of withdrawing with Amaryllis into a meadow, and of letting the wingèd chariot go hurrying past '.   Compare : ' There is [in Milton's *Lycidas*] a clear personal cry question-ing the wisdom of losing amorous joys with Amaryllis and Neaera through the high seriousness of a poetic temperament ' (G. Wilson Knight, *The Burning Oracle*, 1939).

Compare **Phyllis.**

amati.   Concerning violins, Dr Percy Scholes (*The Oxford Companion to Music*) has written : ' The greatest age in the making of these instruments was that of the various generations of the Amati, Guarneri, and Stradivari families (mid-sixteenth to early eighteenth-centuries), all of Cremona, North Italy '; the Amatis belong to the 16th–17th Centuries.

Cf. **stradivarius.**

amazon; amazonian.   ' Lena . . . tall and bronze-coloured and Amazonian,' Warren Stuart, *The Sword and the Net*, 1942 ; compare ' When I heard that the Amazonian blonde was charged with taking part in the badger game, I had a vague idea that she had been annoying animals at the zoo,' Mary Sullivan, *My Double Life*, 1939 ; ' She was a big-boned woman. In her youth she must have had a certain Amazon type of beauty,' Gerald Kersh, *An Ape, a Dog and a Serpent*, 1945.

The Amazons (Greek *Amazōnes* or *Amazōnides*), ' The Breast-less ' (privative *a-* + *mazos*, ' a breast '), were so called, not because they were literally ' breastless ' but because, the better to handle their bows, they cut off their right breasts, so proud were they of—so deadly efficient in—their skill and courage as warriors.   These legendary women, who lived in the vicinity of the Euxine, aided the Trojans against the Greeks, their queen, Penthesilea, being slain by Achilles. Miss Maude Meagher in the 1930's wrote and published a notable novel on the theme of The Amazons.

amazonite.   ' There are no minerals in Babylonia. Yet not only did the earliest inhabitants possess flint and copper, not only had they learnt to grind vases and bowls out of hard stone, but the materials with which they made their beads include lapis-lazuli, . . . which comes from Central Asia, and amazonite, a stone which is found only in Central India and

11

in Transbaikalia!', Patrick Carleton, *Buried Empires*, 1939. Amazonite, an apple-green variety of microline, has been named from the *Amazon* river.

amboyna. Originally *Amboyna wood*, this finely marked wood is grown on Amboyna Island, one of the Moluccas. 'Amboina Town is the capital of the residency of the same name, and at one time was world-famous, when it enjoyed a monopoly of the clove trade ', No. 87 (published in 1920) of the Handbooks prepared by the Historical Section of the Foreign Office— where we further learn that *Amboina* or *Ambon* comes ' from a Malay word meaning " mist " '.

americanium. See **francium.**

ammonal; ammonia; ammoniac; ammonite; ammonium. The second, fourth, fifth of these terms derive from the third; the first constitutes a blend of ' *ammon*ia ' and ' *al*uminium '; and the third—*ammoniac*—incorporates the facts that sal ammoniac affords the material origin of ammonia, *sal ammoniac* the etymological origin of *ammonia*, and that *ammoniac*, an adoption from French, which obtained it from Latin *ammoniacum*, is a term representing Greek *ammōniakon*: the neuter singular of an adjective meaning ' of *Ammon* ' has become a noun meaning ' gum of Ammon '; the gum being reputed to exude or distil from plants growing near the famous shrine (with attendant oracle) of Zeus Ammon, often called Jupiter Ammon, whose name signifies ' Zeus the African ' or ' African Zeus '. The Africa known to the Greeks consisted mostly of desert, the shrine stood on an oasis in Libya, and Greek *Ammōn* derives from *ammos*, ' sand ' or ' a sandy place '; Africa, therefore, was etymologically ' The Country of Sand '.

amontillado. This deep-golden, dry Spanish sherry, form- ing the subject of one of Poe's grimmest *Tales*, comes from vineyards in the hilly district around *Montilla*: *a*, ' from ' + *Montilla* + *ado*, a common Spanish suffix. The town of Montilla, which lies twenty-three miles south-south-east of Cordova, is ' believed by some to occupy the site of the ancient Baetic fortress of *Munda*, where Caesar defeated the sons of Pompey in 45 B.C., and in the neighbourhood are numerous remains of the Roman period ' (George Chisholm, *Gazetteer*).

ampère; often shortened to **amp.** This unit of electrical current has been named after André Ampère (1775–1836), a French scientist famed for his researches into physics, especially in magnetism and electricity, in both of which he made some very important discoveries; *Ampère's law* forms the foundation of the entire study of electro-dynamics. He invented the astatic needle, without which the astatic galvanometer would have remained undiscovered.

Compare **farad, maxwell, ohm, volt, watt.**

anabasis is a military advance, especially one that entails a long march. This purely Greek word would not have been adopted on its own merits : its acceptance into literary English is entirely owing to Xenophon's *Anabasis*, which recounts the ' going up ', from the sea-coast to the interior of Asia, of Cyrus the Younger. Cyrus had with him, on his march in 401 B.C. from Sardis to near Babylon, an auxiliary force of 10,000 Greeks, among them Xenophon, the author of its history.

anacreontic, ' convivial; amatory ' or, in a technical sense, ' written in the metre of the lyrics of *Anacreon* ', a Greek poet of the 6th Century B.C. Only fragments of his poems survive, but we know that, in the main, his verse was light, playful, musical, dealing with wine or love—or both; devoid of passion, all; some, satirical. In style, however, they were perfectly adapted to their subject. Anacreon has had many imitators, the most persistent English emulator being the Irish Thomas Moore (1779–1852), even apart from his very free translation of *The Odes of Anacreon* (1801).

Ananias is still, though much less than in the 19th Century, used for ' a liar '—strictly, for a male liar, his wife Sapphira, equally a liar in the fact, having failed to capture the public fancy. These two early Christians were struck dead for lying to the Apostle Peter, as we know from *Acts*, v, 1–11. The lesson so went home to the neighbours that ' great fear came upon all the church, and upon as many as heard these things '.

andalusian is short for *Andalusian fowl*, which is bluish-black of hue. The andalusian was originally a native of *Andalusia* (the Spanish spelling is *Andalucia*,) an ancient province in the south of Spain, a region better known for its horses and sheep, the latter yielding a very fine wool; *Andalusian wool*, indeed, has become almost generic.

anderson (*Anderson shelter*). An outdoor shelter against bombs; usually an arched top of corrugated iron over a dug-out, the whole strengthened with sandbags. Named after Sir John Anderson (b. 1882), the Cabinet Minister at the head of

13

home security at the time (1940) of its inception. Compare **morrison.**

'I scrounged an Anderson from an empty house,' Robert Greenwood, *The Squad Goes Out*, 1943.

andesite; hence the adjective, **andesitic.** '"What," I inquired humbly, "is andesite?"' "It's a volcanic effusive rock of porphyritic texture," explained Start helpfully. . . . "Well, I'll put it this way. Andesite is a type of basalt. In other words, very ancient, hardened, once molten lava, common in the Andes, less so here. It's found at the surface only occasionally "', John W. Vandercook, *Murder in Fiji*, 1936.— 'A weird gorge of andesitic and basaltic lava ', Nard Jones, *Swiftly Flows the River*, 1939.

Andrea Ferrara. A broadsword: mostly in Scotland. (Whence, at least once in the 17th Century, an *Andrew*.)

When, in *The Lone Adventurer*, 1915, Halliwell Sutcliffe wrote, ' His trust was keen and bright, like the sword-blade that old Andrew Ferrara had forged in Italy for Prince Charles Edward,' he was somewhat astray in his facts. The ' facts ' are thus set forth by Ernest Weekley in his *Etymological Dictionary* : ' *Andrea dei Ferrari*, i.e. Andrew of the armourers, was a famous 16 cent. swordsmith of Belluno, but it seems unlikely that any great number of his costly blades could have got to Scotland. According to some Sc. authorities the native blades were made by *Andrew Ferrars* or *Ferrier* (? of Arbroath), who again, according to a popular legend, may have been the Italian in exile.' Note that the surname may have derived from the city, or the province, of Ferrara in Lower Lombardy, and that ultimately it represents Latin *ferrum*, ' iron '.

Andrew. See **Andrea Ferrara.** (2) See **merryandrew.**

andrewsite. A phosphate, hydrous and composed of copper and iron, it was named after the Irish physicist and chemist, Thomas *Andrews* (1813–85), who, educated in Scotland, became a Professor at the Queen's University, Belfast. He is remembered especially for his experiments in the liquefaction of gases and for his establishment of scientific conceptions of critical pressure and critical temperature. (Webster BD.)

angelus. For that form of Catholic devotion which commemorates the Incarnation and which commences with the words *Angelus Domini nuntiavit Mariae* (the angel of the Lord announced to Mary), the correct spelling is *A—* : and the term

14

is ineligible. Deriving therefrom, however, is *angelus*, 'the Angelus bell': its summons forms the subject of one of the two most famous paintings by Jean François Millet (1814–75).

Angelus is the Latin form of the Greek *angelos*, 'a messenger' —hence 'a messenger from God: an *angel*', itself from *angellein*, 'to bear a message, bear tidings'.

anglaise is a vague 18th-Century musical term for a hornpipe or country-dance tune. Probably short for French *danse*, or *pièce*, or *musique*, *anglaise*. See *The Oxford Companion to Music*.

angora = *A. cat—goat—rabbit*; it also = the fabric made from the wool-like hair of the goat, and in this sense (with variant *angola*) it is always lower-cased. *Angora* (or—going back to the Greek *Angkura*—Ankhara) is a city in the midlands of Anatolia or Asia Minor, and speaking of the Angora region and the lake region lying to the south, Professor Lyde has remarked that 'There is a curious difference in the quality of the wool and the mohair [from the Angora goat] from these two areas. . . . The real "Angora" fibre is very long and white, but is *less* fine; and the fineness of the "lakeland" fibre seems to be due more to the presence of shady trees in summer than to the very low temperatures in winter' (*The Continent of Asia*).—The cat and the rabbit are long-haired, like the goat.

'"It really is *my* supper," she reasoned as she zipped on her white Angora dressing-gown,' Ethel Lina White, *Midnight House*, 1942.

The form *angola* is a corruption.

angostura. '"Hallo, Gilt Kid. Siddown. Watchew going to have? . . ." "Sorry I'm late, pal." The Gilt Kid sank into a chair. "I'd better have an angostura and soda",' James Curtis, *The Gilt Kid*, 1936.—'Arthur was . . . the dash of angostura in the Soho cocktail,' Mark Benney, *The Scapegoat Dances*, 1938.

Short for *Angostura* (originally *Angustura*) *bitters*, derived, as was the febrifuge known as *A. bark*, from the bark of the tree growing at Angustura (now Ciudad Bolivar) on the Orinoco river.

angstrom. Originally, *Ångström unit*. Like the names of other units (e.g., *ohm, volt, farad*; *gauss*; *joule*; *curie*), it has dropped *unit*; for convenience, it has also discarded the accents, either both of them or at least the Scandinavian one over the *a*. Abbreviation: *A.U.*

This unit of wave-length in spectra—by the way, it is one

15

hundred-millionth of a centimetre—honours its deviser, the Swedish physicist and astronomer, A. J. Ångström (1814–74), who studied light, made spectrum-analyses, and, in 1862, identified hydrogen in the solar atmosphere.

anno domini, slang for ' age ' or ' advancing years ' or ' old age ', is properly written *anno Domini* (' in the year of our Lord ').
' His honour was a voluble man of about fifty, who kept *anno domini* at bay with a light grey suit,' Rex Grayson, *Snatch and Grab*, 1938.—' Innings closed by *anno domini*,' cricketer's epitaph.

anselmo. ' Wolfe in bed was a remarkable sight. First the low footboard of streaky anselmo, yellowish with sweeping dark brown streaks', Rex Stout, *The Silent Speaker*, (English edition) 1947. Not—at least until the end of 1948, not—in the dictionaries, *anselmo*, I can merely surmise, is either a wood or a decorative technique; possibly from Giorgio Anselmi (1723–97), a facile, prolific yet able Italian decorative painter, especially of churches.

antimacassar. ' A setting of faded velvet, samplers, antimacassars, and portraits of Queen Victoria,' David Hume, *Good-Bye to Life*, 1938.
Literally ' (a piece of drapery serving as a protection) against Macassar oil '—beloved of the Victorian male, for the beautification of his manly locks. Obviously, Macassar oil comes, or originally came, from Macassar (a corruption of the native *Mangkasar* or *Mangkasara*), the capital of the presidency of the same name in the Celebes; the city is one of the chief ports in the East Indies.

antinomian, ' denying the doctrine, or the belief, that the moral law is binding ', comes from Latin, itself from Greek, *antinomia*; *anti*, ' against ' + *nomos*, ' law ', *-ia* being a characteristic Greek suffix implying abstractness. But the English use on the word springs from the *Antinomians*, certain Gnostics (see **agnostic**) of the 2nd–3rd Centuries A.D.

apache, whether it means ' the colour of cocoa ' or designates ' a criminal tough, especially of Paris ', recalls *apache dance*, ' a violent dance for two heterosexual partners ' (of the kind once popular in certain low dance-halls and cafés of Paris), and derives from *Apache*, ' a member of the Apache tribe of Red Indians '; the word itself is probably a particularization of— and from—the Suñi *ápachu*, ' an enemy '. The Apaches, related to the Navajos, formed predatory bands; unsettled and ferocious, they ranged ' throughout the southern Plains and the Southwest ' and ' were known to the Spaniards as early as 1540, and their guerilla warfare terrorized these regions until the surrender of Geronimo [in] 1886,' Hart. The numerous Frenchmen in North America encountered them and some lived to tell a thrilling tale in Parisian salons.

aphrodisiac; Aphrodite. ' It's all there in his music. It's a dope he's peddling, a narcotic, a nepenthe, an aphrodisiac,' Mark Benney, *Low Company*, 1936.—' Compress and express. Squeeze all the voluptuous images into a lump and, in the act, squeeze out of them a liqueur-glassful of juice, at once astringent and heady, tart and aphrodisiac,' Aldous Huxley, *Time Must Have a Stop*, 1945.

' In Aphrodite, mother of Eros, he '—the Greek of the Classical Age—' incarnated the passion of love, placing in her broidered girdle " love and desire of loving converse that steals the wits even of the wise ",' G. Lowes Dickinson, *The Greek View of Life*, 1896.—' Obviously there is something called sexual appetite, desire, passion or emotion. Obviously, too, it plays an important part in human life. This power personified becomes the goddess Aphrodite. She is perfectly real and genuine, as a natural power; nothing could be more so. If any people worship sexual power, then they worship Aphrodite. If they lack the Greek language, they call her by a barbarian name,' A. D. Ritchie, *Civilization, Science and Religion*, 1945.

By the Romans identified with **Venus,** Aphrodite (? ' Foam Dweller ') is also known as ' The Cyprian ' and ' The Cytherean ', names that relate to place-legends. As Aphrodite Urania, she typified pure love, the higher love—compare **Psyche**; as Aphrodite Pandemos (' of all the people '), she became the goddess of lust; Lowes Dickinson's ' the passion of love ' goes nearest to characterizing her general reputation, influence, nature.

apocryphal, ' of doubtful authenticity; hence, false, sham; hence, invented by one person to foist upon (the memory or the literary *corpus* of) another ', comes direct from *Apocrypha*, the Apocryphal Books of The Bible. The Jews account them false; not originally written in Hebrew, they were, at the Reformation, excluded from the Biblical canon : ' Certain writings accepted by the Church under the heading " Apocrypha " (i.e. " hidden ", from the ordinary reader) do not exist in Hebrew. . . . The " Apocrypha ", accepted by the Roman Council of Trent (1546) and also by the Vatican Council of

1870, was printed in Coverdale's Bible (1535) somewhat apologetically,' Stanley Cook, *An Introduction to the Bible*, 1945. *Apocrypha* represents the Late Latin *apocrypha scripta*, ' hidden writings ' : Greek *apokrupha*, from *apokruphos*, from *apokruptein*, ' to conceal, to keep hidden ', itself from *kruptein*, ' to hide ' (whence *cryptic*).

apollinaris; slangily, **polly.** Introduced into England ca. 1870, the ' water ' came from *Apollinaris-brunnen*, ' Springs of Apollinaris ' or ' Apollinaris Springs ', near Remagen in the Province of the Rhine; the region is noted for its deposits of iron ore, which has beneficially affected the water of these springs. The name *Apollinaris* suggests that at this spot there was anciently an altar of Apollo : *Apollonis ara*, corrupted, might easily yield *Apollinaris*.

apollino is an American musical instrument that was popular ca. 1810–20. Invented by one Joseph Plimpton, it was said in 1819 to combine ' the music of a Church Organ, a Grand Orchestra, a Martial Band, and a Harp ' (The DAE). Compare—and see—**apollonicon.**

Apollo, in its transferred sense ' an extremely handsome man ' (cf. **Adonis**), occurs, for instance, in this sentence, in reference to the year A.D. 210, from Conan Doyle's ' Giant Maximin ' (reprinted in *Tales of Long Ago*), ' A soldier might know that it was the little weary [infantrymen] . . . who were the real terror of the enemies of the Empire, but to the eyes of the wondering Thracians it was this [cavalry] troop of glittering Apollos who bore Rome's victory upon their banners, and upheld the throne of the purple-togaed prince who rode before them '.
  The divinity of Apollo is lightly hinted in a passage from Helen Waddell's *The Wandering Scholars*, where, concerning the Irish scholars in medieval Europe, she says that ' A good many of the exiles had more scholarship than sanctity, and some little of either, with Bacchus '—the wine cup—' nearer their elbow than Apollo ' (god of poetry). Both the religion and the philosophical significance are more emphatically implied in an aphorism by ' Palinurus ' : ' Where Apollo reigns, Dionysus will follow ' (*The Unquiet Grave*). *Apollo*, Greek *Apollōn*, is important not only in Greek mythology—god of music, lyric poetry, medicine, prophecy, archery, and, as Phoibos Apollōn, Phoebus Apollo (Apollo the Radiant, of light, youth, the sun)—but also in Roman religion, the earliest temple to him in Rome being erected in 432 B.C.; near the end of the Christian era, Augustus strengthened and officialized his cult.

18

apollonicon, either a sort of harmonium or a mechanical organ, pays tribute to **Apollo** as god of music, especially the lyre (hence of poetry, especially the lyric). See *The Oxford Companion to Music* for further information on the instruments concerned. Compare **apollino.**

appeal from Philip drunk to Philip sober. See **Philip . . .**

applejohn. This apple, a wonderful 'keeper', said to attain to perfection only when it has become shrivelled, matures—or rather, has matured—at about St *John's* Day (December the 27th). The variant *John apple* is obsolescent.

arab or **A—** (= *A. horse*); **street arab; arabesque; gum arabic; arabis.** Only in the first is the capital letter held to be obligatory, and even *arab* (as 'synthesizing' *Arab horse*) might well, for it could logically, be adopted; in the other four, the capital would now be absurdly pedantic.

'You were described as abounding in the witty sallies of the street arab, as if courage consisted in demeaning oneself to schoolboy banter in the midst of danger and the hour of death', Antoine de Saint-Euxpéry, *Wind, Sand and Stars*, 1939 : not 'the street Arab', which could mean only an actual urban Arab.

'The tortured arabesques of [Henry James's] later manner', John Buchan, *Memory Hold-the-Door*, 1940 : from the scrolls, the leaves fancifully intertwined, characteristic of Arabian decorative work. Compare *arabesque* (or *-eske*) in music : a florid figure or piece.

In relation to *gum arabic* (originally *g. Arabic*), a gum exuded by certain acacias, Lionel W. Lyde has remarked, 'The general character of that region—from the Aegean and the Levant to the Thar Desert—is African rather than Asiatic; for the combination of heat and drought shows itself . . . in resinous and aromatic plants, the best gum-*arabic* being, literally, African' (*The Continent of Asia*, 1933).

Arabis, a kind of water-cress, gets its name 'probably from growing on stony or sandy soil suggesting Arabia' (W).

arachnid. A member of the Arachnida (spiders, scorpions, mites). Lydian Arachne challenged goddess Athene to a contest in weaving : the goddess, disliking Arachne's subject, slapped her : Arachne hanged herself, but Athene, not satisfied with that finality, turned her into a spider (Greek *arachnē*).

aragonaise or **aragonesa** is a Spanish dance—or dance tune—originating in *Aragon* (Spain); the latter form, the Spanish form, seems preferable.

19

aragonite, a mineral similar to calcite, also derives from *Aragon*, one of the ancient provinces of Spain and now divided into the provinces of Huesca in the north, Zaragosa midway, and Teruel in the south; the region is rich in minerals.

'Among these ruins' of a residence excavated at the pre-historic Babylonian mound of Jemde-Nasr 'were found the typical polychrome-decorated pottery, fine vases of porphyry, granite, aragonite and alabaster,' Patrick Carleton, *Buried Empires*, 1939.

araucaria, a plant, a tree, of the genus *Araucaria*; the tree is also called 'monkey puzzle' and 'Norfolk Island pine'. The word is a latinism, formed from *Arauco*, a province of Chile (formerly *Chili*), where the natives speak the Araucan language —or rather, dialects of that language. The province, capital Arauco, ends westward at the bad-anchorage Arauco Bay.

arcadian; Arcady. 'These cows, faintly steamy, beyond a hedge, were a picture of arcadian innocence. Were there cows in Arcady, or only goats and sheep?': 'Michael Innes', *The Weight of the Evidence*, 1944: which neatly exemplifies the trans-ferred sense of *Arcadian*, characteristic of (or an inhabitant of) *Arcady* or, as in the original, *Arcadia*. Though not more neatly than does the following passage from William McFee's dis-tinguished novel, *Spenlove in Arcady*, 1942: 'Was it a fallacy on his part to think that he could live in Arcady without being an Arcadian? . . . In Arcady one worshipped Pan and Diana.'

Arcadian, 'ideally pastoral or rustic' and, as a noun, either 'a figurative inhabitant of Arcady' or 'an ideal rustic'; *Arcadia* or, the more English form, *Arcady*, 'a pastoral or rustic paradise'; these words come from the Greek *Arkadia*, a mountainous district in the central Peloponnese, the highest mountains being in the north, the largest plains lying to the south. At least one tradition has it that Zeus was born there; Pan was originally an Arcadian god; Apollo was worshipped in a famous temple, sited at Bassae in a solitary splendour of scene. The country takes its name from a mythical *Arcas*, the son of Zeus and Callisto (a nymph in Dian's retinue).

For the almost too often quoted *Et ego in Arcadia vixi* (or *fui*), 'I too once lived—or, was—in Arcady', see my *A Dictionary of Clichés*: whereof the predominant connotation is, 'I too have loved, ah! long ago, in youthful, romantic fashion. . . . Ah, me!'

archie; Archibald. To *archie* an aeroplane was, in the war of 1914–18, to shell it from the ground with anti-aircraft fire;

and the originating *Archie* was an anti-aircraft gun. Certainly by personification and perhaps immediately derived from *Archibald*, ' the air-bump over the corner of the Brooklands aerodrome next to the sewage farm ' (W)—aviation slang of ca. 1910–14. The transition from *Archibald* to *archie* would be : ' to air-bump a 'plane '.

archipelago. ' Greece is specially interesting, as its extraordinary proportion of coast was as conducive to piracy as to legitimate trading. Moreover, the belt of mountains across its northern frontier so isolated its people from the rest of Europe that they were almost bound to expand into Asia—by the natural bridge of islands from which the Aegean sea has given its alternative title of " Archipelago " to any " sea studded with islands ",' Lionel W. Lyde, *Man and His Markets*, 1896.

Literally ' (the) chief sea ', the term originally emphasized ' sea ' (Greek *pelagos*) ; this particular sea happens to contain scores of islands, large and small.

arctic, ' very cold indeed ' (familiar English) ; ' an overshoe, especially for wearing when the ground is snow-covered ', hence, e.g., *a pair of arctics* (American usage). Like the derivative *subarctic, arctic* is also used figuratively, as in ' That woman used to be positively arctic, but she's thawed out a lot, for now she's merely subarctic—threatens to become almost human quite soon ; well, in five years' time, say '.

' The contrast between the eastern and western [island] " fences " [of Scandinavia] is repeated on the coasts behind them. For the hinterland is a block of very old rock—too old for coal—which was tilted down to the south-east when the old continent of Arctis sank under what is now the North Atlantic ' (L. W. Lyde, *The Continent of Europe*, 4th ed., 1930). That old continent of *Arctis* is connected with Greek *arktos*, ' a bear ' : it was the habitat of the great white bear.

argand may, as the context indicates, mean an *Argand burner*, an *Argand diagram*, or an *Argand lamp* : of these, the second refers to J. R. Argand (1768–1825), a French mathematician, whereas the first is the burner used in the third, which was invented by Aimé Argand (1755–1803), a Swiss physicist. The second term is the least used, the least known.

argonaut is a tentacle-headed mollusc ; also, an adventurous voyager by (land and) sea. In the U.S.A., it signifies a seeker after gold in the Klondyke ; and in his very readable *The Rise of the City*, Professor A. M. Schlesinger says of these intrepid gold-seekers, ' The argonauts braved incredible hardships presented by a frozen and forbidding country in order to reach the new El Dorado '. Earlier, the term *Argonauts* had been given to ' The Forty-Niners '—those adventurers who, despite difficulty and danger, forced their way in 1849 to the gold of California, as in Bret Harte's *Tales of the Argonauts*; ' at that time three of the routes to the goldfields from the Eastern States involved passages by water ' (H. W. Horwill, *A Dictionary of Modern American Usage*).

In Classical mythology, the Argonauts (Greek *Argonautai*) were those who sailed (*nautai*, ' sailors ') in the good ship *Argo*: under the leadership of Jason they sought to recover at Colchis —a district at the east end of the Black Sea—the romance-famous golden fleece. For the legend, see especially Apollonius Rhodius's *Argonautica* (The Deeds of the Argonauts), William Morris's *Life and Death of Jason* (one of the most vivid long poems in the English language), and Robert Graves's historical novel, *The Golden Fleece* (1944).

argosy. ' The canoe seemed to hang between water and stars, a motionless argosy in a sea of dreams,' Meredith Nicholson, *A Hoosier Chronicle*, 1912.

The 16th-Century form was *ragusye*, which represents Italian *ragusea* (*nave*), ' (ship) of *Ragusa* ' in Dalmatia. Chapman's spelling is *argosea*, and early English spellings of the town-name are *Aragosa, Arragouse*, etc.; compare also the form *Aragousey shippe*, cited by W from the Privy Council Acts of 1545–46 and, for the sense-development, *ship of Tarshish*, Biblical (*Psalms*, lxxii, 10; *Isaiah*, ii, 16—xxiii, 1, 14—lx, 9—etc.) for a large merchant-ship, of the type originated at Tarshish (*Tarsus*, chief city of Cilicia in Asia Minor and, B.C., a Greek settlement), that port which stood in the far north-eastern corner of the Mediter-ranean: ' Like a stately ship Of Tarsus . . . With all her bravery on, and tackle trim, Sails filled, and streamers waving ', as Milton phrases it in *Samson Agonistes*.

' The strategic strength of such a coast '—the Dalmatian— ' is illustrated by the history of such cities as Spalato and Ragusa, " the city of freedom " . . . for long an independent republic. . . . The Romans worked gold and silver, iron and lead [in what is now Jugoslavia]; and the merchant princes of Ragusa made fortunes out of the Servian mines,' Lionel W. Lyde, *The Continent of Europe* (4th ed.), 1930.

The word is archaic, poetic. It means more than ' ship ': ' ship richly freighted ': the vessel implied in the proverbial *When my ship comes home* (or *comes in*); compare Antonio's ships in *The Merchant of Venice*. Sometimes *argosy* connotes ' a com-mercial venture of a perilous, romantic kind '.

22

Ariel, of Shakespeare's *The Tempest*, is often employed to personify the British Broadcasting Corporation. Shakespeare took this delightful 'sprite of the air' from medieval folklore, which took it from the Arabic demonology. The name occurs in The Bible: Hebrew *Ari'el*, 'lioness of God'; but Shakespeare's Ariel, like the medieval Ariel, has been influenced by *aerial* (Latin *aer*, Greek *aër*, 'the air').

Spelt with a small *a* are the derivative Australian flying phalanger and the petrel so named; likewise the *ariel toucan*, a brilliantly plumaged Brazilian bird.

aristarchus and **zoilus** (or with capitals). An *aristarchus* is a severe, but just critic—a careful, but not hair-splitting scholar— a penetrating, but not remote grammarian, whereas a *zoilus* is a carping fellow, addicted to minutiae and thrice-split hairs, one who gazes so hard at the trees that he ignores—indeed, he forgets—the forest. The latter term preserves the opprobrium with which the Greeks of the 4th Century B.C. regarded this defiler of Homeric sanctities, this belittler of the Homeric invention. But the former term commemorates that Aristarchus who, at the head of the magnificent Alexandrian Library ca. 180–145 B.C., has, by the notable historian of scholarship, Sir J. E. Sandys, been described as 'the founder of scientific scholarship': a great critic, commentator, grammarian.

arlequin. See **harlequin.**

armageddon. 'He gathered them together into a place called in the Hebrew tongue Armageddon' (*Revelation*, xvi, 16), the scene of that decisive, that ultimate battle at the Judgement Day: a place that, geographically, is rather the mount of Megiddo than the valley of Megiddon, for Canaan fought there (*Judges*, v, 19), Josiah was slain there (2 *Kings*, xxiii, 29–30), and a levy was, earlier, raised by Solomon to build what was perhaps a walled town there (1 *Kings*, ix, 15): in short, many of its associations were warlike and bloody. 'That plain of Esdraelon or Megiddo, which has been red with the blood of battles all through history' (*The Daily Chronicle*, Nov. 29, 1917, cited in Ernest Weekley's fascinating *Etymological Dictionary*).

The term *Armageddon* was used of the expected First World War long before it commenced. Did Kipling foresee it when, in 1893, he wrote, 'In the day of Armageddon, or the last great fight of all'? It has often been applied also to the Second World War. The Third may, it would seem, be truly Armageddon—for Western civilization, at least.

armagnac. 'They had dined at d'Elboeuf's expense before coming out, the cold night air acted powerfully on his warmed Armagnac,' Margaret Irwin, *The Gay Galliard*, 1942.—' There was a cobwebbed bottle of Armagnac on the table,' Georges Simenon, *The Shadow Falls*, translated by Stuart Gilbert, 1945.

This superior brandy is made in the *département* of Gers in south-west France, a district formerly known as Armagnac. Armagnac is also the name of an ancient French dukedom.

aronoko. See **oronoko.**

arras. 'Behind the curtain hanging across his mind like an arras something of tremendous importance was trying to shine through,' Margery Allingham, *Traitor's Purse*, 1941.

'The *Nativity Ode* has many typically Miltonic images. Here are some : the sun's " burning axletree ", " the well-balanced world on hinges hung ", the " enamell'd arras of the rainbow ",' G. Wilson Knight, *The Burning Oracle*, 1939.

Tapestry or *arras* was first made at *Arras* in Artois (Northern France)—a small town familiar to British and American soldiers and airmen in 1914–18 and 1939–45. The French place-name derives from the Latin *Atrebates*, that people of Artois which Caesar mentions in his Gallic Wars, the Latin itself coming from an old Celtic word meaning ' district '.

Compare **artesian.**

arronoca. See **oronoko.**

'Arry and **'Arriet.** Typical Cockney man (esp., young man) and girl : from the frequent Cockney pronunciation of these predominant Cockney font-names, popularized by *Punch* : The OED quotes '*Arry on* '*Orseback*, which appeared in that weekly so early as 1874. See, too, PS.

'The last, named Kate, was a typical " Harriet ", eighteen years old, tall, strong, well built, and pretty too ' (Graham Grant, *The Diary of a Police Surgeon*, 1920).

artemisia is American, with dialectal variants *artemisie* and *artemishy*, for the garden chrysanthemum (a loose sense, The DAE implies) and a kind of aster, particularly the sage-bush, whose flower enlivened the 19th-Century prairies. Of the English varieties, The OED tells us that they have a bitter savour and that the name derives from the Greek goddess *Artemis*—but not why. The reason is that Artemis-Diana often behaved rather bitterly towards mere men : compare the entry at **Actaeon** (in the secondary list).

24

artesian; sub-artesian. Artesian wells were worked as early as the 17th Century in the north of France—to be exact, in the province of *Artois*. The word *artesian* is the Englishing of *artésien* ('of Artois'), which derives, not from the French but from Latin *Atrebatensis*, 'of the Atrebates'. For these Atrebates, see **arras.**

arty-and-crafty, a humorous description of, e.g., furniture less comfortable than artistic—and more artistic than beautiful. The already existing pejorative facilitated this coining from the name of the *Arts and Crafts* Exhibition Society, founded in 1888. Originally, the phrase was written *Arty-and-Crafty*.

asclepiad. Of Antimachus of Colophon, it has been said that his *Lydë*, a collection of short love-poems, 'was imitated by Asclepiades of Samos (*c*. 300; lyrics rather than elegiacs), who invented the verse called " Asclepiad ". . . . This sort of love poetry did in form influence Propertius; but in Greece its future was to be the epigram, of which Asclepiades was a master ' (W. W. Tarn, *Hellenistic Civilization*, revised edition, 1930). Strictly, there are two *Asclepiadean metres*; both are modifications of the **glyconic.**

ascot is short for *Ascot tie*. A fashionable tie or perhaps rather a neck scarf scrupulously knotted and fastened with a pin; worn in the U.S.A. and supposed to evoke memories of the English Ascot (*Ascot week*, held in June, at Ascot Heath in Berkshire).

'A " made-up " ascot tie, termed by one of Van Tomp's kind a "puff"' (George Bronson-Howard, *An Enemy to Society*, 1911).

Aspasia. ' To love other than uprightly was . . . impossible—yet she had secretly tired of the hollow part of an Aspasia without a Pericles,' Arthur Stringer, *The Silver Poppy*, 1903.

' Aspasia, . . . the mistress of Pericles, was famous for her powers of mind. According to Plato she was an accomplished rhetorician, and the real composer of the famous funeral oration of Pericles; and Plutarch asserts that she was courted and admired by the statesmen and philosophers of Greece. But Aspasia cannot be taken as a type of the Hetaerae of Greece,' G. Lowes Dickinson, *The Greek View of Life*, 1896. Dour biographers call her an adventuress: she wasn't that, for she has much benefited mankind. She died, aged sixty, in 410 B.C.

Literally, *Aspasia* is a Proper-Naming from Greek *aspasios*, ' well-pleasing; welcome ' or ' well-pleased; happy, glad '.

Compare **Beatrice, Dulcinea, Egeria.**

asti spumante ('foaming wine of Asti') is 'the poor man's champagne'. See **chianti.**

astrakhan (superior to *astrachan*) takes a capital only when it shortens *Astrakhan apple*. The fur, or wool, of the young lamb of a karakul sheep takes its name either from *Astrakhan*, the capital, or, more probably, from the province itself of *Astrakhan*, situated on the Lower Volga. This fur was formerly obtained wholly from this region, but now in the main from Bokhara.

atchison. See **bawbee.**

athenaeum; Athene. The latter strictly belongs to the 'border-line' glossary, but is included here as the origin of the former. An *athenaeum*, 'a literary or a scientific or a literary and scientific club', 'a library; a reading-room', is simply a general-purposing of Latin *Athenaeum*, which represents Greek *Athenaion*, that great temple of *Athene* (Pallas Athene), the goddess of wisdom and learning, which stands on the Acropolis at Athens; the Romans identified her with their own Minerva. She was the patron goddess of Athens (Greek *Athenai*), to which she gave her name.

'The war between Athene and Aphrodite that is the conceit of so many of their songs'—i.e., of the scholars flourishing in the earlier decades of the 12th Century—'and that beguiled Shakespeare himself into writing the undergraduate comedy of Love's Labour's Lost, had already begun' (Helen Waddell, *The Wandering Scholars*, 1927).

Atkins. See **Thomas Atkins.**

atlantes, atlantosaurus; Atlantis.

> 'I am but mortal still,
> And seek, all else above,
> The Atlantis of my love,
> Amid the seas of wrath,'—

thus sings Patric Dickinson in *Theseus and the Minotaur and Poems*, 1946.

Atlantis is a legendary island off the Atlantic coast of Africa: a figment of Plato's visionary imagination, it has a basis in geological fact. It has become synonymous with 'an earthly paradise'—but also with 'an earthly civilization (B.C.) that has been submerged and, therefore, utterly lost'. A paradise for romantic poets and fanciful moralists.

Etymologically, it derives from the Proper Name origin of:—

26

atlas. Atlas, in Greek mythology, was the son of a Titan and of one of Oceanus's daughters. As a penalty for his share in the revolt of the Titans against Olympus (compare the revolt of Lucifer and his followers in Heaven), he had, somewhere in the west of the known and imagined earth, to support the heavens on his shoulders—some of the weight being eased with head and hands. According to a later legend, he was, by Theseus whom he received ungraciously, turned into a mountain (hence the Atlas Mountains). ' The malevolent Atlas, who . . . with his own shoulders supports the great columns that hold earth and sky apart ' (E. V. Rieu's translation of *The Odyssey*).

' The application to a map-book is said to be due to Mercator, who used a figure of *Atlas* supporting the globe as a frontispiece (16th Century) ' : W.

The name *Atlas* probably signifies ' upholder ' or ' sustainer ' (compare *Darius* at **daric** : the radical *tel* appears in Greek *tlenai*, ' to bear or endure ', and Latin *tollere*, ' to raise '. (Skeat.)

atropine is a toxic alkaloid found in thorn-apple seeds and in the deadly nightshade, the other names of the latter being *belladonna* and *atropa* (*belladonna*). ' Might be some mydriatic drug '—a drug causing excessive dilatation of the eye's pupil—' like atropine or hyoscine,' J. J. Connington, *Jack-in-the-Box*, 1944.

Now *atropa* has been derived from *Atropos*, ' She who cannot be turned aside ; the inflexible ' : one of the three Fates—the only one by whom we have profited to the extent of a common-noun derivative, the other two being Clotho and Lachesis. Old women spinning, Clotho held the distaff, Lachesis withdrew the thread, and Atropos cut the thread to the required length : metaphorically, she cuts the thread wherewith we are tenuously attached to life.

attic ; Attic salt ; atticism, atticize. An *attic*, ' that part of a building which lies immediately below the roof and, at least in part, within the framing of the roof ', is properly ' a room—or rooms—behind a wall above the main order or orders of a façade in the Classical style of architecture ' ; in English, *attic* (from French *attique*) began by being that wall. Clearly, then, *attic* = *Attic*, ' in the Attic style ' (of architecture).

Attic salt is delicate, pointed wit, in the manner of the Classical Greek writers ; it translates the Latin *sal Atticus*. Likewise, *atticism* means a combination of elegance and wit and polish, and *atticize* is to write or to speak wittily and elegantly. ' *Attic*, or Athenian, has always connoted the civilized and

27

urbane' (WWN). In Greek, *Attikos*, 'Athenian', generated *attikizein*, ' to live like an Athenian '—with all the psychological and cultural concomitants that the phrase implied.

aubrietia; incorrectly, **aubretia.** This plant, or its violet or purple flower, of a genus of originally Mediterranean herbs of the mustard family, does honour to Claude *Aubriet*, who, dying in 1743, was a French painter of animals and notably of flowers.

Augustan is merely the English form of *Augustanus*, ' of—characteristic of—resembling the first Roman emperor, *Augustus* Caesar ', with special reference to the literature written during his reign; the best period (Virgil, Horace) of Latin literature, especially if, as is often done, it be taken to cover the period from the death of Julius Caesar in 44 B.C. to that of Ovid in 17 A.D., for it then includes also Tibullus, Propertius, Livy and Ovid himself; during the period, writers enjoyed the patronage both of Augustus and of such liberals as **Maecenas** and Messalla. Whence the meaning with which we are concerned : of any later national literature, that period which is ' the most like to the Classical Augustan, especially in atmosphere and temper ' and which, only too often, is named Classic in opposition to Romantic; for instance, the 17th Century in France, the 18th ('The Augustan Period') in England.

' He had been Octavius; by adoption as Caesar's heir he became Gaius Julius Caesar Octavianus; now he is Augustus as well as Caesar, and the name is to hint at good auguries, at everything august, at restoration and development,' T. R. Glover, *The Ancient World*, 1935 : wherein that great Classical scholar glances at the *augur* etymology of *Augustus*, ' venerable ', the other proposed etymology being that from *augere* (' to increase '). The title *Augustus* was conferred precisely because, free of monarchistic connotations, it yet elevated Octavian above the ordinary citizens. Living 63 B.C.–14 A.D., he reigned throughout his last forty years.

' The rules which Rockstro had in mind were the grammatical rules of a musical dialect that attained its Attic, or Augustan, purity at the end of the sixteenth century ', Donald Tovey, *A Musician Talks*, vol. I, 1941—a delectable and stimulating book.

aurignacian (or **A—**) is a division of the Upper Palaeolithic Period or the Later Old Stone Age : the period of *cromagnon* man, distinguished for his cave-paintings and wall-engravings at Altamira, and characterized by his use of flint gravers and scrapers, many of which were discovered in a cavern at *Aurignac*, a village that, in the *département* of Haute-Garonne, lies some forty miles south-west of Toulouse.

'The real revolution in Europe, according to Elliot Smith, was not from Old Stone to New Stone, but when Aurignac supplanted Le Moustier, and Homo Sapiens ousted Homo Neanderthalensis,' S. E. Winbolt, *Britain B.C.* (1943).

Compare **solutrian.**

aurora; aurora borealis; auroral. Like **austral,** these three terms have been included because the physical or climatic feature whence they all derive has, by the myth-making Greeks and Romans, been personified into a god. At first, *aurora* was the Latin for 'the dawn': and then it became a personification, *Aurora*, the goddess of the dawning.

In origin, *aurora* is cognate with *austral*, for it seems to come from the Sanskrit *ush-*, 'to burn': the dawn brings the heat of the day, much as *Auster* brought a hot wind.

austral, 'being in, or characteristic of, the south', represents the Latin *australis*, 'southern', from *Auster*, the (god of the) south wind—or, more accurately, the south-west wind; the *Notos* of the ancient Greeks, the **sirocco** of the modern Italians. Deriving from Sanskrit *ush-*, 'to burn', it means, literally, 'the hot, desiccating wind'.

Cf. **aurora.**

automedon, 'a charioteer' or, strictly, 'a skilful charioteer', hence even 'an "ace" driver of a motor-car', recalls that Automedon was the friend and charioteer of Achilles and, after the death of Achilles, the companion of the great hero's son, Pyrrhus. (Homer's *The Iliad*.)

Avernus. *Facilis descensus Averno* (not *Averni*), 'easy is the descent to [not 'of'] Avernus,' as Virgil pithily remarks in *The Aeneid* (vi, 126): to the nether regions: to Hell ('The road to Hell is paved with good intentions').

The Western Avernus is the relevantly allusive title of a most readable book (1887) of reminiscences by Morley Roberts. In *Ups and Downs: A Story of Australian Life* (1887), by 'Rolf Boldrewood', we find the comfortable, illustrative passage, '*Facilis descensus Averni*—which means that it is very easy to "settle oneself" in life—the "down train" being furnished with "palace-cars" of Pullman's patent, and gradients on the most seductive system of sliding scale'.

But the 'nether regions' sense of Classical literature derives

29

from the sense prevalent in Classical mythology, where *Avernus* or, in full, *Avernus lacus*, was a lake set in the crater of an extinct volcano, and near the entrance to the lower world. This Campanian lake (modern *Lago Averno*), situated close to Cumae, Puteoli, Baiae, was shut in by steep, wooded hills; from it issued a noxious exhalation, a mephitic vapour (*aestus*) that killed the birds flying over it; the Cumaean Sibyl dwelt in a grotto near the lake.

The fate of those birds explains the etymology of *Avernus*, which is the Latin version of the Greek *Aornos*: *a*, 'without' + *ornis*, 'a bird': without birds: that is, where no birds can pass and survive.

axminster, or **A—,** is short for *Axminster carpet*, a hand-woven carpet that imitates Oriental rugs or carpets, the warp being of either cotton or linen and the pile of woollen threads tied in by hand. Formerly (1755–1835) it was made at Axminster, a Devonshire town situated twenty-four miles east by north of Exeter. 'The names of Bethel and Holy Island, Kirk-wall and Dun-kirk, Ax-minster and Kidder-minster, speak for themselves,' Lionel W. Lyde, *Man and His Markets*, 1896: in other words, Axminster is 'The *minster* (originally a monastery church) on the Axe'—a Devon and Dorsetshire river flowing into Lyme Bay.

Compare **kidderminster,** q.v.

(2) Hence, a machine-made carpet; also called *chenille Axminster*, because the chenille thread forming the pile serves as weft thread in the actual weaving.

azilian or **A—.** 'With the Azilian, Tardenoisian and Maglemosian transition periods we are taking leave of the Old Stone [Age]', S. E. Winbolt, *Britain B.C.* (1943). Belonging to, characteristic of, resembling (the products of) the mesolithic or transitional period between the palaeolithic and neolithic ages— between the Old Stone Age and the New Stone Age. Bone and flint implements, inferior to those characterizing the preceding magdalenian period, and painted pebbles—purpose unknown, but perhaps for counting or as a means of exchange—were discovered at the village named 'Mas d'*Azil*', Ariège, in the French Pyrenees. Compare **acheulean.**

Azilian-Tardenoisian is Azilian in the variety characterized by finds made at Fère-en-Tardenois, in the *département* of the Aisne and sixteen miles south-east of Soissons.

B

babbitry; Babbit(t). 'Recording and receiving the various rackets devised by the boys of Broadway for the Johnny Babbitts of the suburbs is rather an interesting pastime,' John O'Connor, *Broadway Racketeers*, 1928. (The hero of the novel is not Johnny but George Folansbee Babbitt.)

'He beamed at me, a benevolent Babbitt with a parcel of real-estate to unload,' Eric Ambler, *Cause for Alarm*, 1938.

'Back in 1924 there appeared . . . *The Man Nobody Knows*, by Mr Bruce Barton, . . . which proved that Christ Jesus was not a rebel or a peasant, but a society gent, a real sport, a press agent and the founder of modern business. This Epistle to the Babbitts,' Sinclair Lewis, *Gideon Planish*, (English edition) 1943 : it was Sinclair Lewis, America's best satirical novelist, and Nobel Prize winner in 1930, who followed up the successful *Main Street* (1920) with the successful, the even better *Babbitt*, which, in 1922, enduringly pilloried the smug, smart business man and his self-delusive, hearty, tin-pot ' ideals ' (*babbitry*).

'The philosophy of action for action, power for the sake of power, had become an established orthodoxy. " Thou hast conquered, O go-getting Babbitt ",' Aldous Huxley, *Time Must Have a Stop*, 1945 : if only to note that Aldous Huxley, one of the most allusive of writers, felicitously alludes to the Emperor Julian's apostrophe to the immanence of Christ, ' Vicisti, o Galilee '.

(For **Babbit-metal,** see the secondary list : ' Border-liners . . .')

babel ; Tower of Babel. ' [Men] must share basic assumptions about [their relation to the universe and their relations with one another]—otherwise it's the Tower of Babel. Babel is the state in which there are no basic assumptions about any-thing—in which every man is isolated ' (Claude Houghton, *Passport to Paradise*, 1944).

' These [Sumerian] *ziggurats*'—artificial knolls, sometimes seventy feet high and always crowned with shrines—' are the originals of the Scriptural Tower of Babel (which in Hebrew means " Tower of Babylon "), the tower reaching heaven. . . . It was probably in the year 2057 B.C. . . . that a man with the pure Amorite name of Suwuabum . . . made himself master of an unimportant Akkadian city . . . which the Sumerians called Kadingirra and the Akkadians Bab-Ilim, " the Gate of God ",—a name which, as Hebrew Babel or Greek Babylon,

31

is as familiar to us to-day as that of Athens or of Rome ',
Patrick Carleton, *Buried Empires*, 1939.

Compare **Babylon** (subsidiary vocabulary).

baby. In South African diamond-mining language, *the baby*
is a sifting machine and *to baby* is to sift the soil with this
machine. Both terms date from ca. 1880 and both come,
by affectionate perversion, from *babe*—or rather, from *Babe*,
the name of that American who invented the machine. (C.
Pettman, *Africanderisms*, 1913.)

bacardi. (Big gangster—*Big 'Guy*, *Big Shot*—speaks:) ' My
marine department brought me up a load of [cigars] with the
last cargo of bacardi before repeal,' Howard McLellan, ' A
Recipe for Muscle '—in *Detective Fiction Weekly*, Sept. 29, 1934.
A form of rum—Cuban in provenance—much appreciated by
the Americans during the Prohibition days of 1920–33, and
still much used in the making of cocktails. Osbert Sitwell, in
that no less delectable than informative collection of essays
entitled *Sing High! Sing Low!* (1944), alludes to it thus:
' The drinks [of Cuba] are for the most part constructed on the
sure foundation of bacardi rum, one of the most powerful of all
liqueurs, and a produce of Cuba '.

Bacardi, as it is properly written, is a Spanish surname
(perhaps derived from *Bacchus deus*) : that of the firm of distillers specializing in this aid to conviviality. Having been
distillers in Spain for some three hundred years, the family in
1862 transferred the business to Cuba, where Facundo (d. 1932)
and Luis have made famous the rum that is trade-marked
Bacardi.

**bacchanal, bacchanalia, bacchanalian; Bacchant, Bac-
chante; Bacchic; Bacchus.** The last—*Bacchus*—has given
rise to all the others, which, this being not an ordinary but a
perdicious dictionary, there is no need to define; they all
spring from the observance of the rites, the ritual of the priests,
of Bacchus.

Bacchus (Greek *Bakkhos*), the god of Wine, is but one of the
names of Dionysus (Greek *Dionusos*). The name Bacchus, in
its Greek form, is factually identical, and philologically cognate,
with *Iacchus* (Greek *Iakkhos*), the latter being the mystic name
of the former ; *Iakkhos* derives from *iakkhein*, ' to cry, to shout '
(whether in joy or in grief).

For mythological information concerning Bacchus, see the
entry at **dionysiac.** An interesting modern offshoot is
Bacchus wine, which, one of the Greek wines, is made on the

32

island of Santorin ('corruption of the Italian *Sant Irene*, the patron saint of Thessalonica,' Chisholm), one of the Cyclades in the Aegean Sea; the island is also called Thera.

bacharach or **Bacharach** is a wine made in the neighbourhood of Bacharach, a small town that, on the left bank of the Rhine, is situated eight miles north-west of Bingen; although small, Bacharach is the centre of an important wine-producing district. 'Mostly white wines. Two of the best white wines of Bacharach are those of the Dell and Wolfshoehle vineyards' (André Simon).

baddeleyite. See entry at **brazil.**

badminton. 'Badminton has so long represented English life in its widest, no less than its most individual aspects, that it is impossible for any Englishman who can read or write to approach the Muniment Room there without a sense of mounting excitement,' Osbert Sitwell, 'The Red Folder'—in *Sing High! Sing Low!*, 1944. This Badminton is the seat of the Duke of Beaufort at Great Badminton, which is a Gloucestershire village six miles south-south-east of Wotton-under-Edge.
Thence comes *badminton*, the drink (claret mixed with soda water, with sweetening added) served to ducal parties, and the game (originally played in the magnificent ducal park). Disraeli, in 1870, spoke of someone being 'soothed or stimulated by fragrant cheroots or beakers of Badminton' (The OED); the game became popular ca. 1870. The fame of the ducal interest in sport—there is, for instance, a Badminton Hunt in the district—gave rise to the most famous of all series of books on sports and games—The Badminton Library.

baikalite must not be confused with **bakelite.** *Baikalite* is that dark-green variety of **hedenbergite** (named after Ludwig Hedenberg, a Swiss chemist) which was discovered in or near Lake *Baikal* in Eastern Siberia.

bain-marie (in chemistry and in cookery), according to Littré (1801–81), the French counterpart of Noah Webster and Sir James Murray, is so called from the mildness, the gentleness, of this sort of heating. Short for *bain de Marie* (medieval Latin *balneum Mariae*), 'bath of Mary': the Virgin Mary.

bakelite. 'One brass pillar and a bit of the bakelite casing remained, and Rollo saw at once that the pillar and scrap of

33

bakelite found originally . . . might have belonged to this plug,' Freeman Wills Crofts, *Enemy Unseen*, 1945.

This synthetic resin was invented by Leo Hendrik *Baekeland* (1863–1944), a Flemish chemist, who in 1889 went to the United States. He was also the manufacturer of photographic papers he had himself invented.

baku or **Baku** is short for *Baku rug* : a fine rug with somewhat angular designs of fighting animals or of palmettes, to name the two most usual motives. Originally they were made at or near Baku, the capital of Baku province, bordering the Caspian Sea. It is one of those Caucasian rugs which fall within the generic term, *Khila rug*, the others being *Kuba rugs* (Kuba in Aberbaijan) and certain *Dagestan rugs* (the Dagestan district of Caucasia ; also *Daghestan*)—in fact, the finer sort, known as *Kabistan rugs* (*Kabistan*, a phonetic variant of *Dagestan*). *Khila*, by the way, is not strictly a Proper Name : it seems to represent a specialization of a Caucasian word deriving from Turkish *khali*, ' a carpet '. (Webster.)

balaam. In the **balaam-box,** a newspaper keeps *balaam* or stop-gap matter for slack days or seasons. Disappointing stuff ; but then, *Balaam* is occasionally used for a disappointing prophet or, derivatively, ally, in reference to *Numbers*, xxii, 28, ' The Lord opened the mouth of the ass, and she said unto Balaam, What have I done unto thee, that thou hast smitten me these three times '—or perhaps to verses 37–38, ' Balak said unto Balaam, Did I not send earnestly unto thee to call thee? wherefore camest thou not unto me? am I not able indeed to promote thee to honour? And Balaam said unto Balak, Lo, I have come unto thee : have I now any power at all to say anything? ' Bribed by Balak to curse Israel, he blessed the Israelite cause : verse 38 ends with the significant statement, ' The word that God putteth in my mouth, that shall I speak ' : chapters xxiii–xxiv set forth the outcome. Balaam, of course, was rather a magician and a specialist in divination than a prophet ; his name perhaps means ' man, or priest, of Baal '.

balaclava = *B. cap* or, originally, *helmet*. This woollen covering for head and shoulders forms part of the issue of clothing made to a British soldier and worn on wintry field-service. During the Crimean War, which involved two winters (1854–55 and 1855–56), the British Army suffered rather severely from the cold prevalent in the inclement region of the Crimea.

Balaclava, which lies, a village and a harbour (the ancient *Palakion*), on the shores of the Black Sea and some eight miles

34

south-east of Sebastopol, was the scene of the famous-infamous charge of the Light Brigade on October 25, 1854. The irony in calling the headgear a *helmet* was not irrefutably intentional : the bungling that led to the charge being made at all, caused a deeply unfavourable impression.

balas or, now usually, *balas ruby*, comes, by way of Old French *balais*, from Arabic *balaksh*, which probably derives from *Badakhshan*, a Persian name for that region of central Asia which lies between the Hindu Kush mountains and the River Amu (or Oxus). ' In the Badakhshan hills, gold, silver, iron, copper, and lead abound ; there are also mines of lapis lazuli, emeralds, rubies, and a variety of other valuable stones ' (Chisholm).

balb ; balbo. The former signifies ' to manoeuvre (an enemy aircraft) into a bad position '—Royal Air Force slang of 1918. The latter, ' a large formation of aircraft '—R.A.F. slang since 1929, when Italo Balbo (1896–June 1940), killed in an air crash over Tobruk, commanded mass flights from Italy to Brazil. In the war of 1914-18, he proved himself a brilliant aviator : whence *balb*. As a statesman, he exercised a vision rather less keen.

balboa is the monetary unit—equivalent to the United States dollar—of the republic of Panama. It commemorates the Spanish explorer, Vasco Nuñez de *Balboa* (1475–1517), who discovered the Pacific Ocean, which he named *El Mar del Sur*, ' The Sea of the South ', and claimed for Spain ; he made other explorations. Owing to his quarrel with the Governor of Panama, he was—falsely, it seems—accused of sedition, condemned, and, *pour encourager les autres*, executed.

balbriggan is either the fine unbleached fabric of hosiery made at Balbriggan or, resembling it, a cotton knitted fabric used for both hosiery and underwear ; also it shortens *Balbriggan hose*.

Balbriggan, which is a small market and seaport town, ten miles south-east of Drogheda and in the north-west of the county of Dublin, Ireland, has long been noted for its hosiery and, not so long, for its power-loom weaving. The name resembles that of the near-by town of Balrothery : the Town of the Bridge?

baldachin or **-kin** or **-quin.** The word is French in its *-quin* form : to French it came from Italian *baldacchino* (whence the *-chin* form), a derivative from Italian *Baldacco*, itself from Medieval Latin *baldakinus*, the adjective of *Baldac*, which refers

35

to *Baghdad* (*Bagdad*). Bagdad, on the Tigris, a city known originally as Medinet-es-Salam, ' The City of Peace ' (sacked in 1258), exported the medieval fabrics (*baldachins*), made of silk and gold and much used ecclesiastically; consisting of these fabrics, and later others, were the canopies (*baldachins*) borne, in ecclesiastical processions, over a dais; thence came the architectural *baldachin*, shaped like a canopy.

baldric, ' a shoulder-strap that descends across the breast and supports a sword or dagger or bugle ', is held by Webster to derive, perhaps, from Latin *balteus*, ' a belt '; W, however, compares **goblet, nickel, tankard,** and remarks that, ' as the baldric was very ornamental, the word may represent the Old High German name *Baldarih* or Anglo-Saxon *Bealdric*, bold rich, whence the French surname *Baudry* and our *Badrick*, *Baldry*, etc.'

baldwin, a yellowish-red, slightly acid winter apple of, especially, New England, is so called from the given name and surname, *Baldwin* (Old High German *bald*, bold, and *wini*, friend); that, in particular, of the first grower, Loammi Baldwin (1740–1807), an American engineer and army officer.

balkanize. ' The Moslems appear in the part of civilized though helpless onlookers at the spectacle of Christian barbarity. They were then the dominant power in the [Iberian] Peninsula, and the one which quarrelsome " Balkanized " states tried to involve in every family vendetta,' J. B. Trend, *The Civilization of Spain*, 1944.
    To *balkanize* a region, a country, is to divide it into parts, or states, inimical one to another : from the internecine quarrel-someness of the states of the Balkan Peninsula. Because first used in that part of the world, a surgical frame (overhead bars and pulleys) for the treatment of fractured long bones is called a *Balkan frame* or *splint*.

ballyhoo, ' propaganda; excessive advance-publicity ', is usually associated with, as it is popularly and, I think, correctly derived from, Ballyhooly, a small township and parish in the north-east of County Cork, Ireland; on the left bank of the Blackwater, it stands five miles west of Fermoy. In Erse, *bally* (or *bal*) means ' a dwelling, a village ' and it occurs in scores of Celtic place-names. The precise relationship to this glorified village is uncertain : but American colloquial and slangy speech is ' full of ' references to Irish joviality and noisy high-spirits.

36

Perhaps also from Ballyhooly is *bally*, euphemistic for 'bloody', as in the music-hall tag, *Ballyhooly truth* ('whole bloody truth'?), as W suggests.

balmoral, whether as 'a figured woollen petticoat visible where the skirt is looped up' or as 'a boot, or high-uppered shoe, lacing in front' or as 'a flat round cap, with top projecting all round', comes from *Balmoral* Castle, Aberdeenshire, the Scottish residence of British royalty, particularly, in this instance, of Queen Victoria, in whose time the various articles became popular, thanks partly to the example of Her Majesty and her staff. 'The estate was purchased by Queen Victoria in 1848, and in 1853 the present castle was built in place of the old one' (Chisholm); *Balmoral* = 'majestic dwelling' (compare the origin of Ballyhooly—see **ballyhoo**).

baloney. See **boloney.**

baltimore may be either the phaëton butterfly or short for *Baltimore bird*—*heater*—*oriole* (same as the *B. bird*)—*truss*—or *yellow* (chrome yellow). Then there are the *Baltimore Belle*, a hardy American climbing rose with double pink flowers, and *baltimorite* (compare **bostonite**), a serpentine likewise named from *Baltimore*, that Maryland city and seaport (after the Irish seaport thus named) which lies on the left bank of the Patapsco River, some twelve miles before it enters Chesapeake Bay. The first element, *bal*, recurs in **ballyhoo** and **balmoral**.

banksia. 'The banksia, with its orange-red flowers, in shape like the cone of a pine, and perfuming the air with a scent as delicious as that of the honey-suckle' (J. W., *Perils, Pastimes and Pleasures*, 1849—a book dealing with New South Wales), was named after Sir Joseph Banks (1743–1820), that English naturalist who in 1768–71 accompanied Cook on his voyage round the world, who took a prominent part in the settlement of New South Wales, and who was President of the Royal Society from 1778 until his death.

bant, banting. The former, a verb, is a back-formation from the latter, which represents *Banting*, after a man so named, and which, by its form, resembles a verbal noun equivalent to 'slimming on a diet'. William Banting (1797–1878) was a cabinet-maker and (?) undertaker, who, convinced that many deaths resulted from heavy eating or from a wrong diet, turned author—on the subject of dietetics. In 1864 he published a book wherein he set forth his method (*Bantingism*) of reducing corpulence by adopting a sane diet; in England its popularity was brief, for it excluded butter, sugar, and—would you believe it?—beer.

bantam, whether ' any dwarf breed of domestic fowl ' or derivatively ' a very short person ' (with a connotation of combativeness) or used for the derivative *bantam-weight*, derives from *Bantam*, in Java : that breed of fowl which was, originally, so called is supposed to have come from the district about the present town of Bantam, at which site, some forty-five miles west of Batavia, the Dutch founded, in 1602, their earliest Javanese settlement.

' Among Hakluyt's treasures which he displayed to Purchas were the great Jesuit map of China, brought home by Captain Saris from Bantam in 1614, and the Mexican History in Pictures, with its English translation by Lok,' E. G. R. Taylor, *Late Tudor and Early Stuart Geography*, 1934.

banting. See **bant.**

barb; barbary; Barbary ape. The first is short for the second, the second for *Barbary horse*, a breed that, resembling the *arab*, was introduced into Spain by the Moors, who brought them from Barbary, as North Africa, from Egypt to the Atlantic, was once called; mentioned thus in David Pilgrim's *No Common Glory*, 1941, in reference to the mid-17th Century : ' A barb from the Sultan of Algiers' stable ' and ' One day he would have a barb . . ., all fire and courage, riding the air rather than the base earth '. *Barbary* = French *Barbarie*, derived from *Barbar*, the name given by the Arabs to the people of North Africa. The ape—the only wild one in Europe—is a native of North Africa and Gibraltar.

barbadoes. To transport convicts abroad—originally and correctly, to *Barbadoes*. A 17th–early 18th Century usage. ' To [the West Indies] and also to Spain and the Canaries, she ' —New England—' sent salted fish and sawn timber. The poorest quality of fish went for the slaves of the Barbadoes, better qualities to the Catholic populations of Southern Europe,' Rodwell Jones & Bryan, *North America*, 1946. *Barbadoes* may represent Portuguese *las barbadas*, ' the bearded ' —a Portuguese description of the Indian fig-trees. Formerly, always *the Barbadoes* ; now *Barbados*, although *the* is prefixed by some writers.

Whence such derivatives as *Barbadoes leg* (tropical elephantiasis)—*B. nuts—B. tar—B. water* (a cordial).

38

barbaresque ; barbarian, barbaric, barbarism, barbarous,
etc. For the differences and distinctions, see any thoroughly
good dictionary and Fowler's *Modern English Usage* and my
Usage and Abusage.

They all either come directly from or are at least cognate
with Latin *barbarus* or rather the Greek *barbaros*. To the
Romans, a barbarian was one who spoke neither Latin nor
Greek ; to the Greeks, everyone who did not speak Greek and
who, therefore, was of an inferior race—in short, ' a bloody
foreigner '.

A clue to ' the time-honoured contrast between Greek and
Barbarian ' (V. Gordon Childe) is afforded by *Barbar*, the
14th–17th Century English shape of *Barbarian* in its technical
Hellenic sense, for The OED cites these two quotations, ' The
Barbar rude of Thrace or Tartarie ' (ca. 1590) and ' Goths,
Vandals, Franks, and other Barbars ' (ca. 1639).

That *barbarian* and *barbaric* come to us via French, and
barbarous direct from Latin, is irrelevant. In the 16th–17th
Centuries, *barbarous* synonymized *barbarian* in its primary sense :
' non-Hellenic '. The Latin *barbarus* is cognate with Latin
balbus, ' stammering ' ; or rather, the latter is cognate with the
former. But the clue resides, obviously, in the Greek *barbaros*,
which is both noun and adjective for ' non-Greek, foreign(er) ' ;
hoi Barbaroi, ' foreigners ', were opposed to *hoi Hellenes*,
' Greeks '. Although *barbaros* does not occur in Homer (said
by Herodotus and Thucydides to have lived in the 9th Century
B.C.), *barbarophonos*, ' speaking a foreign tongue ', occurs in *The
Iliad*. Herodotus has *barbarizein*, ' to behave or speak like a
Barbarian ', and a later Greek author uses this verb in the sense
' to speak gibberish—unintelligible nonsense ' ; *barbarismos*
(whence our *barbarism* : cf. **solecism**) appears in various
Greek writers, in the two senses ' a foreign use ', hence a
foreign mode, of speech ; hence, a misuse of one's own
language.

But neither in the recension of ' Liddell & Scott ' for the
several Greek words, nor in ' Lewis & Short ' for *barbarus*, nor
yet in The OED for the aforementioned English words, do we
find a forthright theory of the origin of the basic *barbaros*,
although The OED does commit itself to the statement that
' the Greek word had probably a primary reference to speech '.
Skeat, however, dares—after G. Curtius (*Greek Etymology*, 1876)
—to say that ' the name was applied by Greeks to foreigners to
express the strange sound of their language ' ; and Weekley
goes further : ' With reference to unintelligible speech (*bar-bar*) ;
cf. *Hottentot* '—*Hottentot* being a name given by the Dutch to
these aboriginals on account, as a Dutch lexicographer of 1670

explains, of their 'clucking speech'—speech imitated, in one of its essentials, by the very word *Hottentot*.

But the clearest theory of all—so clear, direct, forcible that it almost certainly contains the true explanation—is propounded, cursorily, by Professor Lionel W. Lyde, in *The Continent of Asia* (2nd edition, 1938), in the following passage, which occurs in the chapter entitled 'The Heart of Asia' :— 'The "Turks" came to "High Tartary"'—approximately, Zungaria—'from the steppes of Northern Mongolia. . . . But in the early days the rich and fertile Hwang-ho basin was "very near", and supplied all that the raiding instincts of the tribes wanted; and it was even the Hun control of the *natural* Silk Route [—see **silk**—] *via* Hami and Urumtsi that forced the Chinese to find the *unnatural* ones along the northern and the—still safer—southern margins of the Tarim basin, and that suggested to them the name of "*Tar-Tar*" (exactly the Greek "*Bar-Bar*-os") for the intruders.' (Cf. **tartar,** q.v.)

Reinforcing that quotation is this from Patrick Carleton's valuable *Buried Empires* (1939) :—'They'—the Indus Valley race conquered, ca. 1500 B.C., by the Aryans—'spoke the non-Aryan tongue, and the Aryans frequently applied to them the epithet *mridhravachah*, "hostile-talking", which we may compare with the Greek name for foreigners, *barbaroi*, "jargon-talkers", "stammerers".'

Greek *barbaros*, therefore, would seem to connote either 'unintelligible' or 'uncouth; foreign'—or both 'unintelligible' and 'uncouth'. And in the sounds *bar-bar* and *ta-ta* (pronounced *tah-tah*) or *tar-tar*, as used thus derisively by the Greeks and the Chinese respectively, there may be an implication of the baby-talk sounds, cf. *pa-pa* (cf. *papa*), *ma-ma* (cf. *mamma*), *ta-ta*, *ba-ba* (cf. *baby*, *babe*; *babble*), and so forth : these infantile reduplicated vocables have, for thousands of years, been present in many Asiatic and European languages.

The *Barbarians*, so *barbarous* of speech, were, like the *Tatars*, 'The Unintelligibles' or 'The Uncouth' or perhaps even 'The Babies' (or at least 'The Babe-like').

Postscript. Not identical but at least illustratively similar are the two slang terms, *Wee-Wees* (or *Wi-Wis*), 'the French', so named by New Zealanders and Australians, ca. 1850–1900, because of their addiction to *oui! oui!*, and *Ki-kis*, that American name for Russian-Jew immigrants which sprang from the fact that so many of their surnames ended in -*ki*,—an appellation that led to the low-slang *Kike*, 'a Jew'.

Barbera. An Italian red wine. 'We ate spaghetti and a great deal of bread and drank a tolerable Barbera,' Eric Ambler,

Cause for Alarm, 1939. Having failed to ascertain the origin, I postulate a trade-name or a grower's surname.

barcelona = *Barcelona nut*. Barcelona, the most important commercial and industrial city of Spain, a great Mediterranean seaport, stands in a region noted for its vines and its fruit trees. The name seems to be an elaboration of *Barcina* and the place is supposed to have been founded by the Carthaginian, Hamilcar *Barca*, about 230 B.C.

barége, now usually *barège*, is either a gauze-like fabric for women's dresses, veils, etc., made originally at *Baréges* (now *Barèges*), a large French village situated in the *département* of the Hautes-Pyrénées, or a medicinal water drawn from the sulphurous thermal springs for which Barèges is famous.

barlow is short for *Barlow knife*, a United States one-bladed jack-knife, so named from its maker. ' Barlow pen-knives ' occurs at least as early as 1779 in the printed records of America ; ' Mark Twain ' and Joel Chandler Harris in the 1870's–90's were still attesting its excellence. (See especially The OED and The DAE.)

barney, in slang, means ' a fight, a " row " ; nonsense, foolery ; a pre-arranged sporting—especially, boxing—contest '. Prob-ably it represents *Barney*, diminutive of *Barnaby* (and *Barnabas*) ; *Barney* is a common name among Irishmen : Irishmen love a ' free-for-all ', foolery, a ' leg-pull ' : compare **paddy.**

barnumism ; barnumize, transitive. (To subject to) adver-tisement or talk that is showy, boastful, bombastic—pretentious **ballyhoo.** From Phineas Taylor Barnum (1810–91), Ameri-can showman, who became famous in the U.S.A. in 1842, in Britain several years later ; in 1871 opened at Brooklyn ' The Greatest Show on Earth ' ; in 1881 combined with Bailey to form the Barnum & Bailey Circus ; remained in the circus business until his death.

barrack—' to express noisy displeasure at the course of a game ' —originated in Australia ; both the practice and the word are Australian. In the 1880's and early 1890's, *barrackers* was the Melbourne term for those rough teams which used to play football on the vacant land near Victoria *Barracks* on the St Kilda Road. (With thanks to Mr Guy Innes, letter of March 1, 1944.)

41

barukhzy is another name—introduced into England in the 1890's—for the *Afghan dog* or *hound* (see **afghan**). From the Barakzi tribe, which, in Afghanistan, either first or at least notably reared it.

baskerville, or **B—,** is the printing-type designed by—or a slight modification of the type designed by—John Baskerville (1706–75). A Birmingham man, he began as ' stone carver, writing master, and manufacturer of japanned goods '; feeling his way. It was not until 1750 that he commenced his studies in typefounding, but he soon became known as a pioneer in the manufacture of fine paper and inks for printing, and by 1757 he was printer to the University of Cambridge. His printings of Milton (1758), The Bible (1763), Virgil in 1757 and other Latin authors in the decade-or-so of 1758–68 earned him a well-deserved reputation. The *baskerville* combines dignity with grace, notable legibility with beauty. I am proud to know that by my use of both the roman and the italic in a number of Scholartis publications in 1927–31, I did something toward a repopularizing of Baskerville types.

basque, in dressmaking, almost certainly comes from a Basque fashion (originally, male), although W, despite the evidence of the French *basquine*, ' a Spanish farthingale ', thinks that probably it doesn't. The word *Basque* is connected with ' the Bay of *Biscay* ' and derives from Late Latin *Vasco* (*-onis*).

bass, or **Bass** (still the more usual way to write it), is short for *Bass beer*. The Bass family established their brewery at Burton-on-Trent in 1777 : it was Michael Thomas Bass (1799–1884) who made it a household name, and his son Michael Arthur was in 1886 raised to the peerage as Baron Burton (cf. **Burton . . .** in the subsidiary list). In ' Nonsense Botany ' (*Laughable Lyrics*, 1877) Edward Lear depicts a bibulous bloom that he names *Bassia Palealensis*.

' One double scotch, one guinness, one bass and a Starboard Light [*crème de menthe*] for Gwyneth,' Philip MacDonald, *The Rynox Mystery*, 1930.

bastille. The use of the word in Britain for ' prison ' is explained by the notoriety rather than by the fame of the Bastille, that fortress-prison of Paris which originated in the not very impressive form of two towers on each side of the Porte St Antoine but which, in its historic form, had eight towers. On the outbreak of the French Revolution, the Bastille was stormed and

42

destroyed. July 14, 1789, is commemorated in the most popular holiday of the French year.

Originally, in French, *bastille* signified any bastion-defended fortress—in which there might, or might not be (but usually there was), a dungeon. Political prisoners were sent there, and thence they escaped more rarely than Russian political prisoners from far north-east Siberia. The word derives from Old French *bastir* (Modern French *bâtir*), ' to build '—or rather, from Provençal *bastida*, ' a building ', itself from Provençal *bastire*, ' to build '. The more remote etymology is obscure; Webster, however, credibly adduces Low Latin *bastare*, ' to suffice ; to carry '—from Greek *bastazein*, ' to raise ; hence, to carry '.

From the English use, the underworld derived *steel*, ' a prison '.

batiste, originally lawn or fine linen, came to mean a fine, similar-textured cotton fabric ; a rather later sense is that of a fine cotton, impregnated with caoutchouc, used for compresses and antiseptic dressings. The word doubtless represents the French name, *Baptiste* : and tradition has it that one Baptiste of Cambrai was the first to make it, so long ago as the 13th Century. Compare **cambric** and **lawn.**

baud, ' one dot per second ' in telegraphic signalling, is short for, or rather derived from, Monsieur Jean Baudot, who (1845–1903) was a well-known French inventor. Indeed, he invented the *baudot*, an early form of the teletype.

bauxite. ' It interested me, to see if a mid-ocean volcanic group of the Fijian type mightn't show outcroppings of bauxite, perhaps cinnabar,' John W. Vandercook, *Murder in Fiji*, 1936. ' The manufacture of aluminium from the Aquila bauxite,' L. W. Lyde, *Europe*, 4th ed., 1930 : bauxite being, in point of fact, the chief commercial source of aluminium.

From *Baux* (in France)—the Baux hills above Arles, to be precise—where it was first extensively mined.

bawbee, whether in its English senses—' sixpence ' in the time of Charles the Second, and the later ' halfpenny ' (compare the slang *bawbees*, ' cash, money '), or in its original sense, a Scotch coin, worth about three-halfpence, first issued in or about 1542, probably commemorates the Laird of Sillebawby, a mint-master of Scotland. ' Another coin was called an *Atchison*, from a mint-master who is coupled with the above in Treasury records ' (W).

43

bayonet, which has existed in English since the 17th Century, has, since Tabourot des Accords in 1614, been traditionally associated with, and derived from the name of, the city of *Bayonne*, ' though ', as W rightly points out, ' proof is lacking ' ; Webster, however, says, without reservation, ' Because bayonets were first made at Bayonne ', a statement requiring this modification, that *bayon(n)ette* (the early form of the French *baïonnette*) originally signified ' such a dagger as could be attached to the end of a gun ', Skeat remarking that these daggers were first made at Bayonne. To refuse to accept the *Bayonne* origin of *bayonet* would be to carry a healthy scepticism to the point of ineptitude ; it is difficult to close one's mind to the viability, the cogency, of the evidence afforded by Cotgrave's *French-English Dictionary*, 1611, and that adduced by Hatzfeld & Darmesteter. The truth is that whereas there exists no direct evidence, the weight of indirect evidence is very considerable : and for the sake of those whose knowledge of French history is even less than mine, it is worth recalling that Bayonne, near the south-west corner of France (a strategic position of some importance), was for centuries a famous fortified city, ' though often besieged, . . . never taken ' (Chisholm, 1895).

B.B.C., as adjective. Literally, ' belonging to, connected with the British Broadcasting Corporation,' it has, via the nuance ' characteristic of the B.B.C.', come, among its opponents, to have, in such phrases as ' a B.B.C. accent ' and ' a B.B.C. voice ', the pejorative connotation of ' affected or over-cultured [*can* one be?] or even effeminate '. The B.B.C. aims at the cultivation of nothing more dreadful, nothing more dangerous, than what philologists call ' Southern Standard English '.
  ' " Now the murderer has been bumped off. Whodunit? " —" You mean by whom? "—" Don't be so B.B.C. I mean, who done it," insisted Norman,' Berkeley Gray, *Mr Ball of Fire*, 1946.

Beatrice, whom the one-year-older Dante Alighieri (1265–1321) ' worshipped from afar ', is thought to have been Bice Portinari. Certainly she was Dante's idol of womanhood : and she appears both in the *Vita Nuova* and in the *Divina Commedia*. Perhaps the two best interpretations of Dante's Beatrice are Charles Williams's *The Portrait of Beatrice* and Giovanni Papini's *Dante Vivo*. Literally ' Bringer of Joy ', *Beatrice* has become generic for ' a (beautiful) young woman regarded as the inspirer of great literature or great art '. Compare **Egeria.**

' This [Late Medieval] poetry of love, from its most heavenly
flight in Dante's chaste worship of another man's wife, to the
more usual idealization of courtly adultery, has seldom anything to do with marriage,' G. M. Trevelyan, *Social History of
England*, 1942. ' The Beatrice of temporal conditions became
the " beata Beatrice " . . . of the soul,' Laurie Magnus.

Beau Brummel(l); adjective : **Brummellian;** abstract derivative noun : **Brummelism.** G. R. Brummell (1778–1840)
was called—and usually spelt—' Beau Brummel ', hence the
normal figurative term for ' a leader of male fashion ; hence,
as nearly always in the 20th Century, a dandy, a fop ';
Brummell (that *arbiter elegantiarum* who was more famed for his
manners than for his courtesy) led the fashion in the Regency
world of London and, in the season, Bath.
    ' He was a young dance-hall Brummel, except that his face
was different,' W. R. Burnett, *The Giant Swing*, 1933.
    ' The Chinese Beau Brummell glanced at me again, smiled
secretly, and whispered a word that I could not clearly hear,'
Hendrik de Leeuw, *Cities of Sin*, 1934.

beaujolais. See the quotation at **burgundy.**
    Beaujolais, a type of burgundy, comes from the Beaujolais
district of the *département* of the Lyonnais : ' pellucid Beaujolais '
(' Palinurus ', *The Unquiet Grave*, 1945).
    Compare **beaune.**

beaumontage or **beaumontague,** a composition used by
cabinet makers to conceal holes, cracks, and other flaws in
wood-work or metal-work, does not combine French *beau*
(which it is not) and *montage* (nor is it that). Apparently the
word has been derived from Elie de *Beaumont* (1798–1851), a
noted French geologist, whose ghost still shrieks at the stain
thus cast on his escutcheon.

beaune. The quotation at **burgundy** will help : compare ' the
rich vineyards of Dijon and Beaune and other towns of the
Côte d'Or slopes ' (L. W. Lyde, *Man and His Markets*, 1896).
    This type of burgundy is produced in the Beaune district of
the *département* of the Côte d'Or ; the ' hub ' of that district is
the town of *Beaune*.
    Compare **beaujolais.**

bechamel is short for *bechamel sauce*, itself a popularizing of
Béchamel sauce, which represents the French *sauce Béchamel*.
This rich, white sauce is said to have been devised by a steward

45

of Louis XIV (' Le Roi Soleil ', as he liked to be called) : Louis de Béchamel, who happened to be a *marquis* and a renowned epicure.

bedlam. ' For a moment the [court-]room was plunged in an abyss of surprise ; and then the walls cracked, and Bedlam piled on Babel, so that Judge Newbold pounded with his third gavel of the trial, and the bailiff ran up and down shushing people ' (Ellery Queen, *Calamity Town*, 1942).—Concerning Major Longden's exhibition of Picasso and Matisse paintings at the Victoria and Albert Museum, late in 1945 : ' Having opened the doors, he watches . . . while the whole of London rushes in . . . and he listens to a bedlam of talk . . . *about art*. That is . . . his extraordinary achievement—to get London crazy about art ' (Maurice Collis, ' Art '—*The Observer*, Dec. 23, 1945).

In 1547, the Hospital of St Mary of *Bethlehem* (Middle English *Bethleem*), founded three centuries earlier, was converted into a state lunatic asylum ; even before the conversion, the pronunciation had become *Bedlam*. In the 16th–17th Centuries, a lunatic asylum was, literally and figuratively, a ' mad-house ' : noisy, disorderly, haphazardly conducted : crazy.

bedlamite, n. and adj., derives from the preceding. ' A bedlamite inferno of sound ', Warren Stuart, *The Sword and the Net*, 1942 (a fine war-time thriller).

bedlington = *B. terrier*. ' That sweet little guy who looks like a Bedlington terrier is good,' Erle Stanley Gardner, *The Case of the Careless Kitten*, 1944.

This short-haired, broad-nostrilled terrier with a flesh-coloured nose, takes its name from the Northumberland town of Bedlington, situated on the Blyth. It became popular in the 1870's and has retained its popularity.

Beëlzebub (' a devil incarnate ' or ' a very king among devils ') owes its modern sense to The New Testament : ' This fellow doth not cast out devils, but by Beelzebub the prince of the devils ' (*Matthew*, xii, 24). In The Old Testament he is ' Baal-zebub the god of Ekron ' (2 *Kings*, i, 2). The Hebrew *ba'al-z'bub*, ' Fly-Lord ' or ' Lord of Flies ', has come to us via Greek and Latin. Compare **Baal** in the Appendix.

before one can (or **could**) **say Jack Robinson.** See **Jack** . . .

beg, beggar. In Middle English, *beggen* (' to beg ') comes from Anglo-French *begger*, itself from Old French *begard*, ' a

46

mendicant'; and the Old French word represents a Low German one, which Webster thinks to be probably from Middle Dutch *beggaert*, 'a mendicant'. But Old French *begard*, as W proposes, may well come direct from Medieval Latin *Begardus*, 'a member of mendicant order founded (early 13 cent.) in Netherlands, in imitation of earlier *béguines* . . ., who were of the rule of *Lambert de Bègue* (Liège, 12 cent.)' and the Middle Dutch *beggaert* may equally well be a cognate descendant of the Medieval Latin word; the latter occurs in the *Glossarium* of medieval latinity (1678) as, in the plural, *begehardi* (or *beghardi*) for men and *Beginae* for women. In the name *Lambert le Bègue*, the last element may represent the locality now focussed in the Gironde town of *Bègles*: 'Lambert (the man) of Bègue'.

begonia. 'The rose begonias made a solid pale mass under the front windows and pansies a blur of colour around the base of a white acacia in bloom,' Raymond Chandler, *Farewell, My Lovely*, 1940.

The genus *begonia* was thus named as a compliment to Michel Bégon (1638–1710), a French administrator in the French West Indies and elsewhere: he was famed for his patronage of science.

beguine is a member of that Netherlands lay sisterhood which is not bound by vows; and the word transliterates, in French, the Latin *Begina*. For further details, see **beg.**

behemoth. 'Here was John Dingbat O'Berta, bantam sidekick of the behemoth' (Fred D. Pasley, *Al Capone*, 1931).

Literally 'a mighty beast'—cf. **leviathan**—and derivatively 'any powerful and very large animal', *behemoth* is a Hebrew word, an intensive plural, expressive of (great) size, of *behemah*, 'a beast, an animal'.

'Behold now behemoth . . .; he eateth grass as an ox. . . . He is the chief of the ways of God. . . . He lieth under the shady trees, in the covert of the reed, and fens. . . . Behold, he drinketh up a river. . . . His nose pierceth through snares,' *Job*, xl, 15–24: apparently a hippopotamus.

bel. 'A unit for the logarithmic expression of ratios of power, and also ratios of voltage or current, in wire or radio communication' (Webster). This thoroughly Common Noun rather obviously derives from Alexander Graham Bell (1847–1922), the inventor of the telephone. Bell was not, as the *Encyclopaedia Britannica* somewhat unnecessarily claims, an American:

he left Scotland in 1870 for Canada and did not arrive in ' the States ' until 1873.

belcher, a handkerchief spotted with blue and white and known to the 19th-Century vulgar as a ' bird's-eye wipe ' (neatly descriptive), honours the memory of a great English prize-fighter, Jem or Jim *Belcher*, who (1781–1811) was extremely successful until, in 1803, he lost an eye and, soon after, became —as is the way of retired ' pugs '—a publican. W notes that *Belcher* is a Picard form of French *bel* (= *beau*) + *sire* (= *sieur*), ' fine gentleman '.

belga, the Belgian unit of exchange (five francs), is short for *Belga pecunia*, ' Belgian money ', where *Belga* is the feminine of *Belgus*, itself from *Belgae*, a tribe of which we hear in Caesar and Tacitus ; the Greeks had already named them the *Belgai*. In Liddell & Scott it has been noted that, in Lower Germany, *Balge* is ' a low, swampy region '—compare the origin of **Maglemosian.**

bellarmine, now only historical, was a drinking-jug designed by Dutch Protestants as a caricature of Roberto Bellarmino (1542–1621), better known as Robert Bellarmine, best known as Cardinal Bellarmine. He became a cardinal in 1599, after working on the revision of the Vulgate—yet another great Jesuit scholar. But he forsook scholarship for controversy, and he is famed for his dispute with James the First of England.

bendigo, ' a rough fur cap ', was sporting slang of ca. 1840–1900. The Nottingham prize-fighter, William Thompson (1811–89), went by the ring-name of *Bendigo*. His first challenge was in 1835 ; when he gave up pugilism, he turned evangelist. He affected this sort of headgear. (Ernest Weekley, *The Romance of Names*.)

benedick, benedict. ' *Benedick*, not *Benedict*, is the spelling in [Shakespeare's] *Much Ado* [*about Nothing*], and should always be the spelling when the name is used generically for a confirmed or captured bachelor ; but *Benedict* is often used . . . either (and probably) in ignorance, or on the irrelevant ground that Shakespeare might have done well to use the more etymo-logical form in -ct,' thus the inimitable H. W. Fowler in that evergreen, *A Dictionary of Modern English Usage*. Note too that the latinized form is *benedict*, the English form either *Benedick* or *benedick*. Literally, ' the blessèd ', the Latin *Benedictus* occurs,

48

in appropriate shapes, in all the Romance languages—and even in German (*Benedikt*).

benedictine or **Bénédictine.** 'One of the oldest—if not actually the oldest, and one of the most widely renowned Liqueurs in the world. It is distilled at Fécamp in Normandy, and its origin has been traced to the Benedictine monks of Fécamp, as far back as 1510 . . . the label bears the initials D.O.M. (*Deo optimo maximo*) of the Benedictine Order. Bénédictine is sometimes referred to as *D.O.M.* Liqueur,' André Simon, 1946. St Benedict founded the order in the year 529. (See preceding entry.) Compare **chartreuse.**

bengaline. 'That night [in ca. 1890] she had put on the dinner dress that he always noticed and approved—heliotrope bengaline with jewelled insertions,' George Blake, *The Westering Sun*, 1946. An adoption from French and a derivative from *Bengal*.

benjamin; benjie. A *benjamin* is a kind of overcoat; *benjie* or *benny* is a slangy form. As W has remarked, *benjamin* is 'probably a playful variation of the earlier *joseph*', the reference being to the facts that in The Bible, Benjamin is youngest brother to Joseph (*Genesis*, xxxv–xlv), and that Joseph had 'a coat of many colours' (*Genesis*, xxxvii, 3). 'And it came to pass, as her soul was in departing, (for she died) that she called his name Ben-oni,' glossed, 'That is, *The son of my sorrow*'; 'but his father called him Benjamin,' glossed 'That is, *The son of the right hand*'—the references being to the literal meanings of the Hebrew names; Neil Bell, in *Child of My Sorrow*, 1944, effectively alludes to this Biblical passage.

Derivatively in the U.S.A., *benjamin* is the plant otherwise known as the wake-robin. In the *benjamin bush* (or *tree*), *benjamin* is a folk-etymological corruption of *benjoin*, the earlier shape of *benzoin*; the bush or tree is the spicebush or spicewood.

benzoin, a balsamic resin from a tree abounding in the East Indies, including Sumatra, was earlier *benjoin*, adopted direct from French, which got it either from Spanish *benjui* or from Portuguese *beijoim*—or perhaps from both. The Iberian Peninsulars took it from Italian *benzoi*, earlier *lo-benzoi*, the *lo* being dropped because it was misjudged to be an article like the Arabic *al*. Now, *lo-benzoi* transliterates the Arabic *luban jawi*, literally 'frankincense of Jawa', *Jawa* being not Java but an early name of Sumatra. (Webster.)

From *benzoin* comes *benzene*.

N.I.W.—C

bergamasca, the Italian—the original—form; **bergamasque**
the French; **bergomask,** the English. 'Will it please you to
see the epilogue, or to hear a bergomask dance between two o
our company?': *A Midsummer Night's Dream* (v, 360).
    'This was originally a peasant dance from the distric
around Bergamo in North Italy' (Dr Percy Scholes): *danze*
bergamasca, dance of Bergamo.

bergamot. 'He had cultivated his garden. Literally and in
Marvell's sense: as if his highest lot to plant the bergamot
And in Voltaire's sense too,' 'Michael Innes', *The Secre*
Vanguard, 1940.—'Bergamots and limes, as refreshing and
fragrant as they are decorative,' Osbert Sitwell, *Sing High*
Sing Low!, 1944.
    It is generally assumed that this *bergamot,* like that which
means an essence, a scent, derives its name from *Bergamo* in
Lombardy: only the 'essence' *bergamot* derives from the
Italian town, where it was manufactured.

berlin or, less usually, **berline,** was a carriage introduced, ca
1670, by an officer attached to the service of the Elector o
Brandenburg. It is said to have been used first in Berlin
compare **landau.** The spelling *berline* is customary for the
sense 'an enclosed automobile having at the rear of the driver'.
seat a glass partition with, usually, one movable window
(Webster): compare **sedan** in its derivative sense. With o
without a capital, *berlin* is also short for *Berlin glove, Berlin wear*
Berlin wool, Berlin work, etc.

bertha, berthe. 'Such a quaint, frilly gown it was, with tiny
satin rosebuds sewn into the lace bertha,' Harry Hervey, *Schoo*
for Eternity, 1942.
    A *bertha,* or *berthe,* is a sort of cape, or a deep collar, dependen
from the neckline of a dress (contrast **basque**) and often made
of lace. The original form is *berthe,*—the 'originator' being
Queen Berthe, Charlemagne's mother, who was famed for her
modesty, whereas *bertha* reflects either Germanic or Latin
influence, the German *Bertha* deriving from Old High German
Perahta, whence *Perchta,* a Teutonic goddess of the earth and its
fruitfulness.—But *bertha* (or *Bertha*), usually *big Bertha,* the gun
with which, in 1918, the Germans shelled Paris, comes from
Bertha Krupp of Essen, the name being a translation of *die dick*
Bertha.

besant, bezant. This gold coin, current in Europe from the
6th to the 16th Century, occurs in Wycliffe's translation

of The New Testament—'Lord, the besaunt hath wunne [won: gained] ten besauntis'. The meaning is, 'coin of Byzantium'; and, with suitable variations, this holds good for *besant* (etc.), 'a flat disk used ornamentally in architecture' and, in heraldry, 'a small flat circle' (of gold), with adjective *bezantee*, 'set with besants'. *Besant* comes direct from Old French *besant* (variant, *besan*), from Latin *Byzantius* ('Byzantine'), from *Byzantium*, the city so named, from Greek *Buzantion* —later Constantinople (from *Constantinopolis*, the city of Constantine), now—as always among the Turks—Istanbul (from Greek *eis tēn polin*, '(in)to the city'); the Turks used to call it also Stamboul. The name *Buzantion* may derive from the Greek *buzēn*, 'close-pressed': 'a compact place or city'.

See also **Byzantine** in the subsidiary list.

bessemer = steel Bessemer-processed. 'Guaranteed . . . to go through the toughest Bessemer as though it were cheese,' John G. Brandon, *The Crooked Five!*, 1939.

Sir Harry Bessemer (1813–98), inventor and engineer, took out patents—the first was in 1855—for the manufacture of steel by de-carbonizing melted pig-iron by means—here is the secret of *the bessemer process*—of a blast of air. In 1859, at Sheffield, he established a manufactory specializing, first in guns and then in steel rails.

bethel; bethesda. (Or capital initials.) These words are synonyms for 'a nonconformist chapel'—the former in England, the latter in Wales; the former means 'house of God' (Hebrew *bēth-ēl*: *Genesis*, xxviii, 17, 19, 'This is none other but the house of God. . . . And he called the name of that place Beth-el') and the latter means 'house of mercy' (*John*, v, 2, 'There is at Jerusalem by the sheep market a pool, which is called in the Hebrew tongue Bethesda, having five porches'). Cf. **Ebenezer.**

'An institution which boomed in Victorian days was the "Penny Reading". For an admission fee of a copper or two you could spend an edifying evening in the local Bethel listening to a reading-aloud from English literature ancient and modern,' W. E. Williams, 'Radio'—in *The Observer*, Dec. 16, 1945.

betony, especially the purple (or woodland) betony of Europe, and derivatively any of the various species belonging to the American genus Teucrium, has a name adapted from French *bétoine*, from Latin *betonica*. Now, *betonica* is a phonetic reshaping of Pliny's *vettonica*, the adjective corresponding to *Vettones*, itself a variant of *Vectones*, a tribe of Lusitania, in the

51

modern Salamanca (Spain) and Estremadura (Portugal)
The name *Vectones* being Latin, the tribe seems originally to
have been famous as carriers (ultimately *vehere*, to carry).

betty, whether ' a man occupying himself with womanish matter
or work ' or ' a flask for oil ' or ' a short crowbar used by
thieves ', is communal for *Betty*, the pet-name of *Elizabeth* : with
the first compare *Betty*, formerly a very common name for
maids-of-all-work ; the thieves' term, which has been bestowed
on account of the usefulness of the article, should be compared
with **jemmy** (see especially my *A Dictionary of the Underworld*).

beulah or **B—**. *Beulah* often appears, symbolically, in the mystic
poems of William Blake. In full, *land of Beulah*. In Bunyan's
Pilgrim's Progress, 1678, the Land of Beulah symbolizes the
Christian's spiritual and mental tranquillity : hence (*land of
Beulah*, or, to take the logical linguistic step, *beulah*, has become
synonymous with ' land, or place, where one finds and feels
peace and quiet '. Bunyan doubtless alluded to *Isaiah*, lxii, 4
' Thou [Jewry personified] shalt no more be termed Forsaken
neither shall thy land any more be termed desolate : but thou
shalt be called Hepzibah and thy land Beulah '.

bezant, or occasionally **bezzant**. See **besant.—bezantee**
See **besant.**

biblical. There is a growing tendency to spell the word with
a lower-case initial even where the meaning is ' of—in—in
respect of—*The Bible* '. But would it not, because preclusive
of ambiguity, be wiser to reserve the small *b* for such senses as
' patriarchal ', ' primitive ', ' of a simple dignity ', ' austere '
In a passage concerning a French officer serving in North
Africa and of the Moors he so relentlessly yet chivalrously
opposed, Antoine de Saint-Euxpéry, in that unforgettable book
—loyally translated by Lewis Galantière—*Wind, Sand and Stars*
(1939), has written that ' For years he had accepted their rule
as his rules. He had staked his life against theirs. He had
slept with his head pillowed on their rocks. Like them he had
known Biblical nights of stars and wind in the course of the
ceaseless pursuit ' : there, a direct, unequivocal allusion to
The Bible is intended, not merely a synonym of ' majestic '.
    The origin of *The Bible*, hence of *biblical*, has nowhere been
more neatly set forth than in Stanley Cook's lucid, richly
informative, fair-minded book, *An Introduction to the Bible*, 1945
(Pelican Books). ' Round about the twelfth century B.C.,' he
notes, ' an Egyptian envoy, Wen-Amon by name, visited the

king of the Phoenician town of Byblus. . . . Now, Byblus, to-day the small village of Gebal, was one of the oldest cities of Syria and Palestine. It had been long in close contact with Egypt and, as a trading centre, among the articles of import it included papyrus, a word possibly of Egyptian origin, whence through the Latin comes the word " paper ". . . . From Byblus the Greeks called papyrus *bublos* or *biblos*; and from the plural [*biblia*] of the diminutive *biblion* is derived our word Bible, properly " (the) books "' ; whence that synonym for The Bible: *The Book*, or *God's Book*. ' In Latin the word [*biblia*] was subsequently treated as a feminine singular, and . . . English spellings *bibul*, *bibil*, etc., date from the fourteenth century.'

Compare the origin of **parchment**.

biddy, ' a bed-maker; a woman that cleans up ' : an Irish maid-servant : *Biddy* from *Bridget*, a favourite name for Irish girls : Saint *Brigid*, highly regarded in Ireland : Erse *Brighid* or *Brigit* : compare French *Brigitte* and Italian *Brigida* : all, deriving ultimately from Sanskrit *bṛhati*, ' lofty; august; mighty '.

Shakespeare's—and many later writers'—*biddy*, ' a hen or a chicken ', is a mere affectionate personification.

biedermeier (or **biedermeyer**); also **B—**. Noun or adjective, designating a German style of furniture (1815–48) resembling, though simpler than, its original, ' French Empire '. Named from Gottlieb *Biedermeier*, the imaginary, yet very philistine, author of poems actually written by Ludwig Eichrodt, the pseudonym of Rudolf Rodt (1827–92), who, a jurist, wrote humorous poems that, published in 1848 and 1853, had a considerable vogue.

biggin has two distinct sets of senses, two distinct origins :—As ' hood ' or ' cap ' or ' coif of a sergeant at law ', it derives from *beguine* : for the etymology, see **beg.** The same applies to *biggonet*, ' a woman's hood or cap, with flaps over the ears '— via French *beguinet* (a diminutive).

The second sense (strictly, it constitutes a separate word), ' a coffee percolator ' of a type current about 1790–1830, comes from the surname of its inventor, one Mr Biggin; The OED, in a quotation from *The Gentleman's Magazine* of 1803, informs us that the original form was *coffee biggin*; by 1817, *biggin* was synonymous with ' coffee pot '.

bignonia (not seldom confused with **begonia**) is the flower of the plant so named—a woody vine of North America and Japan;

and it has been named in honour of the Abbé Bignon, librarian to King Louis XV, who reigned from 1715 to 1774. W, however, says that he was librarian to Louis XIV and that the name was given, ca. 1700, by Tournefort (1656–1708), a French botanist: and W is usually right.

bigophone or **bigotphone.** An improved mirliton (a 'Tommy Talker') introduced by one Monsieur Bigot of France and very popular ca. 1890–1914. (*The Oxford Companion to Music.*)

bigot, a (superstitious) hypocrite, hence one who is obstinately and intolerantly devoted to his own religious sect or political party, was in Old French bestowed at least once upon the Normans. The word *bigot* is a gallicizing of a Teutonic oath equivalent to the English *by God!* and is therefore a close parallel to the medieval and early modern French name—as, for instance, in Villon—for an Englishman, *godon* or *god(d)am* (for *God damn it!*).

In this matter I range myself with Webster and W; The OED flouts the oath-origin; Skeat suggests that the French *bigot* may derive from *Beguttae* of the Order of St Augustine (see, e.g., Ducange) or at least that the modern sense has been determined by the influence of the *Beguttae* (or *Béguines*: see **beg**). In the influencing, Skeat is probably right, but the dates rather hinder acceptance of a direct derivation.

bilbo (sword). The variants *bilbow, bilboa, bilboe,* make it fairly clear that the origin is, as Blount affirmed in his mid-17th-Century dictionary and as Moll re-affirmed in his Geography, 1701, the Spanish city of *Bilbao,* which has for centuries been known in England as *Bilboa.* 'The town owes all its prosperity to the neighbouring deposits of valuable iron ore, which have been known since the time of the Romans' (Chisholm).
Compare **toledo.**

bilboes is a plural word, meaning a long bar with sliding shackles and with a bolt at the end, to foot-confine prisoners or offenders, especially aboard ship: and it not unnaturally has the same origin as the preceding term (q.v.): compare in any good dictionary the various derivative senses of *iron* (e.g., to put a man into irons) and *steel* ('Three inches of steel, and you're dead!'). Like the preceding, it occurs in Shakespeare—and earlier. The fact that it antedates the Armada by thirty-or-so years merely disproves the story that bilboes came from Spain with the Armada.

54

bilharziasis (or **iosis**) is a disease, caused by the *bilharzia*, ' a genus of trematode worms parasitic in blood . . . one of the most dangerous human parasites, especially in Egypt' (Webster), the parasite being named after Theodor *Bilharz*, the German physician who discovered the parasite in 1851. The name was devised in his honour by T. S. Cobbold (1828–86), an English biologist well known in his day.

Bill Sikes is often used for ' professional burglar'. As Chief Inspector (of the C.I.D.) W. C. Gough remarked, in 1927, ' since Charles Dickens created the typical criminal of his time in Bill Sikes, the source from which the professional crook is drawn has continued progressively to rise' (*From Kew Observatory to Scotland Yard*). As Oliver Twist asked for more, so Bill Sikes took more, in *Oliver Twist* (1837–38). Dickens knew the London underworld rather well—cf. **Fagin.**

billingsgate is obsolete for ' foul-mouthed person' but extant for the originating sense, ' coarsely abusive language; foul-mouthed vituperation'. At first it was written with a ca·tal *B*, to denote its origin in the Billingsgate fish-market, held near the ancient Billingsgate—a gate (below London Bridge) in the old wall of London; mentioned in ca. 1250. That is, Billing's Gate, although we know extremely little about the builder or, perhaps, a famous burgher. ' Famous for rhetoric since the 17th Century,' as W remarks.

Compare **solecism.**

billy. In all its senses—e.g., Australian *billy* (short for *billy-can*), an open tin can used as a kettle in camping out and at picnics; American *billy*, a policeman's truncheon; obsolete English *billy*, a highwayman's club—this term almost certainly derives from the font-name William. All the commonest font-names have, by their very predominance, generated several common nouns: cf. **bob, charley, cuthbert, doll, jack** (also **john**), **jane, jimmy, moll, nanny, tom, will.**

billy, silly; billy goat. A billy goat is the opposite of, and complement to, a **nanny** goat: *Bill* in contradistinction to *Nan*. With *silly billy* (originally *silly Billy*) compare the synonymous *silly Johnny*; *silly* generated *Billy*, precisely as in the American *hill Billy* (become *hill billy*), a rustic of the hill country, *hill* suggested the rhyming *Bill*, soon affection'd to *Billy*.

billyboy. East Coast English for a buoy. Apparently *buoy* suggested *boy*, and *boy*, ' personified ', naturally added an

55

alliterative *Billy*; *Billy boy* became *Billyboy*, which soon learned to drop the capital letter.

billycock (**hat**). Originally a *bully-cocked hat* (tilted at an aggressive angle), it became a *bully-cock* (*hat*) and then, by personification, *Billy-cock* (*hat*), then *Billycock*, then *billycock*. The same philological process, therefore, is involved here as in the preceding entry.

billyho (or **billyo**), **like**. ' It's raining like billy(h)o ! ' The origin of this intensive is said by The OED to be obscure. Probably it is euphemistic for ' like the Devil ' : the Devil's name has so many euphemistic synonyms ! The *-ho* is a variation of *-o*, so common a suffix in unconventional English.

Bingley. See **airedale.**

bipontine or **B—**. An edition of an Ancient Classic printed, during the 18th Century, at *Zweibrucken* (the town of the two bridges), latinized as *Bipontium*, in Bavaria. Zweibrucken, known in France as *Deux Ponts*, stands at the confluence of the rivers Hornbach and Schwarzbach.

birrellism or **B—**; **birreligion** (now only historical). A cursory comment, kindly though shrewd and pungent, on men and things or on life in general ; the political meaning and significance of Birrell's Educational Bill of 1906.

Augustine Birrell (1850–1933), barrister, entered Parliament in 1889 and became Chief Secretary for Ireland (1907–16). He was a most accomplished essayist, his three series of *Obiter Dicta* (sayings by the way)—whence *birrellism*—appearing in 1884, 1887, and 1924 and his less famous *Et Cetera* in 1930. He wrote well.

Whereas *birrellism* is an ordinary *-isms* and *-ologies* formation, *birreligion* constitutes not only a blend of *Birrell* + *religion* but also a pun on *irreligion*.

bishop, to. To murder ; properly, by drowning. In 1831, one Bishop drowned a boy at Bethnal Green in order to sell the body for dissection. He had probably been influenced by the nefarious exploits of Burke and Hare (see **burke**). W appositely quotes ' I burk'd the papa, now I'll bishop the son ', R. H. Barham, *The Ingoldsby Legends*, 1837.

The sense ' to file or otherwise alter a horse's teeth to make the animal look younger ' comes from the name of a person— probably some early-18th Century horse-dealer of widespread disrepute.

56

bisque, in real tennis, is a French term.   The earlier form *biscaye*
'suggests some connection with the province of *Biscay*, the
inhabitants of which are the great experts at a form of tennis
called *la pelote*,' W.

black guillemot.   See **guillemot.**

blackamoor; blackjack.   The latter = *black Jack*, a pretty
example of personification, as in **billy,** another name for a club
or a life-preserver.   But much more interesting is *blackamoor*,
which, originally, was a dialectal form of the tautological (and
inaccurate) *black Moor*, where the medial *a* represents an inser-
tion made in the worthy cause of euphony.   *Blackamoor* means,
rather a Negro than a Moor; a Moor, though dark, is far from
being black.
    For the *-moor* part of *blackamoor*, see **moresca.**

blackeyed susan.   'Daisy, Noel's wife, was out in a meadow
picking black-eyed susans.   She calls them daisies' (Rex Stout,
Where There's a Will, English edition, 1941).

blarney.   'This story about Phil Marsh might be pure blarney
and invention,' Robert Greenwood, *The Squad Goes Out*, 1943.
    At Blarney, a village near Cork in Ireland, there stands a
castle, wherein is an inscribed stone: difficult to reach, this
stone rewards its kisser by conferring upon him (women require
no such assistance) the gift either of cajolery and flattery, or of a
shameless facility in prevarication: he, so gifted, is then said to
have *kissed the Blarney stone*.   The latter nuance is the later, and
it alone is current in the 20th Century.

bloomer; bloomers.   The former is the American eight-
wheeled street-car (*anglicé* tramcar); the latter, the almost too
famous short skirt and trousers worn by American women in
the 1850's, then, ca. 1890–1910, the even more publicized
female knickerbockers of both the U.S.A. and then England.
The latter owed nothing to Mrs Amelia Bloomer except the
fact that it was she who, ca. 1850, started the earlier fashion
from which the dress-designers developed the latter.   Amelia
Bloomer (1818–94), *née* Jenks, married in 1840 Dexter C.
Bloomer.   A writer upon women's suffrage and the unjust
marriage laws, she achieved notoriety with her lectures (some,
upon dress reform for women), at which she wore the short
skirt and long, loose, at-ankle-gathered trousers correctly
associated with her.

N.I.W.—C*

bluchers, as a name for old-fashioned low boots, or high shoes, was probably suggested by those knee-high rubber boots which we call **wellingtons.** '*Blucher* was also at one time used in London slang for non-privileged cabs which were allowed to pick up passengers at London stations after all the privileged cabs had been hired. The allusion is of course to the late arrival of Blucher at Waterloo' (WWN). Gebhard von Blücher (1742–1819) spent most of his life in the Prussian, after having served in the Swedish, army. Defeated at Ligny, he took a long time to re-group his men and to join Wellington at Waterloo; his absence was compensated by Grouchy's and, on account of his age, the more excusable.

blue bird. 'The blue bird of happiness'—to cite its usual shape —owes its existence to *L'Oiseau bleu*, which, in 1909, symbolized the quest for happiness. This poetic play-romance, by Maurice Maeterlinck, the Belgian poet, essayist and dramatist, has exercised a tremendous influence.

blue dahlia. See **dahlia.**

blue gage. See **gage.**

bluebeard is, strictly, a criminal that murders several women that he has married; loosely, a man that has lured women to his home and murdered them. Landru has been called 'the French Bluebeard', the capital *B* being superfluous except where there is a definite allusion to that fairy-tale, earliest told in literary form by Charles Perrault in 1697, which rests upon a monitory folklore tale of 'female curiosity punished'. In Perrault's story, six wives fall victim to the seductive and fascinating husband and the seventh is saved only by the timely arrival of her brothers, who duly slay the murderer. The original of *Barbe bleue* is supposed to have been a monstrous creature named Gilles de Retz, who died in 1440; but relevant folk-tales antedate this sadistic French general.

bob, dry; wet bob. In these Eton names for summer-term cricketer and summer-term rowing 'man', we almost certainly have the name *Bob* used generically for 'chap, fellow'. There is no need to search for a specific individual Robert Somebody-or-Other: compare the multiple uses of *Jack* and *John*, not to mention *Tom* and *Billy*, and several others.

bobadil, 'a braggart', was originally written *Bobadil*, in allusion to 'Bobadill' in Ben Jonson's *Every Man in His Humour* (1598),

58

a very lively comedy of manners, where the man so named is an old soldier, as cowardly as he is boastful, and as vain as he is decorous, and where he is finally exposed for the baseless boaster he is. Jonson derived the name, and something of the character, ' from *Boabdil*, the last Moorish king of Granada '.

Boabdil represents a ' Spanish corruption of *Abu Abd'illah*, father of the servant of Allah. Compare . . . *Bombastes* ' (W). He ruled in 1482–83 and in 1486–92; Webster BD transliterates the Moorish name as *abu-'Abdullah*.

bobby, ' an English—loosely, any British Empire—policeman ' (but, originally, a member of the London Metropolitan Police), takes the name from the fact that, when, in 1828, the Metropolitan Police Act was passed, the Home Secretary was *Robert* Peel (1788–1850), politician and statesman; *robert* or *Robert* is an occasional variant. Moreover, while in 1812–18 he was Chief Secretary for Ireland, he had established the Irish constabulary: whence the Royal Irish Constabulary's nickname of *peelers*. Loosely, a *peeler* has been extended to mean any British or Irish policeman. All three terms are the more apt in that Sir Robert Peel possessed a courage no less remarkable than his organizing ability and his vision.

bobolink is a development from *boblincoln*; that is, *Bob Lincoln*, a name bestowed on this American songbird because its call was popularly apprehended in that form. The word, therefore, bears an exact semantic resemblance to **whippoorwill.**

bock, short for *bock beer*, translates the German *Bockbier*, itself a corruption of *einbecker Bier*, ' beer of—made at—Einbeck '. Einbeck, twenty miles north-west of Göttingen, lies in the Prussian province of Hanover. ' It is brewed,' in the U.S.A., ' in the winter for use in the spring, *Bock Beer Day* being supposed to herald the arrival of spring ' (André Simon). In France, *bock* signifies a half-pint of draught beer—or the thick-glass tankard holding a quarter-litre (approximately half a pint).

bocking. The fabric—compare **worsted**—takes its name from the village of Bocking (in Essex), where this coarse baize, or woollen drugget, used for protecting carpets, was first manufactured; its manufacture dates from the early 18th Century, but for a generation or two it had only a local fame.

bodle, an obsolete small Scottish copper coin, is ' reputed to be derived from the name of a mint-master *Bothwell*, but no documentary evidence is cited ' (Harvey).

59

bohea (pronounced *bo-he*) is a black tea that, coming from the last crop of the season, is not unnaturally of the lowest grade. In the 18th Century, however, the term was applied to the highest grade of black tea, and in 1701 an English writer said that ' the Bohe . . . is the very first bud gather'd in the beginning of March ' (from a *Voyage* quoted by The OED).

Bohe or *Bohea*, or rather *Bu-i*, is a dialectal variation of the Chinese *Wu-i*, the name of some mountains in the north of the province of Fukien. The Wu-i, or Wu-yi, is a range of the Ta-chin mountains system. ' Fukien is at once essentially mountainous and essentially maritime. . . . Kien-ning and Shao-chow still have an important trade in the real black " Bohea " ' (Lionel W. Lyde, *The Continent of Asia*, 1933).

bohemian, bohemianism, bohemianize; hobohemia.

(Concerning Oxford in the 1890's) ' The massive, bohemian figure of York Powell ' : thus he appeared to John Buchan the undergraduate (*Memory Hold-the-Door*, 1940).

' Verlaine was not a bohemian by choice. No great artist is. Bohemianism is the pastime of mediocrity,' Charles Morgan, *Reflections in a Mirror*, 2nd series, 1946.

' One of the most ancient and universal forms of deception is the fake disease. In Hobohemia a pretended affliction is called " jiggers ",' Nels Anderson, *The Hobo*, 1923 ; ' The hobo, for all his simplicity, is still a phantom man, and Hobohemia still remains a realm too obscure to be interpreted validly by a casual or occasional visitor. . . . Hobohemia is a realm apart from the world. . . . It is a habitat not made by the hobo. . . . The hobo can and does live the life of the consummate artist without being aware of it ', ' Dean Stiff ' (an artist in hobohemian lore), *The Milk and Honey Route*, 1931 ; *hobo + Bohemia*.

In *Sing High! Sing Low!*, 1944, Osbert Sitwell has wittily shown that the maligning of the ancient kingdom of Bohemia into equivalence with the artificial world of faked art and tawdrily gay ' low life ' is to be, in the main, attributed to Henri Murger's *La Vie de Bohème*, 1848 ; a book that became world-famous and, more than a generation later, originated an opera—Puccini's *La Bohème* (1896).

' Bohemia, though only two-thirds the size of Scotland, is the most important province of [Czecho-Slovakia] ; and its importance, political and historic, or economic, is and has been by no means merely local. Much more truly than Switzerland, it is the heart of Europe . . . for centuries a focus of political, intellectual, and ethnic interests, and to-day . . . one of the most important industrial areas in the world ', thus, in *The*

Continent of Europe, (4th edition) 1930, Lionel W. Lyde, who also mentions 'the beautiful Bohemian Forest'.

bohn; usually written *Bohn*. A 'crib' or translation, *bohn* has enjoyed a perhaps wider currency in the U.S.A. than in the British Empire. Henry George Bohn (1796–1884), of German parentage, became an English publisher and translator. *Bohn's Classical Library* (inaugurated ca. 1846) consists of translations, mainly rather pedestrian but mostly pretty accurate, of the Greek and Latin Classics; they were—indeed, in some parts, still are—a godsend to the less ardent student. Compare **Loeb** in the Appendix.

bolivar is the monetary unit of Venezuela, as *boliviano* is that of Bolivia. *Boliviano* is the adjective, used as noun, from *Bolivia* (derivatively, *bolivia* is a woollen fabric), and both *boliviano* and *bolivar* commemorate Simon *Bolivar* (1783–1830), the famous South American statesman, soldier, revolutionary, who lived hard and dangerously; 'never a dull moment' was his subconscious motto.

bolo; boloism. A *bolo* is a First World War fifth-columnist, and *boloism* the practice, the pursuit, of underground activities— especially pacifist propaganda—in favour of the enemy: in favour of Germany. The words are now archaic—but historical.

Paul *Bolo*, a French adventurer and traitor, was in April, 1918, shot for treason of this kind—treason detected in the previous September. He was generally known as Bolo Pasha.

Compare—and contrast—**quisling.**

Bologna sausage. See **boloney.**

boloney or **bolony.** (Cf. **polony.**) 'May be it's baloney,'— an incorrect spelling—'may be it's dyspepsia, and I'm imagining things, but I tell you I'm not happy in my mind,' E. C. R. Lorac, *Case in the Clinic*, 1941.

'. . . "But this isn't the time for it." It is the slogan of discreet Liberalism, as profound as St Francis's "The beasts are my brothers," or Governor Alfred E. Smith's war-cry, "Slice it where you will, it's still baloney",' Sinclair Lewis, *Gideon Planish*, (English edition) 1943.

This Americanism became popular in Britain in about 1936, although it had been known to a fair number of people long before that. The Americans probably adopted it from their

Italian nationals, who got it from those 'culinary artists', the makers of the *Bologna sausage*, a very large kind of sausage—known to the Elizabethans and the moderns ('Red and I ate our bologna and crackers without him': Al Hurwitch in *Detective Fiction Weekly*, May 21, 1932).

Now, sausages have for centuries borne a dubious reputation, and one of several opprobrious names is *bags of mystery* (no; the pun does not operate semantically) : the larger the sausage, the greater the mystery: and much so-called mystery is hocus-pocus: in short, mere nonsense.

bolshevik; bolshie or **bolshy.** The latter is a slangy corruption of the former, and both are slangily used, though much less now than in the 1920's and early 1930's, to mean 'revolutionary' or even 'bloody-minded' or a person so-charactered. The Russian *Bolshevik*, plural *Bolsheviki*, derives from *bolshe*, 'the larger': the Bolsheviki were originally the majority group of that political party which overturned the old regime.

bombasine or **-zine.** The OED derives it immediately from French *bombasin*, representing Latin *bombycinus*, 'silken', from *bombyx* (transliterating Greek *bombux*), 'silk' or 'silk-worm'. But there is another possibility—for this is a twilled dress-material not necessarily containing either silk or, for that matter, cotton at all—and it is undoubtingly posed by Lionel W. Lyde in *The Continent of Asia*, 1933, in the chapter on Syria. 'The descendants of the old Venetian colonists have kept Aleppo famous for all kinds of craftsmanship, especially in silk and cotton textiles and gold and silver "thread"—the two words *bombazine* (Bambyce) and *muslin* (Mosul) coming into English from Aleppo.' Mosul occupies the site of the ancient Nineveh; *Bambyce* is the earliest name for the city (in what is now Syria) better known as *Hierapolis* (earlier *Hieropolis*), which, likewise Greek, means 'the Holy City' (dedicated, in point of fact, to phallic rites)—long a ruin. 'It is interesting,' remarks *The Encyclopaedia Britannica*, 'to note that from Bambyce (near which much silk was produced) were derived the *bombycina vestis* of the Romans and, through the Crusaders, the bombazine of commerce.' It is, perhaps, equally interesting to note that, at first, *bombycina vestis* was probably *bombacina vestis*, one Greek word for cotton—originally known as 'tree-silk'—being *bombax*; either the Romans or some not quite polymathic scholiast may have confused Greek *bombax* with Greek *bombux*, the more readily that, in ancient times in Syria, silk was much coarser, much more like cotton, than it is now.

62

bombast (compare **rodomontade**—and **drawcansir**); **Bombastes**; **bombastic**. ' Sensational lecturers of the Bombastes stripe, that " turba loquax " with their cataracts of declamation . . . dinned into our ears over and over again, avail themselves on pressing occasions more conveniently and opportunely of the adventitious succor afforded by the opium-pellet or the laudanum-draught,' Alonzo Calkins, M.D., *Opium and the Opium-Appetite*, 1871.

In 1810 appeared *Bombastes Furioso*, a verse burlesque by William Rhodes (1772–1826), with excellent illustrations by George Cruikshank : and there *Bombastes* speaks in a *bombastic* manner—with tall and turgid talk.

Both *bombast* (cotton-wool, hence padding, hence inflated language) and *bombastic* existed long before 1810 ; they derive, via French, from Latin *bombax*, ' cotton ', a corruption of *bombyx* (Greek *bombux*), ' silk '—compare, therefore, **bombasine**. But *Bombastes*, as in the quotation, comes direct from the popularity of Rhodes's *Bombastes Furioso*, and both *bombast* and *bombastic* owe to Rhodes something of their post-1810 currency.

Compare **braggadocio**.

bon-chrétien (or unhyphenated). See **codlin**. One variety is the **Bartlett pear**—in the second vocabulary.

bongo—any of three kinds of large, forest antelopes, one of which belongs to East Africa (and the other two to West Africa)—appears to take its name from the *Bongos*, a Negro people of Sudan, noted for their reddish skin ; the antelopes have a reddish coat. But the people may have been named after the animals. *Bongo* is a Negro word.

Boniface, journalistic for ' innkeeper ', commemorates the jolly fellow that was the innkeeper in *The Beaux' Stratagem* (1707), the best of the comedies by George Farquhar (1678–1707), Irishman settled in London ca. 1697. A masculine Proper Name, it came to England, via France, from Italy (*Bonifacio*), and its origin resides in the Latin *Bonifacius* or *Bonifatius*, from *bonifatus*, ' the lucky ': *bonum fatum*, ' fortunate fate '.

bootjack. See **Jack**.

bora is the dry, cold north-east wind that, in the northern Adriatic, blows seasonally. ' Somewhat the same distinction [as that between *sirocco* and *solano*] may be drawn between the

bora (" North Wind ") and the mistral (" Masterful Wind "),
the former being more of a " gap " wind ' (Lyde, *Europe*).

Italian dialect *bora* for Italian *borea*, from Greek *Boreas*,
worshipped as a divine being : see **boreal**.

Bordeaux or, logically, **bordeaux.** The term generically
embraces all the clarets, i.e. the *médoc* (the better clarets) and
the rest of them. They are called *bordeaux* because they are
shipped from Bordeaux, which handles the exportable products
of a considerable hinterland. ' These southern vineyards are
equally famous for red wines and white, and the best of each
. . . are equal to the " first growths " of the north ' (Lyde,
Europe, 1913). Whence the 16th-Century *Bordeaux hammer*,
' headache produced by wine '.

Bordeaux is (*la ville au*) *bord d'eaux*.

boreal ; Boreas. The adjective *boreal* (northern) represents the
Latin *borealis*, which derives from *Boreas*, the God of the North
Wind, hence the north wind itself. *Boreas*, merely the Latin
adoption of the Greek name, may, as Webster has brilliantly
suggested, signify ' the wind from the mountains ' : compare
the Sanskrit *giri*, ' mountain '—and its cognate, the Old Slavic
gora. Compare **austral** and **zephyr.**

bosey belongs to cricketing slang, obsolescent in England but
still used much in Australia. It is the original form of what has
become known as the googly, which, before the Australians
specialized in it, was for some years exploited by such South
Africans as Schwarz and Pegler : but was instituted by the
English cricketer, B. J. T. *Bos*anquet, who flourished ca. 1900–
10 and who, early in 1903, demonstrated its charms to the
Australians. See especially W. J. Lewis, *The Language of
Cricket*, 1934. In *The Observer* of Oct. 20, 1946, the former Test
cricketer, J. H. Fingleton, writes : ' Dooland unloosed a barrage
of " bosies " to Ikin '.

boston. (1) The variation of the waltz, like (2) the breed of
dog, has been named after Boston, Massachusetts. In the
19th–early 20th Century, Boston set the cultural tone of the
United States.

' [Dog] thieves specialize in Bostons, cocker spaniels, and
Scotties, due to the difficulty of identification of these breeds,'
Courtney R. Cooper, *Here's to Crime*, 1937 ; ' He growled like
a Boston Terrier, and told his Father to go Chase Himself ',
George Ade, *Fables in Slang*, 1899.

64

bostonite, an igneous rock consisting largely of feldspar, was found at Marblehead Neck, near *Boston*, Massachusetts. Compare **canaanite.**

boswellize; Boswell, used figuratively. To *boswellize* is to write a detailed, intimate, faithful but indiscriminating account of the life of a friend, after the manner of *The Life of Samuel Johnson, LL.D.* (1791), by James Boswell (1740–95), his friend and recorder. To be 'a Boswell' is to be such a person.

'An ungifted Boswell with a death grip on the coat tails of his betters,' John P. Marquand, *Wickford Point*, 1939—a book delightful to the connoisseur in the stress of family relationships and in the give-and-take of friendship. Compare 'He became a faithful Boswell to the more austere saints, and a whole-hearted admirer of the virtues not his own,' Helen Waddell, *The Desert Fathers*, 1939.

But the following definitions, made by Mr G. W. Stonier in *The Observer*, December 1, 1946, at the beginning of his review of C. E. Vulliamy's *Ursa Major* (Dr Johnson) and D. B. Wyndham-Lewis's *The Hooded Hawk* (Boswell), are far too witty for me to ignore them :—

' BOSWELLIZE. *v. trans.* To immortalise; to render loquacious; to interview exclusively, incessantly, unmercifully; to frisk round and fawn upon; to stimulate by nugacity; to lead (of bears) and red-rag (of bulls); to pump winningly; to importune, with one's weaknesses, the good or great; to find one's Johnson; to huff.

'*Intrans.* To go too far, and then go on, rendering distance no object; to make a friend in order to make a spectacle; to drop bricks that others may hurl them; to catch the words from the lips; to hop in conversation to the " overwhelming question "; to build on the quicksands of temperament; to be an eager, likeable buffoon; to write the whale of biographies in English.'

botany (or **B**—) is short for *Botany wool*, a superfine wool— shipped originally from Botany Bay; or, occasionally, for *Botany card*, a machine for the carding of merino wools, merino sheep being—in Australia—the best for wool, whether Botany or other wool. Botany Bay was so named because, on its discovery in 1770 by Captain Cook, many new plants were found there by Sir Joseph Banks (see **banksia**).

Bottin is the short form, the usual form, of *L'Annuaire du Commerce Didot-Bottin*, the re-naming of *L'Almanach du Commerce de Paris* (1819–53), edited by Sébastien *Bottin* (1764–1853), French official statistician and administrator. The Didot mentioned is the famous old Parisian firm of printers and publishers.

boucherize, ' to impregnate (especially timber) with such a solution of copper sulphate as acts as a preservative ' : from a French chemist, A. *Boucherie* (1801–71). The process was known as *boucherism*. Compare **kyanize.**

Which reminds me. Jacques Boucher de Perthes (1788–1868), notable French archaeologist, gave part of his name to the *boucher* or crude, stone hand-axe employed by Old Stone Age men. In 1847–65 he published a very considerable work, *Antiquités*.

bougainvillaea. ' The path rounded a great pile of bougainvillaea vine that had grown on a dying tree,' John W. Vandercook, *Murder in Fiji*, 1936.

This climbing tropical and sub-tropical flowering vine draws its name from the French navigator Louis Bougainville (1729–1811), who sailed extensively in Oceania early in the latter half of the 18th Century and who took part in the American War of Independence. An island (Solomon group) and two straits (Solomon and New Hebrides groups) bear his name.

bougie, in its medical sense, derives from *bougie*, a candle-shaped filter, itself from *bougie*, a wax candle. The French word, like the candle, comes from North Africa : from the North African town of *Bugia* (French *Bougie*) these candles were earliest imported into Europe. *Bugia*, in Algeria, once a fortified seaport, recalls the *Bejaia*, an ancient tribe of this region ; early in the 12th Century, it was the capital of the Berber empire of the Beni-Hammed. (Chisholm.)

boule (strictly, **boulle**)**;** often incorrectly in the form of *buhl*, which attributes to Germany what is rightly France's, as in ' They all on that side seemed to him museum pieces—their lives led in big cold houses like public galleries with rather dull old pictures and with buhl cabinets in the corridors ' (Graham Greene, *The Confidential Agent*, 1939).

André Charles Boulle, who flourished in the time of Louis XIV and died in 1732, was a French wood-carver, famed for his marquetry or inlaid work, especially on tables and cabinets : *meubles de boul(l)e*.

Cf. **chippendale** and **sheraton.**

bourbon is excellent American for (*a*) an excellent whisky and (*b*) a political die-hard. The former, which takes its name from Bourbon County (in Kentucky) where it was first made, is always small-initialled, whereas the latter, always capitalled, derives from the Bourbon dynasty of France, 'the Bourbons, who forgot nothing and learned nothing' (H. W. Horwill). The political adjective, however, takes a small initial, as in 'the bourbon section of society' (the reactionaries); so, too, the abstract noun *bourbonism* (that is, ultra-conservatism). The so-called *Bourbon* (*sugar*) *cane* may originally have come from the Isle of Bourbon.

'The servants stated that the bourbon had been kept, along with other liquors, in an unlocked cupboard in the pantry,' Rex Stout, *The Broken Vase*, (English edition) 1942.

bourgeois (**type**)—a type of 9 points—has been so named either because it is *bourgeois* or 'middle-class' in that its size lies between brevier and long primer or because a French type-founder and printer, surnamed *Bourgeois*, devised it.

bowdlerize. Thomas Bowdler (1754–1825), an English physician, achieved in 1818 an undying fame by publishing a *Family Shakespeare*, an expurgated version that either omitted or grossly modified those parts 'which cannot with propriety be read aloud in a family', as he himself phrased it. Not content with that piece of literary vandalism, he had to go and serve Gibbon's *The History of the Decline and Fall of the Roman Empire* with the same ineffable impertinence.

Compare **comstockery.**

bowie. 'On March 5, 1836, the [fortified mission house at San Antonio] was carried by assault and every defender was massacred. . . . Among the slain were Davy Crockett and the notorious Bowie of hunting-knife fame,' James Truslow Adams, *The Epic of America*, 1933.

James Bowie (born in 1799) was the reputed inventor of this knife. He became an American soldier—and a soldier of fortune.

[? **bowler.** Not from a maker's name but either from *bowl*, 'a basin'—as W proposes, or, as I suggest, from the fact that, round and stiff-brimmed, it can be bowled along.]

Box and Cox. See **Cox and Box.**

box-calf, says The OED, was named about 1890 by Edward L. White, of White Bros. & Co., Mass., U.S.A., after Joseph *Box*, bootmaker, of London. (The picture of a calf in a box was
67

adopted as an advertising device.) Webster appears to doubt this origin—but doesn't actually say so.

boxer. This ' member of the Chinese anti-foreign movement of ca. 1900 ' embodies a pun : the English, who, dangerous fellows, will have their little joke (see G. K. Chesterton, *The Napoleon of Notting Hill*, 1904), heard that the movement against ' the foreign devils ' had originated with a secret society operating at Shantung and owning the name ' I-Ho-Chuan ' or *I he t'uan*, wrongly interpreted as ' righteous, uniting *fists* ' ; correctly ' righteous harmony band ', a term applied at first to the Chinese militia.

boycott. Of the Rome-Berlin Axis, formed in 1936, Eric Ambler, two years later, remarked that ' They'd agreed on parallel action in Spain. They'd agreed to boycott Geneva. They'd agreed to present a united front to the Western powers ' (*Cause for Alarm*).

The useful verb *boycott* represents the surname *Boycott*, which has become common property because of the treatment meted, in December 1880, to Captain Boycott, of Lough Mask House, in County Mayo, Ireland. Charles Cunningham Boycott, born in 1832, became the agent for Lord Erne's estate ; he was persecuted by the Irish Land League ; the Boycott case was so famous that the resultant verb is to be found in almost every European language (WWN).

bradbury, an English currency note (Treasury note), is a slang word, as is **fisher.** It has been named after Sir John Swanwick *Bradbury* (b. 1872), who in 1913–19 was joint Permanent Secretary to the Treasury ; his name appeared on all Treasury notes.

braggadocio may be either ' a boaster, especially a swaggering braggart ' or ' baseless boasting ; boastful pretentiousness '. In Spenser's *The Faerie Queen* (1589–96), *Braggadocio*, in the original spelt *Braggadochio*, personifies such boasting :

> ' Proud Braggadocio, that in vaunting vain
> His glory did repose, and credit did maintain '.

Spenser coined the name from English *brag* on the analogy of the numerous Italian pejoratives in -*occio* (W).
Compare **bobadil** and **bombast.**

brahmapootra, usually shortened to *brahma*, the very large domestic fowl, with feathered legs and pea combs, is, like the
68

cochin-china, of Asiatic breed—originally of the region lying about the *Brahmapootra* (or *-putra*), the great river that, rising in Tibet, traverses the entire width of the Himalayas, flows through Assam, and joins the Ganges.

braidism; braidist: hypnotism; hypnotist, or believer in hypnotism : a 19th-Century word, deriving from James *Braid* (or Brade), who (1795?–1860), born in Scotland, practised surgery in Manchester and investigated mesmerism, which he proved to be subjective. He coined the term *neurohypnotism* later shortened to *hypnotism*.

braille. ' She told him about the Great Swamp . . . where Indian mounds, like some forgotten Braille, offer clues to the fumbling fingers of searchers,' Harry Hervey, *School for Eternity*, 1942.

> ' Tell him no riddles of a tangled frontier
> Between Life and Not-Life, when the text is braille
> To fingers yet unused to this new contour,'
>   Ronald Bottrall, *Farewell and Welcome*, 1945.

Louis Braille (1809–52), himself blind from the age of three, became in 1828 a teacher of the blind but did not forgo his organ-playing ; he invented a system of raised-point writing and figuring for literature and music—originally *the Braille system*.

brazil, short for *Brazil nut*, strictly is ineligible : see, e.g., The OED, W, or Webster. But *brazilite*, a variety of baddeleyite (named after its discoverer, J. Baddeley), qualifies, for it is found in Brazil.

bren = *Bren gun*; **bren carrier** = *Bren-gun carrier* (a small tracked vehicle). The 1939–45 approximate equivalent of the **lewis** machine-guns ; that is, it uses ·303 ammunition, but is fired from the shoulder. Originally it was made at Brno, a great manufacturing centre of Czecho-Slovakia ; the patent being purchased by the British Government, the gun was perfected and manufactured in the small-arms factory at Enfield on the northern outskirts of London. A blend : *Br*no + *En*field.

bridewell. In London there is a precinct called *Bridewell*, named from *St Bride's* (i.e., Bridget's) *Well*, which was sunk near the spot where stands Bridewell Palace or, as some say, hospital, built by Henry VIII and converted into a house of correction, extant (near Blackfriars Bridge) until 1864. So famous, or so infamous, was it that all houses of correction— and, loosely, many gaols and prisons—came to be known as bridewells.

brie. ' He had some excellent macaroni, delicious brie cheese, then ordered black coffee and lit a cigarette ' (Claude Houghton, *Passport to Paradise*, 1944). Either *Brie cheese* or, better, merely *brie* is preferable to *brie cheese*.

Brie is an agricultural district in the *département* Seine-et-Marne, France ; noted for its dairy produce, especially cheese.

Briton has, in ' He's a Briton ! '—a stout friend, a very good fellow, become a Common Noun and, strictly and indeed sensibly, should be written with a small *b* : compare **christian.** The words *Briton, Britain, Britannic* have an obscure history, clarified by R. G. Collingwood in Collingwood & Myres, *Roman Britain and the English Settlements*, (revised edition) 1937 : ' From the fourth century before Christ, when Britain was visited and described by the Greek traveller Pytheas, the British Isles were called by many geographers, Diodorus Siculus, Strabo, Ptolemy and others, the Pretanic Isles . . . Pretani . . . can hardly be identical with . . . Britanni. On the other hand, there is a name with which it not only can but must be identical : it is the old Welsh Priten, the " P "-form of which the corresponding " Q "-form is Cruithin, the name by which many Irish writers refer to the Picts. The name Picti, painted men, is a Latin translation of this word, appearing in the third century as a general term by which Latin-speaking Britons referred to the barbarian tribes beyond the frontier ; later it was adopted by these tribes themselves, and became the title of the Pictish people. . . . It can hardly be doubted that the true form of the name Britannic, as the name of Great Britain and Ireland, is really Pretanic or Pritenic, and that the inhabitants of these islands . . . were called Pretani or Priteni. It is a very probable conjecture that Caesar, finding himself at the outset of his expedition on the borders of a Belgic tribe called Britanni and knowing that the country he was about to invade had been lately colonized from Belgic Gaul, believed himself able to correct a widespread error by substituting the forms Britanni, Britannia, for Pretani and its Latinized correlative Pretania.' (The philologist's lot is not a happy one —but it has its compensations.)

brobdingnagian. ' He rumbled and thundered again with Brobdingnagian mirth,' Harry Kemp, *Tramping on Life*, 1922.

(The capital letter is no more necessary here than in **lilli-putian**; and the common *brobdignagian* is incorrect.)

In Jonathan Swift's famous satire-novel, *Gulliver's Travels* (1726), Brobdingnag is the island inhabited by giants; its inhabitants, the Brobdingnagians, serve Swift in his purpose of reducing the pretensions and self-conceit of mankind to a healthier proportion: to the Brobdingnagian king, men were 'odious little vermin'.

Coined by Swift, the word, by its length and especially its sound, is evocative and imitative of giants.

brocard, 'an elementary principle or maxim, a brief proverbial rule (operative in, e.g., law or ethics); hence, a pithy gibe', comes, via French, from *Burchard* or *Burkhard*, that 11th-Century Bishop of Worms who compiled a volume of ecclesiastical canons, entitled *Regulae Ecclesiasticae*. The change from *burkh* (or *burch*) to *broc* merely exemplifies the frequent philological phenomenon known as metathesis.

(The *Brocard circle* and the *Brocard ellipse* in mathematics stem from Henri Brocard (1845–1922), a famous French mathematician.)

brodie in 20th-Century American slang is 'a jump; an attempt'; and *do a brodie* is 'to faint; to die' but also 'to try'. The former occurs in, e.g., Godfrey Irwin's entertaining *American Tramp and Underworld Slang*, 1931, the latter in Jack Callahan's moving autobiography, *Man's Grim Justice*, 1929. The origin lies in an obscure or, at the least, disputed episode in the life of one Steve Brodie, who jumped—or failed to jump— from the old Brooklyn Bridge and who afterwards, such being the reward of a national notoriety, became a successful saloon-keeper.

'Nobody will ever know whether or not Steve Brodie really jumped from the Brooklyn Bridge. Steve said he did; many another person says he didn't. . . . On July 25, 1886, something resembling a human form dropped from the Manhattan side of the Brooklyn Bridge . . . Brodie was there and he told his story. It was his story and he stuck to it . . . He immediately became the man of the hour. . . . The expression, "He did a Brodie," meaning "He took a chance," is part of today's idiom,' Charles E. Stills, *Styles in Crime*, 1938.

brodrick is British military slang for the peaked cap introduced into the British Army by William St John Brodrick (1856–1942), 1st Earl of Middleton, while (1900–03) he was Secretary for War. It has other names—less polite.

bronx. See **manhattan.**

bronze, says Webster, is 'of obscure, possibly Persian, origin'. It is at least certain that it comes, via French, from Italian *bronzo*: beyond that point, W is probably right in stating: 'From *Brundusium* (Brindisi). Pliny speaks of *aes Brundusinum.* Compare the history of *copper*.' In ancient times, Brundusium was, as Brindisi long has been, an important seaport.

Brother Jonathan. From Jonathan Trumbull (1740–1809), Governor of Connecticut, affectionately so named by George Washington.

brougham. That eloquent orator, rather dilettante statesman and serious bibliophile, Baron Brougham and Vaux (1778–1868), won such fame—especially by the speech that effectually contributed to the passing of the Reform Bill, 1831—that the carriage was, ca. 1850, named after him.

browning is the logical, the commonsensible shortening of the weapon so charmingly used by an able writer of underworld stories, whether true or fictional, in the following passage: 'Clyde seized a Browning automatic rifle and sprayed the two cars': *Detective Fiction Weekly*, November 10, 1934. This firearm played a useful part in the war of 1939–45, both as a *Browning revolver* (or *pistol*), a seven-bulleted automatic pistol, which represents a development of the **colt,**—a modification introduced, ca. 1904, by John M. Browning of Ogden, Utah, and as a *Browning machine-gun* ('Alkemade swung his four Brownings down and gave a long burst', Brickhill & Norton, *Escape to Danger*, 1946).

bruin. In the medieval beast-epic entitled *Reynard the Fox*, the bear is named Bruin; and so the bear has been Bruin in most fairy-stories, folk-tales, and other popular stories ever since. *Bruin* is the Dutch for 'brown'; *Reynard the Fox* is a Dutch (Old Flemish) poem, *Reineke Vos*; the European bear was, usually, a brown bear.

brum; brummagem. As adjective, 'cheap and showy'; as noun, 'counterfeit coin, or imitation jewellery, or faked antiques'. A *Brummy* is a native of *Brummagem* or Birmingham, noted for its manufactures, some of which used to be made of inferior quality for disposal among ignorant native races abroad. *Brummagem* is a slurring of *Bromwicham*, itself a corruption of *Brimidgeham*. (W.)

72

brunswick is the now merely historical name of a feminine coat, close-fitting, collared, lapelled, of German origin (the Duchy of *Brunswick*), but, in the 18th Century, of European vogue.

brutus. Apart from being a bronze-flowered chrysanthemum (usually *Brutus*), a *brutus* is a wig with hair roughly cropped—hence, derivatively, hair thus dressed.

So named from the rough sturdiness of character exhibited by Marcus Junius Brutus (85?–42 B.C.), ardent upholder of republican principles; he acted ' tough ' with those who owed him money. The modern literary conception of his character and the term *brutus* have been much influenced by Shakespeare's portrayal of him in *Julius Caesar*.

bubbly-jock, ' a turkey cock ' (mostly in Scottish), may just possibly constitute a very early, though isolated, example of rhyming slang. The bird is *Jock* because so many birds and men are Jock or Jack, and the *bubbly* refers to the noise it makes as it *bubbles* over with excitement or indignation.

bucellas is a Portuguese white wine : ' the golden and pleasing wine named after Bucellas, a small town in the midst of vineyards, close to Lisbon. . . . Bucellas wines were popular in England during the earlier part of Queen Victoria's reign ' (André Simon).

bucephalus, ' a high-spirited, much-performing, noble horse ', is the common-property form of *Bucephalus* (Greek *Boukephalos*, literally ' the Ox- or the Bull-Headed One '), Alexander the Great's famous steed, after which he named the city of Bucephala in North India—perhaps the modern Jhelum. Of Bucephalus, ' historians relate details unsatisfactory to a horseman. If Bucephalus was thirty years old at the Jhelum [the ancient Hydaspes] battle, then he must have been already past his prime when Alexander was still a young boy, which is most improbable. And surely his name was not given to him because his head was shaped like a bull's? It is much more probable that he was a handsome and highly-mettled animal who showed a bull-like determination not to be ridden by anyone but Alexander, and that Alexander trained him himself, in which case he might have been a five-year-old when Alexander was fifteen, and twenty years old when he died of wounds or of heart-strain, after swimming across the flooded Jhelum and then carrying his master in full armour throughout the heat and hard fighting of a June day in the Punjab '. This, the kind of etymology I like to see, occurs in a footnote (p. 23

73

of the Services edition) to F. (' Bengal Lancer ') Yeats-Brown's readable and valuable *Indian Pageant*, 1943.

buckram, whether noun or, derivatively, adjective, stems from Bokhara, more correctly spelt *Bukhara* : a region and its capital in Central Asia ; famous in the Middle Ages for its silk, cotton, carpets, and many other things. The Persian *Buchara* became, in Old French, the fabric known as *boquerant* ; hence the Middle English, *bokeram* or *bougeren*.

buddleia. ' There's a garden seat just round the corner behind those buddleias,' Hugh I'Anson Fausset, *Between the Tides*, 1942. Introduced into Britain in the 18th Century, this now ornamental shrub was a native of Asia and America. It has been named after the botanist Adam *Buddle*, who died in 1715. Compare **cattleya, lobelia,** and many other flower and shrub names.

Buffalo Bill. ' There was Pinky Sherman . . . An effeminate sort of killer. Acted like a sissy but could throw lead from a ·45 like Buffalo Bill,' Richard Sale in *Detective Fiction Weekly*, May 29, 1937.

Even more than **Daniel Boone** (subsidiary list), Buffalo Bill has become an American legend : and references to him in American literature and journalism are extremely numerous. William Frederick Cody (1846–1917), whose autobiography (1904) cannot be trusted implicitly, served in the Civil War in the frontier scouts and, later, in the war against the Sioux. In 1883 he became a public figure by instituting his Wild West rodeo and show, which soon won such popularity as to constitute fame : ten years earlier, he had acquired a taste for this sort of thing by acting in Ned Buntline's play, *The Scouts of the Plains*. Ned Buntline—his real name was Edward Judson (1823–86)— by his dime novels, a genre he created ; and soldier of fortune Prentiss Ingraham (1843–1904), by his dime novels ; did more than ' Buffalo Bill ' Cody himself to make him popular and to inaugurate the legend.

bugger, in its colloquial sense, ' a low wretch ; a fellow ;— usually in abuse ; also, sportively, chap ; person,' derives from its legal sense, ' a sodomite ' ; and the legal sense comes later than its religious sense, ' a heretic '. Now, that ' heretic ' sense reaches us, via the French *bougre*, from the derivative meaning of the Medieval Latin *Bulgarus*, which was also employed to mean ' a sodomite '. *Bulgarus* is literally a Bulgarian. From among the Bulgarians came the Albigenses or ' Bulgarian

74

heretics ' : and laymen have always shown themselves unreluctant to impute unnatural vice to monks and nuns, for much the same reason as that which induces landlubbers to impute these habits to seamen.

buhl. See **boule.**

Bumble ; bumbledom. The latter, the asinine pomposity of petty officials, is an offshoot from the former, which is short for *Mr Bumble,* that delectably pompous beadle who figures in Dickens's *Oliver Twist* (1837–38) as a crassly domineering and most consequential parish official. Dickens chose this echoic name—he was a master of echoism—because Mr Bumble and his like waffle and vainly boom their way through life. Compare **dogberry(dom).**

buncombe, bunkum, often shortened to **bunk** (whence **debunk**). Sir Paul Harvey has put the matter thus tersely and clearly :—' Empty claptrap oratory, from *Buncombe,* the name of a county in N. Carolina, U.S. The use of the word originated near the close of the debate on the " Missouri Question " in the 16th congress, when the member for this district rose to speak, and persevered in spite of impatient calls for the " Question ", declaring he was bound *to make a speech for Buncombe.*' This happened in 1820.

bundook or **bandook,** Regular Army slang for a rifle—earlier for a musket (for instance, during the 18th Century in India), originally meant a cross-bow. In Arabic, *Banadik* is Venice, where cross-bows were notably made. Egyptians still refer to Venice as *Bundookia.* (Based on information supplied in 1930 by the late T. E. Lawrence to Mr John Brophy.)

bungalow ; bungaloid. *Bungalow* comes from the Hindu adjective *bangla,* ' belonging to, characteristic of Bengal '—as such dwellings are. For the vowel change, compare that in the preceding entry and that in English *pundit* (from Hindu *pandit*).

bunk, bunkum. See **buncombe.**

buoy is, by Webster, derived from that Teutonic radical which has yielded the English *beacon.* Note, however, that W proposes Dutch *boei,* ' a fetter ; hence, a buoy ' (compare *boeien,* to fetter, to chain) or Old French *boie,* probably from Latin *boia,* ' chain, fetter (by which the buoy was secured), which some would connect with the tribal name *Boii* ' ; it is only fair to subjoin this, that L. *boia*, like *boiae* (a collar), seems to derive from *bos* (an ox), the fetter, like the collar, having originally been of ox-leather.

burberry, a water-proof fabric, hence a light overcoat made thereof, was at first written *Burberry*; the original makers were Burberrys, Ltd. The earliest record adduced by The OED is of 1903. (It is a trade name.) Compare **macintosh.**

burgonet, a light helmet, much used in the 15th–16th Centuries and also by Cromwell's Ironsides, transliterates the French *bourguignotte*. The *Bourguignons* or Burgundians were first in this field as in many another.

burgoynade; burgoyne, v. Capture of a notable person, especially of a general; to capture such a person. General John Burgoyne (1722–92), almost a dramatist not entirely negligible, in 1776 commanded the British expeditionary force sent down from Canada against the colonists and was, in the following year, forced to surrender at Saratoga.

burgundy or **B—.** The term *burgundy* covers the group of (mostly red) wines produced from the grapes of the old French province of Burgundy: regionally, compare **bordeaux**; 'provincially', compare **champagne.** Sometimes the term is used as a colour-name, as in 'A big solid cool-looking house with burgundy brick walls' (Raymond Chandler, *The High Window*, English edition in 1943).

'Once over the Langres plateau . . . the Côte d'Or scarp has the south-eastern exposure so favourable to the vine; and here, where the sheltered Saone basin gets "baked" in summer, the famous Burgundy wines are produced, especially between Dijon and Châlons, e.g. at Beaune. The Beaujolais wines, e.g. from Mâcon and Villefranche, are of the same type' (Lionel W. Lyde, *The Continent of Europe*, 4th ed., 1930).

The French name of the province is *Bourgogne*; the English word derives from the Medieval Latin form, *Burgundia*, 'land of the *Burgunds*'—originally a Germanic tribe.

Burke. See **Debrett.**

burke means 'to stifle or hush up; literally, to murder by stifling', as in 'To say that [in his work on the Albert Memorial] Scott was a bad architect was to burke the problem with a tautology; to say that there was no accounting for tastes was to evade it by *suggestio falsi*' (R. G. Collingwood, *An*

Autobiography, 1939). The term commemorates the fact that Burke and Hare killed a number of persons for the economic reason that they desired to sell—and, for a time, did sell—their bodies for dissection. The casuistry of this procedure did not preclude an execution in 1829. The word may have been strengthened by the murder, in Phoenix Park, Dublin, of Thomas Henry Burke, Under Secretary for Ireland (he was, by the way, an Irishman), by the Invincibles, a branch of the Fenian Society, in 1882.

In *Reminiscences of a Chief Constable*, 1900, W. Chadwick records that in the 1830's a body-snatcher was often called a *Burker*.

Compare **bishop.**

burnettize (incorrectly with one *t*). ' To impregnate canvas, timber, or cordage with Sir William Burnett's fluid, a solution of chloride of zinc,' Smyth, *The Sailor's Word-Book*, 1867. It was he who, in the year of Queen Victoria's accession, patented this steeping process. Compare **boucherize.**

William Burnett (1779–1861), a Scot, became Physician General to the Royal Navy and, in 1835, Physician to the King.

burton. (1) The hoisting tackle (nautical) was, in the 15th Century, *brytton* and also *breton*; the latter indicates that its basic meaning is ' a *Breton* contrivance ' (W)—used and probably devised by those hardy, intrepid, resourceful Breton fishermen.

(2) See **Burton, gone for a,** in the subsidiary list.

busby. In the 18th Century, a large bushy wig; in the 19th, the fur head-dress of a Hussar. ' Probably from surname *Busby* ' (W) : compare **caxon.** The originator—by association —of the former may be the famous disciplinarian pedagogue, Richard Busby (1606–95).

buttinsky and **wisenheimer** are punning names for ' an inquisitive person ', on the analogy of Russian and Polish surnames in *-insky* and German, hence Jewish, surnames in *-heimer*, with reference to *butt in*, ' to interfere gratuitously,' and *wise guy* or ' shrewdy '.

Byronic; Byronism. Literally, ' in the manner of Byron ' and ' imitation of Byron, behaviour or literary manner like Byron's ', these terms also imply ' a striving after—and, indeed,

77

the achievement of—effects picturesque, wildly romantic, eloquently declamatory, courageously and outrageously unconventional, fluent narrative or descriptive or satirical, supermanly heroic, fascinatingly passionate and Eros-energetic, readably restless, widely travelled, exotically attired, melancholy and despairing' and so forth. It used to be the fashion to deride Byron, Sir Max Beerbohm's cartoon not a little contributing to the derision : the 20th Century has, since 1918 at least, arrived at a juster evaluation of his work and character : no less than the somewhat Byronic Disraeli, he was vigorously 'on the side of the angels', however much the 'We are not amused' angels of the 19th Century doubted this spiritual fact. 'As to poor Byron, he's always trotted out by the Philistines who do much more harm in the world than ever he did, and not a tithe of the good' (Hugh I'Anson Fausset, *Between the Tides*, 1942).

George Gordon, Lord Byron (1788–1824), after a lonely boyhood, a stormy adolescence, an affair with the eccentric Lady Caroline Lamb, an unfortunate marriage, and travels on the Continent, left England in 1816—for his own, though not his country's good. Many physical wanderings and much spiritual experiment preceded his venture in the cause of Greek freedom and his death, at Missolonghi, from malarial fever. His influence on Continental literature (see, for instance, my *The French Romantics' Knowledge of English Literature*, Paris, 1924) ranks second only to that of Shakespeare among English writers. The best biography is that by Ethel Colburn Mayne, although the most readable is the very much shorter Life by André Maurois (the French have always adored the Byronic *panache*, as the Italians have paean'd his *bravura*, and the Germans bathed in his *Weltschmerz*) ; the best criticism, the essay in G. Wilson Knight's *The Burning Oracle*—a title that reproduces a Byronic phrase, from *Sardanapalus*.

C

[**cabal** comes, via Medieval Latin and French, from the *qubbalah* ; not, as the too ingenious, too little philological have said, from the initials of the surnames Clifford, Arlington, Buckingham, Ashley, Lauderdale, forming a Privy Council committee in the time of Charles II.]

cabana, as a make of cigar, derives from the name of its Spanish exporters.

cadmia; cadmium. Of the same origin as **Cadmean victory** in the secondary list.

caesarism; caesarist; caesarize. 'Screen Caesar Bans Channel Swim' is a fictitious headline in Gerald Kersh's pro-angelic *An Ape, a Dog and a Serpent*, 1945.

The three terms: meaning respectively 'imperialism; imperialist; to act like Caesar, to imperialize': refer not to Julius Caesar but to Caesar Augustus, who set up an absolute system of imperial and imperialistic government.

Cain-coloured and **Judas-coloured,** applied to human head-hair, signify 'reddish', both Cain and Judas being traditionally reputed to have had a red beard and thatch. Not, as I have heard it stated, because Cain suggests murder—blood—red, nor because Judas's treachery resulted in the shedding of Christ's blood. (Both *Cain* and *Judas* can be employed by themselves to mean 'reddish'.)

cairngorm. This precious stone is found upon *Cairngorm*, a Scottish mountain, and is particularly affected by Scots, especially for brooches. The name Cairngorm is merely a pin-pointing of the Gaelic *carn gorm*, cairn of blue; whence the *cairn terrier*, useful—and used—for hunting among cairns, a fact I mention because the dog is often presented with an unnecessary, unwanted, unjustifiable capital.

cairo is that form of the game of bridge which was devised, as an additional amenity to occidental life at Cairo, by one who preferred the city's commemoration to his own fame: Mr F. Comber.

calabar bean used always to be written with a capital *C*, because, like *Calabar ebony*, this very toxic seed of an African woody vine, a seed that in modern medicine serves a valuable purpose against, e.g., tetanus and that in African trials for witchcraft served the purpose of an ordeal, is connected with the river, the district, the town of **Calabar** in Southern Nigeria. Contrast:

calaber (fur), also spelt *calabar*, comes from the dark-brown squirrel of French *Calabre*, the effectual shape of the Italian *Calabria*, the peninsula lying between the Gulf of Taranto and the Tyrrhenian Sea. The 20th-Century calaber, by the way, is the grey fur worn by a certain Siberian squirrel.

calamander, short for *calamander-wood*, an ebony-like wood of India and Ceylon, may derive from Singhalese *kalimadiriya*,

which is regarded by some as a corruption of *Coromandel* (W) ;
compare *Coromandel ebony* and *coromandel wood*, the latter being
synonymous with *calamander*. Coromandel forms the southern
part of the eastern coast of the former Madras Presidency.

calamine in its Medieval Latin form, *calamina* (compare the
German *Kalmei*), probably represents an alchemists' corruption
—perhaps a deliberate perversion—of the Latin *cadmea*. See
cadmia above.

Caliban. ' We shudder at Caliban when we see him on the
stage, and we tremble for Miranda. But there are dozens of
Calibans in London, and they are free to wander where they
like, night and day ' : this comment upon potential homicidal
maniacs is as true now as when G. R. Sims wrote it in *Mysteries
of Modern London*, 1906.

Caliban, in Shakespeare's *The Tempest*, is apparently either
a particularization, by metathesis, of *cannibal* or an ' easing '
of *Cariban*, a Carib. In the American native languages,
another form of *Caribe* (Carib) is *Galibi* : *r, n, l* are interchangeable in the linguistic group. (The OED.)

calico. ' Sometimes the name of some common article hides
a story. Such words as cambric, damask, muslin, calico may
tell you very little, perhaps ; but to someone else . . . they
might raise questions and, after a little search, might open up
a great history of commerce and adventure, taking him to
Cambrai, and on into Syria to Damascus, and further afield to
Mesopotamia and Mosul, and at last in 1500 to India and
Calicut ' (T. R. Glover, *The Ancient World*, 1935).—' Cotton is
probably a native of sub-tropical Asia ; and, certainly, two of
the most important cotton products take their names from
Asiatic towns—muslin from Mosul, on the Tigris, and calico
from Calicut ' (Lionel W. Lyde, *Man and His Markets*, 1896).

Calico came to Europe from Calicut, which, on the Malabar
coast of India, ranked next to Goa in commercial intercourse
with Europe, and *Calicut* may have become *calico* via the French
Calicot (hence *calicot*, the cotton cloth).

calliope. ' " Come on now, men, we'll make it snappy," said
Slug Finerty. " Join in the song with the calliope " . . .
The crude heavy voices were drowned out by the wail of the
calliope,' Jim Tully, *Circus Parade*, 1928.

Circus Parade is a very American book ; and very good
reading. The calliope is a very American musical instrument
(' the rollicking notes of a calliope,' Harry Hervey, *School fo*

Eternity, 1942), with a keyboard and a series of steam-whistles constituting notes; but not very good hearing. Named after *Calliope* (four syllables), 'the beautiful of voice'—the ninth Muse and the patron-goddess of eloquence.

calmia. See **kalmia.**

calumba (formerly *columbo*; French, *colombo*), a mild stomachic and a gentle tonic, comes from a plant native to the forests of Mozambique—indeed, to Eastern Africa. The derivation from *Colombo* in Ceylon arose from the fact that, in the 18th–early 19th Century, the plant was erroneously supposed to be indigenous to, the medical root to be supplied from, Ceylon.

calvary in its figurative sense, 'a period or, more usually, an experience of intense pain and distress; especially of intellectual and, above all, spiritual suffering', comes either from *calvary*, an open-air representation of the crucifixion of Christ, or from the basic *Calvary*, that place where Christ was crucified, modern scholars tending to associate it with a *skull*-shaped eminence or rock above Jeremiah's grotto beyond the Damascus gate. The word comes from Latin *calvaria*, 'a bare skull' (Latin *calvus*, 'bald': probably from the synonymous Sanskrit *kulva*); the Vulgate *Calvaria* renders the Greek (*tō*) *Kranion*, 'the skull'— an interpretation of the Hebrew *Golgotha* (see **golgotha**).

calvinistic, 'characterized by or addicted to a rigorous, narrow-minded, bleak morality; hence, bleak, grim, forbidding' ('The woods were . . . a solemn place, canopied by Calvinistic heavens': John Buchan, *Memory Hold-the-Door*), springs naturally from the literal sense 'of or like Calvin or his doctrine'. John Calvin (1509–64) systematized and dehuman-ized almost the whole of Continental Protestantism. For him, original sin was inescapable by mankind—and yet man had to be severely punished for it. 'To the Calvinist,' writes Eric Linklater in *Mary, Queen of Scots*, 'dancing was a sin, music an abomination; in Geneva it was a crime to put finery in one's wardrobe or too many dishes on the table. . . . By 1561 the curious insanity of Calvinism had seriously infected Scotland and it was [John] Knox who chiefly carried the infection.'

cambogia. See **gamboge.**

cambrian (or **C**—). ' From Cambrian to Upper Carboniferous (i.e. Pennsylvanian) times, . . . we must conceive of a mountain land of continental proportions,' Ll. Rodwell Jones & P. W. Bryan, *North America*, (7th edition) 1946.

The term refers to a geological period preceding, a system of rocks lying under, the **silurian,** and the name was, in 1836, devised by geologist Sedgwick to classify a system characteristic of Wales, which the Romans called *Cambria* (a variant of *Cumbria*, transliterating the Celtic *Cymru*, Wales, or perhaps *Cymry*, Welshman).

cambric. (Cf. the Glover quotation at **calico.**)
Cambric was first made in Flanders at the town we know by its French name *Cambray* (now *Cambrai*), but the origination becomes clearer when we notice that the Flemish name is *Kamerijk* : *cambric* is, as it were, a blend of *Kamerijk* and *Cambray*. The early French form was *toile de Cambray*. An 18th-Century name for a fine linen made at Cambrai was *cambresine*.

' The textile industries are based on a favourable climate, abundance of coal, hereditary skill that is as typical of French Flanders as of Belgian Flanders, and excellence of local raw materials. . . . There is great division of labour, e.g. Calais and Arras, like Douai and Valenciennes, specializing in lace, —Cambrai and St Quentin in table-linen,—Fourmies and Croix, Roubaix and Tourcoing, in woollens,' L. W. Lyde, (' France ' in) *The Continent of Europe*, (4th edition) 1930.

camellia. This evergreen shrub was introduced to England from Japan ; or perhaps from the Philippines, for Linnaeus named the plant after a Moravian Jesuit, *Kamel* (latinized *Camellus*), who described the flora of Luzon ; the camellia flourishes also in China. Tea, by the way, is botanically known as *camellia theifera* (the tea-bearing, or -producing, camellia).

camembert. ' A roasted mallard duck, thought Soapy, would be about the thing—with a bottle of Chablis, and then Camembert, a demitasse and a cigar,' O. Henry, ' The Cop and the Anthem ' in *The Four Million*, (English edition) 1906.

' Normandy is as famous for its apples and cider as for its cattle and horses, its butter and " Camembert " cheese ' (Lionel W. Lyde, *The Continent of Europe*, 4th edition, 1930). Camembert is a village near Argentan, and the cheese named after it has been well-known in Britain since the late 1870's.

cami-bockers and **cami-knickers.** See **knickerbockers.**

camorra (with abstract noun, **camorrism**), ' a secret organization ', is a generalizing of the *Camorra*, that secret organization

82

which, instituted at Naples early in the 19th Century, was originally political in its aims but soon became also an agency for the extortion of money and protection and for the practice of violence. Perhaps the name arose because its first members wore a kind of smock or blouse : Florio, in his *A World of Words* (an Italian dictionary), 1598, defines *camorra* as ' a Mariners frocke '.

campignian (or **C—**). ' In France the most ancient New Stone culture is the Campignian, so called from Le Campigny, Seine-Inférieur. It is independent of, not developed from, any local Old Stone phase,' S. E. Winbolt, *Britain B.C.* (1943).

canaanite is a pyroxene that consists of either greyish- or bluish-white rock, so named because it was first found at *Canaan* in Connecticut. In 1905 Booth Tarkington published a very readable novel, *The Conquest of Canaan*. In Biblical history, Canaan is Western Palestine, the Promised Land, whence the figurative use of *Canaan* for ' heaven '; Tarkington's story carries a connotation of this figurative sense. *Canaan* represents the Latin and Greek *Chanaan*, for Hebrew *Kena'an*.

canada, whether ' Jerusalem artichoke ' or ' elecampane ', comes straight from *Canada*, by associations of cultivation and of trade. Compare **canuck** and :

Canader is Oxford University and elsewhere widely known slang for a ' Canadian canoe ', the type of canoe favoured by university students everywhere. The inimitable A. D. Godley (1856–1925), scholar, poet and wit, in *Lyra Frivola*, 1899, sang, ' O it's Youth in a Canader with the willow boughs to shade her ' (OED). The word is formed from *Canadian* with the help of that ubiquitous Oxford *-er* which we find in, e.g., *bed-sitter*; for this phonetic frivolity, see especially my *Slang To-Day and Yesterday*.

canary or, formerly, **canaries** is *Canary wine, wine of the Canaries* or the Canary Islands; **canary** is also short for *Canary bird*, found there, and, in Shakespeare, for *Canary dance*, a sprightly French dance based, according to tradition, upon the movements of a dance popular among the natives of those parts.

Via French *Canarie*, from Latin *Insula Canaria*, ' the Island of Dogs ' (*canis*, a dog).

Thomas Nicholas (or Nichols), who flourished in the 1550's and 1560's, was an English merchant; he wrote ' an original book, *A Description of the Fortunate Isles* (the *Canaries*), which he knew at first hand,' E. G. R. Taylor, *Tudor Geography*, 1930 that fanciful name, ' the Fortunate Isles ', reminds us of the legend of the Hesperides (see entry at **Hesperian**).

candytuft, a cultivated plant of the genus *Iberis*, is explained thus : ' The first introduced species . . . was brought from Candia ' (Webster), Candy being an obsolete English name for Candia, which we know as Crete.

canfield (or **C—**). See **saratoga.**

cannibal. In the 16th Century, it existed only in the plural, and that plural was *Canibales*, adopted direct from the Spaniards, who gave this form to the *Caribes* or *Caribs*, the natives inhabiting the West Indian islands of the Caribbean (originally *Cariban*) Sea. The letters *r* and *n*—and, for that matter, *l*— are interchangeable by West Indians ; compare **Caliban** ' The man-eating ' sense derives from the fact that the Caribs a fierce race (the word *carib* signifies ' brave and daring '), are recorded to have been eaters of human flesh : ' He is like a Canibal ' or ' no better than a Canibal ' soon became ' He is a cannibal '. (With thanks to ' The OED ' and to ' Webster '.)

'The first landfall of Columbus placed him within easy reach of the larger West Indian islands, and their size and fertility at once attracted the attention of early colonists, while for a period the lesser Antilles remained neglected. But there was a further reason for this. The warlike and cannibal Caribs, who inhabited also much of the Caribbean coast of South America put up a much more serious resistance to Spanish occupation and exploitation than the Arawaks, those meek cultivators of the greater islands and of the Darien coast ', Ll. Rodwell Jones in *North America* (by Jones & Bryan), (7th edition) 1946.

cantaloup or **cantaloupe,** a variety of musk-melon, comes, via French, from the Italian *cantalupo*, named after the castle of *Cantalupo* in the Italian province of Ancona, where these melons were first grown in Europe from seeds traditionally stated to have been imported from America.

canter derives from *Canterbury gallop*, which, less fast and less furious than a gallop, was the gait and pace adopted, when time pressed, by the pilgrims riding from all over England to the sacred shrine of St Thomas à Becket (murdered in 1170 and canonized in 1172) in the Kentish cathedral city of Canterbury. This pilgrimage, which took place annually for centuries, has been familiarized throughout the world by Chaucer's *The*

84

Canterbury Tales, written during the closing years of the 14th Century.

Compare:

anterbury is a stand that has divisions for music or loose papers and has been traditionally associated with *Canterbury,* the home of cathedral music and ecclesiastical muniments. The cathedral was commenced in the 12th Century.

The name *Canterbury* is an Englishing of Church Latin *Cantuaria,* itself from the Old English *Cantwarabyrig*—the town of the Kentish people. ' In the south-east, the tribes of Kent were united into a single unit with a capital at Canterbury, Durovernum Cantiacorum ', R. G. Collingwood, *Roman Britain,* (revised edition) 1937.

anuck, a Canadian horse, is American slang, from *Canuck,* which, in Canada a French Canadian, is, to the inhabitants of the United States, any Canadian. The word *Canuck* represents an American-Indian corruption of either English *Canadian* or French *Canadien*; *Canada* itself, however, appears to be an American-Indian word.

apuchin. See the subsidiary list.

aracul or **karakul,** usually apprehended in connexion with fur, is—compare **astrakhan**—the product from the wool of the newborn lambs of the *karakul* sheep, a hardy, broad-tailed breed suited to semi-arid regions and, whatever its place of origin, associated with the province of Bokhara. The breed takes its name from a lake in the Pamirs : *Kara Kul,* literally ' Black Lake ' : not far from the city of Bokhara. W cites from Matthew Arnold's *Sohrab and Rustum* (1853) an apposite passage :

> ' And on his head he plac'd his sheep-skin cap,
> Black, glossy, curl'd, the fleece of Kara-Kul '.

arbine. In its earliest form, *carabine,* it seems to have con-stituted the weapon of the *carabin,* or light horseman, although, as W points out, the converse may, as for the word *dragoon,* have been true. Although its origin is obscure, the Medieval French variant *calabrin* (Medieval Latin *calabrinus*) suggests a connexion of earliest use, or of manufacture, in Calabria. (Compare **calaber.**)

arcel, a light-standard common in France, is the light, roughly equal to that of nine British-standard candles, from a *Carcel* lamp, whether the French mechanical lamp with oil pumped by clockwork to the wick or an oil lamp employed in photo metric work. The inventor, ca. 1800, of the former was the French clockmaker, Bertrand Carcel (1750–1812).

cardan joint, cardan shaft; Cardanic; Cardan's solution Cardan's suspension. These mathematical and physical terms all derive from Jerome *Cardan* or, latinized, Hieronymus Cardanus or, native Italian, Geronimo Cardano (1501–76) mathematician, astrologer and physician; lecturer in mathematics, professor in medicine, researcher into astronomy, and writer upon astrology. A very able man, not remarkably ethical.

cardigan is short for *cardigan* (originally *Cardigan*) *jacket*—and derivative for the fabric from which these jackets are made The garment has been named after James Thomas Brudenell (1797–1868), 7th Earl of *Cardigan*. He led the famous charge of the six hundred—the charge of the Light Brigade—at the battle of Balaclava (1854) in the Crimean War. The cardigan is as warm as his temper.
Compare **balaclava** and **raglan.**

carlin or **carline** is that small silver coin which was first coined for Charles d'Anjou, King of Naples and Sicily: Carlo I, who reigned from 1266 to 1285 and who became one of the most potent of European monarchs. The coin was, not unnaturally struck to commemorate this king, the first of a royal line: the European word comes, via French, from the Italian *carlino* and *Carlino*, the derivative of *Carlo*, is ' the little Charles '.
Compare **louis** and **carolus** and **jacobus.**

carlowitz or **Carlowitz** (from the German *karlowitzer*), say André Simon, is ' the only Hungarian wine which ever attained a fair measure of popularity in England, during the 'sixties It is grown on the right bank of the Danube, thirty miles north of Belgrade, now within the borders of Yugoslavia.' That learned wine-drinker, George Saintsbury, did not think very highly of it. It is a strong, sweet red wine, and *Karlowitz* (or *-wicz*)—Hungarian *Karlocza* (from one of the Charleses, King of Hungary in the Middle Ages)—is both a town and its district.

carmagnole is historic rather than current; literary rather than general. Its chief sense is that of a round dance popular in the Paris of 1793—at the end of the Revolution.

86

'Originally this is the name of . . . a short coat, worn in the north Italian district of Carmagnola, and brought into France by workmen from that district. The insurgents of Marseilles in 1792 . . . introduced it to Paris, where it became identified with the Revolution. A round dance of the time was given the name and a song with the refrain " Dansons la Carmagnole, vive le son du canon ", to a very catchy air, became identified with revolutionary festivities such as executions,' as Dr Percy Scholes wittily notes.

carmelite, a light woollen fabric, usually brown or grey, and always plain-woven, derives from the stuff of the robes worn by the *Carmelite* Nuns, instituted in the 15th Century, and by the Carmelite Friars, an order founded, by Berthold in the 12th Century, on Mount *Carmel*—a sacred place already, the site of Elijah's sacrifice. In Hebrew, the place-name means ' the fruitful field ', almost ' the park '.

carolus. Any coin, though usually of gold, issued under a monarch named *Charles*, *Carlo*, etc., but especially a gold coin struck during the reign of Charles I of England. *Carolus* is merely the Medieval Latin form of *Charles*. Compare **jacobus** and **louis.**

carrageen (or **carri-** or **-gheen**) is the ' Irish moss ' of com- merce ; at least carrageen, a deep-purple seaweed, by being dried and bleached, becomes the article of commerce. So named from *Carragheen*, near Waterford, in the Irish Free State ; there, this edible seaweed abounds.

carronade, a short, light cannon, used, mostly on ships, during the approximate period 1779–1860, derives its name from the fact that these mortar-like guns were first cast at Carron near Falkirk, Scotland ; the vast Carron Ironworks opened on New Year's Day, 1760. Marryat refers to them more than once, as also does C. S. Forester in his Hornblower novels ; see, too, G. M. Trevelyan, *Social History of England*.

caryatid, ' a draped female figure supporting an entablature, in the place of a column or pilaster ' (Webster), recalls the historical fact that the priestesses serving in the temple of Artemis or, in Italy, Diana, were known as (Greek) *Karyatides* or (Latin) *Caryatides*, a term strictly applied to those in the temple at *Karyai*, or in Latin *Caryae*, a village in Laconia. Literally, *Karyatides* means ' maidens of Karyai ' : and in their ritual dances they occasionally assumed that attitude in which they figure in the statues.

Casanova. 'Orgiastic promiscuity . . . Each man seemed to think he was Priapus himself, or a Casanova trying to live a whole autobiography in an evening,' Hickman Powell, *Ninety Times Guilty*, 1939.—'I reckon that that Canadian mug is doin' a big Casanova act with some baby. An' I am right,' Peter Cheyney, *I'll Say She Does!*, 1945.

Giovanni Jacopo Casanova de Seingalt (1725–98), born into an Italian theatrical family, set upon his life an adumbration, a veritable sign-manual, by getting himself, aged sixteen, expelled from the seminary at which he had shown wit and a brilliant mind. Soldier, preacher, abbé, alchemist, gambler, violinist in turn, he for twenty years travelled, worked, women-intrigued in various European capitals. In 1755 imprisoned in Venice as a spy, he effected a daring escape and, on the strength of it (for he was a redoubtable raconteur), he dined out and bedded out for another twenty years. He ended up as a librarian in Bohemia, where he wrote his memoirs, no less cynical, sensual, witty than he. The **Don Juan** of real life.

cashmere, 'shawl of fine soft wool of Cashmere goat [or ibex]; the material; imitation of it' (COED). *Cashmere* is the anglicized form of *Kashmir*, a highland state of north-west India. The Indian name 'was, apparently, derived from the inhabitants, Kasmir Naga (? "Tree-Snake" people)'—as Professor L. W. Lyde has conjectured; *kasmir*, 'a tree', and *naga*, 'a snake', as in *Nagpathan*. The obsolete variants *kerseymere* and *cassimere* were respectively influenced by *kersey*, a different fabric, and by the French form *casimir*.

Concerning Mesopotamia but closely relevant is this quotation from Lionel W. Lyde's *The Continent of Asia*, 1933: 'Medinet-es-Salaam, the "City of Peace", was not built—out of the ruins of Greek Seleucia and Parthian Ctesiphon—until c. A.D. 760. The "peace" at which the Arab conquerors of Ctesiphon had wondered so greatly, was the peace of a Persian winter-garden, with its Tree of Life (evergreen) and its Tree of Knowledge (fruit); and so the city was given its *Persian* name of Baghdad, "Garden City", and the map of the garden is still the design of the famous Chashura-Shaki ("Garden-carpet"), as the design of a real Kashmir shawl plots the meanderings of the Jumna.' More immediate is the following quotation from the same book: 'Kashmir probably still stands at the head of all the Indian units in skilled craftsmanship. Some of the artistic inspiration came from Persia . . . ; but much of the development was quite local, e.g. breeding of sheep with different coloured fleeces, use of water-power, and cultivation of vegetable dyes. . . . The " wedding-ring " shawls were made of the underhair of the ibex.'

The poetry the word evokes may be sensed in, for example, this brief passage from Nard Jones, *Swift Flows the River*, 1939 (English edition, 1940) : ' There facing me she stood, one bare arm outstretched from her peignoir. . . . She came forward and lifted her face to mine. The cashmere rustled against me, like the crackling of the white flame of her body.'

caslon, or **C—,** is short for *Caslon type*—an agreeably legible printing-type designed by the English type-founder and printer, William Caslon (1692–1766), and maintained by his son William. The type, becoming popular, was much used both in Britain and in America, and also on the Continent, until ca. 1800 ; it was revived, in the 1840's, by The Chiswick Press, and has on several occasions been modified.

Compare **baskerville.**

Cassandra is allusively employed to signify any such prophetess of evil as meets with incredulity or scorn. The word is the Latin, Italian, English form of the Greek *Kassandra* or *Kasandra*. In Greek mythology, she was the daughter of Priam and Hecuba. Rejecting the advances of Apollo, she was punished by having her prophecies rendered a mockery through the simple Olympian trick whereby her auditors never believed her when she prophesied. For instance, she foretold the doom of Troy. Troy captured, she fell, by lot, to Agamemnon, with whom, at Mycenae, she was slain by the ruthless Clytemnestra.

cassidony. See its doublet, **chalcedony.**

cassimere. See **cashmere.**

cassock. Webster thinks that the word probably comes from the same root as *chasuble* ; Skeat proposes Italian *casa*, ' a house '—an opinion The OED almost endorses. W, however, hits the mark, I think, by saying, ' Probably of Slavonic origin, ? *Cossack* (coat). Compare *dalmatic*, *cravat*, and obsolete *esclavine*, Slav mantle. *Cossack* is regularly *Cassock* in Hakluyt.'

castile = *Castile soap*. This soap came originally from Castile, a province in Spain. The colours *Castilian brown* and *Castilian red* are so named because they were magnificently employed by

89

Spanish painters. The word *Castile* is intrinsically noteworthy in that it represents the Spanish *Castilla*, from Latin *castilla*—the smallish forts built on the frontiers as a safeguard against the Moors. *Castellum* itself is the diminutive of *castrum*, 'a fortified place'.

catacomb, usually in the plural, exemplifies a not infrequent problem. In Late Latin, *catacumba*—apparently a hybrid. Greek *kata*, 'down' + Latin *tumba*, 'tomb'—means a subterranean cemetery; there is no trace of Proper Name origin, but the modern senses of the word derive from the widespread fame attaching to the great catacombs that, on the Appian Way near Rome, were used by the early Christians: '*the* Catacombs'.

catamite, a juvenile pathic, traces his ancestry, via the Latin *Catamitus*, to the Greek *Ganumēdēs*, *Catamitus* being simply an old shape of the Classical Latin *Ganymedes*. In Greek mythology, Ganymede was that son of Tros who was carried off, either by the collective Olympian gods or by Zeus's eagle, or by Zeus himself, to be made, on account of his beauty, cup-bearer in chief to Zeus.

catawba is a light-red variety of American grape, hence the wine made therefrom, hence the colour thereof; and the grape was named after that Siouan tribe of Red Indians which had its original home near the *Catawba* River in the Carolines. In Choctaw, as Webster (unrivalled in these American etymologies) says, Catawba has the shape *Katápa*, 'the Separated'—from the other tribes of the Sioux.

catonism, or **catoism,** means 'stoicism, austerity', and derives from *Cato* (*Catonis*, of Cato), the name of a very famous and remarkable family of Republican Rome. Both Cato the Elder (234–149 B.C.), or Cato the Censor, and his grandson, Cato of Utica (95–46 B.C.), were austere, unbending, stoic, and harsh, of undoubted integrity but deficient in generosity and in human kindness: *Catonian*. The name *Cato* comes from Latin *catus*, 'sagacious'.

cattleya is a plant of the genus *Cattleya*, orchids with a quite imperial bloom; whence *cattleya fly*. Then there is the *Cattley guava*, a widely grown, sub-tropical fruit. The originator is William *Cattley*, English amateur botanist and a patron of botany in the earlier half of the 19th Century.

90

cavendish. (1) That brand of fine virginia (q.v.) which is known as Gold Block carries a label that generically describes it as 'Cavendish or Negrohead'.

'I am an officer of Customs . . . I found on him 5 lbs of cavendish tobacco,' *Sessions Paper* (of the Central Criminal Court, London), February 28, 1872.—'A short while afterwards he rose, filled his clay pipe with cavendish, which he ground fine between his hands, and . . . left the two young people', W. J. Locke, *The Demagogue and Lady Phayre*, 1896.

Named either after a famous Elizabethan family or from the exporter.

(2) A treatise on whist : *Cavendish* was the pen-name of H. Jones, who in 1862 published one.

caxon is archaic for a wig. As W suggests, it may derive from the surname *Caxon* : compare **busby.** (Webster and The OED are of the same opinion.)

caxton may be either any book printed by Caxton and perhaps better written *Caxton*, or a black-letter type resembling that used by Caxton. William Caxton (1422?–91), 'the Father of British Printing', after an apprenticeship on the Continent returned to England in 1476 and immediately established a printing press at Westminster. He translated or wrote some of the books he printed.

cayenne, short for *cayenne pepper*, comes from *kyinha* or *quiynha*, which in the Tupi language of Brazil means 'capsicum' and which, according to Webster, derives from the Tupi name of the island we call *Cayenne*. Despite several etymologists, the connexion with Cayenne is not false but factual.

cayuse, 'an Indian pony' : from *Cayuse*, a member of the Red Indian tribe known as the Cayuses (a Red Indian name), of Waiilatpuan stock. In reference to a folk-tale, Nard Jones (in *Scarlet Petticoat*, 1942) has said that 'Out of the arms of Wishpoosh he [Speelyei] made the Cayuses, famous fighters'. Derivatively, *cayuse* has, since ca. 1880, meant 'a horse of little value, a sorry jade, a nag'.

cecily, cicely. In his delightful and richly informative *Words and Names*, Professor Ernest Weekley, in a few well-chosen words, settles the case of *cecily* and other such terms. 'Though many names of plants (*ragged robin, sweet william, creeping jinny, prattling parnell*, etc.) are actual nicknames, some of them are perversions of more scientific words, e.g. *cicely* or *cecily*, used of several umbelliferous plants, is the Greek *seseli*, and *sweet alison* is a corruption of the Latin *alyssum*. Less graceful, but very characteristic of this tendency is the Kent and Sussex *simpson*, groundsel, French *seneçon*, Latin *senecio*. *Tincture of Queen Anne* (quinine) is a good example of what folk-etymology can do in this direction.']

celadon, both as *Celadon green* and as a grass-green or pastel-green porcelain from China, appears to come from *Celadon*, in pastoral poems a type-name for a rustic lover, itself derived from that *Céladon* who, in D'Urfé's romance, *Astrée*, is Astrée's lover. Honoré d'Urfé's heroic pastoral, 1607–27, had· a tremendous vogue and was imitated throughout Europe: in 1624 an ' academy of true lovers ' was founded in Germany to live the life depicted in *Astrée*; in Thompson's ' Summer ' (1727)—part of *the Seasons*—occurs the touching episode of Celadon and Amelia; to take but two examples.

The French *Céladon* is the Latin *Celadon*, which transliterates the Greek *Keladōn*; the name occurs twice in Ovid's *Metamorphoses*.

celanese is a proprietary name for a certain kind of artificial silk. It is a purposeful perversion of *Ceylonese*, ' of Ceylon '. Not that Ceylon is famous for silk; it isn't. But Ceylon—*Sinhala*, ' the Land of the Lion '; the Hindu *Lanka-dwipa* or ' Shining Island '—evokes the so-imagined exotic Orient. *Ceylanite* or *Ceylonite*, a mineral containing iron, is found there.

celt; celtium. The latter, a postulated chemical element, certainly derives from the Latin *Celtae*, the Celts; the former, a prehistoric axe-shaped stone or a primitive chisel, comes from Late Latin *celtis*, ' a chisel ', which may—or may not—derive from the same radical as *Celta*, a Celt.

Cerberus, ' a vigilant and surly custodian or door-keeper ', is the lineal descendant of *Cerberus*, the latinized Greek *Kerberos* ' akin to Sanskrit *Sábala*, one of the two dogs of Yama ' (Webster), but itself an echoic word. In Greek mythology Kerberos—mentioned by such Latin poets as Lucretius, Virgil Horace, Ovid—is a monster-dog with plural heads (some say a hundred, others fifty, and yet others, the predominant later authorities, three) and the watch-dog guardian of the gates to Hades or the Underworld: a large and fearsome beast with snakes for hair, and with a serpent tail, but no match for Hercules, who, as his 12th Labour, carried him off.

cereal, short for *cereal food*, derives from the idea of *cereal* (or grain) *crops*. Originally an adjective, *cereal* = ' of, from, like grain or the " grasses " producing it ' and represents the Latin *cerealis*, ' pertaining to *Ceres*, hence to agriculture '. Ceres, at first an Italian deity, the goddess of the creative or generative forces in Nature, became identified with Demeter, the Greek goddess of corn in particular and of agriculture in general. The basis *cer* derives from—or is, at the least, cognate with—the Sanskrit *kri*, ' to make ' ; cf. Latin ' *crea*re ', whence our *create*.

ceric ; cerium ; cerous. *Ceric* means ' containing cerium ' ; and *cerium*, named in 1803 after the recently discovered asteroid *Ceres*, so called in honour of the goddess (see the preceding entry), is a metallic element. Likewise, *cerous* means ' belonging to, or containing, cerium '.

cerise (the colour) ; **cherry.** The former is the French for ' a cherry ' and is often used by fashion-formers and fashion-followers to mean ' cherry colour ' or ' cherry-coloured '—' (of) a light clear red '.

' Great enterprise was shown by the Romans in acclimatising Mediterranean or Asiatic fruit-trees, such as the cherry and the peach ', M. Cary, *A History of Western Europe, A.D.* 1–455 (published in 1928). As the **peach** from Persia, so the cherry from Asia Minor. ' . . . Cerasus (modern Kerasunda), whence our word " cherry " is derived to denote the fruit for which the town was famed ', W. W Hyde, *Ancient Greek Mariners*, 1947.

The English apprehended Old Northern French *cherise* as a plural : for them, therefore, only the *cheri* part of the word possessed validity. The French word represents Latin *cerasum*, from Greek *kerasion*, traditionally brought, ca. 100 B.C., by the gourmet Lucullus from *Cerasus* (Greek *Kerasos*) in Pontus, a district in north-west Asia Minor. Nevertheless, it is, as W points out, tenable that the district took its name from the tree : The Land of Cherries. If the latter theory be correct, then Greek *kerasion* may derive from, or be cognate with, *keras*, ' horn '—from its smooth bark (W compares *hornbeam*). I prefer the derivation of the tree (and its fruit) from the place : compare **damson** and **peach** and **quince**.

ceylonite. See entry at **celanese.**

chablis. ' You like trout in chablis, don't you, mother? ' (Georges Simenon, *The Shadow Falls*, translated by Stuart Gilbert, 1945).

This white French wine, a burgundy, which England owes to the Restoration (the Stuarts learned a thing or two while they were exiled in France), is made near the small town of Chablis in the *département* of Yonne.

chalcedony, a translucent quartz, subdivides, if of variegated colour, into agate, carnelian, onyx, etc. The doublet of *chalcedony* is *cassidony* (i, French lavender ; ii, goldilocks), which helps to illustrate its origin. The Middle English form is *cassidoine*, from Old French *cacidoine* or *calcedoine*, from Latin *chalcedonius* (*lapis*), stone of Greek *Chalkēdōn*, a town that, in Bithynia, stands on the Thracian Bosporus and opposite the great port, the metropolis, of Byzantium : compare the Chalcedonic *smaragdi* (emeralds, beryls, etc.) mentioned by Pliny.

challis, formerly an unglossed, soft wool-and-silk dress fabric and now, usually as *challie*, a very light woollen, or cotton and wool usually printed fabric, is, by most lexicographers, said to be ' of uncertain origin '. W, however, proposes an origin, either in **Calais** (pronounced *Chalais* in Northern French dialect) or in the surname *Challis* (itself being ' man from, or of, Calais ') The fabric was first made at Norwich, and I venture to postulate a Challis prominent in its early manufacture or perhaps in its early distribution.

chalon. See **shalloon.**

chalybean, ' of steel ' ; **chalybeate,** ' impregnated with iron '— hence ' a medicine flavoured with iron '. As The OED remarks, ' it is not certain whether steel was named from the Chalybes or *vice versa* ' (the Chalybes being an ancient people of Asia Minor and famous for their working of iron into weapons, instruments, utensils, ornaments) ; but—compare the genesis of **copper**—the probability is that *chalybean*, *chalybeate* derive from the Proper Name.

   ' The most interesting god [in Hellenistic times] was the local deity of . . . Doliche in Commagene, who lived " where the iron grew " ; for he was . . . god of that strange broken people, the Chaldi or Chalybes, the greatest iron-smiths of the world west of China, who had once ruled the kingdom of Van in Armenia, but were now scattered in groups wherever there was iron to enable them to set up their forges and practise their inherited technique,' W. W. Tarn, *Hellenistic Civilisation* (revised edition) 1930.

94

chambertin. A red wine—a superior burgundy—it has been named after the Burgundian vineyard where its vine is grown, eight miles from Dijon. As early as 1775, an historian of wine noted that 'it is generally preferred to any other wine in Burgundy' (The OED).

chambéry. 'We sipped Chambéry as we waited for our soup,' Mark Benney, *The Big Wheel*, 1940.

This wine takes its name from the small cathedral town of Chambéry, which, in the *département* of Savoie in France, is also noted for silk and soap.

champagne is the wine of *Champagne*, a province of eastern France. *Champagne* is cognate with English *champaign*, 'open country', from Old French *champaigne*, from Italian *campagna*, from *Campagna* (Latin *Campania*), the plain south-east of the Tiber—a vast *campus* or 'field' or, basically, 'piece of level ground'.

'Between the two great northward bends of the Loire, . . . the Cretaceous and Tertiary elements are so well mixed, and have been so much enriched for centuries by river-floods, that the area has come to be called "the Garden of France"' (Lionel W. Lyde, *Europe*, 1913); 'The Champagne region possesses the two great requirements of the vine in the northern hemisphere: (1) a slope of 30° to 45° between the actual terraces on which the vines are mostly planted, and (2) a south-eastern aspect, so as to catch the maximum of sunshine in the late autumn' (Lyde).

For another French-Province wine-name, see **burgundy.**

chaney. See **cheyney.**

chantecleer (or **-icleer**). A cock, especially as chanter of untimely aubades, in English owes this fanciful name to the Chantecleer in Chaucer's *Nun's Priest's Tale*; but Chaucer, in turn, owes it to the Chantecler in the medieval French *Roman de Renart*.

charleston. The Charleston fox-trot was popular in America, Europe, and elsewhere ca. 1925–27. It came to the Whites from the Negroes of the Southern States of America.

Hence, to *charleston*, to dance the charleston. Side-kicks from the knee differentiated it from earlier fox-trots.

Charleston, the seaport in Southern Carolina, has always been exposed—and indeed, susceptible—to Negro influences. The centre of the cotton trade, it has a population of about

71,000, half of whom are Negroes. 'The Charleston settlement' (a very early one) 'had characteristics arising from three main factors. Firstly: its intimate relations with the Barbadoes, Bahamas and West Indies generally. Secondly: it represented the only port of call and of refilling between the West Indies and Virginia. Thirdly: the southern temperature made possible the cultivation of rice. . . . The slave economy and plantation system were transplanted . . . bodily to Charleston': Ll. Rodwell Jones in Jones & Bryan, *North America*, (7th edition) 1946. DuBose Heyward (1885–1940), of South Carolina, has written extensively about the Negro, most notably in *Porgy*—novel, 1925; play, 1927; Gershwin opera, 1935—in *Mamba's Daughters*, novel in 1929, play in 1939 —in *Peter Ashley*, 1932—and in *Star Spangled Virgin*, 1939.

charley, or **charlie,** is the fox, from the famous English statesman and orator, *Charles* James *Fox*; a short, pointed beard, reminiscent of that worn by *Charles* I of England and more widely known as a **vandyke**; or a night-watchman before the inception of a regular police force, the name being perhaps associated, by folklore rather than in historic fact, with either *Charles* I or *Charles* II. History, however, does not have to be enlisted: compare the ubiquity of such diminutives as **bob(by)** and **jack** and **tom.**

charlotte; c. russe. The latter is a culinary development or elaboration of the former dish (as in *apple charlotte*), the *russe* being a tribute to the excellence of the cooking at the court of the Czars of Russia; French *russe* = Russian. And *charlotte* itself constitutes a tribute to those excellent Charlottes who have dedicated themselves to 'feeding the brute'. Compare **little Mary** (subsidiary list).

Charon. 'Shadow of Charon'; imminence of death; forms a chapter in Mabel Lethbridge's pleasingly unpretentious autobiography, *Against the Tide*, 1936: which is a much more dignified use of *Charon* than to equate it with 'ferryman', as journalists were formerly wont to do, for, after all, he was Death's ferryman, conveying across the **Styx** to Hades the bodies of the dead. In modern Greek folklore he survives, rather less as ferryman than as the Angel of Death.

The name signifies 'He of the bright, fierce eyes' (*kharopos* is an almost exact synonym).

chartreuse. 'She should never have bought the thing,'—an expensive grey fur coat—'with her light brown hair and the

faint colouring of her skin and her outlandish chartreuse eyes ',
Rex Stout, *Bad for Business*, (English edition) 1945.

Pale apple-green eyes. The colour, *chartreuse*, derives from
the liqueur (brandy flavoured with fragrant herbs), which,
originally, was made at La Grande-*Chartreuse*, the head
monastery (near Grenoble in France) of the Carthusian Order.
La Grande-Chartreuse is *la grande maison chartreuse*; in French,
a *Chartreux* is a Carthusian.

Charybdis. See **Scylla . . .**

chassepot, an obsolete direct-action bolt gun firing a cartridge,
is one of the numerous firearms bearing the inventor's name
(e.g., *martini-henry, gatling, maxim, lewis,* and many others). In
this instance it was the French inventor, Antoine *Chassepot*
(1833–1905), whose musket was adopted by the French Army
in 1866. In his very readable *Quaker Campaigns*, 1899, William
Jones, of the Society of Friends, speaks highly of the efficacy of
the chassepot as used by the French in the Franco-Prussian War
(1870–71).

chaumontel, a European pear so luscious as to justify the slangy
descriptives, ' goluptious ' and ' scrumptious ' and ' lush '. It
takes its name from *Chaumontel*, a village in the *département* of
Seine-et-Oise, France. Dr Johnson, who knew a good thing
when he saw it, mentions the chaumontel in his *Dictionary*.

Chautauqua ; as an adjective, often—in the present century, at
least—*chautauqua*. Growing out of the *lyceum*, the Chautauqua
movement was already strong in the U.S.A. by 1874. Originally religious, it went on to include education, drama, music :
' and " chautauqua " became a generic name for programs
given by troupes of lecturers and entertainers . . . performing
in rural settlements ' (James D. Hart). The name, which is
Indian, has been adopted from that of a county, and a lake, in
the south-west of New York State.

But why *Chautauqua* at all? Because, the movement being
initially a complement to the *Lyceum* movement and *lyceum*
having essentially and markedly urban associations, a rural
antiphrasis was required.

chauvin, chauvinism, chauvinistic. Respectively an intense
patriot, excessively French patriotism (*O, la belle France*, and all
that), and excessively patriotic (*La patrie, c'est tout!*), derive
from a character in Cogniard's too famous vaudeville, *La
Cocarde Tricolore*, 1831 (' Je suis français, je suis Chauvin ') :

a character based upon an actual person, Nicolas Chauvin of Rochefort, that veteran of *La Grande Armée* who rendered himself ridiculous by his inordinate protestations and demonstrations of loyalty to Napoleon and of devotion to Napoleon's France.

cheapjack. See **Jack.**

cheddar. Writing in 1906, John Ross (*Masques and Phases*, 1909) has noted that ' an enterprising American syndicate was once formed for manufacturing Stilton cheeses on a large scale ; like the pirated Cheddars from similar sources ' ; ' I went forward and begged a bottle of water, two slabs of meat pasty, three currant buns, one slab [i.e., slice of bread] and gorgonzola, one slab of cheddar and one mince turnover. After consuming those I was myself again ' (but for how long?), Hippo Neville, *Sneak Thief on the Road*, 1935 ; and, in his witty novel, *The Horse's Mouth* (1944), Joyce Cary tells us that ' Mr Barbon came in. Middle-sized walrus with a squeezed up face and a head like a wedge of cheddar.'

Short for *Cheddar cheese*, made at and in the neighbourhood of Cheddar, a Somerset village near the Mendip Hills.

cheddite, an explosive much used for blasting, commemorates the fact—compare the history of **lyddite**—that it was first made at *Chedde*, a town in the La Haute-Savoie in France, a region particularly suitable to experimentation with blasting.

Chelsea is often used as a synonym for ' the " world " of British art ', ' the artists' district '. Many artists have, in the 20th Century, lived and worked there. In 1925, Stanley Scott could write in *Tales of Bohemia*, ' Chelsea is looked upon nowadays as the playground of a lot of mediocre young men and women playing at Art, dressing the artist, and generally aping the Quartier Latin. . . . The genuine artist, who has no time to bother about velvet jackets and flowing ties, is wondering whether he can take out an action for criminal libel against a type ! ' Chelsea, London, S.W.3, has its charm. (Also see the subsidiary list.)

cherry. See **cerise.**

cheshire, i.e. *C. cheese*, is so called because it is made, for the most part, in the county of Cheshire, England. By itself, but always with Capital *C*, *Cheshire* is also used for a medium-sized white pig, bred mostly in Cheshire.

For **Cheshire cat,** see the subsidiary list.

chesterfield. ' Sitting down on the roomy chesterfield, he talked easily enough ' (E. C. R. Lorac, *Case in the Clinic*, 1941), as well he might on this comfortable form of couch, named after a 19th-Century Earl of Chesterfield ; like a sofa, it has a back, but unlike a sofa, it has two raised ends. The word bears the connotation of solid yet elegant comfort, as, for instance, in ' There were Louis XV chairs, . . . a heavy leather chesterfield, and an expensive radiogram ' (James Curtis, *The Gilt Kid*, 1936—a novel, however, dealing with the underworld of London, one of the best and most authentic of all the books on that subject).

The Earl of Chesterfield understood the art of living and the appeal—and value—of comfort, for it was after him too that the *chesterfield* garment, a man's overcoat, was named ; as in ' He had a black felt Homburg on, an oxford grey suit, a velvet-collared Chesterfield ' (Richard Sale in *Detective Fiction Weekly*, March 5, 1938). But then the Chesterfields always have believed that life should, so far as possible, be an art—not a mere, inglorious muddle.

With the overcoat, cf. **raglan** and **spencer.**

cheviot. ' He wore a small-rimmed derby hat and a double-breasted coat of blue cheviot,' Arthur Stringer, *The Man Who Couldn't Sleep*, 1919.—' He was always neatly dressed in English suitings . . . dark Cheviot, with a stripe ', Gerald Kersh, *I Got References*, 1939.

The ' blue cheviot ' was a blue-dyed fabric made from the wool of the famed sheep of the Cheviot Hills (the Anglo-Scottish border-land), these short-wool'd creatures bearing a thick-set fleece of a kind that yields a strong and agreeable cloth, suitable for men's suitings and even for women's gowns. ' Climate, hill-pastures, and soft water are '—to the woollen industry—' favourable along the Cotswolds and the Cheviots ', L. W. Lyde, *The Continent of Europe*, 1913. Compare :

chevy, chiv(v)y, ' to pursue ; hence, to badger ', seems to derive from *Chevy Chase*, a corruption of *Cheviot Chase* : in English dialect, *Chevy Chase* signified ' a chase or pursuit '. The origination is twofold : by a pun on Chevy Chase itself and, by allusion to the extremely popular 16th-Century ballad of *Chevy Chase*, from the hunting-cry, *chevy!* A later version of the ballad, W tells us, is called *Cheviot Hunting*.

cheyney is china (i.e., China) ware. Until well into the 19th Century, *china* was pronounced *cheyney* (*chanee*). Therefore see **china.**

99

chian is *Chian wine*; Chios, a large Ionian island off the coast of Asia Minor, was celebrated for its wine—and its figs. Certain writers have confused *chian* with *coan*, the more so that both of these wines were famous during the Hellenistic, and not unknown in the Classical Greek, period. ' Wine was produced everywhere, but the finest wines were a speciality of two countries : North Syria . . ., and Ionia with the coastal islands (except Samos) ; Lesbos, Chios, Cos, Cnidus, Ephesus, Smyrna, Tmolus, and the volcanic Katakekaumene were all famous. Alexandria insisted on Syrian and Ionian wines, as London insists on champagne,' W. W. Tarn, *Hellenistic Civilisation*, (revised edition) 1930.

chianti and **asti spumante.** ' By a brilliant night march on December 8–9th [1940], the 4th [Indian] Division surrounded Nibeiwa Camp, where the Italians were drinking their chianti,' F. Yeats-Brown, *Indian Pageant*, 1943.

' A waiter spread caviar and opened a bottle of Asti Spumante. . . . She took her glass of Asti,' Eric Ambler, *Cause for Alarm*, 1938.

' The waiter brought a big flask of Chianti, a rarity, a treasure, a privilege,' John Brophy, *Target Island* (Malta), 1942.

' The best " export " wines ' (of Italy), says Professor L. W. Lyde, *The Continent of Europe*, (4th edition) 1930, ' come naturally from the least backward provinces, e.g. the Asti of Piedmont and the Chianti of Tuscany '—that is, from the Chianti Mountains. Chianti, a dry red wine, though not, by connoisseurs, held to be ' superior ', nevertheless constitutes an excellent bourgeois drink.

chickasaw may be a rose (the Cherokee rose)—a plum (of the Mississippi region)—a grape (delicious, but unknown before ca. 1860) : all of them, American amenities, the word *chickasaw* representing the name of the tribe of Red Indians, whose habitat was, in the main, the area now constituting the State of Mississippi.

chimaera, chimerical. ' Gorgons and hydras and chimaeras dire,' Milton, *Paradise Lost*, ii, 628.—' Rome in 200 [B.C.] . . . was afraid—afraid that Philip and Antiochus would conquer and control Egypt . . . and launch against Italy all Alexander's empire. It was a chimaera ; the two kings, though allies, profoundly distrusted each other,' W. W. Tarn, *Hellenistic Civilisation*, (revised edition) 1930.—' Pure deductive science breaks down because its object turns out to be a chimera, a structure which is the structure of nothing, a law with no instances,' R. G. Collingwood, *Speculum Mentis*, 1924.

The Chimaera (Greek *Chimaira*), in Greek mythology, was dragon-tailed, lion-headed, goat-bodied, and, says Virgil, ' armed with flame '. After causing much consternation, the Chimaera was slain by Bellerophon, aided by the winged horse, **Pegasus.**

china. ' Structural variety has endowed the province [of Kiangsi] with a very valuable coal-field (of good coking coal) in the sedimentary rocks of one diagonal rib, and with kaolin '— a fine white clay—' in the crystalline rocks of another rib, the basis of the most famous *china* industry in the world,' Lionel W. Lyde, *The Continent of Asia*, (revised edition) 1938. The Imperial Porcelain works were founded in the 11th Century.

As silk is ' the Chinese fabric ', so *china* is ' the Chinese ware '. Originally (early C. 17) *China* (often spelt *Cheney* or *cheney*) *ware*, it soon became *china ware*; *China* occurs ca. 1650 ; and, from ca. 1690, the word is often lower-cased. Thence by a natural transition, *china* came to mean no more than ' made of china or porcelain ' : indeed, by one of those oddities of philological recording, the attributive or adjectival use of the word occurs, apparently rather than really, much earlier than the substantival. (With thanks to The OED.)

For the relations of china to silk, turn to **silk.**

China ink. See the entry at **India paper.**

china orange was originally *China orange*, this fruit—the ' sweet orange ' of the fruit trade—coming, at first, from China. Pepys, in his diary, speaks of ' china oranges . . . a great rarity ' : they were brought to Europe by the Portuguese in the 16th Century : cf. the German name, *Apfelsine*, literally ' apple of China ' (W).

china white. ' Mist breaking into round fat shapes, china white on Dresden ', Joyce Cary in a novel about a painter— *The Horse's Mouth*, 1944.

Chinatown is that part of any city where the Chinese population congregates. In some cities it is the official—the topographical —name ; in most, it is a convenient colloquialism. (Never *Chinese Town*.)

chiné ; adj. and n., is ' (a fabric, especially silk) either dyed or woven with a design either mottled or vague after a Chinese fashion—actual or imagined '. The French word *chiné* = ' rendered Chinese ' (in style, etc.), from French *Chine*, China.

Chinese evil, the. Leprosy (*elephantiasis Graecorum*). Of the three million lepers in the world, one million are in China.

' When he, too, was filled with the Chinese Evil, she could not bear to look at him or touch him, and when he went away, he went alone,' Richard Sale, *Cardinal Rock*, 1940—a powerful novel on the theme of leprosy.

Chinese lantern. This type of lantern came to Europe from China, where, originally, it was not merely decorative but utilitarian ; it deeply impressed the early travellers.

Chinese puzzle. ' There are seven of these [silent] cells and they are in fact cells within cells in the same way that chokey is a prison within a prison—a sort of ghastly Chinese puzzle box,' ' Red Collar Man ', *Chokey*, 1937.

These boxes within boxes were made originally in China— and even now, nowhere else so well made.

chinook is short (*a*), for *Chinook wind* ; (*b*), for *Chinook language*, the *lingua franca* (English, French, Chinook and other dialects) among Red Indians themselves and between Red Indians and white traders. The latter arose as a means of communication between the Hudson Bay Company factors and the Columbia and Oregon Indians. There was, in the region watered by the Columbia river of North America, a tribe known as the *Chinooks* : the Company early established a trade contact with them. ' Both the Clatsops and the Chinooks . . . had the short thick legs and the powerful yet misshapen shoulders and arms bespeaking of generation upon generation in canoes,' Nard Jones, *Scarlet Petticoat*, 1942.

chippendale or **C—.** ' The fine sideboard, the laid oval table with candles unlighted, the four good Chippendale chairs,' James Gould Cozzens, *A Cure of Flesh*, 1933.

Thomas Chippendale (1718–79), son of a Yorkshire picture-frame-maker, set up a furniture factory in London in 1749 and, in 1754, set forth the theory of his craft in *The Gentleman and Cabinet-maker's Director*, wherein he folio-illustrated the designs of his solid, comfortable, yet ornate and graceful styles. His son Thomas, who died ca. 1822, carried on his father's worthily flourishing business.

Concerning *The . . . Director*, Oliver Brackett has, in his

English Furniture, 1928, remarked, ' The book served as a useful key to the elements of the subject. . . . Consequently the term " Chippendale " was adopted by dealers and others as an explanatory label for a vast amount of mahogany furniture of the eighteenth century, and the public made use of the expression without bothering much about its meaning.' See too the same writer's *Thomas Chippendale*, 1924.

chittagong or **malay,** (1) a domestic fowl of the Malayan type, was introduced into England somewhere about 1820—probably rather earlier. Obviously the name is short for *Chittagong fowl*, Chittagong being the name of a district and town in Bengal.

Compare **brahmapootra.**

(2) And *chittagong* also = *Chittagong tea*, a noted tea from India.

choctaw is a step, a movement, in fancy ice-skating, and the name comes from the *Choctaw* Indians of North America. The Choctaws or Chahtas, an agricultural tribe, formerly occupied the south of the present Mississippi, and the west of the present Alabama State ; they have long been settled in the reserved Indian Territory. They fought against the British during the American Revolution and, in the 19th Century, again assisted the Americans—this time against the Creek Indians.

chow is a dog of Chinese breed ; rather like a **pomeranian,** it has a black tongue and its coat is usually either black or brown.

The OED says that the word is short for *chow-chow*, a Chinese preserve of ginger, orange peel, and several other ingredients ; and Weekley says that it comes from *chow*, a pidgin word for ' food '. But to me it seems more probable that the *chow* dog has the same origin as the Australian slang *Chow*, ' a Chinese ' : that the dog is ' *the* (or at least *a*) Chinese dog ', *Chow* being a survival of the name of an ancient race in China, the (*Chu* or) *Chou* Dynasty, mentioned in every reputable account of China and in such works as Lyde's *Asia* and Childe's *What Happened in History*.

christen; christian; christianize. When we debase *Christian* to mean ' a civilized person ; a " decent " chap ', we reduce its status to that of a mere slang derivative and should, as ' decent chaps ', spell it with a small *c*. But *christianize* might also be written with a capital.

In *christen* we have a reference to Jesus *Christ*. In New Testament Greek, *Christos* is ' (the) Anointed (One) ', itself a translation of the Hebrew *Mashiah* (our *Messiah*) and a synonym of the derivative Greek *Messias*.

Christian name is, I believe, ineligible, for one does not receive it because one is a Christian : Jews, who use these names, understandably refuse to call them Christian names : the front name is, as Americans neatly say, ' a given name '; it is a font-name, a baptismal name, a christening name, and in *Christian name* the word *Christian* represents *christen* or *christened*. On *christen(ed) name*, folk-etymology has been at work. It is pleasant to find the late Wilfrid Ewart, in one of the best of all First World War novels, *Way of Revelation*, 1921, writing, ' Rosemary—Upton—what could they possibly have in common? Yet here they were calling each other by christian names at her bedroom door ! '

christiania (colloquially **christie**) is the wood of the Norway spruce, shipped from *Christiania*, now Oslo, the capital city : hence a standard size of that wood. Not irrelevantly, it is a cathedral city—therefore see the entry at **christen.**

christmassy or **C—**. ' It was supposed to be her birthday, but with the decorations and presents and good things to eat, it really was all very christmassy '—like Christmas, characteristic of Christmas, suitable to or reminiscent of Christmas. *Christmas* is literally ' the Mass of Christ ', where *Mass* tends to mean ' festival ' rather than ' communion '.

chubb is a *Chubb* (or *Chubb's*) *lock*. There died in 1845 a famous locksmith, Charles Chubb. Much used by banks, it was originally called *Chubb's detector lock*. Compare **Yale lock** in the subsidiary glossary.

church. ' This unity and fellowship with God through Christ constitutes the " Body of Christ ", the New Israel, the Israel of God. It is, as it were, a spiritual organism, a " Church " '; and the footnote accompanying ' Church ' reads thus, ' The term (lit. " the Lord's ") has its Old Testament root in the " congregation ", the natural body of Israel, and the more restricted " assembly " of the people in their religious capacity,' Stanley Cook, *An Introduction to The Bible*, 1945.

That parenthetical ' lit. " the Lord's " ' requires elaboration. *The Lord* is Christ : *the Lord's* is short for *the Lord's house* (or, less probably, *temple*) : Greek *to doma tou Kuriakou*. W and several other noted etymologists, however, seem to prefer a slightly different origin—*to kuriakon doma*, ' the divine house '. The latter is perhaps the more probable, for *kuriakos* is the adjective corresponding to *kurios*, ' master, lord ', and *ho Kurios* is ' the Master, the Lord ' in The New Testament ; *to kuriakon doma*, therefore, is literally ' the house belonging to the Lord ' ; compare Greek *hē kuriakē hēmera* (usually shortened to *hē hēmera*), ' the Lord's day ' : Latin *dies dominica* (whence French *dimanche*) : Sunday. Shortened, it becomes *to kuriakon*, whence Old English *cirice*, whence the modern English *church* and the Scottish *kirk*.

chypre. ' A rather too emphatic trace of chypre hung in the air . . . Sandalwood chypre,' Raymond Chandler, *The Lady in the Lake*, (English edition) 1944. This perfume, a non-alcoholic compound of oils, resins, etc., bears the French name, *Chypre*, of the island of Cyprus, so closely associated with ' the **Cyprian** '—Aphrodite Pandemos—Venus—the goddess of sexual love (*nuit d'amour* and all that).

cicely. See **cecily.**

cicerone, verb, is a natural development from the noun, which, via the Italian *cicerone* (whence the learned, the perhaps pedantic plural, *ciceroni*), derives from *Cicero* (genitive, *Ciceronis*), the famous Latin orator and writer : see **Ciceronian** in the second glossary. The name *Cicero* is traditionally derived from Latin *cicer*, ' a chick pea ' : compare the Roman name *Lentulus*.

cilice, a hair-shirt, and its obsolete adjective *cilicious*, comes, by way of French, from the Latin *cilicium*, a transliteration of the Greek *kilikion*, cloth made from the hair of the goats of *Cilicia*, a province of Asia Minor. Strictly, *kilikion* is the neuter of the adjective *Kilikios*, ' Cilician ', from *Kilix*, a Cilician. This is the cloth implied in ' They would have repented long ago in sack-cloth and ashes,' *Matthew*, xi, 21 (W). Compare **dalmatic.**

cinchona or **cinchona bark** was originally *Cinchona bark*, which contains quinine ; it is also called *Peruvian bark* or *Jesuits' bark*, because it was originally discovered in Peru and much used, medicinally, by early Jesuit missionaries in South America. *Cinchona* was, by Linnaeus, named in honour of the Condesa *Ana Chinchón*, wife of the Conde de Chinchón (ca. 1590–1647), viceroy of Peru in 1629–39. But *quinine* is not so derived : it comes, via the Spanish *quina*, from Quechuan *quinaquina*.

Cinderella; C. (or **c.**) **dance** (one that ceases sharp at midnight).

'Western Australia is the Cinderella of the South,' John Boyle O'Reilly, *Moondyne*, 1889.

'Geography is notoriously the Cinderella of the sciences. Although one of the oldest, it has been treated, until recent years, with unbecoming and wholly unmerited disrespect,' G. H. T. Kimble, *Geography in the Middle Ages*, 1938.

This heroine of a fairy-tale of probably eastern origin bears a name that translates French *Cendrillon* (from *cendres*, ashes). The English word represents *cinder + ella*, a feminine diminutive: The Cinder Girl, or The Little Lady of the Ashes. Compare German *Aschenbrödel* and *Aschenputtel*, a (female) domestic drudge.

cinzano. An Italian wine, as in 'On the other walls were Cinzano posters, a lithograph of Mussolini, and a poster advertising Capri,' Eric Ambler, *Cause for Alarm*, 1938. From the name of the manufacturer, the worthy Signor Cinzano, of Turin.

'. . . That unique tonic wine which is such a pleasant aperitif and which has . . . attained world-wide renown, namely the *Vermouth* of Turin, originally made by Carpano in 1786', Arturo Marescalchi, *The Wines of Italy*, 1933.

cissy or **sissy.** 'An effeminate boy, youth, man.' Usually derived from *sister* (The OED and elsewhere). Perhaps correctly. But, originally slang and still a colloquialism, it may well be derived from *Cicely* (or *Cecily*) or even *Cecilia*.

Cities of the Plain, the. See **Sodom and Gomorrah.**

clarence, a closed four-wheeled carriage with the driver's seat outside, honours the Duke of Clarence (1765–1837), who in 1830 became King of England after many jovial years' service in the Navy: 'The Sailor King'. Less respectfully, 'Silly Billy' (see **billy . . .**), despite the fact that, though in the best sense 'simple', he was not a simpleton.

clarendon, the heavy-faced, narrow-bodied printing-type, takes its name, not from The Clarendon Press, Oxford, but from a 19th-Century printer or type-designer of that surname, although 'R. Besley & Co. originally introduced the Clarendon Character' (*Specimen-Book of Types*, 1848, cited by The OED).

clarkia, 'a small genus of showy annual herbs of the evening primrose family' (Webster), is a native of the Pacific slope of

106

North America and was discovered by William Clark, an American explorer. Captain Clark in 1804 accompanied Captain Lewis on the first governmental expedition across the Rockies—see, e.g., Nard Jones, *Swift Flows the River*, 1939. After him, too, was named *Clark's nutcracker* (or *crow*), a North American greyish-white bird with black-and-white wings.

Cleopatra, that ' serpent of old Nile ' (as serpent-wise politically as she was sexually) whom age withered not nor custom staled, has become—has for centuries been—the symbol, the personification, the exemplar of feminine allurement, charm, fascination, as, for instance, in Gautier's *Une Nuit de Cléopâtre*, 1839. For four notable portraits, see Shakespeare's, Dryden's (*All for Love*), Jack Lindsay's *Last Days with Cleopatra*, an historic novel, and the chapter by W. W. Tarn in vol. X of *The Cambridge Ancient History*. This brilliantly able Egyptian queen, who was of Macedonian descent, died in 30 B.C. at the age of thirty-eight.

' I'm tellin' you that this dame has got everything that Cleopatra ever had an' then a truckful,' Peter Cheyney, *I'll Say She Does!*, 1945.

clerihew. Of a school friend—a lifelong friend—G. K. Chesterton has, in his *Autobiography*, 1936, remarked, ' He could write clear and unadulterated nonsense with . . . serious simplicity. It was he who invented that severe and stately form of Free Verse which has since been known by his own second name as " the Clerihew " (his name is Edmund Clerihew Bentley) ; which dates from our days at school, when he sat listening to a chemical exposition, with his rather bored air and a blank sheet of blotting-paper before him. On this he wrote, inspired by the limpid spirit of song, the unadorned lines :

> Sir Humphrey Davy
> Abominated gravy.
> He lived in the odium
> Of having discovered sodium.'

cleveite is—to quote The OED's citation of 1879—the ' hydrated oxide of uranium, iron, erbium, cerium, yttrium, in cubic forms from Norway '.

Named after Professor P. T. Cleve, a Swedish chemist, who in 1895 lectured to the British Chemical Society on the rare-earth elements ; on these elements he was one of the leading authorities.

clumber is short for *clumber*, originally *Clumber*, *spaniel*, used, in the sport of shooting, for finding game ; and very good it is

107

thereat!   Imported from France in 1720, the dog was 'cultivated' by Thomas Pelham-Holles (1693–1763), who in 1715
was created 1st Duke of Newcastle; one of his estates bore the
name of *Clumber*.   This became the seat of the dukedom, with
a park of 4,000 acres, lying two and a half miles from Worksop,
Nottingham.

clydesdale.   'Henry was a ponderous, Clydesdale kind of Man,
with Warts on his Hands,' George Ade, *More Fables in Slang*,
1900.—' " Me managing great big Clydesdales with tempers
just like his (an' his temper was something fierce).   Why, I
didn't come up to the horses' belly ! " ' : Kylie Tennant, *The
Battlers*, a notable Australian novel, 1941.
   The clydesdale is a heavy draught-horse that came originally
from *Clydesdale*, the valley of the River Clyde in Scotland.
They are justly famous for their strength and their endurance
(' And where else will you find such horses and such men? ').

coalport is a kind of china, the vases, in especial, being famed
for their fine shapes, delicate paintings whether of scenery or of
figures, and rich colouring.   The Shropshire village of *Coalport*
has, since 1814 (when the factory established at Caughley in
1751 was moved to Coalport), been rightly famous for its
pottery.   The village is fifteen miles east-south-east of
Shrewsbury.

coan or **Coan.**   A Roman, speaking in A.D. 92, ' I longed for a
glass of my own rich Falernian or the mellow Coan that was
bottled in the year that Titus took Jerusalem,' Conan Doyle,
' An Iconoclast ', reprinted in *Tales of Long Ago*.
   The island of *Kos*, one of the Sporades, was celebrated for the
cultivation of the vine : and in Roman poetry, notably in
Horace and Persius, *Cōum*, i.e. *Cōum vinum* or ' wine of Cos '
(usually *Coan wine*), is mentioned with affectionate appreciation.
   Compare **chian** and **falernian,** and see also **cos.**

cobalt.   ' Sunlight turned [the adobe walls] into the battlements
of an oriental fortress, standing out pale gold against a cobalt
sky and the snow-capped indigo of Tecos Mountain,' Margaret
Armstrong, *The Blue Santo Murder Mystery*, 1943.
   Cobalt represents German *Kobalt*, earlier *Kobold*, a goblin—
a special application of personal name *Kobold* (Old High
German *Godbald*, God-bold), bestowed in much the same way
as *Old Nick* ; compare **goblin.**   The kobold is a mischievous
sprite (cf. **Puck**) : and the metal was so called because, like
nickel, it was regarded as harmful and useless.   ' Like other
108

German mining terms *cobalt* has passed into most European languages ' (W).

The metal itself is reddish-grey, but the pigment derived from it is deep blue—as in the quotation from Margaret Armstrong.

coburg; coburg loaf. The former, a thin fabric of worsted and either cotton or silk and, on one side, twilled, derives from *Coburg*, which, in Germany, was closely associated in its early manufacture. The latter, a loaf of bread, was introduced into England soon after the marriage, 1840, of Queen Victoria to Prince Albert of Saxe-*Coburg*-Gotha.

Compare **albert.**

cochin-china, often—especially in the U.S.A.—shortened to *cochin,* is a large domestic fowl, thickly and softly plumaged, small-winged, with densely feathered legs, and it originally came from Cochin China. There is also a *Cochin* (better *cochin*) *bantam.*

Compare **bantam** itself and **brahmapootra.**

codlin or **codling** is the *codlin*(*g*) *apple.* The early forms, e.g. *qwerdelyng* in the 15th and *quadling* in the 16th–17th Centuries, ' correspond exactly with those of the surname *Codlin.* Hence the origin is *coeur-de-lion* '—compare Richard Coeur-de-Lion— ' a fancy name for an esteemed apple. Cf. French *reine-claude,* greengage, from the wife of Francis I, and the pear called *bon-chrétien,* from St Francis of Paula ' (W).

coehorn is an obsolete weapon of war—a small mortar, made of bronze and used for throwing light shells or bombs ; provided with handles, it was set upon a wooden block. Its inventor was the Dutch Baron Menno van Coehoorn or Cohorn or *Coehorn* (1641–1704), soldier and engineer. He was a noted authority upon the construction of forts, ramparts, and so forth, and his mortar was first used at the siege of Grave in Holland.

cognac, loosely any French brandy, is to connoisseurs that brandy which is made from wine produced at or near *Cognac,* a town on the bank of the Charente River ; the *entrepôt* of the brandy of the *département* of Charente. The three best vineyards for brandy are, M. André Simon tells us, the Grande Champagne, the Petite Champagne, and Borderies, names that correspond to geographical features.

cointreau. ' In response to my companion's query, Señor Lopez said he would be pleased to take a small Cointreau. Jerrard told him he could have it all right, but not to be so darned aggressive about it (the liqueur was about the most expensive thing in the place) ', Cecil de Lenoir, *The Hundredth Man*, 1933.

Conscientiously omitted by the best English and American dictionaries, *cointreau* appears in M. André Simon's comprehensive and conscientious *Wine*, 1946 : wherein it is elucidated as the name of ' one of the best known French distillers of Liqueurs. Their best known Liqueur is an Orange Curaçao . . . *Triple Sec Cointreau.*'

colchicum. ' Spring seems by some magic to have come round again when one sees the Meadow Saffron or Autumn Crocus, *Colchicum autumnale.* . . . The medicine *Colchicum* derived from the plant is well known as a cure or alleviation of gout and is said in large doses to be an irritant poison. In literature it is often applied to irritable old gentlemen,' Vernon Rendall, *Wild Flowers in Literature*, 1934.

Colchicum is the Latin form of Greek *Kolkhikon*, ' a thing of *Kolkhis* ' : Colchis is a country that, in ancient times, lay at the east end of the Black Sea and immediately south of the Caucasus : thither sailed the Argonauts, and there lived Medea.

colemanite, a calcium borate, brilliant-crystalled, is named after one W. T. *Coleman* of San Francisco. William Tell Coleman (1824–93), a pioneer in California, concerned himself in the manufacture of borax.

Colin, in pastoral verse, or romance, denotes a shepherd. For English, the fashion was set by Edmund Spenser. The name is French : a diminutive of *Col*, itself a shortening of *Nicolas*. See **collie** and compare **Corydon.**

coliseum, in England usually a music-hall, in America often a sports building or a stadium, is a New Latin form—compare Italian *coliseo*—or rather, development of *Colosseum*, that great Roman amphitheatre completed ca. A.D. 80, a name that, as *colosseum*, came to be applied to any Roman amphitheatre. The word represents the neuter of *colosseus*, huge, from *colossu.* (see below).

collation, a light meal, especially a *cold collation*, was earlier a light evening meal in a monastery, notably and originally after the reading aloud of *collations*, lives of the Fathers of the Church, in particular the *Collationes Patrum in Scetica Eremo Commorantium* (lives of those Fathers who dwelt as hermits in the North African desert), by John Cassian, ca. A.D. 400. (Paraphrase of W.)

collie. ' He rode on with his own dog, a strong knowing colley, to . . . where the cow and calf were moving along,' Alexander Harris, *The Emigrant Family* (a tale of Australia), 1849 ; ' Rolf Boldrewood ', greatest of 19th-Century Australian novelists, has, in *In Bad Company and Other Stories*, 1901, a sanely attractive article on ' Australian Collies '.

' Webster ' says : ' Probably from *collie, colie, coaly*, coal-black ' : but the collie is not coal-black ; far from it. And it is a sheep-dog, of Scottish origin : ' Much more probably,' says W, ' from common Scottish name *Colin*. *Collie*, as proper name for a dog, occurs in Chaucer (v, i). With *collie dog* cf. *robin redbreast* ' : nor can there, I think, be much doubt that W's etymology is the correct one. See, therefore, **Colin.**

Collins = ' roofer ' = ' board-and-lodging ' = ' bread-and-butter (letter) ' = a letter written, by a departed guest, to thank one's hostess for a pleasant visit entailing bed-and-board. ' This is a Collins, and a Collins should not wade into deep places. It should be loving but neat,' Sir Walter Raleigh, the belovèd Oxford don, in a letter written in 1911 and cited by The OED.

Although the term did not become general until the 1890's, it is taken from ch. xxiii of Jane Austen's *Pride and Prejudice* (1813), where William Collins, a smug and pompous and obsequious young clergyman, writes to Mr Bennet a solemn, complacent letter of thanks for his stay with the Bennet family ; unfortunately, the inimitable Jane does not provide us with the text of the letter.

colophony is that dark resin which is distilled from turpentine mixed with water. From the Latin *colophonia*, short for *resina colophonia*, ' resin of Colophon ', Colophon being one of the twelve Ionian cities of Asia Minor B.C. and standing, near Ephesus and on the river Halesus, a little inland from the coast. Colophon's name is probably a particularization—almost a personification—of the Greek *kolophon*, ' a top, a summit ' ; hence, ' an end, a finishing ' (whence the bibliographical term, *colophon*).

colossus. ' Quite heedless of chaos and clamour, a man stood in the doorway of a first-class smoking-carriage, one foot within, one on the platform, in the manner of a colossus ' : which passage occurs in *Rimingtons*, published in 1904 and written by

H. C. Bailey, the author of some extremely readable historical novels, many equally readable detective novels, and several good 'straight' novels; H. C. Bailey, Classical scholar, historian, and dignified journalist.

'The city [of Rhodes] was adorned with works of art including . . . the well-known colossus . . . and many other colossal statues. . . . Lysippus' influence lived on at Rhodes, where his pupil Chares of Lindus, to commemorate Rhodes' resistance to Demetrius in 304 [B.C.], carried that colossal statue of the Sun which was one of the wonders of the world; it was destroyed by the earthquake of 225, and nothing remains to suggest what it was like,' W. W. Tarn, *Hellenistic Civilisation* (revised edition) 1930.

The Colossus of Rhodes, dedicated to Apollo, stood at the entrance to the harbour. The Greek *kolossos* is a common noun meaning 'statue'; especially, a huge statue: but the currency of the word in Romance languages and in English is due to '*the* colossus', the Colossus of Rhodes.

colt; often, though now illogically, *Colt*; originally *Colt's revolver*. This 'repeating pistol', patented in 1835, was invented and for many years manufactured by the American Samuel Colt (1814–62).

'I started, as if she had presented a Colt's revolver at my head,' W. W. Dobie, *Recollections of a Visit to Port-Phillip in 1852–55*, 1856.

'Along came young Samuel Colt, of Hartford, Connecticut, with the first really successful revolver, on which fighting men learned to rely. . . . The percussion cap, young Colt's persistent genius, and the conquest of the West were responsible for the development of the revolver as we know it to-day. . . At twenty-two he had patented his revolver on a wooden working model and had actually begun manufacture in a Jersey factory,' John Stuart, 'Do you Pack a Gun' (*Flynn's*, November 15, 1924).

'Colonel Colt makes all men equal, you know,' Don Castle, *Do Your Own Time*, 1938 (compare a quotation at **smith-and-wesson**).

columba, colombo. See **calumba**.

columbiad, ' a heavy, long-chambered, muzzle-loading gun . . . designed for throwing shells and shot at high angles of elevation' (Webster). An American gun dating from 1844, used in the American Civil War, and long obsolete, it resembles the

112

dahlgren. From *Columbiad*, ' an epic of America ', *Columbia* being the Latin name for North America.

Columbine, as a character in pantomime, is *Colombina*, who, in Italian comedy, was the mistress of Harlequin. A given-name, it represents Italian *colombina*, the feminine of *colombino*, ' dove-like ': Latin *columba*, ' a dove '.
Compare **harlequin.**

columbite; columbium. *Columbium* is one of the chemical elements; it derives from Latin *Columbia*, the poetic name for (North) America. It occurs in the ore columbite (itself named from the element—not *vice versa*) and was discovered so long ago as 1801; obviously in the United States; by a scientist, one Hatchett.
Since the mid-19th Century, *columbium* has been called **niobium**; *columbite* has retained its name, though it is also *niobite*.

Comptonia; incorrectly with a capital letter in ' The scarlet *Comptonia* ' (J. W., *Perils, Pastimes, and Pleasures*, 1849); is a shrub and its flower named after Henry *Compton* (1632–1713), an English prelate, a leader in the revolution of 1688, and a notable collector of rare, especially of exotic, botanical specimens.

Comstockery. ' I pled " guilty ". I had to. I was no noble soul, nor was my private life a thing that would have been a joy to Anthony Comstock,' Don Castle, *Do Your Own Time* (as readable as it is moving), 1938.
Anthony Comstock: Roundsman of the Lord, written by Heywood Broun and Margaret Leech and published in 1927, tells the story of this bigoted moral censor, who (1844–1915) in 1873 saw the Comstock Law enacted by Congress, to prevent immoral periodicals, etc., from passing through the post. He headed movements and founded societies for the suppression of vice. So far, so good; the trouble was that he was almost incredibly narrow-minded, intolerant, and self-righteous.

Congo is short for *Congo minuet* or *Congo dance*, the former being only a variety of the European minuet, the latter being either that variety of minuet or a sort of fandango. Performed originally by the Negroes, it soon ' caught on among the whites ', who were dancing it before the end of the 18th Century; by the end of the Civil War, it was as dead as Southern hopes. In American English—until the 20th

Century, anyway—*Congo* was a synonym of Negro, though originally and strictly one from the Congo. Compare **charleston.**

congreve = a *Congreve* (*friction-*)*match* or what was also, a trifle later, called a **lucifer.** This 19th-Century, evil-smelling 'means of ignition' was invented by Sir William *Congreve* (1772–1828), the inventor of the famous *Congreve rocket*.

In December 1842, a match-manufacturer says, 'The lowest price at which we sell congreves is 2*s*. 9*d*. a gross' (*Central Criminal Court. Minutes of Evidence.*)

conkers. See **hong-kong.**

constantia shortens *Constantia wine*. This dessert wine, very popular in England in the earlier half of the 19th Century, 'came from the vineyards of Constantia, at Wynberg, Cape Province. There are still three vineyards bearing the name . . . Groot [Great] Constantia, the oldest vineyard of the Cape Peninsula . . .; Klein [Small] Constantia and High Constantia' (André Simon). As a place-name, *Constantia* is to be compared with *Constance*: they constitute the Latin *constantia*, 'firmness, constancy'.

coolie, a cheap Indian, or Chinese, or occasionally Japanese, or Egyptian native unskilled labourer, hence any poorly paid labourer, is, according to Webster, from a Hindu word (*quli* or a Tamil word (*kuli*), meaning 'hired (labourer)'; W, however, believes it to come from *Kuli* or *Koli*, the native name of an aboriginal tribe of Guzerat (or Gujarat), the northern *maritime* province of the Bombay Presidency.

'He would take up the defence of an obscure native, some miserable coolie whose fate could not affect him personally in the least,' Henry de Monfreid, *Hashish*, 1935.

copenhagen, from *Copenhagen*—'the Merchants' Haven' (cf. 'horse-*coper*')—the capital of Denmark, is 'a sweetened hot drink of spirit and beaten eggs' and 'a game in which a circle of players holding a rope try to escape being touched by "it" who is in the centre' (Webster); also, with variants *copenhagen blue, copen blue*, and simply *copen*, a blue colour of low brilliance.

copper; cupreous, 'of—or like—copper'; **cupric, cupriferous,** 'containing or yielding copper'. *Copper* (in Old English *coper*) comes from Low Latin *cuprum*, which represents

114

Classical Latin (*aes*) *Cyprium*, ' (metal) of Cyprus '; the Latin transliterates the Greek *Kuprios*, ' of Cyprus ', from *Kupros*, ' Cyprus '.

Of prehistoric Egypt, J. L. Myres (*The Dawn of History*) has written that ' for the first copper ores, Sinai and Nubia are very probable sources, and the identity of the forms of the earliest daggers, axe-heads, and pins, with those which long remained characteristic of the copper-island, Cyprus, makes it possible to regard this as an alternative source, especially in view of the close technical similarity of the first Egyptian and Cypriote pottery '; and Gordon Childe (*What Happened in History*) speaks of ' the island's exceptional wealth in copper—the metal takes its name from Cyprus '. Compare the following observation by Lionel Lyde (*The Continent of Europe*) :—' In early days the easy access to copper (the " Cyprian " metal), and the ease with which it was melted, encouraged the use of bronze ; and this again was adverse to the success of the Eurafrican when he came to blows with the iron-using Eurasian.'

cordoba is the monetary unit of Nicaragua. A Spanish term (*córdoba*), it derives from Francisco Fernandez de Córdoba (1475?–1526), that Spanish soldier and explorer who in 1522 took possession of Nicaragua, who founded Granada and León, and who, disclaiming allegiance to his superior officer, Pedrarias, ' was surprised and killed ' (Webster BD). The surname means ' of Córdoba (or Córdova) ' : the term *cordoba*, therefore, is closely related to :—

cordovan is ' (leather) of Cordova ', in modern Spanish always *Córdoba*; the Spanish adjective is *cordovano*, and the Spanish name for the fine-grained, coloured leather (whence the reddish-yellow brown we call *cordovan*) made, during the Middle Ages, chiefly at Cordova or Cordoba, is *cordobán*; the name of the Spanish city represents the Latin *Corduba*, itself from Greek *Kordubē*. '. . . Córdova, a brilliant city in Roman times, as it was under the Moslems, and famous for its poetry and its olive oil,' J. B. Trend, *The Civilization of Spain*, 1944.

? **corduroy** may come from French *corde du roi*, ' king's cord '; if that be indeed the origin, then probably the French term was originally *corde du Roi*, ' cord of the King '—that specific King of France in whose reign the name was bestowed ; the records concerning the first use of the French term are too scanty to allow us to specify an actual sovereign. W mentions the alternative possibility that the word derives from the Middle English nickname *Corduroy* or *Corderey* ('king's heart'), used as a surname: the surname of the maker of corduroy.]

Coridon. See **Corydon.**

Corinthian. 'The classics [of Greece and Rome] corrected a young man's passion for rhetoric. This was in the 'nineties when the Corinthian manner was more in vogue than the Attic' (John Buchan, *Memory Hold-the-Door*, 1940), the reference being to an over-brilliant style, whether literary or oratorical; a sense deriving from the elegance of ancient Corinthian art. Of the three orders of Greek architecture (Doric, the simplest; Ionic, the most graceful—the most 'Attic'; Corinthian), the Corinthian is the most ornate. Also, *Corinthian* (n. and adj.) is '(a) profligate; (one) addicted to elegant profligacy and dissipation': in reminiscence of the famed, the notorious, the proverbial licentiousness, luxury and wealth of ancient Corinth. *Corinthian*, from ca. 1818 to ca 1832, was a dandy, a 'swell', a man-of-fashion (and sport) about town, and from ca. 1870, especially in America, a wealthy amateur of—and in—sport. 'The Corinthians' are a famous team of amateur players of Association football.

Corinthianize (literary and obsolescent) is 'to live licentiously' from Greek *korinthiazesthai*, 'to be—hence, to act like—a prostitute'. And *Corinthian brass* (or *bronze*), Latin *Corinthium aes*, figures in English literature of the late 16th–mid 18th Century; an alloy of gold, silver and copper, it was a Corinthian product, much prized for its employment in costly ornaments.

'Wealthy Corinth'—as both Homer and Pindar described it—was for some centuries (say 650–150 B.C.) the most important commercial town in Europe, a cosmopolis; destroyed in 146 B.C., it was refounded, a century later, by Julius Caesar; the apostle Paul addressed two epistles to the Corinthians— 'unto the church of God which is at Corinth'.

corybantic; corybantiasm: (of, especially, dancing) 'noisy and extravagant', hence 'frenzied'; (in pathology) 'that type of frenzy in which the sufferer has fantastic visions'.

The Corybantes—Greek *Korubantes* (singular *Korubas*)— were those companions of Cybele, the Phrygian goddess, who followed her with music and wild dances, partly religious, partly martial. Asiatic in origin, Cybele was by the Greeks identified with Rhea.

116

Corydon. 'They were just a silly, simple pair of sweethearts, like Corydon and Phyllis; they were crazy about each other,' Mary Fitt, *Clues to Christabel*, 1944.

Also *Coridon*. The Latin form is *Corydon*, as in Virgil and Propertius; the Greek original is *Korúdōn*, notably in Theocritus. In Classical poetry, it does duty for 'a shepherd', whereas in English and Continental poetry it signifies a male rustic (contrast **Phyllis**), after Virgil's *rusticus es Corydon*. It is tempting to think Greek *Korúdōn* cognate with *korudos*, the crested lark.

cos is the shortened, now usual form of *Cos lettuce*, introduced from *Cos* (Greek *Kōs*), modern Stanchio, an island—one of the Sporades—opposite Halicarnassus (modern Budrum) on the south-west coast of Asia Minor. In Classical times, Cos was favoured, as a place of residence, by men of letters : it had good doctors, fine clothes (*Coae vestes*), and, above all, excellent wine (see **coan**). The lettuce, grown also on the Turkish mainland, was mentioned by diarist John Evelyn in 1699 and, at *lettuce*, in Chambers's *Cyclopaedia* in 1753.

cosaque, a cracker bon-bon (originally imported from France), popular ca. 1850–1910, represents French *Cosaque*, a Cossack, 'probably in allusion to the sudden and irregular firing' (OED) of bands of Cossacks : cf., therefore, **cossack.**

The term also = a *Cossack dance* (a two-time).

coslettize; coslettizer. To treat—especially a bicycle frame—with a rust-preventing process named, ca. 1907, after its inventor, a Mr Coslett; a chemical bath in which the treatment is effected.

cosmatesque is the adjective corresponding to *Cosmatic work*, which 'consists of surrounding colored marble slabs with borders . . . made up of small pieces of marble and glass cut into various shapes' (H. Gardner, *Art through the Ages*, 1927), a decorative style either devised or perfected and popularized by the Cosmati family of sculptors, architects and, most pertinently, mosaicists flourishing at Rome in the 13th Century. (The OED.)

cossack; Cossack post; cossacks. A *cossack* is a Cossack pony; *Cossack post*—familiar to Boy Scouts—is an outpost adopted from Russian military practice and consisting of a few men commanded by an N.C.O. or a senior soldier; *cossacks*, a mainly shop-name for a kind of trousers. In 1941–45, *Cossacks* tended to be equivalent to 'Russian cavalry': most of the Russian cavalry were Cossacks. The Cossacks, originally Tatars, were Turkish subjects (in the region immediately north of the Black Sea) before they came under Russian rule. 'The Cossacks are really Kaizaks [or Kazaks], "wanderers," and are certainly not Kirghiz; but the Russian Government persistently classified them as Kirghiz, apparently in order to keep the name Cossack as a purely military title,' Lionel W. Lyde, *The Continent of Asia*, (2nd edition) 1938.

From Turki (the Turkish language) *quzzaq*, which means 'freebooter', 'predatory horseman', hence 'adventurer'.

costmary, whether the common tansy or the pot-herb known to botanists as *chrysanthemum balsamita* and used in salads and formerly in ale and beer, was early known also as *cost*, from Latin *costus*, from Greek *kostos*, from Sanskrit *kustha*, a plant found in Cashmere. The second element is *(St) Mary*. W compares the Old French synonym *herbe sainte Marie* and the German *Marienblättchen*.

coulomb, that amount of electric current which passes a certain point in a given time, honours the fame and now the memory of Charles Augustin de Coulomb (1736–1806), French military engineer become physicist, who did much work on electricity and magnetism; he formulated the *Coulomb's law* of physics.

Compare **joule** and **maxwell.**

covelline, covellite. See **alisonite.**

coventrate or **C—.** Whereas to *rotterdam* a city is to attempt to air-bomb a specific quarter out of existence, as the Germans did with a district of Rotterdam (during the Blitzkrieg, 1940), to *coventrate* is to attempt to air-bomb a city out of existence, as they did with Coventry late in the same year. The latter verb merely anglicizes the German *coventraten*. These two word should be kept alive, as salutary reminders.

Cox and Box. 'Of cave dwellings more in particular. The mouth of a cave is shown by excavation to have been the favoured spot; farther in it was darker and damper. . . Sometimes from season to season it was a case of Cox and Box man and hyena alternating as tenants,' S. E. Winbolt, *Britain B.C.*, 1943.

In 1867, Sir F. Burnand produced his operetta (music by Sullivan), *Cox and Box*: but the effectual origin and the correct form of the phrase were established in 1847, when J. M. Morton produced his farce (adapted from the French), *Box and Cox*, wherein the most absurd alternations take place.

cracovienne or, less usually, **krakowiak.** This sprightly Polish dance, ' a sort of simple polonaise, but . . . in two-in-a-measure time—with some syncopation ' (Scholes), would seem, by its name, to have originated in the city, or at least the district, of Cracow. Disraeli speaks of it in *Coningsby*, 1844. Compare **polonaise.**

Short for *danse cracovienne*, French for ' dance of Cracow ' (French *Cracovie*).

cravat, a neckcloth, hence a necktie, and derivatively a form of bandage or a flesh-wrinkle in a dog's neck, came into English from French *cravate*, the adjective of *Cravate*, a Croatian. In short, it was originally a scarf worn by Croatian soldiers in the Thirty Years War (1618–48). The French *Cravate* is equivalent to the German *Krabate*, and both of these words transliterate the Croatian *Hrvat* (W).

creeping jinny. See **cecily.**

cremona. A violin—any violin—from *Cremona* in Lombardy. ' In string music Italy was inspired by the wonderful productions of the Cremona violin makers ' (Scholes), especially the *Amati, Guarneri, Stradivari* families. ' The cause of the superiority of the old Cremona violin has been much discussed ' (Scholes). 20th-Century makers can, however, produce an instrument as good as—and, unseen, indistinguishable from— a cremona of 1550–1750.

cretaceous ; cretic. ' The coastlands of the Middle and South Atlantic States are developed on cretaceous and younger rocks ' (Jones & Bryan, *North America*, 1924) ; ' In his verse he employed the cretic foot '.

The former is only apparently *Cretan* (*cretaceous* coming from Latin *creta*, chalk ; but note that *creta* = *Creta* = *Cretan earth*, i.e. chalk), whereas the latter actually has the alternative name *Cretan*. The cretic is one of the *paeonic* measures ; $- \cup -$; and this particular measure was, throughout the Classical period of Greek poetry, associated with the island of *Crete*. See also separate **cretic.**

cretic is the metrical foot known otherwise as an amphimacer. The term comes from Latin *Creticus* (*pes*), for Greek *Krētikos* (*pous*), literally ' Cretic (foot) ', from its traditional association with *Crete*. See also the entry at **cretaceous.**

cretin. ' " That woman," he said viciously, " is an imbecile, a cretin ",' Eric Ambler, *Cause for Alarm*, 1938.

Properly a deformed idiot, chiefly and originally in the Swiss mountains. Via French from Swiss dialect, where *crétin* ' means (1) a Christian, (2) a Christian being, one who is not a brute animal merely ' (Skeat) : the implication is that even a deformed idiot is ' not a brute animal merely '. And *crétin* comes from Latin *Christianus*, a follower of *Christus* (Christ), which transliterates Greek *Christos* (literally, ' the Anointed ').

cretonne, as used for curtains and chair-coverings, was originally made at the village of *Creton* in Normandy. As the feminine of the adjective *breton* (Breton) is *bretonne*, so the adjective of *Creton* is *creton*, of which the feminine is *cretonne*—via *toile cretonne*, ' cloth of Creton '.

Crichton, admirable. To begin with, the surname Crichton probably has a place-name origin, for in Scotland there is a parish called Crichton ; nearby stand the ruins of Crichton Castle.

In 1603, John Johnston, in *Heroes Scoti*, bestowed the epithet ' the admirable Crichton ' upon James Crichton (1560?–82), a Scot, who in Paris (1575) disputed scientific questions—so rumour has it—in twelve languages, served in the French Army, and in Italy vanquished almost everyone in formal disputations upon philosophy and mathematics. He was also a prodigy in athletics.

crimmer. See **krimmer.**

crispin, archaic for a shoemaker, and *St Crispin's lance*, jocular archaism for an awl, owe their names to Saints Crispin and Crispinian, who, brothers—and shoemakers by trade, went as missionaries to Gaul ; beheaded at the orders of the Emperor Maximian in ca. 287, they thus became Christian martyrs and, in the natural course of things, the patron saints of shoemakers and, by extension, of saddlers and tanners.

criss-cross, in all its senses and nuances, is explained by its original form *Christ-cross*, applied originally to ' John Doe, his mark : x ', although the effective source may reside, as W has noted, in *Christ*- (later *criss*-)*cross row*, a child's horn-book (not a

book but an alphabet-sheet), whereon the letters of the alphabet
are preceded by a cross.

Croesus. ' Even in the days when Croesus held his court at
Sardis, on the banks of the " gold-bearing " Pactolus, the local
resources were the basis of busy industries, e.g. the silver work
of Ephesus, the wine of Chios, the pottery of Samos ' (Lionel W.
Lyde, *The Continent of Asia*, chapter on ' Anatolia—Natural
Regions ').

Croesus reigned (560–546 B.C.) as the last King of Lydia.   He
conquered the Greek cities of Aeolia and—except Miletus—of
Ionia, states on the coast, respectively the northern and the
western, of Asia Minor : partly as a result of these conquests,
partly by a sound economy, he became very rich, proverbially
rich, and, like the legendary **Midas,** fabulously rich.   Foolish
enough to oppose Cyrus, King of Persia (Cyrus the Great), he
was utterly defeated ; Cyrus philosophically spared the life of
Croesus, who doubtless spent his remaining years in philo-
sophizing about the fickleness of fate and the transiency and
miragery of wealth.   Nevertheless, his shade has the satisfaction of knowing that, like **Dives,** his name has become
generic for an extremely wealthy person.

' He is at once, to use his own phrase from *Manfred*, a
" Croesus in creation " [i.e., creativeness], and, to use Shelley's
remarkably precise title, the " pilgrim of eternity ",' G. Wilson
Knight, ' The Two Eternities : An Essay on Byron ' in *The
Burning Oracle*, 1939.

Cf. also **Rockefeller.**

cromagnon or **cro-magnon** or **Cro-Magnon.** In 1868, at
Cromagnon, a rock shelter situated in a limestone cliff set in the
valley of Vézère, *département* of Dordogne (western France),
were discovered five human skeletons of a tall prehistoric,
perhaps negroid race, belonging—or, at the least, corresponding—to the **aurignacian** culture. See *passim* S. E. Winbolt,
Britain B.C. (1943).

croydon, whether a kind of calico (or of cotton sheeting) or a
light carriage, a sort of gig originally with wicker-work body,
but later with body made of wood, is named from Croydon
in Surrey, England ; the gig was used ca. 1870–1900. Compare **berlin, landau, tilbury.**

cubana is a West Indian dance, originated in *Cuba*, which
country it has not abandoned to join with the other West Indian

and Negro dances that, in the United States, lose few of their orgiastic characteristics.

'The warm drone and drumming of tango, rumba, and cubana,' Osbert Sitwell, *Sing High! Sing Low!*, 1944.

Compare **habanera.**

cuddy, mainly a Scots word, means primarily an ass, a donkey and secondarily and derivatively a blockhead. Not from *cuddy*, a swain, for that word and ' our ' cuddy both represent *Cuddy*, the pet-form of the male given-name *Cuthbert*, which owe much of its (former) popularity to St Cuthbert.

culvert is of obscure origin. W pertinently queries whether it might be the ' name of some engineer or bridge-builder (cf *macadam*) ' ; Webster suggests Medieval French *coulouer* (French *couloir*), a channel, a gutter, but the word seems to have arisen too late in English to come from Medieval French Perhaps—a big perhaps—' Culver's bridge '.

cupid ; Cupid ; Cupid's bow ; cupidity. The second afford the ' key ' to the other three terms, although the fourth come straight from Latin *cupiditas*, which derives, not from *Cupido* but from the same source as *Cupido* : *cupere*, ' to desire '. The name *Cupido*, for the god of love, is a personification of *cupido* ' desire '—especially the desire of, and the desire for, love Strictly, Cupid, the son of Venus, is the boy-god of love. He is a Romanization of the Greek Eros, but usually apprehended as less urgent, less lustful : as mischievous rather than all-compulsive

Compare **Eros, Psyche, Venus.**

curaçao ; incorrectly, *curaçoa*. This liqueur, manufactured in Holland (see the quotation at **hollands**), is named after tha small bitter-rinded orange from which it is made—the oranges of *Curaçao*, which happens to be an island lying off the coast of Venezuela in South America ; a place charmingly described by Osbert Sitwell in *Sing High! Sing Low!*, 1944. ' Curaçao, he says, ' is predominantly Dutch in feeling.' Compare :—

curassow. A bird that, resembling a **turkey,** came from the island of *Curaçao* (see the preceding entry), of which it repre sents a ' phonetic ' spelling, the *çao* being pronounced *sow (sau)* Alternatively called *Curaçao* bird, it inhabits also central and northern South America.

curie (or **curiegram ;** little used). The unit of radioactivity The name was given, in 1910, to honour and commemorat M. Pierre and Mme Marie Curie, the discoverers of radium.

Pierre Curie (1859–1906), brilliant French chemist, worked in Paris and in 1895 married Marja Sklodowska (1867–1934), who, born at Warsaw, went to the Sorbonne in 1891 and then to the School of Physics and Chemistry, where, with her husband, she investigated radioactivity; for their discovery of **polonium** and radium, they in 1903, conjointly with Becquerel, received the Nobel prize for physics. In 1911, Mme Marie Curie was awarded the Nobel prize for chemistry. Their more than merely talented daughter, Irene Curie-Joliot, shared with her husband the 1935 Nobel prize for chemistry and in 1937 published a *Life* of that genius, her mother.

curieum. See **francium.**

curlicism; originally—and strictly—**Curllicism.** This erudite synonym of 'literary indecency' was coined in execration of Edmund Curll (1675–1747), who, ostensible bookseller and surreptitious author, was in 1728 fined for publishing *De Usu Flagrorum* (flagellation) and *A Nun in Her Smock*. But if he had not, 'a fly in amber', been satirized by Pope in *The Dunciad* (1728), he would soon have been forgotten; Swift, perhaps, in the poem 'On the Death of Dr Swift', contributed to Curll's preservation.

currant. Speaking of Greece, Professor L. W. Lyde (*Europe*, 4th edition, 1930) says, 'Another result of substituting the vine for the olive has been gross over-production of currants and sultanas, especially currants, which come mainly from the west of Morea'.

The Old English name for currants was *raisins of Corauntz* (i.e., of Corinth), after Anglo-French *raisins de Coraunte*. Perhaps it would be fair to say that *currant* corrupts French *Corinthe*, which represents Latin *Corinthus*, which transliterates Greek *Kórinthos*.

cyclopean; Cyclops. ' Nor was the district [of Florence] much thought of by the Etruscans—though relics of an old cyclopean fortress still crown the hill of Fiesole (970 feet)—because it is away from the metalliferous strata,' Lionel W. Lyde, *The Continent of Europe*, 1913.—' Mountain and valley, river bed and plain, razor-back hill and wind-lashed dune, rock and tree and red-walled gorge, all were in that stupendous and haunting panorama. Here, too, below the long slopes on which I stood, lay that Cyclopean corridor of the wilderness gods—Redbank Gorge, probably the most spectacular of all the gorges of the

Macdonnells,' Archer Russell, *A Tramp-Royal in Wild Australia*, 1934.

The adjective *cyclopean* means 'made with huge, irregular stones'—hence 'huge', 'Cyclops-like': in reference to the Greek mythological one-eyed giant, *Cyclops*—Greek *Kuklops* (*kuklos*, 'circle' + *ops*, 'eye'). In Homer, there was a race of one-eyed giants; but the allusion, usually, is specifically to Polyphemus, whose eye the crafty Odysseus put out with a burning stake. In the U.S.A., *cyclops* is the title of a grade of officer in the Ku Klux Klan.

cynic, cynical, cynicism. *Kunikos* means 'dog-like' (from *kuōn*, a dog); *Kuon* was the Greek nickname for Diogenes, because of his churlishness, as though he snarled like a dog! But Diogenes—see the subsidiary vocabulary—was a late representative of the philosophic school founded by Antisthenes (born ca. 460 B.C.): and Antisthenes set up his school in the gymnasium of *Cynosarges* (Greek *Kunosarges*), just outside Athens. Many scholars prefer the latter origin. So do I, for the philosophic school soon became known as that of the Cynics.

Of the Cynics, Dr W. W. Tarn has remarked that 'everyone dissatisfied with the existing order was called a Cynic. . . . [The Cynics'] appeal was largely to the poor, and their roughness and studied neglect of ordinary decorums and courtesies rather discounted the manliness of their attitude towards life, though they did affect the early Stoa . . . Zeno's teacher the Cynic Crates . . . seems to have been a man' (*Hellenistic Civilisation*, 1930).

Cyprian; Cytherean. (Both are nouns as well as adjectives.) 'Nor did Prisk appear to be a mere passive collector of anecdotes of Cyprian experience. Much . . . took the form of personal experience' ('Michael Innes', *The Weight of the Evidence*, 1944).

'The contaminated embrace of a modern Cytherean' (J. Johnson, 1807, quoted by The OED).

In those two quotations, the sense of the Proper Name is 'prostitute' in the latter; in the former, 'connected with non-marital physical love': and the words might have been transposed from the one quotation to the other.

We get back to the original in 'Yea, the gods fear thee, O Cyprian, Stronger art thou than Jove'—Helen Waddell's translation (in *The Wandering Scholars*, 1927) of a passage from a medieval Latin poem by the brilliant, dissolute Englishman, Serlon of Wilton.

'The Cyprian'—'The Cytherean': epithetical synonyms of Venus, or rather of **Aphrodite** Pandemos.

czar, czarist, used figuratively; **kaiser.**

A *czar* is a tyrannical despot, absolute and ruthless; *czarist*, one who believes in such monarchy as *czar* implies; *kaiser*, figuratively, a king, a monarch, an emperor.

'To our ears Pompey Wilhelm or Sulla Nicholas is merely ludicrous; Kaiser and Tsar wake no laughter, they suggest an immense vista of history. At this very day King George is Caesar—Kaiser-i-Hind [Emperor of India] . . . *why* did *Caesar* come to be a name so significant for a thousand years and more of modern history, from Charlemagne to [the present]?': T. R. Glover, *The Ancient World*, 1935.

'She didn't slip the oil'—the bribe money—'to the cops herself. That was taken care of by a Sicilian boss, Tony Gabardo, czar of the Beantown underworld,' Howard McLellan in *Detective Fiction Weekly*, August 31, 1935.

Cf. **caesarism, caesarist.**

D

daedal; daedalian (or **D—**). 'The character of my friend Bernard O'Hagan is a maze within a maze, a daedalian labyrinth', says Sax Rohmer in his sparkling book, *The Exploits of Captain O'Hagan*.

Daedalus, Greek *Daidalos* (which means 'a skilful craftsman, a cunning worker'), is legendary—a figure in Classical mythology.

Exiled from Athens for a grave crime, Daedalus flew to Crete, where he devised, and supervised the construction of, the prototypical **labyrinth.** To prevent him from leaving Crete, his royal employer, Minos, confined him and his son **Icarus** to the labyrinth. But, still the cunning deviser, he effected his own and his son's escape and his own safe landing in Sicily.

dagestan or **daghestan;** or capitalled. See **baku.**

dago. This term—usually a pejorative—was originally American for a man of Spanish parentage, but it was soon adopted by the British and used of a Spaniard, a Portuguese, or, especially, an Italian or, generically, for a South-West European. The word is credibly said to be a corruption of the Spanish *Diego*,

125

an equivalent of James and a very common name; moreover, St Diego is the patron saint of Spain.

dago red, 'cheap red wine', is American slang, originally low but, since ca. 1930, reputable enough. 'So called because it is red wine of the sort usually drunk by Italian labourers' (Godfrey Irwin, *American Tramp and Underworld Slang*, 1931). See **dago.**

'So Ignaz the Wolf and his mob do very well for themselves and are able to wear good clothes, and jewellery, and sit around eating spaghetti and drinking dago red and having a nice time generally,' Damon Runyon, *Take It Easy*, 1938.

daguerreotype. 'I can see on each side of the mirror examples of the art of Daguerre, which have already begun to produce in us the same sentiment we get from the early Tuscans,' John Ross, *Masques and Phases*, 1909.

A hybrid word from Greek *tupos*, 'impress' + French *Daguerre*, the name of the inventor (Louis Daguerre, 1789–1851; a scene-painter for the opera) of the Daguerreotype process, published in 1838; the earliest photographic process.

Cf. **dallastype.**

dahlgren is short for *Dahlgren gun*, a smooth-bore gun made of cast-iron and invented in 1856 by Lieutenant, later Admiral, John Dahlgren (1809–70); used, during and after the Civil War, by the United States Navy. His best-known writings are *The System of Boat Armament*, 1852, and *Shells and Shell Guns*, 1856.

dahlia. 'Tall dahlias flaunted their extravagant beauty: giant sunflowers bent beneath the weight of haloed glory,' Claude Houghton, *Six Lives and a Book*, 1943.

Dahl + the botanical Latin -*ia* found in so many modern flower-names. Discovered by Humboldt in Mexico in the year of the French Revolution, it was sent to Madrid, where Professor Cavanilles, of the Botanic Garden, named it in honour of the 18th-Century Swedish professor and botanist, Anders *Dahl*, a friend of Linnaeus.

Hence, *blue dahlia*, which, like 'a white crow,' synonymizes the impossible or the unattainable, there being no blue dahlias.

daler. See **dollar.**

dallastype is a process of photographic engraving, perfected in 1875 by D. C. *Dallas*. Compare, therefore, **daguerreotype.**

dalmatian is short for the long *Dalmatian dog*, that spotted and elegant coach-dog (formerly it was kept to run alongside coaches and carriages) which is sometimes, though now very rarely, called 'the smaller Danish dog'. *Dalmatia* is an Adriatic-coastal district of Yugoslavia and was once a Roman province; the name is Latin (from Greek).

dalmatic, the vestment assumed by priests for the celebration of Mass, under the chasuble by bishops, by a king or an emperor at his coronation. It represents the Latin *dalmatica vestis*, 'Dalmatian vestment'; in Late Latin, *dalmaticatus* signifies 'clothed in a dalmatic'. Compare **dalmatian** (q.v.).

daltonism, colour-blindness (usually the inability to distinguish between red and green), has been so called because this inability was experienced by John *Dalton* (1766–1844); we adopted the French *daltonisme*. This English chemist and physicist was the first person to describe in detail, 1794, the disability of colour-blindness, from which his brother suffered too. His most notable published work is *A New System of Chemical Philosophy*, in three parts, 1808–27.

damascene. (For its fruit sense, turn to **damson.**)
The term *damascene work* refers to steel, or other metal, that has been *damascened*, which may mean either 'inlaid with gold or silver designs' or 'having the dark-lined pattern of *Damascus* blades (or *hilts*)'. The origin appears in *Damascus*, or Italianate *Damasco*, 'Damascus steel, especially a Damascus sword', also called *damask* (*steel*). Damascus was anciently the capital of Coele-Syria and famous for its steel.

damask. (Cf. the Glover quotation at **calico.**) The *damask rose* probably came from Damascus, and from it *damask powder* and *damask water* were respectively scented and distilled; for the 'steel' sense of *damask*, see the preceding entry; and *damask*, the fabric, may be 'a rich silk elaborately figured' or, derivatively, 'a similarly figured twilled linen'. Since ancient times, *Damascus* has been as famous for its fabrics as for its steels.
Damascus stands for Greek *Damaskos*, which transliterates the Hebrew *Dammesek*—compare its modern native name, *Dameshk*.

damson. 'The dried figs of Antioch on the Maeander, the raisins of Berytus, and the prunes of Damascus were celebrated,' W. W. Tarn, *Hellenistic Civilisation*, (revised edition) 1930.
The *damson* is small and with a sub-acid tang, whereas the *damascene* (or *damson plum*) is sweetish and larger.
Grown in and around Damascus in Syria, these plums were

very early introduced into Greece, thence to Italy, thence to Spain and France, whence to Britain.

Perhaps via French, *damson* represents a weakening of the earlier *damascene* (originally applied to *damsons* and *damson plums* alike), which 'translates' Latin *Damascenum*—short for *prunum Damascenum*, 'prune of Damascus' (alternatively *prunum Damasci*).

Compare **cherry** and **quince**.

dan, ' small buoy used by trawlers '. Of obscure origin, it probably, as W proposes, comes from *Daniel*; I propose the prophet Daniel, who withstood the roar of the lions as this buoy withstands the roar of the winds and the disagreeable attentions of the edacious sea.

dandiprat, ' an insignificant and very small person ', probably belongs to the family of *Jack Sprat*, as W has suggested. The word, therefore, may represent *Dandy* (i.e., Andrew) *Pratt* : compare the next term.

dandy, ' an exquisite ', is either short for *Jack-a-dandy*, which in the 18th Century signified ' a beau ', or, as *dandy* was first used in Scotland, the pet-form of *Andrew*; the latter, like *Johnny* a century later, being arbitrarily employed to give a particular personality to a class of men.

Daniel come to judgement, a; Daniel in the lions' den. (Mulcted at a night club) ' " I feel like Daniel among the bloody lions," he said,' James Curtis, *You're in the Racket Too*, 1937; ' Mr Kipter peered round the door, like a Daniel pausing to count the lions, and came in reluctantly,' Desmond Hawkins, *Hawk among the Sparrows*, 1939. The former phrase means an upright judge—and a very wise one.

The Biblical *Daniel* as a whole and the Apocryphal book of *Susanna* have generated the former, chapter vi the latter phrase : and the popularity of the former owes much to Shakespeare's *The Merchant of Venice*, IV, i, 223 and 333, Shylock's ' a Daniel come to judgement ' deriving immediately from *Susanna*.

danse macabre. See **macabre**.

daphne, ' a flowering shrub (i.e., the spurge laurel) ', derives from the Greek *daphne*, ' the laurel, the bay-tree ': but whether the laurel took the name from *Daphne*, that nymph of Greek mythology, who, beloved of Apollo, was transformed into a bay-tree (or laurel), or whether the laurel (or bay-tree) gave it

128

name to the nymph, is uncertain. Certain it is, however, that *daphnean*, 'shy as, or like, a virgin; pertaining to virginal timidity or shyness', derives from *Daphne*, the nymph, who, to escape Apollo, herself begged that the transformation should be made.

darbies ('handcuffs') derives from *Father Darby's bands* or *Darby's bands*, a late 16th- and early 17th-Century phrase for a rigid bond shackling a debtor to the mercy, or mercilessness, of a money-lender. Although it cannot be proved, there was probably some notorious usurer named *Derby* (often pronounced *Darby*), who, like **Shylock,** became generic for all money-lenders; or it may have been some too officious officer of the law with a phobia against debtors.

Darby and Joan. This mutually affectionate old married couple appeared first in a song published in *The Gentleman's Magazine* of 1735 and may have been drawn from two well-known characters in humble life. The connotation of 'humble life' has almost disappeared, but the phrase has become a part of idiomatic English. Hence, mainly in dialect, a pair of china figures, usually set upon the chimney-piece.

daric. 'Darius [King of Persia, 521–485 B.C.] was, if less of a conqueror [than Cyrus], a greater administrator. He . . . gave his empire a gold currency of very remarkable purity,' T. R. Glover, *The Ancient World*, 1935. The *daric* was a gold coin, and on it was set an archer: the Persians, 'bowmen rather than swordsmen', taught their sons three things, 'to ride the horse, to shoot with the bow, to tell the truth' (Glover). The coin *daric* represents *Dareikos*, 'of Darius'; hence it is 'the coin of Darius': and the King's name means 'the upholder of the empire'.

For king-named coins, compare **carolus, jacobus, louis, napoleon.**

davenport, in England, 'a drawered writing-desk with a hinged writing-board'; in the U.S.A. the same article, and also a very big divan or couch. 'Helen led the way into the big living-room and dropped down on the davenport,' Erle Stanley Gardner, *The Case of the Careless Kitten*, 1944.—'At one of these curious Victorianisms known as a Davenport, Mary Hoy sat writing letters,' Humfrey Jordan, *Landfall Then Departure*, 1946.

The term is said to commemorate the name of an English furniture-maker of ca. 1820–40, for the writing-desk; for the couch, that of the makers of a large one for a fat man.

129

daviesite, in mineralogy, has been named after Thomas *Davies* (1837–91), a mineralogist on the staff of the British Museum.

davit, as a nautical term, with variant *david*, seems to be a special application of the Biblical name (perhaps merely as a font-name) ; in French, *davier*, designating several tools, comes from *David* ; compare the use of **jack** in English.

davy (lamp) **; davite,** a variety of alunogen. Both the lamp— in full, *Davy lamp* or *Davy's lamp*—and the mineral ore have been named in honour of Sir Humphrey *Davy*, who, in fact, invented the former. Moreover, *davine*, from *davina*, the Italian name for a nephelite, and *davyum*, a supposed metal, were scientists' names bestowed in honour of the same great English chemist (1778–1829), who invented much, discovered much. He devised the miner's safety-lamp in the year of the Battle of Waterloo.

dearborn is a four-wheeled carriage, light, usually covered, and furnished with side-curtains; much used in the United States from ca. 1820 to ca. 1860 and much affected in Boston and Philadelphia. Its inventor was an American surnamed Dearborn—probably either Major-General Henry Dearborn (1751–1829) or a son. The DAE records *dearborn* for 1824 and its original, *Dearborn wagon*, for 1820.

Debrett, which has been jocularly called ' the stud-book of the British aristocracy ', is sometimes referred to as *Debrett's Peerage* : and so *to be in Debrett* has come to mean ' to be of noble birth '. John *Debrett*, an English publisher who died in 1822, issued in 1802 his compilation, *A Peerage of England, Scotland, and Ireland*, and, six years later, *A Baronetage of England*. The name has ' caught on ' far more widely than that of John Burke (1787–1848), who in 1826 compiled the first alphabetical dictionary of peers and baronets, known as *Burke's Peerage*, annually re-edited (1847–92) by his son, who also re-issued his father's *Landed Gentry*, originally issued in 1833–38.

' Berkeley or Grosvenor Squares, . . . around and about which the owners of names to be found in *Debrett* or *Burke's Peerage* lived and had their august beings,' John G. Brandon, *The Blue-Print Murders*, 1942.

debunk. See **buncombe**.

de-Gauss ; better *degauss*, known to the general public in the form *degaussing belt* (used to counter the magnetic mine). For the man whose name is incorporated, see the entry at **gauss**.

deipnosophist, ' a master of, one skilled in, the art of dining ', is an academic word. Athenaios of Naucratis, a Greek writer usually known as Athenaeus, flourished ca. A.D. 200 and wrote a voluminous work entitled *Deipnosophistai*, sometimes rendered as ' Sophists at Dinner ', but more correctly as ' Connoisseurs in Dining ' or simply ' Gourmets ' or, better, ' Gastronomes ' : The Greek word has been formed from *deipnon*, ' dinner ' + *sophistes*, ' a learned fellow '—perhaps the genitive *deipnou*. This erudite, gossipy anecdotage does, in the form of dialogues that take place among a number of scholars (a sort of dons' dining club), treat of food under many aspects and of a multiplicity of other subjects.

Compare **Brillat-Savarin** in the subsidiary list.

delf or **delft.** ' It was only near the sea that [in Holland]—in the earlier ages—the clay became the basis of industries, some of which, e.g. the clay pipes of Gouda and the earthenware of Delft, still survive, but import English clay,' L. W. Lyde, *Europe* (4th edition), 1930.

Delf—the name means ' canal ' (cf. *delve*, to dig) and the *t* is intrusive, unnecessary—was founded in the 11th Century and the Delf earthenware was first manufactured there early in the 14th Century.

Delilah allusively signifies : properly, a wife or mistress who turns to treachery ; loosely, a temptress ; improperly, a mistress as such, with no connotation of treachery ; as in ' Big Brogan, having made such a fool of himself over this blonde woman Ritz, probably talked a little too much. Here was a case of Samson and Delilah,' Gerald Kersh, *The Weak and the Strong*, 1945. Literally, her name signifies ' delicate '.

Of Samson it is said (*Judges*, xvi, 4–29), ' He loved a woman . . . whose name was Delilah. And the lords of the Philistines . . . said unto her, Entice him, and see wherein his great strength lieth ' ; having thrice tried in vain, she cajoled him into disclosing that the secret of his great strength lay in his unshaven locks ; guilefully, she had him shorn of the hair of his head, and he was undone ; her woman's purpose accomplished, the Philistine money hers, she passes out of his life and the story.

Saint-Saëns's opera, *Samson and Delilah*, produced by Liszt in 1877, was banned in England until 1909—not a very great loss, for it is not one of the greater operas.

Delphian, Delphic. ' He had been about to say that the human mind was a curious and wonderful instrument. But it occurred to him that this was a two-way phrase, a **Delphic hedge**' (or evasion), Ellery Queen, *Calamity Town*, 1942.

Delphian, Delphic, is allusively employed for 'oracular'— with the emphasis upon obscurity and ambiguity. Apollo had at Delphi, a town on the slope of Mount Parnassus, an oracle that was famous throughout the ancient Greek world. The oracular utterances were delivered by the high priestess (the Pythia), and on matters of religion the Delphic Oracle was accounted the supreme authority in Greece; on matters of morality, it often rivalled the Sophists; on mere worldly matters, it mingled charlatanism with wisdom; on the future, it aimed at a nice combination of obscurity with clarity, of ambiguity with verdicts quite unmistakable—in short, its pronouncements thereon were such as to be susceptible of interpretation in the light of events.

demarara; better **demerara.** This brown-crystalled cane-sugar came originally, as it still does in the main, from *Demerara,* the cane being grown in that district—that county of British Guiana which lies between the Berbice and Essequibo rivers; the district owes its name to the Demerara River, which flows into the Atlantic at Georgetown.

'While the best cacao is grown on the sheltered plain of the Orinoco, the best sugar is grown on the coastal plain of the Demerara,' Lionel W. Lyde, *Man and His Markets,* (edition of) 1919.

demijohn would seem to be a folk-etymological shaping of the French *damejeanne,* which rationalizes the folk-name *Dame Jeanne,* 'Dame Jane' or 'Lady Jane'. The folk-name, in addition to exemplifying the general folk-tendency to bestow personal names upon things, bears a particular reference to the fact that this large bottle has a bulgingly buxom body, like that of a prosperous housewife with a comfortable figure.

'In Granada, the new music [especially of Manuel de Falla, b. 1876] and the new poetry [typified and pinnacled in Federigo Garcia Lorca, war-killed in 1936] sometimes met. On summer nights, in the gardens, there would be a party beside the fountains and the demijohns—*damajuanas*—of native sherry,' J. B. Trend, *The Civilization of Spain,* 1944.

denia = a *Denia grape* or, more generally, a *Denia orange.* Denia is a Spanish port in the province of Alicante and on the Mediterranean. Compare **valencia** and **seville.**

denim. ' Pacing up and down the grim [death] chamber, in her neatly fitting but simple blue denim prison dress, Margaret had,

132

oddly enough, little fear,' Harry Stephen Keeler, *The Iron Ring*, (English edition) 1944.

This affords a particularly interesting example of aphesis: *serge de Nim*: i.e., Nîmes in France, ' Nîmes serge '.

For the formation, compare the dress material known as *delaine*, which, made of wool, is simply the French *de laine*.

deodand, in English law, is a personal chattel that, having contributed to somebody's death, became forfeit to the Crown and was affected to pious uses, especially for distribution as alms; in general, a thing forfeited or given to God.

From the Anglo-French *deodanda*, itself from Medieval Latin *deodandum*, it represents the Latin phrase, *Deo dandum*, ' (something) to be given to God '.

derby, which, short for *Derby hat*, sounds so very English, is American for a narrow-brimmed felt hat with a rounded crown; a version of the bowler hat, it became popular ca. 1880 and still has a considerable following in many parts of the world. It is permissible to surmise that originally it was a hat for informal wear, perhaps especially on sporting occasions, and that it bore a reference to the most famous of all English horse-races, the Derby, instituted in 1780 by the 12th Earl of Derby; whence *Derby dog*, allusive for a trifling interruption, from that dog which, after the course has been cleared, so often appears there just before the race—or as it is being run. The Earls of Derby have retained their interest in race-horses.

Spelt with a capital, the term may also designate: (1) a low-heeled, soft sporting-boot; (2) with variant *Derbyshire*, a shortening of *Derby(shire) cheese*, a pressed cheese that, made from milk partly skimmed, is manufactured chiefly in Derbyshire.

derrick. A hangman, from a noted Tyburn hangman of ca. 1600 (compare **Jack Ketch**); hence, a gallows; hence, a hoisting device or machine. As ' hangman ' and ' gallows ' the term did not outlive the 17th Century, and as a hoisting contrivance, it did not arise until the 18th. In the language of the 20th Century underworld, *derrick* means either ' shop*lifter* ' or ' shop*lifting* '.

derringer. ' One of the lads dropped a derringer and I picked it up,' *Sessions Paper of the Central Criminal Court*, November 21, 1907.—' The knuckle-gun is a single-shot derringer—a little gun only about five inches long . . ., but shooting a ·45 caliber cartridge,' Bob Eichberg in *Detective Fiction Weekly*, June 22, 1935.

This pistol, small in size but large of bore (and very effective at short range), entered upon the American scene in the middle 1850's. It was named after its inventor, the American gunsmith Derringer.

Cf. **colt** and **gat** and **roscoe** and **smith & wesson**.

deutzia. This very pretty white-flowered shrub, a native of China and Japan, and of northern India, was, in 1781, named after a well-known Dutchman : J. *Deutz* of Amsterdam. (The OED.)

devon is short for ' one of the Devon breed of cattle '—as in ' " One of those little Devons is kind of sick ",' James Gould Cozzens, *A Cure for Flesh*, 1933. *Devon*(shire) is noted for its cattle and its sheep, its cream and its scenery ; and the mineral *devonite* is so named from having been discovered near Barnstaple in that county.

devonian (or **D**—), in geology, designates that system of rock formation (including the old red sandstone so characteristic of the southern part of the English county of *Devon*) which lies between the **silurian** and the carboniferous.

' If we look at a geological map of the area just to the west of . . . the Cumberland plateau, we notice that the surface exposure of carboniferous (Pennsylvanian–Mississippian) rocks which form most of the surface is interrupted by inliers of Devonian, Silurian, and Ordovician rocks,' Ll. Rodwell Jones in *North America*, by Jones & Bryan, (7th edition, 1946.

dewitt, ' to mob-slay, to lynch ' (somebody), is a literarism now, whereas it used to be primarily an historical allusion. The term dates from 1672, when the Dutch mob-murdered the brothers De Witt. Cornelius (born in 1623) had assisted the great Dutch admiral de Ruyter against the English, but he was of less importance than Jan (born in 1625), for Jan ranks as a considerable statesman, who advocated and upheld the authority of the states against the encroachments of the prince of the House of Orange. A list of his achievements would be impressive. When Louis XIV invaded the Netherlands and the Dutch called William III to the leadership, they, angered by the de Witts' opposition to William, slew the two brothers that had served their country so well.

Diana.

> *Dum Dianae vitrea*
> *Sero lampas oritur:*

> ' When Diana lighteth
> Late her crystal lamp,
> Her pale glory kindleth
> At her brother's fire '

(Helen Waddell's translation of a medieval lyric).

In modern literature, *Diana* is used allusively for two allied types of girlhood or young-womanhood : the Artemis type, so athletic that she has few amorous feelings (' If you play games, you won't think about boys '), a horsewoman, a girl that hunts ; the emancipated young woman, who, very independent, yields her liberty only when she has had enough of it, as in Meredith's *Diana of the Crossways* (1885), where Diana is the actual name of the very intelligent, charmingly prudent Diana-like heroine who, owning ' The Crossways ', long stands at the cross-ways, hesitant about marriage and jealous of her chastity and her single-heartedness alike.

Diana, Latin goddess, became invested with many of the characteristics of the Greek Artemis and hence a moon-goddess (Diana, as in the initial quotation, personifies the moon itself) ; also of Hecate, hence she was also an earth-goddess, with the title of Trivia, she, like Hecate, being worshipped at the cross-ways : Diana of the Cross-Ways. Originally, she was a spirit of woods (*Diana nemorensis* : Diana of the Groves) and of wild life, of Nature uncultivated ; she came to be the especial object of worship by women, who—at least the intelligent among them —have always resented male possessiveness and men's tendency to regard them as a quarry of the chase. Her purity has in the main generated the conception of the moon as the pale goddess of chastity but also, in part, been influenced by the qualities with which primitive mankind invested the moon—so cold in contrast to the sun. This matter of light is central to the origin of the name itself and to the function—one of the functions— of the goddess, the first syllable of her name being identical with the first syllable of *dies*, ' day ' (the light as opposed to the dark : hence, illumination as opposed to ignorance) ; the radiant light of a Mediterranean full moon is as nature-remarkable as the pellucidity of a cloudless Mediterranean day.

dianthus, the colour yellowish red, derives from *dianthus*, the flower. That flower means ' the flower of Zeus ' : Greek *anthos* + *Dios*, ' of Zeus ' ; the name as a whole is not Classical

Latin but Neo-Latin or, if you prefer, the so-called ' scientific ' Latin; one of Linnaeus's neologisms.

Derivative is *dianthine*, an aniline dye—and a brilliant colour.

dick, in its various slang senses, represents *Dick*, the familiar form of *Richard*. So common a name has almost as wide a derivative currency as **billy, bob, charley, jack, john, sam** and **tom.**

dickens. As the Scott of *great Scott!* has nothing to do with the great Sir Walter Scott, much to do with the American General Winfield Scott (1786–1866), a notoriously fussy, bustling candidate, luckily unsuccessful, for the presidency in 1852, so *the dickens!* has nothing to do with Charles Dickens but is a euphemism (via *Dickson*) for ' the devil '.

dick(e)y, whether a garment or a stuff for garments—animal or bird—a seat or the second mate on a ship, goes back, precisely as **dick** goes back, to **Richard**; and for precisely the same reasons.

The slang adjective *dick(e)y*, ' weak, shaky ', probably derives from the noun in the sense ' a false shirt-front '.

diddle, to cheat or swindle; hence, to ruin or even to kill; and, as *diddle away*, to waste (e.g., time); yes, and also the American slang sense ' strong liquor ': all these senses spring from the character of Jeremy *Diddler*, constant borrower on the never-never system of repayment, in James Kenney's farce, *Raising the Wind*, 1803. W notes its probably relevant similarity to dialectal *duddle*, ' to trick '.

dido(e)s, cut up, ' to play tricks, cut a caper ', is by Webster implied to have its origin in *Dido*. A probable etymology. That is, if we accept, not the pre-Virgilian mythological but the Virgilian version of *The Aeneid*, Book iv, wherein she falls in love with Aeneas. He ' loves and leaves her ': and she, distraught, curses him and his race and takes her own life. The phrase debases a passionate love-story.

diesel. A Diesel engine: that type of oil engine which was built by Dr R. *Diesel* (1858–1913) of Munich in the years 1893–97, after having been patented in 1892. Rudolf Diesel received much assistance from the famous Essen firm, Friedrich Krupp.

Concerning post-1920 Burma, John L. Christian has said that ' Electric lighting spread from Rangoon to nearly all cities of 5000 inhabitants or more, each city having an independent lighting plant usually operated by diesel power' (*Modern Burma*, Berkeley & Los Angeles, 1942).

digby shortens *Digby chick* (or *chicken*), a nickname for the herring caught off and cured at *Digby*, town and port, some 150 miles west of Halifax in Nova Scotia; fairly 'in the middle' of the great herring trade of that part of the world.

dionise. This precious stone was, in the Middle Ages, held to be an anti-intoxicant: an amulet against the wiles of *Bacchus*. From Old French *dionise*, from Medieval Latin *dionysia*, from Latin *dionysias*, from Greek *dionusias*, from *Dionusos*, i.e. *Dionysus* or Bacchus. Compare :—

dionysiac or **Dionysian.** (Concerning Joseph Guinta, dance-mad American gangster shot to death in May 1929) 'His elegant little person . . . was, when inspirited by the grape and the ululating saxophone, motion lyricized. His zeal was dionysiac. He was bacchanalian,' Fred D. Pasley, *Al Capone*, 1931.—' My first Dionysian or rhapsodic experience was . . . connected with light; light which has always meant so much to me, its quality even affecting my writing,' Osbert Sitwell, *Left Hand, Right Hand*, 1945.—' For all we duller mortals know, may there not be wild dionysian orgies at night on the Pons Asinorum as the poor inhibited isosceles triangles beat their luminous sides in vain trying to make their three angles add up to more than two right angles,' Ian Mackay in *News-Chronicle*, April 11, 1946.

'Of or like, or belonging to or reminiscent of Dionysus': hence, 'Bacchic; erotic; wildly exalted; ecstatic; dithyrambic; rhapsodic': the reference being not only to *Dionysus*, or, as the Romans called him, Liber, or after a Greek name, Bacchus, but also to the *Dionysia*, the festivals (and worship) in his honour.

In Greek mythology, Dionysus was the son of Zeus and Semelë. Probably Thracian in origin, he appears in post-Homeric times, when he was of scant importance, ' as a god of vegetation, a suffering god, who dies and comes to life again, particularly as a god of wine, who loosens care . . . and inspires to music and poetry. . . . With him were introduced into Greek religion the elements of ecstasy and mysticism that are found in his cult'; he is intimately linked with the Orphic, hence often called the *Dionysiac* or *Dionysian* mysteries. For an excellent account—whence comes the quotation—see Sir Paul Harvey's *The Oxford Companion to Classical Literature*. And that admirable scholar W. W. Tarn has, in *Hellenistic Civilisation*, remarked that ' far the most important Greek God of the age

137

outside Greece was Dionysus, whom the Dionysiac artists carried all over the world; art and literature gave him a triumphal progress across Asia on the model of Alexander's'.

directoire or **D—**. Both the hat and the gown, the latter a blend of Ancient Greek mode and Parisian modishness, take their name from the period of the French *Directoire* (1795–99), when women's dresses affectedly imitated Greek (and Roman) styles; these styles survived the Directoire; and Madame Récamier, and in the 20th Century her famous portrait, have done much to revive and perpetuate them.

dittany. This plant, medievally famous for its medicinal virtues—rather alleged than actual—represents Old French *dita(i)n*, *dictame*, *dictamme*, etc., from Medieval Latin *dictamus*, from Latin *dictamnus* (or *-um*), from Greek *diktamnon*, said, with good reason, to derive from *Diktë*, that Cretan mountain where (as elsewhere) the herb grew. The *-any* ending probably anglicizes the Old French *-amme* ending.

Dives (cf. **Croesus** and **Midas**); **Dives costs.** The latter is a Chancery Law term for 'costs on the higher scale', sometimes recoverable by a poor man from a rich man—a *Dives*.

In *Luke*, xvi, we find the parable of Lazarus and the 'rich man, which was clothed in purple and fine linen': in the Latin version of The New Testament the rich man is *dives*, not *Dives*, for *dives* = 'rich (man)', but, by the pressure of public opinion, the word has come to be apprehended as a Proper Name; hence as a synonym for 'a rich man'.

Dixie = *Dixie Land* (formerly often *Dixie's Land*) and it has come to mean either 'the Romantic South', although the Southern States of the U.S.A. are not so romantic as all that, or even a sort of Negro paradise, although it is far from being that, either! 'Dixie Debunked' is the title of a witty article in *The American Mercury* of April 1938. Properly, the Southern States, despite the fact that originally it signified the North to slaves shipped south from Manhattan Island, where they had belonged to one Dixie, a wealthy slave-owner. The sense-change may have been caused 'through some confusion connected with the "Mason and Dixon Line" that defined the division between the free and the slave states'. The famous song *Dixie*, written in 1859 by the Northerner Daniel Emmett, became a marching song of the southern troops. (Dr Percy Scholes.)

dobbin and **dobby.** A farm horse, a draught horse, is often called *Dobbin*, which, with small or capital *D*, may also be used

138

generically; *dobby* (or *dobbie*), a much later word, is a term in weaving—it helps to *drive* the machine. Both terms are pet-names from *Robert* : *Dobbin* and *Dobbie* are diminutives of *Dob*, an alteration of *Rob*, which, like *Bob*, pet-forms *Robert*. (*Robin* was a diminutive of *Rob* before it became a font-name in its own right.)

Doctor Pangloss. See **Pangloss.**

doctrinaire. ' If he wished to be doctrinaire, we might try to estimate what effects would flow from the ending of the frontier experience and from the closing of that avenue for the out-pouring of the surplus energies of our restless and surplus population. . . . We might expect, . . . talking as doctrin-aires and playing with our interpretation of conditions, that, irrespective of conditions in Europe, we should see a change in the type of our immigrants,' James Truslow Adams, *The Epic of America*, 1933.

Both as noun (a person obsessed by theory, especially in the art of government, whether national or international) and as derivative adjective, the English *doctrinaire* is a form-adoption, a sense-adaptation of the French *Doctrinaire*, ' a member of the party of speculative politicians whose central doctrine of idealistic compromise was, by conservatives and radicals alike, held to lie outside the scope, the range, the potentialities of political practice '; the party arose either in late 1815 or in 1816.

dogberrydom; Dogberry. Blundering officialdom; a blundering, talkative, self-satisfied petty official, especially if a policeman : the terms come from Shakespeare's *Much Ado about Nothing*, where Dogberry and Verges are absurd, officious constables. Dogberry enjoyed a subsidiary, left-handed notoriety because of his anticipation of Mrs Malaprop (see **malapropian**) in the misapplication of words. *Dogberry* was suggested by the *dog-berry* or chokeberry, fit only for dogs.

doily, obsolete for a kind of woollen stuff, obsolescent for a small table-napkin (' coarse Doiley-napkins, fringed at each end,' Swift) for use with fruit, and current for a small ornamental piece of lace to protect a polished surface, commemorates the name of a London draper, one Doily who, in the 17th Century, had a shop in the Strand. ' The name is of French origin, from *Ouilly* (Calvados),' as W reminds us.

139

doll; dolly. The Proper Name *Doll* is the pet form of *Dorothy*, and *Dolly* is a diminutive of *Doll*. In the sense, a child's toy, compare the synonymous French *marionnette*, doubly diminutive for *Marion*, and the Scottish *doroty*. In its various applications to mechanical conveniences or contrivances, compare the use of **jack** and **peggy**, and for its applications to persons compare **moll**.

dollar (16th-Century *daler*). Originally the German *thaler* (now *taler*), then the Spanish and Spanish American peso, and finally the United States *silver dollar*, first issued in 1794. From the Low German—and Dutch—*daler*, from German *thaler*, itself short for *Joachimst(h)aler*, a coin first struck, 1519, in the valley (German *thal*) of St *Joachim* in Bohemia; Joachimsthal is a small mining town, with mines of silver, nickel, and zinc blend. This saint was an Italian mystic of the 12th Century.

The English use of the term for ' the sum of five shillings ' and of *half a dollar* for ' half-a-crown ' is a colloquialism.

dolly. See **doll**.

dolly varden. ' A style of dress made with a pointed bodice and a skirt of bright-colored flowered material draped over a skirt of plain color.—A large hat for women, having one side bent down '—the hat, not the women—' and trimmed with many flowers ' (Webster).

All because a certain fictional young woman happened to wear a cherry-coloured mantle and similarly coloured ribbons? Ah, but what a girl was Dolly Varden, who, in Dickens's *Barnaby Rudge* (1841), was beautiful and coquettishly lively—a man's dream and a woman's nightmare.

dolomite, whether a calcium magnesium carbonate or, deriv-atively, a limestone—or marble—rich in such a carbonate, fittingly recalls the man after whom it was named, the French geologist and mineralogist, Déodat de *Dolomieu*, *dolomieu-ite* becoming, by the principle of ease of pronunciation, *dolomite*. Dolomieu (1750–1801), much-travelled professor, discovered the mineral. He also, while a prisoner of war, wrote two treatises on mineralogy. He was, indeed, one of the heroes of the scholarship of science.

Don Juan. See **Juan**.

Don Quixote. See **quixotic**.

donkey, thinks Webster, may be the colour *dun*, with a diminutive suffix : originally the word rhymed with *monkey*. Skeat is strongly of this opinion. Neither The OED nor W wholly rejects it, but both of them prefer to regard it as a personification —*Dunkie*, the diminutive of *Duncan*—and adduce the synonymous **cuddy** and **neddy.** The latter is much the more probable etymology, in that the word arose in slang and in dialect. Compare also **moke.**

dorcas. 'I thought the stranger within your gates might have transformed you to a model housewife. What a damnable thing—Venus into Dorcas!' (Helen Simpson, *Under Capricorn*, 1937) : which conveniently exemplifies the half-way stage between the Biblical character and the transferred sense, 'a sewing-circle for the benefit of the poor'.

'There was at Joppa a certain disciple named Tabitha, which by interpretation is called Dorcas : this woman was full of good works and almsdeeds. . . . All the widows stood by [Peter] . . ., shewing the coats and garments which Dorcas had made,' *Acts*, ix, 36, 39.

Doric = vernacular language in general, broad Scots in particular. The Dorian dialect, 'the Doric', of Ancient Greece was despised by the speakers and writers of the Attic dialect, the latter deeming it rustic and uncouth ; certainly it was less supple, subtle, mellifluous than Attic.

(Concerning Greece) 'The Dorians and other invading tribes were frankly barbarians,' V. Gordon Childe, *What Happened in History*, 1942 ; compare, therefore, **barbarian.**

dorking. This hen (short for *Dorking fowl*), an excellent layer, despite its five toes, takes its name from the Surrey market-town of *Dorking*, twenty-five miles south of London. It became popular in the 1820's–1830's, although its excellent qualities had been widely recognized locally since long before that.

doubting Thomas. See **Thomas.**

dowlas, a coarse kind of linen, was mentioned in the Acts of Henry VIII and in the plays of Shakespeare (1 *Henry IV*, III, iii, 79). It was made in Brittany and the name refers especially to the township—in the 15th–16th Centuries, a village—of *Daoulas* (often written *Doulas*) situated, some ten miles from Brest, on the coast and in the *département* of Finistère. Compare **cambric** and especially **lockeram.**

doyley. See **doily.**

draconian or **draconic.** 'Nash's draconian edict against the wearing of steel [i.e., swords] within the liberties of Bath was still in full force,' Alice & Egerton Castle, *Incomparable Bellairs*.—'His life revolved round one simple, Draconian principle : he hated cowardice intensely, and venerated "guts",' Mark Benney, *The Scapegoat Dances*, 1938.

Draco is the latinized form of Greek *Drakōn* ('the serpent') : and Draco was that Athenian legislator who, in 621 B.C., codified and promulgated the laws of Athens. For private vengeance he substituted public justice : hence, in the main, the proverbial fame attaching to the Draconian laws, the severity having doubtless been exaggerated by later generations. Draco's laws were, however, abolished by Solon only some thirty years later.

drambuie or **D—.** As liqueur brandy is to ordinary brandy and as Napoleon rum is to ordinary rum, so is drambuie to whiskey. A Scottish liqueur, it is based on Scotch whiskey.

drawcansir, 'a boastful swashbuckler' (ca. 1672–1830), is the lower-casing of the vainglorious blade, Drawcansir, in George Villiers the 2nd Duke of Buckingham's *The Rehearsal* (1672), a character parodying that of Almanzor (in Arabic, 'The Victorious') in Dryden's *The Conquest of Granada*; Dryden 'got his own back' in *Absolom and Achitophel*, where he satirized Buckingham as Zimri. In view of Drawcansir's drinking abilities, The OED is almost certainly right in deriving his name from '*draw* a *can* of liquor'; I should go further and suggest that the question Drawcansir liked best to hear asked of him was, 'May I *draw* you a *can* of ale, *sir*?'

Cf. **bombast** and **rodomontade**—derivatives from the names of braggarts.

dreadnought; whence **super-dreadnought.** This, the largest, most heavily armed and armoured type of battleship of ca 1906–12, was named after the first of its class : H.M.S. *Dreadnought*, launched early in 1906. The *super-dreadnought* was rather a journalistic than a Naval elaboration. There had been a *Dread-naught* in Queen Elizabeth's fleet; nor, as the designation of a type of warship, was the term new to the British Navy.

Cf. **monitor** for a class of warship derived from a Proper Named naval archetype.

druidic is eligible only in its transferred senses 'given to prophecy' and 'barbarously ritual or religious'.

142

The Latin plurals, *druidae* or *druides*, occur in Caesar and Tacitus as translations of the Old Erse *drui* and Gaelic *draoi*, 'magicians'. W compares the Cymric *derwyddon*, 'sooth-sayers' (literally, speakers of the truth), from *derw*, 'true'—cognate with *true* itself.

dryasdust, a dry, pedantic fellow, especially if he be a professor or an antiquarian or an historian, owes much of his currency to the Rev. Dr *Dryasdust*, that fictitious writer who supplied the prefaces to some of Scott's novels and the conclusion to *Redgauntlet*, a tediously prosy antiquarian.

dubonnet is, I feel, the correct form of the more usual *Dubonnet*, so famous is this French appetizer, of which the foundation has been built, surely and dependably, on potent wine flavoured with herbs. Named after its manufacturer (compare, e.g., **cinzano**), it lends itself to puns (*C'est du bon, eh ?*) and to clever advertising (*Du—Dubon—Dubonnet*).

'The guy who told me that Dubonnet mixed with rye was a good drink certainly knew his vegetables,' Peter Cheyney, *I'll Say She Does!*, 1945.

duffel, a coarse, thick-napped woollen cloth, hence an American colloquialism for 'outfit' (for camping, etc.) or 'kit', is another of those names for fabrics which, like **cambric** and **muslin,** come from the town of their first manufacture. In this instance, *Duffel*, which, on the Nethe river, lies some ten miles from Antwerp.

Dulcinea is the heroine of *Don Quijote de la Mancha*, published in 1605 (Part I) and 1615 (Part II) and written by Miguel de Saavedra Cervantes, who, born in 1547, died in 1616—three days after Shakespeare. She was loved, nay, worshipped, by Don Quijote: 'sweet' her name (Latin *dulcis*), sweet her nature. Figuratively: a woman beloved, a sweetheart revered, the lady of one's fervent devotion.

(Concerning Loyola, another very great Spaniard :) 'The ambition of his generous heart . . . was moving on a higher plane [than that of sentimental chivalry], though for a while longer his Dulcinea would by no means capitulate. . . . Remembrance of her and sweet plotting for the favour of her eyes alternated in his mind with grim prospects of fasting and faring barefooted to Jerusalem,' James Brodrick, *The Origin of the Jesuits*, 1940.

'He had a Dulcinea there [at Cape Town], whose former

143

scruples would most likely vanish on seeing him in command,'
William Kelly, *Life in Victoria*, 1859.

With this idealized mistress, cf. **Beatrice** and **Egeria** and
contrast **Aspasia.**

dumdum, short for *Dumdum bullet*, a man-stopping bullet of a
sinister expansiveness, was first manufactured at the important
military station of *Dum Dum*, six miles from Fort William (the
citadel of Calcutta).

'Dumdums? Well, yes! The —— things do everything
but weep. *You* do that.'

dunce, one who is slow to learn, a 'dim-wit', provides us with
the best example the English language affords of ironical
derivation, its earlier sense being 'sophist; metaphysical hair-
splitter', deriving from '*Duns* man', a disciple of *Duns Scotus*.
Now John Duns Scotus (? 1265–? 1308), so named because he
was born at *Duns*, a Scottish market-town, spent much of his
life in Europe, where, as a Franciscan, he studied, thought,
wrote, disputed. As Aquinas, whose tenets he opposed, was
'the Angelic Doctor', so Duns Scotus was 'the Subtle Doctor'.
He founded *Scotism*. 'Stubborn opposition of Scotists to
classical studies of Renaissance and their obstructionist and
cavilling practices gave rise to the use of *dunce* for a sophist,
pedant, or blockhead' (Webster BD).

dundrearies are *Dundreary whiskers*, 'long flowing side-whiskers
separated by a clean-shaven chin'—known in slang as
'Piccadilly weepers'. They are of the kind worn by E. A.
Sothern (1826–81) in the role of Lord *Dundreary*, a brainless
idiotic feather-head in Tom Taylor's comedy, *Our American
Cousin* (1858). The play had a great success in New York;
the English-born Sothern had gone to 'the States' some six
years earlier.

dunstable, whether the noun—a straw hat, or the plait thereof—
or the adjective ('plain, direct'), refers to the town of *Dunstable*
in Bedfordshire, where the hats were formerly made and whence
the Dunstable Way or Road led to London. Part of the ancient
Roman-built Watling Street, the Dunstable Way was noted for
its evenness and for its many long straight stretches (*plain as
Dunstable way*).

duralumin, a proprietary name, constitutes a blend of *Düren* and
aluminium; thus *Dür(en)alumin(ium)* drops the capital and the
accent. Düren, the ancient *Marcodurum*, 'Marcus's hill-fort'

144

(Sanskrit *durga*), is in Prussia; a manufacturing town, with a productive zinc mine nearby. (Chisholm.)

dutch. In American slang, *in dutch* means 'in disgrace or disfavour', and it reflects the general pejorative nature of *Dutch* in such phrases as those which are cited in the second glossary.

In Cockney slang, *my old dutch* = 'my wife'; it shortens *my old Dutch clock*, with a pun on *dial*, 'face'.

In Standard American and English, *dutch*—more usually *Dutch*—represents a breed of small rabbits native to Holland.

E

eau de cologne (or **Cologne**); **eau de luce** (or **Luce**); **eau de nil** (or **Nil**); or **eau-de-** etc. At Cologne, the commercial centre of Prussia, scent is a favoured industry: the *Kölnische Wasser*, or *eau de Cologne* or 'Cologne water', was originally, as it is still mainly, prepared at Cologne. The German *Köln*, French and English *Cologne*, derives from the Latin *Colonia*, '*the* Roman colony' of Germania.

The second term, *eau de Luce* (a snake-bite antidote, used also as smelling-salts), means 'water—or scent—of Louis', in reference to one of the French kings: compare **fleur-de-luce.** For *eau de Nil*, the colour otherwise known as 'pale green', see the subsidiary list.

Ebenezer. 'How irritating are the janglings of sect against sect, Bethel's cracked note trying to outvoice the plaintive tinkle of Ebenezer,' Ronald Knox, *An Open-Air Pulpit*, 1926. A Nonconformist term, both in this sense 'house of worship' and in the lower-cased sense 'memorial stone' (1 *Samuel*, vii, 12), it springs from the literal meaning of the Hebrew masculine name: *eben-ha-'ezer*, 'the stone of help'.

Cf. **bethel** and **bethesda.**

Hence, in the U.S.A., *set-up (one's) Ebenezer*, 'to make up one's mind firmly'; hence, too, *ebenezer*, 'anger, temper'—slang of ca. 1820–60. (DAE.)

écossaise is short for *danse écossaise*, 'Scottish dance'. But on this tricksy subject, it is mere commonsense to cite, not an ordinary dictionary but that eminent musicologist, Dr Percy Scholes, who himself cites a great Scottish musician, Sir Alexander Mackenzie, as saying 'It is difficult to believe that the *Ecossaise* is of Scottish origin, for it bears no resemblance either to the strathspey or to the reel . . . which solely represent the dance music of Scotland,' and himself continues, ' The fact of a French name being used would seem to point to an origin in the ball-rooms of Paris ' (in the late 18th Century).

edam. ' The cheese ' of Holland ' is made chiefly west of the Zuider Zee, e.g. at Alkmaar and Edam, and the butter chiefly east of it, e.g. at Gröningen and Zwolle,' Lionel W. Lyde, *Man and His Markets*, 1896.

This cheese, yellow-hued (with a dark-red outside) and fine-flavoured, was made originally at, and still in the district around, Edam, a village eleven miles north-east by north of Amsterdam.

Eden. Either as *the Garden of Eden* or simply as *Eden*, the term has come to possess, beside its literal meaning, the sense ' an earthly paradise; a scene, a life, of much felicity; a realized Utopia—with the emphasis on personal happiness rather than on the common weal '.

For a witty commentary, see the first two or three pages of Rose Macaulay's light satirical novel, *Going Abroad*, 1934.

' Here through many an hour of rapt reading of poetry she had returned to Eden ', Hugh I'Anson Fausset, *Between the Tides*, 1942.

In Hebrew, *eden* means ' pleasure, delight ' : ' Paradise is a place lying in the eastern parts, whose name is translated out of the Greek into Latin as *hortus* (i.e. garden) '—some scholars render *eden* as ' orchard '. ' It is called in the hebrew tongue Eden, which is translated in our language as *Deliciae* (i.e. place of luxury and delight). Uniting these two gives us Garden of Delight,' Isidore of Seville, who flourished ca. A.D. 600–36. (With thanks to G. H. T. Kimble, *Geography in the Middle Ages*, 1938.)

Egeria has come to be equated with ' a gracious woman counsellor of much wisdom and not a little charm '. In Roman mythology, she was the goddess of fountains : near the Porta Capena of Rome, she had a sacred spring, where, by night, she met King Numa and gave him much sage advice : there has been, among godless moderns, a tendency to surmise that she bestowed more than advice, yet this cynicism may have arisen from the fact that, according to one legend, she was Numa's wife.

The name may derive from Latin *egerere*, ' to bear ' : for Egeria was also the goddess of childbirth. More probably Etruscan.

146

It is worth noting that of the four inspiring mistresses known in legend, history, literature, only Egeria belongs to mythology —Roman mythology ; Beatrice is historical—Italy of the 13th Century ; Dulcinea is imaginary and Spanish ; Aspasia, through Pericles, forms part of Greek history of the 5th century B.C.

Compare **Beatrice** and **Dulcinea ;** contrast (and compare) **Aspasia.**

ldorado (strictly, **El Dorado**) **;** or, as a genuine Common Noun, *eldorado*. ' Four-wheeled wagons . . ., superb stone vessels, golden daggers, spears and axes of electrum (gold-silver alloy), lovely miniature animals of gold, soldiers' helmets of copper, curious inlaid gaming-boards, beads and ornaments of every description are amongst the . . . precious objects yielded in staggering profusion by this El Dorado of the dead ' (the Royal Cemetery at Ur), Patrick Carleton, *Buried Empires*, 1939.

Eldorado (Spanish, ' the golden '; strictly, ' the gilded '), ' legendary country of tropical America, which early explorers believed, according to native rumours, to lie in different parts of the vast region between the Amazon and the Orinoco. In the centre of this country stood, according to tradition, a city with roofs of gold, known as *Manoa del Dorado* ' (George Chisholm, *Gazetteer*). Some very interesting, though cursory, information on the medieval phase of the El Dorado legends is to be found in G. H. T. Kimble, *Geography in the Middle Ages*, 1938.

ecampane is the plant known also as horse-heal. The word comes by metathesis from Medieval Latin *enula campana ;* in Classical Latin, *enula* is *inula*, which means the plant ' elecampane '. Why, then, the *campane* element of *elecampane*? Probably it represents *campana*, which signifies either ' of the fields ' or ' Campanian ' (of the Campania in Italy).

oïsa (French : Héloïse) and **Abelard** have become, like **Romeo and Juliet,** typical of hapless love : but the love of the former was deeper, stronger, nobler, and their tragedy much the greater. Since the early 12th Century, they have typified the love of a famous man, the intellectual glory of his age, and a beautiful, intellectual young woman. They adored each other as they adored their God. Perhaps the warmest and loveliest tributes to them occur in Rousseau's *La Nouvelle Héloïse*, in Pope's *Eloisa to Abelard*, and in Helen Waddell's *Peter Abelard*—especially in the last.

ysian ; elysium. ' It was an elysian evening indeed, the air light and warm, and the sun still lingering among the foliage '

(W. L. George, *The Triumph of Gallio*); 'Who as they sung would take the prisoned soul And lap it in Elysium' (Milton *Comus*).

The adjective comes from the noun, which has been adopted direct from Latin, which takes it from the Greek *Elusion* (*pedion*), 'the Elysian plain' or *the Elysian Fields*, in Greek mythology the abode of the happy dead, especially of heroe and patriots, placed by Hesiod and Pindar in 'The Isles of the Blest' (see **Hesperian . . .**), where they live a full life and delectable.

elzevier or **elzevir**. The strictly correct form, says W, is that in -*ier*. Originally a book printed and published by the *Elzevier* family in Holland, especially at Amsterdam and Leyden, during the period 1583–1680, and then a style of type both roman and italic, used by the Elzeviers for their publications. Founded at Leyden (or Leiden) by Louis Elzevie (1540–1617?), the business was carried on by his five sons and by two succeeding generations.

Compare **aldine.**

Emma was, ca. 1900, an alternative name for the sport more widely known as *Aunt Sally*, or rather for an elaboration thereof (W.)

emmenthaler is a Swiss cheese, resembling **gruyère** (q.v.). is made in the valley (*Thal*) of the Great *Emmen*; this valley 'famous for its pastures', and there is a large cheese-depot 'Bugdorf at the mouth of the Emmenthal' (L. W. Lyde, *T Continent of Europe*, (4th edition) 1930).

Enfield. The *Enfield rifle* was, as its successors are still, made the famous small-arms works—a Government factory— Enfield, immediately outside 'postal' London on the nort Enfield rifles were used by the Americans during the Civil Wa

Compare **Lee-Enfield.**

english, n.; **English side.** The former, beginning as slan was by 1945 a technicality—part of Standard American an Canadian; the latter, still slang and much less usual, decidedly obsolescent.

The use of *english* in baseball, where the longer synonym unknown, derives from its use in billiards. The term mea 'spin'—spin imparted at or from the *side*. What *bias* is bowls, *english* is in billiards.

So much nonsense has been written upon the subject that feel I cannot do better than to quote from a letter dat

August 23, 1937, and sent to me, as a contribution to *A Dictionary of Slang and Unconventional English* (a much shorter account appears in the 3rd edition), by Mr D. E. Cameron, Librarian to the University of Alberta. His explanation is much the best I have seen.

'One very odd case of the development of slang, which without knowledge of the stages would remain an insoluble mystery, is found in the use of " english " as " spin " on a ball (as in billiards or baseball) . . . Stages, all still '—in 1937— ' co-existing, are :

' 1. Language ekes out its own deficiency by gesture, hence gesture equals " body English " [i.e., English expressed by means of physical signs or gestures].

' 2. By direct transference, any gesture or contortion (as in trying to perform a difficult physical task) becomes " body English ".

' 3. In a game (e.g. billiards), effect and effort, as thus described, on the ball becomes " body English " on the ball.

' 4. By natural contraction, this becomes " English " on the ball, or " spin ".

' For example, when a ball fails to be drawn enough by the spin imparted to it to effect the desired result, the remark is : " Not quite enough English " (can be written with a little *e* also). Or of a baseball pitcher, " He sure puts (the) english on his ball ! " '

To which Mr Cameron appended this comment. ' I have heard this use of *English* objected to, as if it were a derogatory reference, using the word " side " to remind Englishmen of the social uppishness or affectedness sometimes attributed to them by others ; this, however, entirely ignores the heredity of the word in this sense of " spin " or " side ".

' If, however, the intermediate steps were lost sight of, some future lexicographer would be almost certain to conjecture an oblique reference to a supposed characteristic of Englishmen, and would be cleverly wrong.' (I admit that, without Mr Cameron's entirely convincing account of the genesis of this the billiards sense of *english*, I should have gone wrong—not at all cleverly wrong.)

english, to ; better, *english*. To translate into English—or into American. Short for *turn into English* or *render in(to) English*.

English horn. See **cor anglais** in the Appendix.

entellus, the long-tailed monkey of the East Indies, derives its name—somewhat unflatteringly to him—from a Sicilian hero,

Entellus, who, famous as a pugilist, figures in *The Aeneid* (v. 38
et seq.).   He, presumably, was an inhabitant of *Entella* (now
Rocca d'Entella), in the interior of Sicily—literally, *in* the *tellu*
or country.   (Lewis & Short.)

epicure; epicurean, epicureanism.   ' L'épicuréisme bie
compris est la fin de tout,' Sainte-Beuve (1804–69), quoted b
' Palinurus '.—' Death is the very life of undertakers, and it'
churlish for a layman to resent their epicureanism,' R. C
Hutchinson, *Interim*, 1945.

   ' Epicurus himself, who died in 270 [B.C.], was a gentle
frugal man, who bore his last painful illness with quiet fortitude
his personal success in Athens was considerable, and the lives c
his own circle, which included women, were not only exemplar
but a fragrant oasis in a stormy age ; and if his doctrine c
pleasure was sometimes abused, this was not done by those wh
really followed his teaching.   The real reproach against hi
philosophy was that it taught men to shirk living ; it was
running away,' W. W. Tarn, *Hellenistic Civilisation*, (revise
edition) 1930.

   To equate *epicure*, *epicurean*, *epicureanism* with ' gourmet
' connoisseur ', etc., is going too far ; to equate them wit
' selfish hedonism ', etc., is worse ; to equate them wit
' glutton ' or with ' sensuality ', etc., is ludicrous.   Yet th
vagaries of language have done precisely those things.   Com
pare the less objectionable distortion of **stoic.**

erbium.   Discovered in 1843, it is one of the 92 chemica
elements ; its earth is *erbia*.   *The Chemist* (vol. I, 1843)
' [Mosander's] close examination of Yttria has led him t
discover . . . two oxides, to which he has given the name
terbium and erbium ' (quoted by The OED) ; but he did no
examine yttria closely enough, for **ytterbium** remained to b
discovered.

   A foreshortening of **terbium,** which, like *ytterbium* and it
prototype *yttrium*, derives from the Swedish town of *Ytterby*
where deposits of all four elements are found.

ermine.   The fur comes from the animal of that name ; a
animal whose widespread habitat did at least include *Armenia*
it was, at first, known as *armenius mus*, ' mouse(-like) animal o
Armenia '.

Eros; erotic, eroticism.   The Greek god of love, so lon
associated with romantic love, has come to be apprehended a
the personification of physical love—of passion—as opposed t

Psyche, spiritual love. Eros is the male counterpart of **Aphrodite**—likewise opposed to Psyche. The Greek word is allied to *eramai*, ' I desire (sexually), I love '. In psychology, *eros* signifies ' the principle, the power, the function of physical love as a driving force in the affairs of men ' : physically, mentally, spiritually.

' The first half of Shakespeare's work concentrates on two primary emotional positives : (i) the normal romance interest of human love, and (ii) the king-ideal. Both are approached with a profundity too easily missed. The two are related imagistically as eros-charged symbols : love is often compared to a kingly presence, and both love and kings are associated with the sun, repeated age-old religious associations,' G. Wilson Knight, *The Burning Oracle*, 1939.

' One of [Shakespeare's] major themes . . . is the gradual recognition by his heroes of their own deepest selves ; which is, normally, a kind of love ; a kind of eros-music, at once a humility and a royalty,' *ibid.*

' The two Aphrodites, *Agapé* and *Eros*, the maternal-sisterly and sexual impulses,' *ibid.*

escallonia is a plant belonging to a large genus of shrubs native to South America and discovered by a Spanish traveller named *Escallon* ; *-ia* is the typical ending, in scientific Latin, for flower-names formed from Proper Names. Compare :—

eschscholtzia, a gaudy herb of the poppy family, recalls the German botanist, Johann Friedrich von Eschscholtz (1793–1831), who accompanied Otto von Kotzebue on a round-the-world voyage in 1823–26. Kotzebue, son of the famous German dramatist, was a first-class navigator and an ardent explorer ; on his third great voyage, Eschscholtz was his botanist.

esclavine is an obsolete name of a Russian mantle. Literally, a *Slav* mantle. So W tells us, at *cassock* ; Webster and The OED omit this interesting word, which should be compared with **cassock** and **dalmatic.** See also **slave.**

etna. A vessel consisting of a cup set in a saucer of alcohol and serving to heat liquids, *etna* derives from *Etna*, a volcanic mountain on the east coast of Sicily ; its first recorded eruption took place in 467 B.C. In Latin, it is written *Aetna*, a transliteration of the Greek *Aitnë*, from *aithein*, ' to burn '. Vulcan is, in Roman mythology, known also as *Deus Aetnaeus*, the god of *Aetna*, where he is reputed to have had his forge.

' Above us in the blue mist we could just glimpse Mount

Etna with its scarred upper slopes and its rich vine-clad foot-hills,' Brigadier James Hargest († August 12, 1944), *Farewell Campo 12*, 1944.

euclid, 'geometry', is short for 'Euclid's geometry'—'the geometry of Euclid'; **euclidean** (from *Euclidean*), 'geometrical' or, derivatively, 'lucid and orderly in the exposition of geometrical evidence and in the elucidation of geometrical problems'. The Latin form of the Proper Name is *Euclides*, from the Greek *Eukleidēs*, literally, 'the renowned': compare the synonymous *eukleēs* and *eukleia*, 'renown'. This Greek mathematician, who flourished ca. 300 B.C. at Alexandria, wrote one large work, the *Stoicheia* or 'Elements', dealing with geometry and the theory of numbers. His geometry held the field until ca. 1900, and his fame rests secure upon his warning to Ptolemy I that there is 'no royal road to geometry'.

'The Euclidean geometrician supposes the existence of Euclidean space, but he does not suppose that he supposes it; he knows that he supposes it,' R. G. Collingwood, *Speculum Mentis*, 1924.—'Thomas's'—i.e., Thomas of Aquinas's—'writings display an almost Euclidean clarity and rigour' (they are almost diagram-lucid), Meyrick H. Carré, *Realists and Nominalists*, 1946.

euhemerism is usually defined as 'the reference of myths to, and their explanation by, an historical basis'—especially in respect to the origin of the gods. 'Two prominent gods of the time, Apollo and Dionysus,' writes the great historian W. W. Tarn in *Hellenistic Civilisation*, 'had had mortal mothers . . . ; others, like Asclepius, had been men ; and Euhemerus's theory that *all* had once been men was widely known.' Euhemerus, who flourished ca. 300 B.C., was a Sicilian Greek : he held that the gods had been kings or heroes deified by those who had been their subjects or their beneficiaries. Euhemerus also created a true Utopia—on an island in the Indian Ocean.

euphorbia; euphorbium. The latter is a gum resin, drawn from the euphorbia, a cactus-like African plant (*euphorbia resinifera*) ; euphorbium, which has for many centuries been used medicinally, is a late Latin form of *euphorbeum*, itself transliterating the Greek *euphorbion*, which derives from *Euphorbos*, a Greek physician.

euphuism, 'high-flown style', derives from *Euphuism*, style affected and artificial in the manner of the *Euphues: the Anatomy of Wit* (1578) and *Euphues and His England* (1580) by

John Lyly (1554?–1606). In these sequel-romances, the two chief stylistic excesses were those of antithesis and historical or mythological allusion. Psychologically, euphuism is trivial when compared with **gongorism**. The name *Euphues* is of Greek origin and it means ' (The) Well-Born (One) '.

Compare also **guevarism** and **marinism**.

europium. A chemical element: Latin *Europa*, Europe. Belonging to the rare-earth group, it was spectroscopically discovered in 1896 by Eugène Demarçay (1852–1903), a noted French chemist.

eusol, ' an antiseptic solution, used especially for war wounds ', is said by Webster to constitute a blend of the Greek prefix *eu*, ' well ', and ' *sol*ution '. The COED, however, in the 1944 Supplement, states that it is from the initial letters of ' *Ed*in-burgh *U*niversity *sol*ution *of l*ime ': which, in view of the actual discovery, is true and which, therefore, is to be preferred.

Eve = generic woman. Waldo Frank, an American writer born in 1889, wrote ca. 1913, of the Catalans: ' It is a subtle and gracious people. Its secret of survival is manifest in the women: delicate daughters of Eve, perhaps the fairest of all Europe, hued like April orchards, and with eyes like twilight ' (cited by Dr J. Trueta in his *The Spirit of Catalona*, 1946, in a passage quoted in that gracious Oxford University Press quarterly, *The Periodical*, April 1946): a tribute worthy to be set alongside Milton's mellifluous description in *Paradise Lost*.

' When Adam delved and Eve span, Who was then the gentleman? ': Eve, traditional mother of mankind, is in Hebrew *Hawwah* (later pronounced *Havvah*), literally ' life; or, the living one '.

every man Jack. See **Jack, every man.**

Everyman. Every man and every woman. A generalization from the 16th-Century morality play, *Everyman*, and the central character therein: Everyman. Not only is the play available in ' Everyman's Library ', but it has been produced, more than once, in the present century.

F

abian, ' cautious in politics ', as in ' The Fabian Society ', which, formed in 1883, had as its dominant personalities the Sidney Webbs and G. B. Shaw, inculcated an evolutionary

Socialism, based upon 'the inevitability of gradualness' and opposed to the doctrinaire, revolutionary tenets of Marx,—*Fabian* takes its name from Quintus *Fabius* Maximus, who, as Roman dictator, harassed Hannibal's army yet avoided open battle, finally (209 B.C.) defeated the Carthaginians, and by his 'tip and run' tactics earned himself the agnomen, or official nickname, of 'Cunctator', the Delayer.

faërie, -ry; or without the diaeresis. 'The subtle and transforming art of what is faery,' as H. M. Tomlinson phrases it in *Tidemarks*, 1924.

In the sense, 'The world of fairies; especially, a visionary, romantic world', *faërie* may justifiably be derived immediately from *The Faerie Queene* (1590–96) by Edmund Spenser (1552?–99); in Shelley's phrase, 'some victor knight of faëry', the reference is direct, as also in Keats's 'in faery lands forlorn'. The word comes from the Old French *faierie* or *faerie*, 'fairy folk; enchantment', from *faie* or *fae* (modern French *fée*—compare English *fay*), from Late Latin *fata*, 'one of the *Fata* or *Fates*', Classical Latin *fatum*, 'fate'—that which is said or uttered, from the defective verb *for*, 'I speak', past participle *fatus*.

Fagin. Of a Chicago crime-school she attended at the age of fifteen, 'Chicago May' (May Desmond, at the font; later May Churchill Sharpe) wrote, 'Years afterwards, in jail, I read about Fagan, the thief-trainer, in Dickens' "Oliver Twist"; but he was a piker, compared with my teachers' (*Chicago May—Her Story*, 1928); and Henry Hyatt, ex-crook, in 1931 spoke scornfully of those writers who pictured 'old-time crooks as Fagins . . . A real crook seldom boasts of his accomplishments' (*Detective Fiction Weekly*, January 31). The word is also used as a synonym for 'keeper of a thieves' kitchen' and 'a receiver of stolen goods'. Cf. **Bill Sikes.**

Fahrenheit is eligible only in the colloquial 'What's the fahrenheit?' = 'What is the temperature?'; and perhaps better written, here, with a small initial. The other four person-named temperature scales, Celsius, De L'Isle, Réaumur, Kelvin, are not thus used (in English, at least) and are therefore ineligible. Fahrenheit, a German physicist, lived 1686–1736, and invented the mercurial thermometer.

faïence probably derives, via the obsolete French *Fayence*, from Italian *Faenza*, a centre of the 16th-Century ceramic industry; the term covers the various glazed porcelains and glazed earthen wares, and its full shape in French is *poterie de Faïence*. The process long antedates the Christian era. In the chapter on ' Early Bronze Age Civilization ' (*What Happened in History*), Gordon Childe remarks that ' the chemistry of glazing was discovered and faïence was made '.

Falernian = *Falernian wine*. Concerning the Oxford of his day (the later 'nineties), John Buchan, in his distinguished auto-biography, *Memory Hold-the-Door*, 1940, has written, ' There was the Horace Club, which . . . met in summer . . ., when we supped on nuts and olives and fruits, drank what we made believe was Falernian, and read our poetical compositions '.

Horace speaks more than once of Falernian wine, as (*vinum*) *Falernum* ; and Tibullus mentions it in the form (*cadi*) *Falerni*, literally ' Falernian wine-jars or flasks ', in the phrase *fumosi Falerni*, where *fumosi* implies that the wine has been kept in the smoke-chamber (*fumarium*) to mature. This wine came from grapes cultivated in the district known as the *ager Falernus* in the northern part of Campania (Italy) ; a celebrated wine.

Compare **chian.**

Falstaff ; Falstaffian. ' A very Falstaff of a man ! '—' I could stand and gloat over this kind of show ; it was enormous, Falstaffian ; it suggested large appetites, needs and fulfilments of needs ', W. L. George, *The Making of an Englishman*, 1914.

Sir John Falstaff, in Shakespeare's *Henry IV*, is robust, witty, self-indulgent, boastful—yet lovable. The complexity of his character was first indicated by Maurice Morgann in 1777.

Fanny, in American, hence in English slang, is a much-used word for ' backside ' ; it captured the British fancy when Clare Boothe's *The Women* was performed in London late in 1938. Obviously it is a personification : *Fanny*, diminutive of *Frances*. But why *fanny* rather than, say, *doll* or *molly* or *peggy*? Probably by a pun on ' fundament ', whereof *fun* is an obsolete slang abbreviation : *fun* becomes *fan*, which becomes *fanny* : less by conscious wit than by subterranean, folk-etymological growth.

Fantee, go. The variant *go fanti* explains why the phrase should, applied to an European, signify ' to go native ', for *Fanti* is the name of a region and a tribe in the middle of the Gold Coast of West Africa. Originally the phrase seems to have meant ' to run amok '—hence ' to turn savage '—hence ' to go savage, to go native '.

farad ; faradaic, adj. ; **faraday.** Whereas the third belongs to physics and chemistry, the first belongs to electricity. Both of the nouns do honour to Michael *Faraday* (1791–1867), born at Newington in Surrey. Chemist and physicist, he made many discoveries relating to electricity. His *Experimental Researches in Electricity*, published in 1844–55, made him world-famous, although he had been known to scientists ever since 1821, when he successfully investigated certain potentialities of the magnetic needle.

faro was a card game-of-chance very popular in the 18th Century, when—until the 1790's—it was usually spelt *pharaoh*; it seems to have come from either France (*pharaon*) or Italy (*faraone*)— but travellers may have pooled their knowledge. Obviously from the *Pharaoh*, kings of Egypt: precisely why, nobody knows for certain; but compare *nap(oleon)*. *Pharaoh*, by the way, was, like *Kaiser*, a generic name, ultimately from an Egyptian word meaning ' great house ': and that explains why, in *What Happened in History* (1942), Professor V. Gordon Childe always writes the word *pharaoh*, as in ' In Egypt . . . the great land-lords . . . made themselves independent of the pharaoh '.

faun comes from Latin *Faunus*, a woodland deity—a god wor-shipped by country folk and later identified with the Greek Pan; hence, *faunus*, a satyr-like creature: compare Mallarmé's *L'Après-midi d'un faune*.

The Latin word derives from *favere*, ' to favour '. In journalism and in careless writing, a handsome, lustful young man is often called a faun; that is, when he's not a ' wolf '.

fauna, animal life in general, or the animals of a given country or region, especially as the complement to **flora.** In 1746, Linnaeus adopted *Fauna*, who, in Classical mythology, was the sister of Faunus (see **faun**).

fedora. ' A sage-green fedora ' (Stephen Leacock, *Moonbeams from the Larger Lunacy*, 1916) ; ' The man in the centre was tall, well-built, smooth-shaven, wearing a brown overcoat and a brown fedora hat' (Fred D. Pasley, *Al Capone*, 1931).

A fedora is a hat of soft felt, low crown, curled brim: and it gets its name from *Fédora*, a drama (1882) by Victorien Sardou (1831–1908), an extremely slick dramatist with an excellent sense of ' theatre ': he owed much to the acting of Mlle Déjazet and, later, of Sarah Bernhardt; in England, Henry Irving contributed notably to his foreign success. Compare **trilby,** which owed more to the fame of Du Maurier's master-piece on the stage than to its literary success.

fenugreek, used in curry-making, is an aromatic-seeded Asiatic herb. The English word has come to us, via French *fenugrec*, from Latin *faenugraecum*, earlier *faenumgraecum*, which represents *faenum Graecum*, ' Greek hay '. True; it is an annual herb, but it does not look much like hay, nor is there anything Greek about it other than its importation into Italy from Greece; it is mentioned both by Cato and by Pliny.

fergusonite, ' a niobate and tantalate of yttrium, erbium, etc.', has been named after R. *Ferguson*, a Scot; and *fergusite*, ' a plutonic equivalent of leucitite,' from *Fergus* County in the State of Montana. (Webster.)

fermorite, in mineralogy, commemorates L. L. *Fermor*, of the Geological Survey of India.

feronia is the fruit of that genus of the rue family which is known as *Feronia*, after an ancient Italic goddess, who, perhaps at first a fountain goddess, seems to have been the protectress of freedmen; her chief sanctuary was at Terracina, in Latium; ' several groves were dedicated to her '. The word seems to be of Sabine origin.

Ferrara. See **Andrea Ferrara.**

fescennine. ' A fescennine temperament,' John Ross shrewdly remarks in *Masques and Phases*, 1909, ' is too often allied with religiosity.' The word signifies ' scurrilous ' or, as in the quotation, ' obscene ': and it derives from *Fescennine*, ' of or like Fescennium '—an ancient city of Etruria. With this city has been associated that ancient form of Italian verse known as *versus Fescennini*, ' Fescennine verses ': not an immoral city, it has suffered from an imputed derivation of *fescennine* from *fascinum*, ' the phallus '. (Harvey.)

fiacre is a small hackney coach of the 17th–18th Centuries, a cab of the 19th, both popular in France. These vehicles were first hired out in 1648 by an innkeeper residing at the sign of St *Fiacre* in Paris. *Fiacre* is a gallicizing of the Irish nobleman *Fiachrach*, who founded a monastery at Breuil, near Paris, and who died ca. 670.

fifth column; hence **fifth(-)columnist.** ' Philip [of Spain], if the Invincible Armada had been successful enough to allow him to land troops [in England], would have found a ' fifth column ' of Catholics waiting to receive him, and a sufficient

157

number of Englishmen ready to act as quislings. Neither Spanish propaganda nor Spanish gold had been idle; . . . there were men in high places in England who were in Philip's pay,' J. B. Trend, *The Civilization of Spain*, 1944.

The allusion is to the Spanish Civil War of 1936–39 (see especially J. Alvarez del Vayo, *Freedom's Battle*, 1942). Derivatively ' secret sympathizers and subverters ', *fifth column* was, originally, ' the Franco sympathizers within Madrid . . . so described in a radio address by General Mola when he was leading four columns of troops against the city ' (Webster).

There is even a verb, as in ' When he was fifth-columnising, he wasn't doing anything criminal from his point of view. He was merely being patriotic according to his lights,' Miles Burton, *The Three Corpse Trick*, 1944.

Compare **quisling.**

filbert, the nut from either of two European hazel-trees, is a Norman word that shortens the French *noix de filbert*, and *filbert* is a ' telescoping ' of **Philibert** (from Old High German *Filuberht*, ' very bright '), a Saint whose day fell on August 22, in the nutting season.

Hence *filbert*, short for *filbert brown*, hazel-colour.

finnan, short for *finnan haddock* (Scots *haddie*), i.e. a smoked haddock, is traditionally stated to derive either from *Findon* or from *Findhorn*, both of which are seaport villages in Scotland; Findon, however, has the closer connexion with fishing.

fisher, ' a currency (i.e., Treasury) note '—compare **bradbury,** is a slang term, derived from the fact that, born in 1879, Sir Norman Fisher in 1919 became Permanent Secretary to the Treasury and therefore (October onwards) all Treasury notes bore his name.

flamingo; fleming. The former comes from the Spanish *flamenco* or the Portuguese *flamengo*, literally ' Fleming '. W remarks that ' the choice of the name ' is ' due either to a kind of pun on *flame* [Latin *flamma*] or to the medieval reputation of the Flemings for bright dress and florid complexion '. A *fleming* is, in Pembrokeshire, a soft clam.

Fleming is in Middle Dutch *Vlaming*, ' from the source of *Fland*ers '. (Webster.)

flash, ' the language of the underworld ' or, as adjective, ' relating to the underworld, or to its language ' (18th-Century meanings), hence, ca. 1805–40, ' the slang of the man-about-town ', comes, I believe, from *flash*, ' a sudden flame ': but

158

Canon Isaac Taylor (1829–1901), in his interesting *Words and Places*, advances the theory, it may—despite the dates—be the correct theory, that ' In a wild district of Derbyshire, between Macclesfield and Buxton, there is a village called Flash, surrounded by unenclosed land. The squatters on these commons, with their wild gipsy habits, travelled about the neighbourhood from fair to fair, using a slang dialect of their own. They were called the Flash men, and their dialect Flash talk; and it is not difficult to see the stages by which the word Flash has reached its present signification ' (i.e., showy, ostentatious). Certainly John C. Goodwin may be right when, in *Sidelights on Criminal Matters*, 1923, he states that ' " Flash notes " . . . is . . . from Flash . . ., where, several generations ago, the manufacture of spurious notes was carried on on a wholesale scale, the notes being put into circulation at the neighbouring fairs ', for, in this sense, it is a 19th–20th-Century term.

flemish eye; flemished (or **Flemish**) **coil.** ' Already the snow was thick enough . . . to blur the outlines of objects on the deck. On its forward side the square base of the binnacle was now a rounded mound; the flemished coils of the falls were now merely white cylinders'; ' Rodgers, the boatswain, kept a select party doing neat work in the rigging—knots and flemish-eyes and pointings ': C. S. Forester, *The Captain from Connecticut*, 1941—a novel, dealing with the earlier half of the year 1814. There are also the verb *flemish*, ' to lay (a rope, etc.) in a flemish coil ', and *flemish* (or *F—*) *knot*, shaped like the figure 8. The Flemings are related to the Dutch, who have given to English a host of nautical terms.

fleur-de-luce. ' There are two wild sorts of Iris, the Yellow Flag . . .; and the stinking Iris, also called the Gladdon. . . . Both plants are unmistakable in the form of the flower, but the first has led to much dispute about the " Flower-de-luce ". This is explained as the " flower of Louis ", adopted with the shield of France by Louis VII, or the " flower of the lily ", " fleur-de-lys ",' Vernon Rendall, *Wild Flowers in Literature*, 1934.

flindersia, an Australian timber-tree of the genus *Flindersia*, commemorates, as also does the sea-navigational term *Flinders bar*, that very able English navigator, Matthew Flinders (1774–1814), who in 1795–1800 explored and charted the coast of New South Wales, who in 1801–02 first surveyed much of the west coast of Australia, and who in 1814 saw his *Voyage to Terra Australis* published.

159

flip, in the sense 'a spiced and sweetened drink', as, e.g., in *egg-flip*, may perhaps derive from *Philip*, as W suggests—without adducing any evidence. Nor can I, yet I propose that there may be a pun on 'to appeal from *Philip* drunk to *Philip* sober' (which see at **Philip . . .**).

flora. (A list or a methodical description of) the plants of a given region—or a particular epoch. *Flora* is the Roman goddess of flowers (Latin *flos*, a flower) and her name formerly appeared in Latin titles, hence in English titles, of books on botany, as, for instance, in Dr Robert John Thornton's *Temple of Flora, or Garden of the Botanist, Poet, Painter, and Philosopher,* 4 vols, 1799–1804, described by Geoffrey Grigson in *Lilliput,* May 1945, as 'splendid, sumptuous, ornate, magnificent' and 'usually bound in scarlet morocco, too large for a bookshelf'.

'Latin is the language of the medieval commonwealth, in Paris, in Bologna, in Orleans, in Oxford: the scholar's "realm of Flora and old Pan"' (Helen Waddell, *The Wandering Scholars,* 1927).

florence; florentine. Both the former, a dress material (thin taffeta or a corded barège), and the latter, a close-fitting head-dress for a child or, obsoletely, a kind of tart or pie, come, the one direct from, the other from the adjective of, *Florence* in northern Italy: via the Latin *Florentia* and its adjective *florentinus.* A *Florence flask* is a pharmaceutical chemists' name for a *betty* or pear-shaped, straw-wrapped bottle in which olive oil used, in the 18th–19th Centuries, to be brought from Italy.

florin comes, via French, from Italian *fiorino;* compare the Spanish *florín,* for the French-English form has been influenced by *florence,* another name for the coin. Struck at *Florence* in 1252, the florin bore the design of a lily, the city-emblem; *fiorino* is 'a little *fiore* or flower'.

Flossie. In R.A.F. slang, *Flossie* is any girl or young woman; compare the *Flossie*-derivative *floosy* (or *-zy*), low slang for a none too reputable female. Compare the fate that has overtaken *Katy* and *Moll.*

flower-de-luce. See **fleur-de-luce.**

flushing, a fabric for sailors' coats, comes undoubtedly from *Flushing* (Vlissingen), the Dutch seaport that has for centuries had a close commercial and social connexion with Britain; but it is uncertain whether the origination is that Flushing was at first the place of manufacture or whether it is that coats made thereof were first worn by the Flushing pilots. (W.)

föhn is that dry, warm-to-hot wind which, on the northern side of the Alps, blows along and down the valleys. Via Romansch *favugn*, the word derives from the Latin *Favonius*, the West Wind (also known as Zephyrus)—associated, in Europe, with spring-time ; *föhn*, therefore, carries the root-idea, ' favouring ; hence, beneficial ' : Latin *favere*, to favour. ' It is hailed with joy in the spring . . .; it is . . . so dry and so warm that it becomes a veritable " eater of snow " ' (Lyde, *Europe*).

' The Fön, if it then existed, may be responsible for the destruction by fire of so many of the prehistoric Swiss lake settlements,' Norman Douglas, *Together*, 1923.

fontange, an old, polite name for a commode, honours the memory of ' Mlle de *Fontanges* ', who flourished ca. 1679, i.e. at the height of the earlier phase in the splendour of ' Le Roi Soleil '. Brief mistress of Louis XIV, she had a too brief life : 1661–81. Marie Angélique de Scorraille de Roussilles was created Duchesse de Fontanges by her royal lover.

Ford, a Ford motor-car ; often—and now better—*ford*. Also it is, and indeed has since ca. 1915 been, a synonym of ' cheap car, cheap van ', for the sufficient reason that, despite its cheapness, this American make is agreeably dependable.

' He was a decent-looking fellow, Fording it West with his family,' Margaret Armstrong, *The Blue Santo Murder Mystery*, (English edition) 1943.

For the influence of the name upon slang, cf. **tin Lizzie** in the supplementary list and see Godfrey Irwin's fascinating combination of lexicography and sociology, *American Tramp and Underworld Slang*, 1931 (Oxford University Press, London ; Sears, New York).

forsythia.

' Belbroughton Road is bonny, and pinkly bursts the spray of prunus and forsythia across the public way '—

so, entertainingly and unerringly, sings John Betjeman in *New Bats in Old Belfries*, 1945.

This flowering shrub was thus named, at the beginning of the 19th Century, after an English botanist : William *Forsyth* (1737–1804). Note the typical -*ia* ending, seen also in, e.g., **camellia, fuchsia, lobelia.**

161

forum, whether 'public meeting-place for open discussion'—'medium for discussion'—'tribunal—or court', is a common-propertying of the Forum of Rome (*forum romanum*), that open place lying in the hollow between the Capitoline and the Palatine Hill which served as the centre of public business: compare the Athenian agora. The Latin word is cognate with Latin *foris* (or *fores*), 'a door', and especially with the derivative adverb *foris*, 'outside': out of doors, the ablative denoting not only 'at' but 'away from' the doors.

fournier = *Fournier type*. In 1742, Pierre Simon Fournier (1712–68) published his *Manuel des caractères de l'imprimerie*. A French engraver and type-founder, he designed a type that, although now out of fashion, has its merits; the *Fournier point* belongs to the esoterics of printing.

franc is the monetary unit of France, the land of the ancient Franks (French *Francs*). Originally a gold coin, the *franc d'or*, it was first struck in 1360, the silver franc ensuing about two centuries later and becoming the monetary unit only at the Revolution. See **frank.**

francium. 'It seems that some new elements have been discovered lately, including No. 87, Francium; No. 95, Americanium; and No. 96, Curieum. But whether "They Came to Stay" or not, I should not care to avouch for a while, until we see if they stand the tests of other workers than their discoverers . . . . . . Masurium has turned out to be a pure fake by a German . . . The discoverer—one Noddack—was pushed into the Strasbourg chair by the Nazis during their occupation of the place; and when the Allies arrived, they found in his lecture-room a large wall-map of the Table [of Elements], on which "Masurium" was given type far larger than that used for the ninety-odd other elements,' thus one of the leading British research chemists in a letter of February 23, 1947, to the author. (The late Professor A. W. Stewart.)

With *curieum*, compare **curie.** And with *francium*, compare **germanium**: as the latter from *Germania*, so comes the former from *Francia*, the name used by the Latin poets Ausonius and Claudian for Franconia, the region inhabited by the Franks. And as the discoverer of *francium* is a Frenchman, so the discoverer of *americanium* is an American.

frangipane or **-i.** 'The wave of perfume which had met her emerging from the forest path eddied gently in the garden space about the open cups of many moon-pale blossoms, blossoms o.

a white moon-flower from which the scent named frangipani is distilled : and although she was happily unaware of this perfume's associations, Eva felt that she hated it, that its cloying sweetness robbed the air of life,' F. Brett Young, *The Crescent Moon*, 1925.

'. . . Frangipani, which resembles an oleander that has been both blessed and cursed ; blessed in its flowers . . . of an overwhelming sweetness, cursed as to its bare, ugly, thick branches,' Osbert Sitwell, *Sing High! Sing Low!*, 1944.

This perfume has come, traditionally, to be associated with Continental courtesans. The COED says, ' Probably from *Frangipani*, maker '; but Weekley notes that the perfume is ' said to have been introduced into France (temp. Catherine de Médicis) by one of the famous Italian family *Frangipani*, lit. break-bread, a name earned, according to tradition, by benevolence '—the breaking of bread, to give it to the poor.

frank ; derivatively or perhaps independently, **frankincense.** In both words, the allusion, ultimately, is to *les Francs*, that Germanic tribe, or confederacy of tribes, which conquered Gaul and gave its name to France and *les Français*. *Franc* is the Gallic form, via Latin *Francus*, of Old High German *Franko*. The adjective came to mean ' free ' because ' in Frankish Gaul full freedom was possessed only by those belonging to, or adopted into, the dominant people ' (The OED).

In *frankincense*, the *frank* element would appear to mean either ' pure ' (Skeat) or ' of high quality ' (The OED) : compare *racially pure* and *of great national worth*.

Frankenstein. ' If Vortigern '—a British prince, flourishing ca. A.D. 450—' appears in history as the Frankenstein of Roman Britain, it is not because what he did was in principle wrong. It was because his invitation '—his being invited to rule Britain —' unwittingly opened the floodgates of one of those mass migrations of which the British movement to Armorica was already giving an example,' R. G. Collingwood in Collingwood & Myres, *Roman Britain and the English Settlements*, (2nd edition) 1937.

In Mary Shelley's *Frankenstein, or the Modern Prometheus*, 1818, Frankenstein, a Genevan Natural Philosopher, creates a monster, which, huge and repulsive, gets out of control, murders his creator, and disappears. Very often ' Frankenstein ' is misapprehended as ' Frankenstein's monster ': see especially my *Usage and Abusage*, 1947.

Compare **robot.**

163

frankfurter ; occasionally *frankforter* ; also *frankfurt* (or *-fort*) *sausage*. This sausage, as popular in the United States as fish-and-chips in England, represents German *Frankfurter*, ' of or from *Frankfurt* ' (anglicé *Frankfort*) in Germany. In other parts of the world it used to be called a *German sausage*.

Compare **hamburg(er)**.

franklin, (1) in the 14th–15th Centuries a middle-class land-owner (see, e.g., Chaucer's *The Canterbury Tales*), derives from Anglo-Norman *fraunkelain*, from Medieval Latin *Franchelanus*, the Latin *Francus* with a latinizing of the Teutonic suffix *-ling* (W).

See **frank.**

(2) A lightning-conductor : from Benjamin *Franklin*, who devised it : only ca. 1770–1820.

(3) Short for *Franklin stove* (Appendix).

Compare :—

franklinia is a tree of the species *Franklinia*, related to the moun-tain bay. It was thus named, in honour of Benjamin *Franklin* (1706–90), scientist, inventor, philosopher, statesman, writer. As a writer he is remembered chiefly for *Poor Richard's Almanack* (1732–57), a store of acute aphorisms and practical precepts. During his sojourn in France (1776–85), he became an international figure.

franklinite, an oxide of iron or zinc or manganese, was dis-covered in the country around *Franklin*, New Jersey ; Franklin was an iron-smelting centre.

freesia, a sweetly scented herb of the **iris** family, is an adaptation of *Friesia*, named after Elias Magnus *Fries* (1794–1874), who, a Swedish botanist, was a notable authority upon the classification of cryptogams—especially fungi. (Webster BD.)

' The table was covered with brocade, with a waxy fountain of freesia in the centre,' Harry Hervey, *School for Eternity*, 1942.

french windows ; french polisher ; frenchman (the red-legged partridge). In these three terms, the *French* origin of the objects designated has been almost forgotten, simply because the terms themselves now form an inseparable part of the English language. So, too, *french beans*, which we no longer need to write with a capital *F*. In cookery, the verb *french*, ' to prepare, or to cook, food in the French manner ', does not require a capital.

164

friesian or **frisian** is short for *F. cattle*. *Frisian* means 'of Friesland': and Friesland, a province of the Netherlands, has for centuries been famous for its dairy cattle.

frieze derives, not from French *friser*, 'to curl', as Webster seems to propose, but from Old French *drap de Frise*, cloth from Friesland, as W makes quite clear. This simple explanation is preferable to the theory associating the cloth with the curly heads of the Frisians; W, indeed, cites, in support of his Old French origin, an irrefutable passage belonging to the date 1390–93.

frontignac. This drink has a name that is a blend of the words *Frontignan* and *cognac*. Not a spirit but a wine, 'the best dessert wine of Languedoc and one of the best of the naturally sweet wines made in France,' it bears the variant names *Frontigniac, Frontiniac, Frontinac*, and *Frontignan*, as M. André Simon informs us. Frontignan, in the *département* of Hérault, stands on the site of the ancient *Forum Domitii* or 'forum of Domitius'.

fuchsia, so often misspelt *fuschia*, is that decorative shrub with edible fruit which has been named after Leonhard *Fuchs* (1501–66), a German botanist. Hence a colour, a bluish red, as in 'The tea-rose in the west had deepened to fuchsia, and the window bathed her in the soft reflection,' Harry Hervey, *School for Eternity*, 1942.

fudge, 'nonsense, humbug', is of obscure origin. The best guesses are those made by W: 'This'—the interjection—'may be German *futsch*, no good, corrupted from French *foutu* . . ., ? a reminiscence of Goldsmith's wanderings in Germany. . . . The noun *fudge* may owe something to *Captain Fudge*, a 17th Century mariner, known in his day as *Lying Fudge*.'

fulham or **fullam** or, occasionally, **fullom,** 'a loaded die', was originally a term used in the 16th–17th-Century underworld. *Fulham*, in south-west London, was a notorious resort of crooks; probably it was also the site of the chief manufactory of cogged dice. In the 19th Century, *Fulham virgin* was what we nowadays call an 'enthusiastic amateur'.

furphy. Joseph Furphy (1843–1913), native-born Australian, under the pen-name of 'Tom Collins' wrote a classic, *Such Is Life*, 1903, and an amusing novel, *Rigby's Romance*, also some

165

short stories and verse. Certain of his tales sound 'tall': hence, a 'furphy' is, in Australian slang, a rumour, a baseless report.

furry dance. The furry dance—a farandole, or processional dance, through the streets—of Helston (Cornwall) is also called 'the Flora' or 'the floral dance' (Scholes); celebrating the arrival of spring and therefore announcing the coming of flowers, the advent of the reign of Flora, that goddess of fertility and flowers in whose honour the *Floralia* or *Ludi Florales* were held, the furry dance is seen to be a folk-etymological form of either *Flora* or, more probably, *floral*, perhaps via *flowery* (the flowery dance).

fury; Furies. When you ungallantly describe a woman as a fury, you liken her to one of the Furies of Greek mythology, where their name was Erinyes or, euphemistically, Eumenides ('the kindly') or, propitiatorily, Semnai ('the Holy'). There were three of these avenging spirits—avengers, especially, of crime against kinship; Allecto, Megaera, Tisiphone.
'The pangs of guilt took shape,' for the Greek, 'in the conception of the avenging Furies,' G. Lowes Dickinson, *The Greek View of Life*, 1896.

fustian is a literary term for 'bombast' or 'claptrap', but originally it designated cotton-and-linen cloth and now, though obsolescently, corduroy or velveteen. By Webster derived from Latin *fustis*, 'a stick', it is by The OED and W derived from Old French *fustaigne*, from Medieval Latin *fustaneus*, probably the adjective corresponding to *Fostat*, that suburb of Cairo where cloth was made; W compares the Spanish *fustán* and the Italian *fustagno*. 'The suburb of Masr-el-Atiqa or Old Cairo (first called *Fostat*, " tent-town "), was the site of the original Cairo, founded about 624 by the sultan Amru' (Chisholm).

G

gadolinite; gadolinium. The former is a black mineral: silicate of yttrium: first analysed by the mineralogist *Gadolin* and, in 1802, named after him; its adjective is **gadolinic**. The latter was not discovered until 1880 (by that very able scientist, Marignac); as its name indicates, in gadolinite; metallic, it forms one of the 92 chemical elements.

gage (plum); **greengage.** The former is short for the latter, a high-quality, luscious, yellow-green plum imported, ca. 1725, from France by Sir William *Gage*, of Hengrave, Suffolk; he, by the way, popularized also the *blue gage* and the *purple gage*.

Galahad or **Sir G—.** 'This book,' says Vachell Lindsay of *A Handy Guide for Beggars*, 1916, ' is dedicated to all the children of Don Quixote who see giants where most folk see windmills: those Galahads dear to Christ and those virgin sisters of Joan of Arc who serve the lepers on their knees and march in shabby armor against the proud, who look into the lightning with the eyes of the mountain cat.'

' " If he's so torn between his new duties and his old loyalties perhaps he does want to kill himself—but not this way he suggests—it's a mixture of Galahad and Quixote and . . . and Hitler ",' Warren Stuart, *The Sword and the Net*, 1942.

This son of Lancelot, this chaste and virtuous Knight of the Round Table, was—so one tradition has it—' added by Walter Map [fl. 1200] to the Arthurian legends ' (W); Map spiritualized those legends and added thereto several of their finest episodes, including the Quest of the Holy Grail, wherein Sir Galahad appears as the hero, to the immense benefit of Malory and Tennyson. Galahad has become the prototype and the archetype of chivalrous male chastity and of male sexual decency, despite the efforts of the Freudians to debunk that which he champions.

galatea, a superior-quality cotton fabric, used for children's sailor suits and women's dresses, takes its name from H.M.S. *Galatea*, a British warship commanded, in 1867, by the Duke of Edinburgh. (The OED.)

The warship recalls that Galatea who, in Greek mythology, was a nereid or *sea* nymph, beloved by Polyphemus. She figures in Gay's libretto to Handel's *Acis and Galatea* (1732).

Galen; Galenic; galenicals (the study of medicine; medical practice). Galen, a Greek physician (*Galēnos* in Greek), born at Pergamon in Asia Minor, settled in Rome in A.D. 164— at the approximate age of forty-five. He wrote many treatises upon medical theory and practice: for more than a thousand years his works were accepted as authoritative in Roman and Greek and also in Arabic medical practice; moreover, in Western Europe and in Britain he was esteemed well into the 16th Century.

167

galilee, a chapel or porch—often used for accessories—at the entrance to a church, comes, via French, from Medieval Latin *galilaea*. W aptly cites *Matthew*, iv, 15, which runs : 'The land of Zabulon, and the land of Nephthalim, by the way of the sea, beyond Jordan, Galilee of the Gentiles '. The Lake of Galilee is also known as the Sea of Tiberias or the Sea of Gennesaret ; in modern Arabic, Bahr-et-Tubariya. The fact that it lies some 680 feet below sea-level, in a great basin, cosmically creates the effect of a vast room, sky-vaulted.

gallegada. A Spanish dance, and song, in six-in-a-measure time ; known also as the *mu(i)ñeira*. The word is short for *danza gallegada*, ' dance of Galicia ' : Galicia was the Celtic province of Spain, the *Gallic* province : originally it was, therefore, ' a Gallic dance '. But its modern characteristics are predominantly Spanish.

(Dr Percy Scholes, *The Oxford Companion to Music*.)

gallery is, in French, *galerie*, from Italian *galleria*, which Webster holds to derive from Medieval Latin *galilaea* and to be, therefore, cognate with **galilee.**

galliambics, or **galliambic verse,** is a variation of iambic ; and the word, by its division *gall + iambic*, recalls the fact that the former element derives from *Gallus*, ' a priest of Cybele ' ; compare *galliambus*, ' a song of the priests of Cybele '. *Gallus* is a personification of the *Gallus* (Greek *Gallos*), a tributary of the Sagaris of Phrygia ; a stream whose imbibers went mad ; the Cybelic priests raved and acted with mad extravagance.

Gallic ; gallicé ; gallicism ; gallicize. French ; in French ; an expression, esp. a phrase or a trick of style, imitative of or derived from French ; to render French.

Gallic comes from the Latin *gallicus*, of or belonging to the *Galli* or *Gauls*. (*Gallia*, ' Gaul is divided into three parts ' and all that, is a derivative from, not the origin of, *Galli*.)

The word *Gallic* merits a place in this the main glossary chiefly on account of *Gallic wit*, which is the Western-European equivalent of ' Attic salt '.

galligaskins, ' breeches ' in the 16th, ' leggings ' in the 17th–18th Centuries, is, in part, a corruption of 16th-Century French *greguesques*, *gargesques*, Venetian breeches, i.e. *alla grechesca*, ' in the *Greek* fashion '. W, however, points out that ' *gaskins*, *gascoynes*, found equally early, were associated with *Gascony* ' ; also that *galley-gaskins*, sailors' long hose, and *galley breeches*

168

existed at about the same date. Very wisely, W concludes thus:—'Possibly all three (*greguesques*, *Gascony*, *galley*) have contributed.' Such an accretion and such an accumulation of origins are not so very rare in etymology, especially in the etymology of common nouns derived from Proper Names.

Gallio. A conscious indifferentist, a philosophical *je-m'en-fichiste*: 'What care I?' or, at most, *pococurante*. 'When Gallio was the deputy of Achaia, the Jews made insurrection against Paul, and brought him to the judgement seat, saying, This fellow persuadeth men to worship God contrary to the law. And . . . Gallio said unto the Jews, If it . . . be a question of words and names, and of your law, look ye to it; for I will be no judge of such matters. And he drave them from the judgement seat. Then all the Greeks took Sosthenes, the chief ruler of the synagogue, and beat him before the judgement seat. And Gallio cared for none of those things' (Revised Version, '. . . these things'), *Acts*, xviii, 12–17.

The best adjectival form is *Gallio-like*, which usefully serves as an adverb too; *Gallionic*(*ally*) has a pedantic ring.

In W. L. George's uncompromisingly adult novel, *The Triumph of Gallio* (1923), the final chapter-title is 'And Gallio Cared for None of Those Things . . .' and in the penultimate chapter the chief character says, ' I suppose I can call myself a Gallian; . . . I consider happiness unnecessary, and . . . I look upon [life] as . . . merely a fact. . . . Galliosophy is sweet, for while it does not deny pain, it sets aside envy, it ignores the lusts, annuls regret. It is always by me, sweet denier, always setting a question to my desire, and always readily consoling me. It reminds me that what I desire will do me no actual good, since I have so easily survived desire denied; that loss and loneliness will do me no harm, since both I have survived. There lies serenity.'

gallium. One of the chemical elements: from Latin *Gallia*, ' Gaul '—approximately France. (Its name, therefore, should be compared with the other nation-honourers: **germanium, polonium, scandium.**) Perhaps also with a pun on Latin *gallus*, ' a cock ': the metal was, in 1875, spectroscopically discovered in a Pyrenean zinc blende by *Lecoq* (' The Cock ') de Boisbaudran.

galloway, ' small horse or large pony ': from *Galloway* (*horse*), a small, very hardy breed of horses, originating in *Galloway*. Also short for *Galloway cattle*, likewise a hardy breed—medium-sized, rather than small—hornless—usually black, native of

south-west Scotland. Galloway, a district in south-west Scot
land, consists of Wigtownshire and the Stewartry of Kirkcud
bright; a geographical, not a political division. The origin c
the Proper Name is pointed by its adjective, *Gallovidian*, fron
Medieval Latin *Gallovidia*, the land of foreign *Gaels*.

galvanic; galvanism; galvanize. (' *Galvanized iron* is no
galvanized ': W.) *Galvanism* (Italian *galvanismo*) is so name
because it was discovered, or founded, by Luigi *Galvani* (1737
98), who, Italian physician and physicist, researched into tho:
twitchings in the muscles of frogs' legs which, caused by
current of electricity, he in 1791 thought to be induced h
animal electricity. The true reason was later determined b
Volta.

gamash, normally in the plural (*gamashes*), is a pair of gaiters c
leggings, worn especially by horsemen, to protect the leg
The word derives from the French dialectal *gamaches*, whicl
like the Provençal *galamacha* or *garamacha*, appears to come fro:
the Spanish *guadamecí*, itself from Arabic *ghadamasi*, '
Ghadamas'. Ghadamas, in African Tripoli, was former'
famous for its leather-work. Now *Ghadames* or *Rhadames*
a Berber oasis, situated at—or rather, causing the existent
of—a cross-roads of important trade-routes.

gamboge. ' It was variegated in colour like a patch-work qui
—flame-colour, ultramarine, crimson, orange, gamboge, an
violet,' C. S. Lewis, *Perelandra* (a Charles Williams fantas:
esoteric and philosophical), 1943 : where *gamboge* signifi
' bright yellow '. The pigment derives from the gum-res
obtained from Garcinia trees of Siam and *Cambodia* (a distri
of Annam) ; the resin also yields that drastic purgative no
called, by pharmacists, *cambogia*.

Whence also **gambogic acid;** and **gambogiate** (·
-odiate), gambogic acid with a metallic base. (The OED

gambroon. See **gombroon.**

gamp; Mrs Gamp. In slang, *gamp* is an umbrella. M
Sarah Gamp, a disreputable yet likable old nurse, figures
Dickens's *Martin Chuzzlewit*, 1843–44. In ch. xix we read th
' Mrs Gamp had a large bundle with her, a pair of pattens, ar
a species of gig umbrella '.

Sairey Gamp is independently famous, both for her consta
references to her supposititious friend ' Mrs Harris ' and, thoug
less, for her addiction to liquor.

Sarah (or *Mrs*) *Gamp* is also used allusively for ' midwife '.

170

Ganymede has two apparently dissociated senses, 'a cup-bearer or potboy' and 'a catamite'.

In Greek mythology, Ganymede (*Ganumēdēs*) was translated from Troy to be the male cup-bearer in chief to Zeus : according to *The Iliad* (xx, 234–35), by the gods ; according to later 'authorities', by the eagle of Zeus or even by Zeus himself. Sexually, Zeus had almost as much time for a handsome boy as for a pretty girl.

Garden of Eden, The. See **Eden.**

gardenia. 'I'll be there with a gardenia in my buttonhole and a song in my heart,' David Hume, *Cemetery First Stop!*, 1937.

Named, in 1760, after Dr Alexander *Garden* († 1791), the Vice-President of the Royal Society.

Compare **camellia, fuchsia, lobelia**—and a century of other flower-names that commemorate either their discoverer or some important person.

gargantuan. 'Dr Reinach divided his energies between gargantuan inroads on the viands and copious drinking,' Ellery Queen, *The New Adventures of Ellery Queen*, (English edition) 1940.—'Those who specialize in millennia . . . forget that man was born to be loved or hated, to plough a field or write a poem, to win a battle or lose it, to take a risk, to make his soul ; he is not on this earth to be counted as though he were one of a million beads on the adding-machine of some gargantuan and idiot child', as Charles Morgan, who so eloquently champions the need for spiritual values and who so luminously indicates what some of those values are, has pertinently remarked in that memorable collection of Essays, *Reflections in a Mirror*, 1944.

To Rabelais, satirical romancer, whose *The Great and Inestimable Chronicles of Gargantua*, a giant, appeared in French in 1531 (there was a re-cast some twenty years later), we owe *Gargantuan repast*, 'a huge meal', and *gargantuan*, 'enormous'. See **Rabelaisian** and compare **pantagruelian.**

garibaldi. 'I stared, strangely entranced, at her Garibaldi blouse, at her full crinoline, her hair gathered in the chenille net,' Nard Jones, *Swiftly Flows the River*, 1939 (in reference to a girl in north-west America in the early 1860's).

A garibaldi is a shirt-waist, and it was so named because it resembled the red shirt worn, as it were a tunic, by Giuseppe Garibaldi (1807–82), who, with his 1000 Redshirts, did so much in 1860 for Italian freedom.

As a synonym of the red perch, an edible Californian fish, it is usually written with a capital: the name was bestowed by Italian settlers in reference to its colouring of deep-crimson or deep-orange.

gascon; gascon(n)ade. A *gascon* is a swashbuckler, a braggart, especially a boastful, swashbuckling fellow, and *gasconade* (gallicé, *gasconnade*) is 'a boast, to boast; bravado'.

The *Gascons* or natives of *Gascony*, French *Gascogne* (from the Medieval Latin *Vasconia*), until 1789 a province of south-west France, had a reputation for boastfulness and a rather showy assurance. The original *Vascones* (did they practise urn (*vas*) burial?)—see Pliny and Juvenal—were of Spanish stock, and from them have descended the Basques. Notable Gascons in the tradition were D'Artagnan, of Dumas's *The Three Musketeers* and *Twenty Years After*, and Cyrano de Bergerac, of Rostand's poetic drama, which bears little reference to the actual 17th-Century French soldier and poet, even though he was a famous duellist.

gat; gatling. A *gat*, 'revolver', originally a term heard only in the American underworld but since about 1935 familiarized in England by 'the talkies', is short for *gatling*, which is not a revolver at all but a machine-gun invented by Dr R. J. *Gatling* and first used in the American Civil War (1861–65) and discarded before the beginning of the First World War.

'The upshot of the whole thing was, the guard'—a San Quentin prison warder—'was transferred from the mill to one of the outside posts, a gatling post' (i.e., manned by a guard armed with a gatling): Donald Lowrie, *My Life in Prison*, 1912.—'Now whenever I . . . went into the dining saloon for supper I might hear a discussion of Gatling's new battery gun, or a typing machine,' Nard Jones, *Swiftly Flows the River*, 1939.

Cf. **lewis** and **maxim** and **nordenfelt.**

gauss. A magnetic unit—cf. **maxwell.** More precisely, the C.G.S. unit of intensity of the magnetic field; whence *gaussage*, the gauss-expressed degree of intensity of a magnetic field. Named after Karl Friedrich *Gauss* (1777–1855), a German mathematician—whence *Gaussian* in mathematics—and astronomer. Investigating magnetism and electricity, he 'proposed an absolute system of magnetic units' (Webster's BD).

gaussbergite is one of the most interesting of the words that, deriving from Proper Nouns, have come to stay. This obtrusive lava, containing olivine, recalls the fact that it was discovered on *Gaussberg*, a mountain in Kaiser Wilhelm II Land, Antarctica, so called in contradistinction to Kaiser-Wilhelm's Land, which, on the east coast of Greenland, was explored by the German North Pole Expedition in 1869–70. *Gaussberg* itself is a compound, German *berg*, ' mountain ', and *Gauss*, the name of the ship used by the German Antarctic Expedition. (Webster; Chisholm.)

gauze, a thin, transparent fabric of silk or cotton or linen, derives from French *gaze*, which, on the analogy of *damask* and *muslin*, may come from *Gaza*, Arabic *Ghazzah*, a city in Palestine. *Gaza* is mentioned in both the Old and the New Testament, and the modern Ghazzah or Ghuzzeh lies, twenty-six miles north-west of Beersheba, at the foot of that height on the crest of which stands the ancient town.

gavotte, a French-peasant dance presented at Court in the 16th Century and later shaped to the needs of a theatrical dance, is, as a word, an adoption from French, which takes it from Provençal *gavoto*, derived from *Gavots*, the Provençal name of the mountaineers operating in the Alps. Thus Webster; Dr Percy Scholes slightly modifies that etymology by defining *gavotte* as ' a dance form coming originally from the Pays de Gap, . . . where the inhabitants are called Gavots '. To clarify: *Gap*, the ancient *Vap*icinum, is the capital of the *département* of the Hautes-Alpes.

gay Lothario. See **Lothario.**

gehenna. ' The whole region [about Jerusalem] had sacred associations. . . . At Jerusalem the valley of Rephaim (the " shades " of the dead?), the valley of Hinnom (= " sleeping " [?], the later Gehenna), and the infamous Topheth speak for themselves,' Stanley Cook, *An Introduction to the Bible*, 1945.

In other words, *gehenna*, ' place of torment or misery; hell-fire; torment ', derives from *Gehenna*, Late Latin for the New Testament Greek *Geénna*, itself representing Hebrew *Gehinnom*, which in the New Testament means ' hell '; *gehinnom* itself derives from *Ge Hinnom*, the Valley of Hinnom (as above), a place of horrible memory: there, the worst malefactors had been burnt; there, certain Israelites had sacrificed their children to **Moloch;** by the time of Christ, the valley was regarded as a place of abomination.

geikia; geikilite. Both the former, ' a small toothless reptile from the New Red Sandstone of Scotland ', and the latter, 'magnesium titanate, in the form of bluish- or brownish-black pebbles', commemorates the fame of Sir Archibald *Geikie* (1835-1924), that deservedly famous Scottish geologist who, in addition to being the director-general of the geological survey of the United Kingdom, was a scholar and a writer—*The Story of a Boulder* (1858), the excellent *Textbook of Geology* (1882), *Landscape in History* (1905), and several other books.

genappe, that smooth worsted yarn which, in fringes and braids, is used in combination with silk, recalls that originally it was made at *Genappe* in Belgium. It was at this small town that, on June 15, 1815, the Prussians defeated the French.

[**Geneva,** the spirit; whence *gin*. Strictly, *geneva*, the old name for gin, comes from Old French *genevre*, from Latin *iuniperus* (apprehended as *juniperus*), a juniper-bush, this spirit being flavoured with juniper berries. But the word became confused with *Geneva* in Switzerland : and, by folk-etymology, derived therefrom, even though the spirit is more likely to have been first manufactured in some other country—say Holland.]

genoa. '. . . the sails. The boys had a light genoa and spinnaker, and a strong storm jib and topsail, roped all round, for dirty weather', Cecil Lewis, *Pathfinders*, 1943.

That is, a *genoa jib*, often called a *genoese jib*—when not called a *Swedish jib*. Genoa, the fortified seaport of north-western Italy, has a fine harbour and a long, honourable record of maritime achievement. Cf. *all ship-shape and Bristol fashion.*

gentian. 'In twenty years . . . the sketch will be something to glance at with the rest of one's sentimental junk : the pressed gentians, a shoulder strap with a hole through it, the concert programmes,' R. C. Hutchinson, *Interim*, 1945.

'The Gentians, named from *Gentius*, King of Illyria, their first discoverer according to Pliny, are well known in medicine for their bitter, astringent quality,' Vernon Rendall, *Wild Flowers in Literature*, 1934. Gentius was defeated by the Romans in 168 B.C.

[**geography,** the science—the description (Greek *graphë*)—of the earth (*gē*) and its life, is one of those words which may have a common noun, may have a Proper Name, origin, for in Greek mythology *Ge* or *Gaia* was the personification of the earth, sprung, according to Hesiod, from Chaos.]

174

George, an automatic pilot. Strictly, this is slang—of the R.A.F., who named it thus because as *Tommy* is the generic soldier and *Jack* the generic naval sailor, so *George* is the generic airman. 'Let George do it!'

George Washington has become the type, the very exemplar, of the utterly truthful person, as in ' He's no George Washington!' or 'You're like George Washington—you just *cannot* tell a lie '. 'The Washington legend owes much to the biography of M. L. Weems [in the 5th edition, 1806], which first tells the cherry-tree story ' (*The Oxford Companion to American Literature*) : wherein, confronted by his father with a felled cherry-tree, the boy Washington said ' Father, I cannot tell a lie. *I* did it.' The present writer remembers that, as a boy, he was deeply impressed by this tale, which he read in a collection of stories about boy-heroes.

georgette, a fine-textured thin silk crepe (formerly called *georgette crepe*), was originally *Georgette*, a trade-name and trademark for this dress material : and *Georgette* perpetuates the skill, the fame, of a celebrated French modiste of the late 19th–early 20th Century, Madame *Georgette* de la Plante. (Webster.)
Compare **jerkin.**

Georgia buggy is American slang for a wheelbarrow. ' " Y'nearly caused a riot in that dining-room this morning," he roared. " Now let's see if y'can cause a riot with one o' them ' Georgia buggies '. Git one o' them Georgia buggies in yer hands and step about ",' Jack Callahan, *Man's Grim Justice*, 1929. Georgia contains many Negroes, and Negroes do much of the heavy work, and some of that work requires wheelbarrows, which, by the way, are, in the North, slangily called *Irish buggies*.

gerardia is a plant, or its flower, of the genus *Gerardia*, American plants of the acanthus family. There are several kinds—for example, the *yellow gerardia*, a showy woodland flower ; the *purple* ; ' the dainty *rose gerardia* '; the *salt-marsh gerardia*. It is named for John *Gerard* (1545–1617), that English botanist who is remembered chiefly for the *Herbal* he published in 1597.

german = *German cotillon*. Mainly in American usage, as, for instance, in ' The cherry-tree figure in the german ' (Meredith Nicholson, *A Hoosier Chronicle*, 1912). *German*, from Latin *Germanus*, was probably, like *Alemanni*, in its origin the name of

a tribe; probably, too, it comes from a Celtic stem, the precis
original being still undiscovered.

German measles. We might imitate W. L. George and small
initial it as he does when, in *The Triumph of Gallio*, he write:
' There was a good deal of competition for these visits, particu
larly in the case of german measles, because german measles wa
a nice painless thing to catch, and produced about a fortnight
holiday [from school] '.

Here, as in the unimportant *German silver*, German implie
' spurious ': *German measles* resembles a mild form of measle
proper.

German polka. See **schottische.**

germanium. One of the elements in chemistry; discovered
ca. 1885, by a German scientist.

Latin *Germania* (approximately the modern Germany).

germantown or **Germantown** is either a *Germantown wagon*
a small covered wagon made at *Germantown* in Pennsylvania, o
short for *Germantown wool*, used in knitting and weaving and firs
manufactured there. This State was largely settled by Germa
immigrants.

gerrymander, to manipulate electoral divisions; hence, i
argument or discussion, so to manipulate facts as to obtain a
unfair advantage; is a blend of *gerry* and *salamander*, the latte
a queer, crawling, lizard-like animal, the former being Elbridg
Gerry (1744–1814), who, in 1812, during his second term in th
governorship of Massachusetts, had the State so re-districte
that the Republicans might remain in power.

For several amusing senses of the noun, see especially th
DAE.

geyser, with its derivatives *geyserine, geyserite,* etc., takes its nam
from *Geyser*, a certain hot spring in Iceland. *Geyser* spring
from Icelandic *geysa*, ' to rush furiously '—cognate with Ol
Norse *gjosa*, ' to gush ', hence with *gush* itself.

The form *geysir* is a mere variant.

ghetto, the Jewish district in a city (originally Venice), derive
like **gipsy** and **gitano,** from the Latin *Aegyptus*, Egypt. Th
word *ghetto* itself is Italian. Probably because the Jews dwe
so long in Egypt, perhaps also because so many Eastern Jew
are swarthy—like the gipsies. See especially Israel Zangwill

176

The Children of the Ghetto, 1892 ; *Ghetto Tragedies*, 1893 and 1899 ; and *Dreamers of the Ghetto*, 1898.

ib (cat). For centuries *Gib*, the pet-form of *Gilbert*, the surname and hence the male given-name, has been a nickname or a term of address for a male cat ; thence, a name for a male cat—or, in the 19th–20th Centuries, a castrated cat. The original *Gilbert* comes from Old English *Gislbeorht*, ' bright pledge '.
Compare ' *tom*-cat '.

ibbon. Like *gib*, *gibbon* is—via *Gibbon*—a familiar form of *Gilbert*. But why should an ape be named *Gibbon*? For the same reason, or glorious unreason, that a cat should be called **gib** or **tabby** or **tom.** The OED does not record *gibbon*, ' ape ', before Buffon, who apparently so named the animal in his magistral and monumental *Histoire naturelle* (1749 ff.) ; yet, as W points out, ' the tombs of the Gybbon family at Rolvenden (Kent), dating from ca. 1700, are surmounted by an ape's head, the family crest '. Maybe M. le Comte Georges Louis Leclerc de Buffon had a sly sense of humour : as Americans say, ' It *could* be '.

ibraltar is an American name for a *rocky*, i.e. hard, white candy, popular at least as early as 1830. ' The Gibraltar is the aristocrat of Salem confectionary,' H. L. Bates, *Old Salem*, 1886 ; the same author, however, remarks that it is ' so unutterably flinty-hearted that it is almost a libel upon the rock whose name it bears ' (DAE). The name derives from the Moorish *Jebel-al-Tarik* bestowed in 711 ; ' Mount of Tarik '—Tarik being the Moslem invader of Spain ; the rock is the Classical Mons Calpe.

ibus, an opera hat, the collapsible ' gimick ' that looks so well on the cinematic screen, commemorates its inventor, a Parisian hat-maker in the earlier half of the 19th Century. Thackeray in ' The Snobs of England ', which appeared in *Punch* in 1846–47 and was republished as *The Book of Snobs*, 1848, speaks of a dandy ' with his gibus-hat and his little glazed pumps ' (The OED).

ilbert is the C.G.S. unit of magneto-magnetic force, named after William *Gilbert* (1544–1603), physician and physicist, whose *De Magnete*, 1600, has been called ' the first great scientific work published in England ' and who has himself earned the title of ' the Father of Electricity ' : to him we owe such terms as *electric attraction, electric force, magnetic pole* (Webster BD).
Compare **joule, maxwell** and **oersted.**

Gilbertian. In its transferred sense, 'richly and wittily comical or 'comical, fanciful and witty', it might well be written *gilbertian*.

'A Gilbertian Situation': a chapter-heading in John C Goodwin's novel, *The Zig-Zag Man*, 1925.

W. S. Gilbert (1836–1911), in dramatic form a 19th-Centur John Gay, constitutes but the verbal half of the phrase in 'Sh adores a Gilbert and Sullivan': the comico-satiric operas these two—Sir Arthur Sullivan (1842–1900) was 'just the man for Gilbert—covered the effective period from 1875 (*Trial Jury*) to 1896 (*The Grand Duke*) and included such suigeneric masterpieces as *The Pirates of Penzance* (1880), *Iolanthe* (1882 *The Mikado* (1885), *Ruddigore* (1887), *The Yeoman of the Guar* (1888), and *The Gondoliers* (1889).

Giles; Farmer Giles. Like **Hodge**, *Giles* is used 'for a simple minded chawbacon' (WWN); *Farmer Giles*, however, althoug implying rural simplicity, also connotes sense and substanc Compare also **hick** and **rube.**

Giles derives from Old French *Gilles*, which, strange as it ma sound, comes from the Roman name, *Aegidius* (Greek *aegis*).

Gill or **gill; Jill.** As a girl, hence a sweetheart, it comes fror —is the diminutive of—*Gillian*; derived from French *Julian* from Latin *Juliana*, which was originally applied to a woman the Julian *gens* or clan. 'Every Jack has his Gill'—mo usually 'Jill'.

gin is a shortening of **geneva,** which see!

giottesque is both adjective and noun, '(in) the style Giotto': the famous Giotto, whose full name was Giotto Bondone (1276?–1337?). A Florentine, he was architect ar sculptor as well as painter. The pupil of Cimabue, he was th chief Italian painter in the period before the Renaissance. I excelled in the art of the religious—especially the allegoric religious—fresco.

gip, to; **gipsy; gipsy moth.** 'Cleopatra was Greek, n Egyptian in any sense, even if Shakespeare calls her a " gypsy " T. R. Glover, *The Ancient World*, 1935.—' Momentarily, Har rigg imagined that these were nomads from the moors. The he saw that they were fair and unlike the olive-skinned gypsi whose long powerful stride he had so often admired,' F. Green, *A Song for the Angels*, 1944.

The variant spellings *gyp*, *gypsy*, make it clear that *gip*, '

178

cheat', as obviously derives from *gipsy* as that *gipsy* or *gypsy* comes from *Egyptian*. On their centuries-long travels from India to Western Europe, the gipsies sojourned in *Egypt*.

gitano, plural *gitanos*, is merely the Spanish term for a *gipsy* and, derivatively, it also means a trickster; literally, *Gitano* is an Egyptian. The word, therefore, presents several illuminating —even if, to the professional etymologist, rather obvious— parallels to the terms in the preceding entry.

gladstone is short for *G. bag* or *G. claret* (or *wine*). In 1860, W. E. Gladstone reduced the tariff on the cheaper French wines: *Gladstone claret, Gladstone wine*, therefore signified inferior claret or wine. Gladstone did not invent the Gladstone bag: intoxicated with the exuberance of his own verbosity, he liked the sound of his own voice, which he freely exercised upon the hustings; to do so, he travelled much about the country. Less widely known is *gladstone* as the name of an (internally) two-seated four-wheeled pleasure carriage: a commemorative term, for William Ewart Gladstone (1809–98), four times Premier, was a 19th-Century institution.

glauber's or **glauber** is short for *Glauber's* (or *Glauber*) *salt*— not, by the way, *salts*; a colourless crystalline salt.

Johann Rudolf *Glauber* (1604–68), German physician and chemist, investigated the decomposition of common salt; the name honours his memory.

glengarry 'shorthands' *Glengarry bonnet* or *Glengarry cap*, originally worn by the Scottish Highlanders and imitated by the Sassenachs. *Glengarry* is a narrow valley in the west of Inverness-shire: the glen of the river Garry.

Compare **tam.**

glenlivat or **glenlivet.** 'Had ta mixture been only half glenlivet,' as the vigorous ballad-writer W. E. Aytoun feelingly says, all would have been well, for was it not an excellent whiskey? It was earliest manufactured at *Glenlivet* (or -*at*), an ecclesiastical parish in Banffshire, Scotland. In 1594 a sectarian battle took place there. It is the glen of Livet Water, a small river that runs into the Avon.

Compare **glengarry.**

gloucester, single and **double,** is short for *single* or *double Gloucester cheese*, a sort of pressed cheese made originally in Gloucestershire, England—such part of the country as is rich

in cheese (compare **cheddar**). 'The vale of the Severn is
noted for its cornlands, rich pastures, and general fertility; in
the hills sheepfarming forms an important industry' (Chisholm).

gloxinia, to botanists a leafy-stemmed, violet-flowered American
herb, and to horticulturists a related popular greenhouse herb,
especially the Brazilian genus *sinningia*, very good-looking and
attractive. It takes its name from Benjamin *Gloxin*, an 18th
Century German physician and botanist.

glyconic is *Glyconic (metrical) verse*, usually of three trochees and
a dactyl. The word is an adjective, representing the Greek
Glukōneios, 'of or from or like *Glukōn* or *Glycon*', its deviser.
A Glyconic stanza consists of three of these verses, to which
several poets added a **pherecratean.**

go fantee. See **fantee.**

gobelin is loosely used for any tapestry that resembles the true
gobelin, or *Gobelin*, *tapestry*; derivatively, *gobelin* means *Gobelin
blue*, a greenish blue of a sort often used in these tapestries—
compare *Gobelin green*, always written in full and with a capital
G. The *Gobelin* family set up, near Paris, a very distinguished
tapestry business in the 16th Century; in 1662, Louis XIV,
who always had an eye to the main chance, caused the work
to be converted into a royal manufactory, now the Manufacture
Nationale des Gobelins. See also **goblin.**

gobi, in geology, 'the lenticular mass of sedimentary deposit
that occupies a tala or down-warp basin' (Webster), comes
straight from 'the *Gobi* Desert', where this particular formation
abounds. In Mongolian, *gobi* means 'desert'; 'the Gobi' is
therefore '*the* desert'; the Chinese call it *Shamo*, 'sea of sand'.

goblet, which The OED declares to be 'of uncertain origin' and
which Webster accords a problematic Common Noun etymology,
is explained thus by W: 'Old French *gobelet*, diminutive of
gobel, *gobeau*. All these words are common French surnames;
Old High German *God-bald*, god-bold (cf. English Godbolt),
and the vessel is no doubt of the same origin. Cf. English
dialect *goddard*, goblet. Old French *godart*, Old German *Gott-
hart*, god-strong, named in same way. See *goblin* and cf
demijohn, . . . *jug, tankard*.'

goblin represents French *gobelin*, diminutive of the French
surname *Gobel*; *gobelin* is *Gobelin*, likewise a surname—see the
etymology of *goblet*.

Parallels are **harlequin, jack o' lantern, kobold, will o' the wisp**; but especially **kobold**. W adduces a very informative comparison: the German *Heinzelmännchen*, a little *Heinz* man, i.e. a gnome, *Heinz* being a pet-form of *Heinrich*.

goddard. See **goblet**.

godetia, an annual plant, hardy and free-flowering, is a 'botanical Latin' formation from the man after whom it was named, Charles H. *Godet*, a Swiss botanist.

godfather, godmother; god-parents. 'There can only be fairy godmothers because there are godmothers; and there can only be godmothers because there is God,' G. K. Chesterton, *Autobiography*, 1936. At baptism, god-parents sponsor the god-children (godson or god-daughter): they undertake, before God, to interest themselves in the god-children.

godfrey! An American exclamation, euphemistic for *God*, the surname and given-name *Godfrey* being utilized for the purpose. Compare the British euphemism *christmas* and the American *for crying out loud* for *Christ*.

golconda. A mine of actual, or a source of figurative, wealth. From *Golconda*, which it is not quite correct to describe (for some dictionaries do thus describe it) as 'the old name of Hyderabad'. Of the Hyderabad plateau, L. W. Lyde in *The Continent of Asia* (2nd edition, 1938) remarks that on it 'stand the present capital . . . and—half a dozen miles away—the old capital of Golconda, where there sprang up a famous diamond-cutting industry', foot-noted thus: 'The diamonds seem to have come from the sandstones and shales of Kurnool and Cuddapah'.
    Compare **Eldorado**.

golgotha, 'a charnel-house or a cemetery; a place of martyrdom or merely of anguish or torment' (for slang usage, see PS), derives from *Golgotha*, which is but another name for Calvary. Via Greek, it comes from Aramaic *gulgultha*, itself from Hebrew *gulgoleth*, 'skull'.
    'And when they were come unto a place called Golgotha, that is to say, a place of a skull, They gave him vinegar to drink' (*Matthew*, xxvii, 33–34); 'And he bearing his cross went forth into a place called the place of the skull, which is called in the Hebrew Golgotha: where they crucified him' (*John*, xix, 17–18).

181

goliard; hence **goliardic.** 'Diverse as the authors are, from the Chancellor of Paris to a nameless goliard, they '—the poets of the *Carmina Burana*—'belong alike to the *ordo clericalis*, Helen Waddell, *The Wandering Scholars*, 1927.

Probably of common noun origin, but perhaps from the mythical *Golias*, who, often said to be a bishop, is represented both as the hero and as the author of numerous goliardic poems. Presumably Golias was created to account for the poems, but our records of the 12th–13th Centuries may be defective : it isn't impossible that a certain poet took the pen-name *Golias*, in allusion to the not wholly mythical *Golias* (a medieval variant) or *Goliath* of the next entry.

Goliath. See **David and Goliath** in the Appendix.—(1) A *Goliath beetle* is a very large beetle, a native of Africa.

(2) **goliath** = *G. crane.* A travelling crane that is powerful and Goliath-large.

In Hebrew, the name is *Golyath.*

gombroon, or **gomroon,** is short for *Gom(b)roon ware*, a white semi-porcelanic ware, made originally at *Gombroon* or *Gambroon*, now Bandar Abbas, a town in Persia—on the Persian Gulf.

The form *Gambroon* has generated *gambroon*, a twilled cloth of linen or of wool or of linen and wool, manufactured there.

Gomorrah. See **Sodom and Gomorrah.**

gongorism. 'The word Gongorism is generally used to mean that it is artificial, involved, and affected in poetic style. In fact, however, many of Gongora's best poems happen to be written in the direct, " popular " tradition. . . . It is only in the last few years that readers have begun to recapture the beauty of those longer poems in which he worked out the baroque manner that is called Gongoristic. They are not easy to read : the syntax is distorted . . . to make a chosen word sparkle . . .; the imagery is coiled into conceits, to create a world far from nature,' J. B. Trend, *The Civilization of Spain*, 1944.

Luis de Góngora y Argote (1561–1627) adopted his mother's name, Gongora. In his earlier period, he wrote some fine lyrics and many sonnets that have never been bettered ; the gongorisms belong to his later period.

Compare **euphuism, guevarism, marinism:** to all of which, gongorism is superior—probably in intellectual, certainly in spiritual significance and subtlety.

good-bye! Webster very neatly traces its divine origin in a convincing table of probabilities:

> *Godbwye* or *godbwye* (16th Century)
> *God bw'ye*
> *God be wi ye*
> *God be with ye.*

The phrase has been brought into line with *good day!* Compare **adieu**.

gordonia belongs to that genus of North American trees, the *Gordonia*, which has two species, the mountain bay and the loblolly bay. In *Philosophical Transactions*, 1770, J. Ellis writes, ' I desire it may have a place among your [Linnaeus's] genera, by the name of *Gordonia*, as a compliment to our worthy friend, that eminent gardener Mr James Gordon, near Mile-end '— Mile End Road in the East of London (DAE).

gorgon; gorgonia; gorgonize. A terrible (and ugly) person, especially a formidable repellent woman; a sea-fan; to turn into stone (especially, as though to stone), to stare at (a person) as if one intended to paralyse him.

' To hear myself pleading what I knew instinctively to be a hopeless case and to be gorgonised in the process from head to foot with a Medusa-like stare which would have turned anything born of woman to stone was too much ' (Francis Beeding, *The Twelve Disguises*, 1942).

The three *Gorgons*, of whom the best known is **Medusa,** are dread women of Greek mythology. Hideous of face, glaring of eye, and with serpents in their hair, they petrified all those human beings who were so foolish, or so unlucky, as to meet their gaze. Hence *gorgoneion*, a protective figure, especially upon walls or armour.

Speaking of the Iron Age, Professor Gordon Childe notes that ' Athenian potters ' traditions . . . still taught them to fear the demon who cracked pots in the kiln and to mount on it a gorgon mask to scare him away ! ' (*What Happened in History*, 1942).

gorgonzola. (See also the entry at **parmesan.**)

This pressed milk cheese, which resembles *roquefort*, is known in full as *Gorgonzola cheese*, so named from a Lombardy village (and commune) some thirteen miles east-north-east of Milan. The name itself probably has some connexion with the Gorgons—see **gorgon**.

183

gosport, in an aircraft, is a flexible speaking-tube for communication between pilots, or between pilot and the rest of the crew or between instructor and student, and it is named after *Gosport*, a formerly fortified seaport in Hampshire, England, a town with extensive barracks, a powder magazine, and one of the largest naval hospitals in the world.   Hampshire, like Kent, contains many airfields.

goss or **G——.**   (1) A felt hat fashionable in the 1830's and 1840's : *à titre de curiosité* only, for it does not, as I've seen it stated, derive from the name of either the manufacturer or of a fashionable shop ; it shortens *gossamer hat.*

(2) A ' crest ' china and porcelain, made at Stoke-on-Trent : the bright idea was that of W. H. *Goss* of that city, and it struck him ca. 1900.   Not in the same order of merit as, say, **spode.**

gossip, originally ' a sponsor, whether male or female, at baptism ', has, from the fact that at christenings, as at funerals, there is usually a spate of chatter, both benevolent and malevolent, come to mean ' a newsmonger, or an idle tattler '. Its original sense appears in the etymology, *gossip* being a corruption of *godsip*, which represents *God-sib*, ' related to God ' and therefore, to the child being baptized, standing in a spiritual, not merely a spirituous relation.   As for *sib* : well, it is at least cognate with German *sippe*, ' family ' ; and both the English and the German word may spring from Sanskrit *sabha*, ' an assembly ' ; for the earliest assembly consisted of a single family (even unto second cousins).

Goth.   ' With the fifth [century A.D.] began a new series of invasions which finally broke down the Roman frontiers.   The attack was now opened by the Goths, an East German people who had been moving westwards under pressure from the Huns and in 378 had won a memorable victory over the Emperor Valens at Adrianople,' M. Cary, *A History of Western Europe*, A.D. 1–455.

The Goths were in Late Latin *Gothi* (Greek *Gothoi*) from *Gut*, the radical in Gothic *Gutthioda*, ' the Gothic people '—literally, ' the good—or the brave—people '.   Whence :

gothic = *Gothic type*, *Gothic art*, etc.   The printers' type is that which they use for printing German in ' German ' characters ; rather like black letter, it is, *non*-technically, synonymous with it.   In the sense ' uncouth, barbarous ', it had achieved the small initial so early as 1782 (OED) ; a sense it derived from that of ' characteristic of the Middle Ages in Europe ' ; the

184

Goths were often associated with the Vandals (see **vandal** and cf. **Hun**). See the preceding entry.

' " Did he hang himself before? "—" He started. But . . . just before he lost consciousness, he " '—a sculptor—' " had an idea for a piece of modern gothic and knocked on the wall and the neighbours came in and cut him down " ' (Joyce Cary, *The Horse's Mouth*, 1944).

gouda is (1) a *Gouda clay pipe* of the sort made originally at Gouda, ten miles from Rotterdam in Holland : see the quotation at **delf.**

(2) A flat, round cheese—rather like **cheddar** in flavour—likewise made at Gouda ; often of skimmed milk.

Gouda ' has manufactures of pipes and pottery, and an extensive cheese mart ' (George Chisholm, 1899).

goulard is short for *Goulard's cerate* (a surgical lotion) and for *Goulard's extract*, used for the alleviation of bruises and sprains ; in both, lead sub-acetate is present.

The term commemorates Thomas *Goulard*, a French surgeon that died during the French Revolution.

Gradgrind, a hard, matter-of-fact utilitarian, is another of the numerous debts we owe to Charles Dickens, who, in *Hard Times* (1854), depicted just such a character in Thomas Gradgrind, a hardware merchant of ' Coketown ', a drab industrial centre. Believing himself to be an ' eminently practical man ', he systematically repressed the aesthetic and spiritual potentialities of his children, Tom and Louisa. The name constitutes a grim alliterative pun on *grind*.

Compare **Chadband, Mark Tapley, Micawber** and **Micawberish, Mrs Gamp, Pickwick, Podsnap, Scrooge, Spenlow and Jorkins, Stiggins, Uriah Heep,** and those two rogues, **Bill Sikes** and **Fagin.**

grahamize. (Of, usually, the Civil Service) to edit a Civil Servant's report or other official communication. With reference to Richard Cobden the economist's accusations against Lord Dalhousie, Governor-General of India, in the matter of the Second Anglo-Burmese War (1852–53), John L. Christian, in *Modern Burma*, 1942, remarks that ' Dalhousie defended his action by pointing out that Cobden's information was based upon the official Blue Books, which while composed from the official despatches, had been severely edited by Sir James Graham, the Chief Secretary in India, and by the Home

Government'; for this 'editing', see J. G. A. Baird, *Private Letters of the Marquess of Dalhousie*, 1910, at p. 423.

Sir James Graham (1792–1861) was Home Secretary when, in 1844, Mazzini's letters were, at the former's instigation, opened in the post.

granadina. A fandango that originated in *Granada* (southern Spain), 'with the same harmonic and vocal peculiarities as the **malagueña**' (Dr Percy Scholes). Compare also **murciana.**

Grandisonian (or g—) is 'in the manner of Sir Charles *Grandison*', the hero—the author's ideal of a perfect hero and of a Christian gentleman—of *The History of Sir Charles Grandison* (1754), a novel by Samuel Richardson (1689–1761). Not a good novel, his *Pamela* (1740) and especially *Clarissa* (1747–48) being much superior.

The name *Grandison* would appear to be a disguised particularization of *grandee's son*.

grangerize is either 'to extra-illustrate' (a book) or 'to mutilate books or magazines to provide material for such illustrations'.

In 1769, the Rev. James Granger (1723–76), print-collector and biographer, issued his *Biographical History of England . . adapted to a Methodical Catalogue of Engraved British Heads*, wherein the letterpress was poor relation to Dives-illustration. To obtain the 14,000 engraved portraits he collected for his daunting purpose, he often pillaged and ravaged other (some of them very fine) books. As a writer,—well, one does not wish to be unnecessarily unkind.

graves or **G—.** See the quotation at **sauterne.**

This light and usually white wine comes from the vineyards of that south-western French district known as *Graves*. The wine was well-reputed in England as early as the early 17th Century, Taylor the Water Poet (the reference is to his occupation, not to his favourite tipple) mentioning it. Etymologically, *Graves* is related to the gravelly, sandy parts of the Bordeaux country. Compare **médoc** and **bordeaux.**

greek, in slang, is a swindler, a sharper—especially at cards; a boon companion; an Irishman; and in American universities, member of a Greek-letter fraternity—e.g., Phi Beta Kappa. The modern commercial Greek has the reputation of being a shade too sharp: perhaps in the cut-throat competition of the Mediterranean, most notably in the Levant, he had to be, or the Syrians and Arabs and the Italians would have ' bested ' him.   Contrast **trojan.**

greengage.   See **gage.**

grevillea.   ' You'll see five miles of the finest grevillea trees in the world ' (in California), Raymond Chandler, *The Lady in the Lake*, (English edition) 1944.

The *grevillea*, a native of Australia, was in 1809 named after the Rt Hon. Charles Francis *Greville*, who at that time was the Vice-President of the Royal Society.

grig, whether cricket, grasshopper, small fowl, or small eel, is thought by W to have a Proper Name origin.   He points out that originally it meant a boon companion and in this sense bore the synonym *merry Greek*.   ' Quite possibly it is the pet-form of *Gregory* (cf. surname *Grigg*) and *merry Grig* may go with *merry Andrew*, *zany*, etc.'

grimalkin is simply *grey malkin*; that is, *grey Malkin*.   *Malkin* is a nickname, or a term of address, for a she-cat : contrast **gib** and **tom.**   Aptly so, for *Malkin* is a centuries-old diminutive of *Matilda* and also of *Mary*.   W appositely quotes from Shakespeare's *Macbeth* :
' I come, Gray-Malkin '.

grimthorpe, coined by *The Athenaeum* in 1892, signifies ' to restore (an ancient building) ', as Lord Grimthorpe restored the Abbey at St Albans, England.

Sir Edmund Beckett (1816–1905), who became 1st Baron Grimthorpe, was an architect famous in his day.   He interested himself particularly in ecclesiastical architecture, one of his printed works being *A Book of Building, Civil and Ecclesiastical*, 1876.

gringo, among Spanish Americans ' a foreigner, but usually a " Saxon " American, or an Englishman ', and mostly contemptuous in usage, is an American Spanish word, sense-distorted from Spanish *gringo*, ' gibberish ', itself a corruption of Spanish *Griego*, ' a Greek ' (compare ' It's all *Greek* to me ').

The first notable American writer to use the word, although it had appeared, among Spanish Americans, in the late 18th Century, was Ambrose Bierce, who, in 1913, deliberately sought death in war-rent Mexico : in one of his latest letters, he spoke of dying there as a Gringo ; he probably did, at the hands of a firing-squad.

187

grobian or **G——,** noun and adjective, is a literarism for ‘ (a) boorish, slovenly, clownish (person) ’, and it comes from *Grobianus*, the name of a mythical character often mentioned by German writers of the 15th–16th Centuries as the generic boor. *Grobianus* is facetious Latin, derived from the German *grob*, ‘ surly, coarse, uncouth ’—with which our English *gruff* is cognate. (The OED.)

grog ; groggy. *Old Grog* was the nickname of Admiral Edward Vernon (1684–1757), because, in dirty weather at sea, he wore a coat of *grogram* (French *gros grain*, coarse material). In 1740 he achieved an unenviable reputation among naval men by being the first to order the Navy’s rum to be diluted with water, a drink known as *grog*. He was a ‘ character ’; in 1746 he got himself dismissed the service for pamphlets attacking the Admiralty. From *grog* comes *groggy*, unsteady upon one’s legs, hence ill.

Grub Street, allusive for the ill-fed corpus of literary hacks, comes, not from an actual Grub Street but from that street in Moorfields, London, which has, since 1830, been known as Fore Street : in the approximate period 1660–1800, it was inhabited by literary *grubs* ; there is, moreover, an ironic pun on the slang *grub*, ‘ food ’.

See especially Beresford Chancellor’s *Annals of Fleet Street*.

Grundy, Mrs ; grundyism. ‘ The prurient and feeble-minded Mrs Grundy ’ (H. L. Adam, *Woman and Crime*, 1914) ; ‘ a sort of grammatical grundyism ’ (*Journal of Education*, 1889 : OED).

Thomas Morton (1764?–1838) wrote three successful comedies, of which the third, *Speed the Plough*, 1798, concerns us, for it contains the character of Mrs Grundy, who is several times mentioned in the now famous ‘ What will Mrs Grundy say? ’

The name is, I think, echoically allusive to *grumpy*, influenced perhaps by the *grunt* of excessively puritanical disapproval. In 16th-Century colloquialism, by the way, *grundy* was ‘ a short fat person ’—though rarely a woman.

Derivatively, *grundyism* is ultra-conventional behaviour or social criticism.

gruyère. In Switzerland, ‘ cheese—made up on the alp—is the great product, especially Gruyère and Emmenthaler (both full of holes and with hard rind). . . . The Gruyère type of cheese is coloured and flavoured with yellow melitot,' Lionel W. Lyde, *Europe*, 1913. Gruyère is a town.

'At the local restaurant there would be one or two "plats à emporter", to which I would add some wine, sausage and Gruyère cheese,' 'Palinurus', *The Unquiet Grave*, 1945.

Compare **emmenthaler** (q.v.).

guarneri is a *Guarneri violin*. The Guarneri family made, at Cremona in North Italy, very fine violins in the 17th–18th Centuries; cf. **amati** and **stradivarius.**

guelder = *G. rose*, a cultivated variety of the cranberry with globe-shaped flowers. Compare the Dutch *Geldersche roos* and French *rose de Gueldre*, the effective origin residing in *Guelders*, the old capital of *Guelderland* (the Netherlands), formerly a province of Prussia.

guernsey. 'I bought a guernsey and changed a sovereign,' remarked a witness at the Old Bailey on January 13, 1885.— 'The room fitted him as closely as the grey guernsey he was wearing,' R. C. Hutchinson, *Interim*, 1945. The garment has been so named because, originally, it was worn by seamen: apparently first made in France, it naturally became the wear of French sailors, hence of Channel Island sailors (cf. **jersey**).

It is usually spelt with a capital *G* when it means a breed of cattle characteristic of the Channel Islands, as also are Jerseys.

guevarism, guevarist. Euphuism; a euphuistic writer. Antonio de Guevara (ca. 1480–1545) was that Spaniard whose writings would seem to have fathered **euphuism.** Moralist and romancer, he had a style characterized by allusiveness and alliteration, vivacity and wit, erudition and, occasionally, involution. Compare **gongorism** and **marinism.**

guillemot is a narrow-billed auk of the northern seas, the smaller being known as *black guillemot* because in summer its plumage is, in the main, black. The name is a common-propertying of French *Guillemot*, a pet-form of *Guillaume* (William). Why this particular given-name? No particular reason. Why the comparable **robin**? Why **tomtit**? Compare:

guillotine is a French term, short for *la machine guillotine*, i.e. 'machine of Guillotin', for a French thing. The name *Guillotin* afforded a linguistic convenience: the ending in *-in*, feminine *-ine*, is a common French-adjectival termination. In 1789, Joseph *Guillotin* (1738–1814), a French physician and a

189

deputy to the States-General, proposed, on humanitarian grounds and despite—perhaps because of—his belief in the efficacy and desirability of capital punishment, the substitution of his invention, a beheading device with a sharp blade, for the clumsy and barbarous sword.

His surname was originally a double diminutive of *Guillaume*; compare, therefore, **guillemot.**

guinea; guinea fowl, guinea hen; guinea pig. The coin minted from 1663 until 1813, was so called because, originally at least, it was struck from gold mined in *Guinea*, a region that on the west coast of central Africa, was once famous for its gold and infamous for the export of Negroes; it includes the Gold Coast. The earliest form of the name was *Guine*, applied by the Portuguese ' to the region near the Senegal from a native kingdom with a similar name ' (Chisholm).

Occasionally *guinea* is short for *guinea fowl*, of which the feminine is *guinea hen*; it inhabits West Africa, including *Guinea*. The *guinea pig* is of South American origin, but it was brought to England by *Guineamen*, ' merchants, or their ships trading with Guinea ', and engaged in the slave-traffic.

guinness or **G—.** ' I don't mind if I do take another " Guinness ", I'm just about dead-broke,' W. N. Willis, *The White Slaves of London*, 1912. A *guinness* is a (drink of) stout manufactured by those famous brewers, the Guinness family at Dublin; the business, established ca. 1820, has been in the family ever since—a family almost as remarkable for its philanthropy as for the excellence of its stout.

gum-arabic. See at **arab.**

gum-mogador; gum(-)senegal. The former (also simply *mogador*, or *mogadore* or *mogidore*) is Morocco gum, so called from its exportation from *Mogador*, a seaport on the west coast of Morocco. And *gum-senegal* is simply Senegal gum, exported from the region about the Senegal River in central West Africa. *Senegal* is a Portuguese name, derived from *Senega*, a Berber tribe.

gun is of obscure or, at the least, of complex origin. First recorded in 1309 in the plural, *gonnes*, it perhaps comes, as W suggests, ' from female name *Gunhild*, recorded as applied to a mangonel, " . . . *Domina Gunilda* [Mistress Gunhild] " (1300–1). *Gunhild*, an Old Norse name of which both elements mean war . . ., was a common name, with pet-form *Gunna*

190

in Middle English, and there are many historical guns with names of the same type, e.g. the famous 15th Century *Mons Meg* of Edinburgh. Compare *Brown Bess, Long Tom, . . . Bertha.*'

gun moll. See **moll.**

gunnera, a plant of that small but widely distributed genus of herbs known as *Gunnera*, gets its somewhat odd-looking name by substituting a ' Latin ' *a* for the masculine Latin ending *-us* in *Gunnerus*. Johan Gunnerus (1718–73) was a Norwegian : a botanist, a friend of Linnaeus, and in the latter part of his life a bishop ; an interest in botany having never constituted an obstacle to ecclesiastical preferment, for a garden is a lovesome thing, God wot.

gunter ; Gunter's chain ; Gunter's line ; Gunter's gradient ; Gunter's scale ; according to Gunter. The first is the ' shorthand ' synonym of the fifth ; the last is the American equivalent of **according to Cocker** ; and all of them were invented by or are related to Edmund *Gunter* (1581–1626), an English mathematician and, in 1619–26, the Professor of Astronomy at Gresham College, London.

guy. In English, the term denotes ' an effigy of Guy Fawkes ; hence, a person that looks ridiculous, especially in attire (mostly : ill-dressed ; dressed old-fashionedly) ', the transition appearing clearly in ' Allis looked a positive Guy Fawkes. Cardby burst out laughing when he saw him,' David Hume, *Toast to a Corpse*, 1944 : in American, it signifies ' a chap, a fellow ' (a *regular guy* is the English *decent chap, decent fellow*)—compare the pun in the title of Damon Runyon's sparkling collection of stories, *Guys and Dolls*, 1931 : and the American verb *to guy* is ' to make fun of '. Clearly, both the American usages derive from the English *guy* in the former nuance. Also English is the slangy *do a guy*, ' to run away ' : Guy Fawkes expected to escape, but someone divulged his picturesquely hare-brained Gunpowder Plot : a pleasantly ironical phrase.

Guy Fawkes in 1605 attempted to blow up the Houses of Parliament and thus enriched both history and language. Sellars & Yeatman, in *1066 and All That*, have gaily stated that Guy Fawkes was executed because he failed in his venture, but some think that this statement constitutes ' unparliamentary language '.

gypsy. See **gipsy.**

H

habanera. A Cuban dance, slow, voluptuous and in two-time, that became popular in Spain about the middle of the 19th Century. From Habana or, as the English call it, Havana, whither it was imported from Central Africa. Compare **havanaise** and **cubana.**

hack, a horse let out for hire, is short for *hackney* in the same sense. *Hackney* derivatively means a *hackney coach* or *carriage*, let out for common hire (whence *hackneyed*, ' trite '). Either these horses were first bred in Middlesex or they were sent from Middlesex for hire in London : for some topical reason, now lost, they were originally associated with *Hackney*, formerly outside but now a borough of north-east London ; Skeat suggests that they were raised on the pastures about Hackney and taken, via Mare Street, to Smithfield horse-market. Other Hackney place-names are *Hackney Downs*, *Hackney Marsh* (reclaimed in the early 1890's) and *Hackney Wick*.

hades or **H—.** In *go to hades*, it means no more than a somewhat vigorous request to make oneself scarce, but it recalls the loose association with hell. The Septuagint employed it to render the Hebrew *sheol*, the abode of the spirits of the dead. In Classical Greek it meant the underworld (the *sheol* sense of the word), whence only a few fortunate souls passed to **Elysium** ; this is a derivation from the Homeric sense, ' the god in charge of that underworld, inhabited by the ghosts of the dead ' : *Hadēs* or *Aïdēs* or *Aidoneus*, ' the Unseen ', from *aïdēs*, ' unseen ' : Greek privative prefix *a* + the passive participle of *eido*, ' I see ' (compare *eidos*, ' the seen ').

hafnium, one of the chemical elements, is, more precisely, a metallic element ascertained in 1923.

An entirely ' elemental ' reshaping of Latin *Hafnia*—or what is now known as Copenhagen.

half joe; half johannes. The former shortens the latter. The *johannes*, originally *Johannes* or *Joannes*, is a Portuguese gold coin that circulated in North America in the 18th–19th Centuries ; occasionally affectioned to *Johnny*. It was struck in commemoration of King Johannes V of Portugal (1703–50). The word is the Portuguese form of *John*.

192

hallelujah. See **alleluia.**

hallstat (or **H—**). Of—in—characteristic of—the period of transition from the Iron Age to the Bronze Age. In Upper Austria there is the village of Hallstatt, where relics of this early civilization were first discovered : see, for instance, V. Gordon Childe, *What Happened in History*, 1942. Hallstatt, 'famous for its lake fishing', as was that ancient civilization, has 'salt-mines . . . worked for 2000 years' (L. W. Lyde, *Europe*, 1913).

hamadryad, a wood nymph, comes, via the Latin *Hamadryas*, from Greek *Hamadruas*, traditionally a blend of the preposition *hama*, 'together with'—hence 'associated with', and *drus*, 'a tree'—originally 'an oak', the tree that is sacred to Zeus. The life of each nymph was dependent upon that of the tree she inhabited ; when it died, she died.—In the 19th-20th Centuries, the name has been applied also to the sacred baboon and the king cobra.

hamburg or **hamburgh; hamburgher.** 'He had a police dog back there—and that mutt went after me like I was a juicy hamburgher,' Mark Hellinger, 'Tops in Tough Luck,' *The* (New York) *Mirror*, September 2, 1937.

Usually, *hamburgher* means *Hamburg steak* ; and so does *hamburg* ; the former may also be a type of *German* sausage, or a kind of black grape (usually *H—*) or a small domestic fowl (*H—*). Literally, *Hamburgher*, noun and adjective, signifies '(inhabitant) of Hamburg'—greatest of German seaports.

hammer of Thor. See **Thor.**

Hampden, or **village Hampden,** is a defender of the liberties of the people against royal or parliamentary or bureaucratic tyranny and imposition.

> 'Some village Hampden that with dauntless breast
> The little tyrant of his fields withstood,
> Some mute inglorious Milton, here may rest,
> Some Cromwell guiltless of his country's blood'
> (Gray, *Elegy*, 1751).

John Hampden (1594-1643) resisted forced taxes and other injustices. He died in the service of the Parliamentary army. See especially G. J. Whyte-Melville's historical novel, *Holmby House*, 1860.

hansard; hansardize. *Hansard* is collective for 'the official reports of the Parliament at Westminster'; the derivative

193

hansardize is ' to confront a Member with his earlier statements as recorded in Hansard '. In 1774, Luke *Hansard* (1752–1828) commenced to print these journals; his eldest son, Thomas (1776–1833), succeeded him in 1803. Thomas was a very able fellow: he patented an improved hand press and in 1825 published *Typographia*, a text-book on printing.

hansom. In reference to the London of the 1890's, Claude Houghton employs this evocative phrasing, ' A West End of tinkling hansoms, lovely ladies with eighteen-inch waists and muffs attached to jewelled chains ' (*Passport to Paradise*, 1944).

Joseph *Hansom* (1803–82) was an English architect. In addition to designing the Birmingham town hall in 1833, he invented, in 1834, a safety cab, which had many modified successors.

harlequin; harlequinade. In the old Italian comedies, a harlequin is the buffoon; in English pantomime a mute actor; he dominates that part of a pantomime which takes its name from him—the harlequinade. The *harlequin* came, via French *(h)arlequin*, from Italian *arlecchino*, the last word being perhaps the same as Old French *Hel(l)equin* or *Herlequin* or *Hennequin*, a devil-horseman riding by night. ' It is a Flemish diminutive of some personal name, perhaps of *Han*, John ' (W). The longer word represents French *arlequinade*.

harpy comes to us by way of French *harpie*, from Latin *harpyia*; the Greek original is usually the plural, *harpuiai*. In mythology the Harpies were winged, clawed, female-bodied monsters (' The female of the species . . .') and they derive their grimly apposite name from *harpazein*, ' to carry off; to seize and overpower '.

Derivatives: *harpy bat* and *harpy eagle*.

Harriet, Harry. See '**Arry** . . .

harrisbuck or **Harrisbuck** or **Harris buck,** otherwise known as the sable antelope, is a native of South Africa. It was first described by Sir William Cornwallis Harris (1807–48), who discovered it in 1837. An engineer, he travelled in South Africa in 1835–37 and in 1840 he published *Portraits of the Game Animals of South Africa*.

harrisia, a flower, white or pink, of the genus *Harrisia*, tropical American cactuses that are spiny and slender, commemorates a Jamaican botanist named William Harris. Contrast:—

194

harrisite, a plutonic rock containing olivine, was discovered at *Harris*, a parish on the Isle of Rum in the Hebrides; a rocky part of the world. Compare **Harris tweed** in the Appendix. The more Scottish form *Herries* has not affected the derivatives.

harveyized, especially *h. steel*, a steel treated by the *Harvey process*, concerns the hardening of armour-plating. The process was devised by an American inventor, Hayward Augustus Harvey (1824–93), who was also, and primarily, a manufacturer of steel.

haussmannize, ' to reconstruct (a city) on liberal and beautiful lines ', forms a tribute to Baron Georges *Haussmann* (1809–91), who, while Prefect of Paris in 1853–70, effected far-reaching municipal improvements, among them being a new sewage-system and water-supply, the creation of wide boulevards (the boulevard Haussmann was named in his honour), and the landscape gardening of the Bois de Boulogne and the Parc de Vincennes.
    Compare **grimthorpe.**

havana; havanaise. The former is a Cuban cigar; the latter a Cuban dance (see **habanera**), based on French *Havane*, English *Havana*, Cuban—i.e., Spanish—*Habana*. With the dance, compare **cubana.**
    ' Havana, as its name implies, is a splendid " haven " [harbour]. The characteristic product of Cuba is . . . tobacco; and the best quality in the world—at least, for cigars —is grown west of Havana. There, in the celebrated Vuelta-abajo district, the soil is a light, sandy loam, very rich in lime, potash, and forest refuse; and, as both the heat and the humidity are great, it is an ideal site for the tobacco plant,' Lionel W. Lyde, *Man and His Markets*, (edition of) 1919.
    ' The cigars are still [Cuba's] chief glory, unequalled else-where,' Osbert Sitwell, *Sing High! Sing Low!*, 1944.

havelock, a light cloth cap or helmet-covering that, hanging over the neck, is worn by soldiers as a guard against the sun in very hot climates, commemorates General Sir Henry *Havelock* (1795–1857), who distinguished himself by relieving Lucknow in September 1857, and by holding it until the arrival, in November, of ' The Campbells are coming, hurrah, hurrah ! ' and who had an equally notable son—winner of the V.C. in 1858.

Hebe, which is the same in Latin and in the originating Greek, is a personification of *hēbē*, ' youth(fulness) ' : Hebe, in Classical mythology, is the goddess of youth. Daughter of Zeus

195

and Hera, she was cup-bearer to the gods (hence the somewhat facetious use of *Hebe* for a barmaid—or even a waitress)
until Ganymede supplanted her in Zeus's—to us—heterodox
affections.

> ' Nods and becks and wreathèd smiles,
>   Such as hang on Hebe's cheek '
>
> (Milton, *L'Allegro*).

hector, n. and v.   ' Caillaux turned upon his judges, hectored
them haughtily, and more than once made them look like
culprits cowering before indignant righteousness ' (leading
article in *The Times Literary Supplement*, December 29, 1945).

A *hector* is a bully, a blusterer ; to *hector* is to bully, to brow-
beat, to bluster : and formerly at least the noun was spelt with
a capital initial, in deference to the unwitting originator,
Hector, who, the son of Priam and Hecuba, was the Trojan
hero of Homer's *Iliad*, where he is represented as the leader of
the forces besieged in Troy and as being killed by Achilles.
In Homer, Hector is not a bullying braggart, and in English
literature of the 14th–early 17th Centuries, his name stands for
' a gallant warrior ' : the derogatory conception of his character
dates from the latter 17th Century, when the Hectors, a gang of
disorderly young fellows that fancied themselves as very
Hectors, disturbed the streets of London with their hooligan-
ism ; popular drama took up this topical cue.   Etymologically,
Hector means ' the prop, the stay, the support ' of Troy, as
Darius—see **daric**—was of Persia.

hedenbergite. See **baikalite.**

Helen, i.e. Helen of Troy, has, ever since the siege of Troy in the
late 12th Century B.C., been the archetype and emblem of
female beauty so breath-taking as to become her country's
bane.   For instance, Eric Linklater in his sympathetic study,
Mary, Queen of Scots, refers thus to the earlier woman, ' Mary,
who is Scotland's Helen and Scotland's Deirdre, was something of a prude under her beauty ', and Lady Dorothy
Wellesley in ' The Scholar ' (*The Observer*, June 17, 1945) says
of the titular character :

> ' Like ghosts upon life's outer rim
>   Live women moved, withdrawn,
>   The breast of Helen glowed for him
>   As certainly as dawn ' :

gleaming not with noontide splendour but with a merely
penumbral beauty.

196

Helicon; heliconian. Whereas *helicon* is 'a huge bass tuba used by military bands' (a derivative sense), *Helicon* is poetry in general and poets collectively, and *heliconian* is 'poetic'. In Greek mythology, *Helicon* (Greek *Helikōn*) is that mountain in Boeotia which formed the home of Apollo and the Muses and from which gushed the springs of Aganippe and Hippocrene.

helium (first isolated by Ramsay) is one of the 92 elements, and the name derives from Greek *hēlios*, 'the sun': but, on the analogy of *selenium* and *tellurium*, *helium* comes from a personified sun: the Sun, giver of life, the male-principle apotheosized: in brief, a god. Helios was the son of Hyperion and the sister of Selene; he came to be identified with **Apollo**.

Héloïse and Abelard. See **Eloïsa and Abelard**.

helot. In Rex Stout's diverting 'deteccer', *Where There's a Will*, (English edition) 1941, Archie Goodwin, who is detective Nero Wolfe's adroit and witty assistant, asks, 'What am I? I'm a helot. A damn flunkey.' With a small *h*, it means 'a bondsman, a serf, a slave'; whence **helotism,** 'serfdom' (with a derivative sense in biology). Historically, the *Helots* were that class of serfs in Sparta which ranked between the citizens and the full slaves: from Latin *Helotes*, which represents Greek *Heilōtai*, traditionally—and probably correctly— derived from *Helos*, a Laconian town whose inhabitants were forced into serfdom.

'Revolution broke out at Sparta in 207 [B.C.] under the lead of Nubis; he carried out . . . the revolutionary programme, freeing many Helots, though he too never dealt radically with the Helot question,' W. W. Tarn, *Hellenistic Civilisation*, (revised edition) 1930.

helvetium (also called *alabamine*) is a chemical element that, named after Switzerland in its Latin dress of *Helvetia*, has yet to be irrefutably proved to exist. A note thereon may be read in *Annual Reports of the Chemical Society*, 1935 (vol. xxxii), where there is also one on the supposititious **virginium.**

Henry. See **martini-henry**.

henry; plural **henries.** Like **amp(ère), coulomb, farad, joule, maxwell, ohm, volt,** and **watt,** it comes from the name of a scientific pioneer in electricity—and, like them again, it forms the name of an electrical unit; it is, to be precise, the unit of (electro-)magnetic inductance. The term has become almost popular : it occurs in the theory, as the unit does in the practice of wireless.

Joseph Henry (1797–1878) was an American physicist of very considerable note.

Hercules (including **pocket Hercules**)**; Herculean** or, preferably, **herculean.** A *hercules* is a very powerful machine, used for pile-driving, and *herculean* means ' possessed of tremendous physical strength or requiring tremendous strength ' (*a herculean task*).

In Roman mythology, *Hercules* is a romanization of the Greek **Hēraklēs,** the son of Zeus and Alcmene. Herakles was so strong that he inevitably attracted the envy of the weaker : and in the performance of ' the twelve labours ' he had to call upon his brains as well as his brawn.

hereford is the name of the red-coated, white-faced and white-marked, hardy beef cattle, first bred in Herefordshire, England, but now reared extensively in New Zealand and the United States also. The county has been named from the ancient town of Hereford (not far from the Welsh border) : and *Hereford* means ' the ford of the army '.

hermaphrodite comes from the Latin *hermaphroditus*, Greek *hermaphroditos*, derived from the legend of *Hermaphroditos*, the son of *Hermes* and *Aphrodite*. He spurned the love offered by Salmacis, the nymph of the fountain wherein he bathed. Closely embracing him, she prayed the gods to make them one —a request they granted quite literally. The resultant was a being with the genitals of both sexes : which is the strict, the medical sense of *hermaphrodite*.

Whence the *hermaphrodite*, short for *hermaphrodite brig*, a brigantine : a two-masted vessel that, square-rigged forward, is schooner-rigged aft.

hermetic. The *hermetic art* is another name for alchemy, and a *hermetic seal* is an air-tight sealing by fusion. From the Greek god *Hermes*, thus : On Thoth, an Egyptian god virtually identified with Hermes, the alchemists, mystics, Neoplatonics bestowed the name *Hermes Trismegistus* (thrice great). Messenger of the Olympian gods, he conducted to Hades (purgatory, not hell) the souls of the dead. A cunning and secret fellow—a true hermetic.

Probably derivative, in Greek, from *Hermes* is *hermeneuein*, ' to interpret ' : whence, via *hermeneutikos* (' interpretative ')

198

comes our *hermeneutics*, (the art of) interpretation, especially of the Scriptures.

Herod. See **out-herod Herod.**

Hesperian; Hesperides and **the Garden of Hesperides; hesperis.** *Hesperian*, poetical for ' western '—*Hesperides*, Isles of the Blest (compare **canary**)—and *hesperis*, a botanical genus including Rockets and Dame's Violet, all three derive, via Latin, from the Greek *Hesperos*, the Evening Star, from *hesperos*, ' of the evening ; western '. *Hesperian*, therefore, explains itself; *hesperis*, besides being a genus, is specifically the ' *night*-scented gillyflower ' ; and *the Hesperides* are those islands which, in Greek mythology, lay—were they not the Sunset Land?—at the *western* extremity of the then known world, the *Garden of the Hesperides*, where grew ' the apples of gold ' (mundanely : oranges), being situated in the Fortunate Isles and guarded by the Hesperides, or daughters of Hesperus—the Daughters of the *West*.

Later, philosophy rationalizing the ancient poesy, ' the gardens fair of Hesperus ' were set in ' the broad fields of the sky ' ; and medieval theology transferred to the garden and the islands some of the properties of the Christian heaven, or rather, reinvested them with these properties, for St Ambrose's description of the celestial fields of bliss owes much to Pindar's account of the Elysian Isles, as other Christian descriptions owe much to the same, or to some other, Classical source. (See an erudite and sympathetic letter from Robert Eisler in *The Times Literary Supplement*, September 22, 1945.)

hessian; Hessian; Hessian boots; Hessian fly. All from (the former Grand Duchy of) *Hesse*—German *Hessen*—in Germany : *hessian* is ' a coarse, strong cloth made from jute or hemp ', because originally made there ; *Hessian* is American for ' a mercenary ' (whether military or, derivatively, political), because in the American War of Independence, the British employed nearly 30,000 Hessian soldiers,—and it also has a mathematical sense (see **Jacobean**) ; *Hessian boots* (better : *hessians*), high boots tasselled at top front, were first worn by Hessian troops, to become fashionable in England early in the 19th Century ; the *Hessian fly*, destructive to wheat, is incorrectly said to have been carried to North America by those already mentioned Hessian mercenaries.

hessite, a silver tellurite, often auriferous, takes its name from a Swiss chemist, G. H. *Hess* (1802–50).

hick, ' a rustic ; hence, rural, rustic ' : *hick* represents *Hick,* which, like *Dick,* pet-forms *Richard*; cf. **rube.** For ' a rustic ', *hick* was used by the English underworld so early as 1690 : and, like so many other English obsoletes and subterraneans, it has reappeared in the U.S.A.

Of a rural newspaper-editor, Ellery Queen says, ' " He's more what you'd call a hick Horace Greely " ' (*Calamity Town,* 1942).

hill billy. See the **billy, silly** entry.

hippocras is an archaism for a spiced and sweetened wine extremely popular in medieval and early modern times. After being treated, it was passed through a woollen bag, a ' *Hippocrates*' sleeve ', originated as a filter by the 5th-Century (B.C.) Greek physician of that name. The Middle English and the earlier Old French form of *Hippocras* was *Ypocras.* In his invaluable *Wine,* 1946, the great connoisseur (and delightful writer), André Simon, sets forth a recipe for making a ' white hippocras ' (*nunc est bibendum*).

hippocrene is used for a draught of such water or, derivatively, other liquid, as inspires one to write verse or even poetry. In Greek mythology, *Hippocrene* is that spring or fountain which is fabled to have gushed from the slope of **Helicon** when **Pegasus** struck the ground with his hoof. Literally, *Hippocrene* is ' the fountain (*krēnē*) of the horse (*hippos*) '. Keats speaks of ' the blushful Hippocrene ', Longfellow of ' maddening ' draughts.

hob. ' One name for the *will o' the wisp* is *hob lantern. Hob* is, like *Bob,* a rimed diminutive of *Robert,* and we find it familiarly prefixed to words meaning demons in *hobthrush* and *hobgoblin* . . . the *thrush* of *hobthrush* is a perversion of *thurse,* once a common name for a goblin, and *Hob* just gives the personal touch, like *Old Nick.* By regular association with *goblin,* the name *hob* itself came to mean fairy, imp, etc.' (WWN.)

hobbledehoy. W, speaking of ' the mysterious *hobbledehoy* . . first recorded from 1540, with a bewildering number of variants ', thinks that the first syllable may well be that of **hob.** Not improbably it is a *Hob* afflicted with a hobbling gait, and, as the term refers to a youth, ' neither man nor boy ', the *hoy* element rhymes on *boy*; *-de-* I surmise to be an intrusive, meaningless element, perhaps introduced for ease of pronunciation. The 16th–17th-Century forms in *hob*(*b*)*er-* do not invalidate that suggestion.

hobby, an inferior hawk, comes from French *hobet*, of which the origin is unknown. But, since *Robert* is a French given-name, *hobet* may signify ' the little *Hob* ', the hawk thus being such a personification as we have in **robin.**

hobgoblin. See **hob.**

hobohemia. See **bohemian.**

hobthrush. See **hob.**

hock is short for *hockamore*, the English form of German *Hoch-heimer* (*Wein*), the wine of *Hochheim* in the Rheingau district of Hesse-Nassau, Germany. It is a fine white wine, and the term *hock* has, in the language of commerce, been extended to the entire group of German delicate white wines. Hochheim, by the way, stands on the River Main.

   Compare **johannisberger** and **rudesheimer.**

hocus-pocus is a quack's word in imitation Latin, ' perhaps suggested by *hotch-pot* or *hotch-potch*; compare obsolete *hiccius doccius* (? *hicce est doctus* [here is the learned man]) in same sense,' W. Nevertheless, W continues thus, ' But the fact that *hokuspokus-filiokus* is still used in Norway and Sweden suggests that there may be something in the old theory of a blasphemous perversion of the sacramental blessing, *hoc est corpus* (*filii*) '— ' This is the body (of the Son of God)'. I share W's opinion, despite the opposition of the pundits ; compare, for instance, the perversions in the Black Mass.

Hodge, n. ; **hodge,** adj. A farmer (*Farmer Hodge* is any or every farmer), a farm labourer ; rustic, rurally simple. As **hick** comes from *Richard*, *Hodge* comes from *Roger*.

   ' There was something infinitely amusing in the sight of this burly " hodge " policeman ', Edward Wyrall, ' *The Spike* ' (i.e., workhouse), 1909.

   Compare *Jacques Bonhomme* (in the entry at **jacquerie**) and **rube** and **Giles.**

Hogarthian, ' uncompromisingly realistic (though not exagger-atedly so) in manner or style, in subject or treatment, especially in literature and, as originally, in painting ', e.g. in ' A " mixed " dosshouse is a den . . . which affords harbour . . . to male and female vagrants who have contracted permanent or temporary connubial ties. All the depravities of the social abyss are concentrated in its Hogarthian atmosphere ' (Joseph

201

Augustin, *The Human Vagabond*, 1933). I.e., in the social-satirical manner of the English painter and caricaturist, William Hogarth, who flourished in the earlier part of the 18th Century. *The Rake's Progress* is the most frequently mentioned, though not the best, of his satirical series.

holland. ' The older industries [of Holland] were in flax and wool, e.g. the " brown holland " of Tilburg and Eindhoven, in the great flax-growing area,' Lionel W. Lyde, *The Continent of Europe*, (4th edition) 1930. This *holland*, therefore, is but another name for ' Dutch linen ', the *brown holland* being the unbleached version thereof.

Skeat says that the original form of *Holland* was *Holt-land*, i.e. woodland : but when was Holland so famous for its trees as to be named ' *the* land of trees '? Is not *Holland* equivalent to *Hol-land*, i.e. ' hollow land ', as Lyde proposes?

hollandaise shortens *sauce hollandaise* (Dutch sauce). See, e.g., Escoffier's *Modern Cookery*, 1907.

hollands. A grain spirit—a gin—made in Holland. The owes its existence to the fact that the origin resides in the Dutch *hollandsch genever* (' Holland gin '). ' Rye is the typical grain [of the country] . . .; and it is the base of the typical food and drink of the people, the bread being made mainly of rye . . . and both the " Hollands " gin of Schiedam and the curaçao liqueur of Rotterdam having a rye base ' (Lyde).
Compare **schiedam.**

Hollywood, adjective, tends to mean or, at the least, to imply ' extravagant—whether in expenditure, in clothes, in manner or in theme '—' the acme of *non sequitur* '—' romantic in a modern, or even a modernistic, way '—' sentimental '—' impossible, wildly improbable '.

' In most of America and in the whole of Europe the word " Hollywood " is pejorative,' Evelyn Waugh, ' Why Hollywood Is a Term of Disparagement ', in *The Daily Telegraph*, April 30 1947.

Hollywood was chosen to be the centre of the American film industry because of the climate, the quality of the light, and the scenery. In a famous gazetteer of 1899 the place (*horribl dictu*) was not even mentioned. But then, Hollywood ha probably failed to hear of the gazetteer.

holmia; holmium. The former is a rare earth, the latter a rar element (discovered in 1880 by Clève). Near Stock*holm* (fo

202

that is, truly, the origin of both of these scientific words), many yttria-bearing minerals are found; holmium belongs to the **yttrium-cerium** group of elements residing in **gadolinite.**

homburg; or **Homburg hat;** the former is preferable. It is a **trilby** and was popularized in Britain by King Edward VII, who ' took the waters ' at *Homburg* in Prussia, where the hat was first manufactured.

' You didn't get a moon or stars like this in London, but there you weren't followed by Italian detectives in Homburg hats,' Eric Ambler, *Cause for Alarm*, 1938.

Concerning the Rhineland, Professor L. W. Lyde has written that ' the southern scarp . . . is generally much less rich than the northern both in metal and in fuel; but it has some compensation in the greater area of volcanic formation, the bleak Eifel being much less important than the fertile Taunus, as the hot-springs of the latter, e.g. at Wiesbaden, Ems and Homburg, are more numerous than those in the north, e.g. at Aix ' (*The Continent of Europe*, 4th edition, 1930).

homeric combat—homeric laughter. The *combat* is almost, the *laughter* entirely, a cliché. Both are hearty, unreserved and unreserving, and both recall the *Homeric* heroes, whether in their fighting (especially in the single combats) or in their moments of hilarious ease. They had more to laugh at than has the 20th-Century soldier.

In *The Iliad*, Homer, who flourished—we suppose—in the 9th Century B.C., wrote of that ten years war between the Trojans of Ilium and the besieging Greeks which certainly took place, though at an uncertain date (perhaps ca. 1200). From among the mighty warriors we may select Hector and Achilles, both of whom have influenced the English vocabulary, as also did the Greeks and the Trojans in general.

hong-kong; usually in the plural : **hong-kongs.** The fruit of the horse-chestnut, as in ' He went among the branches . . . For a time he jigged up and down to make a hong-kong fall ' (Dan Billany, *The Opera-House Murders*, 1940). The horse-chestnut tree, which came from the East, reached England in the middle of the 16th Century; indeed, it is probably indigenous to Asia and the earliest shipments may well have been from Hong-Kong.

The OED derives *conkers*, the children's game, from dialectal *conkers*, small snail-shells : but it has yet to be proved that, in general, the game was not originally, as it has been in the 20th Century, played with horse-chestnuts. I propose : *hong-*

203

kongs > *hong-kongers* > *hong-konkers* > *konkers* > *conkers* (whence the variant *conquerors*).

hoodlum. Webster essays no etymology ; The OED, remarking that soon after its arrival ca. 1870 many fictitious stories were current to account for its origin, itself attempts no etymology, and the DAE follows suit. W, however, suggests that it may be a 'perverted back-spelling (cf. *slop*) of *Muldoon*' and supportingly adduces **hooligan** and **larrikin**, which are like-wise of Irish origin. To amplify : as *police* becomes *ecilop*, corrupted rather than perverted to *slop*, so *Muldoon* becomes *noodlum*, corrupted to *hoodlum*. For the prominence of Irish-men in American gangs, see Herbert Asbury's books on New York, San Francisco, Chicago, and Fred D. Pasley's and E. D. Sullivan's on Chicago.

hoodoo is synonymous with **voodoo** (in both its strict and its debased senses, its original and its derivative meanings), of which it seems to be an alteration. Careful writers tend to reserve *voodoo* for the body of superstitious belief and practice, *hoodoo* for the senses ' the opposite of *mascot* ; a person or thing bringing, or regarded as bringing, misfortune ' and ' to bring misfortune or bad luck to ' (a person). See **voodoo.**

Hookey Walker or simply **Walker.** An expletive, implying derision and incredulity. ' The reason for the choice of the name is unknown ' says W, who adduces an artfully allusive quotation from Dickens's *The Pickwick Papers* (1836–37) : ' Mr Weller senior ventures to suggest, in an undertone, that he [**Stiggins**] must be the representative of the united parishes of Saint Simon Without and Saint Walker Within '. But surely the origin is this : ' to take (or sling) one's *hook* ' is ' to depart ', —compare *play hooky,* to play truant ; ' to get out ' is ' to walk out ', and ' to get away ' is ' to walk away ',—compare *Get out!* and *Get away with you!,* ' You don't say so ' or ' I don't believe you ' ; this *hook* is affectionately diminished to *hook(e)y*, this *walk* is converted into an agential noun, *walker*, the two words become phrase-associated instead of being merely sense-associated. Probably some such injunction as ' Be a Hookey Walker ! ' or ' Make yourself a Hookey Walker ! ' is understood. Can I prove it? I have no proof, but if I searched long for one I should almost certainly find it.

hooligan is, Webster says, derived from ' an Irish family named *Hooligan*, in Southwark, London '. The family's actual sur-name was *Houlihan*, as W was, I believe, the first lexicographer to point out. The *locus classicus* on the subject is journalist Clarence Rook's sociological masterpiece, *The Hooligan Nights*, 1899. Rook says that ' there was, but a few years ago, a man called Patrick Hooligan, who walked to and fro among his fellow-men, robbing them and occasionally bashing them. This much is certain. . . . But with the life of Patrick Hooligan, as with the lives of Buddha and of Mahomet, legend has been at work, and probably many of the exploits associated with his name spring from the imagination of disciples . . . . . . He lived in Irish Court . . . . . . He left a great tradition. . . . He established a cult.' For fuller details, see PS, 2nd or 3rd edition.

Compare **hoodlum** and **larrikin.**

hoover. ' Mrs Briggs, the charwoman, was doing the passages and the stairs with the Hoover—an excellent invention, but so *very* noisy. I always go out on Saturday morning when the Hoover is operating,' E. C. R. Lorac, *Case in the Clinic*, 1941.

A *hoover* and ' to *hoover* ': from *the Hoover vacuum cleaner*, an American ' boon to housewives '. It is a proprietary name.

Horace. See **'Orace.**

Horatian, in its derivative and eligible sense, means ' kindly and tolerant, shrewd and sensible, worldly yet upright, pleasure-loving yet lovable, cultured yet not " superior ", witty, and possessed of an admirable style—terse, compact, pithy, elegant, polished, pellucid '.

' Provence, lovely land of olives, sunshine, dusty houses with yellow tiles, and the old Horatian view of life ' (Francis Beeding, *Eleven Were Brave*, 1940).

' What is the secret of his appeal that he can be something to all men? . . . Is it the tone and the philosophy behind the Odes, the genial but tempered outlook . . .? the human warmth and with it the control? or is it the atmosphere of " golden mediocrity " [*Auream quisquis mediocritatem Diligit*, whoever loves the golden mean] in the Golden Age of Rome, where Virgil and the Sabine farm and the Augustan peace, the gilded youth . . . are in the background? or is it the lapidary restraint and mastery of those perfect verbal mosaics? *Omnes eodem cogimur*; we may each compose our answer ': thus, in *The Times Literary Supplement* of September 22, 1945, the reviewer of L. P. Wilkinson's notable book, *Horace and His Lyric Poetry*.

Quintus Horatius Flaccus (65–68 B.C.), the Roman poet characterized by a most distinctive felicity (*curiosa felicitas*), has

205

been well translated by John Conington and subtly, charmingly written about by Gaston Boissier, Sellar, Mackail.

hotchkiss is usually taken to be short for *Hotchkiss machine gun*, but it may also shorten *Hotchkiss magazine rifle*. Both of these weapons sprang, fully armed, from the fertile brain of Benjamin Berkeley *Hotchkiss* (1826–85), a native of Watertown, Connecticut.

Compare **gatling, lewis, maxim, tommy gun.**

Hottentot is used, by transference, for a person uncultured or uneducated or uncouth (or all three); also for a depraved person, a vicious hooligan. From the *Hottentots*, a native race, small and stupid, formerly inhabiting the region about the Cape of Good Hope.

For the etymology of *Hottentot*, see **barbarian**, para. 5 (especially) and para. 6.

houdini, do a. To wriggle out of handcuffs and thus escape from arrest or captivity; hence, to get out of ' a tough spot ' : ' I was put in the patrol wagon, and handcuffed to two policemen. . . . I having escaped him so many times, he was afraid I would do a " houdini " on the way to his district, and he wasn't taking any chances with me,' Edward Martin in C. R. Shaw, *Brothers in Crime*, 1938.

Erich Weiss (1874–1926), American magician of Hungarian Jewish extraction, took the name of Harry Houdini in emulation of a French magician : Houdin. Houdini became world famous for his skill in extricating himself not only from handcuffs but also from locked or sealed or locked-and-sealed containers of many kinds.

houstonia is a plant of the genus *Houstonia* of the madder family; it has a delicate, bluish-purple flower. Its name commemorates an English botanist, William Houston (1695?–1733).

howlet is traditionally and understandably associated with *owl* : if the form were *owlet*, it would obviously be a diminutive, but since it is *howlet*, W is probably right in saying that ' it is really a diminutive of the name *Hugh*. Compare French *hulotte* in same sense, and dialect *houchin*, *how-howching*, owl. The surnames *Howitt*, *Howlett*, *Hullett*, *Hewlett*, *Houchin*, *Hutchin* similarly represent Old French diminutives of *Hugh*. Compare *robin*, *jackdaw*, *dicky*(*bird*), etc.' Compare also :—

huguenot, a French Protestant, comes immediately from Bezanson *Hugues*, a syndic and a party leader at Geneva,

Huguenot being a diminutive of *Hugues* and Geneva ever a stronghold of Protestantism. *Eiguenot*, a Swiss dialectal form of German *eidgenoss* (*eid*, oath + *genoss*, comrade), 'an oath-companion, a confederate', became assimilated to French *Huguenot*, which, like the more usual *Huguenet*, had been a French surname since long before the Reformation. (W; Webster.)

humpty-dumpty. It has not been irrefutably proved whether Humpty-Dumpty of the nursery rhyme is the personification of *humpty-dumpty*, a short (or small) *dumpy* person, or whether, as seems probable, from the antiquity of such rhymes, the generalized short person is a common-propertying of Humpty-Dumpty. If the latter be correct, then *Humpty-Dumpty* is a duplication of *Humpty*, a pet-form of *Humphrey*, as W has acutely proposed.

Hun, 'a very objectionable person; an uncultured brute', arose in 1914–18, died out in the late 1920's, and was revived soon after Hitler's accession to power early in 1933.

The use of *Hun* for 'a German' originates in a speech delivered by the Kaiser on July 27, 1900, to German soldiers on the eve of their departure for China; he invoked the merciless conduct of the Huns under Attila in the Dark Ages ('Let all who fall into your hands be at your mercy'); and the German soldiers did, in fact, act 'Hunnishly' in China. In 1902, Kipling wrote, 'With a cheated crew, to league anew With the Goth and the shameless Hun'. (The OED.) The Royal Flying Corps, with a nice sense of humour, called flying cadets of the 1915–18 period: 'Huns'.

On the *Hünen*, in Medieval Latin *Hunni* (or *Chunni*), known to the Chinese as *Hiong-nu* or *Han*, the race that overran Europe in the 4th–5th Centuries of the Christian era ('In A.D. 450 widespread alarm was created in Western Europe by an invasion of the Hun monarch Attila. Hitherto the Hunnish tribes, which had temporarily settled in Hungary, had been on fairly amicable terms with the Romans,' M. Cary, *A History of Western Europe, A.D. 1–455*), Professor Lionel W. Lyde has, in *The Continent of Asia*, 1933, afforded us this sidelight: 'These abrupt [geographical] contrasts are . . . reflected in the whole history of Asia. On the one side, there emerges swarm after swarm of savage steppe men—Scythians, Sarmatians, Oghuz, Huns, Bulgars, Avars, Magyars, Mongols, Tatars, Kirghiz, Kalmucks, an interminable procession of raiders into Europe, meteoric in their movements, but in their effects most of them as ephemeral as the steppe grasses—for nomadism forbids accumulation. On the other side, there brood the creeds of calm and contemplation—Hinduism and Buddhism.' The trouble came when the Huns and Goths and Vandals consolidated into States and Nations: and these three sets of savage intruders formed a large part of *Germania*; Classical scholars have recalled what Tacitus said of the brutal warriors of that country ; compare Victor Hugo's verses : *Les Turcs on passé là, Tout est ruine et deuil.*

Compare **Goth** and **vandal.**

husky (dog). Not, by the way, just any Arctic dog, but an Eskimo dog of unstandardized breed. Webster, on the ground that *Husky* is American slang for an Eskimo, thinks that *husky* is a corruption either of the Tinneh (or north-Athapascan Indian) *uskimi*, ' an Eskimo ', or of *Esky*, English slang for an Eskimo. W inclines to a ' corruption of *Eskimo* ', yet he mentions the significant fact that ' A Scotsman resident in Canada suggests . . . that it may be the personal name *Husky* (? for Hugh), as in *Huskisson*, given by early Scottish immigrants. Compare *collie* ' (q.v.).

hyacinth. The colour and the mineral probably derive their names from the plant and its flower, *hyacinth* or *hyacinthus*. *Hyacinth* comes, via French *hyacinthe*, from Latin *hyacinthus*, which transliterates Greek *huakinthos*. In Greek mythology, the flower is said to have issued from the blood of Hyacinth (Huakinthos) : ' that sanguine flower inscribed with woe ', as Milton phrases it. Hyacinth, a too handsome youth, was loved by Apollo and Zephyrus ; he loved the former ; the latter, jealous, slew him.

Compare **jacinth,** which is a doublet of *hyacinth* ; *jacinth*, once both the flower and the gem, is now only the gem.

hydra is ' a multiple evil or danger ', not to be overcome or circumvented by a single effort ; especially, *a hydra of error*. Like the technical sense, ' a thermometer that, possessing a compound bulb, acts quickly ', it derives from *Hydra* (adopted direct from Latin : Greek *Hudra*), that serpent or other monster of Greek mythology which, inhabiting the marsh-like lake of Lerna in the Peloponnesus, was slain by **Hercules.** It had nine heads—hence the common phrase, ' a many-headed Hydra ' ; any head, lopped off, would, unless it were cauterized, immediately become two. This mythological tale is, in essence, a highly moral allegory on the insidious growth of permitted evil.

The creature took its name from the fact that it inhabited

a body of water (Greek *hudōr*). Compare, therefore, the etymology of *otter*, a water animal.

Iygeia or **Hygiea; hygeian; hygiene.** The second and (via *hugieinē tekhnē*, ' the healing art ') the third obviously derive from the first, Hygeia being the Greek goddess (*Hugieia*) of Health. Fittingly she was the daughter of Asklepios (see **Aesculapius**).

The personification of health, Hygeia was worshipped as a goddess, and the myth-makers soon came to associate her with Asklepios. Compare the Greek verb *hugiazein*, ' to render sound or healthy; to heal ': probably both *Hygeia* and *hugiazein* derive immediately from *hugiēs*, ' sound, healthy '.

Iymen, hymen; hymeneal; and, either a derivative or a cognate, **hymn.**

Clearly, *hymeneal* (connected with a wedding) derives from *Hymen*, the god of marriage. *Hymen* is the Latin transliteration of Greek *Humēn*. It is not certain whether *Humēn* is a personification of *humēn*, ' a membrane '—especially the vaginal membrane (poetically, *maidenhead*), or whether *humēn*, that membrane, follows from *Humēn*, that god, for the rupture of the *hymen* is, or used to be (and in Oriental countries is still), regarded as an integral—nay, the quintessential—*hymeneal* rite. The Greek word, i.e. the common noun, may come from—or be at least cognate with—the Sanskrit ' sy*uman* ', a suture.

Now, *hymn* represents Latin *hymnus*, Greek *humnos* : one of the earliest nuances of the Greek word is ' wedding song '; and one of the earliest nuances of *humēn* or perhaps *Humēn* is ' wedding-cry '—a nuance rich in physiological and psychological implications.

I

carus; adj., **Icarian.** *Icarus; or, The Future of Flying*, by J. H. D'Albiac (who became an Air Marshal).

Icarus, Greek *Ikaros*, has been described as ' the earliest airman ': as he was mythological, the claim can be neither denied nor substantiated. Confined with his father Daedalus (see **daedal**) in the Cretan **labyrinth,** he and his inventive sire, wafted on wings attached with wax, flew away. Icarus, however, flew too near the sun : his wings melted : he fell into the sea reminiscently named *Icarian*. The adjective is therefore

applied to presumptuous ambition that ends either in ruin o
in ignominious failure.

ichabod! or **Ichabod!** Alas!; a parenthetic or interposed
'I regret to say'. Also it occurs allusively in Barbar;
Goolden's novel, *Ichabod*, 1945: whereon *The Times Literar,
Supplement* (November 3, 1945) provides a gloss in the opening
sentence of its review. 'Miss Goolden's theme . . . is th
departed glory of the upper-middle-classes.'

The origin lies in 'She named the child Ichabod, saying
The glory is departed from Israel : because the ark of God wa
taken' (1 *Samuel*, iv, 21). The literal meaning of Hebrew
ichabod is 'inglorious'.

idrialite; whence **idrialin.** Idrialite is 'a dark, earth,
mineral consisting of idrialin mixed with cinnabar, clay, etc.'
idrialin, 'a colorless crystalline compound' (Webster). The,
are found in the neighbourhood of *Idria*, a small north-Italia;
(formerly Austrian) mining city, noted for its quicksilver.

ikey, in slang, means 'addicted to sharp practice—or, at th,
least, excessive keenness—in business'. It is the adjectiva
use of *Ikey* (cf. *Ike*), a pet-form of the frequent Jewish given
name, *Isaac*.

iliad. *An iliad of woes* (or *misfortunes*) is, or was, a fairly commor
phrase among the literary-minded; there the sense is 'a long
series' or 'a tragic series', and *iliad* is a common-propert,
noun from 'The *Iliad*'—Homer's epic on the fall of Troy o
Ilium (Greek *Ilios* or *Ilion*), so named from *Ilos*, the son of Tros
the founder of Troy. Commencing with the quarrel of Achille
and Agamemnon, it deals with the siege of Ilium, ending wit|
the burial of Hector.

Compare **odyssey.**

illinium. This is postulated as one of the 92 chemical elements
but—Professor A. W. Stewart once informed me—its existenc
is doubtful.

From the State of *Illinois*—or rather from the Universit,
whose scientific staff 'discovered' this rare earth so late as 1926

ilmenite, known also as titanic iron-ore, is an iron-black minera
that, in form and habit, resembles haematite. It was firs
found, in notable quantities, in the *Ilmen* mountains—one c
the ranges in the southern Urals.

Hence *ilmenitite*, consisting mostly of ilmenite, and *ilmenorutile*, a reddish-brown mineral (Latin *rutilus*, golden red).

mmelmann. ' Quayle pulled upward and came over in an Immelmann turn, and saw tracers dive past him . . . . . . Quayle pulled up with the throttle wide open and he knew they would think he was going to Immelmann out of it. . . . The 42 did an Immelmann and was nearly on Tap's tail,' James Aldridge, *Signed with Their Honour*, 1942 : a novel of the R.A.F. in Greece.—' Low over their heads an ecstatic lightning of strange birds manoeuvred, looping-the-loop and immelmaning at unbelievable speed, acrobatic as new-born dragon flies,' Malcolm Lowry, *Below the Volcano*, 1947—a very remarkable novel.

A flying manœuvre, so named from that German airman (Max *Immelmann*, 1890–1916) who, in the war of 1914–18, hit upon it. It is designed to enable evasive action to be so taken that the aircraft quickly reverts to an offensive (or a defensive) position.

mpeyan is short for *Impeyan pheasant*. This bird ranges from Afghanistan to Bhutan ; and Lady, wife of Sir Elijah, *Impey* tried to acclimatize it in England. The name was bestowed by Latham in 1781 in their honour. Sir Elijah Impey (1732–1809) was Chief Justice of Bengal (1774–89) ; like Warren Hastings, with whom he had co-operated, he was impeached ; thanks to his able self-defence, he was acquitted.

ndia paper; Indian ink. Properly, *India paper*, soft and absorbent, is a paper used for proofs of engravings—and it comes from China ; the relevant paper for printing is *Oxford India paper*, which is very thin, but tough and opaque—nor has it any intimate connexion with India, for it merely imitates paper made in the East. Obviously, India has meant far more to the British than China has done.

Compare this :—' In the days of Marco Polo, Hwei-chow seems to have been the home of the literary and professional (banking) leaders of Kinsay (Hang-chow) ; and there may be a hint of that in the fame of the city to-day as the greatest ink-market in the world. For the supreme excellence of the real " *Chinese* ink "—often miscalled " *Indian* ink "—is due to the extreme care with which the most resinous timber of the Hwang-shan is reduced to an absolutely pure soot, and to the quality of the sesame oil ; the actual works are 25 miles away from Hwei-chow, in the hill-town of Sui-ning ' (Lyde, *Asia*, 1933).

Indian clubs, bottle-shaped and used in athletic exercises, ar[e] so named because the Red Indians' native weapons were bows[,] tomahawks, clubs.

Indian corn. Maize. Native of North America and cultivate[d] by the Red Indians, maize naturally came to be so named i[n] that continent.

' Whichever way I looked I could see fields of the tall gree[n] Indian corn (maize), with its tassel tops, bending and wavin[g] under the fresh breeze,' Alexander Harris, *Settlers and Convicts* 1847, in reference to the Hawkesbury River Valley of Ne[w] South Wales. (A very readable and instructive autobiography[.]

Indian file, in. In single file. The Red Indians of Nort[h] America, forced to traverse immense distances on foot (the[y] had no ridable animals), for much of the way through forest[,] were forced to walk thus : and thus were the narrow India[n] trails formed.

Indian ink. See **India paper.**

Indian summer. See the Weekley quotation in the **india[-] rubber** entry.—' Athens enjoyed an Indian summer of materia[l] wealth ' (ca. 146–88 B.C.), W. W. Tarn, *Hellenistic Civilisatio[n]* (2nd edition) 1930.—' The Indian Summer of a Forsyte[ ]formed one of the interludes in John Galsworthy's *The Forsy[te] Saga.*—' The rule of the Elamite kings of Larsam was . . . th[e] Indian Summer of Sumerian culture,' Patrick Carleton, *Burie[d] Empires*, 1939.

Literally ' summer weather in the late autumn in th[e] Northern Hemisphere ', it has come to mean ' material o[r] intellectual or moral or spiritual well-being that comes late i[n] a person's, institution's, nation's life '.

Indian weed. Tobacco. The term is short, not for *Red India[n]* but for *West Indian, weed,* **tobacco** having been first smoke[d] and by the Europeans first discovered, in the West Indies.

indiarubber. Caoutchou ; an eraser made of caoutchou. I[n] the late 18th and early 19th Centuries, *indiarubber* was know[n] as *Indian rubber* ; ca. 1830–80, the usual form was *India(-)rubber*[.] Rubber is the coagulated juice of certain trees and plants tha[t] grow in South America (*Cayenne resin* is an early name), Africa[ ]the East Indies. As W has remarked, ' The early explorer[s] thought America the back-door of India, whence *West Indies*

212

Red Indian, Indian corn, india-rubber etc.'; C. S. Forester's *The Earthly Paradise* reinforces the ' thought '. Compare, too, the preceding entry.

indigo. ' All the west was rose-colour, deepening by almost imperceptible gradations to the indigo shades of night. About the zenith were strata of pale gold, amethyst green and deep turquoise blue. A phantom moon sailed into the sky. The evening star glimmered like a jewel ' (Wilfrid Ewart, *Way of Revelation*, 1921).—' In Luxemburg, I met a half-breed who told me that money was to be made smuggling indigo into France and saffron into Holland ' (this was ca. 1900), F. S. Stuart, *Vagabond*, 1937.

In the 16th Century we called it *indico* (perhaps direct from Spanish), which represents Latin *indicum*, which in turn represents Greek *indikon*; that is, Indian (dye). It is ' *the* Indian dye ', as **peach** is ' *the* Persian fruit ' and **copper** is ' *the* Cyprian metal '.

indium. This very rare, soft, silver-hued metal was spectroscopically detected, in 1863, by Professors Reich and Richter, in a zinc ore of the Harz Mountains : and it owes its name to the indigo-band that characterizes its spectrum. On the analogy of *sodium*, it represents the radical of ' *ind*igo ', hence of ' *ind*icum ' : see **indigo.**

ingersoll is the common-property form of *Ingersoll watch*. Robert Hawley Ingersoll (1859–1929), noted American industrialist, developed the chain-store and mail-order business, and in 1892 introduced ' the one-dollar Ingersoll watch '. Becoming insolvent, he in 1922 sold his assets to the **Waterbury** Clock Company.

inverness is the common-property, the sensible, form of *Inverness cape*. Strictly, an *Inverness cape* is that removable cape which goes with an *Inverness cloak* (or overcoat) ; and its name comes from a Highlands of Scotland town and district, where they were manufactured, especially ca. 1860–1914.

iridium, a white metal that, resembling burnished steel, belongs to the platinum group ; **iris ; iritis,** inflammation of the iris. All three come, the first and the third by derivation, the second by adoption, from *Iris*, who, in Greek mythology, was the daughter of the rainbow and hence the personification of the rainbow, with its *iridescence*. Messenger of Hera, she travels along the *iridescent* hues of the rainbow to deliver her messages, as Virgil relates. She made a suitable marriage, for she becam the wife of the mild west wind, Zephyrus (whence **zephyr**).

Irish or **irish** = hot temper (cf. **paddy**). Slang. The Iris are Celts—apt to become fiercely indignant (Juvenal's *saeº indignatio*); high-spirited. This is a national characteristic s marked that even ' British [i.e., English] phlegm ' and ' Scottis caution ' have paid the Irish the compliment implicit in th slang term.

' She had a perfect right to demand an explanation . . . an I should not '—says the speaker, Carrie Murphy, begorra !– ' have got my Irish up,' Rex Stout, *Bad for Business*, 1945.

Irish bull; Irishism. *Irish bull* is so widely understood tha we often shorten it to *bull*; nevertheless, it is only fair to remar that *bull* was used in the senses ' an obvious contradiction i terms ' or ' a laughable inconsistency unperceived by th speaker or writer ' long before it came to be associated with th Irish. As early as 1802, there appeared *An Essay on Irish Bulls*– from the pens of Maria and Richard Edgeworth, who, daughte and father, lived for years in Ireland; and in 1928, Walte Jerrold published his *Bulls, Blunders and Howlers*.

Here are two examples, taken from my *Usage and Abusage A Guide to Good English* (New York, 1942; London, 1947) ' the entrance out '; ' If there was twelve cows lyin' down i a field and one of them was shtandin' up, that would be a bull

Irishism, as well as bearing a more general sense ('a usag characteristic of, or belonging to, the Irish variety of English ' is synonymous with *Irish bull*, as in ' I'd have said that Majo Grendon was the type to hang on to his life like grim death– if you'll allow me an Irishism ' (E. C. R. Lorac, *Case in th Clinic*, 1941).

isabelline, ' greyish-yellow in hue ', **isabel** or **isabella** bein the noun; the history of the noun is obscure. Also, *isabella* the *Isabella grape*, often called the ' fox grape '; and the *isabellin bear* is greyish-yellow (or buff). Tradition has wrongl associated the colour with the underwear of the Archduches Isabella (daughter of Philip II of Spain), who flourished ca 1600. Yet it may be she who originated the name.

Ishmael; Ishmaelite. An *Ishmaelite* is simply an *Ishmael* in th figurative sense of the latter word—an outcast; especially a outcast at war with society: see *Genesis*, xvi. The nam *Ishmael*, in Hebrew, means ' God hears '.

Concerning the primitive patriarcho-pastoral stage

214

civilization, J. L. Myres, in *The Dawn of History*, writes thus, ' A woman who knows her business is . . . worth many cattle ; and it may be good business to exchange superfluous cattle for additional women, who are of course added to the family during good behaviour. If there has been a bad bargain, the family cuts its losses : Hagar, and Ishmael [her son] with her, is cast out, to find her way back whence she came, *if she can* '. —' The pathetic story of Hagar and Ishmael is . . . a slight but recognizable . . . proof that the tradition of Abraham's migration from Ur *via* Haran into Palestine is based on historical fact,' Patrick Carleton, *Buried Empires*, 1939.

It, in *gin and it,* is short for ' Italian vermouth '. Compare the less truncated **scotch.**

italic, italicize. Italic type was devised by Aldus Manutius (see **Aldine**) and first used, in his printery, for an edition, issued in 1501, of Virgil : that lovely book was dedicated to *Italy*, which in Latin is *Italia*, with adjective *Italicus* (transliterating the Greek *Italikos*). Compare, therefore, the complementary **roman.**

In manuscripts, *Italian hand* is the plain sloping handwriting as opposed to the finicky upright Gothic. And in allusive speech, *a fine Italian hand* formerly connoted either a stiletto or a stabbing with a stiletto.

J

jabberwock, ' a weird monster ' ; **jabberwocky,** ' nonsensical or meaningless talk or saying '. *Jabberwocky* is the title of a brilliant nonsense poem in Lewis Carroll's *Through the Looking Glass,* 1872.

Obviously an apparently nonsensical elaboration of *jabber*—with a shrewdly oblique glance at ' to *gibber* ' and *gibberish*. See especially ' The Nonsense Words of Edward Lear and Lewis Carroll ' in my *Here, There and Everywhere,* 1950.

jacconet is a variant of **jaconet,** q.v.

jacinth. See **hyacinth.**

Jack ; such words as **bootjack, cheapjack, lumberjack, steeplejack.** Jack is, indeed, a man of many trades ; and of as many personifications—see, e.g., *jack knife*. Sometimes he is shrewd, sometimes a simpleton.

215

In a ' Song.   Sung by Mr Incledon, at Vauxhall ', found at pp. 32–34 of a song-book entitled *The New Vocal Enchantress* 1791, a song upon the catch-word *quoz*, current in the 1790's we find this stanza :

' There's a jack [1] to roast your meat, a jack [2] to hold your liquor,
Jack [3] upon the green, to amuse the vicar ;
Jack of various sorts—Jack's a quiz, because
Jack gives way to Gill, and so does quiz to quoz '.

Jack is the commonest pet-form of *John*, much the commonest of all given-names in the British Empire and appreciably the commonest in the United States and, in one form or another (*Johann*, *Johannes*, *Jan*, *Jean*, etc.), in the Indo-European world.

See especially PNTC, Weekley's *Jack and Jill* (a study of given-names), and E. G. Withycombe's *The Oxford Dictionary of Christian Names*.

Compare the ensuing entries.

jack.   See **jacket**.

Jack, every man.   ' Tell you one thing about that book.   The fellow who wrote it has discovered a new kind of intoxication . . . permanent intoxication.   And that's what we all want— every man-jack of us,' Claude Houghton, *Six Lives and a Book*, 1943.

The addition of *Jack* to *every man* simply gives a familiar tang to the idea in *mankind* : *Jack*, generic for ' a male human being ', becomes double-sexed.

Jack Frost is merely the personification of frost, for the almost childish reason that *Frost* was already a well-known surname and Jack the best-known of all given-names.   Originally, it would seem, a pun.

Jack in office.   A fussy official, ' much too damned officious ! '

' But man, proud man ;
Drest in a little brief authority,—
. . . .
. . . like an angry ape,
Plays such fantastic tricks before high heaven
As makes the angels weep '
(Shakespeare, *Measure for Measure*).

[1] A device for turning the spit, i.e. a turnspit.
[2] A pitcher, originally, of leather ; called also *blackjack*.
[3] The small bowl that, in the game of bowls, serves as the mark.

216

jack-in-the-box is a toy; a little-man figure that springs out of a box whenever the latter's lid is raised. Punningly used in J. J. Conington's ' deteccer ' published early in 1944 : *Jack-in-the-Box* : wherein an oddity of murder springs to the thinking mind whenever the legal case is opened.

Another application of the ubiquitous, generic **Jack**.

Jack Johnson was in the Great War of 1914–18 a German 5·9 howitzer, its shell, or its shell-burst : and it got its name from the fact that the smoke emitted by the explosion was black and the detonation formidable. Jack Johnson, a *Negro* born in 1878, was in 1908–15 heavyweight boxing champion of the world.

Jack Ketch. See **Ketch.**

Jack Mormon is a non-Mormon that, especially on terms of friendship, lives in a Mormon town or city. Here *Jack* is gently depreciative.

jack o' lantern, like **will o' the wisp,** is an ignis fatuus—a phosphorescent light seen on marshy ground and therefore deluding a traveller into marsh or quicksand. That is, *Jack of the lantern*, the apparent light requiring a fellow, any fellow, *Jack*, to hold it.

Jack of all trades (and master of none). Properly, one who can turn his hand to anything; derivatively, a handyman, also one who has passed from one livelihood to another. Here, as in so many *Jack* (or *jack*) phrases, the font-name signifies little, if anything, more than ' man, chap, fellow ' (cf. American **guy**).

Jack pine is a fir which grows well in the U.S.A. Not named after anyone surnamed Jack, nor after any other person. Merely another personification and a tribute to *Jack's* insidious influence.

jack rabbit. ' Any of several large hares of western North America, having very long ears and long hind legs ' (Webster). Here *jack* = *Jack* and is probably depreciative.

' The open country abounded with large-eyed jackrabbits that sometimes took prodigious leaps to escape us, but more often stood frozen as we passed,' Nard Jones, *Swiftly Flows the River*, 1939.

Jack Robinson, before one can say. Literally, before one can utter the four easy syllables of that name—only a shade

longer than is implied in *in a trice*. Who the originator was
nobody seems to know. Probably the name is a mere combination of the very short and common *Jack*, with a very
common surname.

Jack Tar or **Jack tar** or **jack tar** or **jack-tar** or even **jacktar**,
as a colloquialism for a sailor in the British Navy or—though
no longer in Britain—for any sailor, is a *Jack* personification
and elaboration of *tar*, the latter being, in the old sailing ships,
a constant preoccupation of the crew.

jackanapes. A silly, conceited fellow; an impertinent
'puppy'. *Jackanapes* was originally the name often given to
a monkey; hence, a monkey; hence, a coxcomb.

> *Jack a Napes* :
> *Jack o' Napes* :
> *Jack of Napes* :
> a monkey from Naples.

jackaroo, a young fellow acquainting himself, especially as an
apprentice, with colonial life—properly, as originally, in
Australia.
  Here, *jack* = *Jack* = any Jack = a fellow : and as he is
working in a land famous for its kangaroos, *jackaroo* is obviously
a blend of *Jack* and *kangaroo*.

jackass is a *Jack* or male *ass*. Donkeys being noted for their
obstinacy, perversity, and seeming stupidity, the transition to
'obstinate or conceited blockhead or fool' is easy. Hence, in
reference to cacophonous cry, the *laughing jackass*, or kooka-
burra, of Australia.

jackdaw. As *magpie* is *Mag pie* (with which compare the not
quite analogous yet relevant *Dicky bird*), so *jackdaw* is *Jack daw* :
pie existed before *magpie*, *daw* before *jackdaw*. The *pie* being
a bird addicted to chatter was feminized; the *daw* being a
thief, and most thieves—or, at least, burglars—being men, was
masculinized.

jacket represents French *jaquette*, a diminutive of Old French
jacque; from the latter comes the now only historical
jack, 'a leather jerkin; a leather drinking vessel'. Now,
jacque has the alternative *jacques*, which clearly points to
Jacques, the very common French given-name. Another
example of personification.
  Compare **jacquerie** and **jerkin**.

jack-knife. Perhaps simply a knife used more by a man—a *Jack* —than by a woman, but perhaps, as W suggests, ' for obsolete *jackleg*, corruption of Scottish *jockteleg*, said (1776) to be for *Jacques de Liège*, a cutler. This may be a myth, but has a parallel in French *eustache*, knife carried by an apache, from *Eustache Dubois*, cutler at Saint-Etienne.'

jackstraw, ' a man of straw—a figurehead of a fellow ', and **jackstraws,** ' a game known otherwise as spelicans ': both owe something to *Jack Straw*, who was one of the ringleaders in Wat Tyler's rebellion against the English king in 1381. It is worth noting that *Jack Straw* may have been only a nickname. In any event, the *jack* element of *jackstraw*—compare **jack in office**—is contemptuous, a point rendered the clearer by the apparently earliest sense of the term *jackstraw*, ' an effigy, stuffed with straw that it may catch fire the sooner '.

jacob, in the 16th–19th-Century underworld, meant a ladder (compare the botanical *Jacob's ladder*), the reference being to *Genesis*, xxviii, 12 ; ' And he '—Jacob—' dreamed, and behold a ladder set up on the earth, and the top of it reached to heaven ; and behold the angels of God ascending and descend- ing on it ' : as the ladder symbolized the hopes of Jacob for his descendants, so, to a burglar, a ladder may lead to wealth for himself.

The name *Jacob* (from Latin, from Greek *Iakobos*) represents the Hebrew *ya-'aqob*, ' one that takes by the heel '—see *Genesis*, xxv, 26.

jacobean and **hessian;** or **J**— and **H**—. In mathematics, these terms are derived from two German mathematicians, Otto *Hesse* (1811–74) and Karl *Jacobi* (1804–51). The former is known especially for his work in elliptical functions, differential equations, the calculus of variations ; the latter, a shade less notable, showed in 1844 the importance of the Hessian co-variant, his work therefore linking with Jacobi's.

jacobin = *Jacobin* pigeon and, later, a tropical American humming-bird that bears certain resemblances to the pigeon. The pigeon got its name from the fact that its fluffy neck- feathers resemble the cowl of a *Jacobin*—a Dominican—friar. The Dominicans became known also as Jacobins because they built their first convent near the church of Saint *Jacques*, which stands back from the rue Saint-Jacques in the Rive Gauche district of Paris.

jacobus. As **carolus** was a gold coin of Charles I of England, so *Jacobus*, Latin for James, yields King James's coin: *jacobus*. See also **jacob**.

jaconet, a dress fabric between cambric and muslin, was originally made in India; to be precise, at *Jagannath*; a Jagannath stuff or fabric. Jagannath, now usually called Puri, is in Cutch—and it is intimately connected with **juggernaut,** q.v.

jacquard is short for *Jacquard apparatus—Jacquard fabric* or *weave—Jacquard loom*, all named after Joseph Jacquard (1752–1834) that French inventor who, closely associated with the great manufacturing city of Lyons, devised the Jacquard apparatus (with its Jacquard cards) used in the Jacquard loom, used for weaving figured stuffs.

jacquerie, 'a peasant revolt', derives immediately from *la Jacquerie*, the great French revolt, in 1358, by the peasant against the nobles, the latter thus naming the revolt; already the latter had contemptuously called the typical French peasant 'Jacques Bonhomme', which might be anglicized as 'goodman James' or 'simple, easy-going James'.
Compare **Hodge**.

jaegers. Woollen underclothing, as in Thorne Smith's boisterously, naughtily amusing and witty novel, *The Bishop's Jaegers* From Dr Gustav *Jaeger*, who 'invented' the garments which included nightdresses, slippers, dressing-gowns, as well as 'undies', manufactured originally by Dr Jaeger's Sanitary Woollen System Co. Ltd; the garments came on the market in England, ca. 1890.

jaffa. A Jaffa orange—properly an orange grown in or in the vicinity of the Palestinian port of Jaffa; hence, loosely—but in accordance with the elastic tenets of commercial ethics—applied to any orange of approximately the Jaffa type. See the Lyde quotation at **latakia**.

jakes, 'a privy', probably represents either French *Jacques* or English *Jack's place*, or, perhaps, *Jack's house* (compare the euphemistic *little house*), but the pun in Sir John Harington's *An Anatomie of the Metamorphosed Ajax* (1596; wittily edited 1928, by Jack Lindsay) suggests the possibility that there may in *jakes*, be a reference to that Ajax of Greek mythology of whom C. M. Bowra has noted that 'his prowess was nobly celebrated by Homer, who . . . made him the greatest Achaean after

220

Achilles and . . . stalwart in battle, gigantic and beautiful, a match for Hector, the peer of Ares, the bulwark of the Achaeans' (*Sophoclean Tragedy*, 1944).

jalap is a powdered drug, extracted from the *jalap* or tuberous root of a Mexican plant. Via the Spanish *jalapa*, the word comes from *Jalapa*, a small Mexican town some twenty miles south-south-east of San Juan Bautista; there the drug was first obtained. The Spanish *Jalapa* represents the Nahuatl *Xalapon*, which literally means ' Sand in the Water '. (Webster.)

jamaica is short and lower-cased for **Jamaica rum,** rum made in Jamaica in the West Indies. The name *Jamaica* is the Indian *Xaimaca*, ' Island of the Springs '—in reference to the abundance of spring-water. For the change in the word, compare that in **jalap.**

jamake. Ginger; especially as an ingredient in intoxicating drinks, thus ' There ain't nothin' better in th' booze line than pure alky mixed with jamake ', as an American tramp might have said at any time in the present century. Clearly, *jamake* represents *Jamaica*, whence comes much ginger.

james has at least three meanings in slang : a sovereign coin —compare **jacobus**; a burglar's small crowbar, the word being a jocular dignifying of **jemmy**; a sheep's head, by personification.

Jamestown weed. See **jimpson.**

jamocha, jamoke. Like *jamake*, this is an Americanism; originally a tramps' word, it is now slang—and in the middle 1930's it was adopted in England, where, however, it has remained a low term. It means ' coffee '.

A blend of **java** + **mocha,** *jamocha* has, by the process of philological economy, become *jamoke*.

jane was, in the England of the 14th–17th Centuries, a small silver coin, introduced from *Genoa*. Later, it was a variant of **jean,** a fabric made at Genoa (Latin *Genua*: cf. **geneva**).

In American slang—and since ca. 1930 in Britain—it signifies ' a girl, a young woman; one's sweetheart ': the given-name *Jane* used generically. Compare **moll.**

janissary or **janizary,** usually in the pl. Only in the transferred sense, ' bodyguard ' or ' household troops ', is *janissaries* eligible. Originally, the word designated the Sultan of Turkey's guard, the flower of his standing army: and in Turkish the word means 'the new or modern soldiery or militia': *yeni-tsheri* comes into English by way of the Romance languages—Italian *giannizero*, Portuguese *genizaro*, French *janissaire*.

'From Orchan's time onwards'—he reigned in 1329–59—'it was [the Turks'] habit to select the likeliest of their Christian captives, . . . young men, convert them forcibly to Islam, educate them in the use of arms, and entitle them Janissaries ("bright faces")': R. G. Collingwood, *The New Leviathan*, 1942.

japan, n. & v.; **japanner**; **japanesque**; **japonica.**
'Another process of decoration which became fashionable after about 1660 was lacquer work or "japanning", the taste for this work lasting throughout the eighteenth century. In furniture ornamented in this manner panels were sometimes sent out to the East to be lacquered, and afterwards made up in England; in other cases the lacquer work was done at home in the Oriental style,' Oliver Brackett, *English Furniture*, 1928. The Japanese have for many centuries excelled in lacquer work. *Japanesque:* quaint or unusual in a manner reminiscent of Japan. *Japonica:* camellia; Japanese quince: from Late Latin *Japonia*, Japan. *Japonia* comes either from the Malay *Japang* or from the Chinese *Jih-pün* (sun-rise), corresponding to the Japanese *Ni-pon*, whence the European *Nippon*. (W.)

jarvey; jarvie; Jarvis. All three, in colloquial English, mean a hackney-coachman, hence a hackney coach. The earliest form, recorded by Captain Francis Grose in *A Classical Dictionary of the Vulgar Tongue* (late 18th Century), is *Jarvis*, a personal name applied with jocular affection (compare **jehu**); the other two, being diminutives, soon followed.

jasey or **jazy** is a wig, especially if made of worsted. An early authority—Forby, 1825—says that *jasey* is a corruption of *Jersey*, as if the wig were made of Jersey yarn, yarn manufactured from Jersey flax in Jersey. People even said *dash my jasey!* instead of the more usual *dash my wig!*

java, (1) among American tramps, is coffee, in obvious allusion to Java.
'"So long", said the derelict, "thankee fur the java and rolls, too"', Jim Tully, *Emmett Lawler*, 1922.—Godfrey Irwin, *American Tramp and Underworld Slang*, 1931.—'Now if I have

any idea Rusty Charley is coming my way, you can bet all the coffee in Java I will be somewhere else at once, for Rusty Charley is not a guy I wish to have any truck with whatever,' Damon Runyon, *Guys and Dolls*, 1931.

(2) A Javan melody, dance, air, tune, as in ' In the doorways [on a June evening in Paris] sit families on their wooden chairs, while from the Bal Musette where *Fiesta* began the Java fades on the sultry air,' ' Palinurus ', *The Unquiet Grave*, 1945.

jawbation. See **jobation.**

jay. W agrees with The OED that the word is ' of uncertain origin ' but pertinently remarks that ' the analogy of *robin*, *jackdaw*, etc., suggests that it may be the Latin *Gaius*, a name which was used very much as *Jack* is in English to designate persons familiarly. In French the *jay* is also called *jacques*, *richard*, *cola* (*Nicolas*).' Webster uncompromisingly states that *jay* derives, via Old French, from Vulgar Latin *gaius*, itself ' perhaps from Latin *Gaius*, proper name '. The weight of the circumstantial evidence, dangerous though such evidence be, justifies the jury in finding *Gaius* guilty of the pleasant crime of foisting his name upon an unsuspecting bird.

jazy. See **jasey.**

jeames, at first *Jeames*, is a common name for a flunkey, especially a footman, *Jeames* being a corruption of—it sounds like an affectation for—*James*. Its currency in literature dates from the appearance of Thackeray's *The Diary of Jeames de la Pluche* in *Punch*, 1845–46, and reprinted in *Miscellanies*, 1856. The ' hero ' of that short story is *James* Plush, a footman.

jean; American **jeans.** Either a twilled cotton cloth, or derivatively a garment—especially a pair of trousers—made thereof as in ' My friend in the jeans and white hat informed me that my failure to meet my appointment had caused great consternation,' Sol. Smith, 1846 (DAE). Two revealing early forms are *jenes* and, above all, *geanes*, from French *Gênes*, Genoa : where this cloth was first manufactured.

Compare **bombasine, calico, cambric, muslin.**

jehu. ' Gone for ever are the old roystering days of the hansom cab, when jovial Jehu, cracking his long whip, would whirl you home through the crowded streets at 1 a.m. with never a protest at the lateness of the hour,' Sidney Felstead, *The Underworld of London*, 1923.

In the 20th Century, *jehu* is sometimes used of a taxi-driver, as in David Hume's *Come Back for the Body*, 1945 : 'The jehu had slumped over the steering-wheel '.

'The driving is like the driving of Jehu the son of Nimshi; for he driveth furiously ' (2 *Kings*, ix, 20). Many a cab-driver did drive his cab furiously as though it were a chariot.

Jekyll and Hyde, 'a dual personality : the one, good ; the other, criminal or otherwise evil ', comes from Robert Louis Stevenson's ' psychological thriller ', *The Strange Case of Dr Jekyll and Mr Hyde* (1886), wherein the doctor was average, lovable, and Hyde a noxious villain. The term did not become generic until ca. 1900, some six years after the death of R. L. S., who had a pretty taste in the **macabre.**

(Concerning Pepys's diary) 'There is perhaps no record in the English language in which the truth stands revealed in such stark nakedness as in these " Jekyll-and-Hyde " confessions,' Oliver Brackett, *English Furniture*, 1928.

'Burgling night after night . . ., leading a Dr Jekyll and Mr Hyde existence of which my unfortunate family were profoundly ignorant,' George Smithson (' Gentleman George '), *Raffles in Real Life*, 1930.

'Kelly had the stuff in him to be honorable and right, and . . . to be evil and bad. His was a blending temperament, a Dr Jekyll and Mr Hyde controlling his thoughts and actions according to his mood,' Lee Duncan, *Over the Wall*, 1936.

jemimas. 'I aim at presenting the common idea of a Nonconformist clergyman, and I dress him in " Jemima " boots, white gloves, very short sleeves, and a top hat with a sash round it,' A. Neil Lyons, *A Market Bundle*, 1921. These elastic-sided boots are derisively personified by the non-aristocratic feminine name *Jemima*, which in the Hebrew means 'a dove'; perhaps, in part, because they are often dove-grey.

jemmy or **jimmy** is a burglar's small crowbar; in the British Empire, both forms are used, in the U.S.A. only the latter. But ' the States ' also has the verb *jimmy*, ' to open (esp. a door) with such a crowbar '. Whether *jemmy* or *jimmy*, noun or verb, these terms originally belonged to the language of the underworld ; they are still slang.

From the pet-form of *James*: cf. the remarks at **billy.**

jennet, a jenny (i.e., female) ass, derives from *jennet*, a small Spanish horse, *jennet* representing the French *genet*, which transliterates the Spanish *jinete*, a soldier mounted on such a horse, hence the horse itself. The Spanish word comes from the Arabic *Zanátah*, the name of a Berber tribe. ' *Sanhaja*, or *Senaja*, in Berber *Zanaga*, or *Zenaga*, two small tribes of Berbers, Algeria, formerly the most numerous and powerful of the Berber tribes ' (Chisholm).

jenneting has nothing to do with the preceding term. A variety of early apple, it has a name that derives from French *Jeannet*, little *Jean* (John) ; more strictly, French dialect has *pomme de Jeannet* (Jeannet's apple), the Standard French being *pomme de Saint-Jean* (St John's apple). The fruit was so called because it attained maturity at or about St *John's* Day, June the 24th. The ending *-ing* has been assimilated to that of *hasting* and *codlin*.

jenny, whether short for *jenny ass*, *jenny wren*, or *spinning jenny*, whether the compasses or the crane, whether singly or in combination (e.g., Scottish *jenny-long-legs*), is the pet-form of *Janet* or, confusedly, of *Jane*. For its mechanical applications, compare **jack.** ' [The Spaniards] shipped in so many cattle and horses and jennies for breeding mules that within a few generations these were running wild all over the country and were hunted instead of being bred,' James Truslow Adams, *The Epic of America*, 1933.

Jenny or *Jennie* is also a training aircraft—'from the designation JN ' (Webster).

jeremiad, a (lengthy) lamentation or dolorous complaint, comes from the French *jérémiade*, from *Jérémie*, from Latin *Jeremias*, the Jeremiah of the Old Testament. Jeremiah, a major Hebrew prophet, excelled in denunciation, severe judgement, dire prophecy : and his inveighings are to be found not only in *Jeremiah* but also in *Lamentations*. ' Jeremiah wrote in a book all the evil that should come upon Babylon ' (*Jeremiah*, li, 60).

jerkin. ' Perhaps from *George* (cf. *jacket*), of which the popular Old French form was *Joire*, *Jour*, preserved in name *Jorkins*. Compare German dialectal *jürken*, jacket, apparently from *Jürg*, popular form of *Georg*, and Old French *georget*, in similar sense ' (W).

Compare **georgette.**

jeroboam. ' . . . The Saintsburyan hospitality in the grand days of his professorship in Edinburgh . . . when each dish in a ten-course dinner was accompanied by a distinct and appropriate vintage ; and when the jeroboams of champagne were

225

wreathed as centre-pieces for the table ', remarks the writer of
' The Ideal Professor ' (George Saintsbury) in *The Times
Literary Supplement*, October 27, 1945. A *jeroboam*, a very large
goblet, bowl, bottle, has been named after *Jeroboam*, the *first* of
all the kings of Israel : see especially 1 *Kings*, xiii, 22.
Compare **jorum.**

jerry, slang for ' chamber-pot '. W thinks that this *jerry = Jerry* :
such a personification as appears in the various **jack** terms.
Diffidently I propose a slangy corruption of **jeroboam.**

jerry-built. ' The A.V. [of the Bible] became part of English
literature and left its imprint in a thousand ways upon English
idiom and usage—*e.g.*, Tarry at Jericho till your beards grow,
Adullamites, safe and sound, old wives' tales, pride goeth before
a fall, and perhaps jerry-built houses (cf. the walls of Jericho,
Joshua, vi, 20),' Stanley Cook, *An Introduction to the Bible*, 1945 :
' So the people shouted when the priests blew with the
trumpets : and it came to pass, when the people heard the
sound of the trumpet, and the people shouted with a great
shout, that the wall fell down flat, so that the people went up
into the city, every man straight before him, and they took the
city '.

jerry-hat and **jerry-shop** would, as W has suggested, appear to
have resulted from the influence of Pierce Egan's *Life in
London*, which, published in 1821, became ' the rage ': it
affords a picture of high life and low, of the fast fashionable
(Tom and *Jerry*), the sporting gentry, the drinking.

jerrymander. See **gerrymander.**

jersey is that kind of knitted jacket of which the wool was
originally made of *Jersey cloth*, cloth manufactured in Jersey, the
largest and southernmost of the Channel Islands. The Latin
name for the island is (*insula*) *Caesarea* : Caesar's Isle.
(For *Jersey justice* and *Jersey wagon*, see Border-Liners—i.e.
the 2nd List.)

jerusalem is short for *Jerusalem pony*, obsolete slang for a donkey,
with reference to Christ's ride into Jerusalem on a donkey.
Jerusalem comes from the Greek *Hierousalem*, itself from the
Hebrew *Yerushalaim* ; *Hiero-* of the Greek form of the name has
been assimilated to Greek *hieros*, ' holy '.

Jesuit ; jesuitical (in transferred sense—the literal sense
obviously being spelt *J*—).

A Dissenter, in 1688, is in Jane Lane's historical novel, *England for Sale*, 1943, represented as saying, ' I am no Jesuit, and I will not use evil means to accomplish a good end '.

Owing to the tendency of a very few but influential Jesuits to concern themselves with English politics of ca. 1550–1710, *Jesuit* came, in the minds of many, to bear the secondary meaning, ' underground political intriguer ', and because of the Jesuits' skill in debate, the term still, to some, connotes ' casuist ' or ' sophist '; likewise *Jesuitical* came to connote ' unscrupulous in argument, unscrupulous in intrigue; casuistical '. To at least one non-Catholic, these terms appear to have become obsolete and invidious and unjust.

Concerning the erroneous belief held by many Protestants that ' The end justifies the means ' is a Jesuit tenet, *The New Catholic Dictionary* (New York, 1929) has this entry : ' *End Justifies the Means*, a maxim which is true if the end and the means be good, not if either be evil. This maxim, or practice, was attributed to the early Christians in the sense that they were doing evil in order to obtain something good. " And not rather (as we are slandered, and as some affirm that we say) let us do evil, that there may come some good? " (*Romans*, iii). The Jesuits were accused [by Protestants] of approving any evil means, in order to attain their end.' In 1903 Count Hoensbrach alleged that the slander was well founded and, when challenged, ' submitted passages from thirteen leading Jesuit theologians . . . . . . The Supreme Court of Cologne, 30th March, 1905, decided that in no one of the citations was the maxim employed in the sense attributed to the Jesuits.'

' They would call themselves " of the Company of Jesus ", using the word in the military sense of a compact fighting force under one direct command. That form of the title is still in use in some languages, but in Latin it became " Societas " '— in English, the Society of Jesus (abbreviated *S.J.*)—' and the name " Jesuit " (" Jesuita ") for its members was really an accident, being at first applied as a nickname in derision of their supposed arrogation to themselves of a specially favoured intimacy with Our Lord ' (R. H. J. Steuart, S.J., *Diversity in Holiness*, 1938). *Jesuit* = Latin *Jesuita*, i.e. *Jesu* + the agential *ita*.

For the rise and early vicissitudes of the Society, even a Protestant cannot do better than to read *The Origin of the Jesuits*, by James Brodrick, S.J., 1940.

jet, the black mineral, comes from that river and town of Lycia (part of Asia Minor) where first it was mined : *Gagas* or *Gangai*. The Greek name was *gagates*, ' (mineral) of Gagas '; a name adopted by the Romans. Gallicized, this name appears as *jayet*: hence Modern French *jaïet* or *jais*, and English *jet*.

Jezebel is often used figuratively for a bold-faced, evil prostitute or a bedizened woman of not invincible virtue, a harridan.

' And when Jehu was come to Jezreel, Jezebel heard of it; and she painted her face, and tired her head, and looked out at a window . . . . . . He trode her underfoot . . . and said, Go see now this cursed woman, and bury her,' 2 *Kings*, ix, 30–34.

Wife of Ahab, she had a name that appropriately means ' Oath of Baal '.

Jill. See **gill.**

jilt. The early forms of the word, *gillet* or *jillet*, show that it is a diminutive of *Gill* or *Jill*. Like that of *flirt*, its sense has been softened by the passage of time. (W.)

Jim Crow. From an old (pre-1838) Negro song and a character therein, *Jim Crow* (from his colour)—later *Jim crow*—came to mean a Negro, and *to dance Jim Crow* to jump or dance in accordance with the words and the music of the song. *Jim Crow* became an adjective, with many senses, the two most important being, ca. 1830–1900, ' dexterous; tricky; double-dealing' and *Jim Crow car*, a car that, on train or tram, is set aside for compulsory use by Negroes.

jim-dandy, ' excellent '; **Jim Dandy,** ' a fine or admirable person or, derivatively, thing '. The adjective comes from the noun, which is a personification of the American national adjective *dandy*. *Jim* reflects the popularity of *James* as a given-name.

jimmy. See **jemmy.**

Jimmy Valentine. A master burglar; properly, a diabolically adept safe-opener. This 20th-Century Americanism arises from a story by O. Henry (1862–1910) : that story, ' A Retrieved Reformation ', was, by Paul Armstrong in 1909, turned into a play, *Alias Jimmy Valentine*, wherein the handling of the reformed-burglar theme reinforced the already considerable popularity of the story : before the end of 1910, Jimmy Valentine had been admitted to the American pantheon. The conception of this burglar owes something to the professional career and attractive character of a fellow convict, and all film

228

land references to Jimmy Valentine imply a burglarious Robin Hood, a knight among 'box-men', an otherwise upright and a quite romantic figure.

'The yeggs'—the safe-breakers of ca. 1890–1914—'smiled at the "Alias Jimmy Valentine" brand of fiction,' says Jim Tully, who knew this species of American fauna, in *The American Mercury* of April 1933.

'If anyone ever tells you a Jimmy Valentine story about a screwsman with sensitive fingers, opening a peter by listening to the tumblers falling, call him a liar,' Charles Prior, *So I Wrote It*, 1937, the author nevertheless admitting that perhaps a certain bank-robber did once possess this aptitude.

jimpson is loose for *jimson*, short for *jimson* (originally *Jimson*) *weed*, a colloquial re-shaping of *Jamestown weed*, from *Jamestown* in the old colony and state of Virginia. *Jamestown weed* is recorded by the DAE for as early as 1687. This poisonous Asiatic weed—often mentioned as *datura*—was early naturalized in North America, and Jamestown was the early capital (1607–98) of Virginia and 'the first permanent English settlement within the boundaries of the present U.S.' (Hart).

jingo, 'a noisy, blustering, fire-eating patriot' and, as obsolescent adjective, 'noisily and vulgarly dashing', comes from *by jingo* in popular songs—for instance, 'We don't want to fight, but, by jingo! if we *do*'; the interjection sometimes takes the form, *by the living jingo!*

The OED holds that *jingo*—like **hocus-pocus**—originated in a piece of that gibberish or patter with which a conjuror distracts the audience's attention from his sleight-of-hand. I prefer Ernest Weekley's explanation. 'Perhaps Basque *Jinko*, *Jainko*, God. It may have been picked up from Basque sailors, who were always employed as harpooners by the early whalers.' Dates are against the possibility that the origin lies in the name of 'the soldier-queen Jingo, still worshipped by the chivalrous sailors of the Mikado' (L. W. Lyde, *The Continent of Asia*, 1933).

Joan of Arc. 'She felt something of a Joan of Arc. Hers had been a high purpose . . . Fearlessly she had endeavoured,' Charles Francis Coe, *G-Man*, 1936. Joan of Arc, born in 1412 of peasant stock in the village of Domrémy (now Domrémy-la-Pucelle: of the Maid), near the Lorraine frontier, led the French army, recovered the French crown for Charles VII, and, betrayed to the English, was burnt at the stake in 1431. Jeanne d'Arc, la Pucelle, 'The Maid of Orleans', was not canonized until 1919. Inspired, fearless, self-dedicated, she still awaits an adequate biography : despite the rationalists, the psychologists, even the historians, she remains an enigmatic figure.

joannes. See **johannes.**

Job; Job's comforter; jobation (by folk-etymology : **jawbation**). ' *Job*, one of the greatest of the world's writings, is an arraignment of God's rule, a passionate discussion of the justice, or rather the lack of it, in the world, by a man undeservedly tormented and suffering . . . . . . The drama of Job, one of the three typically righteous men of old . . ., is set in a popular prose frame which describes how the Satan . . . was permitted by God to afflict him in body and estate,' Stanley Cook, *An Introduction to The Bible*, 1945.

Job's comforter comes from the Book of *Job*, xvi, 1–2, ' Then Job answered and said, I have heard many such things : miserable comforters are ye all ' ; the ' lectures ' delivered by these comforters have likewise given us *jobation*.

Job's turkey, used for comparison, is an imaginary bird *as patient* and *as poor as Job*. The *patient* phrase, which is recorded for 1824, seems to have been originally a euphemism, as also was the *poor* one (1830). In *The Valley of the Moon*, 1913, Jack London referred to the Dalmatian immigrants as being ' poorer than Job's turkey ' (DAE).

jockey. In 1698, one B.E., Gent., issued his *Dictionary of the Canting Crew* and in it he defined *jockeys* as ' rank horse-coursers, race-riders [jockeys in the modern sense] ; also hucksters or sellers of horses, very slippery fellows to deal with '—whence *to jockey*, ' to swindle '. The word is a personification, *jockey* being *Jockey*, diminutive of *Jock*, the North Country and Scottish form of *Jack*. (W.)

Compare, therefore, **jack.**

jockteleg figures thus in Webster : ' *jockteleg*. A large clasp knife. *Scottish*.' The OED cold-waters the theory mentioned by W : ' Said (1776) to be for *Jacques de Liège*, a cutler. This may be a myth, but has a parallel in French *eustache*, knife carried by an apache, from *Eustache Dubois*, cutler at Saint-Etienne.' Tentatively I suggest that *jack* (Scottish *jock*) is used for so very many tools and implements that the origin is a *jack de Liège*, a knife of—made at—Liège, famous for its manufactures, even in medieval times ; the close connexion between Scotland and France is notorious. See **jack-knife.**

jodhpurs, baggy-seated riding breeches fitting the leg closely from knee to ankle, is short for *Jodhpur breeches*. Now Jodhpur is the name of a state in Rajputana (India) : the breeches were not made there, but they have, through the pleasure-riding sahibs and memsahibs, become associated with that state. Neither The OED nor Webster nor W can tell us the reason for that traditional association. Probably there is no reason more precise than that kind of reason which lies behind the association of Poona with ultra-martial, rather ' dim ' Army officers.

joe. See **half joe.**

Joe Miller, a jest-book, a jest—especially a stale one, commemorates the fact that a jest-book published in 1739 and achieving a very considerable success was entitled *Joe Miller's Jest-Book,* or *The Wit's Vade Mecum,* by one John Mottley, who tells only three stories about Joseph Miller (1684–1738), an English actor attached to Drury Lane from 1709 onwards—a famous actor of comedy. The title was an unwarrantable publicity stunt.

joey means a fourpenny-piece : *joey* equals *Joey,* diminutive of *Joe,* itself familiar for *Joseph,* the reference being to *Joseph* Hume (1777–1855), English politician and an authority upon finance. The American *joey* for a circus-clown comes from *Joseph* Grimaldi (1779–1837), the most famous of all English circus-clowns. The Australian *joey* for a young kangaroo is a ' Hobson-Jobson ' for the Aboriginal *joè.* (For other senses, consult my *A Dictionary of Slang.*)

johannes; also **joannes.** See **half joe.**

johannisberger. This delicate white wine takes its name from *Johannisberg* in the Rheingau region of Germany. ' The volcanic area is much the most important in Hesse-Nassau, with its characteristic springs . . . and its magnificent vineyards—in the shelter of the Taunus, on rich volcanic soil, and facing full on the Rheingau " lake ", off which sunshine is reflected or mist is sent up to the slopes of Hockheim, Johannisberg, Geisenheim, Rudesheim, Rauenthal, etc.,' Lionel W. Lyde, *The Continent of Europe,* 1913. *Johannisberg* means ' John's mount '; and the name passed from the castle to the dependent village and to the surrounding district.

John, like its hypocoristic or familiar or diminutive form, or pet-name **Jack,** is used in so many ways, singly and in combination, simply because it is the most popular of all given-names in

231

the British Empire—and, in one form or another, in the world. See, e.g., PNTC.

John a'Dreams ; J. a'Nokes and a'Stiles ; John Barleycorn. In all these terms, *John* (cf. **Jack**) is simply a personification of the final element ; *a'Nokes* is ' at the oaks ', *a' Stiles* is ' at the stiles '—two surnames of the same type as *John Doe* and *Richard Roe*. *John Barleycorn* humorously alludes to *barley* as used in whiskey and in malt liquor.

John apple. See **applejohn.**

John Bull. In reference to the New Stone Age, S. E. Winbolt, *Britain B.C.* (1943), has written, ' In essentials the modern conditions of life begin : the distant prototype of John Bull, the farmer, comes on the scene '. *John Bull* originally typified the farmer, the pastoralist, the *John* (or *every man Jack*) that kept a bull. As a symbolic figure, he very rapidly became popular after the publication of Arbuthnot's set of satirical pamphlets, *The History of John Bull,* 1712.

John Doe and **Richard Roe** are the complementary signatories to any legal agreement : *John* and *Richard,* because they are such common given-names ; *Roe* rhymes with *Doe* ; and *Doe* is a gentle, agreeable, doe-like fellow. Compare the earlier *John a' Nokes* and *John a'Stiles,* at the oaks and at the stiles.

John Hancock. ' All I want you to do is to sign your John Hancock at the bottom. We'll do the rest,' Rex Grayson, *Snatch and Grab,* 1938.

The origin of the American slang-become-colloquial *John Hancock,* ' one's own name ; especially, one's signature ' resides in the fact that the American patriot John Hancock not merely signed the Declaration of Independence but was the first signer. Hancock (1737–93) was later to be the first governor of Massachusetts.

johnny ; Johnny. The former is slang for ' chap, fellow ; in U.S.A. : guy '. The latter, short for *stage-door Johnny,* has almost become Standard English ; the type he represented flourished ca. 1888–July 1914.

See the quotation ushering-in the Introduction.

Johnny not only pet-forms *John* but softens it : renders it familiar : causes the person to be regarded with a friendly or, at least, a tolerant or an amused eye and mind.

232

Johnsonese; Johnsonian. 'Byron's religious intuitions are based on a preliminary acceptance of the conventional, seen in the robust Johnsonian phraseology—as well as thought—of

> I speak not of men's creeds : they rest between
> Man and his Maker '
> (G. Wilson Knight, *The Burning Oracle*, 1939).

'Southey's moral fervor . . . sharpened the Johnsonian ring of some of the sentences' (Raymond D. Havens, in *Publications of the Modern Language Association of America*, December 1945).

Whereas *Johnsonian* has, in the 20th Century, come to bear the predominant senses ' manly; forthright; filled with good, as opposed to mere common, sense ', *Johnsonese* retains its 19th-Century meaning, ' a sesquipedalian terminology and a riotous licence of latinisms '. *To die very poor* is good English, *to expire in circumstances of dire indigence* would be Johnsonese. If at times he appeared desirous of popularizing his Dictionary, Johnson could, and often did, write tersely and ' Anglo-Saxonly ', whether in verse or in prose.

As *Williamson* is *William's son*, and *Jackson* is *Jack's son*, so *Johnson* is *John's son*.

Jonah, ' a bringer of bad luck '. The prophet Jonah, *en route* for Tarshish, met with a tempest : ' And they said every one to his fellow, Come, and let us cast lots, that we may know for whose cause this evil is upon us. So they cast lots, and the lot fell upon Jonah ' (*Jonah*, i, 7). Meredith, felicitous neologist, used *Jonah* for ' to cast (a person) overboard '.

' They say that that guy Jonah in the whale's belly had a tough time, but I'm willing to lay anybody a million to one that Mr Jonah's experience was a cakewalk compared to what I endured on that railroad barge on the Chesapeake Bay,' Broadway Jack (really, Jack Callahan, author of *Man's Grim Justice*, 1929) in *Detective Fiction Weekly*, May 2, 1936.

Jonathan. See **David and Jonathan** in the Appendix.
A **jonathan** is a red apple, maturing in the late autumn, presumably because, originally, it was topically associated with a well-known gardener. Whence *jonathan* (or *J.*) *freckle*, a discoloration and disease that affects apples, especially jonathans.

Jordan. In slang, *jordan* is a chamber-pot. The reference is to the Palestinian river Jordan and its valley. The valley contains the river, as the pot the urine. It so happens—most

relevantly to our purpose—that the Jordan valley is a tru
river-valley, from a quarter to a half a mile wide and also tha
the Jordan river (literally, the plunger-down) flows swiftly, it
average fall, between the Lake of Galilee and the Dead Sea
being ten feet in every mile. See especially L. W. Lyde, *Asi*
(1933), where, moreover, we hear of ' the saline and mudd
flood of Jordan '.

As a transitive verb, *jordan = Jordan*, ' to refine (pulp—fo
papermaking) in a Jordan engine ', invented by Joseph Jordan

jorum, loosely a jug or a bowl, strictly a large drinking-vessel (o
its contents), is a bonhomous colloquialism.

' Then Toi sent Joram his son unto King David, to salut
him . . . And Joram brought with him vessels of silver, and
vessels of gold, and vessels of brass,' 2 *Samuel*, viii, 10.

Compare **jeroboam.**

joseph in the 18th and early 19th Century meant either
woman's riding coat or a man's overcoat. ' Perhaps wit
obscure allusion to *Genesis* xxxix, 12 ' (W) :

' And she '—Potiphar's wife—' caught him '—Joseph—' b
his garment '. Because *joseph* is recorded earlier than *benjami*
(q.v.), the latter term owes its origin to the ' prompting ' of th
former.

josie is either a bodice or a woman's close-fitting outer wais
An Americanism, it derives from **joseph** and is therefor
eligible only at second-hand.

joskin, a country bumpkin, a yokel, a boor, may be a diminutiv
of *Joseph* (cf. **Hodge**), much as *rube* and *hick*, American slan
synonyms for a ' hayseed ', are diminutives of *Reuben* an
Richard.

joule, unit of work or energy in electricity, owes its origin t
James Prescott Joule (1818–89), who in 1840 published paper
concerning his attempt, with a unit of his own, to measur
electric current and, in the same year, *On the Production of Hee
by Voltaic Energy*, wherein he propounded what has come to b
known as Joule's Law. English physicist, he owed much, a
a student, to John Dalton.

Compare **ampère, coulomb, farad, maxwell, volt, watt**

jovial; Jove, by; Jovian. ' I found Dinah Mason sittin
there in Jovian '—Olympian—' superiority, looking dow
benignly on the struggling masses on the floor below ' (as th

234

gods did on struggling humanity), Richard Sale, 'A Hearse for Hiawatha', in *Detective Fiction Weekly*, January 29, 1938.

In Greek mythology, *Jove* was not conspicuously *jovial*, except perhaps towards those country wenches whom he deigned to tumble in the hay; French, from the Italian *gioviale*, 'born under the planet Jove' and therefore generous, big-hearted. The exclamatory *by Jove* began as a euphemism for *by God!*

Juan, Don. Don Juan (i.e., John), irresistible to women as a refined, hedonistic, cynical wooer, love-maker, lover (and, finally, heartless leaver), comes into all the literatures of Europe, thence to America and elsewhere, from a Spanish tradition wherein, as Don Juan Tenorio, of Seville, he kills in a duel the father of the girl he has attempted to ravish. Visiting the tomb, Juan invites the statue to a banquet; accepting, the statue seizes him and delivers him to hell. Don Juan appears in *El Burlador de Sevila*, by Tirso de Molina (1571–1641), in Molière's *Le Festin de Pierre* (1645), also in plays by Thomas Corneille, Shadwell, Goldoni, in Mozart's great opera, *Don Giovanni*, and above all—for 19th–20th-Century Europe—in Byron's *Don Juan* (1819–24).

Compare **Lothario** and **Lovelace.**

Judas and **judas:** 'ineffable, infamous traitor, especially against spirituality' (hence **Judas-kiss**) and 'peep-hole in a door'. 'I allowed the traitors to pay for my lunch, and reflected over the cigar of Judas that Judas has at least one merit: he can afford to buy good cigars' (W. L. George, *The Triumph of Gallio*, 1924).—'He spied me, slid out, and with an indescribable Judas look at me, fled away' (Stanley Weyman, *The Red Cockade*, 1908).

Judas Iscariot, who sold Christ for thirty pieces of silver. His case has been ably put by R. H. Horne in a poetic drama named after The Arch-Vendor.

For **Judas-coloured,** see **Cain-coloured.**

judy. As *Judy* (the pet-form of *Judith*), it means a woman resembling the Judy of the puppet-show 'Punch and Judy', especially a ridiculous-looking woman. As *judy*, it is, in 19th–20th-Century slang, a girl or young woman, especially if less good than is advisable: compare **doll** and **moll, Flossie** and **Katy.**

jug, a ewer or a pitcher (derivatively, in slang, a prison—hence, 'to put in prison'), derives from *Jug*, a pet-form of *Judith* (compare **judy**) and of *Joan*, both being names of women, especially of maid-servants; it is mostly women who deal with jugs. Moreover, personification of vessels is frequent, as we see from such terms as **goblet** and **Jack**.

juggernaut, rather more usual than—and preferable to—*Juggernaut car*, is figuratively employed for an institution, a custom, an idea to which one insensately sacrifices oneself—or somebody else. ' One hope was theirs as a people : to put themselves beyond the pursuit of a juggernaut,' Jane Lane, *He Stooped to Conquer*, 1944.

The old Dravidians built on the Puri sands a great pagoda—the Jagannath or Juggernaut. ' Their most famous king, Kharavela (200 B.C.), was a devout Jain, a great musician, a shipbuilder; and an architect . . . He seems to have begun the processions connected with the Juggernaut, but the first " car " carried a wooden image of King Ketu, his predecessor by 1300 years ' (L. W. Lyde, *Asia*, 1933). This image, which came to possess the attributes of an idol, was annually drawn through the streets of Puri : and under the wheels of this monstrous car, devotees cast themselves—or, at least, are legendarily supposed to have done so : for Lyde would seem to be correct in declaring that, ' so far from the " Juggernaut Car " procession being a scene of merciless sacrifice of human lives, a single drop of blood from some hysterical suicide defiled the ceremony and made it ineffectual ! ' In 1360, Firuz, the Sultan of Delhi, ' a rigid Muslim ', marched an army into Orissa, ' his objective being Puri, famous for the great temple of Jagannath. He reached Puri, occupied the raja's palace, and is said to have sent the great idol to Delhi, to be trodden underfoot by the faithful ' (*The Cambridge Shorter History of India*, 1934). The Hindustani *Jagannath* represents the Sanskrit *Jagannatha*, which combines *jagat*, ' the world ', with *natha*, ' lord, master '.

' " I'm not denying it's useful having an assistant with enough private means of his own to afford a death-dealing juggernaut like this tin buggy ", said Cromwell grudgingly ' (and most unfairly of an Alvis sports car), Victor Gunn, *The Dead Man Laughs*, 1944.
Cf. **Moloch.**

juggins is either a jocular, rhyming variation of **muggins** or a diminutive of *jug*, itself being *Jug* (see **jug**) : in either case, it is eligible. The sense ' fool or simpleton ', can, in the latter derivation, be accounted for by the fact that serving-maids are often apprehended as stupid.

julienne comes from the French *potage à la julienne*, soup in the manner of *Julien* (Julian) ; bestowed by the chef of the Comte de Julienne. *Julien* derives from Latin *Julianus*, itself from *Julius* (strictly *Iulius*).

Juliet. See **Romeo and Juliet.**

junkerism is the beliefs, the manners, of the nobles of the Prussian aristocracy ; strictly *Junker* is a young (German *jung*) Prussian noble. The term connotes arrogance, haughtiness, social exclusiveness, unbending conservatism, and martial tradition, and it is often applied to other nations and other circumstances, when only is the small *j* correctly used.

Juno ; Junoesque or **j—.** Any majestic, queenly, handsome, large-breasted woman ; feminine in a large and regal way.

In *The Observer* of May 13, 1945, Lionel Hale, in his Cinema review, remarks of a certain character that ' His wife is something of a Juno and something of a Jezebel '.

Juno, the wife of Jupiter, was a stately goddess, possessed of considerably more dignity than her husband, who was constantly assailing the chastity of attractive women and whose motto seems to have been ' Je prends mon bien où je le trouve '. Not that Juno lacked her moments.

jurassic, a geological term, means ' characterized by the presence, in considerable quantities, of granular limestone ' : as are the *Jura* mountains separating France from Switzerland.

' In what is known as the Jurassic period in the geological history of the earth, there suddenly developed in the course of animal evolution a vast number of huge reptiles,' James Truslow Adams, *The Epic of America*, (revised edition) 1938.

Jurassic—spelt with a capital only in the literal sense ' of or in the Jura mountains '—represents the French *jurassique* and has been formed on the analogy of the geological *liassic* (from *lias*) and *triassic* (from *trias*). For a geological parallel, compare **laurentian.**

Juvenalian, in the senses ' indignantly or fierily satirical ', ' loftily or eloquently condemnatory ', with particular reference to morals public and private, might almost be written with a small *j*.

Juvenal, greatest of Roman satirists and one of the world's greatest, was born ca. A.D. 65 and at the height of his powers ca. 98–128. In his sixteen satires, which have been imitated by such English poets as Dryden, Swift, Johnson, he savagely attacks the fatuities, the abuses, the vices of the Rome of his day, in a vigorous, powerful, ironical, terse, epigrammatic style, and with tremendous verve, but too pessimistically and with a too thorough-going concentration upon life's seamier side.

K

kabistan or **Kabistan.**   In full, **Kabistan rug.**   See **baku.**

kaiser.   See **czar.**

kalmia, a dwarf American laurel, takes its name (variant *calmia*) from Peter Kalm (1715–79), the Swedish botanist and a friend of Linnaeus.   In 1748–51 he travelled North America on a survey of its Natural History and in 1753–61 published, in three volumes, an account of his travels and his finds and findings.   'The Mountain Laurel, Kalmia latifolia, is . . . declared to be the state flower of the State of Connecticut' (*Public Acts of 1907*: cited by James Gould Cozzens in *A Cure of Flesh*, 1933).

kaolin is a fine white clay used in the making of porcelain; it results from the composition of feldspar—a crystalline mineral, either white or flesh-red in colour.
   Kaolin receives its name from Mt Kaoling in the Kiangsi province of China.   'The [tea] gardens [of north-east Kiangsi] are rather in the lee of the Kauling—or *Kaolin* ("High Ridge")—crest, with less rain and poorer soil.   And, in any case, the value of this ridge is in its feldspar . . . . . . The Imperial Porcelain works remain where the emperor King-tè founded them in the eleventh century—at King-te-chen' (L. W. Lyde, *Asia*, 1933).

karakul.   See **caracul.**

karst.   'Yucatan is an extension of the Gulf Coastal Plain corresponding in structure to the peninsula of Florida.   Both are developed on limestone and have the characteristics of a low karst region,' Ll. Rodwell Jones & P. W. Bryan, *North America*, (7th edition) 1946.
   From that infertile limestone plateau between the Adriatic and Carniola which is characterized by sudden ridges, caverns, subterranean streams.

238

Katy and **Kitty.**   For the latter, see the separate entry.   *Katy*, familiar for *Kate* (itself from *Catherine*), has been used in many common-property connexions simply because of the prevalence of this given-name.   Compare **moll.**

katydid, a large, green, tree-haunting American insect of the locust family, makes a chattering noise that sounds like a stridulously enunciated *Katy did! Katy did!* : the name, therefore, should be compared with that of the *mopoke*, often called—after its cry—the *morepork*, and with the *whippoorwill* (*Whip poor Will*).
     'The amazing concert of crickets and katydids,' Rex Stout, *Double for Death*, (English edition) 1940.

keen as mustard, as.   This colloquialism springs from good advertising : *as keen as mustard = as keen's mustard = as Keene's mustard*, a very well-known English brand of mustard.   All mustard has a keen impact on the palate.

keeshond.   This small wolf-coloured dog, much esteemed in Holland, would seem to qualify, though the precise etymology is obscure.   The word *keeshond* appears to come from *Kees hond*; *hond* obviously means 'dog'; *Kees* is the diminutive of *Cornelis*, the Dutch form of *Cornelius*.   But why Cornelius?

kennedya, a perennial herbaceous climber, was named, at the beginning of the 19th Century, after Kennedy, a Hammersmith (London) gardener, who has thus earned himself a remote but immarcescible fame. *Kennedy-ia*, *Kennedyia*, becomes *kennedya*.
     'There was the purple *Kennedia*, climbing here, there, and everywhere ; and, also, the scarlet *Kennedia*, creeping along the ground, in the same fantastic forms,' J. W., *Perils, Pastimes and Pleasures*, 1849 (a book dealing with New South Wales).

kerria is a golden-flowered, rosaceous shrub, native to Japan. In this word, William Ker, a well-reputed English collector of botanical specimens, was in 1816 honoured by Augustin de Candolle (1778–1841), a much more notable person—a Swiss botanist.
     Ker + intrusive *r* + the latinized *-ia* that characterizes shrub and flower names.

kerrite, known only to mineralogists and a few eccentrics, is an American property and an American word, formed from the
239

name of Professor W. C. *Kerr* (1827–85), a noted American geologist. Contrast **kerria**.

kersey. This coarse, usually ribbed, narrow cloth, made from wool, may take its name from Kersey, a village situated in the Sudbury division of Suffolk and about ten miles west of Ipswich. In ' Fourteenth Century England ' (*An Historical Geography of England before 1800*, ed. H. C. Darby, 1936), Dr R. A. Pelham uncompromisingly states that ' The village of Kersey . . ., like the more renowned village of Worsted, had given its name to a type of cloth that was not being made exclusively in East Anglia during the fourteenth century '.

' To Venice, Leghorn, Florence, Genoa, Civita Vecchia, and other parts of Italy, 100 Dutch sail '—annually in the 17th Century—' carried herrings, pilchards, lead, tin, and Devonshire kerseys,' E. G. R. Taylor, *Late Tudor and Early Stuart Geography*, 1934.

kerseymere. See **cashmere**.

Ketch, Jack. *Jack Ketch*, as a synonym (now obsolescent) for ' hangman ' or ' executioner ', commemorates a real person : a very notorious fellow, the Government or ' common ' executioner of ca. 1662–86, Jack Ketch became a mark of execration, not because he was a good executioner but because he was a barbarous one. Restoration memoirs tell of his brutality at the executions of political offenders, especially the Duke of Monmouth.

kidderminster = *K. carpet*. Kidderminster, fourteen miles north of Worcester (England), is a market-town. ' The manufacture of carpets . . . was introduced in 1735, but the carpets now made here are no longer chiefly the so-called K. (an inferior kind made wholly of wool), but Brussels, Wiltons, Axminsters and other high-class fabrics,' George Chisholm, *The Times Gazetteer of the World*, 1895.

killick, a heavy stone used as an anchor, hence any small anchor, is of uncertain origin. Not impossibly from some sailor, named Killick and forced in an emergency to adopt the expedient of a large stone used as an anchor ; jests and experiments by others would soon have caused this type of anchor to be called a killick, at first in fun and then in nautical earnest.

kirk. See **church**.

it-cat, a less-than-half-length portrait nevertheless including the hands, derives from the famous Kit-Cat Club of the late 17th–18th Centuries : the dining-room of its chief 18th-Century premises was so low that the members' portraits hanging there had to be less than half-size. The club's name embalms the fragrant memory of Christopher (familiarly *Kit*) *Cat*—or it may have been *Cat*ling—the keeper of the pie-house where, in the 17th Century, the club used to meet.

itty, the pool in certain card games. As *Catherine* became *Kate* and *Cat*, so *Kate* was diminished to *Kitty*; the connexion between *cat* and *kitten* (with its diminutive *kitty*) is obvious. The card-game sense may have originated thus : one throws money into the pool or kitty as a roistering blade threw coins into a wanton's lap—and *Kate*, like *Doll* and *Moll*, is an old name for a prostitute or a wanton.

iyuse is an obsolete variant of **cayuse.**

laxon is short for *Klaxon horn*, from the *Klaxon* Company—its manufacturers. Oddly (?), the very name *Klaxon* suggests an echoic origin : compare the Greek *klazein*, ' to make a sharp, abrupt sound ' (stem *klaz*), from the likewise echoic *klankxo*.

nickerbockers, which yields **knickers** and, at second remove, **cami-knickers** and **cami-bockers.**

The garment is so named from their resemblance to the Dutchmen's knee-breeches in the illustrations made by George Cruikshank (1792–1878) for Washington Irving's *History of New York* (published in 1809), which professed to have been written by Diedrich *Knickerbocker*. The actual Knickerbocker family arrived in America in the 1670's.

obold, a familiar spirit, peculiar to mines—derivatively, to houses—is merely a special use of the personal name *Kobold*. For further details, see **cobalt.**

' The centre-piece showed the Court of the Beer King—a jovial and venerable figure attended by a host of dwarfs and kobolds, all holding on high enormous mugs of beer,' Arthur Machen, *Holy Terrors*, 1946.

kodak does not qualify, for not only is it an arbitrary name but also it is proprietary—and proper only to a particular make of portable camera. The name was arbitrarily formed by Mr

George Eastman (1854–1932), American industrialist and inventor; he devised the Kodak in 1888.]

koepenick, 'a military impostor'. As W has phrased it, ' Th " Captain of Koepenick ", a Berlin cobbler named Voigh succeeded (1906), with the help of a second-hand uniform, persuading the local military to help him raid the bank. good example of the docility of the Prussian soldier.' Th place-name has supplanted the surname.

kohinoor, allusive for any ' very large diamond ', hence figu ative for ' something extremely precious; something that is th finest of its kind ', became famous in 1849, when the Punja was annexed and the Kohinoor diamond joined the glitterin ranks of the Crown jewels of Britain. In the Persian, the wor means ' mountain of light ': a name iridescent with Orient brilliance.

kolinsky. '. . . That morning on Sixth Avenue when Myrt Menchen stole the kolinsky muff,' Arthur Stringer, *The Hou of Intrigue*, 1918. *Kolinski*, the name of a well-known kind fur, is simply the Russian for ' of Kola ', a district in north eastern Russia; otherwise known as *Siberian mink*.

kouiaviak. See the entry at **mazurka.**

krakowiak. See **cracovienne.**

krimmer; also **krimma** or **crimmer.** Fur, grey or black made from the fleeces of young lambs reared in or near th *Crimea*. The name is derived from the form *Krim*, of whic *Crimea* is a latinistic derivation. Compare *Crim Tartary*, whic embodies the memory of the ancient Scythian folk known as th *Gimirrai* or *Cimmerians*.

Compare **astrakhan** and **caracul,** likewise much used fo coat-collars.

kuba or **Kuba.** In full, *Kuba rug*. See **baku.**

kunzite, a gem—a spodumene occurring in lilac-lovely crystal takes its name from George Frederick Kunz (1856–1932), a American expert on precious stones. For many years wit Messrs Tiffany & Co. of New York, and special editor (gem and jewels) for Webster's *New International Dictionary*, he wro *Gems and Precious Stones of North America* and two other works o allied subjects.

242

kyanize, ' to impregnate (wood) with corrosive sublimate, to preserve it from decay ', is to effect a process patented by its inventor, J. H. Kyan (1774–1830); the process is known as *kyanizing*, and wood so treated is said to have been *kyanized*.

L

labrador. ' Among Labradors and creels and mackintoshes in the hall I met my only fellow-guest,' Peter Fleming, *A Story to Tell*, 1942.

Short for *Labrador dog* (or *retriever*), that variation of the **newfoundland** which came originally from Labrador and Newfoundland. The labrador is black, much smaller than the newfoundland, and excellent in hunting.

labradorescence; labradorite. The former means the dazzling coloration and play of colours emitted and exhibited by the mineral known as labradorite, that brilliant feldspar which was in 1780 named *Labradorstein* and which, at its best, comes from Labrador; the English, as is their way, have transmuted the Germanic word to a shape of their own.

labyrinth. ' For the first time, I felt the wonder of the fact that these men and women were living with me on this whirling planet . . . . . . We were marooned together on the island of earth . . . We were partners in the perilous adventure of life: the overarching sky above our heads; the countless dead under our feet. We were sharing a miracle together. We were dreaming in the same labyrinth,' Claude Houghton, *Six Lives and a Book*, 1943.—' The Frozen Labyrinth: An Essay on Milton ': G. Wilson Knight, *The Burning Oracle*, 1939.

The term comes from Greek *Laburinthos*, ' the name given to the maze in Crete, said to have been devised by Daedalus [see **daedal**], where the Minotaur . . . was kept . . . . . . The idea of a maze may have derived from the intricate plan of the great Minoan palace at Cnossus,' Sir Paul Harvey, who also says: ' The word " labyrinth " is of uncertain origin, perhaps from *labrus*, a Lydian or Carian word meaning double-headed axe ' (*The Oxford Companion to Classical Literature*). The Lydian —or Carian—origin seems more probable than the Egyptian suggested by Skeat.

laconic; laconicism or **laconism.** ' It was wrong to condemn a large, laconic man simply because he approximated so nearly

243

to the strong silent heroes of fiction,' Peter Fleming, *A Story to Tell*, 1942.

Via Latin from Greek *Lakōnikos*, ' of or like a *Lakon*—a Laconian, i.e. a Lacedaemonian, or Spartan '. The Spartans affected an extreme brevity of speech and a thoroughly British outward lack of emotion.

Lady Bountiful. ' Tess became a sort of Lady Bountiful to the countryside. Her generosities won true appreciation,' Charles Francis Coe, *G-Man*, 1936.

This pleasant character is a survival from Farquhar's delightful comedy, *The Beaux' Stratagem*, 1707 : W cites an apposite sentence from Chaucer, ' For she herself is honour and the root of bounty ' : in the play, Lady Bountiful ' cures all her neighbours of their distempers ' and spends half her income in charity.

Laïs has, among the literary, come to stand for a beautiful courtesan. In Ancient Greece there lived two hetairai of this name : the first, probably a Corinthian and certainly a **corinthian,** lived at the time of the Peloponnesian War (in the latter part of the 5th Century B.C.) and was as avaricious as she was beautiful ; the second, not at all avaricious but even more beautiful, was a rival of **Phrynë** and was, ironically in the temple of Aphrodite, stoned to death by Thessalian women— of greater virtue, less beauty—maddened with jealousy of her loveliness, which lured their men away to her **circean** charms.

lalique is short for the Lalique glassware mentioned in : ' She signed her name, laid down the bright emerald quill, blotted the page with a roller blotter of Lalique glass, folded the letter . . . and put it into an envelope ' : Francis Beeding, *The Twelve Disguises*, 1942.

And in : ' Imagine the Ritz, the Carlton, and Buckingham Palace rolled into one, a dash of rococo and a spicery of Lalique, and you will have some idea of what I found ' : Eric Ambler, *Cause for Alarm*, 1938.

René Lalique (1860?–1944), a French jeweller and glassmaker, manufactured many beautiful yet inexpensive objects in glass.

lamia, ' a sorceress, an enchantress ', perpetuates the memory of *Lamia*, a fabulous witch, a vampire that, addicted to children, occurs both in Greek and in Latin literature. Horace speaks of her, and Keats has immortalized her in *Lamia* ; Keats took the story from ' Anatomy ' Burton, who took it from Philostratus.

landau, landaulet (a little landau). The kind of coach thus denoted takes its name from the small but ancient Bavarian town of *Landau* ('land—especially a meadow—near water'), some eighteen miles north-west of Karlsruhe and in the palatinate of the Rhine. This coach was first built—in the 18th Century—at that place; its German name was *landauer Wagen*.

'These landaus and victorias at the Piraeus [ca. 1918] were in the last stages of dilapidation, like the evening clothes hanging in second-hand clothes shops,' Henry de Monfreid, *Hashish*, 1935.

For a place-name conveyance, compare **tilbury.**

Laodicean. 'The supremacy of Smyrna . . . pointed to the Gediz valley as the route for railway connexion with the plateau of [Asia Minor] . . ., though the easier route was up the Menderes valley—past sleepy Laodicea' (Lionel W. Lyde, *The Continent of Asia*; 2nd edition, 1938): that 'sleepy' bears upon the modern meaning of *Laodicean*: 'lukewarm, especially in religion (the original application) or in politics', a sense deriving from *Revelation*, iii, 15–16, (to the typical Laodicean) 'Thou art neither cold nor hot . . . So then because thou art lukewarm . . ., I will spue thee out of my mouth.' The Laodiceans were the inhabitants of a Greek city in Western Asia Minor—*Laodicea*, named after the mother of Seleucus I—Seleucus Nicator, founder in 312 B.C. of the Syrian monarchy. One of Thomas Hardy's minor novels bears the title *A Laodicean*; and in *Reflections in a Mirror*, 2nd Series, 1946, Charles Morgan admits, 'I have a reluctance that some may consider Laodicean to enrol myself in any band which claims a monopoly in truth'. Compare, too, the implications of

'His material home was a neutral country,
His stock-in-trade litmus paper,
His spiritual abode a Laodicean chantry,
His badge a chameleon couchant upon a cloud of vapour'
        Ronald Bottrall, *Farewell and Welcome*, 1945.

lapland or **laplander** is a kind of muffin, simple and white; F. E. Owen's American *Cook Book*, 1882, furnishes the recipe: 'One egg, one cup of milk, one cup of flour, pinch of salt; beat well' (DAE). Then there are the magnificent *Lapland azalea* and the slightly less splendid *Lapland rhododendron*; and, among birds, the *Lapland snow-bird* and the *Lapland waxwing*.

Laputan or, as Swift spells it, **Laputian.** In its derivative senses, 'visionary; scientifically chimerical; philosophically

ludicrous; "Heath-Robinsonish"; extravagantly im-
practical; merely theoretical—and remote from the facts'
the word should be written with a small *l*.

In Jonathan Swift's *Gulliver's Travels*, 1726, the third par
deals with the flying island of Laputa and its neighbouring
mainland (and capital), Lagado.

In Laputa, the 'wise' men (erudite, not wise) are so rap
away by their visionary speculations that in all mundand
matters they are more helpless—and much less practical—than
young children. The 'lesson' for the world of to-day is a:
clear, and as necessary, as it was in the 1720's.

Lares and Penates, with capitals: household gods. With
small initials: household goods, especially heirlooms and othe
prized possessions. The Lares—properly, the *Lares Familiare*
or *Domestici*—were Roman tutelary spirits of greater power and
wider scope than the Penates, who protected the store-cup
board. The latter word derives from *penus*, 'a temple
sanctuary', itself related to *penitus*, 'within'. *Lares* is the
plural of *Lar*, which, having an Etruscan origin, is yet cognate
with Latin *larva*, 'a ghost'.

larrikin is the Australian synonym for **hooligan** and the near
equivalent of the American **hoodlum.** Two proposed
origins; (1) from *larking*, (2) from the underworld *leary kinche*
('a wide boy'); may be dismissed with a kindly smile. Prob
ably *larrikin* is *Larrykin*, 'a little Larry', *Larry* being the pet
form of *Lawrence*. The term originated at Melbourne, where
in the 1860's and 1870's there were many Irishmen: and
Lawrence is a name common among the Irish. Compare the
colloquial simile, *as happy as Larry*.

lat is that unit of currency which, at about twenty-five to the
English pound, was established in 1922 by the state of Latvia
lat forms the first syllable of the Lett name of the country
Latvija.

Compare **belga** and **franc.**

latakia. 'The book lay face downwards on his legs, blu
Latakia smoke hung heavy and pungent about his head, whe
Mrs Guildford and Ethel came to him' (H. C. Bailey, *Riming
tons*, 1904).

Now, **latakia** is properly a tobacco of the type grown in o
near the port of, and in the region now known as, Latakia i
north-western Syria; hence, any tobacco of approximately the
same type. 'Sharon is still a fertile and flowery plain, beloved

of bees and Gargantuan thistles; once it was forested, and it grows admirable " Jaffa " oranges and " Latakia " tobacco,' Lionel W. Lyde, *The Continent of Asia*, where, against ' flowery ' (p. 306), we find the illuminating footnote, ' The famous " rose " was really a white narcissus, and the Philistine " lily of the valley " was a blue iris '. (In Latin, *rosa* and *lilium* tended to be generic.)

ateen. This triangular sail, so often seen even now on sailing-ships in the Mediterranean, preserves in its English shape the pronunciation of the French *latine*, short for *voile latine*, which probably answers to the Latin plural *vela latina*, Latin (i.e., Roman) sails. Roman sails were triangular : compare Spanish *a la Latina*, ' triangular '.

latinize; latinized. ' Instinct *originates* action ; reason is merely a " comparing " power . . . . . . So

> Reason raise o'er instinct as you can,
> In this 'tis God directs, in that 'tis Man—

" this " being, of course, " instinct " in Pope's slightly latinized syntax,' G. Wilson Knight, *The Burning Oracle*, 1939 : with a delicate literary instinct, the critic lower-cases ' latinized '.

Literally, ' to render into Latin ; give a Latin shape ', *latinize* represents Late Latin *latinizare*, ' to express in Latin ', from *latinus*, ' of Latium ' ; Latium was the region and country about Rome—the present *Campagna di Roma*—the region whence the Classical language took its name (*latinitas*).

laurentian (formerly *Laurentian*). ' From this shore line, over nearly the whole of the area of the present continent to the west, lay a great sea, which received deposits from this mountain land, as also from that other great positive area, the Laurentian Shield, to the north-east,' Ll. Rodwell Jones & R. W. Bryan, *North America*, (7th edition) 1946.

The laurentian is a geological formation, mostly gneiss and granite, belonging to the archaean period and characterizing the Laurentian Mountains of Canada, themselves named from the St. *Lawrence* River.

lavallière. ' Women's lockets and lavallieres are frequently " lifted " by the stone-getter ' (or thief specializing in the appropriation of precious stones), George C. Henderson, *Keys to Crookdom*, 1924.

In French, a *lavallière* is a loose fancy necktie ; in the U.S.A., it is sometimes applied to a tie-pin used with such a necktie.

This kind of necktie was affected by Mademoiselle Françoise

247

de La Baume Le Blanc, who (1644–1710) became Louis XIV'
mistress (ca. 1661–74) and Madame la Duchesse de L
Vallière; on her supersession (1674) by the Marquise d
Montespan, she suitably retired to a convent, where she ma
have written the *Réflexions sur la Miséricorde de Dieu*, 1685.

lawn. 'Evening comes in "a robe of darkest grain" an
"a sable stole of cypress lawn",' G. Wilson Knight, ' A
Essay on Milton '—in *The Burning Oracle*, 1939.

The word has been used in England since at least as early a
1415; sometimes, in the 15th–16th Centuries, as *Laune* (o
Laun or *Lan*) *linen*. For centuries this clothing material, a fin
linen, was made at *Laon*, a little to the north-west of Rheims
Laon; in Old French, *Lan*; comes from Latin *Laudunum* (itsel
of Celtic origin: compare **arras**).

Closely comparable is **cambric.**

lazar; Lazarus. The former is archaic for a diseased destitute
especially a leper, as in *lazar-house* and *lazaretto*; the latter, a
very poor man, a beggar, especially in contrast with **Dives**
A *lazaret* is also a quarantine ship or building.

' And there was a certain beggar named Lazarus, which wa
laid at his gate, full of sores, And desiring to be fed with th
crumbs which fell from the rich man's table ' (*Luke*, xvi, 20–21)
Lazarus = Greek *Lazaros* = Hebrew *Eleazar*, ' the God-aided '

' Zuta and his mob, kicked around by the Capone monopoly
were '—despite the very considerable money they made by thei
many rackets—' but a Lazarus crew snatching at the ric
man's '—Capone's—' table ': Fred D. Pasley, *Al Capone*, 1931

Lee-Enfield; Lee-Metford. The Lee-Enfield short repeating
·303 rifle was adopted by the War Office in 1904 and thereupo
manufactured at the great Government small-arms establish
ment at Enfield, just beyond the northern boundary of London
it had been invented by the Scottish-born American, James P
Lee (1831–1904). It succeeded the Lee-Metford, which hac
been adopted by the War Office in 1888 and which combinec
the basic invention of the Englishman William Metford (1824–
99) with improvements by Lee.

leghorn ' shorthands ' *Leghorn fowl* and *Leghorn straw*, the forme
reared at and near Leghorn, now Livorno, a port in north-wes
Italy, the latter coming from the wheat of the region. ' Ir
Tuscany [wheat] is grown as a spring crop, and is intentionall
" crowded ", with the result that there is a very quick growth
of the " leggy " and pliable kind needed in the straw-plai

industry of Leghorn, Pisa, and other Tuscan towns,' Lionel W. Lyde, *The Continent of Europe*.

emur, 'nocturnal mammal allied to the monkey and native to Madagascar', recalls its mythological, its penumbral origin in the *Lemures* or Roman maleficent spirits of the dead (in contrast to the Parentales), their festival being the *Lemuria*: ' Nocturnos lemures . . . rides ' (You will laugh at the night-haunting Lemurs), says Horace. ' Once a year as on our All Souls Eve, [the Lemures] hungrily revisit their loved ones,' says ' Palinurus ' in *The Unquiet Grave*, 1945; and of his pet lemurs Palinurus remarks, ' At last we would go to bed, bolting the doors while the lemurs cried in the moonlight, house-ghosts bounding from the mulberries to the palms, from the palms to the tall pines '.

eninism should not be summarily equated with ' communism '; if it could, then it would be spelt with a small *l*. It stands for that particular set of communistic principles predominating in the Union of Soviet Socialist Republics which was propounded by Nikolai Lenin (1870–1924), whose real name was Vladimir Ilich Ulyanov. The study of Marx and the political execution of an elder brother started him on the career that has a per-petual sequel, for his embalmed body lies permanently on exhibition in Moscow.

eonine (**verse**), ' verse in which there are both middle rhyme and end rhyme ', probably takes its name from some medieval poet: perhaps *Leo*, a 12th-Century Canon of St Victor, Paris. Literally, *leonine* signifies ' of the lion ' (Latin *leo*).

esbian, -ism ; or small initials. ' Lesbianism or Sapphoism ' —usually *Sapphism*—' is as old as Pompeii . . . Sadism and masochism have survived,' Joseph F. Broadhurst, *From Vine Street to Jerusalem*, 1937.

' The Restaurant . . . with its Burgundy and Lesbians,' *The Unquiet Grave* (1945), by ' Palinurus '.

Sappho, the greatest poetess of the Ancient World, who flourished in the latter half of the 7th Century B.C., passed much of her life in the island of Lesbos, where she gathered about her a circle of young women, probably for instruction in poetry, legendarily for the cult of **Aphrodite** :

> ' The isles of Greece ! the isles of Greece
>   Where burning Sappho loved and sung ',

as Byron put it with that characteristic combination of energy and eloquence.

Whether she practised unnatural vice has never been proved : but slander has foisted upon her this practice, maybe on account of the amorous ardour of some of her poems.

Sapphism answers to *Lesbianism*, but *Sapphic* or *Sapphist* is a rare, literary, and—as to the second form—infelicitous synonym of *Lesbian* the noun ; *Sapphic* may, but rarely does, answer to *Lesbian* the adjective.

Lethe ; lethean ; letheon (sulphuric ether used as an *anaesthetic*)
'America has always been a land of dreams, the " land of promise ". The Atlantic has ever been a vast sundering Lethe which has shut out the influence of the past,' James Truslow Adams, *The Epic of America*, 1933.

'Opium is mentioned again and again by writers of the classical age . . . In the Georgics there is a line about " poppies soaked with the sleep of Lethe "—*Lethaeo perfuse papavera somno*,' Margaret Goldsmith, *The Trail of Opium*, 1939.

In Roman mythology, *Lethe* (personification of *lēthē*, ' forgetting ; oblivion '—from *lēthanō*, ' I cause to forget ') was that river in Hades of which the water, drunk by souls about to be re-born, induced forgetfulness of the life they have just left. Ovid and Lucan, Virgil and Horace, Propertius and Statius have sung its story and its virtues.

levant ; levanter. To abscond—an absconder—especially with betting or gambling losses unhonoured. Perhaps from Spanish *levantar el campo*, ' to strike camp ; hence, to decamp '— but almost certainly with the connotation that the Levant used to be the favourite refuge of fleeing swindlers. And *levanter*, a strong wind blowing in the eastern Mediterranean, is quite certainly derived from *the Levant*, originally ' the East in general ', then the land immediately east of the Mediterranean. Compare *le levant*, ' the sunrise, the East '.

leviathan, ' anything large (and monstrous) of its kind ; a person, a nation, of vast power or wealth or ability '—as in ' Fashioning of Leviathan : The Beginnings of British Rule in Burma ', by J. S. Furnivall in *Journal of the Burma Research Society*, vol. XXIX (1939)—is a generalizing of the *Leviathan*, a sea monster, in The Bible (*Job*, xli, 1, ' Canst thou draw out leviathan with a hook? ' ; *Psalms*, lxxiv, 14, and civ, 26 ; *Isaiah*, xxvii, i, ' Leviathan the piercing serpent, even leviathan that crooked serpent . . . the dragon that is in the sea '). The word, which may mean ' The Twister, The Tortuous One ' (compare Hebrew *lawah*, ' to twist or bend '), has formed an allusive title to two very considerable works, Thomas

Hobbes's *The Leviathan* (later he wrote a *Behemoth*), 1651, and R. G. Collingwood's *The New Leviathan*, 1942.

The Ras Shamra tablets, discovered in 1929, ' tell of . . . Baal (often in the O.T.) . . . and the slaying of the many-headed serpent Lotan—*i.e.* Leviathan', Stanley Cook, *An Introduction to The Bible*, 1945.

Compare **behemoth.**

lewis, the son of a freemason; a Lewis machine-gun. The former is an example of esoteric personification. The latter was named after Isaac Newton Lewis (1858–1931), American Army officer and inventor: an artillery range-finder, the machine-gun (1911), a fire-control signal-system. He was also a brilliant organizer of artillery; his organizational system, adopted in 1904, still dominates the artillery corps.

lewisite, the mineral, derives from W. J. Lewis (1847–1926), an English mineralogist, whereas the chemical-warfare *lewisite* was, in 1918, named for Winford Lee Lewis (1878–1943), an American chemist, who, as a captain in the United States Army, had invented it in 1917–18.

lido. ' To make way for a battledore-and-shuttlecock court, combined with the latest " Lido " and soda fountain,' Osbert Sitwell, *Sing High! Sing Low!*, 1944.

From the Lido of Venice. Literally, *lido* = shore: compare the original and transferred senses of the French *plage* (in, e.g., Paris-Plage).

liebfraumilch. See **lachryma Christi** in the subsidiary list.

lilliputian, ' diminutive' or, as noun, ' a tiny " human being ",' comes from *Lilliput*, that island which, in Swift's *Gulliver's Travels*, 1726, is peopled by a race of most diminutive men and women, averaging six inches in height. By making their statecraft and politics, their loves and hates, appear ridiculous, Swift was ridiculing mankind. As *brobdingnagian* by its sound evokes the idea of great size, so *lilliputian* by its sound evokes that of smallness.

limburg(h)er = *Limburg(h)er cheese*, more popular and much better known in America, where it ' caught on ' as early as ca. 1880, than in Britain. The spelling without *h* is the more usual. Originally and properly it is a soft cheese made in the *Limburg* (strictly *Limbourg*) province of Belgium—not Limburg in Holland.

251

'It is some of Mindy's Limburger cheese, and everybody knows Mindy's Limburger is very squashy, and also very loud,' Damon Runyon, *Furthermore*, 1938.

'Just who do you think *is* hired by the people to see that they get good limburger cheese, to see that we have food inspectors who know cheese from Euclid?': Sinclair Lewis, *Gideon Planish*, 1943.

limehouse, denigration of one's political opponents, derives from the fact that, on July 30, 1909, David Lloyd George (1863–1944), at that time Chancellor of the Exchequer, delivered an uncomplimentary speech at *Limehouse*, London. That Parliamentary borough takes its name from a great *limehouse* (where liming of sails or hides is done) that once was situated there.

limerick, usually said to have arisen from the refrain *Will you come up to Limerick?* (an Irish county and city : Erse *Luimneach*, pronounced *liminegh* and meaning 'waste piece of ground' : famous for woollens and flour), sung at convivial gatherings at which it was the custom to extemporize these five-lined nonsense poems. 'But it seems likely ', as W keenly remarks, ' that the choice of the word may have been partly due to the somewhat earlier *learic* coined by Father Matthew Russell, S.J. " A ' learic ' . . . is a name we have invented for a single-stanza poem modelled on the form of the ' Book of Nonsense ' for which Mr Edward Lear has got perhaps more fame than he deserved " (*Irish Monthly*, February, 1898).' *The Book of Nonsense* appeared in 1846; Edward Lear (1812–88) followed it up with *Nonsense Songs, Stories, and Botany* in 1870.

limousine. ' When I beat it away from the small town where my father was a general painter . . . I had big ideas about coming back in a limousine with a driver in uniform and thousand dollar bills stuck in every pocket I owned,' Charles Francis Coe, *Swag*, 1928.

A motor-car with closed body : from French *limousine*, ' a closed carriage '—itself a sense-development from *limousine*, that kind of hood which was worn by the inhabitants of *Limousin*, one of the French provinces.

lingua franca. The use of this term has become so general—for instance, the ' Bazaar Malay ' of Malaya is often called the lingua franca of those parts, and a simplified form of Malay has almost established itself as the lingua franca of Borneo—that its original sense, ' that medley of Italian, Spanish, French, Greek which constitutes the most popular means of communication in the Levant ', is in danger of being overlooked. *Lingua franca* is Italian for ' the Frankish tongue '. In the Levant, it should be remembered, a Frank was any person of West-European nationality.

The term *lingua franca* occurs, in English, first in Dryden, 1678, 'A certain compound Language, made up of all Tongues ' (OED), but this composite was in use centuries earlier.

linnaea, ' a small, creeping, woody plant ', directly commemorates the great botanist *Linnaeus*. See **Linnaean** in the secondary list.

linsey-wolsey is an elaboration (on *wool*) of *linsey*, which, dating from the 15th Century, is derived by Skeat from *Lindsey*, a village parish near Kersey (see **kersey**) in Suffolk, England—a district famous in the Middle Ages for its manufacture of fabrics.

lisbon. A sweet, light-coloured wine that, produced in Estremadura, is named *lisbon* because it is shipped from Lisbon. *Lisbon* derives from the Phoenician *alis ubbo*, ' delectable bay '. (Chisholm.)

lisle ; lisle thread. When you say *lisle* to a woman, she usually thinks of lisle stockings, made of lisle thread. The word *lisle* represents *Lisle*, the old spelling of *Lille*, the great manufacturing city of north-east France. *Lisle* itself is *L'Isle*, the original town—literally ' the Island '—being so named from its dominating centre, ' an insulated castle ' (Chisholm).

listerine ; listerize. The former is an antiseptic solution named after, the latter is to treat operations antiseptically in the manner devised by Lord Lister, Joseph 1st Baron Lister of Lyme Regis, who (1827–1912), a surgeon, studied inflammation and suppuration consequent upon wounds and injuries and who, much influenced by the teachings of Pasteur, founded antiseptic surgery.

lobelia, any one of the flowering herbs of many species of the genus *Lobelia*, was named for Matthias de *Lobel* (1538–1616), that Flemish botanist and physician who became physician to King James I of England. James loved these learned fellows.

lockeram or **lockram.** As **dowlas** comes from Doulas in Brittany, so lockram, another cheap sort of linen mentioned by

Shakespeare, comes from *Locrenan* (Breton *Lokronan*) in Lower Brittany—a few miles north-west of Quimper.

The place-name means ' St Ronan's cell ': Breton *lok*, ' a cell ' + *Ronan*, i.e. St Ronan; Locrenan is alternatively known as *St Renan*. (Skeat.)

loganberry; colloquially shortened to *logan*. Discovered in 1881, this berry, shaped like a blackberry, coloured like a raspberry, and with a flavour that combines those of both, was at first described as *Logan berry*, after James Harvey Logan (1841–1921), American jurist and horticulturist, who produced it in his own garden in Santa Cruz County, California.

logie, a piece of imitation jewellery, especially as a theatrical property, is said to have been named after its ' inventor ', David *Logie*, ca. 1860.

looby, a clumsy fellow, may come from *lob*, a dull, heavy fellow, but it equally well may come from French *Lubin*, a Proper Name that in the Middle Ages was abusively applied to a monk or a friar. In its earliest use (Langland's *Piers Plowman*, written ca. 1362–92), *looby* is a loafer. (W.)

loosestrife, any plant of the genus *Lysimachia*, is the early herbalists' translation of Late Latin *lysimachion*, from Greek *lusimachion*, generalizing the Proper Name *Lusimachos*, itself formed of the elements *lúein*, to loose, and *makhë*, a battle, a quarrel : ' loose strife '.

Lothario or **gay Lothario.** ' Youthful Lotharios may use the pilfered automobiles to take their " sweeties " for a ride,' George C. Henderson, *Keys*, 1924.—' The Lothario of the club, a young Wall Streetman,' William McFee, *Spenlove in Arcady*, 1942.—' I had never thought of my elder brother as a Lothario, Romeo or Don Juan,' Gladys Mitchell, *The Rising of the Moon*, 1945.

Lothario, callous libertine, is proverbial as ' the Gay Lothario '—a character in Nicholas Rowe's *The Fair Penitent*, a blank-verse play, produced in 1703. In revivals, David Garrick often played the part.

louis, the coin, is short for *louis d'or*, a *Louis d'or*—of gold. Struck by Louis XIII in 1640, it was superseded in 1795. Louis was the name bestowed upon the Bourbon monarchs of France. In Medieval French, *Louis* was *Loeis* or *Loöis*, forms that indicate the origin in Old High German *Hluthawig*, ' famed in war ': *Louis* is therefore a doublet of *Clovis*.

254

ouisine.   A twilled silk that, thin and soft and usually woven in stripes or checks, serves to make dresses.   Either from *Louis* or more probably from *Louise* (cf. **georgette**), perhaps topically from some once famous modiste, but otherwise certainly a pretty personification.

ovage is that European herb which once was cultivated as a domestic remedy.   The word comes from Old French *luvesche*, from Late Latin *levisticum*, a corruption of Classical Latin *ligusticum*, ' lovage '—a plant native to Liguria ; *ligusticum* is the generalized neuter of *Ligusticus*, Ligustine or, as we should say, Ligurian, i.e. of *Liguria*, in the north-west of the present Italy.

ovelace.   In Samuel Richardson's lengthy novel, *Clarissa Harlowe* (1747–48), Robert Lovelace, an attractive and versatile but heartless and unscrupulous man of fashion, woos and abducts Clarissa, who, belonging to a good family and remembering its good name and her own, dies of a shamed and broken heart ; but ' the wages of sin is death ' at the duelling hands of her colonel cousin.   Richardson intended the book as a warning to parents :   and Lovelace survives as the rival of Lothario and Don Juan.   His name is designed to indicate the lace adorning, and therefore emblematic of, the attire of fashionable men about Town in the 1740's.

ucifer, a ' friction match ', takes its name, not from the arch-rebel Satan (*as proud as Lucifer*) but from the morning star, ' the Light-Bringer ' (*lucem ferre*) ;   the word, like the thing, belongs to the approximate period 1830–70.
  ' "Lucifer hath set," said Philippe of Harvengt when he [Peter Abelard] died,' Helen Waddell, *The Wandering Scholars*, 1927 :   the star.   The other Lucifer, who likewise merits a place here, receives recognition in Neville Cardus's reminiscences of Old Trafford cricket-ground ;   having mentioned Ernest Jones, he goes on to say, ' Another great Australian fast bowler, the most beautiful Lucifer of them all, found his own element at Old Trafford ;   McDonald . . .' (*The Manchester Guardian Weekly*, July 13, 1945), the reference being to the diabolical grace and power of his bowling.

Lucretia—or **Lucrece**—has, thanks to Shakespeare's narrative poem, *The Rape of Lucrece*, 1594, become the prototype of female married chastity.   Raped by Tarquin, she took her life.   The story belongs to Roman history :   that rape led to the dethronement of Tarquinius Superbus in 510 B.C. and the establishment of consular government.
  Compare **Penelope.**

Lucretian, in its transferred—its eligible—sense, means ' poetic
ally philosophic ' or ' philosophically poetic ' and relates t
philosophy written not in prose but in verse ; it connote
grandeur softened with a profound understanding of th
Virgilian ' tears of things '. The Roman poet Lucretiu
(ca. 99–55 B.C.) wrote, in eloquently weighty hexameters, *D*
Rerum Natura (on the nature of things) ; his philosophy is tha
of Epicurus, with emphasis upon the atomic theory of th
universe ; there is a noble prose rendering by H. A. J. Munr
(1819–85), notable also for his work upon Catullus and for som
admirable Latin translations of English verse.

Lucullus ; Lucullan or **-ian.** The noun signifies ' wealthy *bo*
viveur and gourmet ' ; the adjective, ' gastronomically splendid
varied, refined '. Lucius Licinius *Lucullus* (ca. 119–57 B.C.)
general and administrator, fought for eight years agains
Mithridates and Tigranes, amassed money as well as success
and on his return to Rome in 66, lived luxuriously and magnifi
cently ; he gave the most superb banquets, hence *Lucull(i)a*
banquets, dinners, feasts ; it was he who introduced the **cherry** t
the Romans, the Romans to the cherry.

Of the same origin is *lucullite*, also—after Latin *Luculleu*
marmor—called *Lucullan marble* : an Egyptian marble of
blackish hue, it seems to have become known in Rome throug
the agency of Lucullus, who discovered it on an island set in th
Nile.

lumber, ' old useless things ' : from ' things stored away ' : fron
' store-room ' or ' pawnbroker's shop ' : from *lombard* in thos
last two nuances : from *Lombard,* ' a Lombard's bank or pawn
shop ' : from the *Lombards* or famous bankers of *Lombardy,* th
North-Central part of the Po Valley in Northern Italy
' capital ' Milan. The *Langobardi* or *Longobardi* (whenc
Italian *Lombardi*) were a Teutonic tribe that settled in thi
region in A.D. 568 ; *Langobardi* means ' the long-bearded (men)'

lumberjack is the colloquial and more usual form of *lumberman*
a feller, rough-hewer, and conveyor of timber. This *lumbe*
exemplifies a sense derivative from **lumber** ; and this *jack* i
that ' Jack ', or man, we find also in, e.g., *steeplejack.*

lundyfoot is a snuff named after a tobacconist, *Lundy Foot.* H
lived in Dublin and flourished in the latter half of the 18t
Century.

lunel. ' What could literary men mean by ordering lunel?
asked Thackeray in 1841. This sweet, tawny-coloured musca

wine had been well-known in England since ca. 1760, and 'it comes from the vineyards of Lunel, in the Languedoc, on the French side of the Pyrenees' (André Simon).

lunkah, a strong cheroot, derives from Hindi *langka*, generalized from the *Lankah* islands in the delta of the Godavery (or Godavari) River, in the Madras Presidency of India; tobacco is grown on those islands.
Compare **trichinopoly.**

lushington, a man with a thirst (especially for beer) much bigger than his brains, is a personification, on the analogy of *simpleton* and *singleton*, from the slang *lush*, of which the most probable origin is the Shelta (Irish tinkers' language) *lush*, ' to eat and drink '—as W proposes; a process aided by the fact that there is a surname *Lushington*.

lutetium. One of the elements; discovered in 1907 by the French scientist, Urbain. It was he who proposed that this element, which rather closely resembles ytterbium, should be named after the ancient—the Latin—name of Paris (la Ville Lumière)—*Lutetia* or *Lutecia*.

lyceum. In Britain, a literary institution or a lecture-hall; in the U.S.A., ' a lecture system, once '—ca. 1835–80— ' extremely popular but nowadays superseded by the Chautauqua movement' (H. W. Horwill, 1935); the first lyceum was founded in 1826 at Millbury, Mass., and it was not until ca. 1890 that the supersession took place.
The word represents the Latin form of the Greek *Lukeion*, that garden in which Aristotle taught at Athens: it lay next to the temple of Apollo, one of whose many descriptive addenda was *Lukeios* (Lycian).
Compare **athenaeum** and **academy.**

lyddite. In 1888, this explosive, invented by Turpin, was tested at—or rather, near—*Lydd*, a picturesque old Kentish town at the southern extremity of Romney Marsh. Lydd, a few miles from the sea, has long possessed a Government artillery range.
Compare **turpinite.**

Lydian.

> ' Sweetly soft in Lydian measures,
> Soon he sooth'd his soul to pleasures ',

as that great poet and great man, Dryden, once sang. In its transferred senses, *Lydian* means either ' effeminate ' or 'voluptuous'. The kings of Lydia in western Asia Minor, especially **Croesus,** were famed for their wealth and luxury. In music the Lydian mode was 'plaintive and pathetic' (Harvey).

lyncean; lynx-eyed. Although Skeat and W, The OED and Webster, all derive *lynx* from Greek *lunx* (probably from *leussein*, to see) and relate it to certain Teutonic words meaning 'to shine', yet there can be little doubt that the keen-sighted *lynx* owes something to *Lunkeus* (latinized as *Lynceus*), who, in Greek mythology, was an Argonaut so sharp of sight that he could see through the earth.

'Kadigeta, the lynx-eyed young Dankali, lay in the prow, trying to pierce the darkness,' Henry de Monfreid, *Hashish*, 1935.

lynch. 'The gambling gentry [on the Mississippi river-boats] frequently abused their privileges, and the term "lynch law" seems to have been coined about 1834 to meet the need of dealing with them, and in particular of hanging one of them at Vicksburg' (on the west bank of the Mississippi, and in the Warren County of that State), James Truslow Adams, *The Epic of America*, revised edition of 1938.

Webster's Biographical Dictionary, however, says of Charles Lynch (1736–96), a Virginian planter and Justice of the Peace, that 'During disorganized conditions accompanying American Revolution, presided over extralegal court to punish lawlessness, in which convictions were frequent and followed by summary punishment, usually flogging; hence the term *lynch law* or, formerly, *Lynch's law*'.

lynx-eyed. See **lyncean.**

lyonnaise. 'He had ordered cold guinea hen and lyonnaise potatoes had come with it,' John P. Marquand, *So Little Time*, 1943. That is, *pommes de terre à la lyonnaise*, in the fashion of Lyons—with sliced (or flaked) fried onions. The citizens of Lyons know a good thing when they taste it.

M

mac or **mack; macintosh** or **mackintosh.** The correct forms are *mac* and *macintosh*, for in 1823 Charles Macintosh patented the 'Macintosh capes and cloaks' he had so considerately invented to enable the British to endure, with a patient

258

smile instead of an uncomely scowl, the vagaries of the English summer.

'To indulge in it '—that is, in ' the habit of sensuality and pure aestheticism '—' is to become a spiritual mackintosh, shielding the little corner of time, of which one is the centre, from the least drop of eternal reality,' Aldous Huxley, *Time Must Have a Stop*, 1945.

macabre ; danse macabre. Gruesome or grim ; the Dance of Death.

'A macabre and novel means of smuggling heroin into France came to light to-day. . . . A zinc-lined coffin hailing from the Levant was found to contain many score pounds of the deadly drug instead of the corpse, which had been abstracted *en route*,' Ferdinand Tuohy, *Inside Dope* (an able exposure of the drug traffic), 1934 ; ' Death's macabre mockery comes too late to prevent Cordelia's reunion with Lear,' G. Wilson Knight, *The Burning Oracle*, 1939.

' The idea of Death as a dancer, or as a fiddling inciter to the dance, is very old. A dance of skeletons has been found on an ancient Etruscan tomb, and pictures of Death fiddling whilst people of all sorts and conditions dance to his music were extremely common in many parts of Europe during the Middle Ages ' (Dr Percy Scholes).

French *macabre* is a legitimate alternative of Old French *macabré* (in *danse Macabré*, 14th Century) ; and *macabré* = *Macabré*, itself not impossibly a popular corruption of *Macabé*, which = Latin *Maccabaeus*. 'Apparently corruption of *Maccabaeus* ; cf. Medieval Latin *chorea Machabaeorum*, . . . dance of death ' (W). The adjective *macabre*, therefore, is, even in French, considerably later than *danse macabre*, whence it derives ; and in English the adjective does not appear before ca. 1880. The Maccabaeus concerned is presumably Judas Maccabaeus (' The Hammer '), leader of the Maccabees, a Hasmonean clan in Palestine : a brilliant maker of guerilla warfare, he in 164 B.C. defeated an army sent against him by Syria.

That admirably erudite scholar, Robert Eisler, however, has shown (*The Times Literary Supplement*, April 27, 1946, and, at great and fascinating length, in *Medium Aevum*, 1946), that the origin of the word *macabre* resides in the *mequaber*, which is ' Biblical Hebrew . . . and Aramaean for '' burier '', '' grave-digger ''. The Aramaean plural . . . *mequabrey* '' the buriers '' is exactly rendered by the spelling '' The Frenshe ' Dance of Machabray ' '' in the edition of 1598 of John Lydgate's and in Chorier's edition of 1659 entitled '' Danse Macabrey '' ' and that the dance itself is ' the funeral dance in honour of the departed ', a dance that may be the ritual one performed by communal *fossores* or grave-diggers.

macadam, macadamize; tarmac (tar-macadam).

' He '—a coach-driver in the Australian ' bush '—' solemnly declared that " when the roads came to be 'cadamised, he would resign his employment and go a-prospecting for another rough-and-tumble drive ",' William Kelly, *Life in Victoria*, 1859.

> ' *Ignore the stale figs, the weevils and the whippings,*
>   *The old men terrified of death* . . .

But that was horribly flat. Steam-rolled and macadamized, like bad Wordsworth,' Aldous Huxley, *Time Must Have a Stop*, 1945.

John Loudon *Macadam* (d. 1836), a Scottish civil engineer who became general surveyor of roads in England in 1827, had published in 1819 an essay in which he set forth the method and the advantages of thus paving a road with small, broken stones. ' The success of his work made the greatest advance in rural communication until the coming of the Ford car,' James Truslow Adams, 1938. His name is sometimes written *McAdam*.

macao. ' The game of macao, a variety of vingt-et-un, one card only being dealt and nine being the total required,' Neil Bell, *Child of My Sorrow*, 1944. This game is still much played by gamblers at Macao, a seaport on the Canton River and in the province of Kwantung.

macartney is short for *Macartney pheasant* (or *cock*), the fire-backed pheasant of the Far East; named in honour of George, the first Earl Macartney (1737–1806). Macartney was an Irish-born diplomat in the British service, and in 1792–94 he had the distinction of being the first British diplomat at the Court of Pekin.

macassar is the common-property form of *Macassar oil*, so much used by 19th-Century dandies and 20th-Century ' wide boys ' for their hair. Probably when first prepared to subserve the noble cause of male beauty, the oil did come from Macassar; since, 'tis but a name.

Macassar (the native name is *Mangkasara*) is a presidency, and the capital thereof, on the western side of the East Indian island of Celebes.

maccaboy or **maccoboy.** A snuff, especially that which is scented with attar of roses. The name, which was bestowed ca. 1730, is indicated in ' The snuff of Martinico, celebrated under the term " Macouba " ' (John Badcock, 1823; cited by The OED), for *Macouba* is a district in Martinique, the French island in the West Indies; mariners know Cape Macouba, in the north.

macédoine, ' a mixture of fruits, or of fruit embedded in jelly ', hence figuratively ' a hotch-potch '. The word—in English, the accent may be omitted—represents *Macédoine*, French for *Macedonia*: '? from empire of Alexander '—Alexander of Macedonia, Alexander the Great—' being regarded as a miscellaneous collection ' (W).

' The social development of the Macedonians—to give various peoples one generic name—had, for certain reasons, not been nearly so rapid as that of their southern cousins ' (the Greeks), D. G. Hogarth, *The Ancient East*, 1914.

machiavel; machiavellian. A *machiavel* is a crafty, devious statesman or diplomat; *machiavellian* signifies ' extremely cunning, tortuous, carefully scheming '.

' The utilitarian form of political action . . . is one which facilitates the concealment of a ruler's purposes from the ruled.

' Such concealment is commonly called Machiavellian; a name originating no doubt from a vulgar inappreciation of that very great man, Niccolo Machiavelli, but expressing a sound enough criticism both of Machiavelli and of the Renaissance political life whose spokesman he was,' R. G. Collingwood, *The New Leviathan*, 1942.

Niccolo Machiavelli (1469–1527) or, in the French mode, Machiavel, was a noted Florentine diplomat and statesman, who, after an eminently practical career, was in 1512, when they regained power, deprived of office by the Medici. After imprisonment, he retired to his estate, studied, wrote on history and war and the art of government, his principal work being *Il Principe* (The Prince), written in 1513 but not translated into English until 1540. Although it countenances breach-faith and cruelty in certain circumstances, *The Prince* is much less immoral than many critics have asserted—and much more profound.

macintosh, mack. See **mac.**

MacKay, the real. See **McCoy, the real.**

mackinaw is short for *Mackinaw coat* (or *jacket*); also, though rarely in the 20th Century, for *Mackinaw blanket*, which origin-

ates the *Mackinaw jacket* or *coat*. 'They all wore heavy blanke
mackinaw coats,' Stewart Edward White, *The Blazed Trail*, 190:
(DAE). In the 19th Century, a *Mackinaw blanket* was ofte⊓
written *Mackinac blanket*, i.e. a blanket resembling those formerl⟩
distributed or traded to Red Indians at *Mackinac*, a trading pos:
in Michigan and a strait between Lakes Michigan and Huron
Mackinac is Canadian French, derived from Ojibway Indiaⁿ
mitchimakinak, 'great turtle'—from its shape. (DAE.)

mackintosh. See **mac.**

mâcon is wine from the considerable wine-producing regio⊓
known as the Mâconnais, which happens to include the canto⊓
and city of Mâcon ; this region of Lower Burgundy lies north o⌐
Lyons, and its chief wine-mart is Mâcon. *Mâcon* is a re⊂
Burgundy.

madaleine. See **madeleine.**

madapollam is a heavier than calico cotton-cloth, manu
factured at *Madapollam*, in the time of the East India Company
But, important then, it has long been a 'decayed weaving and
dyeing village on the banks of the Godavari river in th⊂
Presidency of Madras '.

madeira, a wine made in the beneficent climate of *Madeira*, ca⊓
be very good. '*Sercial* Madeira has a distinctly dry finish
Bual Madeira is rich, and *Malmsey* Madeira is the sweetest o⌐
all ' (André Simon). *Bual* is also *Boal*, and these are thre⊂
distinct wine-names.
  Madeira, the principal of a group of islands, usually called th⊂
Madeira Islands, is so named 'from the abundant timbeⁿ
(Portuguese *madeira*, from Latin *materia*). And *madeira cak⊂
may originally have been flavoured with the wine ' (W).

madeleine ; loosely, *madaleine*, *madeline*. This early-ripeni⊓⅁
pear, a favourite in the United States, is called, in full, th⊂
Madeleine pear. Like the *madeline*, a small, rich cake (Frencʰ
madeleine), the pear represents a personification. The feminin⊂
given-name *Madeleine* derives from *Magdalen*.

madge has three chief senses, a barn owl (*madge howlet*), a leadeⁿ
hammer woollen-covered and used in hard-solder plating, and
in 19th-Century Scots, a woman (compare **moll**) : all, clearly
are personifications, *Madge* being a common name for a girl.

madrileña. A Spanish dance-type arising, and popular, in the province of Madrid. Short for *danza madrileña*, dance of Madrid.

Mae West. This originally slang, now—indeed by mid-1943—official name for an airman's life-jacket was created by the R.A.F., 'because it bulges in the right places', as I saw it phrased in *The Reader's Digest* of February 1941. From the name of a most vital American film actress, who thus joins the very exclusive, very small band of film actors and actresses that have permanently enriched the language. The first dictionary to record it as official was Squadron-Leader C. H. Ward Jackson's entertaining *It's a Piece of Cake*, (late) 1943.

Maecenas, figuratively 'a very generous patron of literature or '—this nuance is derivative—' of art ', has been so used in English since the middle of the 16th Century ; and, in various shapes, for centuries in the Romance languages. The transitive verb *Maecenas*, ' to be a generous patron to ' (a person), is literary and rare.

Maecenas (ca. 70–8 B.C.), a wealthy Etruscan, wrote inferior prose and verse and acted as counsellor to superior men, notably Augustus himself, and as an enlightened patron to a distinguished literary circle, including Virgil, Horace, Propertius. Both Virgil and Horace speak of him in terms at once grateful and admiring : the former owed him at least an idea, the latter his financial independence. It is pleasant to remember that Maecenas did not confine his patronage to condescending and unnecessary advice.

maelstrom (or **maelström** or **malström** or **mälström**) owes its currency in English to the fact that, although it means ' millstream ' and derives from the Dutch *maalstroom* (earlier *maelstroom*), ' a whirlpool '—*malen*, ' to grind ' + *stroom*, ' stream ', it has come to us from the Scandinavians, who adopted it as a literary word as a result of its application by 16th-Century Dutch geographers to the famous and in some ways notorious whirlpool formed by a strong current that becomes dangerous only when the north-west wind blows contrary to the tide between the islet Moskenö and the Moskenoes island, south of the Lofoten group of islands off Norway, its other name being the Moskenström. The danger is often increased by dense fogs. (W ; Chisholm ; Lyde.)

The adoption of the word into English, especially in its figurative nuance, was assisted by the appearance, 1841 in

263

Graham's Magazine and 1843 in *Prose Tales*, of Edgar Allan Poe's tragic and powerful story, ' A Descent into the Maelström '.

maenad is to be used with care, for it signifies rather more than ' mad woman '—even though that is the literalness of the Greek *Mainas* (from *mainesthai*, ' to rave '), a votary of Dionysus, a Bacchante; it rather signifies a woman furied by ' the working of a god ', the god being Dionysus (or, in the Roman hierarchy, Bacchus), a woman possessed and raving : *maenadic*.

' At any moment she might laugh like a child, or run like Artemis or dance like a Maenad,' C. S. Lewis, *Perelandra*, 1943.

maffick, mafficking. ' Walking in silence, I hungered to keep hold of this treasury, untainted by the smell of clothes and oil, the mafficking of pistons,' R. C. Hutchinson, *Interim*, 1945.

' To *maffick* ' is a back-formation from *mafficking*, applied originally to the scenes and spirit of popular rejoicing at the relief (May 17, 1900) of *Mafeking*, which, defended by Baden-Powell, had long been besieged by the Boers. The term was revived in November 1918, and again in May 1945. Apparently it has come to stay.

mag, slang for ' a halfpenny ', is almost certainly, as also is its underworld variation *meg*, a popularization of *Mag*, a familiar form of *Margaret*.

In the sense ' to chatter ', it derives from **magpie,** which is likewise of Proper-Name origin.

magdalen(e), ' a reformed prostitute ', and its perhaps derivative, perhaps original sense, ' a house either of refuge or of reform for prostitutes ' (for both of which the shorter form is much the more usual), comes from the New Testament Mary *Magdalene* (Greek *Magdalēnē*), i.e. Mary of *Magdala*, on the Sea of Galilee.

See *Matthew*, xxvii, 56, 61 ; *Mark*, xv, 40, and xvi, 9 ; *John*, xix, 25–xx, 1 and 18.

magdalenian or **M—** (period, culture). Applied to the culture characterizing the magdalenian period of civilization ; the latest division of the Later Palaeolithic Period or Late Stone Age. In *Britain B.C.*, S. E. Winbolt dates it at ca. 35,000–10,000 B.C. Flint implements, inferior to those of the **solutrian** period, and bone implements, e.g. needles and spears, were discovered at and near La *Madeleine* (Latin *Magdalena*), a rock shelter—Winbolt calls it ' a castle '—near Les Eyzies in the Dordogne, France. Compare **acheulian, azilian.**

magenta. This aniline dye, yielding a brilliant crimson, was discovered shortly after, and named in order to commemorate, the battle of Magenta (North Italy), fought in 1859 between the Franco-Sardinians and the Austrians. It was a *bloody* battle.

In *Matthew Smith*, by Philip Hendy, 1944, the author, having spoken of the picture *Couleur de Rose*, continues thus, ' In *The Model Waking*, though it was painted at much the same time, the colours stand out for the most part in contrasting patches, crimson and ultramarine, magenta and peacock, red gold and aquamarine, which bear out the starker sensuality of the naked, more sculptured figure by their deep translucency, the brilliance of stained glass '.

Compare **solferino.**

maggot-pie. See **magpie.**

magian, figuratively ' magician ' and ' magical ', derives from the *Magi*, those members of a priestly caste or order of ancient Persia and Media who posited good and evil as rival deities, to be worshipped. *Magoi* was the Greek name for a Medic tribe that constituted the priestly caste of Persia : repositories of all knowledge, interpreters of dreams, practisers of necromancy. From *Magoi* came *magos*, ' a sorcerer '; hence *magikos*, ' of or by or like a sorcerer or a magician '. The Greek word *magos*, which fathers the Latin *magus* (whence the English word), derives from Old Persian *magus*, ' member of a priestly caste '.

Its common-adjectival use appears to advantage in the following excerpt from George Santayana's ' Spengler ' in *The New Adelphi* of March–May 1929 : ' Now whenever I stand there [in the Parthenon] I say to myself: This grandeur in unity, this splendour in emptiness, this harmony in silence, this vastness in seclusion—all this is *magian* . . . . . . The realm of truth is magian like the Parthenon. All things, in the impartial light of eternity, show like marbles inlaid richly but unobtrusively in one seamless dome, windowless like a hollow gourd, yet vertically open to the heavenly air and the perfect blue.'

magilp. See **megilp.**

Maginot. A ' Maginot ' is any means of defence or protection that, at the proof, turns out to be a delusion. From *the Maginot Line*, which, devised by Monsieur André Maginot (1877–1932), French Minister of Defence, was not continued to the coast, which could so easily have been ignored by

265

parachute troops, and which could, at selected points, have been obliterated by heavy bombing; the Germans in 1940 rendered it ridiculous by by-passing it.

' The tombstone of France ' (General J. F. C. Fuller, 1927).

' Misguided over-optimistic propaganda in the early days of this war . . . was given the official *cachet* by Ironside and Chamberlain, who said Hitler had missed the bus. It was ourselves and our friends who were bluffed, not the enemy. . . . Hitler outflanked the Maginot Line ' (O. D. Gallagher, *Retreat in the East*, 1942).

In reference to about the 20th May 1940, Francis Beeding (a collaboration of two shrewd, alert, far-visioned officials in fiction that has ' a sting in its tail ') has written, ' . . . The politicians who had spent the last six months thanking God for the Maginot Line, which now seemed to be taking its place as a derelict antiquity beside Hadrian's wall and the Great Wall of China ' (*Eleven Were Brave*, November 1940).

maglemosian (or **M**—). ' Maglemose means a great marsh '— cf. Latin *magnus*, ' great '; and the original sense of English *moss*, ' a morass, a swamp '—' once a lake, in Denmark ' (S. E. Winbolt, *Britain B.C.*, 1943); an actual place-name. ' This culture came in with the ancestors of the blond peoples of North Europe ' (Winbolt).

magnalium (alloy of magnesium and aluminium) and **magneton** (unit of magnetic moment) have the same origin as **magnesia** and **magnet,** q.v.

magnesia; magnesite and **magnesium.** The latter words have been derived from the first, and the first represents the Greek *magnesia lithos*, Magnesian stone, i.e. stone of Magnesia. There are at least three places that, in the Ancient World, bore the name *Magnesia* : a peninsula in eastern Thessaly, between the Aegean and the Gulf of Volo ; and two cities in Asia Minor. The peninsula constitutes the effective source.

magnet, magnetic, magnetism, magnetize; magnetite, etc. ' Creative Imagination, like magnetism, requires two poles, a positive and a negative pole, before it can exist—it is not a single but a mutual act, a giving and a receiving,' Charles Morgan, *Reflections in a Mirror*, 2nd Series, 1946.

The origin of *magnet* has been hinted in the preceding entry : etymologically, *magnet* = Greek *Magnetis lithos*, ' stone of Magnesia ', whence Latin *magnes* (genitive *magnetis*), whence Old French *magnete*, whence—well, you see how it goes !
266

Originally, a piece of magnetite; derivatively, a magnet in the modern sense.

magnolia. ' Mysteries of nature: The properties of the quince . . .; lemons and the smell of lemon-verbena and lemon-scented magnolias, the colour of gentians,' ' Palinurus ', *The Unquiet Grave*, 1945.

The name *magnolia* was bestowed by Linnaeus in honour of Pierre Magnol (1638–1715), French physician and that botanist who originated the family-classification of plants.

magpie; maggot-pie. The *pie* is French, from Latin *pica*, ' a magpie '. To the adequate *pie*, the English have added *Mag* (formerly, also *Meg*); *maggot* is folk-etymology for *Margot*, a French name for the (mag)pie; from *Margot*, obviously, come *Mag* and *Meg*, the diminutives or pet-forms of *Margot* or *Margaret*.

Compare **robin.**

majolica. ' The sun had not yet set, but slanted behind the late blossoming rose-trees and monstrous forms of giant toads and diminutive dragons of green majolica,' Margaret Irwin, *The Gay Galliard*, 1942.

Majolica is Renaissance Italian pottery, or an imitation thereof, made at *Majolica*, the former name of Majorca (in Spanish, Mallorca); from Latin *maior*, ' greater, larger '— contrast *Minorca*, from Latin *minor*, ' lesser, smaller '.

malacca = *Malacca cane*. A walking-cane, of a rich brown, imported originally from Malacca (one of the Straits Settlements of Malaya), but also, and for long, from other Eastern parts. ' Malacca cane sticks—which have always been among the most expensive—come from the rattan palms of the East Indies and Ceylon,' Benjamin Richards, ' Walking-Stick Lore ' in *Chambers's Journal*, July 1945.

malaga, a Spanish white wine, takes its name from the seaport and province of Malaga in the south. The city of Malaga ' stands next to Seville for the export of olive-oil, and has also a large export of wine and fruit (raisins and almonds) ', as Professor L. W. Lyde noticed in 1930. Malaga wine— *Malaga sack* it was called in the early days—has charmed British palates since the late 16th Century, and Malaga raisins (*malagas* to your grocer) have appealed thereto since at least as early as the late 17th.

' The Italian cities and Marseilles were '—in the early 17th

Century—'served by 20 English ships, the Spanish ports within the Straits (and especially Malaga) by 30,' E. G. R. Taylor, *Late Elizabethan and Early Stuart Geography*, 1934.

malagueña is short for Spanish *danza malagueña*, 'dance of Malaga' (in southern Spain : compare **malaga**). It is a kind of fandango.

Compare **granadina** and **murciana**.

malakoff, besides being an ephemeral name (late 1855–59 or thereabouts) for a crinoline, is a restricted game of four-handed dominoes, the unrestricted game being the *sebastopol*, the two words dating from the Crimean war : *Malakoff*, a Russian fortification at *Sebastopol*, was captured by the French on September the 8th, 1855. Moreover, the Crimean War also imposed *malakoff* on 'a small round cream cheese made in Gournay, France' (OED).

Cf. **balaclava.**

malamute or **malemute** is an Arctic dog, descended from the wolf. Originally it was bred—and exclusively owned—by the *Malemuit*, an Arctic tribe. (Webster.)

malapropian; malapropism (or **malaprop**) : of, like, addicted to malapropisms; a ludicrous (yet not displeasing) misuse of words, or an instance of this misuse.

In Sheridan's coruscating comedy, *The Rivals*, 1775, one of the characters is a Mrs Malaprop, who tends to misapply the longer words she ambitiously uses, as in 'as headstrong as an allegory on the banks of the Nile' and 'a nice derangement of epitaphs'. Shakespeare had effectively used the device in several of his earlier plays, but it remained for Sheridan to 'name' it; he felicitously thought of turning *malapropos* (French *mal à propos*), 'inopportunely, unseasonably' into a name. Nevertheless, Sheridan got the idea from Winifred Jenkins in Smollett's *Humphry Clinker* (1771).

maldy. See **maud.**

malkin, archaic for 'a cat', is a Common Noun from a Proper Name : *Malkin* is the diminutive of *Maud*, a doublet of *Matilda*, and also of *Mol*, i.e. *Moll*, i.e. *Mary*. Semantically connected is *malkin*, a slattern, *Malkin* being a name common among maidservants and kitchen-wenches.

Compare **grimalkin** and **tabby** and **tom**(**cat**).

Mallaby-Deelies means 'clothes', but the name did not long survive its wildfire popularity of 1920, when (in March) Mr

Mallaby-Deeley, M.P., inaugurated an ambitious scheme for the supply of clothes at reasonable prices. ' See *Punch*, March 10, 1920,' says W.

For its short life, compare **mervousness** and **zabernism.**

mallard is cited as an instance of that sort of philological, or more precisely of etymological, knowledge in which there is no certainty but only probability or possibility. Here, the probability is that *mallard* has a Common-Noun origin (Old French *masle*, compare English *male*) ; the possibility is that it has a Proper-Name origin (Old High German *Madalhart*, ' strong in the council '), the latter reinforced, though it would seem insufficiently reinforced, by the fact that ' the application of proper names to birds (*guillemot, parrot*, etc.) goes back to pre-historic folk-lore ' (W).

malmaison, as a flower name, may denote either a carnation popular in England or a garden rose of the Bourbon variety, but in both of these senses it originates in *Malmaison* (literally ' bad house '), the Empress Josephine's palace near Versailles. Josephine de Beauharnais was Napoleon Bonaparte's wife from March 9, 1796, until 1809, when he divorced her.

malmsey. Philologically, *malmsey* comes from Medieval Latin *malmasia*, derived from Medieval Latin and Italian *Monemvasia*, representing Greek *Monembasia* (now *Malvasia*) in the Morea, Greece. Historically, it was in the hinterland of this maritime town that the wine was perhaps first produced or, as Chisholm puts it, this town ' was the shipping port for the famous malmsey, or malvoisier, wine of earlier centuries '. The wine has long been produced also in Italy, Spain, Madeira. (See **madeira.**)

maltee ; Maltese. Strictly, the former is the colloquial shape, but it is also the common-property re-shaping, of the latter. Only the context will decide whether *maltee* is a *Maltese ass* or a *Maltese cat*, or whether it means ' the colour of a Maltese cat ' —i.e., blue-grey.

malvoisier, also **malvoisie.** The latter, with variant *malvasie*, is a 14th–15th-Century form of **malmsey** ; it occurs in, e.g., Chaucer.

mamaluke or **mameluke,** small-*m*'d in the senses ' fighting slave ' and, in Mohammedan countries, ' a white, or a yellow, slave ', is capital-*m*'d in its original sense, ' one of a body of
269

soldiers recruited from slaves converted to Islamism' in Egypt and having great political power until exterminated in 1811 and, a little earlier, serving with the French against the British in the Egyptian campaign. *Mameluke* is the French *Mameluk*, from Arabic *mamluk*, literally 'in one's power'.

mammon. 'As America grew she tried to serve, so to say, God and Mammon—that is, she insisted upon clinging to the ideal of Jeffersonianism while gathering in the money profits from Hamiltonianism,' James Truslow Adams, *The Epic of America*, 1933. *Dieu et Mammon* is the title of a novel by François Mauriac (b. 1885).

It is to medieval writers that we owe the conception of mammon as a demon. Our word represents Latin *mammon*, like *mammona* a variant of *mammonas*, an adoption of Greek *mamōnas* or, in late New Testament texts, *mammōnas*, itself from Aramaic *mamon* (compare Syriac *mamuna*), which means 'riches or gain'. From the New Testament passages we see how *mammon* came both to be personified and to be apprehended as the devil of covetousness, greed, passion for money: 'Ye cannot serve God and mammon', (*Matthew*, vi, 24); 'the mammon of unrighteousness' (*Luke*, xvi, 9); 'If . . . ye have not been faithful in the unrighteous mammon, who will commit to your trust the true riches' (*Luke*, xvi, 11).

man Friday is employed allusively for a servile, yet cheerful and hard-working follower or assistant, as the first Man Friday, an aboriginal, was to Robinson Crusoe on his island in Defoe's imperishable *The Life and strange surprising Adventures of Robinson Crusoe*, which, published in 1719, was based on the life of Andrew Selkirk, a voluntary castaway on uninhabited Juan Fernandez in 1704–09, and which influenced Swift's *Gulliver's Travels* and which, furthermore, is part of that vast literature concerning 'the noble savage' which my friend Geoffroy Atkinson has studied so intensively.

man Jack, every. See **Jack** . . .

manchineel, a poisonous tropical American tree or its *apple*-shaped fruit, owes its form to French *mancenille*, which derives from Spanish *manzanillo*, diminutive of *manzana*, 'apple'; the Spanish *manzana* is the Latin (*malum*, apple) *matianum*, a variety of apple named either after some man called *Matius* or *Mattius* or, more probably, from *Matius* as the name of a Roman *gens* (clan).

270

manetti, or **Manetti,** is a variety—a vigorous one—of the China, sometimes called the Bengal, rose : and it has been named for Saverio *Manetti* (1723–84), an Italian botanist.

manganese ; manganese steel (containing 12% of manganese, and very resistant to shock) ; **manganin,** which is a derivative word for an alloy of 83% copper, 13% manganese, 4% nickel, an alloy ' very widely used in resistance coils owing to its very small temperature coefficient of resistance ' ; **manganite** (grey manganese ore).

Manganese is a corruption of *Magnesia*; *manganin* and *manganite* come from *mangan*, the German name for manganese. The ultimate origin of all three words is therefore to be seen at **magnesia.**

mangel-wurzel is a German word, of which the earlier form is *mangold-wurzel*, the second element signifying ' root ' and the first being probably the Proper Name *Mangold*. By folk-etymology, *Mangold-wurzel* was corrupted to *mangel-wurzel* by association with *mangel*, ' want, scarcity ', as though the whole meant ' famine root ', hence ' famine food '. (W.)

manhattan. This American cocktail takes its name from Manhattan Island, the nucleus of—the site of the original— New York City. Compare, therefore, *bronx*, the cocktail named from *the Bronx*, that mainland northern suburb which has become part of Greater New York. Long before cocktails were devised, *manhattan* signified *Manhattan water*, ' the water drunk in New York City before the Croton River was used as a source of supply ' (DAE).

manil(l)a is usually understood to mean either *Manila cigar* (or *cheroot*) or *Manila paper*, the former made from tobacco grown in, the latter being paper originally made at, *Manila* (the better spelling)—the capital of the Philippines ; sometimes it repre- sents *Manila hemp*, often mentioned by its native name, *abaca*. Absolutely, and always with a small *m*, *manila* is a yellowish hue —such a hue as characterizes envelopes made of Manila paper.

' At present '—1896—' the most important rival of Havana in the production of cigars is Manilla,' Lionel W. Lyde, *Man and His Markets.*

mannlicher. The name is applied especially to a breech- loading repeater rifle, much used by German (and other) big-game hunters, but also to a self-loading pistol. Their inventor was Ferdinand Mannlicher (1848–1904), an Austrian

engineer with a practical affection for 'small arms'. See, e.g.,
F. Brett Young's *The Crescent Moon*, 1925, a novel about the
tropical Africa of 1914; in *Death on Herons' Mere*, 1941, Mary
Fitt speaks of the smaller-bored 'Austrian Mannlicher ·256'.

mansard is short for *mansard roof*; compare French *toit en
mansarde*, hence *mansarde*, 'a garret'. This type of roof was
designed by François *Mansard* (1598–1666), a noted French
architect, who did most of his work in Paris, although he also
designed several attractive *châteaux*.

mantua; mantua-maker. The latter makes women's dresses
and cloaks : *mantua*, a woman's stayless gown fashionable about
1700, derives strictly from the French *manteau*, a mantle, but has
been confused with a dress-material named *mantua*, which was
in the 17th–18th Centuries made at *Mantua*, the English shape
of the Italian *Mantova*, a manufacturing city in Lombardy.

manx is short for *Manx cat*, that breed of domestic cat which
has a ridiculously rudimentary tail but is not in the least
ashamed of it. *Manx* represents the earlier *Manks*, a metathesis
(consonant-switch) of the 16th-Century *Manisk*, 'of (the Isle of)
Man'.

marabotin. See **maravedi.**

marathon. 'Frankie was in alimony jail playing marathon
poker,' Cornell Woolrich in *Detective Fiction Weekly*, June 5,
1937.
   'If ever single events have been decisive in history, these
two, Marathon and Salamis, have been. They stand for the
triumph of skill and courage against brute force,' A. D. Ritchie,
Civilization, Science and Religion, 1945.
   The Greeks, ably led by Miltiades, defeated the Persians on
the Plain of Marathon in 490 B.C.; the sea-battle of Salamis
had witnessed the defeat of the Persians a decade earlier. The
modern sense of *marathon*, a foot-race of some twenty-five miles,
derives from the feat of Pheidippides, who, after the battle of
Marathon, carried the news of the victory from Marathon to
Athens without a rest.
   Marathon means 'The Field of Fennel' : *Marathōn* derives
from *márathron* or *márathŏn*, a fennel-plant.

maravedi is a Spanish term for either of two coins, a gold one,
otherwise known as a dinar and worth about two-thirds of a
pound sterling, and a copper, worth less than a farthing. The

gold coin is also called a *marabotin* and was used by the Moors in Spain as well as in Morocco ; the copper one was introduced by Ferdinand and Isabella, joint sovereigns of Castile and Aragon in 1479–1504. The Spanish *maravedi* is really an adopted word from Arabic *Murabitin*, literally 'hermits' (singular, *Murabit*), the name of that Moorish dynasty, the *Almoravides* (an hispanicism, the *al* being originally the Arabic article 'the'), which resided, 1087–1147, at Cordova. The Murabitin were Mohammedan monks of North Africa, and *Murabit* derives from the 'Arabic *ribat*, guard-house on the frontier, often occupied by fanatics' (W).

marcel, to. 'That well-attended (and carefully marcelled) head of dark hair,' George Dyer, *The Mystery of Martha's Vineyard*, 1939.

Early in the present century, a French hairdresser surnamed Marcel (born in 1852) devised *the Marcel wave*—an artificial wave of the hair : hence, *marcel* is 'to treat, to wave hair by this process'; and a *marcel* is hair thus waved.

marcella, a cotton quilting or piqué used for, e.g., waistcoats, was originally manufactured at *Marseilles*—French *Marseille*— Latin *Massilia*—Greek *Massalia*, the Ionians of Phocaea (the most northerly of the Ionian settlements in Asia Minor) having founded a maritime port there in the 7th Century B.C.; for over 2500 years, Marseilles has been a thriving port and manufacturing centre—and for over 100 years it has contained some of the toughest professional criminals in the world.

See also **marseillaise.**

marconigram, a radiogram or, as it was earlier called, a *Marconi radio* (or *wireless*) *message* : compare **marconigraph,** the apparatus used in Marconi wireless telegraphy. They were invented by the Marchese Guglielmo Marconi (1874–1937), whose father was Italian and whose mother Irish. In 1912 he introduced the time-spark system for the generation of continuous waves. A very great engineer and inventor : one of the glories of modern Italy.

marigold.

'And thus she spake to the bright Marigold of Leutha's vale, Art thou a flower, art thou a nymph? I see thee now a flower, Now a nymph' :

William Blake, whom Joyce Cary quotes frequently and appositely in his novel, *The Horse's Mouth*, 1944.

273   N.I.W.—K

This flower is either golden or bright-yellow : the *gold* of The Virgin *Mary* : W compares the obsolete *marybud* (Shakespeare) ; The OED, the Middle Low-German *marienblome* ('Mary's flower').

marijuana is a powerful narcotic, taken in the form of cigarettes, widely known as *reefers*. The word is Mexican Spanish, being *Maria Juana* (Mary Jane), which becomes *Marijuana*, which was bestowed—probably by men—on the plant and the drug ; the latter renders men 'mad for women' and therefore it seemed, to men, to possess a striking degree of sexual appeal.

Note, however, that Webster uncompromisingly derives *marijuana* from Mexican Spanish *mariguana* (or *marihuana*), 'of uncertain origin' ; the DAE derives it, via Mexican Spanish, from (Mexican Indian?) *maraguango*, 'any substance producing intoxication'. But the Mexican Spanish form indubitably prompted the personification.—Slang synonyms are *Mary Ann* and, humorously, *Mary Warner*.

'I found myself on the Mexican border with a bad " yin " [usually *yen*, 'craving'] and nothing to relieve me but the native drug marijuana . . . . . . I would like to warn you that marijuana, cannabis indica, Indian hemp, hasheesh (call it what you will . . .) is the most degrading of all the narcotic groups,' Cecil de Lenoir, *The Hundredth Man*, 1933.

'There are three species : Cannabis Indica, or Indian Hemp, known in that country [India] as bhang, gunjah, ganga, ganza, cherrus, charras, siddhi, etc., but perhaps even better known by its Arabic name of hashish ; Cannabis Sativa, sometimes called dagga, the African form ; and Cannabis Americana [often called Mexican hemp]. It is a weed and grows as weeds do . . . . . . At first it makes you cough. Then it makes you daring . . . . . . Finally it makes you insane. Cannabinc mania, physicians say, is absolutely incurable' (yet Cecil de Lenoir—one man in a hundred—cured himself), Donald Barr Chidsey, 'On Your Way Out' in *Detective Fiction Weekly* January 8, 1938.

Compare the fact that the etymological origin of *assassin* is *hashish*—its Arabic form is *hashshash*—via *hashishiyy*, 'eaters o' hashish'.

marinism is poetry that is extravagant, over-ornamental, florid, flamboyant. Named from Giovanni Battista Marini (1569-1625), commonly known in his own day as Il Cavalier Marino, an Italian poet of exaggerated merit. He set a fashion in verse both gorgeous and empty. 'Marinism may be termed physica

274

in its manifestations, while Gongorism, Euphuism and the rest were largely metaphysical' (Sir Laurie Magnus).

Compare **euphuism, guevarism, gongorism.**

marionette, a small, intricate mechanism in a ribbon loom, derives from *marionette*, a puppet string-moved or hand-moved as in a puppet-show, a sense adopted direct from French, where it common-properties the personification *Marionnette*, the diminutive of *Marion*, itself originally a diminutive of *Marie*, from Latin (and Greek) *Maria*, identical with Hebrew *Miryam* (our *Miriam*).

'They were gaping at me. I saw their jaws drop and their mouths come open as if they were a lot of marionettes,' Lawson Glassop, *We Were the Rats* (of Tobruk), 1944.

marivaudage, highfalutin' gallantry, an affected style, is applied less to English and American writers than to French; naturally enough, since, literally, the term signifies ' affectation in the manner of Pierre Marivaux ', who (1688–1763) was a noted playwright and novelist. At least two of his comedies are graceful, witty, lively reading; his affectations occur more tediously in his novels, yet they too are better reading than many critics affect to think.

Mark Tapley. 'That lady must be a sister of Mark Tapley, who can be happy here,' W. W. Dobie, *A Visit to Port Phillip*, 1856.

In Dickens's *Martin Chuzzlewit* (1843–44), Mark Tapley leaves the Dragon Inn, where he has been a servant, to obtain a position wherein it will be grace, not disgrace, to show how good-tempered, good-humoured he is. He constitutes the type, the very acme, of invincible cheerfulness.

marmalade is usually and, I think, correctly derived from the Greek *melimelon*, a sweet apple resulting from the grafting of an apple upon a quince. The folk-etymological origin has been attractively supported by Margaret Irwin in *The Gay Galliard: The Love Story of Mary Queen of Scots*, 1942 : ' Mary . . . showed Jan how to cook French dishes in the kitchen. Some Spanish oranges had been stored there, and she made a new sort of preserve—called after herself . . ., for the cook at her grandmother's chateau of Joinville had made it to tempt her appetite when she was ill; " Marie est malade ", he had muttered again and again as he racked his brains to invent something for her; and " Mariemalade " they had called it ever since. They ate the bitter orange jam in her honour but preferred honey.' Unfortunately, dates upset that theory, which, philologically, ranks with the derivation of *sirloin* from a hypothetical Sir Loin.]

marocain is both a silk, or silky woollen, ribbed dress-material and, because that material was often dyed red, the colour Morocco red. The word is the French adjective from *Maroc*, Morocco, this fabric having originally been manufactured there. Compare *maroquin*, Morocco leather : see, therefore, **morocco**. The form *maroquin* is an imperfect anglicism of the French *marocain*, *maroquin* having at first been an adjective.

marry! Mere interjections have, for the most part, been omitted from this glossary. *Marry!* is ' by the Virgin *Mary!* ' One of the most interesting is *dear me!*, probably from Italian *Dio me salvi!*, God save, or spare, me.

marsala is the most esteemed of the Sicilian wines, Marsala being a seaport—and district—of Sicily. The latitude of Italy, says Professor Lyde (*Europe*), ' is really favourable only to the heavier type of white wine, *e.g.* Marsala '. This wine resembles a light sherry, but most of us will agree with Thackeray, who, in 1848, said, ' I prefer sherry to marsala when I can get it ' (OED). Nevertheless, marsala is a generous wine, and it was first produced, in 1773, by an Englishman, John Woodhouse.
  Marsala is an Italianate conflation of *Marsa-Allah*, ' The Port of God ' : a name bestowed upon the ancient Libybaeum by the Arabs.

marseillaise ; Marseilles or **marseilles** or, obsoletely **mersailles.** The former has, since the days of the French Revolution, been the song—hence the name—of the French national anthem, ' written and composed (1792) by Rouget de l'Isle, and first sung by " patriots " from *Marseille* ' (W) anglicé *Marseilles*. The latter—occasionally, in the late 18th–early 19th Centuries, *mersailles*—is a stiff strong cloth made of cotton at Marseilles, much exported to Britain and the United States, and frequently used for summer dresses. The French *Marseille* derives from the Latin *Massilia*, itself from Greek *Massalia*, ? ' the City of Craftsmen ' (Greek *massein*, to work with the hands). See also **marcella.**

martaban. With reference to pottery, J. Leroy Christian in *Modern Burma* (Berkeley and Los Angeles, 1942) writes thus revealingly, ' When Europeans first came to Burma they made frequent reference to Pegu jars or " Martabans ", the jars made in lower Burma and holding as much as 150 gallons. They are used for storing rice and other food, for preparing *ngapi* [a rich, highly-seasoned fish-paste], and for holding water for domestic use.'

Martaban, a small and ancient city of Burma, stands on the right bank of the Salween River, opposite Maulmain.

martello is short for—and common'd from—the *Martello tower* mentioned in ' The construction of the Martello towers in the early nineteenth century as a line of defence against the threatened invasion by Napoleon is a later instance of the same coast '—at and near Portsmouth—' being fortified in a manner very similar to that used by the Romans ' (during their occupation of Britain), E. W. Gilbert, ' The Human Geography of Roman Britain ' in *An Historical Geography of England before 1800*, edited by H. C. Darby, 1936. The ' clue ' lies in the early form of the word : *mortella* : in 1794, at Cape *Mortella* in Corsica, the British captured a tower widely held to be, defensively, of great strength : and they actually took the lesson to heart. This region abounds in myrtles ; and *mortella* signifies ' a myrtle ' : compare the origin of **marathon.**

Martha, especially in *the Marthas of this world* and, in Christian allegory of the Middle Ages and later, in *the way of Martha*, the active life as opposed to the contemplative life or *the way of Mary*. In the New Testament, Martha, the sister of Lazarus and Mary, was the friend of Jesus.

' Now it came to pass . . . that he ', Jesus, ' entered a certain village : and a certain woman named Martha received him into her house. And she had a sister called Mary, which also sat at Jesus' feet, and heard his word. But Martha was cumbered about with much serving, and came to him, and said, Lord, dost thou not care that my sister hath left me to serve alone? bid her therefore that she help me. And Jesus answered and said unto her, Martha, Martha, thou art careful and troubled about many things : But one thing is needed : and Mary hath chosen that good part, which shall not be taken away from her,' *Luke*, x, 38–42.

Martha, as Kipling emphasized in one of his short stories, represents the virtue of service : the virtues of the Marthas are too often forgotten or depreciated. It is an ironic twist of chance that, etymologically, her name is the feminine of the Aramaic *mar*, ' a lord '—as in ' lords and ladies gay '.

martial comes from Latin *martialis*, ' military ' (compare *martial law* and *court-martial*) and ' warlike ' or, originally,

'belonging to, hence characteristic of *Mars*', in Roma
mythology the god of war, although at first he had been
spirit of vegetation. In his predominant character, he wa
often called *Mars Gradivus*, where the second element ' prob
ably signifies "he who marches forth " to war ' (Harvey)
Latin *gradi*, ' to go, to walk '. Archaically *Mavors*, the nam
derives from the Sanskrit radical, *mar* (' a gleam '), in *mariki*
' a gleam of light '—hence, *Mars* the Bright God : compare th
so-called *glory* of war.

martin is an adoption straight from French, where the Prope
Name *Martin* (itself from *Mars*—see **martial**) has been applie
to the bird for perhaps no better reason—as though one wer
needed !—than that the birds depart at or a little befor
November 11, *Martinmas*, the festival of a 4th-Century Bisho
of Tours, Saint Martin. In French compare *martinet*, th
house-martin, and *martin-pêcheur*, the kingfisher ; and i
English, *robin* and *dicky*, mere arbitrary personifications.

martinet. ' Some officers . . . were . . . petty, stupid, spite
ful martinets,' Robert Blatchford, *My Life in the Army*, 1910.
  In the latter part of the 17th Century, a French Arm
officer, serving under Louis XIV, invented a new system o
drill for ' the Forces ' ; the drill was named after him ; a stric
and, at first, tedious drill, it caused its deviser's name to becom
proverbial for ' a strict, especially an excessively sever
disciplinarian '.
  Compare **martlet**.

martingale has three senses, ' a strap to keep down a horse'
head ' and the closely related ' a rope for guying down th
jib-boom or the flying jib-boom ' and the less obviously relate
technical term in gambling. The chief authorities think tha
the word probably originated in the Spanish *almartaga*, a rei
or a halter, from Arabic *al*, the + *mirta'ah*, a rein, but the
admit that it may have derived, perhaps via Rabelais's *chauss*
à la martingale (breeches with a strap-belt), from Provenç
martengalo, rather than from the variant *martegalo*, apparentl
from *martengau* (or *martegau*), an inhabitant or native o
Martigues, an ancient town in the *département* Bouches-du-Rhôn
in old Provence. But since such breeches, thus tied, wer
formerly worn in Provence, the latter origin is more probabl
than the former : here, as elsewhere, social history is importan

martini. (1) This cocktail (gin and vermouth, in the main
with orange bitters, etc., just to make it more interesting) ha

been named after a person, the original form being *Martini cocktail*. Probably Martini was a now forgotten, once well-known bar-tender of Italian or Spanish origin.

'The Martini tasted good', Richard Wormser, in *Detective Fiction Weekly*, November 1, 1941.

(2) See :—

martini(-henry). As early as 1868, the U.S. Army had a Henry rifle; the Henry barrel received the Martini breech, and in 1870 the English adopted the Martini-Henry rifle, soon called the *Martini-Henry* (cf. **Lee-Enfield**) and then the *Martini*—at least in 1876, if not earlier; the short name may with propriety be lower-cased. But the excellent Merriam-Webster *Biographical Dictionary* (1943) sets forth the genesis in a different way: '[Martini] invented rifle adopted by British army (1871), used until 1889, and replaced with the Martini-Henry rifle, the invention of Henry'.

'The good and virtuous people who hardly know a Martini from a Snider' (Kipling, 1890—with thanks to The OED).

Benjamin Tyler Henry (1821–98) was an American inventor; Frédéric de Martini (1832–97), born in Hungary and, for much of his life, domiciled in Switzerland, was a mechanical engineer with a marked talent for invention. The facts concerning Henry are confused and obscure: the authorities do not agree: it may not have been Benjamin Henry, American, but something-or-other Henry, a Scottish gunmaker.

martlet, the swift, comes from the French *martelet*, a variant— and a derivative—of *martinet*, a pet form of *Martin*. Compare, therefore, **martin.**

martynia is the fruit or the plant of the small genus *Martynia*; much used, in the warmer parts of the United States, for pickles. The genus takes its name from John Martyn (1699–1768), a practising physician and a keen botanist; indeed, he held the chair of Botany at Cambridge from 1732 to 1762. Also, he translated Virgil's *Bucolics* and *Georgics*, with a botanical and agricultural commentary, and published in 1728-37 his very considerable history of the rarer plants.

marxian (or **M**—) has come to synonymize 'characteristic of dialectical materialism' and, among those who set man's spiritual welfare above his economic status and physical comfort, 'economically doctrinaire' and 'communistically extremist'.

Karl Marx (1818–1883) developed his Communism from the

philosophy of Hegel and the economics of Ricardo : and gave to both a particularly materialist bias, yet with a skill that has made him the most influential economist since Adam Smith.

masochism, -ist, -istic. The delighting—the delighter—characteristic of the delighting—in either pain or humiliation or, indeed, both inflicted upon or suffered by oneself; especially as a form of sexual perversion and often compared or contrasted with **sadism** (etc.). **Masochism** derives from a glaring instance of this weakness described by the Austrian novelist, Leopold von Sacher-Masoch, who died in 1895, and the word first appeared in English in 1893—appropriately, in a medical dictionary. The Viennese pathologists, psychologists, psychiatrists have had much to say upon this painful subject.

' Nearly every public woman '—he means a prostitute—' has customers who are sadists and masochists,' Dr Ben Reitman, *The Second Oldest Profession*, 1936.

' It is not long since it was fashionable to believe that a reader who plunged through the loose shingle of—shall we say?—Theodore Dreiser's prose was by that resounding deed of masochism performing a duty to literature,' Charles Morgan, *Reflections in a Mirror*, 1944.

' There are two great moments in a woman's life : when first she finds herself to be deeply in love with her man, and when she leaves him. Leaving him enables her to be both sadist and masochist,' ' Palinurus ', *The Unquiet Grave*, 1945.

' We are great gluttons for punishment and, time and time again, like docile droves of masochistic Oliver Twists we keep coming up for more. And, time and time again, we get it ! ' : Ian Mackay in *News Chronicle*, April 11, 1946.

massic, preferable to **Massic,** is short for *Massic wine* and named after Mount *Massicus* in Campania. It is thus mentioned in Cyrus Redding's *Wines*, 1833, ' The Falernian . . . grew upon the volcanic Campania near Naples, where also the Massic was produced '; it was a wine of Classic Rome, and Horace refers to it in his *Odes* (I, 1) : *Est qui nec veteris pocula Massici, | nec partem solido demere de die | spernit*, which an anonymous of the mid-17th Century translates, ' In Massic wines some booze their time away '. (With thanks to The OED.)

Cf. therefore **falernian.**

masurium. From platinum ores and by the spectroscopic method, there was, along with **rhenium,** discovered in 1925 by the German scientists, Noddack and Tacke, an element they patriotically decided to name after the Masuren district—

' Masuria . . . forested lakeland ' (L. W. Lyde, *Europe*)—in East Prussia. As the no less readable than dependable *Chambers's Journal* neatly remarked, in the August issue of 1925 : ' From Berlin there comes the news that the same means have been employed to effect the recognition of two other new elements, to which the names *masurium* and *rhenium* have been given, in honour of Germany's eastern and western borderlands ' (quoted by The OED).

matico, a styptic made from the dried leaves of a South American pepper, derives from a shrub that has been prettily personified as *Matico*—a Spanish pet-form of *Mateo*, Matthew. The ' reason ' for the personification is obscure ; probably it was entirely arbitrary.

maud, a plaid that, grey and striped, is worn by shepherds in southern Scotland, hence a plaid-like travelling rug or wrap, is, says The OED (Webster discreetly saying nothing at all and Skeat and W as discreetly ignoring the term altogether), ' of obscure origin '. Yet The OED remarks, ' Compare *maldy* ', which happens to be a 16th–17th-Century Scottish word for ' a coarse woollen cloth, either grey or mixed in colour '. Now *Maldy*, like *Maud*, derives from *Matilda* : *Maud* is a Proper Name of complete dignity, whereas *Maldy*, like *Mal*, is a pet-form. Is there any insuperable objection to the fabrics, woven by the industrious Scottish women, having been called, the one affectionately *Maldy*, the other decorously *Maud* ?

maudlin ; ' foolishly drunk ' : from *maudlin*, ' weakly or tearfully emotional ' : from *maudlin*, ' tearful ' : from *Maudlin* : from Old French *Maudelene* or *Madeleine* : from Latin *Magdalena* : from Greek *Magdalēnē*, Mary Magdalen (or Magdalene), whom medieval—and later—painters have depicted with eyes red and swollen with weeping. Mary of Magdala (see **magdalen**) sat, with Mary the mother of James, by the sepulchre of Christ in the interval between His burial and His resurrection.

maumet ; maumetry. *Maumet*, an odd figure, a ' guy ' (hence, in dialect, a scarecrow) from *maumet*, a puppet, a doll (whence, probably, the obsolete term for a kind of pigeon) : from *maumet*, an idol : from *maumet*, a false god : from *Maumet*, a conflation of *Mahomet*, the term arising from those wars between the Christians and the Mohammedans which Christian historians have dignified with the name of Crusades. *Maumetry*, ' the characteristics and appurtenances of idolatry ' and spelt with a small *m*, is similarly related to *Maumetry* (capital *M*), Mohammedanism; the ending *-ry* is the anglicizing of the French suffix *-erie*, Latin *-eria*.

mauresque, a variant of *moresque* (q.v. at **moresca**), is a gallicism, somewhat archaic.

mauser is short either for *Mauser rifle* or for the later *Mauser pistol*. ' And in one neat stacked flat pile, old German 6·5 mm. Mauser rifles . . . The Mausers were the Kuwait weapons,' James Aldridge, *The Sea Eagle*, 1944.

The rifle, named after its inventors, was adopted by the German Army in 1871 and improved in 1884; it remained the standard Army rifle for a generation. It was in 1867 that the brothers Mauser, Peter Paul (1838–1914) and Wilhelm (1834–82) perfected the breech-loader that became known as ' the Mauser model 1871 '; in 1897, Peter Paul invented the Mauser magazine rifle, which remained in Army use for many years. The great German big-game and sporting rifle was the **mannlicher.**

Compare **Lüger** and **Webley** in the secondary list and **browning, colt, derringer, smith & wesson** in this main vocabulary.

mausoleum, mostly humorous, for a large, gloomy structure (e.g., a bed), room, building, derives from *mausoleum*, a magnificent tomb—such as that monumental tomb erected at Halicarnassus in Asia Minor to the glory of *Mausolus*, king of Caria, and completed ca. 350 B.C. The *Mausoleum of Halicarnassus* was ranked as one of the Seven Wonders of the World. *Mausoleum* is the Latin form of the Greek *Mausōleion*, an adjective (from *Mausolos*) used as a noun; Martial and other Latin writers employed *mausoleum* for ' a splendid sepulchre '.

maverick. In Texas, ca. 1845–56, a certain civil engineer owned many, many cattle: some, through no design of his and, indeed, unknown to him, did not get themselves branded: hence, all unbranded cattle, but especially calves and yearlings, became *mavericks*, and so, derivatively, all masterless persons, all wanderlusters.

mavrodaphne. ' Wolfe unwrapped a bottle of Mavrodaphne . . . . . . They started to drink the wine,' James Aldridge, *Of Many Men*, 1946.

This is ' one of the best known of the modern Greek wines: it is a red wine, fortified, rather sweet and satisfying . . . It

282

is made from the grape of the same name ' (*Wine*, by André L. Simon, 1946—Section VIII of *A Concise Encyclopaedia of Gastronomy*) : and the name of the grape obviously is formed, in part, of **daphne.**

naw-worm is *maw worm*, a worm ' infesting ' the intestines (*maw*, the stomach) ; but the use of *maw-worm* for a hypocrite comes from the character *Mawworm* in the play entitled *The Hypocrite* (adapted from Molière's *Tartufe*—see **Tartufe**—and Cibber's *The Non-Juror*), 1769, by Isaac Bickerstaffe, who, after writing a number of popular comedies, in 1762 fled the country because he was suspected of a capital crime. He died ca. 1812, aged about seventy-seven.

nawkin. See **malkin.**

naxim. ' The marauder of the desert laid away his spear just before the war [of 1914–18], and to-day goes out on his raids with a Maxim,' T. E. Lawrence, ' The Changing East '—in *The Round Table*, September 1920.

' I'm giving you command because I think you can get things done . . . You'll have twelve sailors and a maxim gun from Latona, ten agents from here . . . and fifty Venizelist soldiers,' Wilfred Macartney, *Zigzag*, 1937.

The *Maxim machine gun*, in its early days called also the *Maxim mitrailleuse*, was invented by Sir Hiram Maxim, who died in 1916 ; it came into general use ca. 1885. A well-known modification is the *Maxim-Nordenfelt*.

Compare the more easily handled **lewis** and the **nordenfelt.**

naxwell. A magnetic unit—cf. **gauss.**

From James Clerk Maxwell (1831–79), a brilliant Scottish physicist, who, though he died so untimely young, had already done more than thirty years' work ; at the age of fifteen, he had written a paper on a new method of tracing Cartesian ovals. The first professor of experimental physics at Cambridge, he worked for years upon electromagnetism and in 1873 published his great *Treatise on Electricity and Magnetism*.

Compare also **joule** and **volt.**

nayonnaise is short for *sauce mayonnaise*, wherein the second word would pose a problem—if we were unaware of the variant *sauce mahonnaise*. In French, *mahonnais* refers to *Mahon*, a town on the east coast of the island of Minorca ; *Mahon = porte Mahone = portus Magonis* = port of Mago (a Carthaginian admiral).

In 1782, Louis, Duc de Mahon (1717–96), a very distin-

guished French soldier that had entered the Spanish servic
twenty years earlier, forced the British to capitulate in Minorc
' What's this stuff—potato salad? You know I hate mayon
naise and messes of that kind,' Victor Gunn, *Nice Day for
Murder*, 1945.

mazarine is a dark rich blue. The **mazarine hood** is probabl
connected with the Duchesse de Mazarin, who died at Chelse
in 1699 : thence, perhaps, comes the hue, which may, howeve
derive from Cardinal Mazarin, who ruled France during Lou
XIV's minority. Of Sicilian birth (his real name was Giul
Mazarini : 1602–61), he became a naturalized Frenchman an
succeeded Richelieu as Prime Minister of France ; amassing
very large fortune, he effectually patronized literature.

mazurka. A Polish dance, lively and triple-timed, introduce
into England about the year 1830; hence, a piece of musi
accompanying it. In Polish, the word *mazurka* signifies '
woman of the province of *Mazovia* ': compare the relate
dance, the **kouiaviak,** named from the Polish province c
Kujavein. (Scholes.)

McCoy, the ; often **the real McCoy.** (*Mackay* is apparentl
an Australian and English variation.) ' The real thing '–
something or somebody the best of its kind, the best of his clas
or profession or sport. An Americanism, it would seem—fo
the evidence is less satisfactory than Americans think it—t
derive from ' Kid ' McCoy, American boxer, who was, early i
the 20th Century, for some time at the head of his class. Se
my dictionaries *of Slang* and *of the Underworld*.

meander (to wind in and out—and all about; a sinuou
winding) ; **meandrine** (characterized by many sinuou
windings). Of a river in Central Hindustan, L. W. Lyde ha
written, ' The Gumti, " The Meanderer ", with all the sug
gestions that the name carries ' (*The Continent of Asia*, 1933).
The adjective comes from the noun, and so also does the verl
Via Latin, it derives from the Greek *Maiandros*, the name of tha
particularly crooked river in Phrygia (now part of wester
Turkey) which has long been called the Menderes. There ar
other winding rivers, both in Asia Minor and elsewhere ; bu
concerning the Aegean coastlands of Asia Minor, Lyde ha
remarked that ' westward . . . the rivers . . . deposit thei
burdens of silt, and have built up rich flat plains, over whic
they wander in the way that has given us the word *meander* '

284

the Menderes river has achieved fame because its basin has, ever since 1200 B.C. (or even longer), been economically of paramount importance—rich soil, excellent climate, mineral wealth, easiness of access, a fine harbour.

Mecca (in its figurative senses, including ' the colour Tuscan brown ': preferably *mecca*). Mohammad's birthplace in Arabia, of which it is one of the two holy cities, Medina being the other, represents the Arabic *makkah*. Derivatively, it has, by a very natural development, come to signify ' a place one longs to visit ', especially as a pilgrim, and also ' birthplace of a faith ' or even, rather trivially, of a policy; compare its frequent occurrence in the names of cafés.

' Chicago has always been the mecca of vagabonds and thieves, of thriving wealth and miserable destitution,' Jim Tully, *Emmett Lawler*, 1922.

' The night of the Friday on which the body of the Prophet (on whom be prayer and peace) was brought to rest in the Kabba in Mecca, the Holy City where he had been born, a miraculous star waved its golden hair across the sky,' Henry de Monfreid, *Hashish*, 1935.

' Mecca, which was " Holy " before the days of Mahomet, seems to have owed its importance . . . to its real centrality as a market ', foot-noted thus, ' Its " Feasts " are at times when the different fruits, skins, etc., of the plateau are ready for sale,' Lionel W. Lyde, *The Continent of Asia*, 1933.

' Pilgrimage for the Mohammedan was obligatory. Unless he were incapacitated by illness or circumstance, he had to make the journey to Mecca before he died,' G. H. T. Kimble, *Geography of the Middle Ages*, 1938.

Mechlin. ' The great spinning centre [of Belgium]—for hemp and cotton as well as flax—is in the higher humidity of the Lys-Scheldt confluence; and this site, at about equal distances from the three great lace-making centres of Bruges, Brussels, and Mechlin, and at the limit of the tide on the Scheldt, has made Ghent the textile metropolis of Belgium,' Lionel W. Lyde, *The Continent of Europe*, (4th edition) 1930.

So *mechlin = Mechlin lace*. In the 18th Century, there were *Mechlin cravats*—made of this lace. The term *Mechlin embroidery* is a synonym for *Mechlin lace*; ' The thread that was inserted round the outlines of that lace gave it somewhat the look of Embroidery ' (Caulfield & Saward, *A Dictionary of Needlework*, 1882—quoted by The OED).

The name *Mechlin* is the English form of the Flemish *Mechelen*, corresponding to French *Malines*.

medeola. The ' Indian cucumber root, one of Thoreau's favourite flowers, is named after the sorceress Medea, and is called " medeola ",' John Burroughs (1837–1921 : American naturalist). In Greek mythology, *Mēdeia* (Latin *Medea*)—prominent in the story of the Argonauts—was, like her aunt Circe, an enchantress. (DAE.)

médoc. ' The city of Bordeaux had every opportunity of . . . specialising in shipping the products of the mild Médoc peninsula to the Severn ports of Britain . . . . . The Haut-Médoc clarets are grown on the slopes of Margaux, Lafite, Latour, etc.,' L. W. Lyde, *Europe*; and see the quotation at **Bordeaux.**

In Médoc, a district in the Gironde, are to be found all the best clarets—known collectively as *médoc* (or even *medoc*).

Medusa or **m—,** the jellyfish being *medusa*, the Gorgon being *Medusa*; *medusal* or *medusan*, the common-property forms of the adjective *Medusean*, ' of the Medusa '. The transferred sense, ' a woman whose glances are below freezing-point,' comes from the fact that, in Greek mythology, *Medusa* (the Latin form of the Greek *Medousa*) was one of the three Gorgons (see **gorgon**) : Sthenno, ' the Mighty '; Euryale, ' the Far-Wanderer '; and our particular ray of sunshine, Medousa, ' the Queen ' (from an old verb, *medein*, ' to rule ')—*Medousa* being the Proper-Noun form of *medousa*, the feminine of *medōn*, ' a ruler, a lord, a guardian '. A glance from any of the Gorgons turned mere men and women to stone. Medusa owes her survival in popular (?) language to the fact that, of the Gorgons, she alone was mortal.

meet at Philippi. See **Philippi.**

megilp; in 18th Century, *magilp*, still often used ; there are more than a dozen other variants, including *McGilp*. To take the lexicographers chronologically : Skeat omits the term ; the editors of The OED say, ' Of obscure origin ' and cold-douche the proposal that it derives from a surname ; W admits, although he does not warmly advocate, derivation from a surname ; Webster, ' Origin unknown '. *Megilp* being a colour-vehicle for artists (the verb derives from the noun), I think it very probable that it was devised by some talented manufacturer of ' artists' accessories ' or by an art-dealer with a turn for chemistry, and that his name was, in fact, *McGilp* or *McGuilp* or some variation thereof.

megohm. See **ohm.**

Melpomene is one of the nine Muses—the Muse of Tragedy, as **Thalia** is of Comedy. By derivation, *Melpomene* is 'the Songstress', from *melpein, melpesthai*, ' to sing '; and presumably she was so named for one of two reasons : that primitive tragedy was chanted, or that every Greek tragedy contains a lyric or two or three. See also the entry at **muse.**

melton. ' His body encased in a huge overcoat of blue Melton,' George Bronson-Howard, *An Enemy to Society*, 1911 ; an American novel.

It is a kind of broadcloth, used in men's wear—especially the *Melton jackets* formerly adorning hunters. Melton Mowbray, in Leicestershire, has for centuries been a famous hunting centre : ca. 1820–60, *Meltonian* constituted a sporting synonym for ' an adept at hunting the fox '.

Mendelian; Mendelianism or, better, **Mendelism,** which might well be written *mendelism*. Now mendelism is the operation of *Mendel's law*, or its principles, or again *Mendelian inheritance*. This ' law ' was suspected, checked, formulated by Gregor J. Mendel (1822–84), an Austrian abbot of the Augustinian Order. He began as a botanist, entered the Order at the age of twenty-one, and continued as a botanist; he experimented with peas in the monastery garden at Brünn. The results of his experiments and impeccably careful observation were published in 1865, but did not become generally known until 1900, when several scientists, especially DeVries, publicized them.

mentor, ' a shrewd, experienced (and trusted) adviser ' : as is the Greek *Mentor*, adviser to Telemachus in the early part of *The Odyssey*, where, in point of unpedantic fact, it is Pallas Athene who speaks in the guise of Mentor. The name derives from the radical *men*, ' think ' (as in *menoináo*, I intend), with which the Latin *mens*, ' mind ', is cognate; and ' the currency of the word is due to Fénelon's *Aventures de Télémaque* ' (W), a book that appeared in 1699.

Mephistopheles, Mephistophelean. Generically, *Mephistopheles* is ' a diabolical person, sinisterly crafty and evil and persuasive ', and *Mephistophelean* is the adjective therein implied; often applied to a man sardonic, too worldly-wise and dangerously persuasive—a **Machiavelli** of evil counsel. The medieval-demonological conception of him as one of the seven chief devils and, after Satan, the most powerful of the fallen archangels, was transformed by Marlowe in *Dr Faustus*

(1588) and by Goethe in *Faust* (1808, 1832) into a callous, contemptuous, scoffing and merciless fiend, luring Christians to hell by promising them the world in return for their souls. The name *Mephistopheles* is of uncertain origin—a Germanic abracadabra word of the kind beloved by alchemists, by conjurers and by charlatans, the earliest form being *Mephostophiles*, ‘lover of—hence, addict to—something or other’ (perhaps darkness : Greek *philos*, ‘ friend ’ + *mē̆*, ‘ not ’ + *phōs*, ‘ light ’).

mercerize, to strengthen cotton fabric and simultaneously render it more susceptible to dyes by means of a chemical process, owes its name to John *Mercer* (1791–1866), an English calico-printer, who, chemist as well, discovered this process in 1850. He also discovered such dyes as were suitable for printing calico in hues of orange, yellow, bronze. (Webster BD.)

mercurial; mercury. The former derives from Latin *mercurialis*, ‘ of or belonging to *Mercurius* ’ or Mercury; and *mercury* or quicksilver is so called because, like Mercury, it is quick to move, being the only metal that is, at ordinary temperatures, liquid. In Roman mythology, Mercury, besides being the god of commerce and gain (compare Latin *merx*, merchandise), was, like his Greek prototype, Hermes, the messenger of the gods ; indeed, *mercury* (small *m*), was, in 16th–18th-Century English literature, a synonym of ‘ messenger ’ or ‘ news-bearer ’. For the formation, compare **jovial** and **martial.**

merryandrew is a common-noun shape of *Merry Andrew*, a quack’s attendant, often buffoon (*merry*) as well as assistant (*Andrew*), *Andrew* being very frequently used as the generic name for ‘ men-servants ’ or ‘ serving men ’. Compare **zany** and, despite the sex, **abigail.**

mersailles. See entry at **marseillaise.**

mervousness was a political short-lifer of the 1880’s. In ca. 1882 the Duke of Argyll coined it to describe Lord Roberts’s state of mind, Roberts having warned the British Government that Russia had designs upon *Merv* in Turkestan ; the Russians did, in fact, take possession of the town in 1883–84. I.e., the word is a blend of ‘ *Merv* ’ and ‘ nerv*ousness* ’. (W.)

mesmerism; mesmerize. *Mesmerism* should be compared with **galvanism.** Both *mesmerism* and *mesmerize* were formed from *Mesmer*. Franz Anton Mesmer (1734–1815) was an Austrian physician (compare the 20th-Century body of psychological and pathological thought expressed by 'the Vienna School'). He deluded himself that he possessed occult force, a delusion upon which he erected a theory of animal magnetism. In 1778 he went to Paris. The French Government held an investigation into his séances and declared him to be an impostor. There is, it seems, no such thing as animal magnetism.

The scrupulous writer is careful to distinguish between *mesmerism* and *galvanism* and *hypnotism*.

messianic, especially in *the messianic* (or *M—*), or *Messiah, complex*. The adjective *Messianic* comes from Modern Latin *Messianicus*, 'of the Messiah': and *Messiah* is the Vulgate *Messias* (the same in Greek), representing Aramaic *m'shiha*, Hebrew *mashiah*, 'the Anointed'—from *mashah*, 'to anoint'. (Compare the origin of *Christ*.) A *messianic complex*, therefore, is a person's obsession by the fancy that he, or she, is the Redeemer come again to earth. In his *Hellenistic Civilisation*, Dr W. W. Tarn speaks of 'the growth and modification of the Messianic hope' characterizing Judaea during that pre-Christian period. The 'central thought' of the Apocalyptic literature 'was the Messiah'.

' "You mean Harris, a thin squirt with a Messiah complex?" —"That's him ",' Don Castle, *Do Your Own Time*, 1938.

methuselah. 'If you live to be as old as Methuselah, you won't understand the Theory of Relativity.'

'And all the days of Methuselah were nine hundred sixty and nine years: and he died,' *Genesis*, v, 27; that chapter is full of alarmingly ancient men, the women seeming to have been more fortunate. Hence *methuselah*, an extremely aged man.

In Hebrew, *Methusha'el*. The form *Methusalem* is an illiteracy, influenced by *Jerusalem*.

Micawber; Micawberish or **m—; micawberism.** ' " We weren't satisfied about Gussage's death. We always expected something more would turn up." "Micawber & Co. Bless your sweet innocence ",' H. C. Bailey, *Dead Men's Shoes*, 1942.

Mr Wilkins Micawber is one of the Dickens immortals, one of the characters that maintain the vitality of *David Copperfield*. Micawber was not quite hopelessly mercurial, not quite fatuously optimistic (he not merely hopes, he expects 'something to turn up'); although impecunious and feckless, he was basically no fool and by his abilities and integrity he overcame his fecklessness and justified his optimism. Both *Micawberish* (better with a small *m*) and *micawberism* refer, above all, to his insuperable optimism and cheerfulness.

Dickens, with grotesquely effective irony, has adopted this surname precisely because it derives from, or at the least is cognate with, the second element in the French ' danse macabre ' (see **macabre**).

michelangelesque is an adjective formed from *Michel Ange*, the French shape of *Michelangelo* Buonarroti (1475–1564) ; compare *michelangelism*, his artistic manner or tendencies, or such a manner and tendencies in others. Sculptor and architect and poet as well as mighty painter, he stands second only to Da Vinci among the splendours and excellencies of Italian art.

Midas, especially **the Midas touch.** ' There was a famous king of Phrygia, up country [in Asia Minor], who became a proverb ; for everything that Midas touched " turned to gold " ; but the raiders were too much for him, and he drank bull's blood and died,' T. R. Glover, *The Ancient World*, 1935.

Granted a wish, Midas wished that everything he touched might turn to gold, but when he found that this effect applied even to such things as food and drink, he asked to be relieved of his ' good fortune '. As ordered, he washed in the river Pactolus : thereafter the sands of Pactolus contained gold : whence **Pactolian.**

mike, to ; do a mike. These slang terms, respectively ' to waste time, to loiter, to idle ' and ' to decamp ', are, the former perhaps, the latter probably, connected with *Mike*, for a variant of the latter is *do a mick* (i.e., *a Mick*). *Michael* is a typically Irish given-name, and the attribution of idleness is typical of the English attitude towards Irishmen.

milliner, -ery. Milliner is simply a corruption of *Milaner*, ' an inhabitant of Milan ' ; The OED quotes the enlightening example, ' He was encountered by the Mylleners and the Venicyans ' (1529) ; thence the natural development, ' a dealer in articles made at Milan ', e.g. ' Milan bonnets ' (famous), ribbons, gloves : and *millinery* is collective for all such articles, *milliner* being their maker. Ernest Weekley notes that *millayne* (or *milleyne*) *needles* are often mentioned in the Naval Accounts of 1495–97. *Milan* itself comes from Latin *Mediolaneum*, ' the Middle Plain site ' (Lyde).

miltonia. ' I handed Horstmann the cards. " For that bunch of miltonias and lycastes. The germination dates are already in ",' Rex Stout, *Over My Dead Body*, (English edition) 1940.

A *miltonia* is a plant, or its flower, known also as a pansy orchid—a tropical North American orchid, named after Lord C. Fitzwilliam (1786–1857), Viscount *Milton*, who, in addition to his interest in statesmanship, was a man of parts.

Minerva, owing to Greek influence, is mostly apprehended as the Roman counterpart of Athene, the goddess of learning and wisdom; as the personification of wisdom, she is, according to Webster, obsolete. That is not true. She is merely out of fashion. Among horticulturists, those wise delvers !, *Minerva* is the name of a hardy Ghent azalea.

The word itself is cognate with Latin *mens*, ' the mind '; compare Greek *menos*, ' purpose '.

minié; colloquially **minnie** (or **M**—). A *Minié ball* or *bullet* is used in the *Minié rifle*, which constitutes the origin of the synonymous term that appears in the shorter, often uncapitalled, form at the beginning of this entry.

Claude Etienne Minié (1814–79), the inventor, was a French army officer. The bullet was designed to expand and thus take the rifling. As early as 1855, the Americans knew all about this firearm of merit—and its equally convincing bullet.

' When he was sixteen he ran away and joined the Union Army, and got a minie ball in the leg during a battle that never had a name,' Nard Jones, *Still to the West*, 1947.

minorca is a *Minorca fowl*, a Mediterranean breed of domestic fowl resembling, though larger than, the **leghorn.** *Minorca* is the lesser of the two main islands of the Balearic group in the western Mediterranean; in the 18th Century it was a British possession. *Minorca* derives from the Spanish *Menorca*, itself from Latin *Balearis Minor*, the smaller Balearis : compare **majolica.**

Minotaur. At the beginning of his *Cities of Sin* (1934), Hendrik de Leeuw likens the ravages and outrages of the ' white slave ' traffic to the demands of Minotaur.

The Greek-mythical Minotaur ; *Minotauros*, the *tauros* or bull of Minos ; had a bull's head on a human body. ' It is noteworthy that the Phoenicians had a god, Baal Moloch, of this form,' remarks Sir Paul Harvey. The Minotaur was kept in the **labyrinth,** where it consumed those youths and, especially, those maidens whom Athens sent as tribute ; it was the gallant Theseus who slew the ravening and ungallant monster.

Cf. **juggernaut** and **Moloch.**

mint. ' I sit in my study, and upon the table before me lies a denarius of Maximin, as fresh as when the triumvir of Juno Moneta sent it from the mint,' Conan Doyle in ' Giant Maximin ', reprinted in *Tales of Long Ago*.

Now most dictionaries will tell you that *mint* comes from Latin *moneta*, ' money '; but does this go far enough even for our word *money*? It was in the temple of Juno Moneta that money was coined in Rome, and *Juno Moneta* literally means ' Juno, the admonisher, the adviser ' : in general; hence in that not inconsiderable particular, money: compare *monēre*, ' to warn ', and *monitor*.

Miss Molly; Miss Nancy. See **Molly** and **nance.**

mitchella is a plant, or its berry, of the genus *Mitchella*; a small, creeping evergreen, affecting mossy, shaded banks; named in honour of Dr Mitchell of New York. John Mitchell, who died in 1768, was a physician, a botanist, a cartographer; little is known about him, apart from a famous map he published in 1755. (Webster BD.)

mithridatize. To render immune to poison by increasing tolerance to it with doses gradually increased.

Mithridates VI, King of Pontus, implacable enemy of Rome, was finally driven out of Europe by Sulla. He took refuge in Tauris, where he so fortified himself against poison that, at last wearied by his son's treachery, he committed suicide: but, unable to poison himself, he was forced to beg a slave to stab him to death.

Mizpah or **Mizpeh** sometimes serves as a talismanic inscription upon finger-rings; hence *Mizpah ring*. The Hebrew *mitspeh*, literally, ' a watch-tower ', became the name of several towns in ancient Palestine; hence, *mizpah!*, ' be careful! watch! '

' The name of [this heap of stones] was . . . Mizpah; for he said, The Lord watch between me and thee,' *Genesis*, xxxi, 48–49.

mob-cap; mobled queen. The indoor cap worn by women in the 18th and early 19th Century may, possibly (the origin being very obscure), be a *Mab-cap*, where *Mab* is generic for ' woman '. But Shakespeare's ' mobled queen ' in *Hamlet* had her face and head muffled, not capped; nevertheless, *mobled* may be *mobbled*—hence, a variant of *mabbled*, ' with head muffled up ', and *mabble* not improbably derives from *Mab*: compare *mab*, ' to dress untidily '.

mocha has been current for ' coffee ' since about 1880 in the U.S.A.: at first a tramp's word, it promptly worked its way into general slang; and soon it became a colloquialism. George Ade (*More Fables in Slang*, 1900) says of a married couple that, sweet to each other in public, they threw things at each other in private, ' They did not Mocha and Java '—i.e., agree—' worth a Cent ' (see **jamocha**).

  ' Mocha, whose splendor was once sung by early Islamic poets, was long famed for its export of coffee, but it has now been left literally high and dry by the receding sea ', foot-noted thus : ' Up to the close of the seventeenth century the world's coffee supply had come from this part of Arabia ' : W. W. Hyde, *Ancient Greek Mariners*, 1947.

modena, as a colour, means ' deep purple '; sometimes the hue is described as *modena red*. That is, *Modena-red* or the red of Modena. The artificial colouring was first devised and manufactured at Modena, the capital of the Italian province thus named; a university town and an archiepiscopal see. The colour was required for dyeing academic and ecclesiastical hoods, gowns, head-gear.

moët, ' champagne ', is a lower-cased generalization from *Moët and Chandon champagne*, made by the firm of *Moët et Chandon* of Reims (anglicé *Rheims*). Reims, in western Champagne, is famous for its vast and numerous champagne-cellars. As early as 1841 Thackeray, a connoisseur of wine, wrote it with a small *m* : ' real moët '.

  Compare **widow.**

mogador. See **gum-mogador.**

Mogul; moguls. A *Mogul* (better *m*) is ' an important man; a magnate '; *moguls* are playing cards of quite the best quality.

  ' Among the neighbours he became aware that he was, in a sense, back among the producers and the executive moguls of Hollywood. He was a minnow among tritons,' William McFee, *Spenlove in Arcady*, 1942.

  A Mogul, properly, is a Mongolian: Persian *Mugul*, from *Mongol*, which is itself a native Mongolian word : see **mongol.** But the figurative sense of *mogul* comes either from *the Grand*

Mogul, the Emperor of Delhi (*the* Mongolian *par excellence*), or from the *Mongol dynasty* of rulers in India.

mohock. The mohocks (or Mohocks) were a gang of aristocratic roughs that, early in the 18th Century, terrorized Londoners at night : ' A race of rakes . . . that play the devil about this town every night, slit people's noses, and beat them,' Swift in his *Journal to Stella*, March 18, 1711–12 : whence the **yahoo**? Hence, *to mohock*, ' to assail in the manner of a mohock '.

Occasionally spelt *Mohawk*, in reference to the origin of the term. The *Mohawks*, who were the easternmost Red Indian tribe of the Iroquois Confederacy, lived mainly along the Mohawk River. They bore an unenviable reputation for their bellicosity and ferocity ; they conquered even the Delawares. The women, however, were more gentle ; the historical hero, Hiawatha, somewhat resembled them in this.

Compare **tityre-tu.**

moke, colloquial—originally slang—for a donkey, is, according to The OED, of obscure origin ; but W hits the etymological nail right on the head when he says, ' Perhaps from some proper name (? *Moggy*) applied to the ass. Compare provincial . . . *Mocke hath lost her shoe* (Skelton). *Mocke, Mok, Mog, Mug* all occur as personal names in 13 Cent. and survive in surnames *Mokes, Moxon* ' ; *Mog* is an extant pet-form of *Margaret*. With *moke*, compare the synonymous **cuddy** and **neddy** and **donkey** itself.

moll; gun moll. ' Here, said everyone, was a true gun moll, " the kind that would go to hell for a guy ". She was Dolores Delaney, one of three sisters, all of whom had become the molls of vicious criminals,' J. Edgar Hoover, *Persons in Hiding*, 1938. Here *moll* = *Moll* = *Mary*, the commonest of the female font-names.

Originally, both *moll* and *gun moll* were cant : see my *A Dictionary of the British and American Underworld* ; and, for the slang extensions of *moll*, see *A Dictionary of Slang*.

Molly or **molly,** an effeminate man or boy, a milksop, is explained by its alternative form, *Miss Molly*. Compare **nancy** or **nance.** The sense ' a large basket for fruit or vegetables ' is an arbitrary personification ; arbitrary—unless there be a reference to a woman (a *moll*) forming, as it were, a fruit-basket with apron folded to contain the fruit held against her lap ; if ever you have seen women in an orchard, you will know what I mean.

294

molly-coddle, n. and v. The verb comes from the noun, which is an assonantal elaboration of the preceding term; a *molly* coddles himself.

Moloch. 'An idolatrous religion is one in which time is substituted for eternity—either past time, in the form of a rigid tradition, or future time, in the form of progress towards Utopia. And both are Molochs, both demand human sacrifice on an enormous scale,' Aldous Huxley, *Time Must Have a Stop*, 1945.—' The Moloch of war and the Minotaur of The White Slave Traffic ' (any knowledgeable journalist).

'Moloch, a Canaanitish idol identical with Hebrew *melek*, king, owes his fame especially to Milton. His name is often used of a merciless all-devouring force, just as we erroneously attribute to **Juggernaut** . . . the wholesale crushing of fanatical pilgrims ' (WWN).

Cf. also **gehenna.**

molossus is the latinized form of Greek *molossos (pous)*, ' Molossian foot ' in metric : three long syllables. The *Molossi* inhabited, in Epirus (north-west Greece), a country named after them *Molossis* or *Molossia*. 'Epirus . . . exhibits a long . . . conflict between . . . federalism and monarchy; by 300 its three stems, Molossians, Chaonians and Thesprotians, had constituted themselves the federal " Epirote Alliance " under the headship of the Molossian king ' (W. W. Tarn, *Hellenistic Civilisation*, 1927).

The metrical foot may owe its genesis to the impressive tread of *the Molossian hounds*, famed throughout Greece and antiquity.

Momus, a carping critic, a censorious fault-finder, is merely a transferred use of *Momus*, that minor ' god ' of Greek mythology who personifies criticism and fault-finding. His name is but the aggrandizement of Greek *mōmos*, ' blame, censure ': compare *mōmaomai* and *mōmeuo*, ' I chide, blame, find fault with '.

mondayish, ' tired, despondent, " fed up " with life, lacking interest in men and things ' : *Mondayish*, ' feeling, as one so often does on Monday, chilled by the prospect of another week of work '—as though work, or at least congenial work, did not afford life's most enduring satisfaction !

money. See **mint.**

mongol or **mongolian; mongolism.** A *mongol* (or *mongolian*) is one who has *mongolian* symptoms or the disease itself, which is

295

called *mongolism*, a cranial malformation and, like a *Mongol*, slanting eyes. But *mongolian*, the noun, may also (usually *M*—) denote a Mongolian rug, more usually called a *Chinese Turkestan*. The word *Mongol* is a native Mongolian term, from *mong*, ' brave ' : Cf. **mogul.**

monitor, ' a small ironclad armed, properly with one heavy gun, loosely with several ', has been generalized from Captain Ericsson's *Monitor*, employed in the American Civil War against the South (' After Ericsson's *Monitor* had overcome the Southern armoured frigate—the *Merrimac*—the James estuary . . . was open to the Northern ships supporting McLellan,' Ll. Rodwell Jones, *North America*, 1924) : Ericsson thus named it because he intended it to constitute a severe warning to the Southerners : from *monitor*, ' something that conveys a warning '. A certain single-gunned English monitor used to steam up and down, a mile off the coast of Anzac Bay in Gallipoli, in the summer and autumn of 1915, and shell the Turkish trenches every evening. From Latin *monēre*, ' to warn '.
Cf. **dreadnought.**

monkey. ' Low German *Moneke*, son of Martin the Ape in *Reinke de Vos*, the 15th Century Low German version of the *Roman de Renart*. Earlier is Old French *Monequin*, *Monekin*, occurring in a French version of part of the epic, and evidently from Flemish diminutive of some personal name. Italian *monicchio* . . . is from Teutonic, and related forms are recorded in Spanish and Portuguese. *Moneke* is a German surname with many variants . . ., derived from a Teutonic name-element which belongs to Gothic *muns*, mind, Old Norse *munr*, mind . . ., English *mind*. Its choice for the ape was perhaps due to association with Low German *monnik*, monk (cf. French *moineau*, sparrow, literally little monk, from brown-capped head, and see *talapoin*). For formation cf. *Reinke* from name-element *Regin* (see *reynard*) and other similar names in the same poem ', the *Roman de Renart* (Reynard the Fox). I quote thus fully from W to recall the excellence of his etymological dictionary, so unfortunately out of print.

monongahela is short for *Monongahela whiskey*, originally that manufactured ca. 1820 in the lands about the Monongahela River in Pennsylvania. From all accounts, it was potent stuff; so were the men that drank it.

monroeism = *Monroe doctrine*. ' In the Monroe Doctrine we had told Europe we would let her alone over there if she would let
296

us alone in our New World,' James Truslow Adams (who is fully alive to the dangers of isolationism), *The Epic of America*, 1933.

James Monroe (1758–1831), fifth President (1817–25) of the United States, promulgated in his annual message of 1823 his Monroe Doctrine of the independence of his country; the Doctrine resulted in part from his convictions at the time of the 1812 war with England.

montbretia is a plant—or its flower—of the genus *Tritonia*. It was named after the French botanist A. J. Coquebert de *Montbret*, who died in 1801. The *-ia* ending is typical of the plant-names of modern or scientific Latin : compare **dahlia, lobelia,** and many other flower-names in this dictionary.

montgolfier, in the late 18th–19th Century, meant ' a balloon '. Named after the French brothers J. M. & J. E. Montgolfier, who invented it in 1783. The *montgolfier*, short for *M. balloon*, was raised, not by gas, but by heated air.

mop. See **mob-cap.**

moresca ; moresque ; morisco. A *morisco* is, loosely, a morris-dance, but properly a Moorish-dance ; *moresque* (or *M*—), in addition to signifying, in French, ' a Moorish dance ', means ' Moorish—in style, e.g. of architecture, or in design, e.g. of furniture ' ; and whereas *moresco* is ' Moorish ' in Italian, *morisco* is ' Moorish ' in Spanish, both coming from *Moro*, ' a Moor ' (in both Italian and Spanish). *Moresca*, therefore, is Italian ; the feminine of the adjective, with a noun understood —probably *danza*. But *moresco* is also used—a synonym of (*danza*) *moresca*.

' In a composition called a *moresca* or *frottola*, Orlando di Lasso has written a certain progression of chords to the text, *miaow, miaow*,' Donald Tovey, *The Integrity of Music*, 1941.

Moor ultimately represents Greek *mauros*, ' dark ', whence *Mauros*, ' an inhabitant of Mauretania '—a country in northern Africa, where, not unnaturally, the people have a skin dark-bronzed by the sun.

morisque, besides meaning ' a Moorish dance ' (compare the preceding entry), means—more usually means—' a morris dance '. This *morisque* is, in fact, the old French form of the morris.

morocco. Leather made—originally in Morocco—from goat-skins tanned with sumac, a North-African shrub, the tan being extracted from the leaves.

Our *morocco* ' communizes ' *Morocco*, and *Morocco* merel⸱
Europeanizes *Marrakesh*, the native form of an Arabic wor⸱
meaning ' Extreme West '. In Italian, Spanish, French, th⸱
first syllable is *Ma-*, which, obviously, goes closer to the nativ⸱
and the Arabic words.

Morpheus, (safe) in the arms of; morphia; morphine
The first is an obsolescent genteelism for ' asleep '; the tw⸱
drugs are opium-derived pain-alleviatives and sleep-inducers
' Have you ever tried experiments of that sort, Mr Ashmun
Ether, atropine, hashish, hyoscine, morphine? They all seen
to set the mental faculties askew in a peculiar fashion,' J. J
Connington, *Jack-in-the-Box*, 1944.

Morpheus, cognate with whose name are also such words a
anthropomorphic and *morphology*, was the Greek god of dreams an⸱
sleep ; and *Morpheus* derives from *morphē*, ' form, shape '.

morris (dance). Both The OED and W explicitly, and Skea⸱
implicitly, derive the term ultimately from Continental term
signifying ' a Moorish dance '—as in Flemish *mooriske dans*
The morris, however, is a very English dance, with Robin Hoo⸱
characters ; as Skeat suggests, ' the use of the tabor as a⸱
accompaniment ' may explain the Moorish origin of this mos⸱
un-Moorish dance, or, as W proposes, it was ' perhaps origin⸱
ally danced by people with blackened faces ' (cf. ' nigge⸱
minstrels ').

Morris, a *Morris* (*motor*) *car*, as well-known in Britain as the **For⸱**
is in North America. The word constitutes one outward shap⸱
of the fame enjoyed by ' Morris of Oxford ', now Lord Nuffield
whose progress from the humble bicycle-shop to the grea⸱
works at Cowley forms one of the romances of the 20t⸱
Century.

morris pike is a Moorish pike. The term occurs in Sir T
Elyot's *Castel of Helth*, 1534, and in Shakespeare's *A Comedy o⸱*
Errors. This kind of pike was merely supposed to be o⸱
Moorish origin.

morrison = *Morrison shelter* (cf. **anderson**). A type of insid⸱
shelter against bombs, it had a steel table-top and frame an⸱
wired sides. Named after Mr Herbert Morrison (b. 1888), th⸱
Cabinet Minister in charge of home security in Britain at th⸱
time ; and very useful in the ' blitz ' of 1940–41. In slang i⸱
was irreverently called a *Morrison mousetrap*.

298

morse. ‘ People in France and Norway were tapping out their
V’s in morse to the annoyance and confusion of their oppressors,’
Francis Beeding, *The Twelve Disguises*, 1942.

Here, *morse* = *Morse alphabet* or *telegraphy*, which, consisting
of dots and dashes, has been used in telegraphy since about
1846.   The telegraph and the alphabet were invented by an
American electrician, S. Morse (1791–1872).   The alphabetic
system is usually known as *the Morse code*.

mosaic. ‘ With a dense and largely vegetarian population
Italy must have an abundance of cheap labour : and this is
generally of a high standard, with centuries of inherited skill,
especially in the handling of stone—from mosaic work and
marble-cutting to road-making and bridge-building,’ L. W.
Lyde, *The Continent of Europe*, (4th edition) 1930.

‘ *L’Allegro* and *Il Penseroso* are mosaics of expression,’
G. Wilson Knight, *The Burning Oracle*, 1939.

‘ The mosaic of the long-forgotten past,’ G. M. Trevelyan,
English Social History, 1942.

The word *mosaic*, signifying a form of art, or work in that
form, comes, via French, from Medieval Latin *mosaicus* (compare Late Greek *mouseion*), which goes back to Classical Greek
Mousa, ‘ a Muse ’: see **muse.**   ‘ For sense-development cf.
antic, grotesque, miniature ’ (W) : in ancient Greece, mosaic work
was aesthetically associated with the Muses.

mosandrite or **mosanderite,** a silicate, was named after Karl
Gustav *Mosander* (1797–1853), that Swedish chemist who has
been credited with the discovery of didymium, **erbium,**
lanthanum and **terbium.**

mosasaurus, a large extinct marine reptile, combining the
characteristics of a saurian with those of a snake, was discovered
at Maestricht (on the Meuse) in 1780 ; in the 19th Century it
was often called the *fossil monitor of Maestricht* (in Holland).
The *saurus* represents Greek *sauros*, a lizard ; the *mosa* element
is Latin *Mosa*, the river Meuse or Maas.

moselle. ‘ The great wealth of the [sovereign Grand-Duchy of
Luxemburg] is in the extreme south, where the “ Gut-land ”
[the rich land] of the Moselle valley grows excellent wine, with
special cellars at Remich and a central market at Greven-
macher . . . . . . The fertile flats of the Moselle . . . a
warm, sunny wineland . . . . . . The lowlands of . . .
Moselle . . ., with an average summer temperature above

66° F. and an average winter temperature above 32° F.,'
Lionel W. Lyde, *Europe*, 1913.

This dry white wine, therefore, takes its name from the region consisting of the lowlands of the *Moselle* river (in Latin, *Mosella*).

moses. A ship's boat, broad and flat-bottomed, at one time used in the West Indies, is *Moses*, a personification that was perhaps originated by the Moses-conducted crossing of the Red Sea by the Israelites.

And see :

mosey, American slang for ' to stroll ' ; may come from *vamoose*, but, no less probably, it may derive from the slouching manner of itinerant Jewish vendors, so many of whom are named *Moses* or *Mose* or *Mosey*. Compare *Moses* as the nickname of any Jewish money-lender or pawnbroker.

mother (or **M—**) **Hubbard.** ' The white men in their drill suits and cork helmets, the native women in their flowing Mother Hubbards, and girls dancing . . .,' Richard Sale, *Cardinal Rock*, 1940.

Originally a long cloak and later a calico dress, the garment was named after the character in the well-known nursery rhyme ; the former was fashionable in the 1860's and 1870's, the latter in the 1880's.

Mrs Gamp. See **gamp.**—**Mrs Grundy.** See **Grundy.**—**Mrs Malaprop.** See **malapropism.**

muggins, a card game or a game of dominoes, derives from *muggins*, a simpleton : and *muggins*, a simpleton, is, like *juggins*, derived from a still existing surname, chosen, like **lushington,** for its phonetic fitness, as W has pointed out. To this I should like to add that, as one pours water, milk, beer into a *mug*, so one can ' pour ' any old story into a *muggins*, for he'll ' take ' anything.

muller. A man's hat, of a kind much worn in London ca. 1855–75. From the name of a murderer.

' You had a little black, and a foreign hat, like a *Muller cut down*, only it came up very high ' (*Sessions Papers of the Central Criminal Court*, London, December 20, 1865).—' He wore a round hat . . ., what they call a deerstalker or a *Muller cut down* ' (ibid., November 21, 1866).—' It was a low-crowned felt hat, sometimes they are called deerstalkers and sometimes wideawakes ' (same law-suit).

300

mumbo-fumbo, meaningless incantations, hence would-be impressive 'hot air', derives from the sense 'a bugbear; an object of superstitious homage', from *Mumbo Jumbo*, who, among the Mandingos, a native tribe of the western Sudan, was the guardian spirit or god that protects a village. ' From *mama dyambo*, in the language of the Khassonke (a Mandingo tribe) in the district of Kayes, on the Senegal, from *mama*, ancestor + *dyumbo*, pompom, wearer of a pompom' (Webster).

Munchausen, a glorious, fantastic lie, derives from *Munchausen*, such a liar, from *Munchausen*, such a travel-book, from (*Baron*) *Munchausen*, reputed author of a book of travel noted more for its 'traveller's tales' than for its veracity. Hence, *munchausenism*, a traveller's fiction, and *munchausenize*, v.i. and v.t., to write such a book or tell such a tale.

In 1785, Rudolph Raspe published a book purporting to relate the wildly improbable travels of a Baron *Munchausen*, a name based upon that of Baron Karl von *Münchhausen*, a German officer (d. 1801) that served in Russia. With the surname itself, compare the English *Monkhouse*.

muntz is the 'popular' form of *Muntz*—or *Muntz's*—*metal*, an alloy of copper (60%) and zinc, used for bolts and sheathing. It was invented by G. F. *Muntz* of Birmingham, England.

murchisonite, a mineral, was named after Sir Roderick *Murchison* (1792–1871), Scottish geologist, director of the Royal School of Mines in 1852 and, twenty-five years earlier, the indicator, to A. Levy, a geologist, of this variety of feldspar.

murciana is a Spanish dance—a sort of fandango. The *danza murciana*, 'the dance of Murcia' (Spain), resembles the **malagueña** (Scholes) : it is the sort of dance you might expect of 'the hot African landscape of Murcia in the south-east' (J. B. Trend, *The Civilization of Spain*, 1944). The modern province of Murcia forms part of the old Moorish kingdom of Murcia : is *Murcia*, then, 'the land of the Moors'?

murphy, like **donovan,** denotes a potato because *Murphy* and *Donovan* are very common Irish surnames and potatoes have, at least in English hearsay, formed for centuries the staple food of the Irish. They are slang terms.

[**muscovado** is short for *muscovado sugar*, unrefined cane-sugar, also called *muscavado* or *muscovade*. The word is only apparently eligible, for it has nothing to do with Russia ; it derives from

301

either a Spanish or a Portuguese word, meaning ' unrefined '. So, too, a *Muscovy duck* is merely a corruption of *musk duck*.]

muscovite, earlier known as *Muscovy glass*, is common mica, a product of Russia, of which the old name is *Muscovy*, *Muscovite* signifying *Russian* (adjective, hence noun) : ' *the* Russian product ' or ' a typically Russian product '.

' It was certainly in the Moskva basin '—*Moscow*—' that the Muscovite germ of the Great Russian people had its race-home ' (Lionel W. Lyde, *Europe*, 1913).

muse, v. ; the Muses—museum—music. The Greek original of the second of these terms is also the original of the other three ; it therefore merits three exemplary quotations : ' The hero of the tale which I beg the Muse to help me tell is that resourceful man who roamed the wide world after he had sacked the holy city of Troy,' E. V. Rieu's translation of the opening of Homer's *The Odyssey* (The Penguin Classics, 1946) ; ' In olden days the Muse cared not for gain ; she was not hired,' Lionel W. Lyde's translation (*A Patchwork from Pindar*, 1932) of a verse and a half from an ode by Pindar ; ' He was a poet. He said : " When I was a young man, the Muses took entire possession of me ",' Melbourne Garahan, *Stiffs*, 1923.

The relation of the third to the second term appears thus : ' Ptolemy I founded the Museum [of Alexandria] . . . Little is known of the Museum, an association of learned men, at their head a priest of the Muses, who lived and laboured in the building,' W. W. Tarn, *Hellenistic Civilisation*, 1927.

The word *museum* is Latin, the Greek original being *mouseion* (temple of the Muses ; hence, seat of the Muses—of art and learning) ; and ' to *muse* ' was originally to meditate upon music or art or literature.

The nine Muses (Greek *Mousai*)—fabled goddesses—' the sacred nine, the Pierid Muses,' as Euripides calls them in the *Medea*—presided over the Greek, hence over all other, art and literature and *music*. They were Calliope (epic), Clio (history), Erato (the lyre), Euterpe (flute-playing), Melpomene (tragedy), Polyhymnia (sacred song), Terpsichore (dancing), Thalia (comedy), and Urania (astronomy). Their mother was Mnemosyne (memory).

muslin, slang for ' women ' (*a bit of muslin*), derives from dresses made of *muslin* : French *mousseline* : Italian *mussolino* : colloquial Arabic *musili*, ' (fabric) of al-*Mawsil* '—*Mosul*, that city in western Mesopotamia which first manufactured it. Mosul was for centuries, though no longer by ca. 1890, famous for its manufacture of cotton goods.

See also the Lyde quotation at **bombasine** and the Glover quotation at **calico.**

myrmidon occurs mostly in the plural. Its original transferred sense was 'loyal retainer or servant', but in the 19th–20th Century it has meant 'hireling' or, as in *myrmidons of the law*, a pitiless minor official or bailiff or police constable. In Greek mythology, the *Murmidones* or Myrmidons were a Thessalian tribe—or rather, a troop or contingent therefrom—that accompanied their king, Achilles, to the Trojan war, wherein they unquestioningly obeyed his orders. In fable, they were ants (Greek *murmēx*, an ant) transformed into men.

N

nagaika, a Cossack whip, thick and tightly twisted, is pronounced *năgīkă*, the Russian being, however, *nagaïka*. Originally it was the whip used by the *Nogaï* Tatars of southern Russia. Tatars 'perhaps named from a famous khan *Nogaï* (13 Cent.),' says W. The *Nogaï* are nomads, found mostly in the north-eastern Caucasus, their language being one of the Ural-Altaic group.

namby-pamby, a person or talk or writing that is weakly sentimental ('Namby-pamby madrigals of love,' as William Gifford the satirist once phrased it), derives from *Amb*rose *Philips* (1675–1749), in derision of the extreme simplicity and sentimentality of some of his poems. This fly in the amber of English verse has been preserved mainly on account of the witty scorn visited upon him by Pope.

nance, nancy, nancy-boy. The original seems to have been *Miss Nancy*: compare **Molly.** As 'an effeminate man or youth, also a passive homosexual or male whore', it merely damns a man by bestowing upon him a feminine name. Compare also *pansy*, named after the flower.

nankeen; nankeens. *Nankeen* is a cotton cloth that in the old days was made from a cotton naturally yellow; and *nankeens*, trousers either yellow or buff-coloured. From the Chinese city of *Nankin* or *Nanking*.

Of *Nankin(g)*—the name itself means Capital of the South—Lionel W. Lyde has written, in his *The Continent of Asia*, that

303

'Its command of the last of the defiles on the Yantze did give i
once some commercial as well as military importance, so tha
all the *yellow* cotton-cloth from China came to be known a
nankeen'.

nanny, a nurse, and **nanny** (or female) **goat,** often shortened t
nanny (contrast **billy goat**), are common-propertyings o
Nanny, a diminutive either of *Nan* or directly of *Nancy,* a given
name more usual perhaps in the 'lower' than in the 'higher
strata of society.

nants or **nantz,** often *right nantz,* i.e. the real thing in Nantz o
Nants, i.e. *Nantes brandy, cognac de Nantes,* which 'came in' witl
the Restoration. In 1706 Ned Ward, who wrote so entertain
ingly of 'the humours of the Town', alluded to its higl
estimation among persons of fashion. Nantes on the Loire i
a great inland port, whence brandy came, as it still comes, t
England.
'Before the Roman period, when Nantes became a grea
administrative capital, the Nannetes had their chief town here
and thus originated the name' (Chisholm).

nap, the game; **go nap; to nap** (in horse-racing). The firs
is short for *Napoleon*—see the next entry; the other two,
merely derivative senses of the first. To *go nap* is, to attemp
the highest score, hence to aim at the best, the highest; *to nap*
is to bet all one's money on (a certain horse), as audaciously as
but often less brilliantly than, Napoleon concentrated on one
point of impact, one goal, one ambition.

Napoleon; Napoleonic; napoleon. A masterly strategist
and tactician ('Napoleonic guile and wide strategic design,'
Dr S. W. Wooldridge, 1936); hence, e.g., 'a Napoleon o
finance'; 'masterly in planning and execution'; a French
twenty-franc piece in gold, commemorating Napoleon Bonaparte, Napoleon I—a sort of top-boot, much like those worn
by Napoleon—the game we now call *nap*—and, in the U.S.A.,
a type of cannon used in the Civil War.
Of the Napoleonic legend, Hilaire Belloc has, in *Napoleon
Bonaparte,* 1932, acutely remarked, 'The legend of a great man
should never be despised. Apart from it, that is apart from
vision, we do not know him at all.' (Of all the books on
Napoleon I happen to have read, I—in no sense an historian—
like best Fisher's and Belloc's and Bainville's.)
'Charles Peace has been called "the Napoleon of the
Jemmy", but the wizened little Yorkshireman was a clumsy

304

amateur in comparison with " the Spider "," W. C. Gough (ex-Chief Inspector of the C.I.D.), *From Kew Observatory to Scotland Yard*, 1927.

napolitana (the Italian form) or **napolitaine** (the French). This sort of madrigal, simple and airy-light, was of Neapolitan origin. The Italian original of *Naples* is *Napoli*.

narcissism, narcissistic; narcissus. ' Narcissus in Greek mythology was changed into a flower ', but only after his death, which he incurred in punishment by Aphrodite, who, angered by his repulse of the nymph Echo, caused him to fall in love with his own reflection in a fountain and to pine away because he could not grasp that image, the figment of self-love. ' With the Greeks the Narcissus was . . . connected with imminent death. . . . In " The Sensitive Plant " Shelley writes of

" Narcissi, the fairest of them all,
      Who gaze on their eyes in the stream's recess,
      Till they die of their own dear loveliness "',

as Vernon Rendall notes in *Wild Flowers in Literature*, 1934.

The psycho-analytical concept of narcissism is Freud's. The word *narcissus*, or rather its Greek original *narkissos*, derives from *narkao*, ' I grow torpid ' (cf. *narkē*, torpor), because of its narcotic properties (Liddell & Scott).

narragansett is short for *Narragansett horse*, a small, hardy, sorrel-coloured breed, developed in the country about Narragansett Bay ; the better ones were known as *Narragansett pacers*. The term also designates an inferior breed of hog. The Narragansett Indians inhabited Rhode Island, and their name means ' People of the Small Point ' of land. (DAE.)

nattier blue. ' His own bedroom with the satinwood furniture and the nattier blue hangings,' W. J. Locke (much more knowledgeable than the majority of popular novelists), *The Rough Road*, 1918 (cited by The OED). This—originally *Nattier*—blue, from French *bleu Nattier*, is a very soft blue, much used by Jean Nattier (1685–1766), a French portrait-painter, one of whose commissions was to paint Peter the Great and members of his immediate circle. Compare **Titian.**

navarraise. A dance, originally of the province of *Navarre*. Spanish in type, it has a French name : *danse navarraise*.

Nazi, transferred sense. *Nazi* shortens ' nationalen Sozialisten ', i.e. ' National Socialists ' ; it arose on the analogy of *Sozi* (short

305   N.I.W.—L

for ' Sozialisten '), a rather derogatory label attached to the earlier Socialists. *Nazi* came to mean ' German ' (noun and adjective), with the corresponding abstract noun, *Nazism*. In the British Empire and the U.S.A., they acquired the same unpleasant senses as the 1914–18 *Hun* and *hunnishness* ' militarist brute ', ' military brutality ', ' barbarian(ism) '. To many, *Nazi* has meant *nasty* in the nastiest, strongest sense.

neddy, an ass, a donkey, is a personification : *Neddy*, diminutive of *Edward*. Such personifications abound, especially in slang and in dialect. The ass is a much, an exceptionally favoured animal, for it has at least three other synonyms, all of Proper Name origin—**cuddy** and **moke** and **donkey** itself.

negrohead is short for *Negrohead tobacco*, dark as a Negro's head (Also called *niggerhead*.) It is a strong tobacco, of low grade which the DAE records for the year 1833, although the name probably goes back a generation earlier.

negus, a perilously persuasive beverage composed of lemon juice and hot water, nutmeg and sugar, upon a meritorious base of wine (usually, either port or sherry), was diabolically devised and joyously compounded by a Colonel of the old school but the modern idea, Francis *Negus*, who, dying in 1732, is ignored by biographical-dictionaries in favour of much less genial benefactors of the human race. M. André Simon benevolently confides to us his own mouth-watering recipe.

The name is an odd one : did, perchance, an ancestor perform some signal service for a medieval King of Abyssinia, or *Negus*, from the Amharic *n'gus* or *negus*, ' king-governed, or king '?

nelly, either the sooty albatross or the giant fulmar, is a sailor's personification, from *Nelly*, the diminutive of *Eleanor*, *Helen*, *Ellen*. Compare **mag** and **robin** and **dicky.**

nelson, double nelson, and **half-nelson** are terms used in catch-as-catch-can wrestling. Apparently they derive either from a famous wrestler named Nelson or from the town of Nelson in the North of England—famous for wrestling.

nemesis. ' What terrible mistake had he made? How had Nemesis overtaken him? ' Freeman Wills Crofts, *The Starv Tragedy*, 1927.

' Side by side in the *Vitae Patrum* with the lives of Paula and Marina and Euphrosyne, holy virgins and faithful widows, ar the lives of the harlots, Thaïs, Pelagia, Mary of Egypt : and on the *Vita S. Thaïsis* Anatole France founded his study of the Nemesis that waits on the absolute denial of the body,' Helen Waddell, *The Desert Fathers*, 1936.

In Greek mythology, Nemesis was the ' personification of the gods' resentment at, and consequent punishment of, insolence (*hubris*) towards themselves ' and, ' according to Hesiod, a child of Night ', as Sir Paul Harvey concisely phrases it. Nemesis may be anglicized as ' the goddess of Retribution ' and the word derives from *nemesao*, ' I feel just indignation, properly at undeserved good fortune ' (Liddell & Scott).

neophron, the white Egyptian vulture or an allied vulture of India, both of them characterized by horizontal nostrils, is derived by Webster from *neophron*, ' childish in spirit ' ; but the immediate origin rests with *Neophron*, which, in the *Metamorphoses* of Antoninus Liberalis, is the name of a man changed into a vulture (The COED).

Neptune; neptunian; neptunium. *Neptune* figuratively = the sea ; in geology, *neptunian* means ' produced by the action of water ; a supporter of the theory that certain rocks are water-caused (contrast **Vulcanist**) ' ; *neptunium* is an element, named after the planet Neptune as plutonium is from the planet Pluto, these two elements ' lying on the confines of the atomic system just as Neptune and Pluto are the outermost members of the Solar System ' (A. W. Stewart, discoverer of the chemical ' isobars ').

Neptune, the Roman god of the sea (*Neptunus*), had most of the attributes of Poseidon, the Greek god of the sea. He is often familiarized as *Father Neptune*.

nereid. Of Ancient Greece, G. Lowes Dickinson has written that ' Nature has become a company of spirits ; every cave and fountain is haunted by a nymph ; in the ocean dwell the Nereids, in the mountain the Oread, the Dryad in the wood ' (*The Greek View of Life*).

In current English, a nereid is a sea-nymph, secondarily a long sea worm : and *nereid = Nereid =* Greek *Nereïs =* a daughter of the sea-god *Nereus* (the deity of the fluid world : the ocean).

Nero; Neronian, Neronic. In *Revelation*, xiii, 18, ' The number of the beast 666 . . ., for which the most fantastic identifications have been found (including Luther and Napoleon), probably refers to Nero Caesar,' Stanley Cook, *An*

Introduction to The Bible, 1945; ' Nero, a fierce persecutor of Christians—he numbered some among his household . . .— claimed to be the world's saviour ' (Dr Cook refrains from pointing the parallel to Hitler) ' and was regarded as a veritable Antichrist '. Nero (A.D. 37–68) fiddled while Rome burned in a conflagration he himself is suspected of having caused; cruelly persecuted the Christians; made himself unpopular and, proscribed by the Senate, took his own life.

neroli, ' an essential oil distilled from the flower of the bitter (or Seville) orange ', commemorates its discovery, supposed or actual, by an Italian princess surnamed *Neroli*, away back in the 17th Century. For an analogous attribution, compare **frangipane.**

Nestor, the type of the outstandingly wise old man, is an adoption of that *Nestor* who, king of Pylos, at an advanced age joined the Greeks in their besieging of Troy and who was consistently noted and, what is more, revered for the sagacity of his advice, despite his garrulity. He appears much in *The Iliad*, less in *The Odyssey*.

A *nestor* is a long-lived genus of parrots in Australasia.

newfoundland is short for *Newfoundland dog*, a very large dog now native to North America but believed to have sprung from a cross, in the 17th Century, between dogs found in Newfoundland and other large dogs brought from England. (Webster.)

' If the voyage [ca. 1577] were carefully timed to reach the . . . section . . . between the New Found Land and Greenland, in late summer, no danger from ice was to be anticipated,' E. G. R. Taylor, *Tudor Geography*, 1930.

newmarket, whether short for *Newmarket coat*, a coat or cloak that is long and close-fitting (the male County still wear it), or the card-game that resembles Pope Joan and probably originated among racing men, derives from *Newmarket*, a town on the borders of Suffolk and Cambridgeshire, where Charles II established a royal stable. The course has long been the property of the almost royally privileged Jockey Club. Still a market-town, Newmarket was, in the 16th Century and earlier, *The New Market* of East Anglia.

nickel is a Swiss shortening of German *Kupfernickel* (copper nickel), whereof the second element is a transferred sense of German *Nickel*, a goblin, from *Nickel*, a diminutive of *Niklaus* (Nicholas). The name was in 1751 bestowed by the Swiss

308

mineralogist Cronstedt on this metal because of its puckish gleam : the simple were deceived into thinking it a precious metal.

nicotian; nicotine, my Lady Nicotine. The third means tobacco, especially as smoked in a pipe : a late-19th-Century fancy ; the first is obsolete for ' tobacco ', obsolescent for ' of or arising from tobacco ', and should be compared with **nicotiana,** an old name for tobacco, with **nicotyl,** a hydro-carbon present in nicotine, and with the equally technical **nicotianin,** the essential oil of tobacco. They all derive from the surname *Nicot* (itself a pet-form of *Nicolas*).

' Many of us are aware that Jean Nicot, Lord of Villemain— whose name is immortalised in . . . *nicotine*—first took tobacco in 1561 from Portugal, where he was French Ambassador, as a present to the Grand Prior of France ; on which account, it was originally called *Herbe du Grand Prieur*,' Osbert Sitwell, *Sing High! Sing Low!*, 1944.

niersteiner is a wine from *Nierstein*, ' the most important wine-producing parish of Rhinehesse. It produces much white wine, some of which is of very fine quality,' André Simon, *Wine*, 1946.

Nierstein, on the left bank of the Rhine, lies some nine miles south-east of Mainz.

Nietzschean. ' What constitutes the spiritual ideal? Is it the Nietzschean Superman, or his opposite, the Buddha? ' : ' Palinurus ', *The Unquiet Grave*, 1945.

Friedrich Wilhelm Nietzsche (1844–1900), Classical scholar and far from Classical philosopher, set forth in *Thus Spake Zoroaster* (four parts, 1883–91), the doctrine of the *Übermensch*, the overman or superman. He championed the ' morals of master men '—but he did not, as so often is said, champion the Prussians as the master race, despite his theory that man is perfectible through self-assertion and the will to power (*Die Wille zur Macht*, 1888).

nigger = nigger brown, dark brown, the hue of a *Negro*. Compare the entry at **negrohead.**

niggerhead. See **negrohead.**

nightingale, a single-piece bed-jacket, especially for use in hospitals, fittingly derives from Florence *Nightingale* (1820–1910), the English nurse, hospital reformer, and benefactor of hospitals and nurses. 'The Lady with the Lamp', with reference to the hospital she supervised at Scutari in 1854–55 : the first woman to receive (1907) the Order of Merit : the subject, as to her later life, of a moving play by my friend Ronald Delderfield.

nimrod. A *nimrod* is a great hunter ; hence, loosely, a great sportsman. General practice, however, still writes it *Nimrod*. ' It is said that in the Crown of Suleiman ben Daood '— Solomon the son of David—' there was a strange and wonderful stone, and . . . that this stone had belonged of old to the giants, to Nimrod the hunter and his children, and by its virtue Nimrod sought to build Babel which was to reach to heaven,' Charles Williams, *Many Dimensions*, 1931.

Of Nimrod, who flourished ca. 2200 B.C., we read in *Genesis*, x, 8–10, that ' He began to be a mighty one in the earth. He was a mighty hunter before the Lord ; wherefore it is said, even as Nimrod the mighty hunter before the Lord. And the beginning of his kingdom was Babel, and Erech, and Accad, and Calneh, in the land of Shinar.'

ninny, a particularly rudimentary simpleton, is generic from *Ninny*, the pet-form of *Innocent*, with especial reference to *innocent*, as in ' the sweet innocent ! ' (adorably ignorant), from the adjective, which, in the Latin *innocens*, radically means ' harmless '.

ninon, ' a light-weight dress-fabric made of silk ', occurs thus in Ngaio Marsh's well-contrived New Zealand detective novel, *Colour Scheme*, 1943 : ' She's got eyes and a profile and a figure, submerged it is true in dressy floral ninon, but there, nevertheless '.

Either a personification, *Ninon* being a French diminutive of *Ann(e)*, or from the glamorous *Ninon* de l'Enclos (or Lenclos), originally mere Anne Lenclos (1620–1705), Parisian *femme à la mode* and *salonnière*.

Niobe, Niobean ; niobium. The third is that metallic element which, in the first half of the 19th Century, used to be *columbium* : rediscovered in the Bavarian tantalites, 1845, by Heinrich Rose, who Classically—and right wittily—remarked, ' I have called it niobium, and its acid niobic acid, from Niobe, daughter of Tantalus ' (OED) ; see **tantalum.** Also, in chemistry, there is **niobite,** ' a niobic salt '. The second (*Niobean*) is merely the adjective of *Niobe*, who, in Greek legend, was so mother-proud of her children that the gods slew them

310

and she, weeping, was changed into a column of stone, whence her tears still continued to flow : ' a monument to grief' : the emblem of grief (whence *Niobean grief—sorrow—tears*). Byron described Rome thus :

> ' The Niobe of nations !   There she stands,
>   Childless and crownless, in her voiceless woe' :

with which compare ' The wrongs and woes of [Ireland], his mother-land, that Niobe of the nations ', as James, Cardinal Gibbons, phrased it in his Introduction to J. J. Roche, *Life of John Boyle O'Reilly* (a great Irish patriot), 1891.

noah's (or **Noah's**) **ark,** a set of toys representing Noah's ark (the animals went in, two by two) as depicted in *Genesis*, vi, 14–20.   The term is also applied to two plants, the lady's slipper and the monkshood.   *Noah*, in Hebrew, means ' rest ' or ' comfort '.

noddy, ' a simpleton ', but not *noddy*, ' a small hackney vehicle ; an inverted pendulum' (presumably from ' *nod* the head '), may, as W has proposed, be a pet-form of *Nicodemus*, for ' *nicodème* is French for a fool, probably a reminiscence of a part played in some medieval mystery '.

noël or **nowell** or **nowel** is a *Christmas* carol, *Noël* being Christmas.   *Nowel(l)* is the English form of the French original, *Noël*. Old French *noel* represents the Latin (*dies*) *natalis*, the birth day of Christ.

noisette is the name given to a race of hardy garden-roses descending from a hybrid between the China rose and the moss rose and including such fine varieties as the **Maréchal Niel** (subsidiary list).   This class of rose was first raised, ca. 1816, in America by John Champney, from whom a Mr *Noisette*, whose own name represents the French *noisette*, ' hazel-nut ', a diminutive of *noix*, ' walnut ; nut ', itself from Latin *nux*, obtained a rose ; cultivated by this Philippe Noisette, like Champney a citizen of Charleston, it was distributed as *blush Noisette*.   (DAE.)

nonius. ' A second important contribution to science made by Pedro Nuñez was contained in his astronomical treatise *De Crepusculis*, 1542 : this was his device for reading subdivisions of the scales on astronomical and other instruments, known after him as the " nonnius ",' E. G. R. Taylor, *Tudor Geography*, 1930. Later improved into the **vernier.**

Nuñez (1492–1577) was a Portuguese mathematician, much interested in the art of navigation.

nordenfelt. A Swedish engineer, Nordenfeld, invented the machine gun named after him. The nordenfelt came into use ca. 1880—some five years earlier than the maxim, and either it or the **maxim** was modified as the Maxim-Nordenfelt. Compare **gatling** and **lewis.**

nowell. See **noël.**

nylon is said by certain dictionaries to be a blend of ' *N.Y.* (New York) ' and ' *Lon*don '. Incorrectly. The word is a blend, it is true; but of ' *ni*trogen ' + a fanciful ' *lon* ', perhaps on the analogy of ' Baby*lon* '.

O

obsidian. Dark glass-like lava; dark volcanic rock that, in appearance, resembles bottle-glass. The word represents Latin *obsidianus*—a misprint, in early editions of Pliny the Elder's *Natural History*, for *obsianus*, the correct adjective from *Obsius*, who discovered the stone in Ethiopia (Abyssinia); there may have been earlier discoveries, elsewhere.

'Homer's heroes put iron heads on their arrows; in the graves and ruins [of excavated Troy] the arrows were pointed with obsidian. (This is a natural glass, of volcanic origin; in the earliest times the island of Melos seems to have been its chief source),' T. R. Glover, *The Ancient World*, 1935.

'The little islands scattered in a belt across the Aegean (the Cyclades) . . . possessed marketable resources—copper, emery, obsidian, marble. . . . So in the Third Millennium they were thickly populated by people who worked metals, quarried obsidian and carved marble vases and traded the products to Egypt, Crete, the coasts of the Dardanelles and Mainland Greece,' Gordon Childe, *What Happened in History*, 1942.

[**Occidental** and **Oriental,** ' Western ' and ' Eastern ', in especial reference to civilizations, peoples, cultures, are not strictly eligible: first, they form the mere latinized counterparts of the other two terms; second, they do not derive from true Proper Names; and thirdly *the Occident* and *the Orient* represent, not places but merely the western and the eastern halves of the world.   In the Latin, they refer to the *occident,* or setting, sun, and the *orient,* or rising sun.]

ocean; oceanic; oceanids; and certain obvious compounds and derivatives.   The second, *oceanic,* is merely the adjective of *ocean*; the good ship *Oceanic* crosses and re-crosses the great, the tumultuous Atlantic Ocean—cf. *Oceania* as the name for the islands (and their adjacent seas) of the greatest of the oceans, the Pacific.   The third, *oceanids,* is the generic scientific name of the marine molluscs, those minor children of the ocean who recall the Oceanids, the daughters of Oceanus and Tethys. To ' telescope ' Sir Henry Stuart Jones's recension of ' Liddell & Scott ', in respect of *Ōkeanos*: ' Son of Uranus and Gaia [or Gē] . . . father of Thetis . . . and of all the Oceanids . . .; god of the primeval water, and source of all smaller waters . . .; conceived as a *Great River* which compasses the earth's disc . . . . . . Later the name of *the great Outward Sea,* [as opposed] to the Inward or Mediterranean.'   The root-idea of the Greek *ōkeanos* is ' that which surrounds ', as its Sanskrit original indicates.

odyssey.   *The Odyssey of an Out-of-Work,* by Terence Horsley, 1931 ; *Historian's Odyssey,* by G. Pratt Insh, 1938.

(A gangster, guilty of numerous murders and soon to expiate his crimes, *loq.*)   ' A guy . . . brought me a book called " The Odyssey ".   It tells about a guy that roamed all over every-where.   That's what the word Odyssey means, they tell me, a long journey.   It kind of struck me . . . that that might be a good title for this story—The Odyssey of a Killer.   Because you see, pal, I'm going on a long journey soon myself,' Vic Whatman, ' The Odyssey of a Killer ' (*Detective Fiction Weekly,* June 30, 1934).

Properly, an *odyssey* is a long, adventurous journey or wander-ing ; usually with the connotation of ' many lands and many peoples '.   From the Homeric epic, *The Odyssey*: Greek *Odusseia,* ' deeds of *Odusseus* ' (Odysseus) or, as he is more often called, Ulysses (the Latin name).   It is a romantic poem. Two famous verse translations are those by George Chapman and Alexander Pope ; the three best prose renderings are those by Butcher & Lang, by T. E. Lawrence and by E. V. Rieu (in ' The Penguin Classics ') ; and Tennyson's *Ulysses* is one of that poet's finest poems, for it possesses a terse vigour lacking in most of his work.   Although the Greek *Odusseia* is unaspirated and *hodos,* ' way; hence, a journey ', is aspirated, I feel that it is by no means impossible that *Odusseus* means ' wayfarer ' and that *Odusseia* implies ' wayfaring, journeying, wandering ', despite the further fact that Boisacq and other etymologists postulate ' he who is irritated ', from an extremely defective verb meaning ' to be angered against '.

Compare **iliad.**

oersted is the C.G.S. unit of magnetic resistance or reluctance; also a special type or degree of magnetic reluctance. Named after Hans Christian Örsted (anglicé *Oersted*), who (1777–1851) was a Danish physicist and in 1819 a notable discoverer in the field of magnetism—the founder of Electromagnetism.

' The neatest, simplest and most accurate solution of the longitude problem (by wireless signals) has come in a way nobody could have dreamt of a hundred years ago, just because Oersted and Faraday played about with magnets and coils of copper wire,' A. D. Ritchie, *Civilization, Science and Religion*, 1945.

ogam or **ogham** or **ogum.** ' At Silchester a tombstone was found, with an inscription in Ogams ' and ' the rude Welsh tombstones, sometimes with Ogam as well as Latin inscriptions ': R. G. Collingwood, in Collingwood & Myres, *Roman Britain and the English Settlements*, (revised edition) 1937.

Erse *ogham*, from Old Erse *ogom* or *ogum*, is traditionally derived from Ogma mac Eladan, the mythological inventor of this system of writing, peculiar to the old Irish alphabet.

ogygian is a very literary word for ' primeval; prehistoric; ancient; very old '. From the Latin *ogygius* (Greek *ogugios*), it means ' belonging to, or characteristic of, or connected with *Ogyges* (Greek *Ogugos*), a legendary king of Boeotia in whose reign a destructive flood took place '.

But the adjective also means ' magic; expressing or resulting from enchantment ' such as that whereby Calypso kept Odysseus for seven years upon her fabulous Mediterranean isle *Ogygia* (Greek *Ogugia*).

ohm; megohm, a million ohms. The ohm is ' the practical unit of electrical resistance '. It was named after Georg Simon Ohm (1787–1854), a German physicist, who, in addition to his discovery of the relationship between the intensity of an electrical current, the electromotive force, and the resistance of a circuit (*Ohm's law*), did good work in mathematics, acoustics, and crystals. Compare **ampère, maxwell, watt.**

Old Newton. See **Newtonian** in the Appendix.

Old Scrooge. See **Scrooge.**

oliver, whether a small tilt-hammer or a smith's hammer, may be ' of uncertain origin ', as The OED and Webster state. But W suggests that it represents the Proper Name *Oliver*, as The OED itself admits may be the case. The earliest recorded instance being of 1686, I suggest that the origin is afforded by *Oliver* Cromwell, who was as a *malleus Dei* to the Royalists. The fact that he commanded the *Roundheads* accounts for the origin of the underworld's *oliver*, the moon, which, at full, resembles a great, shining head.

Oliver. See **Roland.**

olympiad is the four-years interval between one celebration of the Olympic Games and another. The first Olympics took place in 776 B.C. and the ancient Greeks thereafter used this interval as a measure of time. The word comes, via French, from the Greek *olumpias* (case stem : *olumpiad*), itself from *Olumpios*, the adjective of *Olumpos*; for the latter, see :—

Olympian; Olympus or **Mount Olympus.** *Olympian* is simply the adjective (and elliptically a noun) that corresponds to (*Mount*) *Olympus.*

In Greek mythology, the summit of Mount Olympus, which stands at the eastern end of the chain of mountains forming the northern border of Greece proper and Thessaly and which gazes, calm and majestic, over the Vale of Tempe, is regarded as the residence and habitat of the greater gods.

' Olympus is as high as Scafell, Helvellyn and Skiddaw, one on top of the other,' Lionel W. Lyde, *A Patchwork from Pindar*, 1932.

' He beat his gloved hands together, hard, making a sound like Olympian applause while he looked down on the whole white valley,' James Gould Cozzens, *A Cure of Flesh*, 1933.

' Greece—to put a subtle matter crudely—seems for some time to have been challenging our traditional Christian culture, many poets offering an Olympian or Dionysian theology as co-partners with the Christian,' G. Wilson Knight, *The Burning Oracle*, 1939.

onanism; onanist. Male masturbation ; male masturbator. ' Jean Jacques Rousseau—a confirmed onanist whose puerile tendencies are evident in his conclusions,' Harry Hervey, *School for Eternity*, 1942.

Onan, son of Judah, refused to fertilize a certain woman :

315

Genesis, xxxviii, 7–10.   It is but fair to the memory of Onan to say that, in the light of the records, he was not a masturbator.

Ophir, employed allusively for a land of great wealth in precious metals (strictly, gold) and in gems, is mentioned in 1 *Kings*, x, 11, 'The navy also of Hiram, that brought gold from Ophir, brought in from Ophir great plenty of almug trees, and precious stones' from Sheba to Solomon.

'Is this [the Zimbabwe Valley] the fabulous land of Ophir— the land where the Shebans, or Sabaeans, to which race the Queen of Sheba belonged, amassed their gold, a million pounds of which were to go to adorn King Solomon's Temple at Jerusalem?   That, at any rate, seemed not incredible, as from the wild hills I saw the ancient city in the valley below and, beyond, rising like pillared cones [*glossed*, ' " Sheba's Breasts " of Sir Rider Haggard's *King Solomon's Mines* '], the granitic cliffs of the scarped Beroma Range,' Archer Russell, *Gone Nomad*, 1936.

opuntia is that widespread genus of prickly pear which the Romans called by the same name—originally *Opuntia herba* or ' herb ' of Opus, a city (Greek *Opous*) of Locris in Greece.

'Orace is the Cockney's personification, half-affectionate, half-derisive, for the middle-class young man ; often he uses it in address.

ordovician (or **O—**) designates, especially in respect of its rocks, that geological period which, following the **cambrian,** precedes the **silurian.** It is Professor C. Lapworth's name, bestowed in the early 1880's, for what had been known as the *lower silurian* period, and it refers to the *Ordovices*, as the Romans called the ancient British tribe inhabiting what is now northern Wales.

'These are two dissected domes which have suffered a sufficient denudation to expose the older, underlying Silurian and Ordovician formations' (west of the Cumberland plateau), Ll. Rodwell Jones & P. W. Bryan, *North America*, (7th edition) 1946.

orfray.   See **orphray.**

organdie or **-y; organzine.** The former comes from French *organdi*, the latter, via French *organzin*, from Italian *organzino* ; the former is a fine dress-fabric, the latter a double-thread silk used for the warp in weaving : and both derive, the former

316

probably, the latter certainly, from *Urgendi*, in Turkestan, a country famed from of old for its weaving. Perhaps compare the Mongol *uro*, a palace, or even the Mongol place-name *Hurac*, literally an enclosure.

Oriental. See **Occidental.**

orleans. Although short for *Orleans plum* and a synonym of annatto (a dye-stuff), the word is important for only one thing : as the name of a cotton-and-worsted dress fabric, associated with *Orleans*, French *Orléans*, sixty-nine miles south-south-west of Paris, but not, apparently, manufactured there.

oronoko, with variants *Aronoko*, *Arronoca*, *Oronooko*, and a few others, was originally spelt with a capital. Strong-scented, this tobacco (*Oronoko tobacco*) has for centuries been grown in the lands about the Orinoco River in the north of South America. The Orinoco was at first *Oronoque*—that is, among Europeans or the European-born. But *Oronoque* has got itself into the etymologically more suitable shape, *Orinoco* : the Carib original was *Ibirinoco*. (Webster.)
 Compare **tobacco** itself.

orpharion or **orpheoreon.** This musical instrument, inferior to, yet of the same type as, the cittern, takes its name from *Orpheus*, who, in Greek mythology, attempted with his music to recall Eurydice from hell. Gluck's opera *Orpheus and Eurydice* was performed in 1762.

orphibaryton (a kind of bass horn) likewise derives, as to its first element, from *Orpheus*.

orphray (or **-ey**) or **orfray** (or **-ey**), the former being the learned spelling, the latter the historical and normal spelling from Old French *orfreis*, which, perhaps via Provençal *aurfres* (compare Old Spanish *aurofres*), comes from Medieval Latin *aurifrisum*, which debases Latin *auriphrygium*, gold embroidery : Latin *aurum*, gold, and *Phrygium*, of Phrygia : compare Virgil's *Phrygiae vestes*, gold-embroidered—or, at the least, richly embroidered—garments. The ancient Phrygians of Asia Minor were almost as stupid in general as they were skilful at gold-embroidering in particular.

orpington. 'Mr Cook, a poultry farmer then living in the village of Orpington . . . introduced the single-combed Black Orpington to the poultry world in the autumn of 1886,' F. A.

Mackenzie, *Popular Poultry Keeping*, ca. 1891 (cited by The OED).

Orpington, now one of London's dormitories, was in 1886, and for long after, a small township in Kent. Compare **dorking.**

orrery. This clockwork device to show the sun-related movements of the planets, was invented ca. 1700 by George Graham (1673–1751), a brilliant mechanician; a copy was made by John Rowley, instrument maker, in honour of—and by Graham gratefully presented to his patron—Charles Boyle (1676–1731), 4th Earl of *Orrery*. This Orrery had a varied and adventurous career; and, like most of the men of his family, he generously assisted the cause of science. (The seventh son of the 1st Earl of Cork and Orrery was the famous physicist, Robert Boyle.)

osborne, an English biscuit, plain and sweet, was originally *Osborne*, for it is a proprietary name, chosen—for its advertisement value—to ' commemorate ' *Osborne*, which, on the Isle of Wight, was one of the residences of Queen Victoria.

oscar, in Australian slang, means ' cash; money '. It shortens *Oscar Asche*, rhyming slang for ' cash '. Oscar Asche (1872–1936), born in Australia, became world-famous with *Chu-Chin-Chow*, that sumptuous musical comedy which, running for a phenomenally long time, delighted theatre-goers of the First World War. For the less reputable derivations from *Oscar* Wilde (1856–1900), see the Addenda to the 3rd edition of my *Dictionary of Slang*.

osnaburg or *osnaburgh* or *osnaburgs*; or *osnabrug* or *ozenbrig* or . . . Mentioned as early as 1660, this coarse linen cloth was originally made at *Osnaburg* or *Osnaburgh*—the native name has always been *Osnabrück*—in the Province of Hanover in the old kingdom of Prussia; 'formerly linen was the staple product, and gave name to "osnaburgs"' (Chisholm, concerning Osnabrück). In the 19th Century, the name came to be applied to a cotton-made cloth similar to osnaburg proper and, like it, strong and durable.

otto is that primeval bicycle which, invented—or at least named after its inventor—in 1877, is perhaps more truthfully defined as a velocipede. It is mentioned in Bury & Hillier's volume on *Cycling*, 1887, in ' The Badminton Library ' of sports and games. The brave men that performed on it were known as *ottoists*. (The OED.)

ottoman. ' The drawing-room . . . was large and sunny and crowded with heterogeneous furniture of mid-Victorian taste. Whatnots and ottomans abounded,' Thomas Bodkin, *My Uncle Frank*, 1941. Here it signifies a flat, stuffed couch with a back; earlier, such a couch without a back; originally, an upholstered, backless seat of the sort used in Turkey. From *Ottoman*, ' Turkish; a Turk ': via the Romance languages from Arabic *Uthman*, that sultan who came to power ca. 1300.

out-herod Herod. ' Among the Roman client-kings of the transition period he '—Herod—' is the outstanding personality; able, cruel, and utterly unscrupulous . . . . . . He was not a Hellenistic king, but an Idumaean barbarian moderately well varnished . . . . . . He did give peace and prosperity, but he really ruled by fear and held Judaea down by fortresses. . . . [The Jews] rose repeatedly till he became too strong; his last years were a reign of terror,' W. W. Tarn, *Hellenistic Civilisation*, (revised edition) 1930.

Herodes, usually known as *Herod*, became King of Judaea in 40 B.C. and died, aged seventy, in 4 B.C. He figures in The New Testament (*Matthew*, ii) as having ordered the infants of Bethlehem to be slain.

' It out-herods Herod: pray you, avoid it ': Hamlet to the actors (*Hamlet*, III, ii).

oxfords = *Oxford shoes* (low shoes that lace over the instep) of a type once known as ' high-lows '. The type seems to have been created at the end of the 17th or the beginning of the 18th Century.

' She was natty in a dark-brown suit and brown oxfords,' Rex Stout, *Over My Dead Body*, (English edition) 1940.

ozenbrig is the earliest recorded form (DAE) of **osnaburg.**

P

Pactolian, ' golden; fabulously rich; relating to great wealth ', is a literary word; nevertheless, it might well be written with a small initial letter, as in ' pactolian dreams ', ' a pactolian land '.

The reference is to the river Pactolus in Lydia (in the west of Asia Minor)—a river fabled to have sands rich in gold, as a result of **Midas**'s ablutions in its stream. In a chapter on Anatolia, an eminent geographer has written, ' The mineral

319

wealth is of relatively little importance; some in the west, *e.g.* the gold of the Pactolus tributary of the Hermus (Gediz), is probably exhausted', Lyde, *The Continent of Asia*, 1933.

See especially E. G. R. Taylor, ' Pactolus—River of Gold '— in *The Scottish Geographical Magazine*, XLIV, 137.

paddisway is an American variant of **paduasoy.**

paddy, ' a mason's hod-carrier ' (English dialect), derives from the fact that so many builders' labourers have, for ages, been *Paddies* or Irishmen; as ' a rage, a fit of very bad temper ' (*in a paddy*), it is short for *paddywhack*, i.e. a ' Paddywhack ', from the dangerous rages of the Celt (compare **scotty**); as ' an unlicensed almanac ', it shortens *paddywhack almanac*, traditionally associated with Ireland, *Paddywhack* being another nickname for an Irishman, the *whack* element connoting violence or boisterously high spirits, *paddywhack* being colloquial for a *Paddy's whack* or blow, punch, thrashing; and in North Carolina it is a personification for the ruddy duck, probably the result of some early settler's flight of (? Celtic) fancy.

padovana. See **pavan(e).**

paduasoy, a rich, heavy, corded-silk fabric, hence a garment made thereof, was in the 17th Century *poudesoy*, from the French *pou-de-soie*, of which the first element *pou*, or *pout*, remains a mystery: I venture to lighten it with the suggestion that it be an irregular derivation from, perhaps a would-be-erudite workman's corruption of, the Latin *pondus*, ' a weight; hence heaviness ', with which compare French *poids*, ' weight '. The general semantic idea, by the very definition, is that of *weighty* silk. The *soie* is, of course, ' silk '. But the whole term has been ' learnedly ' changed to conform with the obsolete *Padua say*, ' say ' being serge, and ' Padua say ' having originally been manufactured at *Padua* (compare, as W does, the similar corruption of **mantua**), Italian *Padova*, one of the most ancient cities of Italy.

paean; paeon. ' As the days slid by and the sombre muttering of the guns grew more threatening—increasing to paeons of thunder every morning just before dawn—all seemed drawn together in a truer and a deeper companionship,' Wilfrid Ewart, *Way of Revelation*, 1923.

The more usual association is that with joy—adoration—acclamation—triumph: as in ' A few seconds later the song broke out behind him, louder and lovelier than before, as if in a paean of rejoicing,' C. S. Lewis, *Perelandra*, 1943.

In this sense, 'chant of thanksgiving; song of praise or of triumph', *paean* is the usual spelling—from the Greek *paian*, hymn to *Paian*, one of the names of Apollo (invoked in the refrain-words *Ió Paian*); in the sense, 'a metrical foot (one long and three short syllables, the long being variously placed)', *paeon* is usual, *Paiōn* being the Attic form of *Paian* and this foot occurring frequently in the paean, a choral lyric, probably of Cretan origin (compare *cretic*, the name of another metrical foot). Apollo's name *Paiōn* derives from *paiō*, 'I strike', *Paiōn* being 'he who by his magic stroke, or touch, cures the sick' (Boisacq).

paeonic is a metric foot. See the preceding entry.

palladium—whence **palladiumize**, 'to coat with palladium'— is a metallic element, rather like silver and belonging to the platinum group; discovered in 1804 by William Wollaston, an English physicist, who named it after the very recently discovered asteroid, Pallas. Pallas had been named after that image of the goddess Pallas Athene, 'Athene the Virgin Priestess'—the *Palladium* (Greek *Palladion*)—which was supposed to constitute the safeguard of Troy: whence, also, *palladium* in the sense, 'a safeguard; a protective institution', as in 'This insistence on irrefragable proof may be the palladium of the accused man . . . but . . . it's an accursed nuisance to a hard-worked constabulary,' J. J. Connington, *A Minor Operation*, 1937.

palm beach. Earlier *Palm Beach suit*, this is a light summer-weight, suitable to the strenuous leisure of that famed mecca of American playboys and glamour girls.

(It being a very hot morning) 'I kept the shower moderately cool and selected a palm beach for the day's apparel,' remarks Archie Goodwin in *Where There's a Will*—English edition, 1941 —by Rex Stout.

pam. A card-game, similar to nap and fashionable in Europe in the late 17th–18th Century; also the knave of clubs, the highest trump in that game.

Sometimes written *Pam*, because the word appears to be short for *Pamphile*, which is the French shape of the Proper Name *Pamphilus* or, in the Greek original, *Pamphilos*: *Pamphilos* signifies 'beloved by all': ca. 1660–1880, card-games were even more popular than they are in the 20th Century.

pamphlet; in Middle English, *pamflet, paunflet, pamfilet*; comes from French *Pamphilet* (probably a diminutive), a familiar name for *Pamphilus*, a small Latin poem of the 12th Century: *Pamphilus, seu de Amore*. Having a tremendous popularity, this poem gave its name to pamphlets, by the form of its production, its physical shape; the sense ' small polemical brochure ' came later and was not originally French.

See also **pam.**

Pan. See **panic.**

Pan pipes (or **Pandean pipes**). ' Led by the pipes of Pan, I again descended. Once more that sound, almost overtaken, interwove itself with the water's cry, and I merged body and soul with the stream and the music,' Vachell Lindsay, *A Handy Guide for Beggars* (which has precious little to do with beggars), 1916.

' Making Panpipes from the grasses of the grave was an occupation that needed skill and yielded a phantom music,' a reviewer of Walter de la Mare's *The Burning-Glass and Other Poems* in *The Times Literary Supplement*, November 17, 1945: a phantom Pandean music is heard, afar off, in many of that poet's verses.

We might fittingly adopt the form: *panpipe* for *Pan*(-)*pipe*, *pipe of Pan*, *Pan's pipe*, ' a primitive musical instrument made of a series of reeds graduated in length so as to form a scale, the upper and open-ends being level, so as to permit the easy passage of the lips from one to another; its invention was ascribed by Greek legend to Pan ' (The OED). It dates from the days of classical Greece; Pan's own name for the instrument was **syrinx**, q.v. Shelley, in his *Hymn to Pan*, re-told the pleasing fable that Pan once opposed Apollo in a musical contest.

The variant *Pandean pipe* (also written *pandean pipe*) is rare—indeed obsolescent. The *Pandean harmonica* is a mouth-organ similar to a panpipe: hence *pandean*, ' a member of a band playing only the *Pandean harmonica* ', such bands being common during the first ten or twenty years of the 19th Century, and at least one performing, ca. 1805, at Vauxhall Gardens. See especially Dr Percy Scholes's *The Oxford Companion to Music*. Cf. **Pan.**

panama. The *Panama hat* is a misnomer, for it was made in Ecuador, South America, not at Panama in Central America; it is the heat of Central America which has generated the name, and with that heat the compulsive fact that Panama was at first the chief distributing centre.

pandar, n.; and derivatively **pander,** v. ' I would play Lord
Pandarus of Phrygia, sir, to bring a Cressida to this Troilus,'
Twelfth Night, III, i, 53–54; ' Thou art the pandar to her dis-
honour,' *Cymbeline*, III, iv, 31; and from *Troilus and Cressida*
itself (III, ii, 195–200 in the Shakespeare Head Press edition of
the dramatist's works), ' If ever you prove false one to another,
since I have taken such pains to bring you together, let all
pitiful goers-between be call'd to the world's end after my
name; call them all Pandars; let all inconstant men be
Troiluses, all false women Cressids, and all brokers-between
Pandars ! '

To which precision we need but add that Pandar (Greek
Pandaros) occurs in *The Iliad*—though not as a pandar.
Shakespeare may have taken the Pandarus-Cressida-Troilus
story from Chaucer, who developed it from an episode in a
poem by a Frenchman, who got it from the medieval-Latin
version of a Greek original.

Pandean pipes. See **Pan pipes.**

pander. See **pandar.**

Pandora; Pandora's box. Valerie West speaking : ' Tell me,
Louis, I'm as tragically curious as Pandora and Psyche and
Bluebeard's wife, melted into the one and eternal feminine,'
Robert W. Chambers, *The Common Law*, 1911.

In Greek mythology, Pandora loosed from her box all ills, all
evils upon the world, hope alone remaining in the box : the
revenge of Zeus upon mankind—through Prometheus. Ironically, for *Pandora* means ' all gifts '. The musical instrument
known as the *pandora* or *pandore* is not an unmixed blessing ; nor
does it at all certainly derive from *Pan*, for it more probably
derives from some Oriental word.

Pandy might well, in its derivative sense, ' a mutineer ' (strictly,
in the Indian Mutiny), be written with a small *p*. It comes
from *Pande*, a surname very common in Bengal.

Pangloss (or **Dr Pangloss**) is that type of optimist which
believes that ' all is for the best in the best of all possible
worlds '; less reprehensibly, one who believes that the secret
of happiness, and one's true work in the world, is to ' cultivate
one's garden ' (*cultiver son jardin*). In Pangloss, Voltaire
satirized Leibnitz. He is the central figure of the undying
satirical masterpiece, *Candide* (1758).

323

The name *Pangloss* connotes the *gloss*ing or glozing of everything (Greek *pan*).

panic. *Panic* (*fear*), soon to become a noun in its own right, comes direct from French *panique*, itself from Greek *panikos*, ' of, or caused by, Pan '. The rural god Pan, ' by popular association with the Greek *pan*, neuter of *pas*, all, . . . later became the personification of nature, whence *panic* (terror), inspired by the mysterious night sounds of hill and vale ' (WWN). Not only night but also day sounds : witness Robert Hugh Benson's esoteric novel, *The Angel of Pain*, and the following quotation from J. L. Myres, *The Dawn of History*, concerning prehistoric Greece :—' On the hills, half-nomad forest-haunting pastorals— Pan and the Satyrs, of Greek folk-memory—with magic skill in the ways of all cattle and game, and rather like wild things themselves ; kindly or mischievous at will (like our Pucks and Little People), but in either mood incomprehensible to the cultivators, and much to be propitiated in simple ways. Artemis, too, and the nymphs are up there : you can hear their hunting-cry far up when the wind is still, and the mountain goats scurry down, panic-stricken, to the edge of the corn-land.' (Compare : ' Lose your nerve in a wood, she said to herself, and the result is called panic,' ' Michael Innes,' *The Secret Vanguard*, 1940.)

For the full implications of Pan as an ancient god, see especially J. G. Frazer's *The Golden Bough*. For the etymology of *Pan*, see **paean.**

panpipes. See **Pandean pipes.**

pantagruelian ; pantagruelism. In Rabelais's *Pantagruel*, 1532, the name means ' The All-Thirsty One ' : ' The name had been given in 15th Century French mysteries to a demon who provoked thirst, and its primitive sense appears to have been " suffocation " ' (Harvey) : Rabelais pretends to derive the name from Greek (*pan*, ' everything '—as adverb, ' entirely ') and Arabic, and in the Fourth Book he defines *pantagruelism* (French -*isme*) as ' a certain gaiety of spirit steeped in disregard of things fortuitous '. A jolly drunkard and drinking companion, Pantagruel discharges his seemingly unrestrained humour with a serious moral aim. Rabelais, after all, was ' the Curé of Meudon ' (near Paris).

pantaleon (or **-leone** or **-lon**). This musical instrument—an elaboration of the dulcimer—was invented, late in the 17th Century, by a German : one *Pantaleon* Hebenstreit, whom, rumour has it, Louis XIV honoured by bestowing upon the instrument its deviser's font-name. (Scholes.)

Pantaloon (or **p**—); **pantaloons** (which yields **pants** and **panties**); **pantalet**(**te**)**s,** diminutive from *pantaloons*, which were originally worn by the lean, bespectacled, slippered dotard of Italian comedy, wherein *Pantalone* (from *Pantaleone*, patron saint of Venice : *Pantaleōn*, ' all-lion ', a Greek personal name) was the generic name for every such character, strictly and, for many years, predominantly a Venetian.

pantheon, ' a memorial of national heroes ', comes from the Paris *Panthéon*, itself imitative of the Roman Pantheon, built ca. 25 B.C. by Agrippa ; from Greek *pantheion*, ' (dedicated, consecrated to) all the gods '. Concerning Montrose, John Buchan has written, ' I could ask for no greater honour than to help to restore to his country's pantheon the hero of my youth ' (*Memory Hold-the-Door*, 1940).

paraguay is short for *Paraguay tea*, commonly called ' maté ' ; the leaves of the Paraguay ilex are roasted, or sun-dried, and infused in water in the same way as tea. This shrub grows abundantly in, and maté is the most popular drink of, *Paraguay*, that South American republic between Brazil and Argentina of which Chisholm says, ' The most important industry is the collection and preparation of the yerba-maté, or Paraguay tea, in the forests, or " yerbales ", where the tree grows wild '.

parakeet comes, via the Old French *paroquet* (French *perroquet*) from Italian *parrocchetto*, from a diminutive of *parroco*, ' a parson '—from a presumed Vulgar Latin *parochus* (compare our *parish*) : compare the French *moineau*, sparrow, literally ' little monk ' (*moine*). The Spanish word is *periquito*, pet-form of the earlier *perico*, which is *Perico*, familiar for *Pedro*, Peter : compare **parrot.** As W remarks, probably both the Spanish and the Italian words are of the one origin and folk-etymology has been at work.

paramatta. ' There are two kinds of stuff now made, called " Orleans " and " Paramatta " (why so named, it would probably be difficult to say) apparently formed of worsted, but the weft only is of worsted, the warp being cotton,' G. Dodd, 1844, in his book on textile manufacture (quoted by The OED) : ' *paramatta*. Fabric. ? From *Parramatta* (New South Wales) ; but perhaps only fancy trade-name,' W. Fancy, yes ; because the material has never been manufactured there. But in the 1830's and 1840's, *Parramatta* had, to Englishmen in England, a romantic sound. Next to Sydney the oldest town in Australasia, Parramatta ('Head of the Water') was early associated with sheep—now with fruit.

parchment; pergameneous (the erudite adjective = 'of parchment'). *Parchment*, 'sheep-skin or goat-skin prepared for writing—or for painting', englishes the French *parchemin*, which gallicizes the Latin *pergamena* (*charta*), '(paper) of *Pergamum*', a city in Asia Minor—in Greek, *Pergamon*.

Concerning 'the natural vegetation of the Nile' in ancient times, J. L. Myres in *The Dawn of History* cautiously predicates that 'Thorny shrubs and halfa-grass cover the drier margins; papyrus (extinct since the Saracen conquest displaced the agriculturists' "paper" by the "parchment" natural to a pastoral folk) and many reeds thrive by the river edge; and the spring flowers are brilliant'.

'The kings of Pergamon . . . owned large factories for parchment and textiles,' V. Gordon Childe, *What Happened in History*, 1942.

Pergamon was a kingdom, and its capital; its name is cognate with, or perhaps derived from, Greek *purgos*, 'a tower'; if that be so, Pergamon was originally 'The Citadel'. Later, the city became the capital of the Roman province known as Asia.

Of the kingdom and dynasty of Pergamum, T. R. Glover has, in *The Ancient World*, 1935, said that 'It did valiant service for art, literature, learning and civilization. Pergamum had one of the most famous libraries of antiquity . . . When the rival book-collector, the Ptolemy of the day, refused papyrus to his enemy, parchment (Pergamene; the name is still in the commodity, misspelled a little) was devised at Pergamum.'

Compare **biblical.**

pariah. In Tamil, *Paraiyar* is the plural of *Paraiyan*, the name of the largest of the lower castes in southern India. Europeans have grossly exaggerated the original sense to mean 'utter outcast' (here, from 'utter *out-caste*'), thanks largely, says 'Hobson-Jobson' Yule, to Bernardin de Saint-Pierre's 'preposterous though once popular tale, *La Chaumière indienne* (1791)'. (W.)

parkin is a North Country kind of gingerbread. The OED and W suggest that it may derive from the surname *Parkin*; one Parkin may well have been either the cook that hit upon the happy idea or the baker or confectioner originally concerned predominantly with its baking and distribution.

parmesan. ' The natural water-meadows along the banks of the Po are mainly devoted to dairy cattle, especially in Emilia ; and irrigated meadows both in Emilia and in Lombardy are similarly used. The milk is everywhere made into cheese, which in Emilia takes its name usually from the old Duchy of Parma,—though now made especially round Lodi,—and in Lombardy takes its name from the town of Gorgonzola ' (Lionel W. Lyde, *Europe*, 4th edition, 1930).

The word *parmesan* is French for Italian *parmegiano*, ' of Parma '.

Parnassus; Parnassian. Literature in general, poetry in particular, hence an anthology of poetry ; literary, especially poetical. In *Reflections in a Mirror*, 1944, Charles Morgan has, with a dry derision, referred to that ' twist of critical fashion ' which ' caused Virginia Woolf to send Trollope and Jane Austen for a walk hand in hand over those garden-slopes of Parnassus that are weeded of thought and poetry,' and in her delightful book, *The Wandering Scholars*, 1927, Helen Waddell remarked, ' *Dum Dianae vitrea* is the height of secular Latin poetry, even as the *Dies irae* of sacred : the twin paths of the medieval Parnassus '; and in *The Observer* of December 16, 1945, a third notable maker of striking phrases and arresting rhythms and the finest good-sense, Ivor Brown, alluded to the less-known Elizabethan and Jacobean dramatists thus obliquely, ' the little-known glades and thickets on the foothills of Parnassus '.

Parnassus is merely the Latin form of Greek *Parnassos*, the Greek mountain that, north of Delphi, attains a height of 8000 feet. In Greek mythology and in Greek literary convention (whence the modern Occidental echo), Parnassos—from which flowed the Castalian spring (**Castalian** in the Appendix)—is evocative of, indeed almost synonymous with, the Muses and their brilliant conductor, Apollo, the sun-god, the god of light, the god of music.

parramatta. See **paramatta.**

parrot; poll parrot. The latter is *Poll parrot*, and *parrot* is a straightforward personification, *Parrot* or *Perrot* being a common Middle English diminutive of *Pierre*, French for ' Peter '. Compare **parakeet,** which see !

Partington, Mrs. This old lady is the American ' opposite number ' or equivalent of **Mrs Malaprop,** for she has the happiest knack of misusing words. She is the humorous centre

327

and source of *The Life and Sayings of Mrs Partington*, 1851, by Benjamin Shillaber (1814–90), one of the earliest of the long line of 19th-Century American humorists.

partlet, archaic for ' a woman's ruff ', was originally *patlet*, from Old French *patelete*, diminutive of *patte*, ' hand ' : the change was operated by the influence of *Partlet*, the hen—Chanticleer's wife in the *Roman de Renart*—and hence any hen : hens were, in medieval fancy, apprehended as wearing ruffs.

pasquinade. ' Some of this you may read for yourselves in a pasquinade, set up on the bridge yonder,' David Pilgrim, *The Grand Design*, 1944.
  Pasquinade comes from the Italian *pasquinata*, which derives from *Pasquino*, the name of that statue at Rome on which Latin verses were annually placed—from as early as the end of the 15th Century.

pasteurism ; pasteurize ; pasteurization. ' The milk had been taken away for pasteurisation—a measure which had delivered the population of Malta from the recurrent danger of fever,' John Brophy, *Target Island*, 1944.
  Louis Pasteur (1822–95), the greatest French chemist of the 19th Century, invented a method whereby milk can be sterilized ; he also found the cure for rabies and saved the silk industry of France ; he did many other brilliant and useful things.

pat ; especially in *on one's pat*, alone. Short for *on one's Pat Malone*, a Cockney rhyming-slang term. Slang, it is true ; yet astonishingly general—more general than *on one's jack*, i.e. *on one's Jack Jones*.

patavinity is a markedly literary term for ' provincialism in literary style ', especially in prose ; among philologists, a synonym of ' provincialism '. Roman critics applied *patavinitas*, on the analogy of *latinitas*, to Livy's style in reference to the traces they observed of the dialect characteristic of *Patavium* (now Padua), where the great Roman historian was born.
  Compare **solecism.**

patronite. See **vanadium.**

paulownia is a Japanese ornamental tree or its trumpet-shaped, purplish flower, named thus in 1835 in honour of Anna *Paulowna*, daughter of the Czar, *Paul* I.

pavan or **pavane.** An Italian dance, originating at *Padua*, as the alternative *padovana* indicates : *danza padovana*, 'dance of Padua'. For a long time it was 'fashionable' to derive *pavan(e)* from Latin *pavo*, 'a peacock'. The link between *padovana* and *pavan(e)* is found in the obsolete *pavana*.

'The city commenced to shake, like an amateur practising the first measures of a grim pavan,' Harry Hervey, *School for Eternity*, 1942.

paynize is to treat wood with a solution of calcium sulphide and then with one of calcium sulphate, and thus to preserve by hardening it. The process, discovered ca. 1840 by a chemist named *Payne*, is known as *Payne's process*.

peach. 'The peach to this day, in spite of the vagaries of European spellings, carries its origin in its very name—the " Persian " fruit,' T. R. Glover in his fascinating essay ' Persia ' in *From Pericles to Philip*, 1917.

Speaking of the Near East, Professor L. W. Lyde (*The Continent of Asia*, 1933) has said that ' Where the date-palm thrives . . . artificial supplies of water can nearly always maintain other fruit trees, *e.g.* citrus and fig, peach and apricot ; and these can be extended far beyond the limits of the date-palm, as in the wonderful orchards of Damascus and the parts of Persia from which so many kinds of stone-fruit have spread over Southern Europe '.

' [Persis] is that great Persian province of Fars, which has played so notable a part in the history of Iran, and given its name to the whole of Persia,' Sir Aurel Stein, ' An Archaeological Tour in the Ancient Persis ' (*The Geographical Journal*, December 1935). *Persis*, the region, and *Persai*, its inhabitants, are Greek re-shapings of the native *Parsa* (both region and people).

Via Old French *pesche* (modern French *pêche*) from Low Latin *persica*, which corresponds to Classical Latin *persicum* (*malum*), which transliterates Greek *melon Persikon*, ' Persian (apple or, more probably, fruit) '. *Malum* is often generic ; it becomes ' apple ' by being ' *the* fruit '. Compare the origin of **quince.**

pearmain is the same as the warden pear : 13th–early 17th Centuries. Its modern sense is that of a variety of apple. From Old French *permain* or *parmain*, it perhaps derives from a presumed Latin *parmanus*, ' of Parma ' in Italy. (OED.)

peavey ; loosely, **peavy** or **peavie** or **peevy** or **pevey** or **pevy.** This is the timber-lumberer's lever, sharp-spiked and having,

329

under the sharp end, a semicircular grip or hook. It was invented ca. 1875—on the analogy of the shepherd's crook?—by Joseph *Peavey*; its average length is six feet. See especially Stewart Edward White's novel, *The Riverman*, 1908.

Pecksniff; Pecksniffian; Pecksniffism, Pecksniffery. An oleaginous hypocrite that, talking loftily of charity, benevolence, good will, remains content with talk; unctuously hypocritical; such hypocrisy. Mr Pecksniff, one of Dickens's most trenchant creations, appears in *Martin Chuzzlewit* (1844); and Dickens may have known the Warwickshire term *picksniff*, 'insignificant and despicable (person)'.

'The comfortable phrase'—*a servant of the public*—'is one in which the Sophists would have rejoiced, and Mr Pecksniff after them,' Charles Morgan, *Reflections in a Mirror*, 1944.

In his magnificently readable *Autobiography* (1936), G. K. Chesterton recalls 'the blatantly Pecksniffian person' that 'used to go for walks on Sunday carrying a prayer-book, without the least intention of going to church . . . "I do it, Chestie, as an example to others".'

peeler. See **bobby**.

Pegasus.

'Was there such a horse who, winging, curvetting,
  Kicked Helicon and brought forth Hippocrene?
  Did he know the delirium of the brain?
  Had he felt the pangs of desire and forgetting?'
    (Ronald Bottrall, *Farewell and Welcome*, 1945.)

Pegasus (Greek *Pēgasos*) was in Greek mythology that winged horse which, with the stamp of a hoof, created Hippocrene and which aided Bellerophon to destroy the Chimaera (see **chimaera**). This splendid beast, translated to Olympus, became a favourite of the Muses: hence the symbolism of Pegasus equivalent to the poetic afflatus. As *pegasus*, the word denotes any winged horse.

peggy, as bird—as in *peggy tub*—as an effeminate man (compare **molly**)—and in *Peggy-with-her-lantern* (Jack-o'-lantern, will o' the wisp): in all these dialectal or local usages, *peggy* is a personification: *Peggy* is an alteration of *Meggy* (for *Maggie*), *Margaret*. (OED.)

peke; Pekingese. A *peke* is a *Pekingese* (*dog*): this breed was originally the property and the prerogative of the imperial
330

family of China : that family resided at Peking (literally, ' the northern capital '—in contrast to *Nanking*, ' the southern capital '), which the Jesuits spelled *Pékin* and the English either *Pekin* or *Peking*; ' since Peking has ceased to be the (Northern) capital, its name has been changed to Peiping (" Northern Peace ") ' : Lionel W. Lyde, *The Continent of Asia*, (2nd edition) 1938.   By the way, *pekin* is the name of a silk fabric— see **pekin** and cf. **nankeen.**   (In French, there are several extremely interesting senses of *pékin*—e.g., ' a civilian '.)

' Pékin . . . était l'indescriptible splendeur de ses toits d'or . . . les vastes cours de marbre ciselé, chacune d'elles coupée des cinq ponts rituels.   L'ensemble se pouvait bien voir du haut de cette colline artificielle, la Montagne de Charbon, qui domine harmonieusement le rectangle parfait de la Ville Interdite,—la Cité Violette des anciens Fils du Ciel.— Au-delà, le quartier des Légations, la ville mandchoue, la ville chinoise et les créneaux cyclopéens de la Muraille sans égale . . . Et, surgissant de l'horizon, juste au bout de la ligne droite, astronomique, le Temple du Ciel ; avec ses tuiles gorge de pigeon . . . et sa triple enceinte circulaire, sans socle, sans couronnement, nue, pure et surhumaine comme le Parthénon, comme la Grande Pyramide . . . . . Un rêve chinois, immobile et replié, aptère . . . . . [Cette] capitale, la plus belle, la plus impériale et la plus philosophique qu'on ait jamais rêvée . . .' : thus Claude Farrère in *La Onzième Heure* (copyright, 1939 ; visa, February 12, 1940), a remarkable novel of China and, much less, of Japan in the spring of 1936, with a rather disconcerting, because so temperate and so cleverly veiled, preference of the Japanese to the Chinese.

pekin, silk material, striped or flowered, originally from China, is the French *pékin*, for *étoffe de Pékin*, fabric made at *Pekin* or *Peking* (now often Peiping).   But the *Peking duck*, a breed originating in China, if shortened at all is shortened to *Peking* ; and the same applies to *Peking blue*, a dullish blue of a kind traditionally associated with the 19th-Century Imperial Chinese Court at Peking.

Pekingese. See **peke.**

pembroke is a *Pembroke table*, a four-legged table and, apart from the semicircular leaves on two opposite sides, square or sometimes oblong ; it was often used as a work-table, yet often it was inlaid and always it was beautifully finished.   Fashionable in the latter half of the 18th Century, it took its name from *Pembroke*, the capital of Pembrokeshire, Wales.   The ancient castle there was rebuilt by Strongbow in 1109 when he was created Earl of Pembroke.

penates. See **Lares and Penates.**

Penelope. ' My destiny was a Penelope who tore up her good work before it was half done,' Mark Benney, *Low Company*, 1936.
In Homer's *The Odyssey*, Penelope was the wife of Odysseus. During her husband's overlong absence, she was beset with suitors. Faithful to him, she kept them at bay by undoing at night the weaving she had done during the day, for the end of weaving was to be taken as the end of her resistance. Full of feminine guile, she had not the courage to dismiss those suitors; she feared their vengeance. She has, therefore, become allusive for ' a chaste wife ', patient and ingenious, although not quite of the heroic mould of **Lucretia.**

penistone is a coarse woollen cloth (or a piece thereof), made originally at *Penistone*, a small town in the West Riding of Yorkshire. Large quantities were exported to North America in the 17th–18th Centuries, the DAE's terminal records being for 1651 and 1770. Americans often wrote it as *peniston*.
Compare **kersey** and **worsted.**

peony. ' The scent of the famous Chinese peonies and early roses and flowering shrubs reached us in gusts,' Osbert Sitwell, *Sing High! Sing Low!*, 1944.
Also written *paeony*, it derives from Latin *paeonia*, which represents Greek *paionia*, which, says Pliny, commemorates its discoverer, *Paeon*; modern scholars, however, find the origin in Latin *Paeonius*, Greek *Paionios*, ' medicinal ', the god of medicine being *Paion* (compare **panic**).

percheron. ' A huge, old-fashioned cart with high wooden wheels . . . drawn by three magnificent Percheron horses,' Francis Beeding, *Eleven Were Brave*, 1940.
' John Hodge is muscled like a Percheron stallion : his hands are hard and shiny like hoofs,' Gerald Kersh, *They Die with their Boots Clean*, 1941.
The percheron—for the capitalled initial could fittingly make way for the small *p*—is occasionally known as ' the Norman horse ' : the animal comes from *le Perche*, a region south of Normandy; a region famous also for its cattle (see Lionel W. Lyde, *The Continent of Europe*, p. 217). The percheron is a light, stocky, fast-trotting cart-horse, formerly the post-horse

of France and now bred extensively in 'the Far West' of the U.S.A.

pergameneous. See **parchment.**

périgourdine or, in a more English shape, **perigordine.** This lively old French dance, the more enlivened by the dancers merrily, lustily singing the tune, has taken its name from the former province of Périgord, which represents all of the present *département* of Dordogne and part of that of Lot-et-Garonne. (Scholes.)

perique, the colour otherwise known as 'otter brown', is the colour of *perique*, a strong tobacco that, of a tough fibre, gummy in consistency, has long been raised in Louisiana. The word is in Louisiana French and said to be a re-shaping of *Pierre Chenel*, one of the pioneer tobacco-growers, perhaps via *Perico*, diminutive of Spanish *Pedro*, Pierre, i.e. Peter.

permian (or **P—**). 'For the whole period from Permian to Cretaceous times, denudation was active and the great mountain area was reduced to a peneplain,' Ll. Rodwell Jones in Jones & Bryan, *North America*.

So named—compare **silurian**—by Sir R. Murchison in 1841, in reference to *Perm*, that province of eastern Russia in which this geological formation is very noticeable. It constitutes the uppermost division of palaeozoic strata.

pernod or **Pernod.** 'Then we drank a Pernod, real pre-war stuff, I had brought from Massawa—the absinthe which for so long reigned supreme in the distant outposts of our French colonies,' Henry de Monfreid, *Hashish*, 1935. It took the place of absinthe when the latter was banned by the French government. This is a common-propertying of a trade-name: compare **dubonnet.**

perse; persea. The former, usually an adjective, means 'blue'—now a dark blue, resembling indigo; from French *pers*, feminine *perse*. The latter is a fruit, or the tree of the laurel family, the origin being the Greek *persea*, the tree being a native of *Persia*. The name of the colour also derives from *Persia*—or rather from the adjective *persicus*, Persian.

See also **peach.**

persian blind or **persiennes; Persian** (= *P. cat, P. carpet*), and **persian** (= *P. dance*, 'languorous, melancholy'). All are directly connected with Persia : truly native to the country. 'Everywhere were bear-skins, Persian carpets, palm-trees in tubs,' Henry de Monfreid, *Hashish*, 1935. The theme of most Persian rugs and carpets derives from the design of Persian paradises : see the Lyde quotation at **cashmere** and, in the subsidiary list, that at **Kashan.**

petenera. A Spanish song-type, lively, three in a measure; commemorating a 19th-Century singer. (Scholes.)

Peter; peter in cant; **peterman.** The first is short for *Peter-see-me*, a 17th-Century term for a Spanish wine, named after *Peter Xim*enes (or Jimenez), a famous cardinal. In cant—the language of the underworld—*peter* is a portmanteau, a safe : that is, *Peter*, ' as firm as a rock '. Hence, in cant, *peterman* is simply a safe-breaker. But *peterman*, in obsolete Standard English, means a fisherman, as Peter had been before he was called to the apostolate.

petersham, a heavy corded ribbon, used, e.g., for hatbands or belts, derives from *petersham*, a rough and knotted woollen cloth, used mostly for men's overcoats, whence also an overcoat or a pair of breeches made thereof. It was named, ca. 1811, after Viscount *Petersham*. Gronow in his *Recollections*, 1863, remarks that ' the Viscount was a great Maecenas among the tailors ' (OED). A leader of the Dandies, he became Earl of Harrington.

petit suisse is the name of a particular kind of Swiss cheese, white and, to many tastes, rather insipid. It is ' *little* Swiss ' because it is marketed in little boxes, and usually served one-' box '-one-person.
For other Swiss cheeses, see **emmenthaler** and **gruyère.**

petrel. Earlier spelt *pitteral*, it first became *petrel* in Dampier, who, in 1703, states, ' As they fly . . . they pat the Water alternately with their Feet, as if they walkt upon it . . . And from hence the Seamen give them the name of Petrels, in allusion to St Peter's walking upon the Lake of Gennesareth (OED). The name, therefore, would be an anglicizing, not of *Petrus* or *Peter*, but of *Petrellus* or *Petrillus*, diminutive of *Petrus* Compare **Mother Carey's chickens** (secondary list).

phaeton. ' When Charles, the black mustachioed French Canadian coachman, used to hitch my grandfather's bay pair to the light phaeton, it took an hour and a half of good smart trotting to get to town,' John P. Marquand, *Wickford Point*, 1939.

This four-wheeled open carriage was named after *Phaethon*, who, in Greek mythology, was the son of Helios the sun-god; one luckless day he drove his father's chariot, drawn by the ' horses of the Sun '. (This myth has been handled in skilful galliambics by George Meredith in the poem entitled ' Phaethon '.) The name means ' the Radiant One ' : the word represents the present participle of Greek *phaethein*, ' to shine ', itself formed from *phaos* (often contracted to *phōs*: compare *photography*), ' light, daylight '.

Pharaoh or **Pharo** or **Pharaon** or **Pharoan.** The last is slovenly for the third; the third is French for the first, of which the second is merely a written variant that paved the way for **faro,** q.v.

Pharisee; pharisaic(al). ' [In *Measure for Measure*] pharisaic righteousness is shown as superficial and natural instinct treated with sympathy,' G. Wilson Knight, ' The Shakespearian Integrity ' in *The Burning Oracle*, 1939.

The adjective naturally derives from *Pharisee* in its modern sense, ' self-righteous person, a hypocritical formalist ' : from the New Testament usage, ' member of a strict Jewish sect marked by observance of tradition and by pretensions to holiness '. Via French from the Vulgate from Greek *Pharisaios* from Hebrew *parush*, ' apart (from the crowd), separated (from the rest of mankind) '.

pharos. ' The lighthouse [of ancient Alexandria] was counted one of the wonders of the world and gave its name *Pharos* to all lighthouses; it was not at all so far from shore as Menelaus in the *Odyssey* tells Telamachus,' T. R. Glover, *The Ancient World*, 1935. But Glover's ' it ' refers to the small island on which it was built, for the city of Alexandria was founded by, and took its name from, Alexander the Great; Ptolemy II (Ptolemy Philadelphus), who lived 309–247 B.C., caused the lighthouse to be built. ' Over the whole [city, its harbour, its suburbs] kept watch the Pharos, the lighthouse erected . . . by Sostratus of Cnidus for the safety of mariners . . . . . . Sostratus' lighthouse on the Pharos at Alexandria, built as a tower of three diminishing stories, nearly 400 feet high, was unique; the third story was the " lantern ", eight columns supporting a cupola, under which burnt a fire of resinous wood, the light possibly being thrown out by convex mirrors; a lift ran up to it. It perhaps gave Arab architects the idea of the minaret,' W. W. Tarn, in that monument of impeccable scholarship, luminous with intellect and sweetened with humanism and humanity: *Hellenistic Civilisation*, (revised edition) 1930.

pheasant, in Middle English *fesaunt* or *fesant*, from Old French *faisant*, descends, probably through Provençal, from Latin *phasianus*, a transliteration of Greek *phasianos*, i.e. *phasianos ornis*, ' the Phasian bird ', from the region of the Phasis, that famous river of Colchis which flows into the eastern end of the Black Sea; it plays a notable part in the story of the **Argonauts.** The bird is reputed to have been first brought from its banks to Greece, where, particularly at Athens, it afforded a welcome accompaniment to **Attic salt.** Its scientific name is *Phasianus Colchicus*; and its origin has been recalled to us by Henry Williamson in *The Phasian Bird*, 1948.

pherecratean or **pherecratic** is a *Pherecratean verse*; ‿‿ (or ——) ‿‿‿——; devised or invented by the Greek Pherecrates, who, an imitator of Crates, wrote comedies, for which he twice won the prize; he is known to have won it in 437 B.C.
  Compare **glyconic.**

philander; philanderer, -ering. The verb derives from the noun, which has considerably changed its meaning from the literal one of the Greek *philandros*, ' loving (*philos*) one's husband (*anēr*) ', hence ' loving mankind ', to ' a man given to flirting with women ': and that change is largely owing to the influence of the character Philander in Beaumont & Fletcher's early 17th-Century play, *The Laws of Candy*, and of an old ballad wherein Philander is the lover of Phillis (see **Phyllis**).

Philip, a sparrow; **philip,** a coin. The former (also *Phip*) may have been suggested by a sparrow's chirp. The latter was named after certain dukes—French, Burgundian, Spanish—named Philip, and they derived their name from Philip II of Macedon (ca. 382–336 B.C.); the Greek *Philippos* signifies ' horse-lover '. The name of the coin is entirely obsolete, that of the bird survives only in dialect.
  Of Ausonius the Latin poet (4th Century A.D.), Helen Waddell writes, ' There is a vast and pleasing correspondence: to Theon, . . . who will not come because he owes Ausonius 14 philips, witness the I.O.U. written with reluctance ' (*The Wandering Scholars*, 1927).
  Compare **philippic.**

336

Philip and Cheyney was a clothing material, either of inferior worsted or of cheap woollen stuff, popular in the late 16th–17th Century.

The stress is on the common quality : the stuff takes its name from *Philip and Cheyney*, which, with its variant, *Philip, Hob and Cheyney*, was the 16th Century equivalent of *Tom, Dick and Harry* : two or more men, taken at random from—but held to be representative of—the common people.

Philip drunk to Philip sober, to appeal from ; often as a verbal-noun phrase, **appealing from . . .** To appeal to a person's better nature.

Valerius Maximus, that compiler of historical anecdotes who lived in the reign of Tiberius, relates that a certain woman, unjustly condemned by Philip of Macedon while he was drunk, protested, *Provocarem ad Philippum, sed sobrium* (' I should like to appeal to Philip—when he's sober ! ') : as we learn from the late Sir Gurney Benham's admirable *Book of Quotations*.

' To say that [metaphysical] theory must be checked by appeal to experience . . . seems like saying that the rational must prove its rationality by conforming to the less rational, which seems like appealing from Philip sober to Philip drunk,' R. G. Collingwood, *An Essay on Philosophical Method*, 1933.

This is the famous Philip II of Macedon, usually called ' Philip of Macedon ' (382–336 B.C.), who, after a reign of conquest, was murdered in the prime of his age and at the height of his power. Tactician and strategist, he defeated the assembled might of Greece. Immediately he came to the throne, ca. 359 B.C., he imposed upon the Macedonians a strict military discipline and re-organized the army on the basis of the phalanx (the origin of ' the British square '). A well-informed tribute to his military genius is contained in the following passage, ' With tanks invented by the British, with submarines and aeroplanes and automatic weapons invented by the French, British and Americans, with principles of war invented by Hannibal, Caesar, Napoleon and Philip of Macedon, [the Germans] masqueraded as a race of soldiers, sailors and airmen,' Francis Beeding, *Eleven Were Brave*, 1940.

Philippi, meet at, especially as ' Thou shalt see me at Philippi ' and ' We shall meet at Philippi '. To Brutus in his tent at Abydos in 42 B.C., a spectre announced, ' Thou shalt see me at Philippi '. Brutus, nothing daunted, replied, ' I shall meet thee there '. The spectre did ; Brutus, defeated by Antony, died upon his own sword. (Shakespeare's *Julius Caesar*.)

Philippi, named after *Philip* of Macedon, is in Macedonia.

philippic; philippize. 'A bitter, trenchant invective or denunciation; to speak, to write, corruptly—under influence, suggestion, dictation' (loosely, 'to utter a bitter invective').

From Demosthenes the greatest Athenian orator's orations, in defence of Athenian liberty, against Philip of Macedon (see **Philip drunk . . .**); thence applied to Cicero's almost equally eloquent speeches against Antony; thence generally—but especially in a political context.

philistine; hence, philistinism. A person uninterested in art and culture; a materialistic, unspiritual person. 'Carlyle and Matthew Arnold share the responsibility of having introduced it into English' (WWN). Via German-University slang (where it means 'non-student, hence outsider') from the literal sense, 'a member of an alien race that, in southern Palestine, warred upon the Israelites'—cf. the long-established facetious phrase *to fall into the hands of the Philistines*, 'to be taken by bailiffs; later, to be hardly treated by the critics'. For a full, most readable account of the sense-development, see WWAM; but for those who have not the time to read that account, this extract from Lionel W. Lyde's *Asia* may serve to point the geographical origin :—' With its genial climate, its productive soil, its busy thoroughfare, this plain [i.e., the ancient Philistia] became the home of a rich and self-indulgent people of grossly mongrel type and cosmopolitan tendencies.'

Philistine = French *Philistin* = (via Low Latin) Greek *Philistinos* = older Greek *Palaistinos* = Assyrian *Palastu* and *Pilistu*, the Greek word fusing the alternative Assyrian forms. But beyond the Greek, we stand upon uncertain ground, for, in reference to Egypt and the approximate period 1200 B.C., J. L. Myres (*The Dawn of History*), having mentioned that ' there were already half-foreign settlements on the Palestinian coast plain ', remarks that ' the chief of these settlers bore the name Pulishta, perhaps akin to the obscure name *Pelasgi*, borrowed by Greek writers from an ancient pirate-people in the Aegean; and certainly identical with that of the Philistines, and with the name " Palestine " which has spread from the coast to be the name of all southern Syria. Their later history is entwined for ever in that of their Israelite neighbours.'

Phillis. See **Phyllis.**

philomel, philomela. As ' a nightingale ', the word was popularized by Classical scholars : it is so used by Virgil in *The Georgics*. Virgil's use is derived from Greek mythology, where *Philomela* (in Greek, also *Philomelë*), daughter of Pandion,

338

King of Athens, was raped by her brother-in-law Tereus and thereupon Olympus changed her into a nightingale : the lover's plaint of the nightingale recalls the heartbroken plaint of the violated maid.   Thereafter, the bird was known by the name of the princess.

Philomela :   *philos*, 'fond (of)' + *mela*, 'apples (or other fruit)' : 'Fruit-loving'.

phoebe.   'A phoebe has a nest there, so we moved the chairs,' Rex Stout, *Double for Death*, (English edition) 1940.

The *phoebe* is an American flycatcher or pewit : *Sayornis phoebe* of the eastern United States ;   *black phoebe* and *Say's phoebe* (Thomas Say, 1787–1834, American entomologist and zoologist), of the western States.   It probably received this feminine name from the fact that its nest of mud and grass is often found about buildings.   (Webster.)

Phoebus; phoebad.   The latter, 'a prophetess, an inspired woman', is a modern application of the Classical sense, 'a priestess of Apollo at Delphi' ;   that is, of *Phoebus* Apollo, the sun-god.   The name *Phoebus* is Latin, a transliteration of the Greek *Phoibos*, which ('The Shining One') substantivizes the adjective *phoibos*, 'bright, shining, radiant ; hence, pure' : compare *phoibazein*, 'to cleanse ;   to render *pure*'.   From *Phoebus*, 'the sun-god', comes *Phoebus*, 'the sun'—an obsolescent poeticism.

phoenix.   'Among authors of [books of travel], Marco Polo is prince and phoenix, ever arising anew in flames more glorious, a thousand formerly obscure points . . . springing to life again from year to year, lit by the prodigious renewal of those fires, so that in his travellers' tales . . . is to be found an inner core of a strange truth more true than truth itself,' Osbert Sitwell, *Sing High! Sing Low!*, 1944.

The Phoenix and the Turtle (mystic poem and profound), by Shakespeare.

Latin *phoenix*, from Greek *phoinix*.   'Littré supposes that the phoenix was named from its bright colour [—the Greek word meaning also "purple-red "] ;   and that the colour was so named because invented by the Phoenicians' (Skeat), *Phoinix* being a Phoenician—as Homer was the first to record.   A *phoenix* is also a guitar-like instrument invented by the *Phoenicians*.

phosphor bronze is of the same origin as the next.

phosphorus is one of the 90-odd chemical elements and takes its name from *Phosphorus*, literally 'the light-bringer', i.e. the

Morning Star. In 1669, an alchemist, searching for that supreme *ignis fatuus*, the philosopher's stone, obtained it, by happy accident, from urine. Uninterested in anything so mundane, he passed his knowledge to a true chemist, one Kunkel—whence the earlier name, *Kunkel's phosphorus*. (OED.)

Phrynë, a prostitute. From that lovely and famous Greek courtesan who flourished in the 4th Century B.C.: to her, after her death, stood a statue at Delphi; to her, in the flower of her beauty, the great Attic orator Hyperides composed a speech, defending her against impiety and winning the case by unveiling her bosom's glory to the jury. *Où sont les jours d'antan?*

' I like to think that on the jetty at Alexandria, a couple of thousand years ago, Greeks of fashion sat on the parapet, while passed before them a procession, lightly garbed, a ribbon binding their banded hair, the courtesans. The sun set into Lybia; one waited for Phryne, the other for Eutropis,' W. L. George, *The Triumph of Gallio*, 1924.

Phyllis or **Phillis.** A pretty country lass, as in Horace and in Virgil's *Eclogues*; or a deft (and pretty) waitress, as in Milton's *L'Allegro*. Originally a Greek name (*Phillis*): in Greek mythology, a princess transformed into an almond tree; a common Greek given-name, etymologically ' a green bough ': compare *phullas*, 'foliage', and *phullon*, 'a leaf'.

Compare **Amaryllis.**

pickwick; Pickwickian, esp. in *in a Pickwickian sense*. A pickwick was a cheap cigar, ca. 1840–60, as in ' I recollect the squabble and then the fight between Haycock and Lipscomb . . . it arose from Haycock's burning Lipscomb's hand with a *pickwick* which he was smoking—Lipscomb knocked the *pickwick* out of Haycock's hand ' (*Session Paper* of the Old Bailey, July 12, 1850).

A Pickwickian sense is a constructive sense—a technical sense—an esoteric sense. (' Now he could confine himself to the central aspect of the case, to what might be called its Pickwickian core,' ' Michael Innes ', *The Weight of the Evidence*, 1944.) But the adjective is also, and often, used in a simpler sense, as in ' My father . . . had all the Pickwickian evenness of temper and pleasure in the humours of travel,' G. K. Chesterton, *Autobiography*, 1936.

The former comes from Mr Pickwick of Charles Dickens's *The Pickwick Papers* (1836–37); the latter from the opening chapter of that evergreen. ' Dickens took the name from that

340

of the proprietor of a Bath coach (see Chapter XXXV). It is derived from the village of *Pickwick* (Wilts) ' : Ernest Weekley.

piedmont. Foothills, region of foothills, as in ' [The coconut palm] spreads inland too—up to the highland piedmont, *e.g.* as far as Kurunegala ' (in Ceylon), Lionel W. Lyde, *The Continent of Asia*, 1933 ; the ' highland ' is unnecessary, as the author recognizes when, a page further on, he says, ' The densest forest of all was round the piedmont of the montane core ' (of Ceylon). From Piedmont, a region in northern Italy. The word *piedmont* is merely a literal French translation of Italian *piemonte* ' foot [of] mountain '.

Pierian, ' poetic '—' inspiring poetry, or characteristic of poetry or the knowledge of poetry ', was originally an epithet of the Muses : see **muse.** *Pieria* was a region in ancient Macedonia, where gushed the *Pierian spring*, a fountain sacred to the Muses, and, in its transferred sense, ' the source of poetic inspiration '.

pierrette. See :—

pierrot, pierrette, a masculine, a feminine itinerant minstrel face-whitened and loose-dressed in white, debase two stock characters of French pantomime. The latter term is merely the feminine of the former : and *Pierrot* is merely the diminutive of *Pierre* (English *Peter*, ' a rock ').

In reference to Watteau's paintings, George Moore, in *Memoirs of My Dead Life*, 1906, has written thus :—' Pierrot, the white, sensual animal, the eighteenth-century modification of the satyr, of the faun, plays a guitar ; the pipe of Pan has been exchanged for a guitar '.

pigmy. See **pygmy.**

pilsener = **Pilsen beer.** Often spoken of as if it were a German beer, pilsener is brewed at Pilsen in Czecho-Slovakia. In great quantities. Between the wars of 1914–18 and 1939–45, one could, at almost any reputable *brasserie* in London or Paris or Berlin, obtain a pilsener.

Compare **bock.**

Pimpernel, the, or **the Scarlet Pimpernel,** has become a synonym for ' a gallant man concerned to engineer, and successful in engineering, the escape of political prisoners, or prisoners-to-be, from death, an escape attended with difficulties and perils ' : became that in 1905, when the Baroness

341

Emmuska Orczy, born 1865 in Hungary but later an English citizen, brought out her romantic novel, *The Scarlet Pimpernel*. There were sequels and stage and film productions; in one way and another, the Pimpernel, an English aristocrat, handsome, brave, rich, intelligent, resourceful, debonair and nonchalant, who got French aristocrats out of the clutches of the French Revolutionaries, has had a fabulous success, including that of constant imitation.

pinchbeck, ' counterfeit, spurious ': from *pinchbeck*, ' an alloy of copper and zinc used, in cheap jewellery, to imitate gold ': from its inventor, Christopher *Pinchbeck* (1670?–1732), a London toy-maker and watch-maker.

pindaric; pindarics. The former, ' irregular (verse), hence unrestrained (mode of life; character) ', is closely connected with the latter, which denotes ' versification and style in the manner of those of the odes by *Pindar* '. Pindar (522?–443 B.C.) excelled in the writing of magnificent odes in irregular stanzas : his Greek verse is almost as difficult as it is beautiful. The term *pindaric* comes, via French *pindarique*, from Latin *Pindaricus*, Greek *Pindarikos*, from *Pindaros*.

pink (see my *Underworld*) is a slang form of :—

Pinkerton, properly an operative of the *Pinkerton* detective agency, is, in the U.S.A., often used loosely for any private detective. Allan Pinkerton (1819–84), a Scot, went to America in 1842 and, at Chicago, set up a detective agency eight years later. He soon became a national figure, and his *Thirty Years a Detective*, 1884, is still readable.

pinkster is short for *pinkster flower*, originally *Pinkster flower*, the pink azalea, which flowers about Whitsuntide : the Dutch for that season is *Pinkster*, ultimately from the Greek *pentēkostē* (Pentecost).

pipes of Pan. See **Pan pipes.**

pistol derives from French *pistole*. But whereas Webster derives the French word from German *pistole*, and that from Czech *pistal*, originally a pipe, hence a pistol, W, following Skeat, thinks that the French word shortens the earlier *pistolet*, from Italian *pistoletto*, a diminutive from *pistolese*, defined by Florio as ' a great dagger ', and adds, ' ? from *Pistoia* (Tuscany), still noted for metal-work and gun-making '. The OED derives *pistol* from *pistolet*.

platonic, platonic love, platonics (talk, or relation, between platonic lovers); **Platonic year, Platonism, Platonist.** The last three terms are directly connected with the idealist philosophy of Plato, greatest of Greek thinkers, who died in or about 347 B.C. The *Platonic year* is that ' cycle in which heavenly bodies were supposed to go through all their possible movements and return to original positions ' (COED). Plato had many poetical ideas about ' the music of the spheres ' and other ' heavenly ' matters.

In popular usage, *platonic* means ' merely verbal or theoretical —not resulting in action; hence, harmless '; compare the phrase *of merely academic interest* (without practical bearings). This sense of *platonic* has gradually and naturally grown out of the Platonic philosophy, which strikes the ordinary man—*is* there one ?—as highfalutin'. The almost too famous *platonic love*, ' love purely spiritual or purely intellectual for a member of the opposite sex ', has likewise developed, very naturally, from certain tenets of Plato's imaginatively intellectualist philosophy; and *platonics* derives therefrom in much the same way as *laconics* from **laconic.**

In George du Maurier's *Trilby*, 1894, appeared a delightful pen-and-ink sketch and the following pertinency, ' That type so adored by sympathetic women who haven't got much to do; the friend, the tame cat, the platonic lover (with many loves)— the squire of dames, the trusty one, of whom husbands and brothers have no fear !—the delicate, harmless dilettante of Eros—the dainty shepherd who dwells " dans le pays du tendre "—and stops there ! '

pleased as Punch, as. See **Punch.**

Plimsoll = *P. line*; **plimsolls.** ' She was wearing a shapeless cotton frock and old plimsolls,' Jonathan Stagge, *Death and the Dear Girls*, 1946 : rubber-soled shoes with rubber extending about half-way into the uppers and thus ensuring dryness thus far : *Plimsoll's line* (or *mark*) represents the load-line on all British merchant vessels, a measure secured by Parliament in 1876 at the instancy of Samuel Plimsoll (1824–98), ' The Sailors' Friend '—largely through his book, *Our Seamen*, 1872.

Plutonian; Plutonic; Plutonist; plutonium. A *Plutonist* is one who believes in *the Plutonic theory* (or *Plutonism*), by which many, if not indeed most, geological phenomena are attributed to the action of heat inside the earth's crust; *Plutonic rocks* are igneous rocks. Both *Plutonic* and *Plutonian* are used for

343

'infernal' or, literally, 'of Pluto'; Pluto (in Greek: *Ploutōn*) being, in Greek mythology, the ruler of the infernal regions.

Plutonium, an element, is named after *Pluto*, the planet (discovered in 1930): see **neptunium.**

'Our light failed. The opposite hills merged into the night . . . We could hear the river below . . . and we were being left stranded on a high solitude in eternity. Ryan's quiet voice made eternity almost homely. His presence on the Plutonian shore, should we have the luck to meet him there, will instantly cause the thought of the lord of that domain to be of less moment,' H. M. Tomlinson, *Tidemarks*, 1924.

'About this Cavern there is a peculiar femininity: Pluto wanted to play, and picked up a crochet-hook,' Gerald Kersh, *The Weak and the Strong*, 1945.

On May 24, 1945, the Press revealed the secret of 'Operation Pluto', where *Pluto* is popularly explained to mean '*p*ipe *l*ine *u*nder *t*he *o*cean' but where the Classical god is obviously implied in this excellent official pun. (Oh! they have their fun and games in Whitehall.) In *The Daily Express*, on the date mentioned, Basil Cardew writes: 'While the Germans were being hammered back across the Rhine, British and American tank commanders were merely turning on a tap in the front line'—well, not impossibly far from it—'and running petrol direct from Mersey-side and Bristol. This seeming miracle was done by secret pipelines laid across the Channel and '—ultimately—'reaching as far as Frankfurt-on-Main, a distance of 600 miles.'

'For the first time, it is disclosed officially that neither uranium 235 nor plutonium the [atom] bomb's basic materials —give out any radiation that will indicate atomic time bombs planted by agents,' Chapman Pincher in *Daily Express*, March 13, 1946.

Podsnap; podsnappery. The latter is an Abstract Noun deriving from the former: in the Dickensian world (*Our Mutual Friend*, 1864–65), Mr John Podsnap, whom Webster stigmatizes as 'a pompous representative of British Philistinism' and whom British critics call by a four-letter word. Entrusted with the secrets of Providence (happily confirming Podsnap's designs), he constantly protests against the slightest, the remotest indelicacy.

poinsettia. 'She saw Loraine Driscoll carrying a sheaf of poinsettias,' V. Sackville-West (who has the true poet's eye for such scenes), *Grand Canyon*, 1942.

This originally Mexican species of euphorbia has large,

scarlet, decorative leaves encircling small flowers of greenish-yellow hue. In England the poinsettia is also called *Mexican flame-leaf*, in North America also *Easter flower*.

It was, in 1836, named after its discoverer, J. R. Poinsett, who, in addition to being the American Minister to Mexico, was a good botanist.

polacca. See **polonaise.**

poldavy, a coarse canvas used for sails by the Royal Navy of the 16th–18th Centuries, is also known as *poldavis*. It was, at least at first, made in Brittany and is credibly derived from *Poldavide*, which stands on the south side of Douarnenez Bay ; ' about 1548 a warrant . . . was issued to pay for bringing over certain Bretons to teach men here the art of making poldavies ' (OED).

polka ; polka mazurka. The polka, a lively Bohemian dance, arose early in the 19th Century ' and in its forties spread over Europe like an epidemic ' (Scholes) ; in the 1840's and 1850's, *polka* derivatively signified also a close-fitting, usually knitted jacket (compare **polonaise**). The polka mazurka, however, is much rather a mazurka than a polka.

In Polish, *Polka* is ' a Polish woman '—from *Polak*, ' a Polish man ' : note the analogous origin of *mazurka*. (There is another, though less convincing theory.)

Compare **polska.**

poll parrot. See **parrot.**

pollack. W goes closest to the etymology of this puzzling fish-name by suggesting derivation from *poll*, ' head '—with fanciful assimilation to *Polack*, ' a Pole '.

polly. See **apollinaris.**

polonaise (or, in its Italian shape, **polacca**) is, to music-lovers, the music for a slow dance ; to women of the 19th Century, a dress with bodice and with a skirt that opened from the waist downwards—very becoming. The dance, like the dress, was of Polish origin (*danse polonaise, robe polonaise* : French *polonais*, ' Polish ', from Medieval Latin *Polonia*, ' Poland ' : cf. the next entry) ; the dance was, in fact, one of the Polish national dances and, in form, originally a processional dance. Among the composers of polonaises for the piano are Bach, Handel,

Mozart, Beethoven, Chopin, Wagner; and with the dance may be compared the **cracovienne.**

In a policeman's evidence given on September 22, 1876, 'I also found seven coats, six books, one dress, one skirt, one silk polonaise, and other articles' (*Session Paper of the Central Criminal Court*).

polonium. Discovered in 1898 by Professor and Madame Curie, this metallic element—perhaps rather, form of matter—came naturally into their ken: it is radio-active in a high degree. Madame, of Polish nationality, is honoured by the name *polonium*, which derives from Medieval Latin *Polonia* (now Poland). Polonium is a constituent of pitchblende, once described by Sir William Crookes as ' the **uranium** mineral '.

polony, the sausage, comes probably from *Bologna* and is short for *Bologna sausage*: compare **boloney.** But it not impossibly represents *Polony* (i.e., Polish) *sausage*.

In the sense, ' a kind of long coat or gown for young boys ', *polony* certainly derives from French *Pologne*, Poland : compare the dress sense of **polonaise.**

polska. This three-time dance arose at the time of the union of the Swedish and Polish kingdoms in 1587. Deriving from the **mazurka,** it is a Polish dance : *Polska*, in Swedish, means ' Polish ': and there you have your origin. (Scholes.)

Compare **polka** and **polonaise.**

polypheme, a giant, comes from *Polyphème*, the French shape of *Polyphemus*, the Cyclops. See **Polyphemus moth** in the secondary list.

pom, short for **pomeranian,** a *Pomeranian dog*, originally of Pomerania in northern Prussia and known in England as early as the middle of the 18th Century. Capital *P* is unnecessary.

' I like dolls big enough to take a good hold on, and Miss Midgie Muldoon is only about knee-high to a Pomeranian,' Damon Runyon, *Guys and Dolls*, 1931, a sparkling collection of stories as good as the later and much better-known *More than Somewhat* and *Furthermore*.

pomard, pommard. ' We dined, drinking . . . a bottle of Pommard of the 1915 vintage, a trifle young in those days—it was . . . May 1921—but a fine, robust wine, the proper wine for a wet evening,' H. St George Saunders, introduction to ' David Pilgrim ', *The Emperor's Servant*, 1946.

This red **burgundy** comes from the vineyards around the village of Pommard in the *département* of the Côte d'Or.

Pomona, a treatise on fruit-trees, derives from *Pomona*, the Roman goddess of tree-fruit (*poma*). She was wooed by the god of fruits and orchards, Vortumnus, who, as wooer, assumed the forms of a reaper, a pruner of vines, a ploughman, and so forth.

Hence, *Pomona green*, apple green; the apple (*pomum*) gave its name to fruit in general.

pompadour. 'This morning the red hair was Pompadour style,' Darwin L. Teilhet, *The Fear Makers*, 1946: woman's hair dressed high and brushed back. But *pompadour* also means a woman's dress cut square and low in the neck; a brilliantly coloured American bird; and *Pompadour green*. All four senses derive from Jeanne Antoinette Poisson (1721–64), who, some years after becoming Louis XV's mistress, was ennobled as the Marquise de *Pompadour*. She completely dominated Louis.

poohbah, Pooh-Bah. In Gilbert & Sullivan's light opera, *The Mikado* (1885), Pooh-Bah is the personal name of Lord High Everything Else; hence, in transferred use, a politician that, as Hitler did, holds many offices. The term is echoic: it imitates his inarticulate arrogance.

poonah, adjective, as in 'He's an Army officer of the old school, my dear: too too poonah', derives from *Poonah*, or *Poona*, the military capital of the Deccan, traditionally associated with the British Army in India—though for some years with little justification. Poonah has for centuries been a centre for the manufacture of gold and silver jewellery and with the weaving of silk and cotton fabrics. *Poonah paper* and *the Poonah brush* were employed in *Poonah painting*, the picturing of birds and flowers upon rice paper, this imitation of Oriental work being very fashionable in Britain, ca. 1810–70.

poperin pear, as in Shakespeare, *Romeo and Juliet*, II, i, 37–38 (see my *Shakespeare's Bawdy*). Here, *poperin* = *popperin* = *poppering* = *Poperinghe*, that township in West Flanders which old soldiers of the First World War remember so vividly as 'Pop'.

poplarism, a municipal-council or borough policy that falls heavily upon the tax-payers, especially through the extravagant or at least very generous scale of out-relief, derives from the fact that at Poplar, a borough in the east of London, the Board of

347

Guardians for 1919, and after, practised such out-relief. Hence *poplarize*, to subject to poplarism.

port. Concerning Lisbon, Professor L. W. Lyde remarks that, ' as access inland is almost as bad as access to the coast, movement is more or less limited to the shipping of port wine at Leixoes and Oporto and the collecting of salt in the lagoons of Aveiro and Setubal . . . . . . The port wines are grown specially on the northern slope—which is the broader as well as the sunnier—of the deep Douro valley, in the lee of the Sierra de Marao (4665 feet) ; and here they get the " roasting " in summer which develops their " resinous " qualities . . . In this relatively advanced area, too, where a number of British firms—including the Cockburns, Crofts, and Grahams— actually own " quintas ", every legal protection is enforced against deterioration of product.' Elsewhere he speaks of ' the Paiz do Vinho, *i.e.* the port-wine country '. (*The Continent of Europe*, 4th edition, 1930.)

Whence it is, or should be, clear that *port* = ' Oporto wine '. The name *Oporto* = *o porto*, ' the port ' : as *Cologne* is ' *the* (Roman) colony ', so *Oporto* is ' *the* port ' (of Portugal).

pozz(u)olana or **puzzolana.** Dealing with the century or so before Christ, Professor Gordon Childe, *What Happened in History*, 1942, has noted that ' The Romans or their employees discovered an almost indestructible cement made by mixing lime with a volcanic ash (first found near Puteoli and hence still called " pozzolana ") which would set even under water ' : and to this we need add only that the modern name for Puteoli (a large seaport town of Campania) is *Pozzuoli* and that *pozzuolana* is the feminine of the corresponding adjective.

Compare **solfatara.**

praline is omitted by Skeat and W, etymologically dismissed by Webster with a curt ' F[rench] '. The OED, however, provides the information that this luscious confection was devised— one might almost say ' invented '—by a cook, sorry ! a *chef*, in the service of Maréchal Duplessis-*Praslin* (1598–1675) ; *Praslin* is pronounced as the French pronounce *praline*.

prattling parnell. See **cecily.**

priapean ; priapism. The former is short for *Priapean verse*, a Classical Greek metrical verse, consisting of a **glyconic** and a **pherecratean,** evidently a measure deemed suitable for erotic poetry, although, almost scannable as a hexameter, it seems to

348

be no less suitable for heroic. A *priapism*, besides its medical sense, means 'an amorous act' or 'sexual debauchery'. Both *priapean* and *priapism* derive, the former direct, the latter via Late Latin *priapismus*, from Latin *Priapus*, Greek *Priapos*, that deity who, in Classical mythology, represents the male generative power as it operates in Nature. He was, not ineptly, the son of Dionysus and Aphrodite. Uncapitalled, *priapus* synonymizes 'phallus'.

probang, a surgical instrument for the exploration of the throat, has been so influenced by *probe* or by *probant*, 'serving to test or prove', as to exhibit an alteration from *provang*, generally held to be the mere instrumentalizing of the 17th-Century inventor's name. Lacking sufficient evidence, not of that inventor—for there must have been one—but of that inventor being Provang, I feel that we must not be dogmatic.

procrustean; bed of Procrustes. '[Henry] James sees the social order as rigid, imposed on human beings from outside . . ., a bed of Procrustes, upon which victims are stretched or pared down to fit, unless they are fortunate enough to be correct, and wise enough not to move,' Kathleen Raine, 'La Comédie Humaine' in *The Dublin Review*, July 1945.—' This is pure intellectualism, and leads us to look for syllogisms in music, inductions in religion . . . This is what really happens when people attempt to maintain this view of the forms of experience as co-ordinate species : they assert, without in the least realizing it, the absoluteness of formal logic and reduce all alike to that Procrustean standard,' R. G. Collingwood, *Speculum Mentis*, 1924.

Procrustes, a legendary brigand of Eleusis in Greece, used to do precisely what the Dublin Reviewer mentions. His well-deserved death ensued at the stalwart hands of Theseus.

Prometheus; hence, promethean. A good example of the transferred use of *Prometheus* occurs in this brief passage from Meredith Nicholson's quietly effective novel, *A Hoosier Chronicle*, 1912. '. . . Most of whom were Republicans and devout believers that the furnace fires of America's industries were brought down from Heaven by Protection, a modern Prometheus of a new order of utilitarian gods'; and an effective allusiveness distinguishes the following passage from Graham Greene's movingly realistic novel, *The Power and the Glory*, 1940 : (concerning Judas) 'It seemed to him' (the central character, a priest) 'a good thing that the world's greatest traitor should be made a figure of fun. It was too easy

349

otherwise to idealize him as a man who fought with God—
a Prometheus, a noble victim in a hopeless war ', as he tends
to be in, e.g., R. H. Horne's poetic drama, *Judas Iscariot*;
compare ' In Gide's use of the myth, Prometheus must come to
terms with Zeus ' (' Palinurus ', *The Unquiet Grave*, 1945).

In the adjective *promethean* the emphasis is on either the skill
of or the punishment suffered by Prometheus, that audacious
and heroic demigod who, from clay, created man; who con-
veyed to men the fire he had snatched from Olympus; who
instructed them in its use and in various arts; and who, by
a Zeus angered at his presumption and fearful of this power
rendered accessible to human beings, was chained to a rock in
the Caucasus mountains and thereby exposed to the fiercely
predatory vultures of that wild, fierce region. Aeschylus wrote
the tragedy of *Prometheus Bound*: Shelley, almost fanatical in
his noble passion for liberty, wrote a poetic drama of *Prometheus
Unbound*. The name, ' Prometheus ' signifies ' The Fore-
thinker ': compare Greek *promēthēs*, ' foreseeing, fore-thought-
ful ', and *promētheia*, ' foresight, intelligent anticipation '.

The books and periodicals of ca. 1830–60 contain numerous
references to the *promethean*, which, invented in 1828 (before we
had phosphorus matches), was a small glass tube that, containing sulphuric acid and chlorate of potash, had only to be pressed
to burst into flame.

protean; proteiform; proteus, Proteus. ' The paradoxical and elusive Joyce evaded all attempts to reduce him
to a formula. Joyce had a protean personality ' (Claude
Houghton, *Passport to Paradise*, 1944): ' X. was a veritable
Proteus ' (almost any newspaper); ' Man, being a Protean
animal, swiftly shares and changes with his company and
surroundings ' (Robert Louis Stevenson, ' Samuel Pepys '—
in *Men and Books*).

In Greek mythology, *Proteus*, herder of Neptune's sea-calves,
was a sea-god, notable for ability to change his form when-
soever it pleased him to do so. Horace uses the name for
' a fickle person '. But see especially Homer's *The Odyssey*,
IV, 351 ff.

provençale is a rather vague name for any dance originating—
or popular—in Provence.

Prussian; Prussian blue; prussic (acid). *Prussian* has,
since 1871, come to mean ' arrogant '—' cruel '—' excessively
military '—and so forth. ' *Prussian blue* was accidentally discovered (1704) at Berlin by Diesbach. Cf. *prussic acid* . . .,

obtained from Prussian blue ' (W). From the latter derives *prussiate* (familiar to students of chemistry).

' A fog of white light seeping up into the blue air. Overhead the sky was as black as Prussian blue,' Joyce Cary, *The Horse's Mouth*—a realistic novel about a painter—1944.

' The strong colours of the common paint-box, like crimson-lake and prussian-blue,' G. K. Chesterton, *Autobiography*, 1936.

psyche; Psyche task; psychiatry, etc.; psychic; psychology, etc.; psychopath, etc.; psychosis; psychotherapeutic, etc.; psychotherapy, etc.

A *psyche* or *psyche-glass* is a cheval-glass, or tall mirror that swings on uprights : the word comes direct from French, where it arose, perhaps, from the fame of Raphael's full-length painting of the goddess Psyche; also, in imitation of the Greek, a butterfly; both of these senses are obsolescent. The current sense of *psyche* is ' soul ' or ' spirit ' in its psychological conditions and relations, as in this sentence concerning a nasty-minded spinster, ' From the murk of the Dearlove psyche little of illumination emerged ' (' Michael Innes ', *The Weight of the Evidence*, 1944) ; compare ' The conscious personality plays a passive role as far as the development of his '—the schizophrenic's—' psychosis is concerned ' (Dr Devine, quoted by ' Palinurus ' in *The Unquiet Grave*, 1945), and, concerning Australia, ' A national " Psyche " attuned to the " near-enough " standard, and resentful of any efforts to stir up discontent with that standard, is not calculated to make the quick, precise decisions a quick and mortally precise history is forcing upon it,' Brian Penton, *Think—Or Be Damned*, 1941.

A *Psyche task* is an impossible task : Venus, ' profane love ', set Psyche, ' sacred love ', such a task.

' Time to call up Eros armed to his new Psychean task
Of mobilising moving dunes of grainèd sand
Into an adamantine pyramid
Rising upward, upward '
(Ronald Bottrall, ' Salute '—
in The Loosening and Other Poems, 1931.)

Psychiatry and *psychiatrist* (or *psychiater*) : the treatment, the treater, of mental disease : Greek *psukhē*, ' spirit ' + *iatreia*, *iater*, respectively ' healing ' (or ' medical treatment ') and ' healer ' (or ' physician ').

Psychology is the ' ology ' of the non-physical part of man. ' These activities '—i.e., ' seeing, hearing, touching, smelling, tasting, and experiencing the emotions associated with them ' —' were . . . not activities of the " mind ", if that word refers

351

to the self-critical activities called thinking. But neither were they activities of the " body ". To use a Greek word (for the Greeks had already made important contributions to this science of feeling) they were activities of the " psyche ", and no better word could have been devised for the study of them than psychology,' R. G. Collingwood, *An Essay on Metaphysics*, 1940.

Psychic is simply the adjective corresponding to *psyche* in its predominant current sense.

The noun *psyche* is the Latin form of the Greek *psukhē*, ' breath ': from *psukhein*, ' to breathe ': from a radical *psu-* (itself from an Aryan radical *speu-*), ' to blow ': obviously, like the English *spew*, that radical is echoic. From ' breath ' comes the sense ' life '—' spiritual life, the soul ', in contrast with *soma*, ' the physical body '. In Greek mythology, *Psyche* is the poetic and spiritual personification of *psyche*, ' the soul ': for English poets' interpretations of the legends about, and the allegory of, Psyche, see, for instance, Shackerley Marmion, William Morris, Robert Bridges; and Pater deals with her in *Marius the Epicurean*. Beloved of Eros, she is often contrasted with Venus: spiritual as opposed to physical love.

Puck; hence, **puckish.** Puck, alias Robin Goodfellow, is often used in transferred senses—e.g., a mischievous sprite (cf. **kobold**), a playfully malicious person, as in ' " Born Puck, he died Pierrot ", said Mr [D. S.] MacColl [about Aubrey Beardsley] in one of the superb phrases with which he gibbets into posterity an art or an artist he rather dislikes,' Robert Ross, *Masques and Phases*, 1909.

From ' Middle English *Pouk*, frequently used by Langland for the Devil, but, since Shakespeare's *Puck*, a tricksy sprite . . . " Those that Hobgoblin call you and sweet Puck " (Midsummer Night's Dream, II, i) '. (WWN.)

pullman = *P. car*, ' a dining-car '. George Mortimer Pullman, who had, a year earlier, formed the Pullman Palace Car Company, devised in 1868 the railway dining-car. This versatile American inventor (1831–97), patented in 1864 the Pullman sleeping car, designed with the aid of his friend Ben Field; in 1875, chair cars; and in 1887, vestibule cars. He had begun his adult life as a cabinet maker.

See the ' Rolf Boldrewood ' quotation at **Avernus.**

Punch. ' The French'll be as pleased as Punch if we get this Lerouge out of the way,' C. S. Forester, *The Captain from Connecticut*, 1941.

Unaffectedly, unreservedly, unsubtly pleased, like Punch in

352

the Punch and Judy puppet-show, where he gleefully and frequently overcomes his enemies.

Short for *Punchinello*, which earlier was as Pepys records it in his Diary for April 9, 1667—'Away to Polichinello'. The latter form alters the Neapolitan *Polecenella*, which may diminish Italian *pulcina*, a chicken. 'The Neapolitan form is used also of the young of the turkey-cock, the beak of which the Punchinello mask may originally have resembled' (W).

puncheon, a cask, is, in its earliest French and English forms, identical with *puncheon*, a piercing-tool. The Italian *punzone* means both the tool and the cask. W adds, 'I suggest as origin French *poinson*, a common surname (whence English *Punshon*, from *Pontius* (Pilate)). Personal nicknames for vessels are numerous (see *jeroboam, jorum, tankard, demijohn,* etc.), and usually unaccountable.'

purdonion, or **purdonium** or even **purdonian,** is one of those fanciful trade names (compare *bovril*) which have done something to colour the language—not always felicitously. This one for a coal-scuttle was evolved by its introducer, one *Purdon*. An early example was on view at the Great Exhibition of 1851.

puritan; puritanical; puritanism. 'I am afraid there will always be puritans in this mad world. Puritanism is a natural reaction against nature,' George Santayana, *The Last Puritan*, 1935.
'She's so puritanical! so very strait-laced.'
'Spenser's puritanism is . . . a sex-flooded thing,' G. Wilson Knight, *The Burning Oracle*, 1939.

Since the war of the Cavaliers and the Roundheads, the term *puritan* has lost something of the true savour of *Puritan*, 'one of the advanced reformers in the Anglican Church': the word has been twisted—permanently, it would seem—to convey 'narrow-mindedness; excessive rigour of religious observance; blindness to aesthetic beauty'. Strictly, it means 'the pure in heart'.

purple gage. See **gage.**

puzzolana. See **pozzolana.**

Pygmalion; not Pygmalion likely!; pygmalionism. In Greek mythology, Pygmalion (*Pugmalion: pugmë,* 'fist' + *malattein,* 'to render supple' and hence 'to soften by entreaties '), King of Cyprus, ' fell in love with a beautiful statue (according to Ovid, made by himself). He prayed to Aphrodite to give him a wife resembling the statue; and she did more than this, for she gave the statue life, and Pygmalion married the woman so created ' (Harvey). William Morris beautifully re-tells this tale in *The Earthly Paradise*, 1868–70; W. S. Gilbert made it the subject of a comedy, *Pygmalion and Galatea*; G. Bernard Shaw reshaped it in his comedy, *Pygmalion* (1912), where the heroine exclaims ' Not bloody likely '—whence the wit's *not Pygmalion likely*. The abstract *pygmalionism* is that psychological phenomenon whereby a creative artist of any sort falls in love with his own creation.

pygmy or **pigmy,** ' a very short, insignificant person ', derives, for most of us, from the dwarf people of central Africa—the *Pygmies*. For the Classical scholar, it derives, as does the African term, from the Pygmies of Greek mythology, Homer placing them on the Oceanic shores: the *Pugmaioi*, those who are *pugmaios* or ' like to a *pugmë* ', a length-measure of about 13 inches: the distance from elbow to knuckles: from *pugmë*, the fist. Our *pygmy* comes to us via the Latin *pygmaeus*.

pyrrhic; Pyrrhic victory. The former is either a Classical Greek metrical foot (◡◡), named after its supposed inventor, one Purrhikos, or a dance ' symbolizing attack and defence in war ', devised by the Spartans; the latter, a victory more costly to the winner than to the loser, a victory named after Pyrrhos, King of Epirus, who, defeating the Romans at Asculum in 279 B.C., lost his best soldiers and philosophically exclaimed, One more such victory and we are undone! In the event, he had to forgo his campaign in the West. For an engaging account of the man, see Plutarch's *Lives*.

' Not modern education nor indifference has reduced the number of worshippers [in the churches] so pitifully these last generations, but rather that Pyrrhic system of prosperity which ordains that urban wealth accumulate while men decay,' James Leigh, *Fugitive*, 1932.

Compare **Cadmean victory** in the subsidiary list.

python, a boa or an anaconda or, rather loosely, any large snake, derives from *Python* (Greek *Puthōn*), a monstrous serpent that, having arisen from the mud after that deluge which, in Greek mythology, Deucalion survived, dwelt in the caves of Mount Parnassus and guarded the shrine of Mother Earth at Delphi, earlier known as *Pytho* (Greek *Putho*); Apollo slew the serpent and, expelling Mother Earth, set up his famous oracle, but note that even *Putho* was, originally, *Puthōn* : whence it would seem that the place (whether region or town) took its name from the serpent, which perhaps derived its name from *putho*, ' I cause to rot '.

Q

quarenden or **-on** or **-er.** This early apple, deep-red in hue, is in Middle English *quaryndon*. Like the other great lexicographers, W admits that the origin is unknown. He does, however, suggest that *quaryndon* may come either from *Quarendon* in Buckinghamshire or from *Carentan* in Normandy ; the latter is the more likely, Normandy being famous for its apples.

quassia, a drug known in two chief kinds, *Jamaica quassia* and *Surinam quassia*, is extracted from the *Quassia* genus of tropical American trees, a genus named after Graman Quassi, who, a Negro of Surinam, discovered, ca. 1730, the virtues of the drug. That personal name, as *Kwasi*, means, in one of the Ashanti dialects, ' boy born on *Kwasida*, Sunday '. (Webster.)

quince. As, in Greek, *mēlon Mēdikon* or ' Medic fruit ' is the orange or perhaps the citron and as *mēlon Persikon* or ' Persian fruit ' is the peach, so *mēlon Kudōnion* or ' Cydonian fruit ' (poetically ' Cretan fruit ') is the quince.
 Cydonian means ' of Cydonia ', one of the chief cities of ancient Crete and now called Canea. Situated in the northwest of the island, the city takes its name from a tribe, or a race, known as the Cydones ; *Cydonian* is, in Greek, often synonymized with ' Cretan '. From Crete, quinces were introduced into Italy, where they were called *mala Cydonia* or *Cydonia mala*: *malum Cydonium* soon dropped the *malum* and the capital initial. Now, *cydonium* (noun) had a latinizing variant, *cotoneum*, which yields Old French *cooin*, which in Middle English becomes *coyn* or *quine*, which latter, owing to a misapprehension of plurality, became *quines*, whence *quince*.

quisling. (*The Little Oxford Dictionary*, 3rd edition, 1941, classifies it as slang ; but by 1942 it had become good English.) Properly a fifth-columnist (see **fifth column**), it loosely denotes any other kind of traitor—e.g., an informer to the enemy occupying one's country ; hence it may serve as an adjective (' this quisling monarch ' is a phrase used in 1943 by Major F.

Yeats-Brown). ' Quisling . . . has shed his capital letter with a speed unequalled by any of the several hundred other men and women—mostly men—who have entered our dictionaries,' Dennis Yates, ' Words like Quisling ', *The Leader*, July 7, 1945. Writing on Sunday the 20th May a newspaper article published in *News Chronicle* of May 21, 1946, Colin Wills mentions that ' Some time in the coming week Vidkun Quisling, prototype for traitors, will face the justice of the Norwegian people '. Quisling, having—in April 1940—betrayed Norway to the Germans, became the puppet ruler of the country. The little quisling, he of the village or the small town, has been drawn, dispassionately and magistrally and for all time, by John Steinbeck in his short novel, *The Moon Goes Down* (1943). There is also an abstract noun : *quislingism* : Charles Morgan, for instance, uses it in *Reflections in a Mirror* (1944), thus, ' Quislingism and collaboration are not a product of cowardice alone or of selfishness alone '.

Vidkun Quisling, born in 1887, after being an Army officer became a politician ; ' in May, 1933, he founded a Fascist party in Norway under the name of Nasjonal Samling, which remained very small . . . He conspired with Germany to prepare the seizure of Norway by the Germans,' as Walter Theimer concisely remarks in his *The Penguin Political Dictionary*.

Quixote, Don ; quixotic ; quixotism, quixotry. ' My youth is haunted by my father, this romantic Radical, this Citizen Quixote, this most Christian of atheists ' (W. L. George, *The Triumph of Gallio*, 1924) ; ' He went gunning where and when he pleased, and for reasons as quixotic as the snubbing of a friend ' (Fred D. Pasley, *Al Capone*, 1931—but not concerning Al Capone) ; ' He is a mosaic of quixotic splendours : and when he dies the " Middle Ages " of the desert will have ended ' (T. E. Lawrence, ' Arab Portraits '—reprinted in *Oriental Assembly*, 1939).

All allusions to tilting at windmills (cf. the quotation at **Galahad**) constitute a tribute to Don Quixote.

By Miguel de Cervantes Saavedra (1547–1616), soldier of fortune, dramatist, novelist, gallant and, in despite of many misfortunes, gay, *Don Quixote* appeared in two parts—1605 and 1615—respectively translated into English in 1612 and 1620. It rapidly achieved a European and has long enjoyed world fame. Although satirizing the traditional romances of (and about) chivalry, Cervantes has in the visionary, ludicrous knight and in his earthy servant, Sancho Panza, yet created two antithetic lovables. Don Quixote was a fool ; one of

God's fools. Sancho Panza was ineffably pedestrian; and most loyal to his eccentric master. These two connote the ideals of generous, selfless, unworldly chivalry and of common-sensible realism.

R

rabbit seems to spring ultimately from Dutch *Robbert*, Robert, thus: *rabbit*: Middle English *rabet*: Old French *rabot*, ' a carpenter's plane ' and hence, presumably, ' rabbit ', for compare French *rabouillère*, ' rabbit-burrow ', and Walloon *robett* or *robete*, ' rabbit ': Middle Dutch *robbe* (diminutive *robbeken*), ' rabbit ': probably from Middle Dutch *Robbert*. Note that from *Robert* comes the surname *Rabbetts*. (Webster and W.)

Rabelaisian. Concerning his undergraduate days at Oxford, Hilaire Belloc once chanted:

> ' We kept the Rabelaisian plan:
> We dignified the dainty cloisters
> With Natural Law, the Rights of Man,
> Song, Stoicism, Wine and Oysters.'

' A counterpoint of innumerable hilarities—Voltairian voices, yelping in sharp shrill triumph over the bewildered agonies of stupidity and silliness; vast Rabelaisian voices, like bassoons and double basses, rejoicing in guts and excrement and copulation, rumbling delightedly at the spectacle of grossness, of inescapable animality,' Aldous Huxley, *Time Must Have a Stop*, 1945.

Rabelais, the great French humanist, humorist, satirist, who died in 1553, wrote *Gargantua* (see **gargantuan**) and *Pantagruel* (see **pantagruelian**). He was what Huxley implies; he was also a wit.

rachel is short for *Rachel face-powder*, which is of a shade of fawn. It was devised in honour of Elisa Félix, stage-named Mademoiselle Rachel. In her short life (1820–58), she achieved a fame second only, among French actresses, to that of Sarah Bernhardt. She excelled in tragic roles and was a creature of fire and quicksilver.

Raffaelesque. See **Raphaelesque.**

Raffles, ' a gentleman burglar ', dates from ca. 1904. A pleasant conjunction of the literary—and other—stars may be

357

found in George Smithson ('Gentleman George'), *Raffles in Real Life* (Smithson's autobiography), 1930. Concerning his release, in July 1929, after six years in Dartmoor, Smithson says, 'What an ignominious ending to the ambitious ideas that had filled my mind when I set out on the perilous career of a modern Raffles!'

Ernest W. Hornung's collection of short stories popularized his Raffles: *The Amateur Cracksman*, 1899—from ca. 1903, *Raffles, The Amateur Cracksman*; *The Shadow of the Rope*, 1902; *A Thief in the Night*, 1905; *Mr Justice Raffles*, 1909. A German scholar published, ca. 1912, a thesis entitled *Sherlock Holmes, Raffles and their Forerunners*. Hornung also created the famous gentleman bushranger, *Stingaree*, in 1905; Ernest Hornung (1866–1921) knew Australia better than most novelists; his first four or five books had an Australian setting, the earliest being *A Bride from the Bush*, 1890.

rafflesia is a plant of the genus *Rafflesia*, stemless and leafless; in the *Rafflesia arnoldi*, the flower sometimes has a diameter of so much as three feet. The genus was discovered by Sir Thomas Stamford Raffles (1781–1826), who, after a distinguished and exciting administrative career in Penang, Java and Sumatra, founded Singapore in 1819. The world-famous Raffles Hotel was named after him.

ragged robin. 'The woods had been felled in the war years, ragged robin and willow herb flamed over the stumps, only a clump of sycamores remained to shelter the old Farways inn,' H. C. Bailey, *The Wrong Man*, 1946.

Ragged: it has untidy petals; *robin* is a personification, a *ragged Robin* being a tattered vagrant—an idea lying at the back of Oliver Onions's fine novel, *The Story of Ragged Robyn*, 1945.

Also **ragged Robert,** another name for the herb personified as *Robert*, which is often written with a small *r*.

raglan is short for **Raglan overcoat,** named after Lord Fitzroy Somerset (1788–1855), 1st Baron Raglan. Aide-de-camp to Wellington in 1808–12, he lost an arm at Waterloo; military secretary in 1827–52 to Wellington, whom, in 1852, he succeeded as commander of the forces, which office he held in the Crimean War. The naming seems to have signalized his promotion to the rank of Field-Marshal in 1854 for his victory at Inkerman.

ramillie (or **-lie** or **-lies** or **-llies**), or a **ramillied wig,** is a plaited wig tied at the back with a ribbon bow; the single

358

word also denotes a cocked hat and one or two other articles of dress; all named to commemorate Marlborough's victory at Ramillies (Belgium) in 1706 over the French. Compare **steenkirk.**

raphaelesque, or **raff-,** or either with a capital initial, denotes ' in, hence imitative of, that style of painting which was practised by Raphael'. Raffaello Santi or Sanzio (1483–1520) crowded much great work into his too short life; he even practised architecture. A native of Orbino, he went to Florence in 1504; and four years later, to Rome, where in 1514 he became chief architect of St Peter's. As a painter, richly suave, he ranks very high.

real McCoy, the. See **McCoy.**

real Simon Pure. See **Simon Pure.**

rehoboam. In Charlotte Brontë it means ' a shovel hat ' (from its shape), but it normally means a double **jeroboam**; that is, a rehoboam is a very large flagon, holding sixteen quarts. The name was probably suggested by *jeroboam*: both Jeroboam and Rehoboam were Hebrew kings, the former being the first king of Judah, the latter the first king of Israel. Note, too, that the etymological meaning of *Rehoboam* is ' the clan is enlarged ': so was the flagon.

rembrandtesque, or **R—,** as a transferred Art adjective, usually emphasizes that strong, that effective contrast of light and shade in painting which characterizes the work of *Rembrandt* Harmensz van Rijn (1606–69), etcher and painter, the greatest Dutch painter, probably the greatest painter of them all. Quiet yet masterful; masterly yet human; tender yet strong; concentrated yet various; various yet never dilettante.

reynard, generic for ' a fox ', is, in the medieval beast-epic, *Reynard the Fox*, a Proper Noun and the hero of that remarkable narrative-epic poem. The spelling *Reynard*, first used by Caxton, shows the influence of a Middle Dutch form (*Reynaert*), the old French form of the name being *Regnart* or *Regnard*, with variants *Renart* and *Renard* (Modern French *renard*, a fox); *Regnart* derives from Old High German *Reginhart*—compare Old English *Regenheard*—literally, Strong in Counsel; *hart* is the source of *hard*, ' firm ', and with *regin* compare Gothic *ragin*, likewise meaning ' counsel '.

   In the 13th Century *Roman de Renart*, the fox's full name is

359

Renart le goupil, ' Reynard the fox ' ; ' the popularity of the poem was so great that *renard* has quite supplanted Old French *goupil* '.   Other names we owe to *Le Roman de Renart* are **bruin, chanticleer, monkey, partlet** ; and compare *Tybert*, formerly a favourite name for a cat.   A remarkable fact, that so many names have descended to us from one medieval poem ! Originally written in Latin, it was soon turned into French (ca. 1200) ; it was recast several times in the latter language, and there were early versions in Dutch and German ; in brief, the epic became a literary feature and heritage of Western Europe.

Rhadamanthine, adjective, and its noun, **Rhadamanthus**— to adopt the Latin form of the word.

' It didn't take the judge long to pass sentence . . . . . . Another name was bawled out, and some one else passed quickly from our midst into the council-chamber of Rhadamanthus,' Glen K. Mullin, *The Adventures of a Scholar Tramp*, 1925.

Properly, ' a stern, incorruptible judge ', *Rhadamanthus* is often perverted to mean ' a too severe judge ' and *Rhadamanthine* to mean ' excessively severe in the judgements passed '.

Rhadamanthos, in Greek mythology, was the son of Zeus and Europa ; with Minos and Aeacus, he became a judge, in Hades, of the dead, an appointment rewarding the just, the equitable life he (like his colleagues) had led on earth. Rhadamanthos, the most famous of the three judges, also ruled Elysium.   He figures in the writings of Plato and Virgil, to mention only the very best-known of his ' historians '.

rhea, or nandu, or American ostrich (inhabiting Patagonia and Argentina, but there dying out, and, in a smaller species, Brazil, it is not so large as the African ostrich), was so named in 1752 from the Greek-mythological *Rheia* or *Rhea*, for no very good reason, *Rhea* being ' The Mother of the Gods ' and identified with Cybele, ' The Great Mother '—that great nature-goddess of early Asiatic religion who was, to some extent, adopted by the Greeks.

rhenish = *R. wine*.   By 1660 one of the chief imports from Germany into England was wine, almost entirely Rhenish, which had been well-known long before that ; in *Hamlet*, 1602, Shakespeare mentions ' draughts of Rhenish ', after referring to it in 1596—twice in *The Merchant of Venice*.   In the 18th Century these *Rhine*-wines ' began to be called *Hocks* ' (André Simon).

360

rhenium. In 1925 this manganese-resembling element was, together with **masurium,** spectroscopically discovered in platinum ores by two German scientists, who named it after the River Rhine ('The Rhine was for centuries and still is, the chief natural waterway of Europe,' L. W. Lyde)—in Latin, *Rhenus*—in the approved manner: '*Rhen*(us)' + that '*ium*'-which terminates so very high a proportion of the names for the chemical elements. (And see **masurium.**)

rhesus. 'Latham Brooke clambered down the ladder with the agility of a rhesus monkey,' Richard Sale, *Cardinal Rock*, 1940.

This East Indian monkey (cf. **entellus**) was named after *Rhesus*, a mythical king of Thrace, whose story is told in *The Iliad*, Bk X, and forms the subject of a tragedy sometimes attributed to Euripides. There is no compulsive aptness in the naming.

rhinestone. That is, *Rhine stone*, not truly a stone but a highly lustrous imitation stone made either of paste or of glass. The term is merely a translation of the French *caillou du Rhin*, 'pebble of the Rhine': either the rhinestone was originally manufactured in the factories of the Rhineland, or it imitates that variety (*Rhine stone*) of rock crystal which is found there. (Other varieties are called *Brighton diamond* and *Cornish diamond*.)

rhodomontade. See **rodomontade.**

rhondda. In 1917, David Alfred Thomas (1856–1918), Lord Rhondda, became food controller; he may truly be said to have given his life for his country. W cites this apposite passage from *The Daily Chronicle* of February 15, 1918: 'Captain Wright said that the Food Control Department had given a new word to the language. If a soldier lost anything, he said it was "*rhonddaed*".' But by 1925, the term was obsolescent; by 1930, obsolete.

rhubarb comes, via Old French *reubarbe*, from Medieval Latin *rheubarbarum*, an alteration of *rhabarbarum*, literally, 'barbarous *rha*'—'foreign *rha*' (compare *rhapontic*, 'Pontic *rha*'—a species of rhubarb); that is, a foreign drug. That drug was imported into Europe through Russia; the Greek *rha*, with the significant variant *rheon*, is from *Rha*, itself originally Greek and the ancient name of the River Volga; later the name was applied to a cultivated edible species of the same genus as yielded the drug; 'from the correct form comes Italian *rubarbo*, " the drug rewbarbe " (Florio) ', W. Note that the Greek *Rha*, as the river-name, means literally ' The Flow-er, *the* stream ' (*rhéein, rhein*, to flow), from that great mass of waters which is the Volga.

ribald, the adjective, comes from the obsolete noun *ribald*, ' a medieval retainer of the lowest station '—hence ' a worthless person, a rascal '—hence, ' a dissolute man ; rarely, a whore '. The word anglicizes Old French *ribauld* or *ribaud*. Webster derives it from German and compares Old High German *hriba* ' a prostitute ' ; but W, more accurately (I think), says, ' Probably a special application of the common personal name Ribaud, Old High German *Ric-bald*, mighty-bold ; compare Anglo-Saxon *Ricbeald*. This occurs as a surname in the *Pipe Rolls* (12 cent.), i.e. a century older than the dictionary records of the common noun. The choice of the name would be due to Old French *riber*, to wanton, ? from Old High German *hripa*, prostitute.'

ribston is short for *Ribston pippin*, an apple successfully cultivated at *Ribston* Park, an estate near Great *Ribston* in the West Riding of Yorkshire. Literally, *Ribston* signifies *Rib's ton* (originally *tun*), Rib's hamlet or settlement.

Richard Roe. See **John Doe.**

Riesling = *Riesling wine*. ' " Heartburn," he said, shaking his head. " That's the trouble with white wine. I've had to give up Hock and Riesling completely ; and sometimes even champagne," ' Aldous Huxley, *Time Must Have a Stop*, 1945.

M. André Simon defines *Riesling* as ' the finest white grapes grown for the making of high-class white wines in Alsace, Austria, Germany and Hungary '. Ultimately from *Riesa* in Saxony?

rigadoon. A Provençal dance popular in the 17th Century. The French form of the word is *rigaudon*, said to have been named after a Marseilles 17th-Century dancing-master conveniently named *Rigaud*; this theory has received the support of several more than merely competent French philologists—indeed, it is probably correct.

[**right as a trivet,** ' in excellent health, position, situation, circumstances ', originally meant ' as steady as a trivet ' : a trivet (or tripod) stands firm on almost any surface, for three-legged articles possess that virtue. Do not, therefore, be

362

misled by the plausible statement that *trivet* 'is the last century pronunciation of Truefit, the supreme Bond Street wig-maker, whose wigs were perfect—hence the phrase' (J. Redding Ware, *Passing English*, 1909). This theory of Ware's is folk-etymology, the sort of thing that abounds in the earlier editions of Brewer's *Phrase and Fable*.]

Rip van Winkle. ' He was a bit of flotsam on a surging tide of eager humanity. They were all vital. He'—after eleven years in prison—' was a blanched Rip van Winkle,' J. Allan Dunn, ' Once a Crook?'—in *Detective Fiction Weekly*, October 11, 1930.

Here, as in so many other American (and British) allusions, *Rip van Winkle* represents the man who, ' coming back from the dead ' or from secluded solitude, finds that the world has progressed—and passed him by, as in that story in *The Sketch-Book*, 1819–20, by Washington Irving, in which, safe and forgotten in a sleepy hollow, the hero slept for a full score years.

ritzy. ' I shouldn't have thought this was a job for a house dick [detective] . . . Especially a ritzy house dick like you ' : thus the irrepressible Archie Goodwin in Rex Stout's *Too Many Cooks*, 1938.—' On our arrival we decided to be " ritzy " and to put up at the Chateau Frontenac, a magnificent edifice on the Heights of Abraham,' Netley Lucas & Evelyn Graham, *My Selves*, 1934.

There is even a verb ' to *ritz* ', to behave superciliously towards a person, as in ' I don't mind your ritzing me or drinking your lunch out of a Scotch bottle,' Raymond Chandler, *The Big Sleep*, 1939.

The various Ritz Hotels of the world are, or try to be, sumptuous and very expensive : in imitation of the Ritz Hotel in London, the hotel that crowned the English career of the Swiss-born restaurateur and hotel-keeper, César *Ritz* (1815–1918). *Ritzy* merely signifies ' like, or aping, the Ritz Hotel '. Slang (originally American)—but good slang.

roam. The OED summarily rejects the traditional attribution to *Rome* as a place of pilgrimage ; but, apart from the implications of **saunter** and **rum,** listen to what W has to say :— ' Compare Old French *romier*, pilgrim to Rome . . . It is quite clear that *roam* was early associated with *Rome*, the earliest occurrence of *romen* [proposed by The OED, and used by Layamon, ca. 1200] being connected in the same line with *Rom-leoden*, people of Rome ; compare obsolete *romery*, pilgrimage.'

363

roan obsoletely means *Rouen linen*, and as 'leather' it probably means *Roan leather*, *Roan* being the predominant Middle English spelling of *Rouen*, which, the capital of the Normans, was in English hands for two long periods in the Middle Ages. The Romans' name for this ancient and always important city was *Rotomagus*.

rob Peter to pay Paul. '. . . Always paying the bills as they arrived with the money we collected just previous. In other words we were robbing Peter to pay Paul and taking it from Charlie to pay Peter, at the same time selling the stuff we bought from Mike to meet Charlie's bill. And so on down the line so that our buys and sells were making a regular circle,' John O'Connor, *Broadway Racketeers*, 1928.

As W remarks, this is probably a mere joining of font-names, the French *Pierre et Paul* corresponding to English *Tom, Dick and Harry*; the phrase derives from the proverb *Do not rob Peter to pay Paul*. In French, there is a proverbial saying, *Il a ôté à Saint Pierre—pour donner à Saint Paul* and in English (17th Century) *Who praiseth St Peter doth not blame St Paul*: these, however, may be ecclesiastical elaborations.

rob roy. In 1865, 'Rob Roy', as John McGregor (1825–92), the English writer and traveller called himself, invented and designed a light, short, flat-decked canoe for river work: and called it a *Rob Roy*, now usually written with small initials. In 1866 appeared his *A Thousand Miles in the Rob Roy Canoe*.

roband, robbin, raband, and—a perversion—**rope-band.** Usually derived either from Norse or from Dutch, it may, the earliest English form being *robyn*, be merely a nautical application of *Robin*, the diminutive of *Robert*, as W undogmatically remarks.

robenhausian (or **R—**) refers to that stage of neolithic—New Stone Age—culture which immediately preceded the Bronze Age. 'This phase,' remarks S. E. Winbolt in 1943, 'is named from Robenhausen, near Zurich, and includes polished stone camps of refuge, lake villages, agriculture, weaving, pottery and funerary monuments' (*Britain B.C.*).

Robert is slang for a policeman and therefore synonymous with *peeler* and **bobby**: see **bobby**.
See also **robert** and **ragged robin**.

robin; round robin; ragged robin (see separate entry). As a bird-name, *robin* is short for *robin redbreast*, originally *Robin*

364

Redbreast: compare *Jack daw* and the generic *Dicky bird*. The font-name *Robin* came to England with the Normans; *Robin* is the diminutive of *Robert*, which is of Teutonic origin: Old High German *Hrodeberht*, literally 'glory-bright'.

With *Robin Goodfellow*, Puck, compare *Hob goblin* (*hobgoblin*).

The precise reason for Robin's presence in *round robin* is unknown; the choice was probably arbitrary, though an *R*—name was chosen for the alliteration; but *Robin*, being a *good*, easy-going fellow, was a safe choice.

Robin Hood, that legendary figure who, first mentioned in Langland's *Piers Plowman* (ca. 1362–93), may have had an historical basis, has become generic for ' a chivalrous redresser of the wrongs of the people '. See especially Arthur L. Haydon, *The Book of Robin Hood*, 1931.

' Though even judges of the High Court may possibly read delightful stories about Bold Robin Hood to their grand-children, we have no room for Robin Hood, great or small, to-day—though there are divers ways of robbing the poor to give to the rich which have thus far passed scrutiny,' J. C. Squire, preface to F. A. Stanley, *A Happy Fortnight*, 1938.

' " You'll never be able to make people believe that big gangsters are not Robin Hoods," a member of the Department of Justice told him ' (i.e., told J. Edgar Hoover when, in 1933, he was made Director of the F.B.I.), as Courtney Ryley Cooper tells us in his Introduction to J. Edgar Hoover, *Persons in Hiding*, 1938. It was thanks in the main to Hoover and yet notably, by his fearless journalism, to Cooper also, that boot-leggers in 1933–34, and drug-traffickers since 1933, have received so severe a check in the United States.

robot, in its transferred sense, is a ' machine-like, an apparently soulless, person '—from the literal sense, a ' seemingly human automaton; a non-human machine that is both obedient and intelligent ', which has been adopted from the English trans-lation, published in 1923, of Karel Čapek's play, *R.U.R.* (Rossum's Universal Robots), a witty modernization of the theme expounded a century earlier by Mrs Shelley (Mary Shelley) in her novel, *Frankenstein*: man's creation destroying man.

(Of a wooden, unsympathetic character, a Secretary of State:) ' A robot with a non-conformist conscience,' Alan Thomas, *Death of the Home Secretary*, 1933.

' The buildings were crowded with modern ghosts, the terrible robot ghosts of murdered machines,' George Dyer, *The Mystery of Martha's Vineyard*, 1939.

rochelle ' shorthands ' *Rochelle salt*, discovered by an apothecar of La Rochelle; *Rochelle* is also elliptical for wine exporte from La Rochelle, a city on the Atlantic coastboard of Franc and originally named *Rupella* (Latin for ' a little rock ') whereof *La Rochelle* is a precise translation.

Rochelle powders is an occasional synonym of *Seidlitz powder*

rockaway is an American four-wheeled pleasure-carriage that current ca. 1840–1900, had, in its first shape, a canopied top an side-curtains. This type of carriage was first made at *Rockawa* New Jersey; the name comes from Lenape Red-India *regawihaki*, ' sandy island ' (Webster).

Rockefeller is the American equivalent of **Croesus** : from Joh Davison Rockefeller (1839–1937), who, in oil, amassed th fabulous Rockefeller fortune. He organized the Standard Oi Company in 1870 and dominated the oil business until hi retirement in 1911.

' If horses ran to form like women, Beau, I'd be a regula Rockefeller,' G. Bronson-Howard, *God's Man*, 1915.

rodomontade; incorrectly *rhod-*. ' I reply, with rodomontade that for more than twenty years I have collected and mad worlds, both old and new: some that existed, some tha existed only as I saw them . . ., and some that I created, Osbert Sitwell, *Sing High! Sing Low!*, 1944.

Meaning ' vainglorious boasting ', the word comes, vi French (which invests it with the typical *e* ending), fron Italian *rodomontada*, coined from the braggart *Rodomonte* i Book XIV of Ariosto's *Orlando Furioso* (1505–15); Boiardo, i *Orlando Inamorato*, had spelt it *Rodamonte* and thus, as Skea implies, afforded us with the key: Lombard *rodare* (Italia *rotare*, ' to turn about ') + *monte*, ' a mountain ': one wh turns mountains as if they were wheels: Latin *rota*, a wheel.

Roger. (For **jolly Roger,** see the secondary list.) *To roger* i a slang term of long standing for ' have sexual intercourse witl (a woman) ', probably from *roger* (recorded by W), ' penis '— compare synonymous *dick* and *John Thomas*. Moreover, *Roge* was a very common 17th–18th-Century name for a bull, an Captain Francis Grose derives the verb immediately from thi *Roger*. The penis-personification may have been suggested b the 16th-Century-underworld *roger*, a beggar (cf. *rogue*).

rokelay. See **roquelaure.**

366

Roland for an Oliver, a. This phrase dates potentially from Middle English, wherein Roland and Oliver are frequently mentioned together, as they were especially and originally in Old French.

Roland, the nephew of Charlemagne (742–814), King of the Franks from 768 and, *Carolus Magnus*, emperor of the West from 800, and Oliver, nephew of Girard de Roussillon, once fought a duel lasting three days and struck stroke for stroke, tit for tat, without being able to decide which was the better knight ; thereupon, in what was already the best heroic tradition, they became brothers-in-arms and the best of friends. Along with the other paladins, they were slain in 778 at Roncevaux (or Roncesvalles) in north-east Spain in a battle against the Arabs. Historically unimportant, this battle, by those deaths, originated the *Chanson de Roland*, a mighty epic that yet forms but a part of the Carlovingian cycle of medieval French literature.

oman is short for *Roman type* (compare **italic**) as distinct from Gothic type ; *Roman numerals*, however, are opposed to Arabic numerals.

The Middle English (from French) *Romain* was restored to *Roman*, from Latin *Romanus*, by the influence of the Renaissance. And *Romanus* is obviously the adjective from Latin *Roma*, Rome.

Compare **rum.**

oman candles. ' " If you find life a bit dull at home," I said, " and want to amuse yourself, put a stick of dynamite in the kitchen fire, or shoot a policeman. Volunteer for a test pilot, or dive off Tower Bridge with five bobs' worth of roman candles in each pocket ",' Joyce Cary, *The Horse's Mouth*, 1944.

A *roman candle*, first made, or first used, in Rome, has a shape like that of a fat candle, and it emits a succession of stars : cf. therefore, **catherine wheel** and **greek fire** (in the Appendix). In military, especially the Guards' slang, the term means a Catholic : see Gerald Kersh's trilogy of books about the Coldstream Guards : *They Die with their Boots Clean, The Nine Lives of Bill Nelson* and *Clean, Bright and Slightly Oiled*.

oman holiday. ' Jim Haight has been condemned to death by all the smart lads and lassies '—journalists—' sent here to dish out a Roman holiday for the great American mob,' Ellery Queen, *Calamity Town*, 1942 : a neat allusion to Byron's famous verse, ' Butchered to make a Roman holiday ', which occurs in *Childe Harold*, Canto VI (published in 1818), stanza 141, v. 8. The reference is to Christians thrown to the lions or, earlier, malefactors or even gladiators pitted against impossible odds at the circus; *panem et circenses* and all that.

Roman nose. A nose that is high-bridged or outstanding in its upper part; 'a high and eminent nose'; in the manner of so many Roman emperors (and others) in the busts that have come down to us.

'He has a Roman nose, generously modelled, and perhaps even a shade too large for his face,' John Gloag, *Manna*, 1940.

romance; romantic, -icism; romanticize. 'I romanticized him; I created him dreadfully, out of the forgotten horror of childish nightmares,' Dan Billany, *The Opera House Murders*, 1940—a Sapperesque detective thriller of considerable merit.

The third and fourth terms derive from the second, which derives from the French *romantique*. The word *romance* comes from the Old French *romanz*, as in *romanz escrire*, a translation of Latin *romanice scribere*, where *romanice* is an adverb meaning 'in vernacular, as opposed to Classical, Latin', that vernacular which yielded *The Romance languages* (Italian, Spanish, Portuguese, French, Provençal, Rumanian); *romanz* became a noun, whence *roman*, a verse epic, now a novel, or *romant*, whence the obsolete English *romaunt*; *romanz* survives in English *romance*; *romant* led to *romantique*, *roman* to *romanesque*. Compare:—

romanesca. 'Probably it was a kind of galliard originally danced in the Romagna': Dr Percy Scholes, who adds, 'Also . . . the name for a certain melody much used as ground bass in the seventeenth century'. Alternative form *romanesque*.

romanesque. (See preceding.) The noun derives from the adjective, which was originally French and which originally denoted the *Romance* of 'Romance Languages'; *-esque* is the French form of Italian *-esco*, feminine *-esca*. Compare—and see—**romance.**

romanza; romanzero. As musical terms, they derive—as do those in the three preceding entries—from the root idea implicit in *romance-romantic*.

romaunt. See **romance.**

Romeo and Juliet, thanks to Shakespeare's tragedy thus titled, is synonymous with 'a pair of youthful (and hapless) lovers'. The Continent of Europe regards them in much the same way as do the English; for instance, Berlioz composed a dramatic symphony on the theme of their tragic love.

And Romeo and Juliet have, each of them, a separate, an individual existence. Thus Romeo has become the archtype of the youthful, handsome, romantic lover ('He's no Romeo, it is true; but he wears well'), and Juliet the youthful belovèd, beautiful and warm-hearted, as in 'This vision of loveliness was his Juliet, which means in plain English that he had fallen in love at first sight' (Fergus Hume, *The Scarlet Bat*, 1905), or in 'I had taken too long in climbing over the wall for my country-fed Juliet and she had vanished from the footpath' (Joseph Stamper, *Less than the Dust*, 1931). It is perhaps relevant to note that whereas *Juliet* has become an often given font-name, *Romeo* has not, even in Italy, been much used.

omic is the name given by Henry Sweet (1845–1912), the Oxford phonetician, in 1877 (*A Handbook of Phonetics*) to the phonetic notation he based on the *Roman* alphabet. He was, in fact, the chief founder of Phonetics as a science instead of a haphazardry.

ondeña, 'a kind of fandango of southern Spain, with the same harmonic peculiarity as the **malagueña**' (Scholes). The originating place-name is the town of Ronda in Andalucia: 'Ronda has the finest bull-ring in Spain and a most famous breed of horses' (Lyde, *Europe*, 4th edition, 1930).

oneo, to, is to reproduce, or make copies of, with a *Roneo* duplicating machine, manufactured by the *Roneo* Company, formed several years before World War I.

oquefort. 'Sheep and mules are the typical products of the Aveyron valley, the Roquefort cheese being made of ewes' milk'; 'The typical product [of Czechoslovakia] is a sheep's-milk cheese made under exactly the same conditions as the Roquefort product of the Aveyron " crater " pastures' (Lyde, *Europe*, 4th edition, 1930).

This cheese, which resembles **stilton,** is also made from goats' milk. Roquefort is a township on the Larsac plateau of south-western France. The name may be composed of French *roc* (a rock) and *fort* (strong): a town built on a strong rock. Compare **camembert.**

oquelaure, of which *rokelay* is the, in the main, dialectal form. This knee-length cloak or mantle, buttoned in front, was much worn in the 18th Century: and it was named after the Duc de

Roquelaure, who flourished in the reign of Louis XIV and died in 1738.

Compare **raglan** and **spencer**.

Roscius; Roscian, 'like—or in the tradition of—*Roscius*', a Roman actor, who died in 62 B.C. aged about fifty. Quintus Roscius, the friend of Cicero (who defended him in a law-suit : *Pro Q. Roscio Comoedo*) and the ennobled by Sulla, was regarded in his lifetime as a very great actor and has, since his death, been held up as the finest flower of Roman comic acting. That talented young actor, William Betty, who retired in 1824 at the age of thirty-three, was, in his youth, hailed as and therefore called *The Young Roscius*. The name *Roscius* has become generic for an outstanding brilliant actor.

roscoe (Damon Runyon, *Furthermore*, 'He outs with a big John Roscoe and fires six shots into the sack' : but this elaborated form is rare). 'He wanted me to tote a roscoe,' Richard Wormser in *Detective Fiction Weekly*, February 8, 1936. The name presumably comes from either the inventor's or the maker's ; yet neither Webster nor Webster BD mentions the word. (See my *A Dictionary of the Underworld*.)

rosella, originally *rosehill*. This beautiful parakeet, a native of Australia, has, in *rosella*, corrupted *Rose-hiller* and, in *rosehill*, been named after *Rose Hill*, the governor's residence at Parramatta in New South Wales.

rosinante or **roz-,** a worn-out nag, a jade, a sorry steed, derives from *Rosinante*, in Spanish *Rocinante*, the lean, bony, blemishful horse ridden by Don Quixote in Cervantes's masterpiece and by him affectionately regarded as matchless. Cervantes has perhaps invented the name from Spanish *rocin*, a miserable hack, a very jade, and *ante*, before : a wretched animal, even before Quixote decided to ride him on his knight errantry.

Rotterdam (better **r—**), **to.** See **coventrate.**

rounceval (or **-ival**), a marrowfat pea, is so called because of its largeness. A *rounceval* is obsolete for 'a giant', hence 'a termagant' (large in bad temper), and *rounceval* is 'gigantic or, at the least, very large, 'from the gigantic bones shown at *Roncesvalles* as those of the paladins of Charlemagne ' (Webster) compare the entries at **Roland . . .** and **runcible . . .**

round robin. See **robin.**

370

roussillon. ' A rough but not unpleasing red wine of the kind that used to be ',—and doubtless is again—' grown by the square mile in the pleasant land of the Roussillon about the city of Béziers,' Francis Beeding, *The Twelve Disguises*, 1942.

Roussillon (now the *département* of the Pyrénées Orientales), one of the old Provinces of France, is connected with ' a " land of wine and oil "—the wine mainly in the west [of the region comprised by Provence and Languedoc] and the oil in the east, the one merging southward in the market-gardening of Roussillon while the other merges southward in the flower-gardening of the Var ' (Lyde, *Europe*, 4th edition, 1930). Oddly enough, the Proper Name *Roussillon* probably derives from *roux*, ' red '.

roxburghe, as a bookbinding style (backs of plain leather, gilt-lettered ; cloth or paper sides ; leaves untrimmed at edge and bottom), was named after the 3rd Duke of Roxburghe (1740–1804), a famous bibliophile, on the sale of whose books, in 1812, the Roxburghe Club (very select, bibliophiles only) was formed.

roxbury is a *Roxbury russet*, a good-keeping American apple, golden russet in hue, originally cultivated at Roxbury in Massachusetts. Compare **ribston.**

rozinante. See **rosinante.**

rube. ' The abbreviated *Reuben*, taken as a typical name for an American rustic, a *hick*, is usually spelt *rube* ' (WWN) ; *hey, rube!* is the rallying cry of American circus workers. In Hebrew, *Reuben*, both a male given-name and a tribal name, means, ' Behold, a son ' ; men counted for something in those days.

Compare **Giles, hick, Hodge.**

Rubicon, cross (or **pass**) **the ; rubicon** (in game of piquet). ' The force of my present position stilled my fears, and I crossed the Rubicon,' says a bank-robber in Ernest Booth's *Stealing through Life*, 1929.

The river Rubicon (Latin *Rubico* or, in Lucan, *Rubicon*; genitive *Rubiconis*) constituted the boundary-line between republican Italy and its province of Cisalpine Gaul : by crossing it with a legion in 49 B.C., Julius Caesar automatically declared war upon the Roman Senate.

This small river is thought to be the modern Pisatello, which debouches into the Adriatic a little north of Ariminium, the present Rimini. Its name probably derives from *rubēre*, to be rusty-coloured.

371

rudbeckia, a plant or its yellow-rayed flower, of the North American genus *Rudbeckia*, is Neo-Latin formed from Olof *Rudbeck* (1630–1702), a Swedish scientist. In addition to discovering the lymphatic system, he took a lively interest in botany. In his *Atlantica* (1675–98) he tried to show that Sweden afforded the origins of human culture and the site of Plato's Atlantis.

rudesheimer is the wine of Rüdesheim in the Rheingau area of Hesse-Nassau, Germany; a white wine of a fine, delicate quality; rather like **johannisberger.**

The German term, from which the English name derives, is *Rudesheimer Wein*, precisely as *johannisberger* represents German *Johannisberger Wein*.

rugby; rugger. As *soccer* comes from *Association* (Football), so does *rugger* from *Rugby* (Football), by process of what is known as ' the Oxford *-er* ' (see my *Slang To-Day and Yesterday*).

At *Rugby* School in Warwickshire, as famous for sport as for scholarship, W. W. Ellis in 1823, ' first took the ball in his arms and ran with it ', as an inscription on Doctor's Wall informs us (W). The fashion he set has given the world its finest cold weather game.

Compare **badminton.**

rum, adj., is by most authorities (Webster, W, Skeat; The OED saying nothing on the subject) derived from *rom*, a gipsy, and related to a Hindustani or a Hindi original.

Since ca. 1790, it has meant ' odd, queer ': before that date it meant ' fine, good, superior, valuable, great ', an underworld sense, whereas the other is slang. What to a criminal seemed good (*rum cove*, a complete rogue), to the law-abiding citizen seemed bad : hence ' good ' becomes ' bad '.

But whence springs *rum*, ' good, fine, valuable, etc.'? The Hindi origin, proposed by Skeat, simply does not fit the word directly contradicts it. The gipsies, when they left Egypt, went—those at least who passed on to Spain, France, Germany, and ca. 1435, from the Continent to England—to Italy. To Rome where they sojourned for some time. ' The Eternal City ' must have impressed them, so ancient, so proud a race, with its ancientry ; and, with its splendour, these lovers of splendour Briefly, I cannot prove but I believe that the gipsies derived *rum*, ' fine, great ', from the Italian *Roma*, Rome, or from *Romano* Roman. Certainly the word was unheard in England before the advent of the gipsies.

See my dictionaries of *Slang* and *The Underworld*. (In a

commenced work, the term *rum* will, D.v., be exhaustively treated.) Recourse to the Gipsy dictionaries of Sampson and of Crofton & Smart will assist the sceptical to perceive that I'm not burbling.

rummer, traditionally cognate with or even derived from *Römer*, a Roman, derives in fact from Dutch *roemer* (compare the synonymous German *Römer*), this type of drinking-glass, *roemer* coming from Dutch *roem*, glory, a boast—compare *bumper*. W.]

runcible hat; runcible spoon.

> 'He has many friends, laymen and clerical;
> Old Foss is the name of his cat;
> His body is perfectly spherical,
> He weareth a runcible hat.'

Thus Edward Lear in 'Self-Portrait', where the hat is a 'topper' with a sharp rim. Now, a *runcible spoon* (Lear, 1871) is not a spoon at all but a pickle fork, broadly and triply lined, one line being sharp-edged and curved like a spoon.

Concerning the runcible spoon, Webster remarks, 'Perhaps originally in jocose allusion to the slaughter at the battle of Roncevaux, because it has a cutting edge'. The word *runcible* has been built in the architectural style of *fencible*; indeed, it may constitute a blend of *Roncevaux* and *fencible* (capable of defending).

Rupert; Rupert's drop. The latter was either introduced or perhaps invented by the famous Prince Rupert (1619–82), 'the Mad Cavalier', whereas the former, meaning, in 1914–18, a German stationary balloon, probably comes from Prince *Rupert* or *Rupprecht* of Bavaria (b. 1869), in command of a group of German armies.

Rupprecht, whence the English *Rupert*, derives from Old High German *Hrodeberht* (bright in glory).

Ruritania; Ruritanian. *Ruritania* is any imaginary kingdom, usually small and originally—strictly, still—European, with a connotation of picturesque feudality, wild scenery, brave if rather eccentric men and of beautiful if for the most part 'dumb' women; and *Ruritanian* is the corresponding adjective.

Ruritania (Latin *rus*, genitive *ruris*, combining-form *ruri*; on the analogy of *Aquitania*), was discovered by 'Anthony Hope' (1863–1933) in *The Prisoner of Zenda*, 1894, and exploited in the companion romance, *Rupert of Hentzau*, 1898; both of these books had a tremendous success, and their author a not inconsiderable progeny, among whom were George Barr McCutcheon (1866–1928), in the first decade of the 20th Century, beginning with *Graustark*, 1901, and substituting American for English heroes, and a certain English novelist who died in the early 1940's.

russell is short for *russell cord*, which probably was at first *Russell cord*, presumably from the name of its maker—or perhaps of its chief early distributor, for in the 19th Century it was always spelt with a capital *R*, as again by The OED in 1910. Neither The OED nor Webster venture an explanation. It is a kind of rep, made from cotton and wool and used for, e.g., scholastic gowns.

russia shortens *Russia leather*, a very durable leather impregnated with birch-bark oil and originally so treated in Russia, as several 17th-Century books of travel make quite clear; as early as the early 18th Century it was in use for book-binding.
   Russia is a Medieval Latin name formed from the Russians' own *Russi*, which designated both the country and the people; compare the Byzantine Greek *Rhōsia*.

ruthenium is a metallic element, belonging to the platinum group and closely resembling **iridium.** Thus named in 1828 by its discoverer Osann (though not isolated until 1845), this element perpetuates the fact that it had first been noticed in platinum ores from the Ural Mountains of Russia or, to give that country its Medieval Latin name, *Ruthenia* (to be carefully distinguished from the country at present bearing that name). Other country-commemorators are **columbium, gallium, germanium, polonium, scandium.**

S

sabbath, witches'. This term, for a witches' high-noon of revel, is a survival of an oddly ignorant and stupid medieval superstition concerning the practices and rites observed by Jews on their Sabbath (Saturday). The word *Sabbath* in its religious sense comes, via Greek and Latin, from the Hebrew *Shabbath,* itself from *shabath,* 'to rest': the Day of Rest; the 'witches' revel' sense derives from French *sabbat,* meaning either 'Jewish Sabbath' or, secondarily, 'unholy revels'.

sabino. See **savin.**

sadism, sadist, sadistic(ally).

' He would inevitably see this personal and unavoidable disaster as a fiendish crime, sadistically planned and executed by brutal barbarians,' Warren Stuart, *The Sword and the Net*, 1942.—' One of the warders in charge of this tier was an old Dartmoor " screw ", and a sadist,' James Spenser, *Limey Breaks In*, 1934.—' A sadist, without knowing it, he [a detective] got a thrill from gripping savagely the soft of a good-looking boy's arm,' Ernest Raymond, *The Marsh*, 1937.—' [In Shakespeare] sadism . . . is quite absent : that is, cruelty is not presented with pleasing associations,' G. Wilson Knight, *The Burning Oracle*, 1939.

. *Sadism*, ' sexual perversion characterized by love of inflicting cruelty ', comes straight from the French *sadisme*, the other terms being derivatives. The Count—usually but incorrectly called the Marquis—de *Sade* (1740–1814) wrote several infamous books and died in the lunatic asylum to which he had first gone in 1789, after having spent (1778 onwards) some years in the Bastille, where he began to write novels and plays ; he had in 1772 fled from a sentence of death for sodomy and poisoning.

Contrast the complementary **masochism.**

Sahara, figurative. ' Indifference,' remarked the Irish American novelist, Owen Kildare, ' is like a mind's Sahara without a horizon ' (*My Old Bailiwick*, 1906) ; and ' the Sahara of contemporary literature ' is almost a cliché among the *laudatores temporis acti*.

The Sahara Desert is ' *the* desert ' : in Arabic, *sahra* is simply ' a desert '. Compare *Cologne*, originally ' *the* (Roman) colony ', and especially **gobi.**

St Anthony, as the patron saint of swineherds, gave his name to an *Anthony* or **tantony** (q.v.). But here we are concerned with *St Anthony* as the type of ' saintly person tempted sexually by a woman, especially by a beautiful woman ', which derives from the part-story, part-legend of St Anthony (ca. A.D. 250–350), the first Christian monk, born in Egypt, where he spent much of his life on a mountain in the Fayum. With difficulty yet with firmness he resisted the visions rather than actualities of amorous joys. Cardinal Newman wrote eloquently of Anthony.

For **St Anthony's fire,** see the secondary list.

St Bernard. ' I went past the St Bernards, stopped to marvel at some Afghan hounds, and found the Dobermanns,' Richard Wormser in *Detective Fiction Weekly*, February 22, 1936.

This magnificent breed of life-saving dog has been named

from the Hospice of the Great *St Bernard*—a pass between Italy and Switzerland. These dogs are trained and maintained by the monks of the Hospice.

St Elmo's fire. 'The name . . . has been variously explained. Elmo is an Italian corruption of Erasmus, and one of the two saints bearing this name was formerly invoked by Mediterranean sailors in time of danger. There is an Italian legend that the saint, having been rescued from drowning by a shipmaster, promised as a reward to display a warning light for the benefit of mariners whenever a storm was at hand. Another proposed explanation is that Elmo is no other than Helen of Troy, who, like her brothers Castor and Pollux, was associated with corposants in the nautical folklore of classical antiquity, Charles Fitzhugh Talman, in his most informative article, ' St Elmo's Fire ', in *The American Mercury*, January 1936.

The ' Helen of Troy ' proposal can be discounted : the synonymous *corposant* = Portuguese (and Old Spanish) *corpo santo*, ' holy or sainted—hence, a saint's—body '; and Helen was not quite a saint. *St Elmo's fire* = Spanish *fuego de santlemo* or Italian *fuoco di santelmo* ; the German says *Helenenfeuer*.

St Emilion is the wine of St Emilion. Speaking of the wine exported from Bordeaux, Professor L. W. Lyde remarks, ' Soil and situation are of prime importance, the Garonne wine being better than the Dordogne wines . . . The Dordogne wines, *e.g.*, St Emilion, are " hill " wines of cheaper varieties (*The Continent of Europe*, 4th edition, 1930).

St Michael is a *St Michael orange*, grown on St Michael, one of the Azores.

salem, or **S—,** is one of several terms (compare **bethel,** **bethesda, ebenezer**) for a Nonconformist chapel : all drawn from The Bible and all, apparently, bestowed originally by Nonconformists themselves. *Salem* derives from *Jerusalem* : see *Hebrews*, vii, 1.

salleeman, or *sallyman*, is nautical for ' a marine hydrozoan ' and (compare **Portuguese man-of-war** in the secondary list) is a humorous adoption of *Sallee man*, a pirate from *Sallee*, that seaport which was, from the 16th until the early 19th Century, the headquarters of the Morocco pirates.

Sally Lunn, now generally **sally lunn.** In 1827, William Hone stated that this slightly sweetened teacake was first baked by

376

young woman named Sally Lunn, who, ca. 1780–90, cried her ware in the streets of the then extremely fashionable Bath. Oddly enough, Hone has been contradicted by no authoritative lexicographer : but then, this Bath-born bookseller was a recognized authority upon social history and customs.

saluki (the capital *S* is unnecessary). ' . . . His dog, Ouif . . . was as if some amateur Creator had tried to piece together a bull-terrier with odds and ends of Airedale, Saluki, Dachshund, and jackal,' Gerald Kersh, *I Got References*, 1939.

Known also as the gazelle hound, the saluki is a hunting dog, as graceful as it is swift,' bred for many centuries in Persia, Arabia, Egypt. Its place of origin is indicated by the Arabic *saluqi*, ' of or from Saluq '—ancient city of southern Arabia.

sam (oath), as in *'pon my sam*, seems to derive from the 16th–18th-Century underworld *upon one's salmon*, wherein *salmon* shortens *salamon*, i.e. *Salamon* or Solomon, whom the underworld apparently regarded as a human miracle ; in the medieval lyric, *Omne genus demoniorum*, occurs the oath-phrase *per sigillum Salomonis*, ' by the seal of Solomon '—as Helen Waddell renders it in her delightful *Medieval Latin Lyrics*. The 19th-Century slang *to stand sam* (or *sammy*), ' to stand treat ', is probably a derivative.

Sam Browne, a British Army officer's ceremonial leather belt and shoulder-strap, designed and still occasionally used as a sword-belt, takes its name from its inventor, Sir Samuel Browne, V.C. (1824–1901), who passed most of his life in India and much of it in the Army ; he was in 1888 promoted General.

Samaritan, good. ' From my pocket I took out a parcel of food bestowed upon me by a kindly samaritan,' the Rev. Frank Jennings, *Tramping with Tramps*, 1932.

Based upon the parable of the supercilious Pharisee, the indifferent Levite, and the Samaritan, of whom only the third ' had compassion ' upon the wounded merchant left for dead by the roadside and succoured him : *Luke*, x, 30–35.

The Rev. Frank Jennings's lower-casing (*samaritan*) sets an example that could profitably be followed.

samarium. Just one of the 90-odd chemical elements. The evidence for this supposed metallic element rests on spectroscopic deductions : it corroborates certain indications and fulfils certain desiderates.

Not from *Samaria*, but from the decidedly rare mineral named

377

samarskite, which in 1847 commemorated Colonel Samarski, a Russian mine official. Note, too, that *samaria*, the theoretical oxide of samarium, derives from *samarium*.

(With thanks to the late Professor A. W. Stewart and The OED.)

Sambo, as the nickname for a Negro, may perhaps derive from Kongo *nzambu*, 'a monkey', or from Foulah *sambo*, 'uncle'; but, as W notes, 'a West African tribe called the *Samboses* is mentioned repeatedly in the narrative of the Hawkins voyage of 1564, and *Sambo* would be a natural back-formation from this'.

Sammy, or Other Ranks soldier of the United States, was so named by the Tommy in 1917 but was little used during the war of 1939–45, when *G.I.* (from '*g*eneral *i*ssue') held the field. Obviously *Sammy* derives from *Uncle Sam* employed as a personification of the U.S.A.—much as *John Bull* is of Britain.

samoyed, a white breed of Arctic dog, is short for *Samoyed dog*, the Samoyeds being a race of Mongols living in Siberia and the Russian original being *Samoyedu*. A Ural-Altaic tribe, they were driven by Turkish immigrants from their original habitat in the south : and they are gradually becoming extinct.

'Another personal friend [of Samuel Purchas's], William Pursglove, had spent some time among the Samoyeds in north-east Russia,' E. G. R. Taylor, *Late Tudor and Early Stuart Geography*, 1934.

samphire. Perhaps altered on the analogy of *camphire*, an obsolete form of *camphor*, *samphire* was, in the 16th Century, *sampere* or *sampier*, which came from the French *herbe de Saint Pierre*, or rather from the Proper-Name portion of that term. A sea-coastal plant, it often grows upon cliffs and rocks : Saint Peter was, by Christ himself, associated with the rock of faith and, by etymology, with all rocks.

Samson, any exceptionally strong man. From the Biblical character : *Judges*, xiii, 24–xvi, 31 : in the 12th Century B.C. 'Samson is a sort of Hebrew Hercules, heroic, friendly, rather stupid, with a comic streak in him. He carries off the gates, he asks riddles . . . He is a tragic figure, too, as Milton '—in *Samson Agonistes* (Samson the Striver)—'saw . . ., more tragic than Hercules. But there is always a question whether his name is not too like the Semitic word for *sun* (Shemsha) for him to be quite historic,' T. R. Glover, *The Ancient World*, 1935 ;

the Masoretic Hebrew form being *Shimshon*. In *Buried Empires*, 1939, Patrick Carleton remarks of those Semites who settled in ancient Sumer, that 'The sun, under the name of *Shamash* (whence Hebrew *Samson*), was [an] object of their devotion'.

samsonite; Samson('s) post. The latter is a strong stanchion, or pillar, that passes between warship decks or through merchant-ship holds: cf. *Judges*, xvi, 29, 'Samson took hold of the two middle pillars upon which the house . . . was borne up' (see preceding entry).

'A heavy hawser was brought aboard and passed . . . to the short samson post on deck,' Manning Coles, *The Fifth Man*, 1946.

The former, besides being a kind of dynamite, is 'a manganiferous silver mineral', named, however, not after the Biblical hero, but from the *Samson* mine in the Harz mountains of Germany.

'*Soup, juice*. Nitro-glycerine and samsonite (latter used by modern safe-breakers)', Val Davis—*qui s'y connaît*—in the glossary of his *Phenomena in Crime*, 1941.

Samurai. In old Japan, a Samurai was a member of the military caste and, therein, he stood to a *daimio* (great nobleman, literally 'great name'; an obsolete title) much as, in medieval England, an esquire to a knight, with the modification implied in : 'A perfect fighting code—of living and dying, with life dangerous and death speedy. The *daimyo* chief, his *samurai* officers, their serried troops, concentrated all strength of mind and body on the single purpose—helped, no doubt, by the fact that they were true sons of Asia' (Lionel W. Lyde, *The Continent of Asia*, 1933). In modern Japan, a Samurai (the word remains unchanged in the plural) is an army officer —not a mere 'temporary gentleman'. In *The New Utopia*, H. G. Wells used the word for 'the bosses', and in *La Onzième Heure*, Claude Farrere wrote (May 1939–August 1939), 'L'esprit samurai était d'occident, non d'orient. Toutes nos chevaleries, tous nos héroïsmes y étaient enclos. Mais non la morale méticuleuse et la sagesse médiane de la prodigieusement vieille Asie.'

sanbenito, a garment of sackcloth, worn by impenitent heretics at the auto-da-fé and, in a rather different form, by penitents on a related occasion, is derived from *San Benito*, St Benedict, who had introduced a scapular to which this sackcloth garment bore a close resemblance.

379

sancho pedro (or **S— P—**) is a gambling card-game, developed from the game of auction pitch. The trump cards are *sancho* and *pedro*, i.e. *Sancho* and *Pedro* (Peter), and the game is Spanish. Merely a personification, the choice of names for the trumps having perhaps been vaguely suggested by *Sancho Panza*, the squire in *Don Quixote*.

sandwich, as (the ingredient of) a snack, was explained by Pierre Grosley, *Londres* (a Frenchman's description of London), 1770—the term having been recorded some eight years earlier—as deriving from that mighty gambler, John Montagu (1718–92), the 4th Earl of *Sandwich*, who, on one occasion, passed a solid twenty-four hours at the gaming-table without a meal other than pieces of sliced cold beef between two slices of toast. (The OED.) Also named after him were the Sandwich, now Hawaiian, Islands.

A *sandwich man* is one who carries two advertisement boards, the one in front, the other on his back.

Sangrado is a literary and, in the 20th Century, obsolescent term or nickname for an ignorant physician. Le Sage, in his great picaresque novel, *Gil Blas* (1715–35), introduces such a physician under this name, which he derived from the Spanish *sangrador*, literally 'bleeder', i.e. a leech; bleeding was formerly regarded as a panacea.

santonica; santonin and **santolina** are derivatives. *Santonica*, the European wormwood, hence a drug manufactured therefrom, was in Latin *herba santonica*, the herb of the *Santoni* or *Santones*, a non-Celtic people of Aquitania, between the Pyrenees and the Garonne.

sapphic, sapphism; sapphics. For *sapphic* and *sapphism*, see **Lesbian.** The third term, *sapphics*, is a term in prosody : ' Among the principal [lyric] metres [of Classical Greece] were : (1) the *Sapphic* stanza, consisting of the Sapphic verse
$$-\cup|-\cup|-\cup\cup|-\cup|-\underline{\cup}$$
three times repeated and followed by an Adonic . . . (2) the *Alcaic* stanza . . . . . . (3) the *Glyconic* stanza,' Sir Paul Harvey, in *The Oxford Companion to Classical Literature*, 1937. Obviously, therefore, sapphics were named after that mistress of metric : Sappho.

sapphire reaches us, through Old French *safir*, from Latin *sapphirus*, which represents Greek *sappheiros*, which probably derives from Hebrew *sappir*, which W thinks may have come

380

from Sanskrit *sanipriya*, ' dear to Saturn '—not the god but the planet.

sapphism. See **Lesbian.**

saragossa publicizes *Saragossa wine*. A list of imports into England from Spain in 1660 reads thus attractively : ' Wine (Saragossa), raisins and wool (merino), silk, bullion (from Mexico), oil, indigo, iron, cochineal, tobacco,' J. N. L. Baker, ' England in the Seventeenth Century ' (H. C. Darby's *A Geographical History*, 1936). Like the Alicante and Valdepeñas wines, the Saragossa has lost favour in Britain. *Saragossa* is an anglicism for Spanish *Zaragoza*, a conflation of the ancient *Caesarea Augusta*, i.e. *urbs C.A.*, ' town of Caesar Augustus ', situated on the right bank of the Ebro and 160 miles west of Barcelona.

saratoga. ' On the whole " Saratoga Trunk " is something less than a great picture. It is a bulky and impressive piece of luggage, stuffed so full of gauds that the seams almost burst under the strain,' C. A. Lejeune, ' The Films '—in *The Observer*, January 27, 1945.

The lady's large trunk named the saratoga commemorates the popularity of Saratoga Springs, a New York County watering-place and summer resort : compare the semantics of **tuxedo.** ' Saratoga Springs, which for nearly a century had been to America what Bath once was to England—a resort of fashion, a temple of gambling, and a site of health-giving, foul-tasting waters. In the last century it gave its name to two national phenomena, the Saratoga Trunk and the Saratoga Chip, the chip being a form of potato [the English *potato chips*]. Richard Canfield, its first citizen, gave his own name to what became the world's most popular solitaire card game. Canfield ran a lavish, star-dusted gambling casino which is now a public museum,' John Lardner in *Daily Express*, August 22, 1946. *Saratoga* was originally a Mohawk village ; to Mohawks it signified ' place of floating ashes ' ; the famous horse-races were instituted in 1863.

sarcenet. See **sarsenet.**

sard. See **sardius.**

sardana. ' Studio Vingt-Huit—high up a winding street of Montmartre . . . In the hall stands a Surrealist book-stall, behind it a bar where a gramophone plays " Ombres Blanches "

381

and disturbing sardanas,' ' Palinurus ', *The Unquiet Grave*, 1945. —' *Sardana*. The national dance of Catalonia . . . danced to the Spanish equivalent of the pipe and tabor ' (Scholes).

Sardanapalian. ' Asshurbanipal is a difficult name, and the Greeks and Romans turned it into Sardanapalus, and made the warrior king of the Assyrians into a proverb for the extreme of luxury ' (T. R. Glover, *The Ancient World*, 1935), as in ' He would create for you . . . a heavy, scented interior where . . . hedonism . . . effeminacy . . . sensuality . . . were indiscriminately combined to produce a bed-chamber that Sardanapalus himself would not have despised ' (Mark Benney, *The Scapegoat Dances*, 1938).

Sardanapalus (The Old Testament Asnappar : *Ezra*, iv, 10), a very great Assyrian king (' Ashurbânipal, the scholarly and bloodthirsty tyrant of Assyria ' : Patrick Carleton, *Buried Empires*, 1939), came to the throne in 668 B.C. Reigning for over forty years, he subjugated Babylon. Classical historians have depicted him as effeminate, voluptuous, luxurious : the Assyrian state-records show how very false is the Classical judgement, but the derogatory legend remains. (J. G. Frazer, *The Golden Bough*, III, 167 ff.)

sardian. See **sardius.**

sardine (the fish) is found off the coast of *Sardinia*. The word is French ; from Latin (via Italian) *sardina*, ' the fish of *Sardo*, Sardinia '.

Of the Shardana, one of those Aegean races which raided northern Egypt about 1200 B.C., J. L. Myres (*The Dawn of History*) writes, ' It is certainly tempting to regard . . . the Shakalsha and Shardana as having given their names to . . . new homes in Sicily and Sardinia '.

sardius, with its derivatives **sard** and **sardian stone,** the latter often shortened to **sardian.** Actually *sard* comes via French *sarde*, from Latin *sarda*, a synonym of *sardius*, and both *sardian stone* and *sardius* derive, the former via Latin *Sardianus*, and the latter direct, from Greek *Sardeis* (Latin *Sardes* or *Sardis*), the capital of Lydia—once a famous monarchy—in the central west of Asia Minor. This precious stone is often mentioned by the ancient writers. ' The sards of Sardes and Babylonia were noted, and gem engraving flourished at Alexandria ' (W. W. Tarn, *Hellenistic Civilisation*, revised edition, 1930).

sardonic. Immediately from French *sardonique*, the word is unrecorded in English before the 17th Century. The French may have taken it from the *sardonico* of the other Romance languages; *sardonico* is probably an alteration of Latin *sardonius*, whence the 16th–18th-Century synonymous form *sardonian*. That Latin word means 'Sardinian' and represents the Late Greek *Sardonios* (early Greek *Sardanios*). It is to the Greeks that we owe the notion that a certain Sardinian plant (*herba Sardonia* in Latin) would, if eaten, produce grimaces resembling those of a horribly bitter and mocking laughter.

That picturesque theory, however, may be—the question remains an open one—an early instance of folk-etymology. Liddell & Scott, in their Greek dictionary, think that the Greek *sardanion gelan*, 'to laugh bitterly', comes from *sairein*, 'to draw back the lips and show the teeth', as in a dreadful grin. My own opinion (*quantum valeat*) is that those usually cautious scholars are stretching sound-distortion a shade too far and that the 'Sardinian plant' origin is the correct one.

sardonyx is the Latin shape of Greek *sardonux*, an onyx that is in part a sard: see **sardius.**

sarracenia is a plant (or its purple or its yellow flower) of the genus *Sarracenia*, American bog-herbs that beautifully grow on the margins of swamps and in 1700 took their name from that Dr *Sarrazin* of Quebec who sent a specimen to J. P. de Tournefort (1656–1708), a noted French botanist; Tournefort rewarded the compliment with the name.

sarsen is an archaeologists' term for the sandstone boulders found in Wiltshire; The OED cites 'The inhabitants calling them "Saracens' stones"' (1644), from a baseless legend connecting these pagan or heathen monuments with the Saracens—whom they long antedated. Another name for them is *druids' stones.*

sarsenet or **sarsnet;** also **sarcenet,** which, though obsolete, is etymologically the best form. This soft silk fabric, which may be either twilled or plain, was very popular in England in the late Middle Ages; in modern times, it is used mostly for linings. The word comes from Anglo-French *sarzinett*, itself a diminutive from Middle English *sarzin* or *sarsin*, Saracen; probably influenced by the Old French *drap sarrasinois*, which translates Medieval Latin *pannus saracensis.*

satanic; satanism. Devilish, abnormally and maliciously cruel; the creed and the practice. What, in short, might be expected of a human *Satan*.

Roger Fry once described Aubrey Beardsley as 'the Fra
383

Angelico of Satanism'; and, on April 26, 1945, in *The Daily Telegraph*, J. L. Garvin pertinently wrote, 'The organised Satanism of the Nazi concentration camps had been known for long to the Russians and the Poles'.

Satanic has been applied especially to Byron, Shelley and other writers accused of impiety; for instance, 'towering satanic virulence' is G. Wilson Knight's description (*The Burning Oracle*, 1939) of a passage in Byron's *The Giaour*.

In Hebrew, *satan* originally meant 'adversary'; Satan is the traditional enemy of mankind—the personification of man's shelving of his own responsibility.

Satsuma (ware) might fittingly be written *satsuma*.

'On a mantel above the fireplace were bits of Satsuma and Chinese *cloisonné*, for the most part "water pieces", portraying cranes and suchlike fowl, all of the purest white and with misty backgrounds of aquamarine sea and sky,' George Bronson-Howard, *The Devil's Chaplain*, 1924.

Satsuma is a province in the island of Kiusiu (part of Japan) : *satsuma* is a creamy pottery, a typically Japanese pottery despite its debt to China.

saturnalia; saturnian; saturnic; saturnine. The *saturnalia*, the festival of Saturn; *saturnian*, the metre (*versus Saturnius*) used in early Roman poetry before it 'went all Greek'; *saturnic*, suffering from or affected with lead-poisoning, lead being emblematic of Saturn; and *saturnine*, gloomy: all derive from the Italic god *Saturn*, originally the divinity connected with agriculture (his very name may mean 'The Sower'), but in Classical Latin identified with the Greek deity Cronos.

In the Hellenistic period (323–31 B.C.), 'the seven planets—Sun, Moon, Mercury, Venus, Mars, Jupiter, Saturn—were the interpreters of Fate, the seats of the awful Cosmocrators or "rulers of this world", who subsequently became definitely evil and hostile to man's soul,' W. W. Tarn, *Hellenistic Civilisation*, 1927.

saumur is a white wine that resembles champagne. 'To the north the sparkling wines of Saumur are inferior—except in rare years—because the marine influence is too much felt just before the vintage, while to the south . . . the juice of the Cognac grape is unrivalled in the world' (Lionel W. Lyde, *The Continent of Europe*, 4th edition, 1930); 'Saumur—an island town at the confluence of the Thonet with the Loire—had been an isle of refuge for centuries before it became the metropolis of French Protestantism; indeed, its name is probably a corruption of *Salvus Murus* (" Safe Wall "), and the sides of both river valleys are honeycombed with caves ' (ibid.).

saunter was by 17th-Century etymologists derived from French *(la) Sainte-Terre*, the Holy Land, an etymology derided by certain biographers; Webster discreetly says nothing. But The OED, by implication, admits the possibility of connexion with *saint*, and W with Spanish *santero* in its nuance of a hermit's companion that ' goes about questing for him and his chappel ' (J. Stevens, 1706); on the analogy of the etymology-disputed **roam,** the Sainte-Terre explanation is at least as likely as any other that has been proposed.

sauterne. ' The Médoc [district] is slightly more marine in climate than Graves and Sauterne; and the Haut-Médoc clarets are grown on the slopes . . ., while the Graves wines are grown on the flat sandy lands (" Landes "), and Sauternes are grown landward of the Graves ': thus Lionel W. Lyde, *Europe*, 1913, concerning the wines of south-western France.

Sauterne is a sweet, white wine; Sauterne is a district (cf. **médoc**).

savin(e). An evergreen shrub that, small and bushy, grows in Western Asia and in Europe; hence, a drug made from its tops.

The more English form is *savin*, the other having been adopted bodily from Old French; compare Italian *savina*. The Spanish and Portuguese had the word in the form *sabina*, which comes direct from Latin *Sabina*, short for *herba Sabina*, ' Sabine herb '.

The Sabines (remember ' The Rape of the Sabine Women '?) were an ancient Italic tribe, inhabiting the central Apennines.

Of the same origin is *sabino* for the name of several American trees: perhaps a Mexican form of Spanish *sabina*.

savoy, the compact-headed, wrinkle-leaved cabbage and, derivatively, a spinach with wrinkled leaves, is short for *Savoy cabbage*, a translation of the French *chou de Savoie*. Savoie is that *département* of eastern France which was, in 1860, formed out of the old Italy duchy of Savoy (Savoia).

sawney, a simpleton, is ironically from *Sawney*, a Scot, the Scots being anything but simpletons; *Sawney* is a corruption of *Sandy* (likewise generic for a Scot), a pet-form of *Alexander*. Or it may represent a corruption of **zany,** as Webster uncompromisingly states and as W admits to be possible.

sax is the musicians' colloquialism for **saxophone**; *sax-cornet* a former synonym for **saxhorn.**

saxe, applied to porcelain, derives from one or other of the *Saxe*-principalities of Saxony; chiefly the former Grand Duchy of Saxe-Weimar, noted for its earthenwares. *Saxe* is, moreover, the French name for Saxony. As a colour, *saxe = Saxe blue*; compare *Prussian blue.*

saxhorn (originally written **sax-horn,** and, in the 19th Century, sometimes called the **sax-cornet**), **saxophone, saxotromba, sax-tuba.** For the differences between these instruments of torture, see Dr Percy Scholes's *The Oxford Companion to Music*: whatever you do, avoid going to the performing musicians, they'll rhapsodically and hieratically give you the most gloriously incorrect information.

Once upon a time, there lived in Brussels a Belgian family named Sax. Now, they were musical-instrument makers, and very good they were at their making. But then, oh! then, they took it upon themselves, father Charles Joseph (1791–1865) and, the more active, son Antoine Joseph, known, even officially, as Adolphe, took it into their heads to invent instruments, all of the horn or the trumpet kind and all at about the same time, ca. 1840–44: the two principal ones being the saxophone, invented by Adolphe, and the sax-horn, invented by Charles and improved by Adolphe. The saxotromba is now, long has been, very little used, and the sax-tuba an accessory, an incidental; both of these were Adolphe's inventions. One or two of these instruments made their first public appearance in 1844, in France, and by 1852 they were popular in England. 'The saxophone family'—after an honourable career as inciters, in French military bands, to martial ardour—became, in the U.S.A. of 1914–18, unconvincing aids to mastication and jazzy accompaniments to dancing. Since ca. 1930, saxhorns and saxophones have been utilized more economically—and with better taste.

With thanks to Dr Scholes, The OED, and W, none of whom (or which) is, however, accountable for the opinions expressed or implied.

Saxon. There has, since the war of 1914–18, been an increasing tendency to use *Saxon* to mean 'honest, outspoken, manly', especially in reference to the quintet of four-letter words (impeccably Standard English, by the way) for the complementary genitals, the sexual act, the acts of urination and defecation. These words either are, or sound, thoroughly

Anglo-Saxon or Old English, and in the stated context *Saxon* might properly be written *saxon*. For the etymology, see:—

saxony, a fine sort of wool, hence the cloth made therefrom, derives from *Saxony* (German *Sachsen*), formerly a kingdom of the German Empire; there the wool was first grown.

Saxony comes from the Latin *Saxonia*, the land of the Saxons. *Saxon* represents Late Latin *Saxo*, plural *Saxones*, itself from a Saxon or Old High German name traditionally cognate with Old English *seax*, 'knife, dirk; axe'. The Saxons inhabited Holstein in the 2nd Century; by the 7th they had colonized most of England.

Speaking of the 3rd–5th Centuries, J. N. L. Myres, in Collingwood & Myres's *Roman Britain and the English Settlements* (2nd edition, 1937), says, 'To the frightened provincial [in Western Europe and in Britain] the precise ethnology of those who looted his villa was a matter of indifference—Angles or Jutes, they were all Saxons to him', these men 'whose behaviour was associated in the popular mind with desperate valour and barbarity'.

saxophone; sax-tuba. See **saxhorn.**

scalawag or **scallawag** or **scallywag.** An inferior animal; hence, a scamp, a rascal. Webster thinks that the word may derive from *Scalloway*, Shetland, from the fact that both Shetland ponies and Shetland cattle are small. An enticing theory. Unfortunately, *scalawag* more probably derives from, or is at the least akin to, Scottish *skalrag*, 'shabby'.

scamander; skimaunder, in Yorkshire dialect, being a derivative variant. Meaning 'to wander deviously or haphazardly', it derives from the river *Scamander* (Homer's *Skamandros*) and was suggested by the much more usual **meander.** This is that famous river of Troy 'which the gods call Xanthos, men Skamandros' (*Iliad*, xx, 74), now the Bounabashi; the old name is cognate with Greek *skambros*, 'crooked or bent'.

'Even in [Homer's] day there was shortage of grain round the Aegean, and the grain-buyers along the Scamander and the Hermus, the Caÿster and the Meander, and their customers in Athens and Corinth, demanded " the Freedom of the Seas ", *i.e.* of the Dardanelles-Bosphorus route to the Crimean ports,' Lionel W. Lyde, *The Continent of Asia*, 1933.

scandaroon, a carrier pigeon, is so named because shipping-news was transmitted by pigeon-post to Aleppo from *Scanderoon* or *Iskanderun*, a Syrian port. Iskanderun is but one of the many places commemorative of *Alexander* the Great (356–323 B.C.).

scandium. A chemical element discovered, in 1879, by Nilson in the *Scandinavian* euxenite (a mineral). Named in honour of Scandinavia and derived from its Latin name *Scandia* : compare, therefore, **gallium** and **germanium, polonium** and **ruthenium.**

scaramouch is the English of *Scaramouche*, which is the French of the Italian *Scaramuccia*, that personification of a Common Noun meaning ' a skirmish ' who forms one of the stock characters of Italian pantomime (compare **harlequin**). Dressed in black, in derision of the Spanish dons, Scaramuccia was represented as a boastful coward.

Compare **Bombastes** and **drawcansir.**

scavenger's daughter. This instrument of torture (by the State) was invented by one Skeffington, Lieutenant of the Tower of London in the reign of Henry VIII, and was known technically as *Skeffington's gyves* (or *irons*) : whereof *scavenger's daughter* is a jocular perversion.

schenectady, in golf a putter debarred ca. 1919, was an American aid to the royal and ancient game, and therefore not unnaturally named after Schenectady, which, in New York State, is one of the oldest settlements in America.

schiedam is Dutch gin made at *Schiedam*, near Rotterdam. Its base is rye and its old name is **hollands.**

Compare **curaçao.**

schottische is bastard German (the *e* being a French or an English addition) for ' Scottish '—i.e., Scottish dance. ' Perhaps introduced in Paris, which would account for pronunciation ' (W). The schottische is a round dance, rather like, though slower than, the polka, and it must not be confused with the *écossaise* (French for ' Scottish '), a country dance. Against Weekley's suggestion we have to set the fact that ' when first danced in England, about the middle of the nineteenth century (which was the period of the Polka invasion), it was called " the German Polka ",' as Dr Percy Scholes has noted.

scirocco. See **sirocco.**

scotch has, since about 1920, been freely accepted as a Common Noun and general tender for ' Scotch whiskey ', which is more

388

than we can say for *irish*. A slightly pre-war joke runs, ' I don't care what your English is like—so long as your scotch is good '. In *Chambers's Journal* for May 1945 there is, by Dr M. J. Robb, an article entitled ' " Scotch " : The Making of Malt Whisky '.

In the U.S.A., *scotch* is also the name of a **caslon-**like printer's type that was formerly much used in Scotland : for an informative note, see the end of Ernest Booth's *Stealing through Life*, 1929 (Knopf, New York).

scotch pine is the unblushingly modern form of *Scotch pine*, as in ' The evergreens of Britain could be counted on the fingers of one hand ; holly, scotch pine, yew, holm-oak, and juniper compose all the native list that matters ' (Sir W. Beach Thomas, ' The Open Air ' : *The Observer*, December 2, 1945). Also called *scotch fir*, this is *Pinus sylvestris*, ' the pine of the woods '— the pine best known in Britain and growing most happily in Scotland, whence the *scotch*.

scotchman is a building-trade term for a tall crane wherewith to lift girders—a nautical term for a chafing gear or a hooking ring—and a South African term for a florin. Whereas the last alludes to Scottish thrift, the others pay a compliment to Scottish engineering and other technical ability.

scotticé merely signifies ' in the Scots tongue ', as *anglicé* does ' in the English ' ; the ending *-icé* is the Latin adverbial suffix *-ice*, as in *romanice scribere* (see **romance**) ; these terms imply a reference to idiom.

scotty, in slang, means ' angry ' and, as a colloquialism, a ' Scotch terrier '. The former may derive, not directly from *Scotty*, colloquial for ' a Scot ', but from *scot*, slang for ' a rage, a passion of anger '.

Compare **paddy,** which see !

scrimshaw, n. and v., ' (to make) a small neat object, especially an ornament, in one's spare time ', is nautical slang of uncertain origin. Probably there is no connexion with the military-slang *scrimshank*, ' to evade duty, to be a shirker ' ; almost certainly the word comes from some particularly skilful and popular ' scrimshoner ' named Scrimshaw.

Scrooge, Old ; or merely **Scrooge ;** is often used allusively for a curmudgeon, especially by Dickensians. In that perennial Christmas gift to the younger people, *A Christmas Carol*, 1843,

389

Dickens portrays Ebenezer Scrooge, an old curmudgeon, with affectionate trenchancy. Like the names of so many other Dickens characters, *Scrooge* is echoic : to *scrooge* or *scrouge* is to push or jostle, with an implication of ' squeeze '.   It is tempting but probably incorrect to regard *scrooge* as a blend of *screw* and *squeeze*.

Scylla and Charybdis is common currency only in the phrase *between Scylla and Charybdis*, in a dangerous dilemma, confronted by two dangers, hence two grave difficulties, the avoidance of one almost inevitably forcing an encounter with the other.   In *The Odyssey* (XII, 85 ff.), Homer describes the passage of the ship of Odysseus between the dangerous cave inhabited by the monster *Skulla* and, opposite, the whirlpool of *Kharubdis* ; and in *The Argonauts* (see **argonaut**), Apollonius Rhodius describes the passage of Jason's good ship ' Argo ' between the twin perils, situated in the strait of Messina.   In modern times, the sad story of the once lovely, belovèd Scylla has been handled, briefly, by Keats in *Endymion*.

sealyham = *S. terrier*. This particular breed of dog became popular in the early 1890's.   Originally it was the *Sealy Ham terrier*.   In his *The New Dog Book*, 1907, R. Leighton remarks that ' the Sealy Ham derives its breed name from the seat of the Edwardes family, near Haverfordwest ' (Pembrokeshire).

' Dogs have never frightened me the hundreds of times I have been burgling.   Those yapping little brutes, Pekingese, Sealyhams, and such like, are the worst,' George Smithson, *Raffles in Real Life*, 1930.—' . . . O'Reilly was in the small bar, . . . hunting rats with a ·22 and a sealyham,' R. C. Hutchinson, *Interim*, 1945.

sedan. In English it is a vehicle, seating one person and carried, by means of poles, by two chairmen ; of the Oriental palanquin, or the Classical litter, type, it was much used in the 17th–18th Centuries ; ' apparently introduced from Spain by Prince Charles and Buckingham (1623), but popularized by Sir Sanders Duncombe, who secured a monopoly for them ' (Ernest Weekley).   In the U.S.A. it is derivatively a closed automobile—the English saloon—as in ' " You are to go in the sedan to the residence of Mr Hawthorne " . . . . . . I parked the sedan on 67th Street ' (Rex Stout, *Where There's a Will*, 1941).

The origin is obscure : Dr Johnson derived it from the French town of Sedan and, although he may be right, he was, after all, guessing.   On the other hand, it may come from

Latin *sedes*, ' a seat, hence, a chair ' : perhaps from the accusative-case *sedem* : as the Etonian *montem* represents *ad montem*, so *sedem* may represent *in sedem*.

seidlitz = *S. powder*. ' I also found on him two seidlitz powders, purchased from two shops, in different districts,' *Sessions Paper of the Central Criminal Court*, March 8, 1910.

In the composite dose so named, the *seidlitz* element has been bestowed for no better reason than that the mixture constitutes an aperient, as was the water from a spring at *Seidlitz* in Bohemia : a spring whose waters contain carbonic acid and magnesium sulphate.

selenite; selenium. The latter is a non-metallic element, the former is gypsum (a crystalline form of sulphate of lime). The element, discovered in 1818, much resembles the earlier-ascertained **tellurium,** and this resemblance suggested the name *selenium*, for as Tellus is the Earth, Selene is the Moon : Greek *Sĕlēnē*. (Cf. also **helium.**) In Greek mythology, Selene is the Moon-Goddess : the Roman Diana is, not entirely, her descendant. The daughter of Hyperion, she was the sister of Helios (later identified with **Apollo**).

Other *Selene*-derivatives are touched-upon in the following passage from James Innes Mackintosh Stewart's coruscating ' deteccer ', *The Weight of the Evidence*, 1944 : ' Prisk's lips moved. " Selenitic," he whispered. " Selenologist. Seleno-tropic. Selenograph."

' The Chief Constable's chauffeur took off his cap. " Gawd," he said. " A furriner. And calling for his mother, if you ask me."

' Appleby, with a hand beneath Prisk's shirt front, shook his head. " Just a little lunar philology. And he's not much hurt." '

seltzer. ' " Yes," interrupted M. Clary, " you give us Seltzer water instead of champagne, yet you expect us to sing—

> Qu'il avait du bon vin
> Le Seigneur châtelain ;
> Buvons encore
> Pour en être certain ! " ' :
> (*The Times*, July 14, 1941, quoted by
> Osbert Sitwell in *Sing High! Sing Low!*)

(At the old Haymarket theatre, New York City) ' " Champagne ", which was nothing more than seltzer, sold for ten bucks '—dollars—' a bottle,' Jack Callahan in *Detective Fiction Weekly*, May 2, 1936.

The word represents an alteration of German *selterser* (in full *Wasser selterser*), ' water of *Selters* ', that village in Hesse-Nassau which has long been associated with a mineral spring.

senega or **seneka.** This drug, which forms an ingredient in cough mixtures, is made from the root of a plant known also as the *Senega snake-root*. That capital *S* affords the clue : *Senega* is a thickening of *Seneca*, therefore the Seneca Indians of North America. The Senecas once formed a part of the great Iroquois Confederacy of warlike tribes, who supported the British during the Revolution. ' They now live mainly on several reservations in New York state ' (James D. Hart).

sequoia is the giant redwood tree of California. In 1870, Emerson permitted himself this sober hyperbole, ' The mammoth Sequoias rose to their enormous proportions ' (DAE). They are, indeed, the largest trees in the world and in their name they commemorate *Sikwayi*, the Cherokee Indian (ca. 1770–1843) that devised the Cherokee syllabary, which involved a principle employed for other Red Indian languages. Also known as George Guess, he is listed by Hart as *Sequoyah*.

serendipity means the faculty and the habit of making felicitous discoveries by accident. A very literary word, it was coined by Horace Walpole in a letter to Mann on January 28, 1754, from precisely this faculty as possessed by the titular heroes of the fairy-tale, *The Three Princes of Serendip*, an old name for Ceylon, also written *Serendib*, from Aryan *Sarandib*, which appears to denote ' the Singhalese island '. In an interesting book, *An Index of Titles of Honour*, 1880, E. Solly defined the term as ' looking for one thing and finding another ' (cited by The OED).

serge. ' His collar was shrunken and faded, and his thin serge jacket was frayed at the cuffs,' Mabel Lethbridge, *Against the Tide*, 1936.

The word comes from the Latin *serica* (*lana*), ' silk-like wool ' ; the ' likeness ' must not be too pedantically quibbled about ! The *serica* part of the Latin derives from Greek *serikos*, ' silken ' : compare the next entry and also **silk.** Chaucer, who mentions the material, probably heard of it during his travels in France—in its Old French shape, *sarge* (cf. Rumanian *sarica*).

392

In the 19th Century, by the way, there was a material called *silk serge*, a silk fabric twilled like serge.

sericeous; sericin; sericite; sericulture or **sericiculture:** respectively ' of a *silky*, hence of a satin-like, surface '; '*silk*-glue '; ' a mineral, green in hue, and of a *silky* lustre '; ' the rearing of *silk*worms and the subsequent production of raw silk '. The definitions suggest the origin of the terms. The *seric* element in all four represents Latin *sericus*, ' of silk '—a sense dependent on *Sericus*, ' of China ; Chinese ', literally ' of the *Seres* ', the Seres generally being held to be the Chinese. Silk is ' the *Chinese* fabric ' : see **silk** (where an attempt has been made to untangle the centuries-ravelled skein of *silk*, *seric*, *China*) and the mildly divergent **serge.**

sevillana is short for *seguidilla sevillana*, ' a seguidilla of Seville '. The seguidilla is an old—indeed, an ancient—Spanish dance that, of a Moorish type and origin, is paced to the accompaniment of castanets.

seville = *S. orange.* For a place-name applied to a product of the place, compare **jaffa** ; for a derivative name, compare **tangerine.**
   ' Crowds of visitors flock to Seville at Easter, when the orange-trees are in flower . . . ; but its real beauty is best seen at Christmas, when the oranges are ripe, and the violets and carnations in flower, and the white lines of the typical Moorish houses are not glaring ' (L. W. Lyde, *The Continent of Europe*, 4th edition, 1930). The seville came to Europe from India.

Sèvres. ' Faience figures jostled with massive illuminated volumes, Sèvres bowls stood on thick portfolios,' Mark Benney, *Low Company*, 1936.
   Sèvres is short for ' (made of) Sèvres porcelain '. Sèvres is a small and ancient city of the Seine-et-Oise *département* of France : a dainty and costly porcelain has been made there for centuries.
   Compare **delf** and in the Appendix, **dresden.**

Sexton Blake. ' Famous detectives of fiction, Sherlock Holmes, Sexton Blake, and their compeers, are almost invariably depicted as carrying out their investigations by the aid of magnifying glasses and high-power microscopes. In real life, detectives rarely make use of these adjuncts to their business,' C. L. McLuer Stevens, *From Clue to Dock*, 1927. He is the English counterpart of the American **Nick Carter** (subsidiary vocabulary). *The Sexton Blake Library* covers the period 1915–25; a New Series stretched from 1925 to 1941, when a second New Series began.

shaddock. ' Something like a vast orange—a " shaddock ", his partner [at a ball in Martinique, June 1814] called it, otherwise known as " grape fruit ", rather inconsequentially. She even went on to explain that learned men had come to the conclusion that this thing was the veritable forbidden fruit which Eve had given to Adam,' C. S. Forester, *The Captain from Connecticut*, 1941.

Late in the 17th Century, an English Captain Shaddock had, from the East Indies, brought the seed to Barbados, whence it soon spread to the other islands of the West Indies.

Shakespearean or **-ian.** (Concerning Milton's *L'Allegro* and *Il Penseroso*) ' The ethereal and evanescent are rendered weighty (as in " labouring clouds ") by images from human civilization, clothes, sculpture ; something of nature's Shakespearian and dynamic otherness being lost nevertheless in the process,' G. Wilson Knight, one of the most penetrating Shakespearian critics of the 20th Century, *The Burning Oracle*, 1939.

Apart from its literal senses, *Shakespearian* (William Shakespeare, 1564–1616, the world's greatest dramatist, greatest poet) has come to denote or, more subtly, to connote magnificence and splendour, universal and profound sympathy, deepest understanding, the utmost clarity of mind and vision, a pervasive and mighty, yet magistrally directed power, and a glory, a spheral music of phrasing, style, rhythm. The myriad-minded, the all-souled, the word-magicking Shakespeare has left upon the languages, as upon the thinking and the feeling, of the world an impress unequalled by that of any two other writers combined.

shalloon. A material of wool, close-woven and used for linings ; hence, a wig-tie made thereof. It derives from the French *chalon* : and in 14th–17th Century English *chalon* meant a blanket or a bed-coverlet.

The material was manufactured at Chalons-sur-Marne in France. Thence—via the English adoption—*chaloner*, a maker of these blankets or coverlets : whence the surname *Challoner*.

shande(i)an ; shandeism or **shandyism.** (Possessing) the qualities of Tristram Shandy himself or of the Shandy family in Laurence Sterne's long, extremely idiosyncratic novel, *Tristram*

394

Shandy (1759–67). Sterne describes the novel as a 'civil, nonsensical, good-humoured Shandean book, which will do all your hearts good': wherein we hear comparatively little of Tristram, much of his father Walter, much of the delightful Uncle Toby and of his servant, Corporal Trim.

shanghai, v. and n. 'He seemed to think he'd been Shanghaied and dumped in the elephant-house,' Ethel Lina White, *The Man Who Loved Lions*, 1943.

The verb, 'to drug (a man) and then, while he is still unconscious, ship him as a sailor', was originally American; it dates from those days when from the stews and opium-dens and low saloons of Shanghai, many an indiscreet and many an unfortunate were transferred thus from artificial paradises to salty reality.

The noun, meaning 'a catapult', was originally Australian English, into which it crept from the talk of the numerous Chinese resident in Australia since ca. 1850.

It also denotes a breed of domestic fowl (with feathered shanks) introduced from Shanghai; and 'a painter's daub', this American sense being of obscure origin although probably attributable to cursory glances at the cheaper Chinese paintings seen in the shops of the Chinese quarters of San Francisco and New York.

shantung, a soft Chinese silk that is undressed and usually undyed, takes its name from the province of Shantung.

'Shan-tung ("Eastern Mountains"), the home of Confucius, is essentially a mountainous peninsula, ringed round on its three landward sides by the "horseshoe" of the Great Plain —its eastern bulwark, as Shan-si ("Western Mountains") is its western . . . . . . On the Shimen and Meng-shan piedmonts the mulberry flourishes so well as to make Yen-chow and I-chow very important silk-markets,' Lionel W. Lyde, *The Continent of Asia*, 1933. But Professor Lyde adds that 'the so-called "Shantung", the third quality, is really Manchurian silk, imported at Chefoo, and sent to Chang-i to be woven'.

shasta daisy and **shasta fir.** Both the daisy (an ox-eye) and the fir are natives of California, and the origin of the name *shasta* appears in: 'Just over the California border, on the Upper Klamath, we have the higher . . ., slightly more extensive intermont plain of the Shasta Valley (just north of Mount Shasta), largely devoted to stock-raising,' Ll. Rodwell Jones & P. W. Bryan, *North America*, 7th edition, 1946.

Shavian, 'in general, characteristic of George Bernard Shaw (born in 1856), mostly as a dramatist; but, in particular, disquisitively witty in the manner of the G. B. Shaw of the plays', is an Edwardian creation. An informative sidelight is afforded by 'Shavians from Superman', a sketch, written in 1907, included in John Ross's entertaining *Masques and Phases*, 1909. For some, *Shavian* evokes an attitude of Olympian intellectualism devoid of spiritual vision.

sheba, now obsolescent, in American slang is a very attractive girl; the counterpart to the male *sheik* of the same period: the 1920's. From that glamorous Queen of Sheba who dazzled—and dallied with—the wise King Solomon, who, in respect of women, was as big a fool as any man. But then she was, we are told, very, very seductive. See **Ophir.**

Sheffield, which might fittingly be lower-cased, is short for *Sheffield silverware* (e.g., cutlery); that is, made at Sheffield, where art has not been entirely banished by industry. Sheffield was famed for its cutlery even in Chaucer's day, and Sheffield canteens still form a most welcome wedding-present.

sheila is very general Australian—and, derivatively, less general New Zealand—slang for 'girl'. The original Australian form is *sheiler* (or *shieler* or *sheeler*), which represents the English dialectal and low-slang *shaler*, current in the same sense at least as early as 1839 (see PS). But the form of the word has undoubtedly been affected by the feminine given-name *Sheila* (see especially PNTC).

shelty is a predominantly Scottish variant of *Shetland pony*, *Shetland* becoming, by metathesis, *Sheltand*, which is pet-formed to *Shelty*, which, in its turn, is familiarized to *shelty* or *sheltie*. Or perhaps the word comes straight down to us from the Old Norse *Hjalti* (Shetlander), as pronounced in Caithness and the Orkneys.
  Compare **shetland** below.

sheraton or **S—.** 'He may buy old masters, Rembrandt etchings, Sheraton sideboards' (R. G. Collingwood, *Speculum Mentis*, 1924). The term *sheraton* is short for *Sheraton furniture*—chairs, sideboards, cutlery boxes, and so forth; or for 'made by Sheraton'. (Alas! There are imitations.) Characteristically English (compare **chippendale**), it is both severe and graceful in style. Thomas Sheraton (1751–1806) was a maker and a designer of furniture, and his furniture 'caught on' towards the end of the 18th Century.

'Mrs Gabb led the way . . . past the Sheraton cabinet filled with Sevres and Swansea china,' Mary Fitt, *Death on Heron's Mere*, 1941; 'The Sheraton sideboard . . . a fine authentic piece,' John P. Marquand, *So Little Time*, 1943.

Sherlock Holmes, jocularly **Sherlock,** in the generalized sense 'a remarkable amateur detective'; and **Dr Watson,** jocularly **Watson,** his solemn, rather dull assistant ('Elementary, my dear Watson').

'The stoolies' or police informers (narks) 'couldn't help us much and it didn't take a Sherlock to figure the dirty little killer had left town,' Earl H. Scott, 'The Bull Buster', in *Detective Fiction Weekly*, September 6, 1930.

'Wendover was an eager student of criminology, and prided himself on being something better than a mere Watson,' J. J. Connington, *A Minor Operation*, 1937.

'"My dear Sherlock", said Truman . . . "Elucidate!"': James Spenser, *The Wheels*, 1938.

'Which of us has not been amazed by Conan Doyle's *Sherlock Holmes*? We are all "Watsons" really, when we read the usual opening of a Sherlock Holmes adventure,' Inspector Leslie A. Tomkins in *The Police Journal*, January–March 1943.

Conan Doyle (1859–1930) created the figure of Sherlock Holmes in several series of short stories, beginning with *The Adventures of Sherlock Holmes*, 1891, and continuing with *The Memoirs*, 1894, and *The Return*, 1904; many people forget that the detective had already appeared in Conan Doyle's first work of fiction, *A Study in Scarlet*, 1887, and in *The Sign of the Four*, 1889. The detective heroes of S. S. Van Dine, Ellery Queen, Rex Stout, Dorothy Sayers, Margery Allingham, and, by opposition, Ngaio Marsh and Michael Innes, all 'stem' from him.

sherry. 'In the south of Spain the rains of the late winter and early spring are followed by a very dry summer and autumn which, in the marine exposure of Jerez, produce a wine peculiarly rich in organic ethers, the best sherry almost rivalling cognac in this respect . . . . . . The special product inland [in the province of Cadiz], the sherry of Jerez, is one for which the demand is increasing, though it happens to be one of the most wholesome wines in the world,' Lionel W. Lyde, *The Continent of Europe*, 4th edition, 1930.

The original English form was *sherris* (Shakespeare), from *Xeres*, the English shape of Spanish *Jerez* (*de la Frontera*), not far from Cadiz. 'The final *s* was dropped, from a fancy that it was the plural ending, just as in the case of *pea* for *pease*' (Skeat). *Jerez* = Latin (*urbs*) *Caesaris*, '(the town) of Caesar'.

shetland = *S. pony*, by shortening and by common-propertying. This breed of small ponies, stocky and hardy, rough-coated and long-tailed, long-maned, originated in the Shetland Islands; compare the very small Shetland sheep-dog. There is also *Shetland wool*, from Shetland sheep. *Shetland* derives from the Old Norse *Hjaltland*.

Compare **shelty** above.

shillaber, often shortened to *shill*, is (1) a circus employee that, to set things moving, hastens to buy tickets immediately the barker has concluded his 'spiel' or announcement; hence, (2) a catchpenny hanger-on at circus, fair, or race-meeting. Probably from some notorious 'shill' (sense 1) surnamed *Shillabeer* (or *-er*) or *Shillibeer* (compare **shillibeer**), though perhaps from *The Life and Sayings of Mrs Partington*, published in 1854 and written by the American humorist, Benjamin *Shillaber* (1814–90).

shillelagh, an Irish cudgel, is so called because, originally, it was customarily fashioned of a wood—either blackthorn or oak—growing at *Shillelagh* in County Wicklow. Shillelagh is a barony and a township; and within the barony, says Francis Grose in *A Classical Dictionary of the Vulgar Tongue*, 1785, stands 'a wood of that name famous for its oaks'.

shillibeer, a hearse with seats for the mourners, derives from the sense 'an omnibus'. George Shillibeer (1797–1866) was an English coach-proprietor with an Irish surname. He 'introduced London to the omnibus in 1829' (WWN).

shimose is short for *Shimose powder*, a Japanese explosive, consisting mainly of picric acid, discovered by the Japanese inventor, Masashika *Shimonose* Kogakubachi, apparently in the early half of 1904, the Japanese using it against the Russians in 1904–05. Sometimes it is called *shimosite* (compare **lyddite, turpinite**).

ship of Tarshish. See **argosy,** 2nd paragraph.

shrapnel was invented ca. 1802, by Henry Shrapnel (1761–1842), an English artillery officer, who became a general. The shrapnel shell was successfully employed, in 1804, at Surinam.

Henry Shrapnel also made considerable improvements in the construction of mortars and howitzers.

Shylock, the Jewish usurer in Shakespeare's *The Merchant of Venice*, has, by his insistence upon receiving his pound of flesh (creditor Antonio's flesh), come to serve so generally as the type of the money-lender so hard-hearted as to be outrageously cruel that the word might well be written with a small *s*.

' Shylock is in danger not of despisal but of excessive sentiment' (G. Wilson Knight, *The Burning Oracle*, 1939), so sympathetically has Shakespeare treated him.

' The charitable are often no better than Shylocks, they want their money's worth,' George Moore, *Memoirs of My Dead Self*, 1906.

siamese = *Siamese cat*. ' He came over, looking like a Siamese cat, and held out his paw,' Richard B. Sale, in *Detective Fiction Weekly*, November 3, 1934.

Ca. 1830–1910, *siamese* was occasionally used to mean ' to join unseverably '; usually in the passive, as in ' Body and soul are obviously, yet most mysteriously, siamesed '. That is, like *the Siamese twins*, Eng and Chang, who died, at the age of sixty, in the year 1874: these unfortunates were, at the waist, united by a sort of tubular band.

Chapter XXI of Clifford Roe's *Horrors of the White Slave Trade*, 1911, is entitled, ' The Devil's Siamese Twins ', the chapter-contents beginning with the elucidatory words, ' Liquor and Lust—The Inseparable Twins '.

siberian = *Siberian dog*, a breed of dogs well adapted for and much used in sledging (cf. **husky**).

' The name " Siberia " has been accepted . . . as covering all " Russian " Asia north of the Ob-Aral water-parting, i.e. far more than the original area so named in the Ob and Yenisei basins ; and it is significant that the pioneers in opening up the area—who were almost all " destructive " collectors of loot in the form of furs and fish, the cattle of the natives, and the riches of the Kurgans—moved by sledge and by barge ' : ' It was in 1579 that the Cossacks, under Yermak, seized the Tatar fort of Sibir at the Tobol-Irtysh confluence—for the whole country eastward to take its name from the kingdom of Sibir which he tried to set up ' : thus Lionel W. Lyde, *The Continent of Asia*, 1933.

sibyl; sibylline. ' By 140 B.C. the Sibylline books could claim that every land was full of Jews ' : thus does Dr W. W. Tarn refer, in *Hellenistic Civilisation*, to the Apocrypha.

Sibylla is the origin, via French, of the English form, and the Latin derives from the Greek *Sibulla*, said by some to be Doric *Siobolla* for Attic *Theoboule* (literally, divine wish); 'the derivation and meaning are unknown but certainly are not Greek; they are possibly Semitic' (Ency. Brit.).

She was a prophetess, inspired by Apollo, to utter oracles at various places, e.g. Marpessus and Delphi; Varro lists ten of these shrines. She was accredited with the authorship of *The Sibylline Books* (or *Oracles*), kept in the temple of Jupiter Capitolinus at Rome.

The Proper Name became a Common Noun, 'prophetess'; and was further debased to mean 'fortune-teller'.

siciliano and **sicilienne** are respectively the Italian and the French names for an old dance-type tune, the dance being of Sicilian origin; the music resembles that of the gondoliera and the pastorale. (Scholes.)

siena (often written with capital *S*), the colour Venetian red; *sienna*, brownish-yellow when raw, orange-red or reddish-brown when *burnt*; *sienna brown*, cocoa colour; *sienese* (usually *Sienese*) *drab*, a brown that is red-yellow in hue: all derive from *Siena* in northern Italy, the old Roman *Saena* Julia. The colour *sienna* comes from the earthy substance known in Italian as *terra di Siena*. The town is *Siena* in Italian, mostly *Sienna* in English.

The Sienese school of painting forms part of *the Tuscan School*, the other part being the Florentine school. The Sienese paintings are notable for their refinement, delicacy, tenderness, and the chief members are perhaps Duccio di Buoninsegna, Martini, the Lorenzetti.

silene; Silenus. The former is a plant named by Linnaeus from the latter, which is the Latin form of the Greek *Sīlēnos*, the foster-father, tutor and constant companion of Bacchus. Silenus is reported (Virgil, Horace, Ovid)—and in modern painting has been represented—as of short or middle height, bald, plump, flat-nosed, and having two brief horns, riding upon an ass, tipsy and lascivious-leering. The *Sileni* or satyrs, a later development, do not appear in English allusive speech, whereas Silenus has become, among the cultured, a prototype. Literally, *Silenus* means ' (the) flat-nosed (god) '.

silesia, originally, was a linen fabric made in Silesia and imitated elsewhere; then, derivatively, it became also a thin cotton, usually twilled, fabric—used mostly for linings. The former

400

was often spelt with a capital *S*, the latter is normally spelt with a small *s*.   Silesia, the southernmost province of Prussia, has for centuries been famed for its manufacture of fabrics.

ilhouette.   'They could see the tall, stoop-shouldered figure . . . silhouetted in the open doorway like some great bat,' Victor Gunn, *The Dead Man Laughs*, 1944.

This verb derives from the much commoner noun, which takes its name from a French politician : Etienne de *Silhouette* († 1767).   The joke is variously explained, but it may safely be assumed that this *meagre* form of 'portraiture' constituted a typically subtle yet bitter Gallic satire on that Minister of Finance who, in 1759, 'introduced several reforms which were considered unduly parsimonious' (Skeat).

ilk and its obvious derivatives.   (Compare **serge** and **sericeous** for etymology, **peach** for semantics.)   The word, in its present form, dates back to the 14th Century (when *silc* is also found) ; *seolc* and *selc* occur in the 13th ; *sioloc, seoloc, seolc*, in the 11th ; and there are other early variants.   Compare Old Norse *silki* and the Old Slavic *shelkŭ* (modern Russian *shelk'*).   'The ultimate source is commonly supposed to be L. *sēricus* or Greek σηρικός, silken, from L. *Seres*, Greek *Σῆρες*, the oriental people (perhaps the Chinese) from whom silk was first obtained' (The OED) ; 'it is supposed to have passed into Slavonic via some language which confused -*r*- and -*l*- (cf. *plum* [from Latin *pruna*]), and hence via the Baltic trade into Anglo-Saxon and Old Norse' (W).

The OED referred to Latin *sēricus* and Greek σηρικός, both meaning 'silken' : the actual forms would be the neuter *sericum* and σηρικόν used as a noun.   The Greek σηρικός ('silken') derives immediately from σηρικός, 'Seric'—i.e., 'belonging to the Seres' (as above).   In Latin, moreover, *serica* signified 'silks ; silken robes, garments' : in imitation of the Greek τὰ σηρικά.   The singular of Greek *Σῆρες* is *Σήρ* (little used), which, as σήρ, served in Greek of the 2nd Century A.D. for 'silkworm'.   The Seres certainly inhabited eastern Asia, so the 'probability' that they were the Chinese is almost a certainty.   (In the 16th Century, *the Seres' wool* was synonymous with *silk* : cf. **serge.**)

Neither 'Liddell & Scott' (in its recent recension) nor 'Lewis & Short' has the slightest hesitation in defining *Seres* and *Σῆρες* respectively as 'the Chinese' ;   and Ammianus Marcellinus (4th Century of our era) calls the Great Wall of China *aggeres Serum*, 'the ramparts of the Seres'.

Now for the language which confused -*r*- and -*l*- ;   the

language through which the Greek or the Latin word passed
into Old Slavonic and thence to Scandinavia, Iceland, Britain.
Might that language not have been Chinese, whose trans-
mutation of *r* to *l* is almost proverbial? We are dealing,
remember, with a Greek or a Latin, not with a Chinese word!
Either from Greek or Roman merchants trading in China or,
less likely, to Chinese merchants trading in Italy or Greece or
Asia Minor or the Levant or, most probably, between Greek
(or Roman) and Chinese merchants encountering one another
on the common ground of Aryan India, or Persia, the word,
whether σηρικόν (perhaps σηρικά) or *sericum* (perhaps *serica*),
was frequently uttered, bandied about, repeated, shouted, the
Greeks or Romans pronouncing it correctly, the Chinese pronouncing it *selicon*, *selicum*, perhaps *selica*, which became *selcon*,
selcum, perhaps *selca*, which, maybe simultaneously, became—
or had, as alternatives, the forms—*silcon*, *silcum*, perhaps *silca*
If the transit-language had been Aryan-Indian or Persian or
Hebrew—of all the possibles, these are probably the only
potentials—the question of ' *r* mutilated to *l* ' would not have
arisen, for none of these languages shirks an *r*. But we know
that Chinese silk had reached India before Alexander reached
it in 327 B.C. ' Then in 115 B.C. under the Han Dynasty the
Chinese army occupied, albeit only temporarily, the Tarim
basin. At length the civilizations of the Far East and the Near
East were in contact directly, no longer through inter-
mediaries . . . . . . After 115 B.C. the silk caravans, equipped
by the Empire, travelled on roads protected by blockhouses
and police . . . . . . After 114 B.C. a dozen caravans a year
loaded with silks crossed the deserts of Central Asia from China
to Russian Turkestan, whence the fashionable stuff was sent to
Seleucia, Antioch, Alexandria and Rome,' V. Gordon Childe
What Happened in History, 1942.

There is, however, another matter to dispose of : the relation
between **china** ; *sinologist* ; **seric** (and **serge** and **silk**). And
the unravelling of this Seric skein, the sorting of this Chinese
congeries, may be prefaced with a passage from Professor
Lionel W. Lyde's fascinating *The Continent of Asia* [1] (revised
edition, 1938) : ' Early Europe knew of two lands, as some
thought,—or of one land with two sets of names ', a Greek name
and a native Chinese name ; ' the northern land was *Seres*, and
the southern was *Sin*, the latter with several forms—*Sin* and
Sinoe, *Ch'in* and *China*, even *Ts'in* and *Thîn*. According to the

---

[1] What Professor Lyde has to say possesses the triple value of a pronouncement by an excellent philologist, by a good historian, by a super-eminent
geographer.

School of Ptolemy " the Sinoe lie at the very end of the habit-able world "—so that no people or culture could reach them from " beyond " ; Cosmas said that " beyond Tzinista there is neither habitation nor navigation ".'

The First Dynasty of China was the *Hs'in* or *Ch'in* Dynasty ; the people were known as the *Hs'ins* or *Ch'ins* (literally, ' *the* Men '). ' From the eighth century B.C.,' says Lyde, ' a principality of this name was in complete control of the Chinese and of the Zungarian gateways to and from the West, and it gradually spread southward through the Red Basin, until in the 4th Century it had control also of the Yangtze link with the Irawadi. This was at the very time when Persia, on the Indus and the Amu, was controlling the western ends of both these lines of approach ; and from this time onward Ch'in, though it did not conquer the rest of China until late in the third century B.C., completely controlled all natural intercourse between China and the West. It is difficult, therefore,—and quite unnecessary,—to avoid the conclusion that Western Asia and Europe extended to the lands farther east—knowledge of which, and the products from which, they obtained only through and from Ch'in—the name of the great state that they did know directly ' : that, in short, *Ch'in*, a region, became that vast area which we call *China*. ' At any rate it is obvious that Ch'in, both before and after it conquered the rest of China, was far from avoiding intercourse with the West.'

' *The* Chinaware ' is, obviously, *china* ; ' *the* Chinese study or knowledge ' is *sinology*. But whence this variation? *Sinology, sinologist, sinogram* (a Chinese written character), derive from Late Latin *Sinae*, which represents Ptolemaic Greek Σίναι (cf. *Sinoe* above), which, again, derives from Arabic *Sin*, (the land, the empire of) China. Probably the Arabic *Sin* equals Chinese *Ch'in* or rather *Hs'in*.

The Arabs, the Persians, the Aryan-Indians, as well as Greeks and Latins, must have come to hear about, then to see and handle, silk at a very early period. The Silk Roads were among the most used of the great, old, historic caravan routes. ' Bhamo was a silk-market of the seventh century B.C., though the " Silk Road " may have developed out of a " Salt Trail " ' (Lyde). Two main avenues of approach to China from the West were, basically or virtually, Silk Roads—the North Silk Road and the South Silk Road. ' It is almost certain that the silk trade originated with the Tokharians, or Yue-chi ' (Lyde).

Little wonder, then, that the Greek-Latin name (*Seres*) for the Ch'ins, hence the Chinese, should have yielded **sericin, sericite, sericulture,** and so forth ; little wonder that *serge* should likewise have had the same origin ; little wonder, either, that Chinese concern with and interest in '*the* Ch'in fabric' should have transformed *serikon* and *sericum* into the word that has become **silk**!

Perhaps the 'results' may be tabulated thus:—

I. *Ch'in* and *Hs'in*.		II. *Seres*.
A : Ch'in	*B : Hs'in*	1. *Seric* (of the Seres)
		> *seric* (silken); whence
China	Arabic *Sin*	*sericeous*, *sericulture*;
		sericin, *sericite*, etc.
china	Greek *Sinai*	
('*the* China		2. *serika* or *serica*
ware')	*sinogram, sinology*	> *serge*
	('knowledge	
Chinese (from *Ch'ins*)	about *China*'),	3. *serikon* or *sericum*
	etc.	> *selikon* or *selicum*
		> *selkon* or *selcum* or *silkon*
		or *silcum*, etc., etc.,
		etc.
		> *silk*
		('*the* fabric of China')

sillery is that particular sort of champagne which, originally made at Sillery, a township on the river Vesle, near Reims, is now little more than a trade-name; *Sillery sec* is a still, white wine, genuinely made at Sillery.

silly billy. See **billy . . .**

silurian, or **S—,** refers, especially for its rocks, to that geological period which precedes the **devonian.** So designated, in 1835, by the great geologist Murchison.

The name comes from the *Silures*, as the Romans called an ancient British tribe inhabiting what is now South Wales and Monmouthshire; the Romans conquered them in 48 B.C., and founded Isca Silurum—now Caerleon.

Compare **permian.**

Simon Pure, or **the real Simon Pure,** is the real as distinct from the supposed person known by a certain name; hence, the right person, the person one seeks. In Mrs Centlivre's *A Bold Stroke for a Wife*, 1717, Simon Pure is a Quaker that, in part of the play, is impersonated by another character.

I.e., Simon pure-and-simple, Simon none-else.

simoniac, simoniacal; simony. The second is the adjective formed from the first, a *simoniac* being one who practises *simony* or traffic in Church preferment. *Simony* comes, via French, from Ecclesiastical Latin *simonia*, the reference being to *Simon Magus* in *Acts*, viii, 18–19.

simpson. See **cecily.**

sinanthropus is sometimes, among the erudite, used for a very primitive, sub-human sort of fellow. The term is short for *sinanthropus pekinensis*, better known as *the Peking man*.

singleton, at cards, hence for any *single* or sole example or specimen, is a jocular adoption of the surname *Singleton*. W compares *singleton* from *single* with *lushington* from *lush*, but omits to add that there is a pun on *single one*.

sinology, knowledge of Chinese history, customs, language, derives from the Greek *Sinai*, ‘ the Chinese ’. See the entry at **silk.**

sinoper; sinopite; sinople. *Sinoper*, ‘ red ’, ‘ red earth serving as a pigment ’, ‘ red mercuric sulphide; vermilion ’; *sinopite*, ‘ a clayey earth, brick-red with white dots ’; *sinople*, ‘ sinoper ’ in its first and second senses, also ‘ a kind of iron-bearing quartz ’. To these we may add **sinopic earth.**

All four originate in *Sinopë*, in Paphlagonia, the most important of the Greek colonies on the Euxine shores of Asia Minor ; it was the capital of the Pontic kings, and its territory, reaching to the Halys river, was known as *Sinopis*. The ‘ red earth ’— whence the particular shade of ‘ red ’ (both being *sinoper* and *sinople*, the former also the aforementioned *sinopic earth*)—was brought to Greece from *Sinopë*; by association of ideas, we get the mid-19th-20th-Century word, *sinopite*.

‘ Homer . . . speaks . . . sometimes of a ship . . . with rosy cheeks. To have rosy cheeks, a ship needs red paint. This the Greek got from a red stuff he called *miltos*, which was found as a natural product in large quantities up-country in Asia Minor, but he did not go to the obvious ports on the Aegaean shore of Asia Minor ; he went to Sinope on the North Shore, a Black Sea port, and the *miltos* was called *Sinopic*,’ T. A. Glover, *The Ancient World*, 1935.

siren, incorrectly **syren.** ‘ London, the siren, with a dazzling tray of tempting attractions,’ Walter Greenwood, *Only Mugs Work*, 1938.—‘ My wife is a very clever woman, although she does her best not to be recognized as one. She’d rather be a syren. Feminine vanity,’ Ethel Lina White, *The Man Who Loved Lions*, 1943.

'Your next encounter', said Circe to Odysseus, 'will be with the Sirens, who bewitch everybody that approaches them. There is no home-coming for the man who draws near them unawares and hears the Sirens' voices . . . For with the music of their song the Sirens cast their spell upon him,' E. V. Rieu's translation of Homer's *The Odyssey* in 'The Penguin Classics'.

The word comes to us, via Latin, from Greek *Seirēn*, which is cognate with *seira* (Ionic *seirē*), a noosed cord with which the Sagartians snared and then dragged away their enemies.—As a ship's *siren*, the word is a transferred sense.

sirocco or **scirocco.** 'The southerly sirocco of Sicily and leveche of Spain . . . are essentially Saharan winds—hot, dry and full of dust; and the dust collects so much vapour . . that they are almost always hazy or foggy. They may occur at any season of the year, but are most common about the time of the spring equinox . . . . . . The name *sirocco* is, however applied in the northern latitudes of the [Mediterranean] basin as *solano* is in Spain, to the ordinary eddies in the main air current of the Anti-Trade,' Lionel W. Lyde, *The Continent of Europe*, 4th edition, 1930.

In Byron's *Marino Faliero* occurs this passage:

> '*Doge.*   At what hour arises
>   The moon?
>   *Bertuccio.*   Late, but the atmosphere is thick and dusty,
>   'Tis a sirocco.'

The word derives from Arabic *sharq*, 'the East'—itself from *sharaqa* (of the sun) 'to rise'; cf., therefore, *Orient*, from Latin *oriri*, 'to rise'. This wind, therefore, came from the *Near East*.

sisal, the strong white fibre, takes its name from *Sisal* (which in the Maya language, means 'Cold Waters': Webster), once a seaport of Yucatan—that Mexican state which lies on the eastern side of the Gulf of Campeachy. 'Sisal or Sizal being the former place of export of henequen . . . that fibre was long known as "Sisal hemp",' Chisholm.

sissy. See **cissy.**

siwash, 'to travel without equipment', derives immediately from *siwash*, 'to live, act, esp. to camp, like an Indian'; and like *siwash*, 'to draw logs up to the main hauling cable (imitative of an Indian procedure), as well as like *siwash*, 'a breed of dog found in Alaska' and often confused with the Eskimo dog and the **mameluke,** it comes from *Siwash*, 'a

Indian inhabiting the northern Pacific coast of North America '.
Siwash is a word from the Chinook jargon, a trade *lingua franca*
of the Pacific coast; in that jargon the term means ' a Red
Indian; an aborigine; a savage ', whence it is easy to guess
that the Chinook-jargon word represents an ' Indianization '
of the French *sauvage*, ' savage, wild, uncultivated '. It
becomes evident, therefore, that *Siwash* is misused in ' Siwash
Indians ', for it is not a tribal name. The term is correctly
used in *Hiyu siwash mitlite yukwa*, ' Many Indians dwell here '.
(Webster; Edward Harper Thomas, *Chinook: A History and
Dictionary*, 1935.)
Compare **chinook.**

skimaunder. See **scamander.**

skye = *S. terrier.* A very old breed of terrier, originating in
Scotland, the *skye* has been especially associated with the Isle of
Skye, the largest of the Inner Hebrides. ' MacDougall, a
Skye-terrier belonging to me, of so pure a breed that you never
knew whether he was walking forwards or backwards,' Norman
Douglas, *Together*, 1923.
Compare such canine place-names as **airedale** and
bedlington.

slave; enslave. Concerning the Aryan invasion, ca. 1500 B.C.,
of Western India, Patrick Carleton writes, in his fascinating
Buried Empires, 1939, ' The ordinary Sanskrit (*i.e.* Âryan) names
for these [indigenous] folk were *Panis* and *Dâsas* or *Dasyus*, and
there is plenty of evidence that the Aryans regarded them with
a mixture of contempt and fear, as creatures to be either
exterminated or enslaved. *Dâsî* (the feminine of *Dâsa*), indeed,
soon became the ordinary word for a female slave.'
Our *slave* comes to us, via Old French *esclave*, from the
Medieval Latin *sclavus*, ' a Slav captive '—the Common-Noun
derivative from *Sclavus* (' a Slav '), itself from late Greek
Sklabos or *Eskbabenos*, ' a Slavonian, one of the Slavonic race
captured and made a bondman ' (Skeat); the Medieval Latin
name for ' the country of the Slavs ' was *Sclavonia* or *Slavonia*,
once restricted to a district in Austria (compare *Jugoslavia* and,
in Rumania, the township of *Slavitesci*). I surmise that the
Greek *Sklabos* (*Sklab* + the agential *-os*) was originally an
echoic word, imitative, in its radical, of the speech of the Slavs
with its ' fondness ' for the *sk* hard-hissing sound.

sleazy, in ' sleazy cloth ', means ' flimsy; lacking in firmness '.
Webster, noting it to be an English dialectal word, compares

407

dialect *sleaze* or *slease*, ' to part asunder, said of badly woven
cloth '. The term has been included, for there is, as W has
remarked, assimilation to the obsolete *Sleasy*, Silesia, ' as in
Sleasie or Silesia linen cloth (Blount, 1670) '—although only
doubtfully identical with it, *Sleasy linen* not being noticeably
sleazy.

smart alec(k). ' He was a little tired of this unending persecu
tion by smart-aleck students who acted as if they knew more
than he did,' Sinclair Lewis (castigator of **Babbitts** and ' smart
alecs '), *Gideon Planish*, 1943. Originally *smart Aleck*, the phrase
neatly deflates the know-all ; this it commenced to do ca. 1870 ;
it reached England in the 1920's. There's no particular reason
why it should be *Alec* and not, say, *Archie*.

smellfungus, which is obsolescent, and has always been literary,
for a discontented grumbler, an ill-tempered fault-finder,
commemorates Sterne's description, in *A Sentimental Journey*,
1768, of Tobias Smollett, who, two years earlier, had published
a captious work entitled *Travels through France and Italy*. Sterne
attributes ' the spleen and jaundice ' to the robust Smollett,
in this instance, not unjustly. The name implies an addiction
to unpleasant habits.

smith-and-wesson or **smith & wesson** = a Smith & Wesson
revolver, much used by officers in the war of 1914–18 and by
others since those far days. It has to some extent superseded
the **colt.** Daniel Wesson (1825–1906) and Horace Smith,
American inventors, devised in 1854 a new repeating-action for
pistols and also rifles ; in 1857 they founded the Smith &
Wesson Company at Springfield, Mass., to manufacture the
new type of firearm.
    ' Tim Smith '—a gangster gang-killed on June 26, 1928—
' is credited with the statement : " Smith and Wesson made all
men equal ",' E. D. Sullivan, *Look at Chicago*, 1929 ; ' Joe was
a . . . relic of a bygone day, when a fellow who packed a pair
of brass knuckles was a hard egg, and a Smith & Wesson was a
deadly arsenal,' Fred D. Pasley, *Al Capone*, 1931.

smouch, (v.t.) to obtain illicitly, (v.i.) to cheat or swindle, with
a derivative *smoucher*, one who does or practises any of these
illicits, comes from *Smouch*, a Jew, apparently a variant of the
synonymous *Smous* or *Smouse*, from Dutch *Smous*, ' a German
Jew ' (Sewel, 1708), identical or at least cognate with Yiddish
schmus, patter, profit, from Hebrew *shmuoth*, news, tales

' Sewel explains *smous* as formed from *Moses*, with which it has at any rate been associated ' (W).

snark is an imaginary animal, deriving from Lewis Carroll's *The Hunting of the Snark*, 1876; one variety of this charmingly nonsensical creature is the *boojum*. The word *snark* blends ' *snake* ' and ' sh*ark* ': Lewis Carroll excelled in these blends or portmanteau-words.

snider. ' The other was a light and extremely handy Snider— " a tarnation smart shooting-iron ", as one of the station hands, who hailed from the Great Republic, had admiringly expressed himself,' ' Rolf Boldrewood ', *Ups and Downs: A Story of Australian Life*, 1878.—' I thought the boy was busy with some new design which would . . . make our name as famous as Mannlicher or Snider,' Mary Fitt, *Death on Heron's Mere*, 1941.

Not, as the hasty of judgement have often assumed, a German make of rifle. The *Snider rifle* (a breech-loader) was, ca. 1850, invented by the American Jacob Snider († 1866) and, ca. 1860, adopted by the British government.

soccer—compare **rugger**—is the ' Oxford *-er* ' perversion of *association*, or rather of the italicized portion of ' as*soci*ation ', in *Association Football*. The spelling *socker* is unreasonable.

Socrates; Socratic. ' When Plato described thinking as a " dialogue of the soul with itself ", he meant . . . that it was a process of question and answer, and that of these two elements the primacy belongs to the questioning activity, the Socrates within us,' R. G. Collingwood, *An Autobiography* (perhaps the most stimulating autobiography published in this century), 1939.

Plato was a pupil of the philosopher Socrates (470?–399 B.C.), who developed *the Socratic method*, a carefully evolving series of questions and answers, designed to evoke a lucid, consistent expression of some opinion or belief supposed to be known, even if only implicitly, by every thinking person. The Athenian government, fearing his influence, caused him to commit suicide, the human race having an apparently ineradicable tendency to crucify its greatest men.

sod, sodomite, sodomy. The first is short for the second, and both the second and the third have, via French, been derived from *Sodom* (as in *Genesis*, xviii–xix), from Greek and Latin *Sodoma*, from Hebrew S'*dōm*. *Sodomite* and *sodomy* are, in literary and cultured English, preferred to the legal *bugger* and *buggery*;

sod is colloquial in the 'homosexual' sense, slang when used as an almost meaningless term of abuse for a man—as, indeed, is *bugger* also. (*To sod about*, to play the fool, derives from the noun.) Hastings's *Encyclopaedia of Religion and Ethics* has some salutary things to say on the theme.

Sodom and Gomorrah has long been held to typify cities that are 'sinks of iniquity and vice—especially of unnatural vice', Sodom of male (see the preceding entry), Gomorrah of female vice (in the 16th–early 17th Centuries, a *Gomorrhean* was, sexually, a **Lesbian**). *Genesis*, xix, 24–25 : 'Then the Lord rained upon Sodom and upon Gomorrah brimstone and fire . . ., And he overthrew those cities, and all the plain, and all the inhabitants of the cities, and that which grew upon the ground' : hence the synonymous phrase, *the Cities of the Plain*. Even in Biblical times, Sodom and Gomorrah bore a figurative meaning : see, e.g., *Jude*, 7, and *Revelation*, xi, 8.
  'This', says a fanatical missionary concerning the outbreak of war in 1914, 'is the awful result of the world's sin. Europe is like the cities of the plain . . . those places of pleasure. London and Berlin, Sodom and Gomorrah,' F. Brett Young, *The Crescent Moon*, 1925.

Sodom apple is another name for Dead Sea fruit. See preceding entry.

sodomite and **sodomy.** See **sod.**

Soho is used figuratively for (*a*), the foreign part of central London, hence (*b*), for the cosmopolitan, semi-artistic, semi-underworld society frequenting the bars and restaurants in that quarter ; the former sense has been current since ca. 1685, the latter only since ca. 1840. Although the word has an Italian ring, it is not Italian at all ; it may, not quite inconceivably, have originated in some wit's application of *soho!* to the district.

solander, in full *solander box* ; originally *Solander box* (a book-shaped box for pamphlets, maps, etc.), was named after Daniel *Solander* (1736–82), that Swedish botanist who instructed English botanists in the Linnaean system.

solandra, a shrub, is named after the *Solander* mentioned in the preceding entry. He accompanied Sir Joseph Banks on Cook's *Endeavour* voyage (1768–71) ; from 1760 he passed most of his life in London.

410

solecism. 'Under Croesus the Lydian kingdom practically covered all [Anatolia] west of the Ha ys (*c.* 550 B.C.), but its power lay on the Aegean lowland at Sardis; and primitive tribes survived unconquered in the Tauric basin of Caria, Lycia, and Pisidia—making fine mercenaries for the Greeks, and causing great trouble to the Romans as Soli[1] pirates'; footnote 1: 'Soli (from which we get our word *solecism*) was actually in Cilicia, but was the headquarters of the pirates, perhaps as a good *food* base,' Lionel W. Lyde, *The Continent of Asia*, 1933.

Solecism represents the Greek *soloikismos*, from *soloikos*, 'speaking incorrectly'—originally, like an inhabitant of *Soloi*, a settlement, later a town, of Athenian colonists.

Cf. **barbarism, laconic, patavinity, tatar.**

solfatara, a volcanic vent, derives its name from *Solfatara*, a sulphurous volcano situated near Naples, and that place-name has been formed from Italian *solfo*, itself from Latin *sulfur*, sulphur.

Compare **pozzolana.** Pozzuoli stands but half a mile to the west. This region is famous for its sulphur springs, frequented by sufferers from skin-diseases.

solferino, or *solferino red*, was originally *Solferino red*, a bluish red discovered soon after the battle of *Solferino* (1859); Solferino, in Lombardy, witnessed the defeat of the Austrians by the Franco-Sardinian army.

Compare **magenta** for the semantics, **solfatara** for the etymology.

Solomon means, literally, '(the) peaceable': Hebrew *Shĕlōmōh* (from *shalom*, 'peace') became, in Greek, *Salōmōn* or *Solomōn*, which repeated themselves in Latin; the *Sol-* form won to dominance. (Webster.)

'Solomon is singled out for his wisdom, but *Proverbs* and *Wisdom*, which bear his name, are now of the Greek age,' Stanley Cook, *An Introduction to The Bible*, 1945. In 1 *Kings*, iii, 28, we read that 'All Israel heard of the judgment which the king had judged' in that little matter of the two women claiming to be the mother of the baby; 'and they feared the king: for they saw that the wisdom of God was in him, to do judgment'; in iv, 29–32, 'God gave Solomon wisdom and understanding exceeding much [i.e., great, profound], and largeness of heart . . . And Solomon's wisdom excelled the wisdom of all the children of the east country, and all the wisdom of Egypt. For he was wiser than all men . . . and

411

his fame was in all nations round about. And he spake three thousand proverbs,' some of which, by the way, were of Egyptian origin (*teste* Stanley Cook); and compare x, 6-9.

'Solomon . . . King of Israel (c. 973–c. 933 B.C.) . . . Under his rule Israel rose to the height of its greatness; noted for his wealth and his wisdom,' Webster BD. The 'wisdom' factor has yielded the rare adjective **solomonic.**

Solon. A wise statesman, a most judicious lawgiver: thus in Britain. In the United States of America, however, journalists apply it to any member of Congress—and to almost any lawyer, as in ' Ah, your precious law, and its prissy procedure! How you Solons complicate the simple things of life!': S. S. Van Dine, *The Gracie Allen Murder Case*, (English edition) 1938.

Solon, ' the revered father of Athenian laws ' (as Plato called him in *The Symposium*), born ca. 640 B.C., was an aristocratic Athenian, who lived to a ripe age and an even riper wisdom: he gave to Athens its essential constitution and a noble, most charitable and enlightened set of laws: he was also a great economist and the first Attic poet. (For an excellent brief account, see T. R. Glover's *The Ancient World*, 1935.)

solutrean or **solutrian** (or S—) is the term applied to that archaeological and cultural period which, a division of the Upper Palaeolithic—or Later Old Stone—Age, comes between the **aurignacian** and **magdalenian.**

It takes its name from the cave of *Solutré*, near Mâcon, in the French *département* of Saône-et-Loire; there, discoveries of flint implements, of a sort constituting a cultural entity, were made.

' Through the Solutrean and Magdalenian periods the reindeer preponderates among the animals. The cold became more intense, stunting vegetation. Mammoth, rhinoceros, horse, ox and bison became more rare . . . There remained tigers and bears,' S. E. Winbolt, *Britain B.C.*, 1943.

Compare also **acheulian** and **azilian.**

somerset, a padded saddle—especially for a one-legged rider, was so named because Lord Fitzroy Somerset (1788–1855), 1st Baron Raglan, commander of the British forces in the Crimean War, used a saddle of this kind; one was exhibited at the Great Exhibition at the Crystal Palace in 1851. The same Baron survives also in the **raglan.**

sontag is a woman's crochet'd or knitted jacket that has long ends crossing over the front and tying at the back: and (compare **Jenny Lind** in the secondary list) it commemorates Henriette

412

Sontag (1806–54), a German operatic coloratura-soprano singer, ennobled in 1826. In 1828 she married Count Rossi.

sophism, sophist, sophistry. The etymology is suggested in ' the agile acrobatics of the Sophists ', to quote a neat phrase used by C. M. Bowra in *Sophoclean Tragedy*, 1944. The first two words have passed through Latin and then French on their way to us from Greek; the third is a Modern Languages formation from the second. A *sophism* is Greek *sophisma*, and *sophist* is Greek *sophistēs*, originally ' one learned in some art or skilled in some craft '; both of these terms derive from *sophizein*, ' to render wise or intelligent or clever, hence to devise ', from *sophos*, ' wise ', which goes back to an Indo-European root meaning ' intelligent—literally, clear-seeing '. The Sophists were, from ca. 450, the professional teachers of oratory and politics in Classical Greece: and from the ingenuity, sometimes the disingenuousness of their arguments, comes the use of *sophist, sophism, sophistical, sophistry,* in relation to unscrupulously clever arguments and argumentation. Even *sophistication* and *sophisticated* owe something to the bad reputation of the later Sophists. Not that all Sophists were unscrupulous or over-ingenious, some being very able thinkers, such as Protagoras, Hippias of Elis, Prodicus of Ceos.

' It [a certain, very general kind of psychology] is actually teaching that there is no difference between the pursuit of truth, or science [not merely Natural Science], and the pursuit of falsehood, or sophistry,' R. G. Collingwood, *An Essay on Metaphysics*, 1940.

> ' Fears of a rebuff or a maladroit reply
> Nourished a tough membrane of sophistication
> And threatened the gradual atrophy
> Of the most delicate centres of integration '
> (Ronald Bottrall, *Farewell and Welcome*, 1945.)

sorghum, a syrup, is made from *sorgo*, or saccharine sorghum. The genus *Sorghum* contains more than thirty species of grass, the best known being the common sorghum. Now *sorghum* is modern Latin for Italian *sorgo* (Indian millet), which comes from Medieval Latin *surgum*, a shortening of *suricum*, this last being apparently a corruption of *Syricum*, ' of *Syria* ' (Greek *Suria*).

soubise may be either a cravat popular in the latter half of the 18th Century and probably worn by Charles de Rohan (1715–87), Prince de *Soubise*, or a white, or brown, sauce containing onions sliced or purée, named in honour of the same great aristocrat, a distinguished military leader and general, who became, in 1758, a Maréchal de la France through the influence of Madame de Pompadour (see **pompadour**).

Compare **bechamel**.

sousaphone. 'By sheer force of volume does the band in the Cafe of the Winds transcend the normal . . . . . . And always, at the base of everything, you are aware of the Sousa-phone; . . . a booming tonal blunderbuss; a tortuous tunnel of shimmering brass emitting sounds of unimaginable pro-fundity,' Gerald Kersh, *Men Are So Ardent*, 1935.

> 'Inflate the sousaphone! percuss the drum!
> Subject the zither to intensive twanging!
> Let friction fry the urgent harpist's thumb!
> Accord the double-bass a super pranging!'
> (Commander Justin Richardson,
> *The Phoney Phleet*, 1946.)

This large tuba takes its name from John Philip Sousa (1854–1932), American bandmaster and composer, known as 'The March King': he composed numerous marches, from the *Semper Fidelis* in 1888, through *Stars and Stripes Forever*, 1897, to *The Free Lance*, 1906. He enjoyed—literally enjoyed—his tremendous success both at home and abroad.

spa. 'Th' English Bath and eke the German Spau,' Edmund Spenser, *The Faerie Queen*, 1590 (cited by W).

Spa, as it is now written, is a resort in what is now Belgium. '*Spa*, town, . . . province [of] Liège, . . . has long been famous for its mineral springs—chalybeate, sulphureous, and acidulated. Peter the Great of Russia built the pump-room over its principal spring, the Pouhon, in 1717. Since that time Spa has been one of the most frequented of mineral watering-places, and has given its name as a generic term for mineral springs everywhere' (Chisholm)—for example, Leamington Spa.

spagnicoletta, spagniletta; more generally, **spagnoletta** or **spagnoletto.** 'An old Italian round dance probably related to the pavan . . . . . . By its name'—Spanish—'it may have been borrowed from Spain—probably at the time when Spain held Naples' (Dr Percy Scholes).

spaniel derives from the Old French *espagneul* (modern French *épagneul*), literally 'Spanish' (Latin *Hispaniolus*); *espagneul* is

414

short for *chien espagneul*, 'Spanish dog'. *Hispaniolus* is the adjective from *Hispania*, Spain, itself from *Hispani*, that people which was mentioned by Livy and Tacitus and Suetonius; the Greek *Hesperia* ('most western country') may be cognate; or the origin of *Hispani* may be the Phoenician *sapan* or *span*, 'a rabbit'.

Spartacist, which, in derivative use, might well be written *s*—. 'The Sealand kings eked out a dissident existence among the canebrakes and mudflats of the Persian Gulf, an almost impenetrable wilderness whence rebels and Spartacists have always been able to hurl defiance at the central government, until the reign of the thirteenth Kassite king, Burna-Buriash I (probably 1521–1503 B.C.), who sent his younger son, Ulam-Buriash, against them with an army' (Patrick Carleton, *Buried Empires*, 1939), some 1400 years before the historical Spartacists, led by *Spartacus*, a Thracian gladiator, who, in 73 B.C. escaping from a school of gladiators, was joined by many slaves and desperadoes, opposed the Roman armies for a successful two years, ending with his defeat by Licinius Crassus: a struggle often, though carelessly, named 'The Servile War'. In 1918, Karl Liebknecht and others organized a political party on extreme socialist lines; they called themselves 'the Spartacists' or 'the Spartacus Party (or Union)'.

spartan, n. and adj.; **spartanism** (preferable to *S*—).
'He's a spartan: he takes a cold bath throughout the winter.'
'That's spartan, not to say drastic, treatment!'
Of 'the more icy parts' of Thoreau's philosophy, Robert Louis Stevenson († 1894) once said, 'He was affecting the Spartanism he had not; and the old sentimental wound still bled afresh, while he deceived himself with reasons' (Preface to *Men and Books*).
The rulers of Sparta, the capital of Laconia in the south-east of the Peloponnese, possessed the strongest army in Greece in the 6th–4th Centuries B.C.: and this military excellence was achieved by a most rigorous regimen, after the weakling children had been discarded and the others subjected to an ascetic upbringing and a strict gymnastic training; to the latter, even girls were subjected. In spartanism resides the germ of much that was typical of the Germany of 1933–40. Sparta was a good place to live away from.
The Spartans ultimately derive their name from the Cadmean legend of the sowing of the dragon's teeth (see **Cadmean victory**: secondary list): the five survivors generated the

415

five tribes of early Sparta. They were the five 'sown men':
hoi Spartoi, from Greek *spartos*, 'sown or scattered', itself from
speirein, 'to sow' (grain), 'to sow or plant (a field)'.

spencer, a short jacket, without skirts, worn by men; a similar
jacket for women; also a kind of 18th-Century English wig.
The man's jacket was either first worn or at least introduced by
George John Spencer, Earl *Spencer* (1758–1834); the wig was
probably named after Charles *Spencer*, 3rd Earl of Sunderland
(1674–1722); and the woman's garment derives, not as one
might think, from the man's but from Mr Knight *Spencer*, who
flourished ca. 1803 (OED). The two nautical *spencers*, a life-
belt of the early 19th Century and a sort of fore-and-aft sail,
mentioned by R. H. Dana in *Two Years before the Mast*, 1840,
were almost certainly named after their inventors, but those
inventors have been 'lost in obscurity'.

Spenlow and Jorkins, used in the late 19th–20th Century for
two persons that constantly shift each his own responsibility on
to the other, may be seen in Dickens's *David Copperfield* (1849–
50) as that firm of proctors in Doctors' Commons to whom
David is articled. There, Jorkins is a mild, self-effacing man,
and Spenlow, not so mild, nor so retiring, makes of his reported
intractableness a pretext for refusing every such request as it is
inconvenient either to the firm or to Spenlow to grant.

Spenserian; spenserians. The latter is also called *the
Spenserian stanza*, the metre in which *The Faerie Queene* is
written: eight iambics of five feet, rounded off with an iambic
of six feet, the verses rhyming *ababbcbcc*. The adjective
Spenserian, therefore, covers metric, style, outlook, and so forth.
Edmund *Spenser* (1552–99), was the greatest non-dramatic poet
between Chaucer and Milton, yet the term *Spenserian* is too often
taken to mean 'academically poetic' or 'suitable only to other
poets'.

sphinx. ' " I'd seen nothing, heard nothing and knew nothing.
You understand, don't you, mister? . . ." " Surely, Phil.
Maybe if I'd stood in your shoes I'd have made the Sphinx
sound like a loud speaker ",' David Hume, *Five Aces*, 1940.—
' Put [the name of] that Miss Herongate down also, Squire.
Sphinxes are always interesting until you find there's nothing
behind the smile,' J. J. Connington, *Jack-in-the-Box*, 1944.—
' What kind of damned woman was this? What was the secret
of this Succubus, this mirage, this Sphinx . . . words failed
Chinchilla,' Gerald Kersh, *An Ape, a Dog and a Serpent*, 1945.

416

The modern sense, 'enigmatic person', owes much to the Sphinx of Egypt as well as to that Sphinx (literally 'the Strangler') which, a monster woman-headed and bodied as a winged lion, plagued Thebes until Oedipus, prototype of riddle-solvers, solved its riddle: 'What is it that walks on four legs in the morning, on two at noon, and on three in the evening?' If the implied 'day' be understood as 'the period of human life', the answer is 'man': as a baby he crawls on all fours; in his prime, he walks normally; as an old man, he uses a stick or a crutch. 'Just another story' from Greek mythology.

spinach came to England from Old French *espinache* or *espinage*, with which compare Spanish *espinaca* and the Italian *spinace*. Thus far, certainty. Then the etymologists part company, several proposing an Arabic or a Persian origin. But W has probably hit the mark when he says, 'It may be connected with *Hispanicum olus*, Spanish herb (16 cent.); compare Old French *herbe d'Espaigne*, "spinage" (Cotgrave, 1611)'.

spinet we owe to Old French *espinete*, 'a paire of virginalls' (Cotgrave). The word appears to be derived from the name of its inventor, Giovanni *Spinetti*, who, flourishing ca. 1500, was a Venetian manufacturer of musical instruments. The spinet, by the way, is not the early oblong form of the pianoforte.

spinnaker is 'said to have been a fanciful formation on *Spinx*, mispronunciation of *Sphinx*, the name of the first yacht which commonly carried the sail' (OED): because she was, at first, something of a mystery, as owner knew and seamen felt. With the mispronunciation, compare *Fish* for *Psyche*. The owner may have been influenced by the nautical *spanker*, as W suggests.

spitz is a shortening of *Spitzenberg* (or -*burg*) *apple*, occasionally called *Spitzbergen apple*. It grows chiefly—and best—in the region between the Delaware River and Massachusetts Bay. The correct and original form was *Esopus Spitzenberg*, because a seedling was discovered on a hill at Esopus, New York State; the *Spitzenberg* part of the name is Dutch *spits*, pointed, hence a point, and *berg*, mountain. (Webster.)

spode. 'The plate—Nora's precious Spode—crashed on the floor' (Ellery Queen, *Calamity Town*, 1942). *Spode* or *spode* is that sort of porcelain which, consisting of paste made of bones as well as of feldspar, was devised in 1800 by Josiah *Spode* (1754-

1827), the English potter of Stoke-on-Trent. It was he who so notably improved the old willow pattern.

spoonerism. ' . . . Dr Spooner and his bread. " My bread, I think " (sticking his fork into something). " No, my hand," said the lady. I am not going to indulge in " Spoonerisms ", of which I verily believe " Kinkering kongs " is the only true one. That was current in 1884, since which I do not believe the good man has ever been guilty of another ' (the Rev. James Adderley, *In Slums and Society*, 1916).

The Rev. W. A. Spooner (1844–1930), of New College, Oxford, and long its Warden, is said to have often fallen into this sometimes comical transposition of the initial syllables, or other syllables, of two words—occasionally of more than two words. The transposition must be accidental. Spooner has had deliberate imitators; some of them, saucily ribald.

spruce is a corruption of *pruce*, occurring ' in many names of commodities brought over by the Hanse merchants (*beer, board, leather, fir*). Current sense '—both of the adjective and hence of its derivative, the slang verb (to *spruce up*, make oneself smart)—' apparently from use of *spruce leather* in dress ' (W). The old *pruce* = *Pruce* = Prussian.

Squeers is often employed allusively for a somewhat shady headmaster of a school, especially a private school. He comes from Dickens's *Nicholas Nickleby*, 1839.

stakhanovite. One who practises *stakhanovism*, a voluntary efficiency-system among workmen; operated by teamwork, improved technique, competitions, bonuses. Named after a notable Soviet coalminer, Aleksei *Stakhanov*.

' Hard work, like sheep-shearing and cane-cutting, for him is an athletic performance, but he is a poor Stakhanovite on race days,' John Green (' Thoughts on the Australian Character ') in *The Listener*, January 15, 1948.

stambouline, the frock-coat of the (former) Turkish official, obviously comes from *Stamboul*, the Turkish name of Constantinople. Or rather, *Stamboul* is both the old and the new European name, the Turkish being *Istanbul*, which constitutes a Turkish corruption of the Greek *eis tēn polin*, ' into the city '—Istanbul being the great and ancient seaport affording entry into the city-state of Byzantine times. See **Byzantine.**

stanhope, a single-seated, high-set pleasure carriage, was named after an English clergyman, Fitzroy *Stanhope* (1787–1864), for whom originally it was built. The *Stanhope lens* and the *Stanhope press* was invented by the 3rd Earl *Stanhope*; Charles Stanhope (1753–1816) was not only a democrat but a notable scientist, one of the earliest to investigate electricity and the inventor of a tuning-instrument.

It was the 5th Earl *Stanhope* (1805–75) after whom the plant and flower *stanhopea* was named : Philip Henry Stanhope, the historian. The tradition of aristocratic science, as exemplified in the Cavendishes, the Orrerys (especially Robert Boyle), the Stanhopes and others would appear to have died out.

steel. See **Bastille.**

steenkirk or **steinkirk.** 'When the gentlemen-warriors were seen with disordered ruffles after Steenkirk, the fops of London took to wearing their ruffles in exquisite disorder,' Gerald Kersh, *An Ape, a Dog and a Serpent,* 1945.

Voltaire says that ' the looseness of the *cravate à la Steinkerque* imitated the disorderly dress of the *maison du Roi,* household troops, going into action hurriedly ' (W). In 1692 the French defeated at Steenkirk (literally ' stone church ') the English and their allies.

steeplejack is a Jack—a chap, fellow, or ' guy '—that works, especially at repairs, on steeples, chimneys and similar perpendiculars. Cf. **lumberjack.**
See **Jack.**

steinberger (a very fine type of hock) is the adjective formed from *Steinberg* near Wiesbaden in the Rheingau, Germany ; the following noun (*Wein,* wine) is omitted and the adjective becomes a noun, as in so many German names for wines and beers.
Compare **johannisberger.**

steinkirk. See **steenkirk.**

stellenbosch is a late 19th–early 20th-Century term for ' to relegate (an Army officer) to a post where his incompetence will be rendered innocuous or at the least inconspicuous '. *Stellenbosch,* in Cape Colony, was—so it is said—used for this purpose during the Kaffir Wars. Perhaps it was ; but the military sense is a mere continuation and special application of the South African custom, strongly established before 1797 (Lady Anne Barnard's *South African Journal*), of treating Stellenbosch much as the English treat Bath, Cheltenham,

Leamington Spa, Tunbridge Wells : as a place of easeful retirement for a not excessively impoverished old age. And why not? Stellenbosch lies in a very fertile valley, long since noted for its wines and its fruit.

sten. Short for *Sten gun*, a light-weight machine gun or, rather, machine carbine, cheap to manufacture, crude in make, and lacking in delicate accuracy, yet easy to handle and quite effective at short range.

From the initials of the two English inventors' surnames : *S* and *T*; plus the *-en* of **Bren,** or perhaps ' *Eng*land ', the latter being the more probable. The inventors were Sheppard and Turpin.

stentor; stentorian; stentorphone. ' " Hooray ! " bellowed a stentorian voice. " A new shipmate, lads ",' Harry A. Franck, *A Vagabond Journey around the World*, 1910.

A *stentor* is a protozoan with a *trumpet*-shaped body, or a howling monkey ; *stentorian* usually goes with *voice* or *lungs* or *trumpet*, and it means ' extremely loud ; or capable of powerful utterance '; *stentorphone*, an electrical device for increasing sound, especially the sound of the human voice.

In *The Iliad* (V, 785) we meet with a Greek that was cursed with a voice as loud as that of fifty men : a herald in the Trojan War.

stepney; steponey, stepony, etc. A summer drink, made from raisins with sugar and lemon-juice added for sweetness and freshness, very popular ca. 1650–1810. Lexicographer Blount in 1656 affords the key—drunk ' in some places of London in the summer-time '. Stepney is a very old district of London ; one of the divisions of the Tudor Hamlets borough.

stetson = a *Stetson hat*; a hat made by Messrs J. B. Stetson : a man's hat of much the same build as the slouch hat worn by ' Anzacs ': of a soft felt; wide-brimmed; nonchalantly rakish. Among American tramps, by whom it is called a *J.B.*, the stetson is ' prized because the band may be sold for half a dollar ' (' Dean Stiff ', *The Milk and Honey Route*, 1931).

Stiggins. ' You may cheerfully go and lose all your money on a racecourse backing " dead 'uns " and the law will not turn a hair. But just let Stiggins get a whisper of a game of " chemmy " anywhere in Mayfair, or Regent's Park, and it will not be long before Nemesis descends upon you,' Sidney Felstead, *The Underworld of London*, 1923.

Mr Stiggins is one of the less likable characters in Dickens's *The Pickwick Papers* (1836–37): this pious humbug and hypocrite, this godly drunkard, is there discomfited.

stilton is short for *stilton*—originally *Stilton*—*cheese*. Stilton is a parish, formerly a market-town, in Huntingdonshire—in the eastern Midlands. 'Stilton gives its name to a well-known cheese, originally and still made in Leicestershire. In the middle of the 18th Century the cheese made by a Mrs Paulet of Melton Mowbray, was sold by her relative, Thornhill, the jockey, at the Bell Inn, Stilton, and the position of the village on the Great North Road . . . extended the reputation which the quality of the cheese deserved' (Chisholm). Literally, *Stilton* means 'quiet settlement or hamlet'.

stockholm was originally, often it still is, *Stockholm tar*, so named because this tar, made by the peasants from resinous pinewood and much used in cordage and in shipbuilding, has for centuries been exported from Stockholm.

stogie or **stogy.** 'He took out a cigar, bit off the end, and then he started chewing lustily on the stogie,' Richard Sale in *Detective Fiction Weekly*, May 29, 1937. In short a cigar—properly, a long, rough, cheroot-like cigar. But *stogy* also means a rough, heavy boot (labourer's or farmhand's joy).

Both terms were originally *stoga* (cigar, boot), which represents *Conestoga*, a town of Pennsylvania. Perhaps the drivers of *Conestoga wagons*—a typically Pennsylvanian vehicle—'favoured' the cigars and the boots: 'Thousands upon thousands floated and poled their way down the Ohio, after having crossed the mountains on foot or in Conestoga wagons,' James Truslow Adams, *The Epic of America*, 1933. It is hardly irrelevant to note that Pennsylvania, as a whole, is a somewhat Germanic state, for Germans like their cigars and their boots to be strong. So do the miners of that state.

stoic; stoical; stoicism. 'Budge doctors of the stoic fur,' Milton.

The origin of the Stoic philosophy is touched upon in the following quotation from Dr W. W. Tarn's *Hellenistic Civilisation*, (revised edition) 1930:—'The philosophy of the Hellenistic world was the Stoa; all else'—including the Cynics and the Epicureans—'was secondary . . . . . . Zeno came to Athens after 317 and began to teach in the Painted Porch, the Stoa . . . . . . Very different [from Epicurus] was the gaunt ascetic Phoenician who founded the Stoa, Zeno of Citium in

Cyprus, the noblest man of his age . . . . . . The striking decree which accompanied the honours voted to him after death ended with the words, " He made his life a pattern to all, for he followed his own teaching ".'

The *Stoa Poikilë*, or Painted Colonnade (*stoa* being the Greek for a colonnade), stood in the market-place at Athens ; it was fresco-adorned by celebrated artists, including Polygnotus ; these frescoes represented the fall and destruction of Troy.

stovaine is a local anaesthetic discovered in 1903. The word has ingeniously been formed, on the analogy of another anaesthetic, *cocaine*, by turning the first syllable of its French discoverer, *Four*neau's name into the English translation of French *four*, i.e. furnace or *stove*, which in combination becomes *stov*.

strad, stradivarius. The former is colloquial for the latter, which is short for ' a violin made by the Stradivari family ' : Antonio (1644–1737) and his sons, Francesco (1671–1743) and Ombono (1679–1742). The Stradivari lived and made violins at Cremona in north Italy.

Compare **amati** and **guarneri**—and the generic **cremona** ; the Stradivari were perhaps the best, as they are probably the most famous of the three great violin-making families.

' The varnish is of that rich red which [Antonio] Stradivarius used in his best period after he had abandoned the yellow tint copied by him at first from his master Amati,' L. Meade Falkner, *The Lost Stradivarius*, 1895.

strass, a brilliant lead-glass used to make imitation gems, derives from the name of the inventor of the process, an 18th-Century German jeweller, Joseph *Strasser*.

strathspey. This, the national slow—as the reel is the quick—dance of Scotland, takes its name from Strathspey, where apparently the dance originated. (*Strathspey = strath*, ' a wide valley ' + *Spey*, the river thus named.) There is no good reason to doubt this etymology, for the earliest recorded form, *stravetspy*, may be a printer's error or the author's idiosyncrasy.

street arab. See **arab.**

Strega. ' He found a table near one of the heating stoves and ordered a *caffè latte* and a Strega. The spirit he drank at a gulp,' Eric Ambler, *Cause for Alarm*, 1938. ' One of the more popular liqueurs made in Italy ' (André Simon).

A trade-name with a pun on Italian *strega*, ' sorceress '; as though Strega were ' *the* enchantress '.

Strephon, a lover, wooer, swain, strictly a rustic one or at least one in rural surroundings, comes from Sir Philip Sidney's prose romance, *Arcadia,* published posthumously in 1590 : there, Strephon the shepherd's lament for his lost Urania introduces the story. The name has been formed from *strephōn,* the present participle of the Greek *strephein,* as in *hippous strephein,* to guide horses.

strepyan is a learned adjective, meaning ' of the stage of palaeolithic culture represented by remains found at *Strépy* in Belgium ' (COED Supplement, 1944), a small town fifteen miles north-west of Charleroi.

strontia, strontian; strontium. The chemical element *strontium* has been named after the Scots village of Strontian, where there are deposits of strontium salts. The ecclesiastical parish of Strontian stands near the head of Loch Sunart in Argyllshire, and strontianite was discovered there in 1790— *strontianite* being native strontium.

The modern painters, remarks Thomas Bodkin in *The Approach to Painting* (revised edition, 1945), ' have undoubtedly woven harmonies which the ancient masters could never have attempted without the use of . . . cadmium red, oxide of hydrated chromium green, aureolin and strontian yellow. These new harmonies differ from, but are not necessarily better than, the old ones.'

stroud, a coarse woollen material, hence a blanket or garment used in 18th–early 19th Centuries for trade with the Red Indians, as in ' We'll unload the supplies we've got aboard for you . . . Blankets, strouds, guns, powder . . . Tobacco and Brazil tobacco. Some shirts and kettles ', a reference to the year 1813 in Nard Jones's very instructive, and equally readable, novel, *Scarlet Petticoat,* 1942, comes from *Stroud,* ' the centre of the Gloucestershire woollen manufactures ' (Chisholm). And *strouding* is another name for the material; used sometimes as an adjective.

Struldbrug. In his youthful 89th year, George Bernard Shaw once remarked that he feared a few more years might possibly see him become an incipient Struldbrug. (*The Observer,* July 21, 1946.)

In Swift's *Gulliver's Travels,* 1726, the Struldbrugs were those

423

beings who, never dying, remained at the stage of a non-Shavian, i.e. of a miserable and decrepit octogenarian, pensioned by the state and socially, intellectually, spiritually useless. Even in the 18th Century, the word was employed allusively.

Like Swift's other arbitrary neologisms, *struldbrug* yet has a basis in echoic realism : its cragginess evokes the cragginess of the human head in advanced age. Cf. **brobdingnagian** and **lilliputian.**

stuartia is a plant of the genus *Stuartia*, named for John *Stuart* (1713–92), Marquis of Bute—the 3rd Earl. He was the Scottish favourite of George III and Prime Minister in 1762–63.

stygian ; Styx. ' I didn't think it at all likely that Mr Wainwright was the other side of the Styx,' Dan Billany, *The Opera House Murders*, 1940.—*A Houseboat on the Styx*, by John Kendrick Bangs : a fantasy : 1896.—' The Stygian pool of a hideous immorality,' Dean Farrar, *St Paul*, 1879 (OED).

> ' The other side the reedy Styx ;
> Beyond the setting sun ;
> Is there our Beaune of 'twenty-six ;
> Our hock of 'twenty-one?
>
> *   *   *   *   *
>
> Be waiting, then, a book in hand,
> When Charon bears me in his boat,
> To walk with you that twilight land,
> And share your Stygian table d'hôte '

Michael Harrison, ' To Gawen Egremont Brownrigg, obiit 8. VII. 1938 ' (in *What Are We Waiting For ?*, 1939).

The ' hellish, infernal ' sense of *stygian* is dying out ; the predominant 20th-Century meaning is ' dark or gloomy, like—or as black as—the Styx ' : the river *Styx*, in Greek *Stux*, ' the Abhorrent—the Hateful—the Horrible ' : from, or cognate with, *stugein*, ' to hate, to abhor '. In Greek mythology, the Styx is the principal river of the Underworld. *Styx*, not so very oddly, was also the name of ' a little river which falls down a very lofty cliff on Mt Ardanius (modern Chelmos) in northern Arcadia ' (Harvey).

sub-artesian. See **artesian.**

suède. ' The dove suède of her slacks was tight over her thighs ' (Ellery Queen, *Calamity Town*, 1942) ; ' I gave a description to

424

the police . . . in which I said he wore dark suède gloves'
(*Sessions Paper*, February 13, 1904).

Suedette is a woven fabric imitative of suède; and *suède*,
occurring earliest in *suède gloves*—French *gants de Suède*—made
of undressed kid-skin, represents *Suède*, the French name for
Sweden. Such gloves have long been made in Sweden, but it
is to the astuteness of French manufacturers that we owe their
fashionableness.

sukey is, in English dialect, a tea-kettle, and the name clearly
constitutes a personification : *Sukey*, a diminutive of *Susan* or
Susanna.

sultan, figuratively for one who acts as though he were a *Sultan*
with a harem. See the next.—As a synonym for the colour
crimson lake, it derives from the fact that so magnificent a
colour typifies the magnificence of the former Sultans of
Turkey; semantically, the domestic fowl named *sultan* is in the
same class.

sultana, whether the raisin or the pale-yellow, seedless grape from
which it comes, or (also *sultana bird*) a purple gallinule, derives,
as does *sultana*, a king's or a prince's mistress or paramour,
from *Sultana*, the wife of a *Sultan* or ruler of Turkey or other
Mohammedan state. *Sultana* is the feminine of Italian *Sultano*,
a Sultan; and *Sultan*, an Arabic word meaning also
'dominion'. The Middle English, Elizabethan, and Old
French form of *Sultan* is *Soldan* (in French also *Soudan*).

surah is a soft, twilled silk, now used for scarves and linings, but
formerly popular for women's dresses; also *surah silk*. It takes
its name from the city of *Surat*, once very much more populous
than now : in the 17th–18th Centuries the chief port of India,
it lost its trade to Bombay. In other words : *surah* derives from
Surat pronounced French-fashion with the *t* silent. Compare :

surat. This inferior cotton cloth, usually white or near-white,
was, at least originally, made at *Surat*. See the preceding entry.

surrey, a two-seated, four-wheeled pleasure carriage, popular
during the Victorian Age, is so named because it was made in
the county of *Surrey* : compare, therefore, **croydon.** It was
introduced into the United States in 1872.

Surrey is a modernizing of *Suth Rige*, ' the Southern Kingdom
or District ' of the Anglo-Saxons. ' The name Surrey, Suth-

rige, the southern district, is there to remind us that at one time its political connexions were with the regions to the north of the Thames,' J. N. L. Myres, in Collingwood & Myres, *Roman Britain and The English Settlements*, (revised edition) 1937.

swartout, n. and v.   An embezzler (also *swartouter*) ; to abscond with money that one has embezzled.   This solely American usage, obsolete by 1870 and thereafter merely historical, derives from Samuel *Swartout*, who, having embezzled rather more than one million dollars, absconded in 1838.   Washington Irving, by using the term in 1840, made Standard American out of a journalistic colloquialism.   (DAE.)

swartzia is a plant, or its flower, of the genus *Swartzia*, tropical trees named after Olaus Swartz (1760–1818), a Swedish botanist.

swede is **Swede,** which was *Swede turnip*, which had been *Swedish turnip* (or rutabaga) : that is the ladder of ideas.   Philologically, the *Swede turnip* rung could have been omitted.
     The word *Swede* comes direct from Dutch ; compare the German *Schwede* and Old English *Sweotheod*, from the latter of which it may be a back formation.   Compare, too, the Latin *Suiones*, mentioned by Tacitus in his *Germania* (sections 44, 45).

sweet alison.   See **cecily.**

sweet william.   See **william . . .** and also **cecily.**

swiss, a mercenary ; *swiss*, Swiss muslin (compare *Swiss cambric*, a snow-white muslin) ; *swiss*, a so-called Swiss roll : all obviously derive from *Swiss*, noun and adjective for ' (a native) of *Switzerland* '.   The form *Swiss* is an anglicism for French *suisse*, itself from Middle High German *Suiz*.   The ' mercenary ' sense derives from, or rather is short for *Swiss guard*, the Swiss Guards being a body of Swiss mercenaries, formerly employed by the Kings of France and still, as a ' token force ', by the Pope.

sybarite ; sybaritic.   ' We had sailed with no extra store of sugar.   Before the end of the trip we were regretful, for our " spotted dog " puddings came from the galley as effective but unsweetened stop-gaps, not those gastronomic joys which had made us sybarites on previous trips,' Robert Harling, *The Steep Atlantick Stream*, 1946.

426

A *sybarite* or voluptuary descends, via Latin *Sybarita*, from Greek *Subarĭtēs*, an inhabitant of *Subaris* (Latin *Sybaris*), a Greek city on the east coast of Bruttium in southern Italy. Founded in the 6th Century B.C., it was, until its destruction in 510, an important centre of trade, and notorious for its wealth and luxury.

sybil.   Incorrect for **sibyl.**

syenite, anciently a species of granite, modernly (among petrologists) an intrusive igneous rock, was quarried in Classical times at *Syene* in Upper Egypt. The English term represents the Latin ' *syenites* lapis ' (stone of Syene), from the Greek *Suēnē*. Syene, now Assouan, is the site of the quarries from which, in the 18th Dynasty, the Pharaohs quarried their building-granite.

syphilis.   ' Syphilis : Mrs Grundy's Disease ' is the title of an article by Anthony M. Turano in *The American Mercury* of April 1937.
  This neo-Latin word comes from *Syphilis sive Morbus Gallicus*, ' Syphilis or the French Disease ', a Latin poem issued in 1530 and written by Girolamo Fracastoro (1483–1553), an Italian astronomer, who was in some sort a poet too, although only this work is at all generally known, even among scholars. Fracastoro made a disease out of the personal name of a shepherd hero, *Syphilus*, conceivably a name meaning ' a native of *Sypheum* ' (now Montalto), a town of the Bruttii in southern Italy, but much more probably Greek *Suphilos*, ' lover of pigs ' (*sus*, or *hus*, a pig), almost ' swineherd '. In *Traité de la Syphilis* (Paris, 1931), M. Ed. Jeanselme has established a rather good case for the view that Columbus brought this disease to Europe from the West Indies.

syren.   See **siren.**

syringa ; syrinx.   The *syringa* or mock orange takes its name from the fact that its stems, cleared of pith, were used as pipe-sticks for the *syrinx* or **Pan-pipe.**   ' The Greeks gave it the name it still bears, for they evolved the legend of the god Pan pursuing the nymph Syrinx, of her being changed in the nick of time by the Naiades into a bundle of reeds, and of the god Pan, noticing how the wind made these musical, cutting them down and playing upon them,' Percy Scholes, *The Oxford Companion to Music*, in the entry at ' panpipes '.

427

T

tabasco, a pepper sauce, comes from *Tabasco*, a trade-name for a sauce made from a species of capsicum. That trade-name was evidently suggested by *Tabasco*, a river and a Gulf-littoral State in Mexico: in that region, this particular capsicum abounds.

Note: *Tabasco mahogany* is more usually called *Honduras mahogany*.

tabby. As short for *tabby cat, tabby* is ineligible; but as ' an old or an elderly unmarried woman ', it may derive, not from *tabby(cat)*, but from *Tabitha*, which, as Captain Francis Grose noted late in the 18th Century, was already ' a formal anti-quated name '. As an early name of the dress fabric now called ' taffeta ', *tabby* represents French *tabis*, Old French *atabis*, which comes from Arabic '*Attabi*, that quarter of Baghdad where originally it was made—the quarter at first peopled by the *Attabs* or members of the Ommiad family, as Webster has pointed out.

Tadpole; tadpoleonic. The latter is a humorous derivation, on the analogy of *Napoleonic*, from the former. In Disraeli's *Coningsby*, 1844, Tadpole and Taper are scheming political nonentities: and that is the allusive sense of both of these terms, the one from *tadpole*, incipient frog, the other suggestive of a *tapering-off* into nothing.

[**tagetes** is a plant, or its flower, of the genus *Tagetes*, strongly scented tropical American herbs with gaudy flowers. By the fact that Late Latin *traganthes* was misread as *tagetes*, we get a second-hand association with Latin *tageticus*, ' belonging to Tages '—that literally earth-born grandson of Jupiter who became an Etruscan divinity.]

taglioni = *Taglioni great-coat*. Fashionable ca. 1825–50, this type of overcoat took its name from the ballet-dancing family famous in the earlier half of the century; the most famous was Marie Taglioni, whose career lasted from 1822 (at age eighteen) until 1847.

' I saw it was what is commonly termed, I believe, a Taglioni —there was velvet about it, and a silk lining,' *Session Paper*, May 16, 1842.

428

Taj Mahal, literally ' Crown of the Palace ' (which had been one of the living woman's titles), the mausoleum Shah Jehan (Akbar's grandson) erected in 1632–50 to commemorate his departed and beloved wife, has for at least two centuries constituted as much of an emblem as the Parthenon : the acme of ornate memorial architecture in marble : so that one not seldom meets with such phrases as ' the Taj Mahal of architectural elegance ' or ' the Taj Mahal of romantic architecture ', for ' the supreme statement made by man of the mysteries of love and death ' is indescribable in its loveliness and its significance. The famous Rajput marble has been used to such effect that this ' exquisite elegy ', this ' Bubble in Marble which we call the Taj Mahal ' most happily exemplifies the dictum that those who ' designed like Titans finished like jewellers ' and fully merits the description ' a great ideal conception which belongs more to sculpture than to architecture '. It adorns the already lovely city of Agra, ' the residential capital of the Timurid monarchs ever since the days of Babur'. (F. Yeats-Brown, *Indian Pageant*; *The Cambridge Shorter History of India*; E. B. Havell's *A Short History of India* and his *Agra and the Taj*; and L. W. Lyde's *The Continent of Asia*.)

' He was like a man who had been told to make his will in the Taj Mahal. He found it hard to concentrate,' Peter Fleming, *A Story to Tell*, 1942—and how well he tells it !

alapoin, the smallest of the guenon monkeys of West Africa, has yellowish whiskers on a black face : and it brought to the mind of some explorer or scientist a memory or a picture of the Buddhist monks of Indo-China, the *Talapoins*, whose name has come, via Portuguese *Talapoes*, from Talaing (a Burmese language) *tala poi*, ' our lord '.
  Compare **capuchin.**

albot, a dog of a breed now extinct, or a figure representing such a dog, may—probably it does—derive from the famous *Talbot* family, in whose armorial bearings the figure of a dog occurs. The Talbots were originally a Norman family ; they appear in Domesday Book, and the Earl of Shrewsbury and Talbot is the premier earl in England.

albotype is a photographic technicality, otherwise known as ' calotype '. It has been named after W. H. F. *Talbot* (1800–77), an English photographer. Compare **daguerreotype.**
  ' Photography originated as a method of recording silhouettes and the structure of leaves by the action of light upon paper

429

soaked in silver nitrate. Then came the Daguerreotype, with a metal plate as a basis. The Talbotype process followed, in which the first " negatives " and " positives " played their part. Then came the collodion " wet-plate " method, which demanded the use of a portable dark-room. . . . In 1871 a gelatine dry plate with a gloss backing was invented; and thereafter photography as a pastime spread into wider circles,' A. W. Stewart, *Alias J. J. Connington*, 1947 (a few months after his death).

tallboy, in the 17th Century a tall drinking-glass, in the 18th-20th Century a high chest of drawers, is what it seems, a jocosity: *tall boy*. But probably the choice of the term was in part suggested by the surname *Tallboys*, from French *taillebois*, ' a hewer of wood '. (W.)

talma has, since ca. 1815, signified a voluminous cape or a short loose, cape-like outer coat. It commemorates a French actor as famous as Coquelin. François Joseph *Talma* (1763–1826), having made his début only two years earlier, achieved fame in 1789 in Chénier's *Charles IX*. He excelled in tragic and historic roles and won the friendship of Napoleon.

tam o'shanter. See **tammy.**

tambookie or **tambouki,** a South African large shrub or small tree, hence its very light, cork-like wood, derives, as also does the tall and handsome *tambookie grass*, via Afrikaans from *Tembu*, the name of a Kaffir tribe that inhabits the region between Cape Province and Natal, a region known as *Tembuland*.

Tammany; tammanyism. ' W.P.A.—the Modern Tammany ': title of an article by Albert Jay Nock in *The American Mercury* of October 1938.—' The small political bosses in country villages and small towns were but Tammany bosses writ small,' James Truslow Adams, *The Epic of America*, (revised edition) 1938.

Tammany, the New York political society, has long had a ' boss ' system, occasionally interrupted by reforms; in the 20th Century it is virtually synonymous with political corruption—or, at best, an unwarrantable domination of the vote by political bosses.

Tammany, who flourished towards the end of the 17th Century, was a famous chief of the Delaware Indians. He became the patron saint of the anti-British, then of Democracy

430

and finally of the Democrats; founded in 1789, the Tammany society was, by 1850, the New York stronghold of the Democrats. (*The Oxford Companion to American Literature.*)

tammy; tam o'shanter; tam. The second is Standard English, the third is colloquial, the first slang. ' She was a study in brown. On her head was a brown tam,' Freeman Wills Crofts, *The Pit-Prop Syndicate*, 1922.

In full, *Tam o'Shanter bonnet* (or *cap*), the headgear is named after the hero, anglicé Tom of Shanter, in Robert Burns's poem, *Tam o' Shanter*. Formerly a characteristic of Scottish ploughmen, it became, ca. 1887 in Scotland, the wear of factory girls, then of other Scottish girls, then of English girls, then—well, you know how it goes.

Tanagra = *T. figurine* or *T. statuette*, a statuette made of terra cotta found in tombs near Tanagra, a Boeotian town (now Grimadha) of Classical Greece; or of that type. Famous for their delicate grace and exquisite charm.

' The little clay figures they '—the Ancient Greeks—' used as we do china ornaments put to shame some of the most ambitious efforts of modern sculpture. Who . . . would not rather look at a Tanagra statuette than at the equestrian statue of the Duke of Wellington? ': G. Lowes Dickinson, *The Greek View of Life*, 1896.

' I began to compare her beauty with that of a Greek head on a vase, saying that hers was a cameo-like beauty, as dainty as any Tanagra figure,' George Moore, *Memoirs of My Dead Life*, 1906.

tangerine, the reddish sweet orange with easily detachable rind, is, like *Tangerine*, ' a native or inhabitant of Tangier '. *Tangier*, incorrectly *Tangiers*, locally *Tanja*, is that Moroccan seaport which stands at the western entrance to the Strait of Gibraltar and thirty-five miles south-west of Gibraltar itself. The Roman *Tinge* or *Tingi*, Byzantine Greek *Tingis*, now a mere ruin some three miles east of the present city, constitutes the effective origin of the name *Tanja* or *Tangier*.

tankard. Webster compares the Old French *tanquart* and Middle Dutch *tanckaert*, and then says ' Of uncertain origin '. W, however, noting the Medieval Latin *tancardus*, remarks, ' I take it to be a jocular metathesis ' or transposition ' (? due to the fame of the Crusader *Tancred*) of Latin *cantharus*, [from] Greek *kantharos*, suggested by the personal name *Tankard*, once

common and still a surname . . . This is Old High German *Thane-ward*, literally thought-keeper.'
Compare **bellarmine, goblet, jug, puncheon, toby.**

tantalize; tantalus; tantalum. The Greek-mythological *Tantalos* (in Latin, *-us*), the father of Pelops, for one of three sins (the gods have it every way, as the Greeks were among the earliest to notice)—serving his son's flesh as food for the gods, or purloining their nectar, or disclosing their secrets—was penalized: in Hades, he was set, hungry and horribly thirsty, in a pool of water that ever receded as he made to drink; a pool o'ershadowed by trees that, wind-tossed, proved successfully elusive when he went to pluck their fruit. Hence it is hardly surprising that *tantalize* is ' to play tormentingly with a person's apparently reasonable and encouraged expectations '; *tantalus* is that type of spirit-stand in which the decanters are alluringly visible—but locked up (oh! so near, yet so far); *tantalum* is a chemical element—to the everyday world, that rare metal used for the incandescent filament you may have noticed in electric lamps. This element, discovered in 1802, was given its name because of ' its incapacity, when immersed in acid, to absorb any and to be saturated ' (OED); the ore in which it resides is **tantalite.**

' The Banquets of Tantalus ' is an essay in Osbert Sitwell's delightful book, *Sing High! Sing Low!*, 1944.

tantony is usually apprehended as *tantony pig*, i.e. an *Anthony pig* (now current only in English dialect), the smallest pig in a litter. **Saint Anthony** is the patron saint of swineherds.

A secondary dialectal, little-known meaning of *tantony* is ' a hand-bell ', probably from a swineherd's use of one for calling his charges to their meal, but probably from the fact of ' the emblem of [St Anthony] being a bell at his tan-staff, or round the neck of his accompanying pig ' (*The English Dialect Dictionary*).

Taper; sometimes *taper*; incorrectly *tapir*. See **Tadpole.**

Tapley. See **Mark Tapley.**

[**tarantass,** that Russian low, four-wheeled carriage which, when snow falls, is mounted on a sledge, represents the Russian *tarantas*, perhaps originally a now forgotten spelling of a Russian place-name. ' From Tyoorkish ', says W.]

tarantella (the Italian and more usual word; also **tarantelle,** which is bastard French for *tarentelle*); **tarantism; tarantula.**

432

The relation of these three terms one to another, and their origin, have been so deftly and lucidly set forth by Dr Percy Scholes in his *The Oxford Companion to Music* that it were fatuous impertinence to do other than quote him.

' In the heel of Italy is the seaport Taranto. In the surrounding country is found a spider, hence called the Tarantula. The bite of this spider was supposed to cause a certain disease, hence called Tarantism [Italian *tarantismo*]. The malady was supposed to be curable by the patient's use of a particular very lively dance, hence called Tarantella.' Dr Scholes adds that perhaps ' the spider and the dance were independently named after their place of origin '; and probably *tarantism* was independent of the *tarantula*, for this hysterical malady prevailed in the 15th–17th Centuries in, and in the hinterland of *Taranto*, yet one of the symptoms was, in fact, a craving, a mania, for dancing, and the lively dance was widely reputed to be an infallible cure for the disease.—In short, popular belief in Italy, although it may have produced a prettily inter-linked set of folk-etymologies, was not far wrong in its folklore. What emerges as indisputable is that, immediately or ultimately, all three terms derive from *Taranto*, which, by the way, derives from Latin *Tarentum*, which derives from Greek *Taras* (accusative *Taranta*).

ardenoisian (or **T**—) designates a transitional period between the Old Stone and the New Stone Ages. ' La Fère-en-Tardenois is on the Aisne, west of Rheims. This and the succeeding stage, the Maglemosian, are held by some to belong to the New Stone Age. The first remains of this culture were found at La Fère-en-Tardenois and at Martinet, Lot-et-Garonne,' S. E. Winbolt, *Britain B.C.*, 1943. Many archaeologists suppose it to have been a fishing culture.

armac. See **macadam.**

aroc; but usually **tarot.** The former shows the Italian influence : *tarocchi*, ' (the cards of) the Tarot pack ' of playing cards used by the gipsies in fortune-telling : 78 cards, of which 22 are trumps (see *The Greater Trumps*, by Charles Williams, 1932) : compare German *tarock*, ' one such card '. The English *tarot* shows the influence of the Old French *tarau* or *tarault* (modern French *tarot*), ' one such card '. A game played with this pack is, in English, *tarots*.

All the great lexicographers have cited one or two or all of the Continental forms mentioned above and then gracefully retired with a dismissive ' Of unknown origin ' or ' Origin obscure '.

Now, in a Tarot pack, the additional cards represent powers friendly or, still more of them, unfriendly to man.

The gipsies, chief users of these cards, came to Europe from Egypt. The word, therefore, may originate either in the land of the gipsies' origin, India, or in the land where they sojourned so long, Egypt. The languages of India yielding nothing germane to my purpose, I consulted Wallis Budge the famous Egyptologist's *An Egyptian Dictionary* and there I found *tar*, ' a specific fiend ', and, better still, *taru*, which he defines as ' fiends, demons, devils, enemies '. Some of the gipsy ' powers and dominions ' controlling the fate of men were precisely that : and the cogency of the relation of French *tarau* to Egyptian *taru* needs no further emphasis. (See the essay ' Neither Cricket nor Philology ' in *A Covey of Partridge*, 1937.)

tarragona = *Tarragona wine*, a Spanish port-like wine.
' Tarragona [province], though mountainous, is very fertile, and produces quantities of wine and oil, the wine specially round Tarragona itself . . . . . . The old city of Tarragona occupies a typical cone-hill (550 feet) overlooking the sea ; the new one, which has been provided with a good artificial harbour, is famous for its underground wine-cellars, one of the typical exports being the " Grande Chartreuse " liqueur,' Lionel W. Lyde, *The Continent of Europe*, (4th edition) 1930. In Latin : *Tarraco*, genitive *Tarraconis*.

tartan, in Middle English and Old French *tartarin* and in M.E. also *tarterne*, was originally ' a rich material imported from China via Tartary . . . . . . For later application to a coarser material compare *buckram, camlet*, etc.' : thus W, who goes on to note that in the will of Lady Clare (1360), the significant variant *tartayne* occurs.

tartar, as in *catch a tartar*, is the child born of a marriage between two members idyllically suitable to each other : a *Tartarean*, a she-devil of *Tartarus*, or Hell, and a looting, rampaging *Tatar* of the Middle Ages. Or if you prefer it, the word *Tatar*—the correct, the original, the Persian spelling—has been influenced by the *Tartarean* associations and philological form. In either case, the result is that a figurative *tartar* is a savage, intransigent, intractable male or female (those medieval and early modern Tatar horsemen-soldiers really were—in the transatlantic idiom—' tough babies ') ; and if you *catch a tartar*, you encounter someone who is not merely superior to you but who is violently or startlingly so.

For the origin of *Tata* or *Tatar* or *Tartar* in its ethnic sense,

434

there is an illuminating parallel in 'barbarian' (see the **barbaresque . . .** entry). The immediate origin of the *Tata* or *Tatar* tribesmen is constituted by their descent from the *Tata* Mongols.

artuf(f)e; Tartuf(f)ism. 'Odious Tartuffes endowed with all the vices,' Henry de Monfreid, *Hashish*, 1935.

Molière spelt it *Tartuffe*, but the 'official' spelling is *Tartufe*. In *Le Tartuffe* (1664), Jean Baptiste Poquelin (1622–73), who called himself Molière, made his principal character an odious creature named Tartuffe: this hypocrite, affecting an unctuous piety, worms himself into the household of one Orgon, attempts the seduction of Madame Orgon and, repulsed, tries to involve the entire Orgon family in ruin. Hence, he personifies a treacherous hypocrisy (*Tartuffism*).

atar. See **tartar.**

auchnitz, as used for a cheap, paper-covered reprint in English, especially if issued on the Continent of Europe, derives from *Tauchnitz*, a reprint issued by the publishing firm of *Tauchnitz*, operating in Leipzig. The 'Tauchnitz Edition' of *A Collection of British and American Authors* began publication in 1841. Karl Christian Traugott Tauchnitz (1761–1836) founded the printing business; his son, Karl Christian Philipp (1798–1884) continued it; the latter's nephew, Christian Bernard Tauchnitz (1816–95), founded the publishing house in 1837; the Tauchnitz family retired from the business in 1865, but the good old name was retained.

awdry is aphetic (i.e., lopped of the first syllable) for *St Audrey*, the St Audrey of *St Audrey's lace*, which was sold at *St Audrey's fair* held at Ely, of which she was the patron saint, as also were necklets (often of *lace* and either bone or wood), in memory of the fact that St Audrey, i.e. *Etheldreda*, Old English *Aethelthryth*, regarded that tumour in her throat of which eventually she died as a punishment for her youthful love of necklaces. The semantic step is explained by the showy effect of much lace and by the ease with which lace becomes torn or soiled.

eddy. 'He went to Ethel's room and came back with a heavily fringed and embroidered georgette teddy,' Ben Reitman, *Sister of the Road* (the famed 'Box-Car Bertha'), 1941. This is explained by 'Vi was still fully dressed, wrapped tightly in her teddy-bear coat,' Gerald Kersh, *Night and the City*, 1938, and by :—

435

teddy bear. 'An elderly man appeared—a weather-beaten but perfectly intelligent person named Ikey—who . . . walked Ludgate Hill in the Teddy Bear interests,' A. Neil Lyons, *Clara*, 1912.—'A young man in a black Homburg and a teddy-bear coat came swaggering up Piccadilly,' James Curtis, *They Drive by Night*, 1938.

Originally *Teddy bear*, this name for a toy doll or mascot, shaped as a bear and coated with rough plush, arose ca. 1906; the object bears a humorous reference to Theodore (familiarly *Teddy*) Roosevelt (1859–1919). President of the United States in 1901–07 and a mighty hunter of bears and other big game, he once took a number of baby bears to the Bronx Zoo.

telford is an adjective applied to a road that has 'a surface of small stone rolled hard and smooth, distinguished from macadam road by its firm foundation of large stones with fragments of stone wedged tightly in the interstices' (Webster). Named after a Scottish civil engineer: Thomas Telford (1757–1834). Contrast **macadam.**

tellurium. This, one of the rarer chemical elements, was discovered in 1798, i.e. four years before **selenium.** Its discoverer, Klaproth, probably gave it this name in contrast to **uranium,** which he had found in that epochal year, 1789. From Latin *tellus* (genitive *telluris*), the Earth; or rather, from *Tellus*, who in Roman mythology was the Earth-God, closely associated with the religious cult of the soil—with agricultural ceremonies.

Cf. **selenium** and **helium.**

Tennysonian, literally 'of, or in the manner of, Tennyson' (Alfred Tennyson, 1809–92, laureate from 1850), tends to mean the opposite of what we understand by *Browningesque* and to connote a skilful metric subserving a pretty-pretty subject-matter, a strait-laced morality, the traditional, a deeper love for Nature than for man, the essence of Victorianism: a singularly false conception.

tequila. 'You may find *mescal* and *tequila*—the two varieties of intoxicating liquors distilled from the *maguey*, or aloe—to drink,' *Harper's Magazine*, 1882 (DAE). It is a spirituous Mexican drink of the brandy type and very seductive and wit-scattering: and the name derives from *Tequila*, a small town in Mexico.

terai. In Lionel W. Lyde's *Asia* we come upon the phrase, 'a noisome belt of *Terai* swamp'; and upon the sentence—the reference being to Nepal—'Even the *Tarai* is not so unhealthy as elsewhere, and it is very productive, *e.g.* of rice and cane-sugar'. Famous among big-game hunters, the Terai is that huge and marshy jungle belt which, from the Jumna to Assam, runs along the base of the Himalayas, between the foothills and the plains. Thence comes *terai*, a felt hat, wide-brimmed and often double-crowned, that, in sub-tropical country, is worn by white men.

terbium. One of the elements. (Cf. **erbium, ytterbium, yttrium.**) It is metallic and rare, and it appears to have been discovered in 1843; its earth is **terbia.** The name is a modern-latinizing of the Swedish place, 'Yt*terby*'.

termagant, now only a virago but formerly any brawling or turbulent person, derives from *Termagant*, who, idol or deity, was, in the ancient morality plays, represented as a Mohammedan deity, loud-voiced, overbearing, tumultuous. Middle English affords the variant *Tervagant*, from Old French *Tervagan* or *Tervagant*. Old French also has *Trivigan* or *Trivigant*, with which compare Italian *Trivigante*. The anterior history of the word is obscure; but it does seem that *Tervagant* may be a metathesis of *Trivigant*, that the French springs from the Italian, and that *Trivigant* may derive from Latin *trivigens*, 'thrice-flourishing; thrice-vigorous'—as vigorous as any three ordinary persons rolled into one.

Terpsichore; terpsichorean. The latter, 'connected with belonging to, dancing', is merely the adjective of the former. In Greek mythology, *Terpsichorë* is one of the Nine Muses: the Muse of the Dance. Her name combines *terpsis*, enjoyment, delight (from *terpein*, to gladden or delight) with *choros*, dance or dancing. Derivatively, small-initialled *terpsichore* signifies either a dancer or dancing.

tewke. See **tuke.**

Thalia, thalian. Thalia was, in Greek mythology, the Muse of Comedy and, less notably, of bucolic poetry, and in Greek her name is Thaleia, 'the Blooming', cognate with Greek *thallein*, to be luxuriant. Whereas the derivative *Thalian*, 'pertaining to Thalia', is ineligible, most eligible is *thalian*, 'pertaining to comedy as a dramatic form; comic'.

Thames on fire, not to set the, to do nothing very wonderful or startling, to succeed only moderately in life, appears earliest as

437

set fire to the Thames; another early variant was *burn the Thames*. Similar phrases are those enlisting the Liffey and the Spree. W has quoted from the German of Nigrinus, ca. 1580, a sentence one may translate as ' He has set fire to the Rhine and the sea '.

The general semantic idea is that of performing a miracle : men have, we are told, walked upon water ; none has yet set fire to it (sophistries about oil burning on the surface of the sea, apart).

Thebaïd, Thebaïs ; thebaïne. The first is sometimes employed allusively for a long, dreary epic poem, after the *Thebais* by Statius—in Latin and published ca. A.D. 92—and might therefore be written *thebaïd*. The second, preferably written *thebaïs*, may denote a district inhabited by saints, hermits, ascetics, from Latin and Greek *Thebais*, the district surrounding *Thebes* (now Luxor) in Upper Egypt ; there dwelt many Christian saints and ascetics in the 3rd–5th Centuries. The third term, *thebaïne* is in modern chemistry a poisonous alkaloid and it has changed the sense of *thebaïne*, an Egyptian opium made at Egyptian *Thebes*, which, as a word, derives from Latin *Thebae*, from Greek *Thebai*.

theodolite. The origin is obscure, but W has provided us with what may well be the correct explanation. ' It is just possible ' he writes in his fascinating, far too little-known dictionary, ' that Digges '—Leonard Digges (d. 1571), mathematician, seems to have invented and named this surveying instrument—' for some fantastic reason now unknown [compare **syphilis**], named the instrument after the famous Old French theological poem called the *Tiaudelet*, translated from the Late Latin *Theodulus* of the 9th Century.

thersitical or, less usually **thersitean,** means ' loud-mouthed and foul-mouthed ' and comes from *Thersites*, the ugliest-looking the most scurrilous of the Greeks besieging Troy. He reviled even Achilles and Ulysses : going too far, he was slain by Achilles. The English use of *Thersites*, hence of the adjective owes something to the unsavoury presentment of his character by Shakespeare in *Troilus and Cressida*. Literally, his name signifies ' the Audacious '.

Thespian. See the John Ross quotation at **transpontine** ' Arnold Spence was knighted . . . eight years ago. He' . . . the greatest Shakespearian Thespian who ever trod the boards. When you think of Hamlet you think of Arnold Spence,' Richard Sale in *Detective Fiction Weekly*, March 5, 1938

Thespis is a semi-legendary figure, a poet of Icaria in Attica, and he flourished in the latter half of the 6th Century B.C. He is reputed to have introduced into performances hitherto given by only a chorus an actor representing an historical or a legendary person and to have toured the country with his plays.

Probably *Thespis* is an assumed name: Pickard-Cambridge proposes its origin in *The Odyssey*, I, 328–29, where θέσπιν ἀοιδὴν means 'inspired songstress'.

thibet. See **tibet.**

Thomas, doubting. 'Camlet's middle name is Thomas, so he managed to get a look at her car to check her tale,' J. J. Connington, *Jack-in-the-Box* (1944), in reference to a sceptical detective inspector.

St Thomas doubted the resurrection of Christ: 'Thomas . . . was not with them when Jesus came. The other disciples therefore said unto him, We have seen the Lord. But he said unto them, Except I shall see in His hands the print of the nails . . ., I will not believe. And after eight days again . . . : then came Jesus . . . . . . Jesus saith unto him, Thomas, because thou hast seen me, thou hast believed: blessed are they that have not seen, and yet have believed' (*John*, xx, 24–29).

The name *Thomas* derives, via Greek, from Aramaic, in which language it means 'a twin'.

Thomas Atkins. See **Tommy.**

Thor, hammer of, or **Thor's hammer; thorite; thorium.** A flint axe or hammer; a black, hard, compact Norwegian mineral; a rare metallic element found in thorite: Thor + *ite*, *ium*, as in other metal-names.

All from the Norse deity *Thor*, the god of thunder; a god weaponed with a hammer; the strongest and the bravest of the Scandinavian deities. The name itself signifies 'thunder'; and *Thursday* is *Thor's* day.

'No one before Becquerel ever dreamed of radio-activity, and yet it had been going on all the time in thorium and uranium,' J. J. Connington, *Jack-in-the-Box*, 1944.

thrasonical, boastful', is a literary word, now used by few except those who have received, or given themselves, a Classical education. *Thrason* is a bragging captain in Terence's *Eunuchus*; his name is Greek, from *thrasus*, bold. Compare **Bobadil.**

439

'Caesar's thrasonical brag of "I came, saw, and overcame",
Shakespeare, *As You Like It.*

Throgmorton Street is often used allusively, especially by
Londoners, for 'dealings on or with the Stock Exchange'
(situated there), hence for 'speculation in stocks and shares'.
The Street was named after Sir Nicholas Throgmorton (1515–
71), soldier and diplomat.

thug, in the 20th Century often colloquial for a merely 'tough
guy' that, though fundamentally a 'decent chap', is useful in
a 'rough house' ('He's a bit of a thug'), and in mid-19th–
20th Century a Standard English term for a criminal rough, an
assassin, derives from *Thug*, a member of the *Thugs*, a fraternity
that, in India, made a profession of murder by strangling
(*thuggee*, the Thugs' practice of murder and robbery). Worshippers of Kali, they were suppressed by the British ca. 1835.
The term *Thug* comes, via the Hindustani debasement of a
Prakrit word, from Sanskrit *sthaga*, a rogue. The Hindustani
thag, a swindler, was used, as a euphemism, instead of *p'hansigar*,
strangler. (Webster and W.)

Thule; thulium. See **Ultima Thule.**

Tib. 'Thou art the damned doorkeeper to every coistrel that
comes enquiring for his tib,' Shakespeare, *Pericles*, IV, v, 165–66.
    Tib is the pet-form of *Isabel.* Compare *tib-cat*, a female cat—
the opposite to a *tom*cat.

tibet or **thibet.** Properly *tibet* is a heavy stuff made of goat's
hair, but often it is an imitation thereof. Also, derivatively,
the term designates a lighter, woollen fabric. And it may be
a garment made of any of these.
    The original name was *Tibet cloth*, which, in the goat's-hair
or the woollen form, means a cloth made in *Tibet*. In the
mid-1890's Chisholm noted that 'Manufactures of woollens,
sacking, and other woven fabrics are pretty general, and much
cloth is sent from Lhasa into China'.

tiffany, a gauze fabric, originally a very thin silk but now of
muslin or of transparent lawn, comes from Old French *tiphanie*,
from Latin (itself from Greek) *theophania*, 'the manifestation of
God', perhaps with a playful reference to *diaphanous*, the wearing of tiffany being designed not to conceal but discreetly to
display.

440

tilbury. 'At ten o'clock a Tigrean askari came with a carriage to drive me to the Commissioner's house . . . . . . The Greek merchants . . . lolling on the terraces . . . looked at me in astonishment, for they were accustomed to salute this tilbury, belonging to the Commissioner,' Henry de Monfreid, *Hashish*, 1935.

'The old coach-builders showed some degree of inventiveness. The light two-wheeled tilbury was named from its designer [Tilbury of London], ... but the old slang *tilbury*, sixpence, was the fare paid to cross the Thames by the ferry at *Tilbury*. This is probably the origin of the slang *tizzy*, sixpence,' WWN.

tillandsia is a plant of the very large *Tillandsia* genus, which belongs to the pineapple family. It was named for Elias *Tillands*, a late 17th-Century Swedish botanist. One of its species is the **Spanish moss** (in the subsidiary list).

Timon, a misanthrope or an embittered, very bitterly speaking cynic, derives from the hero of Shakespeare's *Timon of Athens*, written ca. 1607, in the period of tragedies and bitter comedies. Shakespeare took part of his historical material from Plutarch's *Antony* and part from Lucian's ' Misanthropos ' in *The Dialogues of the Gods*. Timon was, in fact, a misanthrope living in Athens at about the time of the Peloponnesian War (431–404 B.C.)— enough to make any except a well-balanced man a misanthrope.

timothy (grass) ; timothy hay. The latter is the hay made from the former, a meadow grass valuable˙for forage and named after *Timothy* Hanson, who, flourishing ca. 1720, was an early and notable grower thereof ; Americans speak also of *timothy meadow*, meadowland sown therewith.

tincture of Queen Anne. See **cecily.**

Tio Pepe. 'The General knows something about sherry, and the butler promptly produced a decanter of Tio Pepe, as pale as stacked straw, dry, delicate, remotely resinous in flavour— a hint of cedar-wood, faint and fragrant,' John Gloag (who knows something about wines), *Manna*, 1940.

Tio Pepe derives from the name of the vineyard that produces it ; literally, ' Uncle Pepe '.

Titan (especially, **weary T.**) ; **titanic ; titanium.** All three words, and, obviously, their derivatives, have sprung from the mighty loins of the Titans, who, born of Heaven (*Ouranos*,

N.I.W.—P*

usually called *Uranus* : see **uranium**) and Earth (*Gaia* or *Ge* :
see **geography**), were, according to Hesiod, twelve in number,
six male, six female, the most notable being perhaps Oceanus
(see **ocean**), Cronus, Hyperion. The Titans, gods themselves
and giants, were thrust from Heaven by Zeus, but only after
a ten years' war. (There is a fascinating book to be written
on the Twelve, the Ten, the Nine, the Seven, the Three : and
the One. They dominate mythology and religion, music and
the arts.) The figurative *Titan* and *titanic*, whence the name of
a famous ship, follow obviously enough. And *titanium* is a rare,
metallic element, named in 1795 by Klaproth on the analogy of
uranium; its true discoverer was a Scottish scientist, one
M'Gregor. *Weary Titan* was a once fashionable journalistic
tag for England, as *The Sick Man of Europe* was for Turkey : the
name had been gratuitously bestowed by Matthew Arnold in
Friendship's Garland, 1871, after being used by him in *Heine's
Grave*; Arnold, unlike Meredith, admired German military
power and thought England and France, by comparison, effete.

'[Seneca] was the last of the ancient tragedians, the most
aged and withered in his titanic strength,' G. Santayana,
'Tragic Philosophy'—in *Scrutiny*, March 1936.

'*Timon*, a play whose artistic cumbersomeness joined to
titanic power might well exemplify an imperfectly objecti-
fied experience, displays a universal love of man to men,'
G. Wilson Knight, 'The Shakespearian Integrity', in *The
Burning Oracle*, 1939.

Titian hair; titianesque. Auburn hair of bright golden hue;
of or like, in the style of, *Titian*, that Venetian painter (perhaps
the finest representative of 'the Venetian school') who died in
1576 at the ripe age of ninety-nine. He excelled in frescoes,
portraits, religious pictures; and in mythological themes—
e.g., *Venus and Cupid* and *The Rape of Europa*.

Titian hair is often misused quite ludicrously : even for the
most irrefutably carroty hair. 'Her hair was of the hue sometimes called Titian, but would have made Titian weep blood,'
as Sax Rohmer remarked in *The Exploits of Captain O'Hagan*, 1921.

tityre-tu is eligible only when employed allusively for a brawling
buck molesting people in the street and not in its strict sense and
spelling *Tityre-tu*, one of a gang operating in London in the
Restoration period. It derives from 'Tityre, tu' ('O Tityrus,
thou . . .'), the opening words of Virgil's *Eclogues*, I. In
Greek (*Tituros*) and Latin verse, *Tityrus* is generic for 'a shepherd' : there was nothing rural or peaceful about these roaring
blades, predecessors of the Mohocks (see **mohock**).

442

tizzy. See **tilbury.**

tobacco, according to Skeat, Weekley, and Murray & Craigie, is respectively a Haïtine word, a term from Guarani (a dialect of Brazil), and again a Haïtine word—from the Carib tongue spoken in that West Indian island. The OED, however, does, unlike Skeat and Weekley, not only admit the possibility that *tobacco*—so far from being the Spanish shaping *tabaco* of a Haïtine word either, as one authority has it, for the tube or rudimentary pipe through which the West Indians inhaled the smoke from the ignited weed, or, as another authority has it, for a roll of dried leaves, a rudimentary cigar, smoked by them —represents *Tobago*, ' after which the herb has been said by some to be named ', but also cites Frampton's translation (1577) of *Monardes' Joyfull Newes*, a Spanish work, to the effect that ' This hearbe which commonly is called Tabaco, is an Hearbe of muche antiquitie, and knowen amongest the Indians . . . The proper name of it amongest the Indians is *Piecielt*, for the name of Tabaco is geven to it of our Spaniardes, by reason of an Ilande that is named Tabaco.' The form *tobacco*, although it did not become predominant until ca. 1660, existed as early as the 16th Century; and although the *ta-* form predominates in the Romance languages and in Dutch and German, yet in many German dialects, as in Danish and Swedish, the *to-* form has ousted the other.

' Bananas, cotton, maize, and tobacco were cultivated [in the West Indies] before the coming of the Spaniard, and he soon added sugar to the list of staple crops . . . . . . Eventually the Spaniards made use of convoys for their seasonal treasure ships. These normally entered the Caribbean Sea between Tobago and Trinidad,' Ll. Rodwell Jones in Jones & Bryan, *North America*, (7th edition) 1946.

As silk is ' the fabric of China ', indigo ' the dye of India ', peach ' the fruit of Persia ', copper ' the metal of Cyprus ', sherry ' the wine of Jerez ', cambric ' the linen made at Cambrai ', and so on, so tobacco is the product of Tobago. In default of a more convincing probability, this, I hold, is the most probable explanation of the origin of *tobacco*.

oby; toby jug or **mug; toby collar.** The first is (i) short for the second and (ii) found mostly in *tickle one's toby*, to thrash someone, where *toby = Toby = Tobias* (*Tobi-as*: hence, *Tobi = as*: hence, *toby*, ' arse '). A jug is called *toby*, originally *Toby*, for much the same reason, or lack of reason, as other vessels are called *jeroboam* or *tankard*: mere personification. *Toby Fillpot* (or *Philpot*) is an elaboration. A *toby collar* or *toby*

443

frill derives from Punch's dog *Toby*, usually represented as wearing a frilled collar.

todea; a single plant of the genus *Todea*, ferns of Africa and Australasia, has been named after H. J. *Tode* (1733–97), a German botanist. The botanist's *Todea superba* is known to the ordinary New Zealander by the aptly descriptive name, ' crape fern '.

tokay = *T. wine*. ' The vine is associated with the volcanic banks [of Lake Balaton], *e.g.* at Tokay and round Buda(-Pest), where the light drift-sand that covers the volcanic subsoil has been found curiously unfavourable to the phylloxera ': thus Lionel W. Lyde (*Europe*, 1913), concerning Hungary's most famous wine. Concerning an imitation, he remarks that ' " Tokay " is made from the vineyards near Kaschau and Munkacs ' in Czecho-Slovakia.

toledo is generic for a sword with a very finely tempered blade, as were those which used to be made at *Toledo*, some forty miles south-south-west of Madrid : an ancient city, important as *Toletum* under the Romans, it was medievally and still in the 16th–18th Centuries famous for its sword blades.
Compare **bilbo.**

tolu is short for *tolu balsam*, earlier *Tolu balsam*, earliest *balsam of Tolu*, said to have come from *Tolú* (now Santiago de Tolú) in Bolivia. This balsam is obtained by cutting into the bark of the *Tolu tree*, a leguminous tree of tropical South America ; the balsam was famous in England as early as 1673 (OED).

Tom has become generic in many senses because, like *Jack*, it is so common a pet-form of so common a male given-name. It occurs both by itself, e.g. *tom*, a *Tom*-cat, a tom-cat, and slang *tom*, a prostitute, perhaps from *tomboy*, and in combination, e.g. *tomtit*: compare *jackdaw* ; *tomboy*, a girl that is like a *Tom*, a boy ; *tomfool*, originally *Tom Fool*—compare *tomnoddy*, *Tom Noddy*. See also the latter part of the entry at **Thomas, doubting.**

Tom, Dick, and Harry. ' Man is the subject of the Greek drama ; the subject of the modern novel is Tom and Dick,' G. Lowes Dickinson, *The Greek View of Life*, 1896—probably in reference to the sociological novels of the 1890's.
Pet-forms, diminutives, of three of the five commonest given-names of England, they particularize ordinary people, common

place people, and not only commonplace men as distinct from humdrum women.

tomfool. See **Tom.**

Tommy, a British soldier of the Other Ranks, especially a private, is the pet-form of *Thomas Atkins*, generic for a soldier since 1815, when first it appeared as a specimen name on Army forms of application, much as *Richard Roe* and *John Doe* were in Law.

As *tommy*, food, originally bread, the term was probably suggested by the 17th–18th-Century *brown George*, military slang for a coarse loaf. Food can be obtained ' on the slate ' or, as we now say, ' on the cuff ', at the derivative *tommy shop*.

tommy gun is the slangy but very general form of the *Thomp*son sub-machine gun, invented by J. T. Thompson (1860–1940) of the U.S. Army with the aid of John Blish of the U.S. Navy, and popularized by the Chicagoan gangsters of the Prohibition era (1920–33). It is shorter, more compact than, say, a **lewis**; it can be handled by one person and fired, either from the hip at speed or from the shoulder at leisure. It's a sweet weapon to handle.

' I'd had enough experience back in Chicago when Pareto and his mob were shooting it out with cops, but they had used tommy-guns,' G-man *loq.* in John Gloag's ' thriller ', *Documents Marked " Secret "*, 1938.

tommy shop. See **Tommy,** 2nd paragraph.

tomnoddy. See **Tom.**

tommyrot was earlier *tommy(-)rot*, at first *Tommy rot*, or perhaps *Tommy Rot*, a personification: compare *hell and Tommy* (or *tommy*), an elaboration of *hell*. Jules Manchon, *Le Slang*, 1923, proposed the origin of the name-element of *tommyrot* in **Tommy** (above): the scarlet uniform suggests *bloody*: ' bloody rot '.

tomtit. See **Tom.**

tonka bean; tonquin bean. The latter is generally regarded as incorrect for the former, and the error caused by a false association with *Tonquin* or Tongkin(g). Webster, however, says of *tonka bean* that apparently it is a translation of Dutch *tonquin-boontjes*, the berries (*boon*, a bean; diminutive *boontje*) of a South American tree being used to mix with *Tonkin* tobacco.

tontine. This process or method of life insurance was introduced into France in 1653 by Lorenzo *Tonte*, an Italian-born banker resident in Paris. His son Henry, instead of insuring, risked his life with La Salle in his exploration (1678–83) of the Mississippi Valley.

torreya may be either the California nutmeg or the stinking cedar of Florida. There is also the *Torrey pine*. They are named after John Torrey (1796–1873), an American botanist and chemist. He collaborated with Asa Gray in the first two volumes of *Flora of North America*, 1838–43, and did much independent work in botany.

tournay, a printed worsted used in upholstery, was originally made at *Tournai*, an ancient, and for many centuries a manufacturing, city of Belgium ; noted for its tapestry and for its wool and cotton-spinning.

townsendia is a plant, or its flower, of the genus *Townsendia*, belonging to the thistle family and flourishing in the once wild west of the United States. The name commemorates David *Townsend* (1787–1858), citizen of Pennsylvania. Another American Townsend, John Kirk (1809–51), Philadelphia-born ornithologist, who rendered a selfless assistance to Audubon's *Birds of America*, assistance based in the main upon his work in Oregon in the 1830's, has given his name to a number of American birds : *Townsend's bunting—cormorant—flycatcher—fox sparrow—mocking thrush—solitaire—sparrow—*and *warbler*.

toxophilite, a devotee of archery, takes his (or indeed her) name from Roger Ascham's treatise on archery, published in 1545 : *Toxophilus* (literally, lover of the bow : Greek *toxon*, a bow + *philos*, lover), formed on the analogy of *Theophilus*—for *toxophilos* does not exist in Classical Greek.

tragopan is the name bestowed on the horned pheasant by the famous French naturalist, Baron Cuvier (1769–1832), who adopted it from the Greek, where *tragopan* denotes some now indefinable, because fabulous, Ethiopian bird. The Greek word combines *tragos*, goat, and *Pan*, the god.

transpontine. 'He was wrestling with hideous melodrama, often described to him by patrons of Thespian art at transpontine theatres' (John Ross, *Masques and Phases*, 1909): where *transpontine* may be translated ' Surrey-side ', in reference to the Thames : during the forty-or-so years ending with the

446

outbreak (1914) of the First World War, there were, on the
south side of the Thames, several theatres devoted to the most
gloriously outrageous melodrama. Literally, 'across the
bridge', the term receives a full elucidation in this passage,
spoken in 1940 by an old man, from Margery Allingham's
psychological 'thriller', *Traitor's Purse*, 1941; here its transferred sense, 'melodramatic', is clearly shown : ' I admit quite
freely that I find it very difficult to get used to this—to this
transpontine world we suddenly seem to be living in . . .
. . . Even the word belongs to another era . . . "Transpontine ". Over the bridge. Over Waterloo Bridge to the
Vic and the Surrey, the homes of melodrama. Blood tubs, we
used to call them. That's the world we're living in to-day.'

trappistine is a liqueur (omitted by André Simon) made by the
Trappist monks, whose name is occasionally employed allusively
—as in *Trappist vow*, *Trappist silence*, in reference to their observance of perpetual silence, relaxed only in choir, with confessors,
and—upon formal occasions—with superiors. This reformed
branch of the Cistercian Order was established in 1664 at the
monastery of *La Trappe* (itself founded in 1140), seven miles
north-east of Bazoches-sur-Hoene in Normandy. Compare
chartreuse.

travertin(e). 'He never afterward forgot . . . the days he
spent crawling over its '—the Pont du Gard's—' huge blocks
of travertine,' David Pilgrim, *No Common Glory*, 1941.
   Travertine derives, via French, from Italian *travertino*, itself
representing the Latin *lapis Tiburtinus*, ' stone of Tibur '—that
ancient town of Latium which is now Tivoli, near which stand
the ruins of several aqueducts, travertine-constructed.

trichi; in full, **trichinopoly.** ' While the Indian tobacco is
. . . of medium quality and largely converted into Trichinopoly cheroots, the Virginian and Kentucky product is of
excellent quality and largely converted into pipe and cigarette
tobacco,' Lionel W. Lyde, *Man and His Markets*, edition of 1919.
Trichinopoli (or -*y*), ' noted for its cigars and beautiful gold
jewellery ' (Chisholm, *Gazetteer*), is a district-headquarters town
in the former Presidency of Madras.

trilby, a soft felt hat, derives from *Trilby* as played on the London
stage rather than straight from the novel ; the latter did, however, give us, direct, the now obsolescent slang *trilbies*, feet, from
the beautiful feet of the heroine, *Trilby* (with a pun on a singer's
trills), in George Du Maurier's remarkably successful novel so

447

entitled: for several years after its publication in 1894 this picture of the Latin Quarter of the mid-19th Century was the talk of the town and the cause of many feminine and not a few male fashions. Du Maurier (1834–96), born in Paris, became a professional artist in 1856.

tripoli, a fine earth used as a polishing-powder, is so named because it is found in Syria (from the Syrian town of *Tripoli*) and in North Africa (including the region of *Tripoli*). Often written *tripela*, for instance in the third edition (1797) of *The Encyclopaedia Britannica*. Hence **tripolite,** an opal-silica variation or 'species' of *tripoli*.

Triton among the minnows. 'He was pleased to do his best. The triton condescended to conquer the minnows,' H. C. Bailey, *Rimingtons*, 1904.

In Greek mythology, Triton, son of Poseidon the sea-god, was a merman, who, not unnaturally, caused a considerable stir among the minnows and other small *freshwater* fish.

trivet. See **right as a trivet.**

troglodyte, 'a cave-dweller', comes from the Greek *trōglodutēs*, 'creeper into holes'—hence 'dweller in holes or caves'. Greek geographers bestowed the name *Trōglodutai* (Latin *Troglodytae*) upon the cave-dwellers inhabiting the western coast of the Red Sea, in Ethiopia and Upper Egypt: and our word owes as much to that fact as to the etymology of the Greek Common Noun. Strictly, those specific cave-dwellers inhabited *Trogodyte*, 'commonly misspelt Troglodyte' (W. W. Tarn).

trojan. In *to work* (or *fight*) *like a trojan*, the lower-case *t* is, I feel, preferable, even though the dictionaries do not support me in this attempt to establish the figurative sense, 'one who acts or endures valiantly—and without fuss or self-pity'.

Having spoken of the Siege of Troy, Helen Waddell (*The Wandering Scholars*, 1927) justly remarks, 'Trojan, unlike Greek, remains an adjective of unequivocal praise'.

In literature, we have the legend, various legends, of a real war. 'This real war is believed to have taken place in the first quarter of the 12th c. B.C., and Troy to have fallen somewhere about the traditional date 1184'; Troy is 'an ancient city near the river Scamander on the Asiatic shore of the Hellespont. Its site has been found at the modern Hissarlik' (Sir Paul Harvey). *Trojan* means 'an inhabitant of *Troas*': which

448

Greek word becomes *Troia* in Latin : and *Trojan* is the English
shape of Latin *Troianus*.

trollopize is an Americanism of ca. 1832–1900 : to criticize
particular persons, an entire people, as unrefined, ignorant,
ill-bred. Frances Trollope (1780–1863), wife of Thomas
Anthony and father of Anthony Trollope, accompanied her
husband to Cincinnati, Ohio, where they fared badly, and on
her return to England she published in 1832 her *Domestic
Manners of the Americans*, much resented by its victims. Hence
also *Trollope!*, ' Behave ! ' : addressed to anyone acting not
quite *comme il faut* in a theatre. The Americans, or rather the
less *comme il faut*, made rude puns upon her surname.

troy (weight). The *troy pound = Troy pound* became known in
England during the 14th Century : a French export. From
Troyes, an ancient city on the Seine : ' from weight used at the
fair of Troyes . . . Many medieval towns had their standard
weights and coins ' (W).
   The English dialectal *Troy Town*, a place—hence a state—
of confusion, derives from the Troy of *The Iliad* : there, on its
capture, reigned a state of almost incredible confusion.

trudgen (stroke in swimming) is incorrectly written *trudgeon*, for
it was originated ca. 1868 by an amateur swimmer named John
Trudgen.

truxillic; truxilline. The former, an adjective, relates to
truxilline, an alkaloid discovered at *Trugillo*, loosely *Truxillo*,
in Peru. (Webster.)

tsar. See **czar.**

tuckermanity. Extreme propriety and conventionality in literary—especially the poetic—treatment of love. An American
literary term, from those two qualities in the Petrarchan
sonnets by Henry Theodore Tuckerman (1813–71), American
essayist (*The Italian Sketch Book*, 1835 ; *Characteristics of Literature*, 1849, 1851 ; *Mental Portraits*, 1853) and poet (*Poems*, 1851).
   Formed on the analogy of *humanity* ; perhaps suggested by
Carlyle's *gigmanity* (1831).
   Compare **tupperism.**

tudor is short for *Tudor type*, a heavy and ' medieval ' printing-
type. As *Tudor* it mostly refers, outside of history and literature, to architecture, such architecture being often called

449

Tudoresque. Historically, the period was 1405–1603; owing mainly to its Elizabethan element, its influence still operates. Named from Owen Tudor of Wales, for he married Catherine, the widow of Henry V.

tuke or **tewke.** In Norfolk, ca. 1600, the following fabrics or stuffs were being manufactured : ' bays, frisadoes, naples fustians, grograynes, broad and narrow russets, serge, says, worsteds, tukes (or turks), Spanish and English rugs, Coxsall bayes ', quoted from the Lansdowne MSS by E. G. R. Taylor in H. C. Darby's *A Geographical History of England before 1800*. The implied derivation from *Turk* is disputable ; nevertheless, this fabric may well have been imitative of some Turkish manufacture—or the name *Turk* may, in accordance with commercial amorality, have been chosen for its exotic associations.

tula metal, tula work. The metal, an alloy of silver, copper, lead, is used in making niello (sometimes therefore called tula work) : the alloy was originally wrought at *Tula*, capital of the region of the same name in central European Russia—a region that is very rich in metals.

tulle, a soft, fine, net-like fabric, made usually of silk and popular for veils, scarves, dresses, was manufactured, first and for a long while, at *Tulle*, an ancient town (the *Tutela* Lemovicum of the Romans : ' the Defence of the Limovices ') in the *département* of Corrèze and some fifty miles east of Périgueux.
Compare **cambric** and **lawn.**

tupperism, the principles and practice of a *tupperian* or even of a *tupperish* philosophy, which tends to *tupperize* everything to the trite morality and mental mediocrity of *Proverbial Philosophy* (1st series, 1838 ; 2nd, 1842 ; 3rd, 1867 ; 4th, 1876), which had a tremendous success, by the complacent preacher in so-called verse, Martin Tupper (1810–89), who perpetrated many other ' crimes ' against the intelligence of mankind.

turcois. See **turquoise.**

Turk ; young Turk ; to **round Cape Turk ; unspeakable Turk.** All these (the third is slang for ' to regard women merely as instruments of pleasure ') derive, as does *turk*, a scimitar or the plum curculio (destructive insect), from *Turk*, a native of Turkey or, vaguely, a Moslem. The word seems to have reached England during the 3rd Crusade (1187–92).

The word was originally Arabic or Persian (or both) : compare French *Turc*, Italian *Turco*, and Late-Greek *Tourkos*.

turkey in Canadian slang means a lumberman's kit, bulky and awkward like a turkey long fattened for market ; in slang of the U.S.A., a pompous or haughty way of talking or walking, from the domestic manners of a turkey cock. *Turkey cock* was originally the name of the guinea cock, ' which was imported from Africa through Turkey into Europe and with which the American bird was for a time identified ' (Webster). Compare the French *dindon* (feminine *dinde*), a turkey, for the earlier and explanatory *coq* (or *poule*) *d'Inde*.

turkis is an archaic form of **turquoise**.

turkish is general for *Turkish tobacco* and *Turkish towel*, tobacco grown in Turkey, towels of a kind traditionally associated with Turkey and Turkish baths.

' He took a turkish, preferring them always to smooth ones, got his face dried, and . . . ran his eyes over the array of articles,' Rex Stout, *The Broken Vase*, (English edition) 1942.

turkois is an archaism for **turquoise**.

turneresque. ' In March, 1812, the first part of [Byron's] *Childe Harold* was published . . . The sweep of the rhetoric, its full-blooded romantic pessimism, its glowing Turneresque landscapes, all torrents and ruins, and patches of picturesque foreign colour, alike hit the taste of the time,' Lord David Cecil, *The Young Melbourne*, 1939.

J. M. W. Turner (1775–1851) began as a Classic, formal painter, but, ca. 1835, passed into his personal, his impressionistic period of poetic, dream-like themes and effects, as in *The Fighting Téméraire* and *The Sun of Venice*. Only slightly less notable is his middle period (ca. 1820–35) : therein, having eschewed the imitations of his first, he showed a new wealth, and understanding of the potentialities, of colour and began to idealize Nature ; as in *Ulysses Deriding Polyphemus*, by many held to be his masterpiece.

turpinite, the explosive (for some years the most powerful in the world), was invented, ca. 1894, by a Frenchman named *Turpin*. It was, in 1895–96, said to be so dreadful in its effects that the very fear of it would put an end to war.

turquoise is a French word, defined by Cotgrave in 1611 as ' a turqueise or Turkish-stone ', because it came, not from Turkey but from *Turkestan* (or *Turkistan*), or rather, because, although it came from Turkestan, it came through *Turkey*. The French *turquoise* is an adjective become noun, via *pierre turquoise*, the masculine being *turquois*, with variants *turcois* and (cf. the Cotgrave quotation) *turqueis*. Obsolete English forms are *turkis*, *turcois* and *turkois*.

tutania, an alloy that, consisting of tin, antimony and copper, is silvery white and much used for tableware. The word is a blend of 'tut*enag*' (a crude zinc) and 'Brit*annia*', influenced by the name of its manufacturer, William *Tutin*, who flourished ca. 1770 at Birmingham.

tuxedo, in American usage a dinner-jacket, derives from a place-name. The place occurs thus in *The Common Law*, 1911, by Robert W. Chambers (1865–1933), the very readable and, at one period, extremely popular novelist of New York society, concerning his 'hero', a fashionable painter. 'He . . . dined . . . on Fifth Avenue; he decorated a few dances, embellished an opera box now and then, went to Lakewood and Tuxedo for week-ends, rode for a few days at Hot Springs, frequented his clubs'.

In Orange County, New York State, one Pierre Lorillard in 1814 acquired a 13,000 acres estate. His grandson Pierre formed the Tuxedo Park Association, which founded the Tuxedo Club and, on June 1, 1886, opened Tuxedo Park. The Club was very smart and, for a generation, the Park was, in the main, frequented by the smart.

'Now she began to see the other kind: the Kind that Wears . . . a jimmy little Tuxedo at Night,' George Ade, *Fables in Slang*, 1899.

' " The dinner-jacket has its advantages—the Tuxedo, as an American gentleman once called it, though I've never understood why a dinner-jacket should be named after a Scottish town."—"Tuxedo is in Dixie", said Johnny humorously, "and Dixie is America's lost Atlantis",' Edgar Wallace, *Room* 13, 1924.

twaddell is 'shorthand' for *Twaddell's hydrometer*, invented, for liquids heavier than water, ca. 1830, by the Scotchman William Twaddell, of whose career little is known and who died ca. 1840.

twankay is *twankay tea*, from Chinese *Taung-kei*, a dialectal form of *Tun-ki*, that town in Anhwei province whose name means

'The Camp by the Stream'. *Tun-ki* is also the name of two streams, of which one is in the same region.

tweed; tweeds; tweedy. 'Her accent was all right, and in their rather shapeless tweedy way the clothes were substantial and of good quality,' Aldous Huxley, *Time Must Have a Stop*, 1945.
   'Originated (c. 1830) in a misreading of *tweel* [in Scott's] *Guy Mannering*, XXVI, Scottish form of *twill*, helped by natural association with the river *Tweed*, which runs through a region where the fabric is made' (W).

tycoon, an Americanism for 'an industrial magnate', comes from *Tycoon*, a foreigners' mid-19th-Century title for the Shogun of Japan. In Japanese, the word is *taikun*, which means no more than 'a great lord'.

tyrolienne was originally *danse tyrolienne*, French for 'a Tyrolese dance, or a song or a melody, characterized by the yodel, for it '.
   Compare **cracovienne.**

tzar. See **czar.**

U

uintatherium. Remains of this elephant-like extinct mammal were discovered in *Uinta* County in the State of Wyoming. The second element *therium* is 'scientific Latin' based upon Greek *thērion*, a wild animal.

ulster, a long, loose overcoat, formerly worn by women too, takes its name from the fact that originally it was made, from frieze, in *Ulster*, Northern Ireland; mostly at Belfast. The Proper Name derives from the old Irish personal name *Uladh* (pronounced *Ulla*), with ending as in *Munster*, this -*ster*, from Scandinavian *stadr*, region, being a relic of the Danish invasions (Chisholm).

Ultima Thule; thulium. The latter is a rare metallic element discovered in 1879, by Clève, in **gadolinite**; and **thulia** a rare earth : *thulium* and *thulia* are, the former adopted and the latter adapted, from *Thulium*, the modern Latin form of Classical Latin, *Thule*, which, according to Roman Pliny the Elder (d. A.D. 79), Roman Tacitus (d. A.D. 117) and—very much later—the erudite English Camden, was the Shetland Islands

453 ·

and, according to the Greek voyager Pytheas (a contemporary of Alexander the Great; his travels had been described by Polybius), was the most northerly land: *ultima Thule*, ultimate Thule, Thule the last—the most remote—of all; whence *ultima Thule* used figuratively for 'the furthest limit; the acme', as in 'the *ultima Thule* of stupidity'. The phrase, *ultima Thule*, however, occurs not in the historians but in Virgil (*Georgics*, I, 30).

'Ever since Virgil . . . its location has been a subject of controversy, and the name has existed in all the cultivated languages of the west to designate some mythical locality in the distant north, or, by metaphorical extension, some non-geographical goal to be reached,' W. W. Hyde, *Ancient Greek Mariners*, 1947.

umber. *Raw umber* and *burnt umber* are made from the brown earth called *umber*, which, as a word, derives from French *ombre*, short for *terre d'ombre*, which transliterates Italian *terra d'ombra*, which probably meant, originally, *terra d'Umbria* (Latin *Umbria*, so named from the tribe inhabiting it: the *Umbri*), a region east of Tuscany in northern Italy. There has also been some influence exercised by Italian *ombra*, from Latin *umbra*, shade.

una, a catboat, is so named from *Una*, the first boat of this sort to sail from America to England, as it did in 1853. In the 19th Century, the word was usually written *Una*, and the 1945 revision of Webster records it as *Una boat*. The feminine name *Una* is Latin, the feminine of *unus*, one: 'The One, the Unique; the sole daughter in the family'.

Uncle Sam. See **Sammy.**

undine, a female water-spirit, was, as a term, coined by Paracelsus; an addition to the sense was made by De la Motte Fouqué's German romance, *Undine*, 1814: it is to the latter fact that *undine* owes its place here. *Undina* is neo-Latin, not Classical, from *unda*, a wave.

unparliamentary language is strictly, or at least originally, language unfitting to a Member of *Parliament*—the British Parliament. The Middle English form is *parlement*, adopted from Old French, from *parler*, to speak.

uranium. Found in **uranite** and pitchblende, this rare metallic element was discovered, in or about 1790, by that great

454

scientist Klaproth.   Heavy and greyish, it is highly combustible ;
it burns with an exceeding brightness and whiteness.   It was
named after the planet Uranus (discovered in 1781), itself
named after the Greek god *Ouranus*, Latin *Uranus*, the personification of the heavens (contrast, therefore, *tellurium*) the
husband of Ge (the earth)—and the father of the *Titans* (see
titanium).

[**Urim and Thummin.**   Strictly, ineligible ; strictly, lower-
cased, the capitals arising from the fact that they were sacred
objects mentioned in The Old Testament.   Vague in use and
shape, they are sometimes employed allusively.]

Utopia ; utopian.   Literally, ' (The Land of) No-Place '—
Greek *ou*, ' not ' + *topos*, ' place ', *Utopia* has become ' the
ideal place or country ', as in ' His charting of Utopias ' : Ivor
Brown, August 18, 1946, in *The Observer*, in reference to the
then very recently deceased H. G. Wells.   And *utopian* now
means ' visionarily ideal or perfect '.   The allusion is to
Utopia, by Sir Thomas More ;   published in Latin in 1515–16,
it achieved a European fame ;   a German translation appeared
in 1524, a French in 1530, an Italian in 1548, an English not
until 1551, and a Spanish not before 1790.   More died, a
martyr, in 1535—his death, a judicial murder.
   ' I confess that I look back to the landscape of my first days
with a pleasure that should doubtless be reserved for the
Utopias of the Futurist,' G. K. Chesterton, *Autobiography*, 1936.
' There are many . . . who . . . persist in the old trade
which, throughout history, has always offered a new earth, if
not a new heaven, to peoples engaged in war.   These merchants of Utopia are disappointed by the lack of popular
response,' Charles Morgan, ' This Autumn ' (1944) in
Reflections in a Mirror, 2nd Series, 1946.

V

valance.   ' Perhaps from Old French *avalant*, . . . hanging
down, present participle of *avaler*, to go down . . .; but
probably from the town of *Valence*, France ' (Webster) ; W
prefers the former etymology, as also does The OED.   I
prefer the *Valence* origin, for the old town (Late Latin *Valentia*,
earlier *Ventia*) is famed for its manufactures.

valencia ; valencias.   The Spanish province of Valencia has
given its name both to *valencia*, a mixed and usually striped

fabric, wool as to the weft, silk or cotton or linen as to the warp, and to *valencias*, which, according to the context, may be almonds, raisins, oranges. Of the Levante provinces of Spain, Professor L. W. Lyde has said, ' All the typical crops are irrigated, *e.g.* the rice of the Valencia vegas, the dates of Elche . . ., the oranges of Castellon and Valencia, the raisins of Valencia and Denia, the almonds of Alicante, the onions of Gandia ' (*The Continent of Europe*, 1913).

' The men who knew how to grow wheat on the plains of Castile, apricots in the *cigarrales* of Toledo, oranges in the *huertas* of Valencia, did as much for the welfare of Spain as all the grand captains whose ideas began and ended with conquest,' J. B. Trend, *The Civilization of Spain*, 1944.

valenciennes. See the quotation at **cambric.** The ancient town of Valenciennes lies in the *département du Nord*, France. In 1895, George Chisholm wrote, ' The manufacture of lace, to which Valenciennes gave its name, has for the last fifty years ceased to be carried on in the town itself, which now produces lawn, cambric, hosiery . . .'
Compare **cambric, dowlas, lawn, tournay.**

valentine, a card, a gift, a set of verses, sent on St Valentine's Day, February the 14th, originally meant a person chosen, as sweetheart, on this day, when, folklore tells us, birds mated. *Valentine* is the Latin *Valentinus*, diminutive of the personal name *Valens*, ' The Strong ', from *valere*, ' to be strong '.

valerian. ' Weeds, even the tough, golden-crested boucalaun or the plumy, purple valerian, flourished amid the flowers as equals, never gaining the upper hand,' Thomas Bodkin, *My Uncle Frank*, 1941. This is the common valerian, whence the calmative drug so named. ' Apparently,' says W, ' from the personal name *Valerius* '—famous in Roman history.

valhalla, as ' temple of fame ', is in Norse mythology the hall—the place—where the souls of the valiant dead revelled and feasted. (Old Norse, *valhöll*, the hall of the slain—of those killed in battle.) Popularized by Wagner and other Nietzschean re-shapers of Germany in the likeness of a supposedly glorious pre-history.

' [Westminster] Abbey . . . or what journalists love to call the " National Valhalla ",' John Ross, *Masques and Phases*, 1909.

' She saw that it was open at the page telling of the death of Colonel Newcome—another inhabitant of Dick's very remarkable Valhalla ', H. C. Bailey, *Rimingtons*, 1904.

456

Illuminatingly reminiscent of the original sense is this allusion to a day in Autumn, 1917, on the Western Front: ' The west was crimson with sunset and . . . huge clouds were scudding before the gale. They were for the most part ragged and tawny, like wild horses, but before them went a white horse, the leader of the unearthly cavalry. It seemed to me that I was looking at a ride of Valkyries, the Shield Maids of Odin hasting eastward to the battle front, to choose the dead for Valhalla,' John Buchan, *Memory Hold-the-Door*, 1940.

vallonia or **valonia**. A particular kind of oak; the acorns from it—used in tanning and dyeing and also in making ink. ' The natural products of [Albania] are surprisingly important . . . Not only are there valuable forests of valonia-oak and beech . . .,' Lionel W. Lyde, who, in *Europe*, 1913, footnotes ' valonia-oak ' thus: ' Valonia takes its name from the old port of *Avlona* or *Valona* ': not the traditional etymology, which causes *vallonia oak* to mean ' the acorn oak ' and which I find unconvincing.

vallota, a genus of South African bulbs (of which the sole species is *Vallota speciosa*, ' beautiful vallota '—better known as the *Scarborough lily*), is named after Antoine *Vallot*, a well-known French botanist (1594–1671).

vanadium is one of the elements: discovered in 1801 in Mexico and rediscovered in 1830, in Sweden, by a Swedish chemist, who gave it a ' patriotic ' name—the name that has gained general acceptance. The ore containing vanadium is known as *patronite*, from Antenor *Patron*, a Peruvian engineer, who first noticed the fact.

From *Vanadis*, the Latin name for the Scandinavian Freya, who, like Venus, was the goddess of love and beauty: Freya was one of the *Vanir*, an early race of gods originally associated with fertility.

vandal, vandalism. ' A collection of vessels and utensils, all gold . . ., and all battered and twisted out of their original shapes . . . . . . It's the most shocking piece of vandalism one could well imagine,' J. J. Connington, *Jack-in-the-Box*, 1944. A *vandal* and *vandalism*, a wanton despoiler, wanton despoliation, of the beautiful or the precious: from the *Vandals* (literally, the Wanderers), who, under Genseric, in A.D. 455 sacked Rome.

' The word Saxon, which had once been the name of a small folk on the neck of the Cimbric peninsula, had widened its scope to include all the peoples between the Elbe and the Rhine and eventually became, like our use of " Vandal " and " Hun ", little more than a term of abuse,' J. N. L. Myres in Collingwood & Myres, *Roman Britain and the English Settlements*, (revised edition) 1937.

Compare **Goth.**

vandyke, n. and v. The noun is short for *Vandyke beard* (pointed) or for *Vandyke cape* or *collar*, a cape or collar adorned with *vandykes*, ' large points forming an edging or border ' ; the verb means ' to adorn, especially a cape or a collar, with such points '.

Such a beard, such capes, collars, points are to be seen in almost every portrait by Anthony van Dyke (or Dyck), who (1599–1641), a Fleming, went in 1632 to England, where he was knighted and where he painted royalty, aristocrats, and notables.

varsovienne. This dance, of the mazurka type, was popular in the Europe of ca. 1850–70. The term, which is elliptical for *danse varsovienne*, shows the undisputed influence, ca. 1810–70, of Paris upon the world's dancing, and it means ' danse of Warsaw '. For other Polish dances, compare **cracovienne, mazurka, polka, polonaise.**

vaudeville. In the 15th Century, Olivier de Basselin wrote many very popular satirical songs ; he lived in the *Vau* (Valley) *de Vire* in Normandy ; his songs became *vaux de Vire* ; the songs winning popularity in Paris, the songs became *vaux de ville*.

Alternatively : from *voix de ville* (or *voix de la ville*). In the mid-16th Century, there existed volumes of songs entitled, some *Vaux de villes* and some *Voix de villes*. The latter theory is, superficially, as plausible as the former. But the former is preferable : there exists the illuminating form, *chanson du Vau de Vire*.

venereal ; venery ; Venus ; venusberg. The third is the origin of the other three, if the second be taken in the sense of *ars amoris*, the art of love. A *venusberg* is a court of love, from that *Venusberg* (a German term, signifying mountain of Venus) which, in medieval legend, was a mountain cavern where Venus held her court. The first term (*venereal* disease) constitutes a sad declension : love becoming lust and entailing a sordid infection. ' Ce n'est plus l'amour, c'est la rage.'

Venus, the Roman goddess of love, corresponds to the Greek Aphrodite and is an apotheosized personification of a word that.

458

radically, means ' desire ': it comes from the Sanskrit *vanas*, ' (physical) desire '.

venetian blind. ' I found four circular holes in the glass corresponding with holes in the venetian blinds inside and with the four bullets, which I found in the room,' says a policeman in *Session Paper of the Central Criminal Court*, March 1904.— ' Daylight gleamed through the slats of the venetian blinds,' Christopher Isherwood, *Mr Norris Changes Trains*, 1935.

Obviously *venetian = Venetian*, from Medieval Latin *Venetianus*, ' of Venice (*Venetia*) '; originally, Venetia was the district inhabited by the *Veneti*, a tribe of ancient Italy. This particular kind of blind, composed of wooden and movable slats, has been much used in Venice from early times—perhaps in imitation of **persiennes.**

Venus. See **venereal.**

verdigris. One of the Middle English forms is *vertegrece*, and that form points to the clue : *vertegrece* anglicizes Old French *vert de Grice*, which has an alternative *vert de Grece* (modern French *Grèce*, though the complete term is *vert-de-gris*), with which compare the Medieval Latin *viride grecum*. Literally, therefore, *verdigris* is ' green of Greece '; and basically it is a pigment and a drug.

verdun, that long rapier which was affected by swordsmen in the 16th Century, derives from *Verdun* in France, where it was first manufactured. Verdun-sur-Meuse, to accord it the full official name, is a small but ancient city, long a fortified town and the scene of the bitterest fighting by the French in the war of 1914–18. *Verdun* comes from the Latin *Virodunum*, which may literally mean ' the stronghold (Celtic *dun*) of the men ', the *he*-men, Latin *vir* often connoting ' a man of courage '— compare Sanskrit *vira*, ' hero ', and Latin *virēre*, ' to be fresh, vigorous ', from the radical sense, ' to be green, verdant '.

Vergilian. See **Virgilian.**

vernicle. See **veronica.**

vernier is a device (a short movable scale) by which minute measurements can be obtained. It has been named after its inventor, a French mathematician, Pierre Vernier (1580–1637), who in 1631 published his invention in a tract entitled *Le*

Quadrant Nouveau de Mathématiques. Wrongly called a **nonius,** on which it was an improvement.

veronica. ' " These veronicas make a lovely splash of blue, don't you think? " ' : Christopher Bush, *The Case of the Platinum Blonde,* 1944.

The flower, like the ecclesiastical veronica, derives from Saint Veronica. In an old legend, Veronica was the woman who wiped the face of Christ as He carried the cross, the handkerchief retaining an imprint of His face. Veronica probably represents Greek *Beronikë, Berenikë,* Berénice. The handkerchief, or an imitation thereof, was formerly known as a *vernicle.*

vesta; vestal. The former, originally of wax, later of wood, but always a short match, derives, as does the latter (at first an adjective), from the Roman *Vesta,* that goddess of the blazing hearth (' Keep the home fires burning ') who was ' worshipped in every Roman household ' and who took her name from the Greek *Hestia,* personification of *hestia,* a hearth, a dwelling. The *Vestal* Virgins (*Virgines vestales*) tended the fire in the Temple of Vesta, which, under the Roman pre-Republican kings, constituted the State Hearth. (Harvey.)

vesuvian; vesuvite. The former (also *vesuvianite*) is a basic silicate, plentiful near *Vesuvius*; also, as a trade-name, an eruptive match, or fusee, common in England, ca. 1850. Likewise from Mt Vesuvius (Italian *Monte Vesuvio*) comes *vesuvite,* a leucitetephrite. Pliny mentions *Vesuvius,* which is cognate with **Vesta.**

vichy. Short for *Vichy water,* French *eau de Vichy,* a mineral water obtained from springs at and near the town of Vichy in the *département* of Allier in central France and known in England as early as the 1850's.

' Mr McKiss reached for his vichy and milk, regarding it thoughtfully,' George Bronson-Howard, *God's Man,* an American novel published in 1915.

' " Have another whisky first."—" Thanks. I think I need it."—" Vichy or water? " said the girl. " Vichy, please ",' Eric Ambler, *Cause for Alarm,* 1938.

vickers is short for—and generalized from—*Vickers machine gun,* much used during the Second World War. It represents an evolution from the Vickers m.g. used in the British Army since

1915; the 1915–18 *vickers* was itself a development from the **maxim.**

" He could hear heavy 1·68 Vickers on the left in regular and long bursts,' James Aldridge, *Of Many Men* (the war of 1939–45 in perspective: a novel), 1945.

victoria. ' She is the daughter of King O'Hara, who is hacking along Broadway with one of these old-time victorias for a matter of maybe twenty-five years,' Damon Runyon, *Furthermore*, 1938.

Queen Victoria (on the throne, and very much ' in the saddle ', from 1837 to 1901) saw her name bestowed on a plum, a fabric, a vehicle: Albert, Prince Consort, was similarly honoured. This low-slung, four-wheeled carriage, with seats for two and the driver perched high in front, was introduced by the French, who thus renamed the *calèche*, in the 1840's. Compare :—

Victorian. ' My hold on life is too slight to include any Victorian hypocrisy,' Raymond Chandler, *The Big Sleep*, 1939. *Victorian*, in the senses ' (hopelessly) old-fashioned ; smug ; prudish ; narrow-minded ; intellectually myopic ; spiritually costive ', obviously refers to the reign (1837–1901) of Queen Victoria, who began by being a wholesome influence for cleanliness in private lives and political careers and ended by being an excessively restrictive influence on natural *joie de vivre* : but it is too often forgotten that the Queen did far more good than she did harm, that a literature including such men as Tennyson and Browning, Dickens and Thackeray, Meredith and Hardy, was hardly negligible, and that such scientists as Darwin, Wallace, Huxley are not to be dismissed with an easy and ignorant sneer. (It was perhaps in art that her influence was the most unfortunate.)

victorine. This ladies' fur tippet, adorning the bosom, may, like **victoria,** have come from France : *-ine* is a French suffix, and the naming characterizes the methods of the shrewd French purveyors of feminine apparel and adornment. Though not certainly, we may take it that the *victorine*, which also entered England in the 1840's, constituted a compliment to Queen Victoria.

Virgilian. ' Seen from a sufficient distance, and in the context of a larger landscape, the life of these Elderbrooks among their flocks and herds had a simple pastoral beauty, a virgilian charm,' Gerald Bullett, *The Elderbrook Brothers*, 1945 : there, the adjective has truly become part of the language—or, at least, of the literary vocabulary; there, the reference is to the Virgil of *The Georgics*. In *the Virgilian 'tears of things'*, the reference is to Virgil (70–19 B.C.) as author of *The Aeneid*, where, at I, 462, occurs the famous 'Sunt lacrimae rerum et mentem mortalia tangunt'.

virginia; virginian; virginium. The first is short for *Virginia creeper* and for tobacco grown in Virginia; the second concentrates 'a cigarette made from tobacco of Virginia'; and the third is—at the time of writing (August 28, 1945)—the most recently discovered of the elements, indeed its very existence is doubtful, merely postulated. The State was named after Virginia, 'the Virgin Queen', Queen Elizabeth. 'I had a keen eye for a thrown-away fag-butt and a stump of cigar. My favourite brands were " Virginia de Pick-up " and " Flor de Pavement ",' the Rev. Frank Jennings, *Tramping with Tramps*, 1932.

volcano. 'There was even, for the ancient world, only one *volcano*, viz. Etna, in the bowels of which *Vulcan* and the Cyclopes forged the thunderbolts of Jupiter,' WWN. See also **vulcanian.**

volt; voltage; voltaic. These terms in the theory of electricity all derive from Count Alessandro *Volta* (1745–1827), Italian physicist, who in 1775 invented the electrophorus, an instrument for producing electric charges by induction, and, twenty-five years later, the voltaic pile. He also studied atmospheric electricity.

voodoo, literally 'a corpus of superstitious belief and practice, including witchcraft, current in the West Indies and the Southern U.S.A., and derived from tropical Africa', is by The OED traced to the Dahomey *vodu* and related to **hoodoo;** loosely, but now generally, debased to mean 'a malefic spell' or 'a visitation of (mysterious) ill-luck' and used even as a verb, 'to bewitch, to impose bad luck upon' a person, although *hoodoo* is the commoner term for these 'debasements'. Professor Ernest Weekley, however, thinks that *voodoo* may be Creole French, from *vaudois*: the French *Vaudois* derives from the *Waldenses*, the reforming followers of Peter *Waldo* or *Valdo* (flourishing ca. 1170) of Lyons: 'heretics' represented by the priestly teachers of Negroes in the West Indies as devil-worshippers. A theory not to be scorned.

vosne is short for *Vosne burgundy*, an excellent red burgundy. ' " Nearly all the vineyards of Vosne are small and most of them are good . . . Most of them are famous. There are the three *Romanées* and the *Richebourg*, the *La Tache*, the lesser known *Les Malconsorts* " . . . . . . He went on, his voice as mellow as the grapes of which he spoke,' Margery Allingham, *Coroner's Pidgin*, 1945.

Vosne-Romanée is ' the most famous of the wine-producing Communes of the Cote d'Or . . . The most renowned [vineyard] is *La Romanée Conti* : it is closely challenged . . . by *Les Richebourg* vineyards,' André Simon, *Wine*, 1946.

vouvray. ' There is a choice tavern . . ., and there you may have . . . amber wine of Vouvray, better than in any tavern in Touraine,' Arthur Machen, *Holy Terrors*, 1946. This white wine of Vouvray, ' the most important wine-producing district of Touraine (Loire valley) '—as André Simon notes—is either a still or a sparkling wine.

vulcanian; Vulcanist; vulcanite; vulcanize. All four words (' of or like Vulcan '—' a holder of the Plutonic theory in geology '—' a sulphur-treated kind of rubber '—' to sulphur-process rubber at a high temperature ') and their derivatives come from *Vulcanus*, Vulcan, the Roman equivalent of the Greek Pluto. Vulcan was that god who represented fire and metal-making.

In reference to Hitler, *The Times Literary Supplement* of May 12, 1945, in a leader, says, ' It was a symbolic act when a vulcanian dictator, as a first step in statesmanship, wrote his distaste of books with a lighted torch '.

W

wabash is ' to cheat '; in 1859 lexicographer Bartlett said that it was ' an expression much used in Indiana and other parts of the West '. Another slang sense, written however with a capital *W*, is ' to throw into the Wabash River '; yet another, in the passive, is ' to be attacked with bilious fever in the Wabash River district '(DAE). The Wabash is one of the northern tributaries of the Ohio; Wabash County is in Illinois; the name is Amerindian.

waler. An Australian horse imported into India, originally for cavalry of the British Army. The term arose in India and it

463

indicates that most of the horses came from New South Wales—and nearly all Australian horses were, in fact, shipped at Sydney.

walk delicately like Agag. See **Agag.**

Walker. See **Hookey Walker.**

walloon is (*a*) a leather or, more probably, a heavy cloth imported into the U.S.A. in the late 18th and early 19th Century from Belgium or from one of the neighbouring countries, the Walloons (French *Wallons*, a name of Teutonic origin, perhaps meaning ' foreigners ') inhabiting Belgium and north-eastern France ; (*b*) an American bird—the ember goose or ring-necked loon, perhaps from its predominant colour ; and (*c*) a disease of tobacco, perhaps from association with the Belgian Congo or with Walloon tobacco-growers in the United States.

Wardour Street English is English bespangled with pseudo-archaisms and specious ancientry. Wardour Street, in the West End of London, is—or rather, it used to be—full of shops selling antique, much of it supposedly antique, furniture ; also it houses some important aspects of the cinematic industry.

Washington ; washingtonia. The *washingtonia*, a palm-tree native to and flourishing in California, was named after George **Washington.** And so was Washington, D.C., the Federal Capital of the United States ; the word is often used for ' the American Government '. Compare the *Washington thorn*, first cultivated in the District of Columbia.

Washington, George. See **George Washington.**

waste land, the ; by a natural extension, *the waste lands*. This phrase has, since 1922 or 1923, allusively signified ' a place, a period, an experience (of some length) characterized by aridity of the spirit and by a lack of spiritual sustenance, the latter partly originating the former '.

' The case of T. S. Eliot's poem, *The Waste Land*, which first appeared in 1922, is instructive. When it came out, it won an unexpected and extraordinary popularity ', and probably those who liked it ' followed the moods of the poem imaginatively and emotionally ', C. M. Bowra, *The Background of Modern Poetry*, an inaugural lecture delivered at Oxford on May 10, 1946.

One gets from poetry what one can give to it : and T. S. Eliot, who was in his middle thirties when he wrote *The Waste*

Land, must have been quite startled by what some of the enthusiasts made of it. The most intelligent criticism of this great poem I have yet seen is that by R. G. Collingwood in *The Principles of Art*, 1938.

Wat, Watty, or small-initialled, is an old name, now mainly English dialectal, for a hare. A personification : *Wat, Wattie,* are diminutives of *Walter.*

[**watchet,** n. and adj.; **watchet blue.** Light-blue, sky-blue; a cloth, a garment, thus coloured. The OED derives the word from Old North-Eastern French *watchet,* which denotes perhaps a colour, perhaps a fabric. But The OED's own citations render it equally possible that *watchet* was a fabric or a dye made at the Somerset locality mentioned in '. . . Gimblett . . . discovered in a Somerset holiday [cricket] match at his native Watchet, famed for its blue dye and its blue Bristol Channel beyond ': *The Observer*, August 26, 1945, ' Something Different ', by R. C. Robertson-Glasgow, who, like that other polished writer on cricket, Neville Cardus, is also a scholar.]

waterbury shortens *Waterbury watch*, especially the one-dollar watch acquired in 1922 from Robert Ingersoll (see **ingersoll**). Made by The Waterbury Clock Company of the U.S.A.

Waterloo, meet one's. To meet one's match—one's conqueror; to succumb to a greater man, a stronger force, as Napoleon Buonaparte met his one summer day of 1815 at Waterloo in Belgium.

Watson, Dr. ' Elementary, my dear Watson ! ' : you have only to ask **Sherlock Holmes.**

watsonia is a plant, or its flower, of the genus *Watsonia*, named after Sir William *Watson* (1715–87), an English physician who was also botanist and scientific experimenter. He helped to introduce into England the Linnaean system of botanical classification.

watt, a unit of power or activity, a volt-ampère, owes its name to James *Watt* (1736–1819), the Scottish mechanical engineer and famous inventor, whom it commemorates. He himself invented in 1765 the modern condensing steam-engine, on which R. G. Collingwood has some very acute things to say in *An Essay on Metaphysics.*

Watteau. ' [Theocritus] perfected the pastoral . . . ; his successors are far below him, and Vergil's *Eclogues* seem artificial copies, an artificiality which grew until the end was Watteau and powdered shepherdesses in hoops,' W. W. Tarn, *Hellenistic Civilisation*, 1927.

Antoine Watteau (1684–1721), dainty and most fashionable as a French painter, has given us the *Watteau back—bodice—hat —mantle—pleat* (often simply *watteau*), imitative of fashion-features in his paintings, which are as graceful as they are mannered ; from his ' school ' of painting we have formed such descriptive epithets as *Watteau-like, Watteauesque, Watteauish*.

Watty. See **Wat.**

weary Titan. See **Titan.**

wedgwood. ' Strong egg cups and saucers of Canton china would appear mingled with the Wedgwood that my grandfather had sent for from New York,' John P. Marquand, *Wickford Point*, 1939.

Josiah Wedgwood (1720–95), a most distinguished potter, in 1763 patented and in 1769 improved, indeed perfected, ' a glazed cream-coloured domestic earthenware '. He also, in 1773–80, 'improved marbled ware and invented jasper ware' ; and at his factory ' Etruria ', founded in 1769, the *Etruria*, or *Wedgwood, ware* was made. (Webster BD.) The Staffordshire potteries have long been famous, and Etruria, close to Burslem, has become a village.

weigela, weigelia. ' It was a tall weigela bush among whose low straggling branches I had forced my way, and one of those slender branches that lay by my neck was heavy with its second bloom,' Christopher Bush, *The Missing Men*, 1946. As a colour, *weigela* is a mediumly brilliant red. The bush was named after C. E. Weigel (1748–1831), a Swedish physician.

weismannism (or *neo-darwinism*) is that corpus of theory concerning heredity, affecting chiefly the germ-plasm, which was put forward by August Weismann (1834–1914), a German biologist.

Wellerism, or **w—**, is a saying or an act committed by Samuel— to us, Sam—Weller, Mr Pickwick's man in Dickens's *The Pickwick Papers*, published serially in 1836–37 and as a book in 1837 ; hence an act or saying reminiscent, or in the manner, of that shrewd, impudent, humorous Cockney.

wellington. See **wellingtons.**

wellingtonia, the tree, is synonymous with **sequoia,** but, a New Zealand tree, it has been named in commemoration of the Duke of Wellington (1769–1852). Compare:—

wellingtons. ' She was wearing an oilskin, Wellingtons, an old felt hat,' Georges Simenon, *The Shadow Falls*, translated by Stuart Gilbert, 1945.

Such boots are—as, of course, you know already—named after the Duke of Wellington; the earliest record being of 1817, it would seem to have been less in reminiscence than as a compliment. Compare **bluchers.**—In the singular, it is a variation of the game of **napoleon,** or a bid therein.

Wellsian. As ' belonging to, or characteristic of, H. G. Wells ', the word is ineligible. (' My inherited Radicalism resisted the Wellsian Socialism, I am a born individualist, but here was the most exciting literature a young man could read [in the year 1900]. I was one of the first " Wellsians " or Wells-enthusiasts ': thus the aseptic, astringent, acerb W. L. George in *The Triumph of Gallio*.) But as ' conceived, written in the manner of one of Wells's scientific romances ', hence ' intelligently, or scientifically yet readably, fantastic or highly imaginative ' it qualifies—though only just.

welsh, to; welsher; welshing. As slang terms in reference to horse-racing (hence, any other kind), these may simply be English amenities in respect of the Welsh people: compare **paddy** and **scotty.** They may, as W has suggested, derive from the famous old rhyme, ' Taffy was a Welshman, Taffy was a thief, Taffy came to my house And stole a leg of beef '.

wensleydale is a well-known English cheese (cf. **cheddar** and **stilton**), made in Wensleydale: ' the dale of Wensley '. In Yorkshire, Wensleydale forms part of the valley of the Ure; it extends from the head of that valley to Jervaulx valley, above the parish of Wensley in the North Riding.

With a capital *W*, it designates an English breed of long-woolled sheep—Leicesters crossed with Yorkshire sheep.

Wertherian; Wertherism. (Given to) a morbid—a weak and excessive—sentimentality; at one time a mode, still a symptom of inability to confront life with ' What the hell! '

Werther was the ' hero ' of Goethe's novel, *The Sorrows of the Young Werther*, published in 1774. That young man needed a

467

purge and plenty of hard work; his melancholy emotionalism strongly influenced the European literature of the ensuing half-century. See especially Dr William Rose's translation of the romance—or rather, his admirable introductory essay.

'Blood is necessary to them [the Germans] as a purge; sin as a means to the ecstasy of redemption—they " do not regret war " but believe that " great things will come of it ". The habits of Tarquin are, in them, a necessary whet and prelude to the romantic idealism of Werther,' Charles Morgan, concerning 'A Good German' in *Le Silence de la Mer*, by 'Vercors': *Reflections in a Mirror*, 2nd Series, 1946.

West End is often employed to imply 'the height of fashion, the focus of entertainment and good food and drink'. Both noun and derivatively the adjective come from the West End of London. Its opposite is *East End*.

western or **W—.** A film or a novel dealing with the cowboys, rustlers, sheriffs, ne'er-do-wells of the Western United States—'the wild west'; it no more deserves a capital letter than does *juvenile*, 'a children's book'. For Americans, *the West* connotes 'the wide open spaces' and 'freedom from restraint' and 'a sense of adventure translated into life': see especially that grand American book, *The Pardoner's Wallet*, by Dr S. Crothers.

'It was a big State and up here at the end of the trip, the place was wilder than a Class B western out of a quickie studio,' Richard Sale in *Detective Fiction Weekly*, February 4, 1939.

whatman. Professional painter to amateur, 'What you've got there is just a bit of nothing at all—nicely splashed on to the best Whatman with an expensive camel-hair,' Joyce Cary, *The Horse's Mouth*, 1944.—'Edouard's father, a medical man and an amateur painter' in North Africa, 'lamented that the Germans . . . had taken his Wattman paper and Windsor & Newton paints,' Keith Douglas, *Alamein to Zem Zem*, dated 1946 but published in 1947: one of the five or six best of the War books.

In full, *whatman* is *Whatman paper*, introduced to artists by its manufacturer, James Whatman, in ca. 1767.

whidah bird, sometimes shortened to *whidah*, is the *Whidah bird*, the bird of Whidah. On the Slave Coast on the Bight of Benin, in what is more precisely known as Dahomey, stands the seaport of Whydah or Whidah.

'Saka-bulla birds draggled their long ungainly tails among
468

rain-soaked grass' (glossed, 'Native name for the African whydah'), Archer Russell, *Gone Nomad*, 1936.

whippoorwill. 'Somewhere down by the Konapic Brook a whippoorwill was mewing out its exasperating mating cry,' Jonathan Stagge, *Death and the Dear Girls*, 1946. As the American katydid is supposed to call 'Katy did!', so the whippoorwill, a nocturnal bird, calls 'Whip poor Will!' *Poor Will* evokes the picture of a hapless Negro slave.

Whitehall signifies 'departmental government', for the reason, well-known to all Londoners, that the oldest Ministries are situated in or near Whitehall in the south-west of London proper (S.W.1). In the 15th–17th-Century London, Whitehall and the Strand and Fleet Street connected Government (Westminster) with business (the City).

whitleyism, the use of *Whitley councils* (employers conferring with employees) for the settlement of labour disputes, derives from J. H. Whitley, who in 1916 was chairman of the committee that recommended the establishment of these councils. John Whitley (1866–1935) was an expert in such relations.

whitney. See **witney.**

whydah. See **whidah bird.**

widow, the. In slang, *the widow*, originally written *the Widow*, means 'champagne', with reference to the well-known firm of *Veuve* Cliquot, wine-merchants notable for the champagne they purvey.

wigan, a cotton fabric that, resembling a flimsy canvas, is used to stiffen certain parts of certain garments, was made originally at *Wigan* in Lancashire. On the 20th-Century music-halls, *Wigan* is almost synonymous with 'provincial': you have but to say *Wigan* and every cit will laugh uproariously.

will o' the wisp is **Will o' the wisp,** where *Will*, just such a personification as you find in *Jack Frost*, is chosen instead of Tom, Dick or Harry, because it alliterates with *wisp*.

'. . . The Moslem kingdoms had their hands too full with the pursuit of trade and converts to have much time or inclination for solving mysteries that might, after all, prove to be mere will-o'-the-wisps. . . . We must look elsewhere than to the

Arabs for the urge to explore,' G. H. T. Kimble, *Geography in the Middle Ages*, 1938.

william, sweet; william pear. In the former, *William* represents a girlish fancy: this flower-name is obviously of feminine bestowing. But *william pear* is an error for *Williams* (or *Williams's*) *pear*, a variety of the *Bon Chrétien*. From the name of the first importer (ca. 1814) into England.

'. . . The corner of the garden where she lay in a bower of larkspurs, sweet williams and cool white phlox,' Hugh I'Anson Fausset, *Between the Tides: A Summer Idyll*, 1942.

winchester, (1) short for *Winchester rifle*, has no concern with the old English cathedral and college town except that thence derives the surname of its manufacturer, an American, Oliver F. Winchester, who, at the Biblical age of seventy, died in 1880. The Winchester rifle was introduced ca. 1865 and the pea-rifle a few years later.

' The guards on the stockade runway, directly over the gate through which they tried to drive the locomotive, riddled both Silver Tongue and English Harry with their Winchesters,' 'Frisco Jimmy Harrington, in *Detective Fiction Weekly*, March 23, 1935.

(2) A *Winchester quart*, half a gallon—or a bottle holding it. So named because the standard of the measure, much used by druggists, was originally deposited at Winchester.

winthrop shortens *Governor Winthrop desk*, an American style of desk with an oxbow, or reversed, serpentine front. It was first made after the time of that John *Winthrop* (1588–1649) who became *Governor* of Massachusetts Colony. English-born, he held the governorship for most of the period from June the 12th, 1630, when he and his company reached Salem, until his death. He wrote a notable *Journal*, figures in Hawthorne's *The Scarlet Letter*, and his descendants and collaterals have been prominent in the history of the United States of America. (Hart.)

wisenheimer, See **buttinsky.**

wistaria or **wisteria.** ' A gaunt grey goat standing up on its hind legs to munch the wistaria buds that hung across an expanse of peeling stucco,' Aldous Huxley, *Time Must Have a Stop*, 1945.

This hardy though deciduous shrub with the lilac-blue flowers is a native of China and Japan, but also of North America; indeed, it was, in 1818, named after the American

470

anatomist, Caspar *Wistar* or, as it happens, *Wister*, in the year of his death.

witney; in America, often *whitney*.   Short for *Witney nap*, this heavy woollen stuff, *napped* and shrunk, is much used for over-coats and blankets.   It was first made at *Witney*, a market-town of Oxfordshire : ' the celebrity of Witney for blankets is in part due to the detersive qualities of the waters of the Windrush ' (Chisholm).   Hence, *witneyer*, a textile worker specializing in producing a *witney nap*.

wolffia is a plant, or the flower, of the genus *Wolffia*, named after the German J. F. Wolff (1778–1806)—another of those physicians who were also excellent botanists.   The wolffia is the smallest flowering-plant in the world.

wolfram, wolframite, wolframium.   In the effort to avoid a Proper Name origin for *wolfram*, several extremely ingenious etymologies have been proposed.   Too ingenious.   We have the analogous **cobalt** and **nickel** (and others) to buttress W's suggestion that, *wolfram* being German, the origin is the German personal name *Wolfram*, literally ' wolf raven '.

woodburytype designates a photographic technicality, invented in 1860 by Walter B. Woodbury (1834–75), an English photo-grapher and inventor, who, in Java, used the collodion process and, two years after settling in Birmingham, devised this method of photo-engraving.   Later, he devised other processes and inventions in the field of photography.

worsted.   See the Pelham quotation at **kersey.**
  Worsted was made, during the Middle Ages, at and around *Worsted*, formerly *Worstead*, concerning which Chisholm says, ' Worstead was settled by Flemish weavers in the 12th century, and is believed to have given name to the yarn and fabric so called which were probably first manufactured in England by these settlers '.

wyandotte.   Whereas *Wyandotte* is a variety of Indian corn, *wyandotte* is ' an American breed of fowls, earlier known as Sebright Cochins, said to have sprung from the mating of a Sebright bantam cock and a Cochin hen ' (Hodge, 1910—cited by the DAE).   The name was originally that of a tribe of Iroquois Red Indians, a tribe bitterly opposed to the Iroquois proper : *Wyandotte*, better *Wyandot* or *Wandot*, anglicizes the French *Ouendut*, which transliterates an Amerindian word.

471

X

Xanthippe. Among those whose fathers had the good, not merely the horse, sense to provide them, and among those who far-sightedly provided themselves, with at least some not too pitiably inadequate knowledge of the Ancient Classics, *Xanthippe* is employed allusively as a shrewish, peevish, quarrelsome wife, for that is the relationship in which, womanly-appreciative, she stood to the greatest teacher of philosophy the world has ever known : Socrates, who seems to have borne most exemplarily with her and may have been grateful to her for having facilitated and increased his love of outdoor discussion.

Y

yahoo. ' Swift has found exact equivalents to his intuition in the Houyhnhnms and Yahoos . . . . . . As for the Yahoos, they are nauseating beasts in human form, disposed to " nastiness and dirt ". Ironically they are defended in terms of swine . . . . . . The hatefulness of the Yahoo form is emphasized together with its comparative uselessness and limitations in strength and speed, and subjection to cold and heat,' G. Wilson Knight, ' Swift and the Symbolism of Irony '—in *The Burning Oracle*, 1939.—' I seemed [ca. 1919] to see the reign of natural science, within no very long time, converting Europe into a wilderness of Yahoos,' R. G. Collingwood, *An Autobiography*, 1939.

The references are to Jonathan Swift (1667–1745), Dean Swift, England's greatest satirist, who in 1726 published *Gulliver's Travels*, which, implicitly a satire, is explicitly a book of imaginary travel ; a masterpiece in either form. The last Book of *Gulliver's Travels* deals with the Houyhnhnms (glorified horses—*Whinnims* or whinniers) and the yahoos, the latter now synonymous with ' bestial human beings '. Perhaps the *yah!-who* ?'s : *yah!* being typical of coarse ignorance and brutality, and *who* ? of defiance.

yapock or **yapok,** ' a South American web-footed water opossum ', takes its mildly confusing name from *Oyapock* or *Oyapok*, a South American river. The Oyapok rises in the Tumuc-Hamac mountains and, by a series of rapids, flows, through French Guiana, north by east into the Atlantic. An animal may have given its name to the river : Webster pertinently adduces Tupi *oyapuça*, 'a monkey of the genus Callicebus'.

yarborough, originally (in the 1880's and 1890's) in whist and then also in bridge, a hand—thirteen cards—containing no card higher than a 9: so named because a certain Earl of Yarborough used to wager 1000 to 1 against the occurrence of such a hand; the mathematical, i.e. the theoretical, odds against it being 1827 to 1. *Yarborough* is relevantly a parish in Lincolnshire.

yellowjack. 'The tragic little ports of northern South America . . . Fever-stricken and lethal, those towns are still haunted by the ghost of Yellow Jack, that, only two or three decades ago, would sweep away within a few days an entire population,' Osbert Sitwell, *Sing High! Sing Low!*, 1944.

A colloquial—but very common—synonym of *yellow fever*, which causes a patient to look jaundiced but which is very much more dangerous than jaundice. By personification.

yid; yiddish; yiddisher. The third, deriving from the second, is a sense-variant of the first, which means 'a Jew', derivatively 'Jewish', whereas the second means 'Jewish', from *Yiddish*, that High German dialect which contains many Hebraisms and some Russian or Polish elements. *Yiddish* is an anglicism for German *jüdisch*, short for *jüdisch-deutsch* (Jewish-German) *Sprache* (speech, language); *jüdisch* comes from German *Jude* (a Jew), itself from Latin *Judaeus*, from *Judaea*, Judea, from Greek *Ioudaia*.

yokohama is short for *Yokohama bean*, a Japanese bean that resembles the *Lima bean*; and for *Yokohama fowl*, the Japanese domestic fowl.

Yokohama: because this is one of the principal and most picturesque cities of Japan.

york, to; yorker. As cricket terms, they seem to derive from the ingenuity of Yorkshire cricketers.

Yorkshire (pudding); Yorkshire club; Yorkshire in slang. The first is baked batter, eaten—originally in Yorkshire—with roast beef (*roast and Yorkshire*). 'They went out and ate roast beef and Yorkshire pudding. Or rather—for Hobhouse was a purist in these matters—they ate Yorkshire pudding and gravy first and roast beef afterwards,' 'Michael Innes', *The Weight of the Evidence*, 1944.

The second occurs in 'I think it was a Yorkshire club, that

473

is, we all paid alike—no one stood treat,' *Session Paper* of the Old Bailey, May 9, 1867; the scene—the old Princess's Hotel.

In slang, *Yorkshire* = 'sharp practice', 'commercially shrewd', and 'to overreach (another person)'; the second and third of these have the variant *Yorkshire bite*. Yorkshiremen are shrewd—but most generous and hospitable.

young Turk. See **Turk.**

ytterbium; yttrium. These two chemical elements (cf. also **erbium** and **terbium**) derive, via its Latin name *yttria*, from the Swedish town of Ytterby. The former element was discovered about 1879, the latter about 1822. The corresponding ores are *ytterbite* and *yttrite*; the corresponding earths, *ytterbia* and *yttria*. See **gadolinite, gadolinium**: for it was the mineralogist Gadolin who gave their names to at least *ytterbite* and *ytterbium*. For a complete list of the *ytterby* derivatives, see Webster or The OED at the four element-names.

Z

zabernism, like **mervousness,** may seem too ephemeral to merit inclusion in this selective dictionary; but, like **mervousness,** it preserves in historical amber the memory of an incident of both political and spiritual significance. In 1912, at *Saverne* (German *Zabern*) in Alsace, a German lieutenant, overflown with military dignity and national pride, sabred a lame cobbler that had the audacity to smile at him, one of the potential 'master race'.

zadkiel, an astrological almanac for popular use, derives from the fact that Lieutenant R. J. Morrison, R.N., who lived in 1795–1874, had, in 1831, founded such an almanac, sponsored by his astrological self, 'Zadkiel', and entitled *Zadkiel's Almanac*. In Jewish lore, *zadkiel* is the angel affected to the planet Jupiter.

zanella is a fabric that, of cotton and worsted, has, since 1848, been used for linings and umbrellas. Earlier *zanella cloth*, it may originally have been *Zanella cloth*, for The OED suggests that *zanella* may derive from Antonio *Zanelli*, who in 1878 published his authoritative *Le Lane Italiane* (the Italian fabrics).

zany. 'I got sore. "What makes you think I'm a stoolie [i.e., informer to the police]?" "Don't be a zany. When the vice investigation was on last year, you were around with dough, spending it, and two guys . . . took the collar [i.e., were arrested], and went to stir [or prison]. You fingered them [pointed them out to the police] ",' Frederick C. Painton, ' Stool Pigeon '—in *Detective Fiction Weekly*, December 12, 1936. —' Shakily, under the contemptuous eyes of the village zany, he mounted his bicycle and wobbled down the road,' Anthony Gilbert, *He Came by Night*, 1944.

Zany is the anglicized form of *Zanni*, the pet-form of Italian *Giovanni* (John). John Florio, in his Italian-English Dictionary, 1598, defines *zanni*, in its earlier form *zane* (dissyllabic, of course), as ' a sillie John, a gull, a noddie. Used also for a simple vice, clowne, foole, or simple fellowe in a plaie or comedie '— so does Shakespeare use ' zany ' in *Love's Labour's Lost*. The scholarly, if rather pedantic Ben Jonson speaks of ' Zani to a tumbler '. (W.)

zephyr. This is one of those difficult cases. If the English word derives from Greek *zephuros*, via Latin *zephyrus*, a west wind, it is ineligible, but if it derives from Greek *Zephuros*, Latin *Zephyrus*, the personification—the god—of the west wind, the West Wind as god, then it is eligible.

zeppelin, colloquially *zepp*, is short for *Zeppelin airship*, a long, dirigible, balloon-type German airship, designed and constructed and in 1900 completed by Count Ferdinand von *Zeppelin* (1838–1917), who, on retiring from the Army in 1891 as Lieutenant-General, founded an airship factory. In 1915–18 London was *zepped* a number of times.

zinnia, the State flower of Indiana, was named by Linnaeus in honour of Johann Gottfried *Zinn*, a German botanist and physician (1727–59). Zinn published in 1753 what is reputed to be the first book to deal with the anatomy of the eye.

Zoilus. See **Aristarchus.**

zolaesque; zolaism. ' There is in Rowlandson's drawings and paintings of drunkards nothing that is ominous, as with Degas's absinthe-drinkers, with Steinlen's Zola-esque alcoholics or the café-drunkards of Beardsley,' Osbert Sitwell, in his masterly essay on the greatest of England's socio-satirical painters (*Sing High! Sing Low!*, 1944).

And *zolaism* is the corresponding noun, usually apprehended to signify ' an excessively life-like treatment of the functional and processive aspects of human and animal life ' : which is all right so far as it goes and is not unfair criticism in reference to such novels by Emile Zola (1840–1902) as *L'Assommoir*, 1877, and *Nana*, 1880, and *La Terre*, 1888: but is inadequate in respect of the grim, terse power of *Thérèse Raquin*, 1867, the delicacy of *Le Rêve*, 1888, the battle scenes in *La Débâcle*, 1892. Zola, moreover, was a great champion of liberty.

zombie. ' Rose Medley and that zombie husband of hers had sunk into apathy,' Claude Houghton, *The Quarrel*, 1948. The famous traveller W. H. Seabrook has defined a zombi(e) as ' a dead body . . . made to walk and act and move as if it were alive '; hence, an apathetic, dead-and-alive sort of person. In the Voodoo cult of the Negro religion, a zombie is also the supernatural reanimating power; compare the Congo-dialectual *zumbi*, ' fetish '.

Hence, an American cocktail, as in Richard Sale, *Death Steps In*, 1943.

zouave, ' a woman's short jacket similar to the jacket forming part of the uniform worn by that light-infantry corps (originally consisting of Algerians) which is known as the Zouaves ', ultimately derives its name from that of an Algerian tribe.

That uniform was Oriental: hence it is piquant to find that J. L. Myres, speaking—in the ' Eastern Mediterranean ' chapter of *The Dawn of History*—of ' the dress and armour of the Minoan Age ' (before 1000 B.C.) in Crete, says that ' The women wore shaped and flounced skirts, richly embroidered, with " zouave " jackets, low in front, puff-sleeved, with a standing collar or a peak behind the neck '.—' Beatrice '—ca. 1902—' flaunted a new fashion—something with gold braid, and a short Hungarian jacket called a Zouave,' Neville Cardus, *Autobiography*, 1947.

Zouave is the French form of *Zouaoua* or *Zawia*, a Kabyle tribe living in the Jurjura mountains of Algeria.

zulu is known to anglers as an artificial fly with a *black* hackle and to readers of the history of fashion as a conical straw hat formerly worn by children in summer; it also signifies a two-masted Scotch lugger, from some fancied resemblance to a Zulu in war dress.

The Zulus (or Amazulus), a Natal tribe of the Bantu nation, caused much trouble both to the Boers and to the British, in the South Africa of the 19th Century, first under Chaka, who was assassinated in 1828, and then under his successor, Dingaan, overthrown in 1840.

END OF DICTIONARY PROPER

APPENDIX

APPENDIX

BORDER-LINERS AND POTENTIAL
CANDIDATES

A

Aaron lily, which lingers in English dialect, was originally a folk-etymologizing of *arum lily.*

Aaron's beard is a name given to several plants whose flower resembles a beard (compare the next term), e.g. St John's wort and the Jerusalem star; the strawberry geranium, from its thread-like runners. (Webster.)

Aaron's rod. See **rod of Aaron.**

Abraham (or **Abram**), **sham; abra(ha)m man.** These two terms, which belong to the language of beggars and criminals (see my *Underworld*) derive, the former from the latter, the latter from the fact that the lunatic inmates of the *Abraham* Ward of Bedlam Hospital, London, were allowed to beg in the streets; hence, *Abram* (short for *Abraham*) *man* soon came to denote any city beggar. The name of the ward may have been suggested by the etymology of the Jewish personal name *Abraham*, which in Hebrew means ' exalted father ' : the doctors and attendants being as fathers (we hope) to these childlike brains.

Achilles. See **heel of Achilles.**

Actaeon. ' [George] Moore is one of many literary Acteons who have mistaken Diana for Aphrodite ', John Ross, ' The Jaded Intellectuals ' in *Masques and Phases*, 1909.

In Greek mythology, *Aktaion* came upon Artemis (Roman Diana) bathing; angered, she transformed him into a stag; his own hounds tore him to pieces.

Adam. See **old Adam.**

Adam and Eve is, in the United States, a popular name for the putty root (a kind of orchis). The DAE, for the origin, refers us to *Genesis*, ii, 21-24. Compare **Adam's needle.**

479

Adam style, furniture, architecture, etc. Concerning ' the great Whig country houses ' of the 18th–early 19th Century, Lord David Cecil remarks upon ' their colonnaded entrance halls, whence the Adam staircase sweeps up beneath a fluted dome ' (*The Young Melbourne*, 1939). The brothers Adam, architects and designers, flourished in the 18th Century, Robert —the more gifted—dying in 1792, James two years later. At first *Adams*, in reference to both the brothers, and then, Robert's genius becoming fully recognized, *Adam*, as in ' the Adam mode ', ' the Adam style ', ' Adam residence ', etc. Robert Adam modernized, restrainedly and delicately, the Classic manner in architecture and decoration. Of the Adam private houses, John Summerson has, in *Georgian London* (1946), noted that ' These houses represent, perhaps, the highest point of imagination and artistry in the handling of the London house. They are not mere repositories of delicious ornament ; the basis of their splendour is their minutely considered arrangement.'

Adam's ale or, less generally, **wine ; Adam's apple ; Adam's needle.** In his thriller, *Screaming Fog* (1944), John Newton Chance writes the second, more than once, as *adam's apple*, originally a technicality which became a jocularity. Adam had no beer or ale to drink ; only water, poor fellow. *Adam's needle* (see quotation at **rose of Sharon**), also *Adam's needle and thread*, is a fanciful name for the yucca ; for the origin, the DAE sends us to *Genesis*, iii, 7 : ' They sewed fig leaves together, and made themselves aprons '.

Addison's disease, a chronic, often fatal malady, was discovered in 1855 by Dr Thomas *Addison* (1793–1860), an English physician, while he was senior physician at Guy's Hospital.

Agnus Dei, a small, cloth-covered wax disc, bearing the figure of a lamb and blessed by the Pope and worn as an expression of devotion, derives from *Agnus Dei*, a representation of a lamb (emblematic of Christ) bearing a banner, Cross-marked and attached to a Cross-headed standard, the latter itself deriving from *Agnus Dei*, the Lamb of God ; that is, Christ. John the Baptist called Christ ' the Lamb of God, which taketh away the sin of the world ' (*John*, i, 2).

Aladdin's lamp, has, from a story in *The Arabian Nights*, come to denote a possession conferring magical—hence, any remarkable —powers, much as *Aladdin's window* (a term far less generally known) has come to denote a task beyond human ability, from the same source, which tells of a window made, but left unfinished, by a jinni, and impossible of completion by mere men. Compare **Alnaschar dreams** (p. 482).

Alastor, a sort of Nemesis, a relentlessly avenging spirit, hence any avenger or persecutor, has at least a name-connexion with *Alastor*, one of the front horses drawing the chariot of Pluto, God of the Infernal Regions. Shelley's first important work was *Alastor* (a poem), 1816. Literally, the Greek *alastor* means ' he who forgets not ': the privative prefix *a* + a noun formed from *lanthanomai*, ' forget '.

Albany beef is the flesh of sturgeon, a fish that is plentiful in the Hudson River. Albany, the capital of Albany County in New York State, stands on the right bank of the Hudson. At first (in the 1780's and 1790's) derisive, it came to be an almost affectionate term. Compare **Bombay duck.**

Alberti bass is ' that form of accompaniment to a melody that consists of " broken chords " . . . the simplest sort of moving accompaniment possible . . . It takes its name from the Italian composer, Domenico Alberti (c. 1710–40), in whose popular harpsichord sonatas it is frequent ' (Dr Percy Scholes).

Albury is short for *Albury wine*. ' The Pondor people put a couple of bottles of Albury into the buggy ; and I think we can do one of them now, early as it is,' Joseph Furphy (' Tom Collins') *Such Is Life* (in Australia—a most readable classic), 1903. The town of Albury stands at the head of steam navigation on the River Murray, near the border of New South Wales (within which it is situated) and Victoria.

Aldis lamp. ' Towards the day's end . . . the commodore again talked [to the ships in his convoy], giving out by Aldis Lamp or bunting the orders for the night,' Humfrey Jordan, *This Island Demands*, 1941. A signal lamp for the transmission of morse, from the name of the inventor.

Aleppo pine ; A. stone. The pine is so called because, native there, it flourishes in the Levant ; *Aleppo* is a famous Syrian market-town and a populous vilayet. ' Bright air resinous with Aleppo pine,' writes ' Palinurus ' in *The Unquiet Grave*, 1945. *Aleppo stone*, also called ' eye agate ', is an ancient Oriental gem, supposed to be a cure or a lenitive of the *Aleppo button* (or *boil*), a sore—a skin disease—common in the Orient and known also as the *Baghdad button*.

481

Alhambresque, fancifully and elaborately ornamented. *Alhambresque* refers, on the analogy of *picturesque*, to the fanciful, elaborate ornamentation of the *Alhambra*, the masterpiece of Moorish medieval architecture, the palace of the Moorish kings at Granada, the capital of the old Moorish kingdom of Granada, now a province of Andalucia. The Arabic *al hamara*, 'the red' ('house' understood).

Legends of the Alhambra, 1832, is one of the most celebrated of Washington Irving's works.

Alice blue, an American name for greenish-blue, commemorates *Alice*, who was the daughter of Theodore Roosevelt. Compare **Eleanor blue** (p. 537).

Alice (in Wonderland) is often used allusively for a person in new, strange, fantastic surroundings. From 'Lewis Carroll', Charles Lutwidge Dodgson's two fantasies, *Alice's Adventures in Wonderland*, 1865, and *Alice Through the Looking Glass*, 1872 : works that have enjoyed a posthumous fame comparable with that of Jane Austen's novels. Mathematical don at Oxford, Dodgson (1832–92) wrote them for children and made his heroine a child. Their full savour, tang, bouquet, subtlety can be appreciated only by adults.

Alnaschar dreams are those which, like most, come to naught, fond castles in the air. *Alnaschar*, literally 'the lawyer', is in *The Arabian Nights* a barber, who, inheriting a small fortune, invested in a basketful of glassware, dreamed dreams, and dreaming, kicked over his basket and thus destroyed his wares.

American inevitably forms part of a multitude of names for plants, animals, minerals, manufactures and social characteristics of the United States : e.g. *American Beauty* (below), *American eagle*, *American partridge* (which is a quail), *American turtle* (an early form of submarine). See especially Webster and the DAE.

American beauty is one of the most famous of American roses. These Beauties came in about the same time as 'the Gibson girls' and have, in popularity, long outlived them : they even adorn a detective novel in the 1940's, Ellery Queen's *Calamity Town*.

American cloth, an enamelled oilcloth for covering, e.g. tables, is an English name for an English invention. 'Your American cloth is related to no traditional design,' Michael Harrison, *Battered Caravanserai*, 1942.

482

Americanism; Americanize; americanitis; americanicè.
The first and second need no gloss; the third is humorous for
' a being smitten and bitten with things American '; the fourth
is ' in the American manner; especially, in American speech or
phraseology '. Perhaps it remains but to quote a passage that
implies the origin of the word *America* itself: ' By 1525 . . .
Cabral had discovered the Brazilian coast, and a Portuguese
expedition of which [the Italian] Amerigo Vespucci [1451–
1512] was pilot had disclosed the southern continent to the La
Plata River ', Ll. Rodwell Jones & P. W. Bryan, *North America*,
(7th edition) 1946.

amphitryon, a host whose identity is unknown or, strictly, is in
doubt, derives from Greek mythology, where, in the guise of
Amphitryon, Alcmene's husband, Zeus visits, feasts, and lies
with her (whence Hercules), a theme used by Plautus in his
comedy, *Amphitruo* (genitive *-uonis*). Molière says, ' Le vérit-
able Amphitryon | Est l'Amphitryon où l'on dîne '.

anglicè; anglicism (or **A—**); **anglomania; anglophobia.**
These terms, all connected with ' English ', derive from
Medieval Latin *Anglicus*, ' English ', from *Angli*, ' the English ',
itself from the *Angles*, one of the tribes that settled early in
Britain. See **Saxon** in the main vocabulary.

Ångström unit. See **angstrom** in the primary list and
Balmer Series in this secondary list.

Anne. See **Queen Anne.** In English dialect there are half-a-
dozen flower-names preceded by *Queen Anne's.*

Anne, tincture of Queen. This name for an old domestic
remedy merely stresses its ' oldness '; it was neither used nor
recommended by Queen Anne. (Compare **Queen Anne's
dead!**) Here, *Queen Anne* is folk-etymology for *quinine.*

Antaean; Antaeus-like.

> ' Like these birds, not reckoning hour or minute,
> Rebounding from earth with an Antaean strength
> They are gathered in great cycles of air and fire,
> Finding themselves rapt in acceptance
> Of love's brimming and renewed encounter,'
>   (Ronald Bottrall, ' Freedom Lies in Acceptance '
>   *Farewell and Welcome*, 1945).

Antaeus (Greek *Antaios*: ' He who is *set over against* the
earth ') is that giant with whom Hercules wrestled and who,
483

thrown, rose the stronger from each contact with earth and whom the perceptive hero, raising high in air, crushed to death.

Anthony Eden. A man's black felt hat (Foreign Office style) of the kind so debonairly worn by the Rt Hon. Anthony Eden. 'I thought that they all wore Anthony Edens on stock-exchange,' Michael Harrison, *Higher Things*, 1945.

Anthony's fire, St. Erysipelas, ergotism, and other *inflammatory* skin-diseases were so named because in the Middle Ages they were believed to be curable by the intercession of *St Anthony*.

antichrist; antichristian. Literally, 'one who is *against Christ*' and 'opposed to the Christian religion'. Latin *anti*, against; for *Christ* see **christian** (main vocabulary).

Antinoüs is, to the Classically educated, a young man of pensive yet voluptuous good looks. One of the emperor Hadrian's favourites was a Bithynian youth so named. The word as we have it is Latin, the Greek original being *Antinoos*, from *antinoos*, usually defined as 'opposite in character'.

antisabbatarian is also written *anti-Sabbatarian*, one who denies the moral obligation to observe Sunday. Latin *anti*, against; for *Sabbath*, see **sabbath, witches'** in the main list.

Antwerp is short for *Antwerp pigeon*, a Dutch breed. Other *Antwerp* terms worthy of note are the colours *Antwerp blue*, *Antwerp brown*, names bestowed for obscure reasons, and *Antwerp lace*, a Dutch lace that, resembling **mechlin** (primary list), is of a bolder design.

Apician, a literary and Classical synonym of 'epicurean to a luxurious degree and in a luxurious way', derives from the Latin *Apicianus*, 'of or like *Apicius*'—who, in the reign of Tiberius, was a notorious epicure.

Apollyon is sometimes employed allusively for a destructive fiend. He owes his English survival to Bunyan's *Pilgrim's Progress*, where Christian overcomes the armed fiend in the Valley of Humiliation. Bunyan adapted to his purpose Apollyon, the angel of the bottomless pit. The name is Greek: *Apolluōn*, the destroyer, from *apolluein*, to destroy utterly.

Appleton layer, in radio terminology, is that portion of the **Heaviside layer** (in this vocabulary) which was investigated by the English physicist, Sir Edward Appleton, a specialist in the fields of electricity and wireless telegraphy.

aqua Tofana. ' " Borgia poisons, and Perugia water, and *aqua* Tofana " . . . " The Tofana the doctor mentioned died in Sicily in the seventeenth century . . . . . . She devoted her talents to mixing a liquid which has since come to be known by her name. *Aqua* Tofana was a deadly poison ; and this woman plied her poisoning trade on such a wholesale scale that the name of her concoction has never been forgotten. Though her mixture was probably nothing but a strong solution of arsenic, there's still a lot of mystery attaching to it ",' S. S. Van Dine, *The Gracie Allen Murder Case*, (English edition) 1938.

Arcachon oysters. See **Chesapeake.**

Archimedean drill, pulley, screw (screw of Archimedes), windlass, etc. To Archimedes, a Greek of Syracuse, who died in 212 B.C. at the age of about seventy-five, we owe all these inventions. In Hellenistic civilisation (323–31 B.C.) 'the greatest name of all is Archimedes . . . He wrote monographs on very many subjects ; . . . he calculated limits for the value of π . . . ; invented a terminology for expressing numbers up to any magnitude ; laid the foundations of the calculus of the infinite ; and founded the whole science of hydrostatics . . . . . . He invented the compound pulley, the . . . windlass for moving heavy weights, and the endless screw, used to pump out ships and drain the fields after the Nile flood, which survives in our Archimedean drills . . . . . . During the siege of Syracuse the solitary geometrician kept the whole strength of Rome at bay for three years with his grapnels and burning-glasses and improved catapults. He is the only mathematician who ever became a legend,' W. W. Tarn, *Hellenistic Civilisation* (revised edition, 1930) : which see for a masterly short account of one of the most remarkable men that ever lived.

Argus ; Argus-eyed. The Argus (Greek *Argos*) concerned is not Ulysses' dog, which, after his long absence, recognized him and promptly died, but that far-sighted, keen-sighted herdsman whom Hera, jealous, set to watch Io, the mortal maid whose charms seduced the ludicrously impressionable Zeus. With eyes all over his body, Argus was known as *Argos Panoptes*, ' The All-Seeing '. It is not unpleasant to recall that this ungallant guard was cunningly slain by Hermes.

485

Argos is a personification of *argos*, ' bright, or glistening ' : fleet-footed dogs were, by the Greeks, said to be *podas argoi*, there being an analogy between swift movement and a flickering light : compare *twinkle-toes* as applied to a dancer.

Aristotelian ; aristotelize. Literally, neither qualifies for a place. But *aristotelize*, ' to be dryly formal in one's philosophic opinions ', is eligible—though very rarely used. *Aristotelian*, noun and adjective, may be admitted in its transferred nuances, ' (like, of, in) a methodical, intellectualistic, shrewd, rather unimaginative philosopher '.

Of Aristotle (384–322 B.C.), the greatest Greek philosopher after Plato, Gordon Childe has written : ' In Aristotle culminate in a sense all the philosophical and scientific tendencies of the Classical period. A man of comprehensive interests and encyclopaedic erudition, he lectured on the theory of knowledge, logic, ethics, politics, psychology, mathematics, astronomy, botany, zoology, anatomy, chemistry, physics and meteorology. The vast Aristotelian corpus consists of notes of these lectures . . . . . . As a pioneer in formal logic, positive psychology, comparative anatomy and systematic biology his contributions to later science are invaluable . . . . . . It is his misfortune and ours that his authority grew so great among his Hellenistic successors that his theories were sometimes preferred to observed facts ' (*What Happened in History*, 1942) : if a fact contradicted Aristotle, so much the worse—in medieval Europe—for the fact !

Arkansas toothpick is that sort of bowie knife in which the blade can be depressed into the handle ; Josh Billings defined it as a dirk knife, and for once he wasn't being funny. It was much affected by the wild men of Arkansas and Alabama. Indeed, in 1837 the State of Alabama passed a statute on the subject of bowie knives and Arkansas toothpicks. (DAE.)
Compare **bowie** in the main vocabulary.

Aryan. The Sanskrit *arya* ; in the later languages ' noble ', but in the earlier, ' devoted to, worshipping, the gods of the Brahmans ' ; has yielded *Aryan*, so ignobly used by 20th-Century Germany. The term was introduced by Professor Max Müller, who certainly ' started something ' and, thinking again, did his utmost to disown his theory of an Urvolk. In English, *Aryan* was first bestowed on languages : the Aryan or Indo-European family of languages—a group of languages stretching from Britain to the Indus Valley. Nationalistically, *Aryan* should apply only to those Europeans who, ca. 1500 B.C.,

486

invaded India (the Indus Valley) and Persia; and if it be applied to modern and present-day Europeans, then it applies as much to Greeks and Italians, to Britons and Danes, to Spaniards and Frenchmen, as it does to Germans. In Germany, the word has, since 1933, meant 'non-Jewish', with particular reference to those non-Jews who approximate to Nietzsche's belovèd *blond beast* type.

Claude Farrère has caustically, pertinently written, ' C'est le fait des peuples vaniteux de se targuer d'origines semi-divines, de se dire " aryens," par exemple, encore que la race aryenne n'ait jamais existé, sauf dans des cervelles mi-brumeuses, mi-primaires. Les peuples orgueilleux sont d'une autre classe. Peu leur chaut des cuisses de Jupiter ou des côtes d'Adam. Ils sont fiers de ce qu'ils font ' (*La Onzième Heure*, 1940).— ' Probably no two technical terms have been so consistently and hopelessly misused as *Semite* and *Aryan*,' Patrick Carleton, *Buried Empires*, 1939.

There is, on the subject, an excellent essayette in Walter Theimer's *The Penguin Political Dictionary*. See, too, an essay in my *Words at War: Words at Peace*, 1948.

ass of Buridan. See **Buridan.**

Attila, as a ruthless leader of an army of barbarians, derives from *Attila* (406?–453), who, King of the Huns and ' the Scourge of God ', upset Christendom, both in the East and in the West of Europe, and acted more or less as you would expect.

Auburn system. See entry at **Philadelphia lawyer.**

Aubusson carpet. ' Carpets accounted for most of the total, £7,900, realised at Sotheby's. A Kirkman carpet, nearly 12 ft by 8 ft realised £370. An Aubusson example brought £170. Four Eastern rugs . . . went for £186,' A. C. R. Carter in *The Daily Telegraph*, February 23, 1946.

The Aubusson is a tapestry carpet, made at the town of Aubusson in the Creuse *département* of France; in the carpet world, it spells ' elegance '.

Augean; Augean stable(s). By itself, *Augean* means ' extremely filthy; hence, exceedingly corrupt ', but the term mostly occurs in the phrase *clean* (or *cleanse*) *the Augean stables*, to remove physical filth, hence to suppress moral, especially political, corruption. In Greek mythology, Hercules cleaned in one day, by diverting two small rivers to run through it, the long-uncleaned stables of Augeas (Greek *Augeias*), King of Elis.

Augustine grass, St. This perennial creeping-grass of the southern United States has received its name from *St Augustine* (354–430), a Church Father, a philosopher, and a writer that has, through his *De Civitate Dei* (concerning the city of God) and his *Confessions*, exercised a tremendous religious, literary, philosophical influence; precisely why, I do not know. An 'Indian summer' occurring in September is *St Augustine's* (or *Austin's*) *summer*.

aunt Sally, the effigy at which one throws things at a fair, is a personification: the figure is made to resemble that of a middle-aged or elderly aunt, who must be called by some name, so why not the comfortable one of *Sally*?

Australian slang, in the United States of America, pragmatically means rhyming slang. Probably from that influx of Sydney-siders into California which began as early as 1850 during the gold-rush days and which has never ceased; there have always been numerous Australian tramps and 'con-men' in the Western States. 'In California cities and even as far up as Seattle and Portland, the criminal element converse in a jargon which to the uninitiated must sound rather silly. This is known as "Australian slang," although its users seem unable to state if it originated in Australia. Australian slang is made up of phrases rather than words; but these almost invariably rhyme with the words they represent,' Convict 12627, 'They Talk Like This', *Detective Fiction Weekly*, April 23, 1938. Two examples are *whistle and flute*, 'a suit of clothes', and *twist and twirl*, 'a girl'. Sydney and Melbourne have adopted certain Cockney rhyming-slang terms—and coined a number of others. (See, *passim*, the Addenda to the 3rd edition of my *Dictionary of Slang*.)

Despite the disclaimers made by Sidney J. Baker in his excellent *The Australian Language*, 1945, the rhyming-slang element in Australian speech is far from negligible.

Autolycus. Of the interest, variety, excitement of begging, Glen H. Mullin exclaims, 'Ha! ha! you are a scurvy, unregenerate rogue—and glad of it! It's a heap of satisfaction to be Autolycus and play him at the same time' (*The Adventures of a Scholar Tramp*, 1925).—'The springlike and rebirth quality of the sheep-shearing scenes in *The Winter's Tale* . . . naturally produces Autolycus, whose essence is (i) melody, sunshine, and flowery song, and (ii) shameless disrespect for social values,' G. Wilson Knight, *The Burning Oracle*, 1939.—'In the Constitutions of his Order, St Ignatius
488

laid it down that each of his [spiritual] sons ought to be, as it were, a sort of heavenly Autolycus, with a keen, speculative eye for the unconsidered trifles of humanity, for orphans and out-casts and the disinherited poor,' James Brodrick, *The Origin of the Jesuits*, 1940.

Autolycus, the merry rogue in Shakespeare's *The Winter's Tale*, was ' a snapper-up of unconsidered trifles ' (v, iii) : whence his status in the allusive vocabulary of English : and Shakespeare took the name from Greek mythology, where Autolycus (*Autolukos*), son of Hermes, showed himself an adept in thieving and in trickery.

Averroism is the philosophy, especially the metaphysics, of Averroes of Cordova (1126–98), the principal Arab thinker of the medieval West. He was an interpreter of Aristotle. The greatest Arab philosophy of the East was that of Avicenna (980–1037), an Aristotelian with a neo-Platonic admixture.

Avogadro('s) constant; Avogadro's hypothesis or **law** or **principle.** These technicalities in chemistry are owed to that development of **Gay-Lussac's law** which was made in 1811 by Count Amadeo *Avogadro* (1776–1856), Italian chemist and physicist.

Ayrshire is short for *Ayrshire cattle*, a breed that, valued in dairy-farming, originated in Ayrshire, Scotland, a region famous for its livestock, especially in cattle, and for its crops. ' Recently the Ayrshires have been introduced,' an American official publication, 1856, cited by DAE.

B

Baal. The writer's first recollection, apart from The Bible, of Baal is the following sentence in Conan Doyle's short story, ' The Last Galley ' (reprinted in *Tales of Long Ago*) :—' A brazen, three-pronged ram projected in front, and a high golden figure of Baal, the God of the Phoenicians, children of Canaan, shone upon the after deck.' Figuratively : a false god.

Baal is a personification of the Hebrew *ba'al*, ' lord '. Com-pare the first element of **Beëlzebub** (main list). Compare also this :—' They '—the Semites invading Sumer in prehistoric times—' eagerly adopted the Sumerian deities. An, Enlil and Enki were brought into their pantheon as *Anum, Illil* (also *Bel,*

" the Lord," Hebrew *Baal*) and *Ea*,' Patrick Carleton, *Buried Empires*, 1939.

Babbitt-metal takes its name from Isaac Babbitt (1799–1862) of Massachusetts. In 1839 he patented his invention of a journal box and suggested that the lining consist of what we now call *Babbitt metal*. A soft alloy (tin 20–80%, lead 0–63·5%, copper 1·5–3%, and antimony 10–15%), it is widely used as an anti-frictional material in journal boxes.

Babe Ruth occupies in the annals of American baseball a position comparable with that of W. G. Grace in English cricket: although he retired from big games so long ago as 1935, yet he remains a legend. George Herman Ruth, born in 1894 and known as ' Babe Ruth ' or ' The Bambino ', joined a first-class club in 1914, was at the peak of his form in 1922–30, and in 1927 set up the record of 60 home runs in a season; from 1920 until his retirement, he belonged to the New York American League Club.

' What Babe Ruth was to baseball, the arch-criminal is to the all-too-often moronic main body of a prison population,' Courtney R. Cooper, *Here's to Crime*, 1937.

Babylon; Babylonian. *Babylon* represents—via Latin *Babylon* —the Greek *Babulōn*. The *tower of Babel* was the *tower of Babylon*, and the Greek Proper Name itself, related to Hebrew *Babel*, represents Assyrian *bab-ili*, ' gate of the gods '—compare *Bab-el-Mandeb*, ' gate of the Devil ' (the entrance to the Red Sea : Red because so devilish hot).

The modern sense of Babylon, as in *the modern Babylon* (London : cf. Arnold Bennett's ' thriller ', *The Grand Babylon Hotel*, 1902), ' any great luxury-loving city ', owes much of the ' luxury ' idea—rather the Latin *luxuria*, ' riotous living ', than the current ' excessive comfort; comfort in excess of the normal or the reasonable '—to the metaphorical, indeed the mystical, Babylon of the Apocalypse, Babylon of The Revelation of St John the Divine—' Babylon the Great, the Mother of Harlots and Abominations of the Earth '. Among Protestants, *Babylon* is often applied, polemically, to Rome, the seat of the papal power, as in *the Woman of Babylon* and *the Scarlet Woman* and other amenities of that dreadful *odium theologicum* which disgraces the name of the Christian religion (' Love ye one another ').

Babylonian is the adjective corresponding to the noun in all its senses and in all its shades.

490

Baconian (**theory**) is the theory, arising in the 18th Century, that Francis Bacon (1561–1626) wrote the plays of William Shakespeare. One can easily understand why the theory arose; to understand the ' proofs ' is still easier; to give credence thereto is impossible to any moderately intelligent person that carefully and sympathetically weighs the so-called evidence.

Baddeley cake. This cake is cut every Twelfth Night in the Drury Lane green-room. The cost, with that of the concomitant wine, is defrayed by a bequest of £3 per annum, made by Robert Baddeley (1732?–94), an 18th-Century London actor, who also left property to found a home for infirm actors. A much later Baddeley discovered the mineral *baddeleyite*.

Baedeker raids. German air raids, 1941–42, on such places as Canterbury and York and Bath; places described in much detail in the Baedeker guides to England; raids on antiquities and ecclesiastical architecture.

The Baedeker guides, issued in England, by the old-established firm of John Murray, are translations of the German guide-books issued, from 1839 onwards, by the firm of Karl Baedeker (1801–59).

Those who are addicted to travel have been called ' The Baedeker public ' (Norman Collins in *The Observer*, August 26, 1945).

Baghdad button. See **Aleppo.**

Bailey bridge. ' We had crossed the Volturno by a Bailey bridge that had been built by our own engineers . . . . . . The temporary Bailey structure still spanned the road that crossed the river,' Hammond Jones, *Dead and Alive*, 1946.

' The Bailey Bridge is a thorough-type road bridge, the girders of which are made up from panels 10 ft long by 5 ft deep, coupled together in pairs by means of high-tensile steel panel pins. The roadway is of timber carried on steel stringers . . . . . . The details of the bridge are so arranged that a team of a hundred men can erect a span of 130 ft, capable of carrying the heaviest tanks, in 1½ hours in daylight or 3 hours in the dark without lights, the only erection tackle required being two 15-ton jacks, some leather mallets and spanners, and special chord jacking levers for the two- and three-tier bridges,' *The Welder*, October-December 1946 (with thanks to the Director of Public Relations at the War Office).

The bridge, a marvel of engineering, was designed by Sir Donald Bailey: and the production of its parts, for use by the British Army, began in July 1941.

Bakewell pudding; in England, usually *Bakewell tart*. This confection was originally made and sold at Bakewell in Derbyshire, England. Bakewell is a small market-town, ten miles east-south-east of Buxton. Famed also for its chalybeate springs, Bakewell takes its name therefrom: anciently it was known as *Badecan Wylla*, Bodeca's spring or stream.

Baldwin. ' Tuller can't play the piano . . . and somebody was really going to town on the director's Baldwin a minute ago,' R. L. F. McCombs, *Clue in Two Flats*, (English edition) 1942. A famous American make.

In America it also means ' a variety of winter apple of northeastern America ' (Webster), first grown by Loammi Baldwin (1740–1807), an American engineer and army officer.

Ballyhack !, go to. An American politeness for ' Go to hell ! '; current ca. 1830–1900, and not yet obsolete, though decidedly obsolescent, among Irish Americans. Lexicographer John Russell Bartlett in his *Dictionary of Americanisms*, 1848, remarks, ' I know not its origin. It savors in sound, however, of the Emerald Isle.' To the DAE it is ' an imaginary place far distant or out of the way '. Not so imaginary as all that ! Ballyhack is a fishing village in the south-west of County Wexford; at some considerable distance from Dublin and on a ' coast . . . noted for dangerous sandbanks '. (Chisholm.)

balm of Gilead. See **Gilead.**

Balmer Series, the ; Balmer's Law. ' It has been said that spectra are the language of atoms. Perhaps we may say that [Niels] Bohr first made the language intelligible' in his *Atomic Theory and the Description of Nature*, 1934. ' The way in which his theory interpreted the Balmer and Lyman series forms a most exciting chapter in modern physics, of very great interest to the methodologist,' L. Susan Stebbing, *Philosophy and the Physicists*, 1937. Johann Balmer (1825–98) was a notable German physicist and mathematician. But here is a summary, generously made for me by the late Professor A. W. Stewart, of the Series, the Law, and their relations to the Ångström Unit, Rydberg's Constant, the Lyman Series, etc.

' A light-vibration can be described by means of its wavelength, λ, or by its wave-number, which is the reciprocal of the wavelength. In 1869, Ångström proposed that for purposes of comparison, all wavelengths should be measured in terms of a unit equal to 10^{-10} metres, which is named after him an *Ångström Unit*, and abbreviated to A. or A.U. (Since 1907, a slightly different unit has been employed, which is termed the *International Ångström Unit*, A. or I.A.)

'When the positions of the principal lines in the visible spectrum of hydrogen are plotted on the Ångström scale, they form an arrangement in which, starting from one end, the intervals between the lines grow regularly less and less until the lines become crowded closely together and the series ends at the wavelength 3645·6. In 1885, Balmer showed that the positions of these lines could be calculated from the formula:

$$\text{Wavelength} = 3645\cdot6 \times h \, \frac{m^2}{m^2 - 2^2} \times 10^{-8} \text{ centimetres}$$

in which h is a constant for the whole series, whilst m can be any integer from 3 upwards. When m is made successively 3, 4, 5 . . . etc. in the equation, the value of the right-hand side yields the position on the Ångström Scale of a known line in the series. This relationship is known as *Balmer's Law*, and the lines to which it applies are called the *Balmer Series*.

'*Balmer's Constant*, h, applies only to the hydrogen spectrum; but in 1890, Rydberg worked out a more general expression of the same type, in which Balmer's Constant is displaced by *Rydberg's Constant*, **R**; and this Rydberg Constant can be employed in dealing with the spectrum of any element.

'When applied to the hydrogen spectrum, Rydberg's equation takes the following form:

$$\text{Wave-number} = \mathbf{R} \left(\frac{1}{n^2} - \frac{1}{m^2} \right)$$

in which m and n are integers 1, 2, 3, 4, 5 . . . but m must always be greater than n in order to avoid a negative value in the result. If, now, $n = 1$, whilst m is made in succession 2, 3, 4, 5 . . . etc., the equation gives the positions of a series of lines in the ultra-violet part of the spectrum (the *Lyman Series*). If $n = 2$, and m is successively 3, 4, 5 . . . etc., the equation yields the positions of the various lines in the *Balmer Series* (in the part of the hydrogen spectrum visible to the human eye). When $n = 3$, and m is made in succession 4, 5, 6 . . . etc., the positions of the lines in the infra-red *Paschen Series* are obtained; and when $n = 4$, and m is 5, 6, 7, 8 . . . etc., the positions of the lines in the other infra-red *Brackett Series* are indicated. Experimental work has verified the accuracy of the various equations.'

493

Baltimore, ' the family title of the colonial proprietors of Maryland, and the name of the principal city of that state, founded in 1729 ' (DAE), is famous in American history—see, *passim,* James Truslow Adams, *The Epic of America.* At Baltimore were constructed those fast sailing-vessels known as *Baltimore clippers* (or *flyers*) ; and the *Baltimore bird* or *Baltimore oriole,* the hangbird or hangnest, is ' so call'd from the Colours of Or and Sable, in the coat of Arms, belonging to Lord Baltimore ' (Kersey's *Dictionary,* 1706).

Banagher, beat (or **bang**). ' You take the cake ! . . . . . . Ye beat Banagher—and he beat the devil ! ' John G. Brandon, *Murder for a Million,* 1942. The key is *Banagher,* which, by its sound, suggested *bang,* with *beat* as an alliterative equivalent. Perhaps the inhabitants of Banagher ' loved a scrap '. Banagher is a township in County Londonderry, Ireland. (' Wigs on the green ' and all that?)

Banbury cake. This cake—cf. the origin of **Bakewell tart**— was originally made and sold at the famous old market-town of Banbury, which, in Oxfordshire, lies some fifteen miles from Oxford. Banbury Cross is famed in nursery rhyme and ' Banbury has been noted since Tudor times for cakes which bear its name ' (George G. Chisholm). *Banbury = Banesberie =* Bana's town.

Bangalore torpedo, a long metal pipe filled with T.N.T. and used for cutting wire-entanglements or for detonating mines, is a humorous military term deriving from *Bangalore,* which has, since 1811, been the principal military station in Mysore, India.

Bar-le-Duc. A jam so made from seeded currants that the fruit retains its natural shape. Originally made at Bar-le-Duc (or Bar-sur-Ornain, for it stands on the Ornain River) in the *département* of the Meuse in France.

Barabbas, in The New Testament, was that insurgent and robber whose release the Jewish multitude demanded in preference to Christ's. See *Matthew,* xxvii, 15–16.

Marlowe in *The Jew of Malta* makes Barabas (*sic*) the chief character, a most rapacious Jew. Authors have a suicidal habit of saying, ' Barabbas was a publisher '—as though the fates of authors and publishers were not mutually dependent.

Barbizon school. This school of French (chiefly landscape) painters, including Corot, Rousseau, Daubigny, worked and

494

flourished in the mid-19th Century at the charming village of *Barbizon*, near the forest of Fontainebleau.

Barmecide feast, an illusion of plenty (properly, food), derives from *The Arabian Nights*, where a number of the *Barmecides*, a wealthy family, once served a beggar with an imaginary feast. But, in the story, the beggar's jovial compliance earned him a feast not in the least imaginary.

' The delusive hospitality of your cousin mocks me across vast frozen distances like the banquets of the Barmecide,' Michael Innas, *Appleby's End*, 1945.

Barsac. ' " Light wines like Chablis, Graves, Barsac, and so on, we sell pretty reasonable ",' Gerald Kersh, *Night and the City*, 1938.

After Sauternes, Barsac is the leading white-wine district of the Gironde : the wines of these two French communes are rather alike.

Bartlett pear. ' Once upon a time there was a slim Girl with a Forehead which was Shiny and Protuberant, like a Bartlett Pear,' George Ade, *Fables in Slang*, 1899.

So named from the first distributor of this succulent variety (anglicé *Williams pear*) of the Bon Chrétien pear into the United States : Enoch Bartlett (1779–1860) bought the farm where it was first grown in America—that of Captain Thomas Brewer, who introduced the pear.

Bartram. William Bartram (1739–1823), American naturalist, son of a botanically famous father, published in 1791 an account of his extensive travels in the south-east of the United States in search of plant and animal specimens. (Webster BD.) After him have been named : *Bartram('s) oak* and *Bartram's sandpiper* or *tattler*.

Basedow's disease is a swelling of the thyroid gland—a bronchocele—a goitre—Derbyshire neck. It took its name from a German doctor, Karl von Basedow (1799–1854), who described the disease in 1840. Compare **Graves's disease.**

Bashan. See **bull of Bashan.**

Bath brick (often **bath brick**)—**bun**—**chair** (often **bath chair**)—**Oliver**—**stone.** In all, the reference is to Bath in Somerset ; famous as a watering-place (the very name denotes ' the city at the baths ') since the 9th Century. In detail :

B. brick, a calcareous earth moulded into the shape of a brick and made at Bridgwater, not far from Bath; *B. bun*—because originally it was baked there; *B. chair*: used by the invalids and old people who resorted to or resided in Bath; *B. Oliver*, a biscuit named after a Bath physician, Dr Oliver; *B. stone* (or *B. oolite*) is quarried in the neighbourhood of this gracious city, so severely damaged in a 'Baedeker' raid in 1941.

Baumé scale—Sikes scale—Twaddell scale; also Baumé hydrometer. These three scales of density, used in Hydrometry, derive from the names of their scientific devisers.

> Baumé: See below.
>
> Sikes: B. Sikes's hydrometer was accepted by the British Government in 1817 'for estimating the duties on spirituous liquors', as we learn from an anonymous pamphlet of that year.
>
> Twaddell: William Twaddell (died ca. 1840), Scottish inventor, ca. 1830, of a hydrometer for liquids heavier than water.
>
> 'One method of grading oil [petroleum], and consequently of price-fixing, is to determine the gravity of the oil with the Baumé hydrometer, and to grade it as to price and utility on the basis of its grading on the Baumé scale' (Jones & Bryan, *North America*, 7th edition, 1946). Both the two Baumé scales and the hydrometer were invented by Antoine Baumé (1728–1804), a French chemist.

Bayard, a chivalrous and stainless man, derives from the lifestory of Pierre Terrail (1473?–1524), Seigneur de *Bayard*, a great soldier and a fine man, who died in battle after a life that had earned him the now proverbial 'title', *Chevalier sans peur et sans reproche*.

beat Banagher. See **Banagher.**

Beaufort's scale, a means whereby to determine the velocity of wind, was devised in 1805 by Sir Francis Beaufort (1774–1857), who came to be a rear-admiral. He was a notable surveyor and hydrographer; indeed, from 1829 to 1855 he held the post of hydrographer to the British Navy.

Bechstein. A Bechstein grand piano—from the name of the German maker; the firm of Bechstein was founded at Berlin in the 1850's. 'There was the usual mess. Dust, chips, half a bottle of stout on her ladyship's Bechstein,' Joyce Cary, *The*

Horse's Mouth, 1944. When—if ever—we shall have fully accepted the term, we shall write it *bechstein*.

The **neo-Bechstein** is a semi-electric piano, introduced in 1931.

Becquerel's rays are the rays emitted by a radio-active substance: in 1903, in conjunction with Pierre and Mme Curie, Antoine Henri Becquerel (1852–1908) received the Nobel prize in physics. Famous son of a famous father, whose own father was famous; ca. 1840–1910 was a great period in French science.

Bedfordshire, go to. This pun on *go to bed* dates from the days of Queen Elizabeth. The allusion to the English county of Bedfordshire contains nothing more than the obvious pun: Bedfordshire people are no sleepier than others. Compare *the Land of Nod*.

bedouin, a nomad, affords an easy transition from *Bedouin*, a nomadic Arab of the deserts, whether of the Near East or of North Africa. The English word adapts the French *Bédouin*, from colloquial Arabic *bidwan*, the plural of *badwi* or *badawi*, a dweller in the desert or in ' the open lands ' as opposed to the towns.

[**Bedourie oven.** Concerning an Aboriginal's hole-in-the-ground oven, Archer Russell, in that fascinating book, *A Tramp-Royal in Wild Australia*, 1934, remarks, ' This was to be the oven of early man and . . . as efficacious . . . as a bushman's Bedourie oven, or even a grand electric range '. Problematic.]

Beecher's Bible is a Sharp's rifle, used in the U.S.A. in the 1850's. In February 1856, *The New York Evening Post* reported Henry Ward Beecher (1813–87), the famous clergyman and orator, as having said that ' the Sharp rifle was a truly moral agency . . . more moral power . . ., so far as the shareholders of Kansas were concerned, than a hundred Bibles ' (DAE). The term remained current at least as late as 1914.

Beethoven, as in ' He's no Beethoven '. Of Ludwig van Beethoven (1770–1827), Dr Percy Scholes has written: ' More than any other composer he deserves to be called the Shakespeare of music, for he reaches to the heights and plumbs the depths of the human spirit as no other composer has done '. What Shakespeare is to world literature, Beethoven is to world music.

'Beethoven in a group of yodelers could not have been more solitary than a yegg among men who did not live as dangerously as himself . . . The yeggs moved sardonically in their mysterious realm,' Jim Tully, ' Yeggs '—in *The American Mercury* of April 1933.

Belgravia, together with **Mayfair,** forms the larger, the most famous part of fashionable residential London. To say *Belgravia* is to say ' aristocratic dignity '—with perhaps a connotation of the august charms of yester-year.

From *Belgrave Square*, named after the ground-landlord's estate, Belgrave in Leicestershire.

Belial, man or **son of,** a wicked man, comes from the Biblical *sons of Belial*, as if Belial were a Proper Name (as in fact it may be), although *Belial*, both in Old Testament and in Apocryphal, as well as in rabbinical literature, is a word of doubtful signification; the usual rendering is ' wickedness ', secondarily ' destruction ', the Hebrew *beliya'al* being ' without use, without profit '. There seems to have been an ancient folklore, or folk-etymological, association with *Baal*.

Belisha beacon. A post, topped with a yellow globe, to indicate a street-crossing for pedestrians. Either thought of or approved by Leslie Hore-*Belisha* when, in 1934, he was Minister of Transport.

Bellona, earlier *Duellona*, is the Roman goddess of war, hence a personification of war itself (Latin *bellum*).

belted Swiss. ' '' They're judging Ayrshires and Belted Swiss this morning . . .'' '' . . . Inside were groups of cattle, black, with belts of white around their middles,' Rex Stout, *Some Buried Caesar*, 1939. Webster says nothing about *belted Swiss*, but does mention *Dutch belted cattle* or, for short, *Dutch belted*, similarly coloured and marked—and originating in Holland.

Bengal light; B. stripes. The latter, a striped kind of gingham, was made originally in Bengal, with which compare *bengaline*, a corded fabric of the same origin. The association of *Bengal light* (or *fire*) is more poetical than historical. But a *Bengal tiger* is the tiger proper; it abounds in lower Bengal.

Benghazi cooker. (Military technicality rather than soldiers' slang.)

' They began to brew up their mid-morning cup of " char "

498

or tea on a Benghazi cooker, which is only a petrol tin cut in half and filled with petrol-soaked sand,' George Greenfield, *Desert Episode* (the 8th Army, October 1942), 1945.

Benghazi, a seaport on the Mediterranean coast of Africa, was prominent in the communiqués, whether air or land, of 1940–42. It used to be—and to some extent still is—a starting-point for desert caravans.

Benthamism; Benthamist. Jeremy Bentham (1748–1832), the English jurist and philosopher, propounded and expounded that position in Ethics which is centred in ' the greatest happiness of the greatest number ' as the criterion of moral goodness. Benthamism is, therefore, a form of utilitarianism.

Bergen rucksack. ' Wolfe put his Bergen rucksack on the floor ' (James Aldridge, *Of Many Men*, 1946). This rucksack is in the Norwegian style—from Bergen, a port in southern Norway.

Bergsonian, Bergsonism. The latter is but another name for the theory of creative evolution, set forth by the great French philosopher, Henri Bergson (1859–1941), winner of the Nobel prize for literature in 1927. With a book on Consciousness in 1889, he made his name; with *L'Evolution créatrice* he brilliantly confirmed it. His style possesses a wonderful limpidity.

Berkeleian means ' typical of, deriving from, that subjective idealism which was so ably set forth by George Berkeley (1685–1753) '. His fame rests chiefly upon *The Principles of Human Knowledge*, 1710; he returned to the theme, in a more popular manner, in *Three Dialogues between Hylas and Philonous*, 1713.

Bermudian-rigged is applied to a sailing vessel rigged in the *Bermudian rig*, a fore-and-aft rig employed in *Bermuda*.

Bertillon system refers not only to fingerprints but also to markings and anthropometric evidence, the whole constituting a means to the identification of criminals. It was devised by the Frenchman Alphonse *Bertillon* (1853–1914), anthropologist and criminologist, during his tenure of the headship of the identification department in the prefecture of the Seine.

Bewick's wren abounds in the south and the middle west of the United States; the great naturalist Audubon remarked upon its general similarity to the ' great Caroline wren '. It was named after Thomas *Bewick* (1753–1828), that English wood-

499

engraver who excelled in painstaking representations of British birds and beasts; for the birds, see especially his illustrations to *The History of British Birds*, 1797. It is time that someone should render full justice to this most conscientious and verisimilitudinous craftsman and artist.

Commemorative is that British bird, **Bewick's swan.**

Birretta. 'For ammunition to fit Birretta automatics as much as £5 for 20 rounds has been paid. The Birretta, pocket-sized and easily concealable, is extremely useful to the gangster,' Duncan Webb in *Daily Express*, September 17, 1945. A revolver of Continental make.

black Maria. 'There can be, I suppose, no moment quite so full of loneliness as when she' (a first-timer in prison) 'sets off in the traditional Black Maria with the women officers, who have come to fetch her,' Mrs Cecil Chesterton, *Women of the Underworld*, 1931.
Black: the police van is black. *Maria*: from that self-protective irony with which the unfortunate speak affectionately of something unpleasant.

Blenheim = *B. orange* (a kind of apple) and *B. spaniel*. The former was first grown successfully at *Blenheim* Palace, the seat of the Duke of Marlborough, in Oxfordshire, granted to the 1st Duke in honour of his victory at Blenheim, properly *Blindheim* in Bavaria, in 1704. And the spaniel was originally reared there.

Bloomsbury owes its pejorative nuances: ' (selfishly) high-brow; narrowly intellectualist; " too, too literary "; cheaply Bohemian ': to the fact that Bloomsbury, London, W.C.1, was, during the 1920's, the home or the resort of many authors and some artists. Compare the use of *Chelsea*.

blue Peter. See **Peter, blue.**

Boanerges or **b—,** a shouting, noisy, declamatory orator or preacher, derives from ' James the son of Zebedee, and John the brother of James . . . he [Christ] surnamed them Boanerges, which is, the sons of thunder,' *Mark*, iii, 17, for they were mighty preachers. The word is Greek, ' probably representing the Aramaic equivalent of Hebrew *benāi regesh* (Webster).

Bob Acres. ' It would have been the better part of valor to have emulated Bob Acres—back up and " live to fight another day ",' George Graham Rice, *My Adventures with Your Money*, 1913. Bob Acres is a character in R. B. Sheridan's brilliant comedy, *The Rivals*, 1775; he refuses a duel.

Bodoni is short for *Bodoni type*, the first roman type to merit the name 'modern'. Giambattista Bodoni (1740–1813) was an Italian printer; he was also, as we see, a type-designer.

Boeotian. 'How is it that we are all in this Boeotian fog of ignorance?'—Ronald Knox, *Let Dons Delight*, 1940.

Boeotia (Greek *Boiōtia*), marching with Attica on the northwest, became a by-word for stupidity and ignorance, despite the fact that it produced Pindar, Corinna, Plutarch: as Cicero and Horace—to quote two among many—have remarked.

Bofors is short for *Bofors gun*. 'The shells . . . were those for the twenty-five and forty millimetre automatic anti-aircraft guns . . . made by the Swedish firm of Bofors,' Eric Ambler, *Cause for Alarm*, 1938; 'He was looking directly at a Bofors 4 cm. gun,' James Aldridge, *The Sea Eagle*, 1944.

The Bofors munition works in Sweden were established by Alfred Nobel (1833–96), the institutor of the **Nobel Prizes.**

Bohr model atom, the. The hydrogen atom consists of a positive proton round which revolves a negative electron. According to 'classical' dynamics, the electron might move in an orbit of any radius; but such a system would emit a 'continuous spectrum'—i.e., one containing a series of lines with no gaps between them. Actually, the hydrogen spectrum consists of a series of lines isolated from each other. (See **Balmer Series.**) In order to account for the facts, the Danish physicist Niels Bohr (b. 1885) proposed what is termed the Bohr model atom. He assumed that only certain circular orbits are possible for the electron, orbits having radii in the ratios 1^2, 2^2, 3^2 . . . etc. While moving in any of these so-called 'stationary orbits', the electron neither liberates nor absorbs energy. If, however, the electron jumps from an outer orbit to an inner one, a corresponding amount of energy is emitted from the atom in the form of radiation of a fixed wave-length; and, conversely, if the atom absorbs light, the electron rises from an inner orbit to an outer one of greater radius. From calculations of the energy possessed by the electron when in the various 'stationary orbits', Bohr was able to show that each of the possible 'jumps' corresponded to the emission of one of the main lines in the hydrogen spectrum. This, however, left unexplained the existence of the finer lines.

501

The German physicist, Arnold Sommerfeld (b. 1868) was able to extend Bohr's ideas to these finer lines by assuming that in addition to circular orbits, elliptical ones are also possible for the electron. In both cases, energy is regarded as conforming to Planck's Quantum Theory (see **Planck's constant**). Before Bohr published his theory, the Rydberg Constant (see **Balmer Series**) was regarded as a constant of nature, but Bohr showed that it is merely a calculable number with the value:

$$R = \frac{2\pi^2 \, \mathbf{m} \mathbf{e}^4}{\mathbf{c} \mathbf{h}^3}$$

in which π is the ratio of the circumference of a circle to its radius, $\mathbf{m}$ is the mass of the electron, $\mathbf{e}$ is the charge on the electron, $\mathbf{c}$ is the velocity of light, and $\mathbf{h}$ is Planck's Constant. Bohr's ideas can be applied mathematically to the case of the ionized helium atom, which contains a nucleus with two protons, about which circulates a single electron; but no systems more complex than these—such as the helium or the lithium atom—have as yet been handled mathematically, though possible arrangements of electrons in them have been postulated.

(Owed to the kindness of my friend, the late Professor A. W. Stewart.)

Bombay duck is a folk-etymological variation of *bummalo*, a small fish found in the Indian Ocean; *bummalo* comes from *bombila* in the Mahratti dialect, and *Bombay duck* was originally, as it still is mainly, a sailor's humorous perversion.

Bond Street. ' A London street, especially as resort of fashionable loungers (a B.-S. exquisite) ': the incomparable Fowlers' definition in *The Concise Oxford Dictionary of Current English*.
' Daily the wealthy, fat, and bulging ladies submitted their too, too solid flesh to the Bond Street shrines of vanity,' Walter Greenwood, *Only Mugs Work*, 1938.

Boone. See **Daniel Boone**.

Bordeaux mixture, used for the riddance of fungi, consists of water, blue vitriol, lime : its colour resembles that of claret (see **bordeaux,** main vocabulary).

Border Leicesters. ' Cabell's sheep were all merinoes, th small-bodied animal . . . that grows a weight of fine silky woo out of all proportion to its size, but has next to no meat com pared with the big Border Leicesters and Lincolns and South Downs, which have next to no wool,' Brian Penton, *Landtakers* (Australia, ca. 1840–60), 1934. Leicesters originated in the county of Leicestershire, England. 'The famous L. breed of sheep, which yields one of the finest of " long-stapled " wools . . . was perfected about the middle of the eighteenth century by Bakewell, a noted agriculturist of this county ' (Chisholm).

Borrand water. 'After Miss Karn's Borrand water was poured and iced, I took a sip of my milk,' says Archie Goodwin in Rex Stout's *Where There's a Will* (English edition, 1941). From the name of the American manufacturer.

Boston bag, fern, ledger, rocker, terrier (see **boston,** main list) have all been named from Boston, Massachusetts, itself named from Boston, Lincolnshire; originally *Botolphstown*, from *Botolph*, a hermit that, in the 7th Century A.D., lived on the site. *Boston beans* are navy beans, baked and cooked with pork; Boston has a famous harbour.

'The books . . . were more sensitive than the Chippendale end-chair . . . or the Windsors or the Boston rocker,' John P. Marquand, *Wickford Point*, 1939.

bow down in the house of Rimmon. 'Though individuals might bow down in the house of Rimmon, . . . Jews, as a rule, Hellenisers or otherwise, held fast to their religion,' W. W. Tarn, *Hellenistic Civilisation*, revised edition, 1930 ; ' The most powerful god [of Hellenistic Syria] was Hadad of Damascus (Rimmon of the Old Testament), who absorbed many local Baals ' (same book).

Among the Amorite divinities was ' the weather-god Adad (Biblical Hadad or Rimmon), generally depicted as a horned man bearing an axe and [a] thunderbolt,' Patrick Carleton, *Buried Empires*, 1939.

'[Father] Eadell, with the sly face of Naaman in the house of Rimmon, tugging awkwardly at the Protestant bell,' R. C. Hutchinson, *Interim*, 1945.

'And Naaman said . . . thy servant will henceforth offer neither burnt offering nor sacrifice unto other gods . . . In this thing the Lord pardon thy servant, that . . . I bow myself in the house of Rimmon : when I bow down myself in the house of Rimmon, the Lord pardon thy servant in this thing ' (2 *Kings*, v, 17–18).

Bow Street runner. Apart from loosely meaning a precursor of ' a (London) policeman ', the term is especially and correctly applied to any one of those eight officers who, appointed in 1805, were attached to the *Bow Street* Court and, from their red waistcoats, known popularly as *robin redbreasts* : the forerunners of the modern detective police, notably of the Criminal Investigation Department.

Bowery boy, literally, is the young rowdy or rough that, ca. 1820–95, infested the Bowery in New York; hence, derivatively, a young rough or tough—a **hooligan,** a **larrikin.** The word *Bowery* represents the Dutch *bouwerij,* a farm.

Brackett Series. See **Balmer Series.**

Bradshaw is short for *Bradshaw's Monthly Railway Guide,* first issued in 1839 by George Bradshaw (1803–53), a printer. After his premature death, the publication and the name were continued, going from strength to strength—from complexity to complexity—but always as accurate as it is fascinating.

Bragg angle; Bragg loop. The former (' the small angle between an incident X-ray beam and the planes of a crystal' : Webster) is named after Sir William Henry Bragg (1862–1942), that famous English physicist with the equally famous son, William Laurence Bragg (b. 1890); in 1915 they jointly won the Nobel prize in physics. To them is due also an anti-submarine device, the *Bragg loop,* which, used in the war of 1914–18, is mentioned in *A Minor Operation* (1937), by ' J. J. Connington ', himself a great scientist.

bramah lock (and **key**); **bramah press.** Joseph Bramah (1748–1814), an English engineer, invented a machine, not called after him, for printing banknotes, and in 1784 a safety lock and key and, in 1795, a hydraulic press.

Bramley's seedling, often *Bramley seedling,* is an excellent cooking apple and a good keeper; said to be a Nottinghamshire apple. ' We should be speaking in conformity with the rules of good English if we were to say that the dish contained real apples and imitation apples. But this mode of speaking does not lead us to suppose that there are two varieties of *apples,* namely real and imitation apples, as there are Bramley seedlings and Blenheim pippins,' L. Susan Stebbing, *Philosophy and the Physicists,* 1937.

Mr Bramley is something of a mystery, but probably one would not go far wrong in postulating an enterprising English fruit-grower. Apparently a Mr Bramley, butcher at Southwell

504

in Nottinghamshire, grew a ' sport ' apple, which attracted the attention of the famous Southwell nurseries.

brand of Cain. See **Cain.**

Brasher doubloon. ' It is a gold coin, roughly equivalent to a twenty-dollar gold piece, and about the size of a half-dollar . . . It was made for the State of New York in the year 1787 . . . . . . The Brasher doubloon was coined probably by the pressure moulding process and its maker was a private gold-smith named Ephraim Brasher, or Brashear.   Where the name survives it is usually spelled *Brashear*, but not on the coin,' Raymond Chandler, *The High Window*, (English edition) 1943. There is at least one famous Brashear—as well as at least one famous Brasher—in 19th–20th-Century American annals.

break Priscian's head. See **Priscian's head.**

Breda. A German machine-gun. ' The Bren guns could be heard replying to the M.G. 34's and Bredas as " B " Company fought its way forward,' George Greenfield, *Desert Episode* (the Battle of El Alamein, October 1942), 1945.
  ' In a few minutes we were aboard a sloop . . . with . . . several sets of triple Breda machine guns amidships,' Brigadier James Hargest, *Farewell Campo 12*, 1944.
  Breda is a Dutch town with a royal military academy : but *is* that the clue?

Brewer's blackbird and **Brewer's sparrow,** i.e. the blue-headed grackle and Brewer's bunting, are American birds, named for T. M. Brewer (1814–80), American ornithologist.

Brewster, an American make of hat popular in the 1830's and 1840's, commemorates its maker.

Briareus; Briarean. The latter, loosely ' many-handed ', properly ' hundred-handed ', comes from the former, in Greek mythology a hundred-handed monster or giant.   Strictly there were three of these *hekatonkheires*, the others being Kottos and Guēs (Cottus and Gyes). The Greek *Briareos* derives from *briaros*, strong.

Brigham tea. A medicinal tea, used in the United States. ' For cleaning out the blood in the springtime there is no herb that excels Brigham tea, so named because the Mormon elders have long recognized its vim-giving qualities,' ' Dean Stiff ',

505

The Milk and Honey Route, 1931; the Mormon sect, as not every schoolboy remembers, having been founded by Brigham Young.

Bright's disease ('granular degeneration of the kidneys': The OED) is so named because Dr Richard Bright (1789–1858), by researches of which the results were published in 1827, determined the nature of the malady.
Compare **Graves's disease.**

Brillat-Savarin, 'a gastronome; an authority on cookery', commemorates the fame of Anthelme Brillat-Savarin (1755–1826), that French politician who fled from the French Revolution and that writer who is best known for *La Physiologie du Goût*, 1825: a literary book on cookery and the art of eating; an entertaining, lively, witty book.

Bristol board; Bristol fashion; Bristol milk. The first is a fine pasteboard, associated since ca. 1800 with Bristol; the second, 'in good order', is a nautical term, reminiscent of the days when Bristol was the second port in Britain and its sailors famed throughout the world; the third, an excellent type of old sherry, dates from ca. 1640 and recalls the fact that in the 17th–18th Centuries, nearly all imports from Spain were landed at Bristol and the further fact that in the 18th Century the citizens of Bristol were notable drinkers thereof—see a delightful and witty passage in Sir Ernest Barker's *Essays on Government*, 1946.

Britannia metal, which might well be shortened and small-initialled thus: *britannia*. It is an alloy of tin, hardened by adding 5–10% antimony (T. M. Lowry, *Inorganic Chemistry*), much used, because in appearance it resembles silver, in the manufacture of cheap cutlery: and so a boon to the British poor. Compare:—

Briticism or **Britishism.** The latter is by purists regarded as preferable; strictly, *Briticism*—as opposed to *Americanism*—should be *Britannicism*. For the etymological history of *British*, as of '*Britannia* metal', see **Briton** in the main vocabulary.

broderie anglaise is the technical name for a particular kind of English embroidery: the French have, for centuries, excelled in the art, and the craft, of embroidery; hence the adoption of the French name for the style.

Bronx cheer is the American equivalent of the English *raspberry* (or *rarzer*), a rude explosive noise. From *Bronx*, a New York

506

City borough, where much baseball is played and the ' fans ' are healthily unreluctant to express disapproval.

brown Bess, the old flint-lock rifle of the British Army, was so named because its barrel was of a bronze colour and because the soldier hugged it against his shoulder as though it were his Bess.

brown George was originally a loaf of coarse brown bread, hence a coarse—and hard—brown biscuit. By extension the name was applied also to a small brown wig and a large brown earthenware vessel. The *George* part of the name is merely a personification without any specific reason.

Brownian movement or **motion,** in science, was so named because it was discovered by Robert Brown (1773–1858), a Scottish physician, botanist, naturalist. He accompanied Flinders's expedition to Australia in 1801–05.

Brunswick black—blue—green. These colours were so named because, originally, they were manufactured in the former duchy of Brunswick, especially perhaps in its capital—Brunswick.

Brussells may be either *B. carpet* or *B. sprouts*, the latter being often lower-cased, as in ' How much less awful the man would be, Eustace was thinking, as he ate his mutton and brussels sprouts, if only he lost his temper, or got drunk,' Aldous Huxley, *Time Must Have a Stop*, 1945.

Buchmanism ; Buchmanite. These names are preferable to the synonymous *Oxford Group Movement* and *Oxford-grouper*. ' The moral rearmament ' evangelism, initiated in 1921 by Frank Buchman (b. 1878), proved inefficacious against Nazism, yet the war of 1939–45 does not appear to have destroyed it.

Buddhism ; Buddhist. The doctrine of salvation by suffering was propounded and developed by Gautama Buddha (563–483 B.C.). He preached virtue, wisdom, self-abnegation, and was a great and selfless spirit. His name, which means, literally, ' The Enlightened ', derives from the Sanskrit *bodhati*, ' he awakes ; hence, he understands '.

bull of Bashan. ' She had managed to hold her nerve while Stephen raged around like a bull of Bashan and made himself generally ridiculous,' Margaret Armstrong, *The Blue Santo Murder Mystery*, (English edition) 1943.

507

'Many bulls have compassed me : strong bulls of Bashan have beset me round. They gaped upon me with their mouths, as a ravening and a roaring lion ' : so the Psalmist (xxii, 12–13). In ancient times, Bashan was a small kingdom ; for centuries it was famous for its rams and its bulls.

Bunsen('s) battery—burner—cell—disk—flame—lamp ; bunsenite (a nickel monoxide). All these terms commemorate the fame of Robert Wilhelm *Bunsen* (1811–99), that German chemist who, working as a professor at Heidelberg University, singly discovered much and, with Roscoe the reciprocity law, with Kirchkoff the elements cesium and rubidium.

Buridan, ass of. Jean Buridan (died ca. 1360), a French scholastic philosopher, is reputed, perhaps falsely, to have devised the dilemma of the ass placed between two equidistant trusses of hay, a problem designed to illustrate the will's inability to choose between a pair of equally powerful motives : ' Buridan's ass '. Compare **Occam's razor.**

Burma head. See **Punjaub head.**

Burnham scale. Harry Lawson (1862–1933), 1st Viscount Burnham, in 1903 succeeded his father as director of *The Daily Telegraph*, which he sold in 1927. A Member of Parliament, he took a voluble part in public life and presided over the committee that in 1919–20 established and awarded the Burnham scales of teachers' salaries.

Burton, gone for a. See **gone . . .**

Byzantine ; Byzantinism. ' Mr [Charles] Williams represents an unexpected transformation of the romantic impulse— a transformation conveniently symbolized by the " Byzantine " and " Arthurian " elements in his poetry,' C. S. Lewis in *The Oxford Magazine*, May 24, 1945.

' Italian painting threw off with Giotto the last trammels of Byzantinism,' Dean Milman, *History of Latin Christianity*, vol. IX (1855), cited by The OED.

Both the adjective and the noun imply the characteristics of Byzantine art—especially architecture, distinguished by its use of mosaic and of geometrical figures : intricately ornate. (For a fascinating, most readable, yet scholarly history of the Byzantine empire, see either Auguste Bailly's *Byzance*, Paris

1939, or Norman Baynes' *The Byzantine Empire*, 1925—the latter is brief, a ' Home University Library ' book, but it has been brought up-to-date.)

See also **besant** in the main vocabulary.

C

Cadmean victory is a synonym of the much better known *Pyrrhic victory* (see **pyrrhic** in the main vocabulary). In Greek mythology, *Cadmus* (Greek *Kadmos*), seeking Europe, arrived at the future Cadmea, where he sent his companions for water from a spring guarded by a dragon ; the dragon, slaying them, was therefor slain by Cadmus. He sowed the dragon's teeth, whence sprang armed warriors ; these he set fighting, until only five remained : the probable origin of the *Kadmeia nikë* or *Cadmean victory* (Herodotus, *History*, Book I, sec. 166).

After him is also named the **Cadmean alphabet** : *Kadmeia grammata*, the old Greek alphabet of sixteen letters, afterwards augmented by the eight Ionic letters. In the legend that he taught the ' rude Boeotians ' (see **Boeotian**) the use of the alphabet, there is a trace of historic fact, for the Greek alphabet is based upon the Phoenician script and Cadmus was the son of Agenor, king of Tyre—a city that, like Sidon, formed part of Phoenicia.

Caesarean birth ; Caesarean operation (or **section**). Childbirth effected by the section (or cutting through) of the abdomen-walls, this having been done to bring Julius Caesar into the world he was so profoundly, so trenchantly, to influence.

Cain ; to raise Cain. ' I was mad at the whole thing and I was all for tearing round and raising Cain, and asking for explanations and whatnot,' John Gloag, *Manna*, 1940.

The reference is to the Biblical Cain, the first (Biblical) murderer, as in ' Very large and prominent ears . . . As time passed and I came into contact with scores of murderers, I found that nearly every one had the same distinguishing marks . . . Is it the brand of Cain? ' (H. V. Triston, *Men in Cages*, 1938). Compare the figurative use of murder in ' This is murder ! '—i.e., outrageous. Apparently the phrase originated as an American euphemism for the rude British *raise the devil*. Cf. **Cain-coloured** (p. 79).

509

Calcavella or **Carcavelhos** (or **-llos**) is that sweet, dry, full-blooded Portuguese wine which is 'grown' at Carcavelhos near Lisbon.

Californian honey. 'The coastal valleys of California have a still better soil and climate [than the valley of the Var in south-east France]; and, therefore, the Californian flowers are more burdened with oil, and have a more powerful perfume. Indeed, it is this which causes the Californian honey to rival that of Hymettus or Chamounix or Narbonne in delicacy, and that of Atacama in colour,' Lionel W. Lyde, *Man and His Markets*, 1896. **Californian fruits** are even more famous.

Calippic (or **Callipic**) **cycle, the.** See **Metonic cycle.**

Camberwell beauty. The butterfly known to scientists as *Vanessa Antiopa*: presumably because, in the 1840's (when the topographical name arrived), it frequented Camberwell—now part of London.
'Everyone knows Camberwell. It is famous in farce. " Did you send your wife to Camberwell? " is a stage classic. It is famous in history—Mr Joseph Chamberlain was born there. Its poetical note is sounded in the name given to a dainty butterfly . . . You have hardly passed its famous Green before you are on Denmark Hill, among old country houses with far-stretching gardens and fair lawns and great leafy trees ': thus the once famous journalist, publicist, novelist, G. R. Sims, in *Off the Track in London*; but that was away back in 1911.

Camborne, give (someone). 'During certain riots in Camborne' in the 1870's, ' " Give him Camborne! " originated, and since then it has spread through the county ' of Cornwall: *The English Dialect Dictionary*, 1898.
The market-town of Camborne, noted for its tin-mines, lies nine miles east of St Ives.

campeachy wood, or logwood, is a red dye-wood. It was originally exported from *Campeachy*, and famous in England as early as 1650. Campeachy occupies the south-west of the Yucatan peninsula in Central America; much timber is felled there.

Camponac. 'Into the lower regions of the Citadel they went, into those labyrinthine and gloom-soaked depths that had been the vintries: dim Gothic vaults haunted by the ghosts of

'Château Margaux '47, of Saint Emilion, of Camponac and Lafaurie-Peyraguey,' Harry Hervey, *School for Eternity*, 1942.

Canada balsam (turpentine from the balsam fir)—**C. goose** (a common North American wild goose)—**C. jay** (a North American jay)—**C. pest** (a herb)—**C. plum** (North American)—**C. thistle** (European thistle, naturalized to become a confounded nuisance)—**C. warbler**—**C. wormwood** (a weedy herb),—all these, like **Canadian bacon** (bacon cut from back and loin, and hickory-smoked) and **Canadian golden-rod** (a flowering plant), are tributes—mainly from the U.S.A.—to Canada's fertility.

Canopic jar or **vase.** 'In a corner stood . . . a huge mummy . . . The canopic jars and outer coffins belonging to it were still unpacked,' John Ross, *Masques and Phases*, 1909.

In the burial rites of ancient Egypt these jars or vases contained the entrails of the embalmed body. *Canopic* represents the Latin *Canopicus*, ' of Canopus ', Canopus being an Egyptian town, famed for their manufacture—or perhaps rather for their utilization—and for its luxury. The Greek form is *Kánōpos* or *Kánōbos*, whence the Latin *Canobus*.

' The city [of Alexandria] overflowed its wall on both sides; on the west lay the native Egyptian quarter; on the east, beyond the suburb of Eleusis, the gardens of the wealthy extended to Canopus, Alexandria's playground,' W. W. Tarn, *Hellenistic Civilisation* [323–31 B.C.], 1927.

Canterbury lamb is lamb meat from the province of Canterbury in the east of the South Island of New Zealand, and wonderful sheep-country it is ! New Zealand mutton is highly esteemed, even in New Zealand, and Canterbury mutton stands supreme.

Cape elk (the eland)—**gooseberry**—**jasmine**—**wine.** The Cape that has originated these four terms is the Cape of Good Hope, although the region (Cape Colony), rather than the headland, is understood. In **Cape clouds,** however, Cape Horn is meant; Magellan (1480–1521) discovered the straits named after him, and these clouds are also known as *Magellan clouds*.

With *Cape wine* we may consider **Cape brandy** and **Cape smoke**; the latter is a *cloudy* variety of the former and was in 1879 denounced as ' a poison calculated to burn the inside of a rhinoceros ' (C. Pettman, *Africanderisms*, 1913). In David Collins's *An Account of the English Colony in New South Wales* vol. I, 1798, are the following two interesting items concerning brandy from the Cape of Good Hope (all ships sailing from England to Australia touched at Cape Town for supplies): in December 1793, it was selling ' per gallon from 16s. to £1 '; in reference to March 1795, ' On the 17th St. Patrick found many votaries in the settlement. Some Cape brandy recently imported in the Britannia appeared to have arrived very seasonably; and libations to the saint were so plentifully poured, that at night the cells were full of prisoners.'

' In the early days of New South Wales, . . . my boyish experience familiarized me with various products, animate and inanimate, for this far and oft-forgotten continent [of Australia]. The mention of " Cape " geese, " Cape " wine, " Cape " horses, " Cape " gooseberries was unceasing,' ' Rolf Boldrewood ', *In Bad Company and Other Stories* (' The Australian Native-Born Type '), 1901.

Capehart. 'A dim pleasant room with an apricot Chinese rug . . . deep-sided chairs, a number of white drum lamps, a big Capehart in the corner, a long and very wide davenport . . . and a fireplace with a copper screen,' Raymond Chandler, *The Lady in the Lake*, (English edition) 1944.

Capua. A luxurious, emasculating city, town, place; over-luxurious and enervating. ' How . . . skilfully Gainsborough painted, before at Bath he found his Capua,' *The Athenaeum*, October 29, 1887, cited by W, who remarks, ' From traditional effect on Hannibal's soldiers'. This chief city of ancient Campania seceded to Hannibal.

Capuchin; C. monkey; C. pigeon. The first, better written *capuchin*, is a feminine cloak-and-hood attire, resembling the habit of the austere Capuchin monks (established in 1526); the word is akin to *cape*. The monkey has head-hair that, in its appearance, recalls a monastic cowl, and the pigeon has, on head and neck, a hood-like tuft of feathers.

care a Continental, not to. See **Continental** . . .

Carley float; incorrectly, **Carley raft.** ' I was knocked unconscious and didn't come round until after dark when I found myself lying in a carley raft,' ' Sea Lion ', *Phantom Fleet*, 1946.

This float is a life-saving measure and device, employed by the Royal Navy in the event of loss of ship. ' The Carley float was in use in the Royal Navy during World War I. Survivors of the sinking of H.M.S. Hampshire in April, 1916, owed their lives to Carley floats when the sea was too rough to permit the successful launching of her boats.—The first specification for " improvements in lifeboats " was drawn up on behalf of Mr. Horace S. Carley in 1899 and in 1902 a Carley Lifefloat Company was formed.—Mr. Carley was a designer and decorator of Boston, Mass.' (The Department of the Chief of Naval Information, The Admiralty, letter of December 11, 1946.)

Carlylese, Carlylism; Carlylean. The nouns, like the adjective, imply a literary mannerism, a style, reminiscent of the writings of Thomas Carlyle (1795–1881), especially during the period of *Sartor Resartus, The French Revolution*, and *Heroes and Hero Worship* : prophetic, fiery, violent in manner ; irregular syntax, uncouth neologisms, numerous Germanisms.

Carolina bean. See **Lima Bean.**

Carolina (or **Caroliny**) **swamper.** See the entry at **Pennsylvania ark.**

Caroline refers to the social and literary customs, manners and style of the reigns of the English kings, Charles I (1625–49) and, less usually, Charles II (1660–85) with the emphasis on the non-Puritan elements and features.

Carrara marble. ' The influence of igneous intrusion is . . . seen in the marble of Carrara and Massa ' (Lyde, *Europe*, 1913).
' Evidence of transmarine trade to England comes from London and Richborough, some of whose buildings were faced with marble from Carrara in Italy,' M. Cary, *A History of Western Europe, A.D. 1–455*, 1928.
Carrara is in Tuscany, and the famous statuary marble comes from the marble quarries of Monte Sagro in the vicinity. The very name *Carrara* bears a suspicious resemblance to the Italian *quadrato*, ' a quarry ' : Carrara may be an old Etruscan name from an Etruscan (perhaps dialectal) word for quarry : may, in short, be ' *the* quarry '.

carry coals to Newcastle. See **Newcastle.**

Cartesian barely creeps into even this subsidiary list : in its literal sense, ' in or of Descartes ', it does not qualify, but as ' mathematically interpretative of philosophy ' or ' addicted to the explanation of philosophical problems by the device of

513

mathematical formulas '—well! it is, though only just, a candidate.

Cartesian derives from *Cartesius*, the latinized name of the great French philosopher, René Descartes (1596–1650).

Carthaginian peace is a peace-treaty so severe as to cripple, almost destroy, the defeated nation or party. In *The Carthaginian Peace*, 1946, the late Etienne Mantoux deals with the treaty of Versailles and Lord Keynes' famous book, *The Economic Consequences of the Peace* (1919). The reference is to the treaties imposed on, rather than made with, the Carthaginians by the Romans at the end of the First, Second and Third Punic Wars (3rd–2nd Centuries B.C.); that at the end of the Third reflected and relentlessly expressed the spirit of the famous *Carthago delenda est*, ' Carthage is to be obliterated! '

A *Carthaginian apple*, by the way, is a pomegranate, found in and perhaps native to this part of northern Africa (the region that has Tunis as its centre).

Castalian; Castaly. ' Delphi, now Kastri, sprang up where the sacred Castalian Fount breaks out from the southern slope of Mount Parnassus,' Lionel W. Lyde, *Man and His Markets*, 1896.

Castalia (Greek *Kastalia*) was, in Greek mythology, a nymph : pursued by Apollo—what ' wolves ' were these Olympian gods, exemplar'd by Zeus!—she cast herself into a spring on Mount Parnassus. Thenceforth, with a nice sense of morality and of poetry, Apollo, and in his wake the Muses, held the spring sacred. Hence, *Castalian spring* has come to synonymize ' poetic inspiration '; *Castaly*, ' poetry '—' the land or subject-matter or range of poetry '.

Castor and Pollux, generic for two faithful friends (compare *Damon and Pythias* and *David and Jonathan*), originated in Greek mythology, where they are jointly known as the Dioscuri (the twin ' sons of Zeus ': *Dios kouroi*) ; and Pollux (a Latin name) is properly Polydeuces. On the death of Castor, Polydeuces asked that he might be allowed to die too.

Their exact Greek names were *Kastōr* and *Poludeukēs*.

Catherine wheel ; except in its literal, i.e. its hagiological sense, better written with small *c*. The spiked wheel in the martyr-dom of St Catherine has generated all the derivative senses : circular spoked window ; rotating firework ; lateral somersault. The New Zealander, and romantic novelist, H. B. Marriott Watson, in *Rosalind in Arden*, 1913, conveniently

514

writes, ' A tiny wren went off in song like a fierce catherine wheel '.

Catiline is often employed allusively for a plotter against the State, as was Lucius Sergius *Catilina* (108?–62 B.C.). In 63 this discontented politician formed a conspiracy to kill the consuls and to plunder Rome; Cicero, Consul, spoke most eloquently against him; Catiline fled to Etruria, where he was defeated and slain. See especially Jack Lindsay's fine historical novel, *Rome for Sale*, 1934.

Caudine Forks is used by history-allusive writers for an irretrievable disaster, especially if military. At the *Furculae Caudinae*, near Capua in Samnium, in 321 B.C., the Roman army was obliged to surrender to the Samnites, and its soldiers to pass under the yoke. The use of the diminutive of *furca* refers to the fact that this was a *narrow* mountain-pass; near the small city of *Caudium*.

Cayley. In mathematics there are three or four terms (including the adjective *Cayleyan*) that constitute a lasting memorial to the great English mathematician, Arthur Cayley (1821–95), Sadlerian Professor of Pure Mathematics at Cambridge for the last thirty-two years of his life; he originated Abstract Geometry—the sort of thing that delights great mathematicians such as Poincaré, Whitehead, Milne.

cedar of Lebanon. See **Lebanon . . .**

Celsius scale; C. thermometer. Named after the Swede, Anders Celsius (1701–44): pragmatically what is usually known as ' the centigrade thermometer '. This astronomer invented it in 1742; he also did much good work, both practical and theoretical, in astronomy.

Celtic temperament; Celtic twilight. The latter refers to the almost supramundane, fairy-tending, mistily and often lovelily romantic characteristics of the Anglo-Irish writers of ca. 1890–1930, William Sharp, W. B. Yeats, J. M. Synge, Lord Dunsany and others. The former occurs in, e.g., ' There were those who argued that Celtic art [in the first four centuries of the Christian era] was a product of " Celtic temperament " . . . . . . [but the dependence of this argument] on an occult entity like the " Celtic temperament " forbade me to take it seriously. With entities of that kind we have left behind us the daylight, and even the twilight of history,' R. G. Collingwood, *An Autobiography*, 1939.

Celtic, ' of, belonging to, like a Celt or the Celts ', derives from French *Celte*, from Latin *Celta*; the Greeks speak of the *Keltoi*, later *Keltai* (whence the perhaps preferable *k* pronunciation). Webster suggests that the Latin and Greek words *Celta* may be cognate with *celsus*, literally ' high ', figuratively ' high-spirited, proud '.

Chadband. In Dickens's *Bleak House* (1852–53), Chadband is, with perhaps the exception of Skimpole, the best known of the skilfully drawn minor characters. Chadband is a humbug, seemingly as pious as he is eloquent ; a sanctimonious hypocrite.

Chaldean, Chaldee. ' Danger . . . threatened Assyria from the south. Once again a Semitic immigration, which we distinguish as Chaldaean from earlier Semitic waves, Canaanite and Aramaean, had breathed fresh vitality into the Babylonian people,' D. G. Hogarth, *The Ancient East*, (revised edition) 1945. So much so, that *Chaldea* came to be synonymous with Babylon ; soothsaying and astrology flourished ever at Babylon, especially among men of Chaldean origin ; hence, *Chaldean*, ' a soothsayer ; an astrologer '. In this sense, *Chaldean* is obsolete, except among scholars and journalists.

chancery, put in. This boxing term, meaning ' to get the opponent's head under one's arm and then to pummel him mercilessly and without fear of effectual retaliation ', refers humorously to the fact that a person involved in a Chancery Court Case might as well commit suicide. *Chancery* is an anglicized form of the old French *chancellerie*, from Latin *cancelli*, lattice, a chancellor being originally the keeper of the latticed barrier between choir and nave in a medieval church.

Charlie Chaplin moustache. Whereas Walt Disney (see **Mickey Mouse**) is American, Charles Spencer Chaplin (born in 1889) is English. He went to the U.S.A. in 1910 and first appeared in 1914 in motion pictures, wherein he achieved immediate fame. His moustache has, even more than his cane and his walk, captured and captivated the public fancy. This particular type of lip-wear, known also as ' the tooth-brush moustache ', is a burlesque exaggeration of the curt moustache affected by the Edwardian stage-door ' Johnny ' ; during the Great War of 1914–18, many British Army subalterns sportingly emulated Charlie Chaplin and thereby incurred the derision of their Commanding Officers.

Châteauneuf, short for *Châteauneuf-du-Pape*, is 'the best known and one of the best of the wines of the Rhône Valley. The vineyards . . . are on the left bank of the Rhône, near Avignon'. (André Simon). The red Châteauneuf wines are superior to the white. The *Pape* element is accounted for by the fact that from 1309 to 1376 the Popes resided at Avignon.

Chaucerian; Chaucerism. Geoffrey Chaucer (1340?–1400) composed much verse, but his influence has, in the main, flowed from *The Canterbury Tales*, which, written ca. 1386–99, have set a standard in the very shrewd, seemingly artless art of the long descriptive-narrative poem, with easy yet nervous metre, with kindly yet trenchant characterization, and with a very English humour.

Chelsea bun; Chelsea china; Chelsea ware. The bun (compare **Bath bun**) was first made and purveyed in Chelsea (S.W. London). *Chelsea china* is china, *Chelsea ware* is porcelain, made at Chelsea from ca. 1740 until 1770, when the Chelsea and the Derby factories were merged, to give us *Chelsea-Derby ware*. Compare **Chelsea** (p. 98).

Chesapeake oysters. 'The oyster thrives specially well in the sheltered water of the Chesapeake Bay. There the Susquehanna and the Potomac provide both the percentage of fresh water which is so desirable and even necessary, and the alluvial mud in which the molluscs can burrow for food . . . . . . The oysters can compete in quality with those of Whitstable and Colchester, of Arcachon and Brittany, of Ostend and Texel,' Lionel W. Lyde, *Man and His Markets*, edition of 1919.

Whitstable stands at the mouth of the Swale, in Kent; Colchester ('the castle on the Colne') in Essex, at the head of navigation on the River Colne. Arcachon, on the coast and thirty-three miles from Bordeaux, has the most important of the French oyster-parks; Ostend is the famous seaport and resort; and Texel is a Dutch island at the mouth of the Zuider Zee.

Cheshire cat. 'He was grinning from ear to ear like a Cheshire cat,' Richard Sale in *Detective Fiction Weekly*, January 29, 1938.

The phrase *grin like a Cheshire cat* is first recorded towards the end of the 18th Century; 'Peter Pindar' (John Wolcot, 1738–1819) used it. But its origin is obscure. In *A Dictionary of Slang and Unconventional English*, I have written: 'I surmise but cannot prove *cheeser*, a cat very fond of cheese, *a cheeser* having become *a cheeser cat*, hence *a Cheshire cat*; hence *grin like a*

Cheshire cat = to be as pleased as a " cheeser " that has just eaten cheese.'

' We may drive home to the utmost the significance of *this* world for us here and now, but we should not forget that the account we give of it is, so to say, printed on a white page without which our words would be in empty air, the " grin " of the Cheshire Cat,' Stanley Cook, *An Introduction to the Bible*, 1945.

Chestertonian, e.g. ' C. paradox ' and ' C. wit '. Gilbert Keith Chesterton (1874–1936) was a stimulating and provocative literary critic and historian, a brilliant essayist, a tantalizing novelist (his short stories better his novels), an eloquent poet, and, above all, a man with vision—and a vision. His wit coruscates and devastates.

Chicago piano. This name for a multiple pom-pom was often used by journalists and naval men during the war of 1939–45. *Piano*, because of the merry tune it played ; *Chicago*, in reference to the Chicagoan gang-wars of ca. 1920–33, when machine-guns were employed with a callous insouciance. See especially E. D. Sullivan, *Look at Chicago*, 1929, and *Chicago Surrenders* (to the gangsters), 1931, and Herbert Asbury, *The Underworld of Chicago*, 1941. ' With a population of nearly three millions, and covering more than 200 square miles, [Chicago] is the fourth largest city in the world,' Rodwell Jones & P. W. Bryan, *North America*, (7th edition) 1946.

Chinese blue, white, yellow. These pigments were, all of them, made originally in China, whence they were brought to Europe. To say more were otiose.

Chinese temple block. See **Korean temple block.**

Christiania turn, often colloquially shortened to *Christi*, which occurs also as a verb, meaning ' to do or make a Christi ', is a skiers' term ; from Norway, as are so many such terms. *Christiania*, now Oslo (originally *Opslo*), the capital of Norway, is in Norwegian spelt *Kristiania* : *urbs Christiana*, the Christian city. (See **christian** in the main glossary.)
' You can only go fast and straight on clean snow if you can do a real Christi—and the Christiania turn is the most difficult of all, a jump to clear the skis from their tracks and a right angle turn in mid-air . . . . . . If Mayne could Christi, I wondered if he would realize that I could not,' Hammond Innes, *The Lonely Skier*, 1947.

518

Christmas flower. See **Easter flower.**

Christy minstrels. The Negro-minstrel type of entertainment was very popular ca. 1843-1905. The troupes, including those known as *Christy minstrels* (at first the Virginia Minstrels), consisted of white men with blacked faces and they sang Negro or supposedly Negro songs; superseded by Pierrots, they nevertheless linger as survivals.

Christy (1815-62) was an American song-writer, who popularized his songs by means of his minstrel troupe, which toured England as well as America.

(See 'Negro Minstrels' in *The Oxford Companion to Music*.)

Churchillian. 'Mr. Flint stuck a weed, of Churchillian proportions, in his mouth,' Cecil Freeman Gregg, *Mr Melander's Millions*, 1944. Here, the reference is to those cigars which have proved to be, not merely a pleasure to himself, but a godsend to cartoonists. Usually, however, *Churchillian* is found with *eloquence, oratory, fire, energy, vision, statesmanship, versatility*, qualities which have characterized the life and particularly the 1940-45 Premiership of the Rt Hon. Winston Churchill (b. 1874), soldier, journalist, writer, statesman. He and Franklin Delano Roosevelt (1882-1945), often associated, stand out as the two greatest statesmen of the 20th Century.

Ciceronian; Ciceronianism. Figuratively, *Ciceronian* = 'eloquent, rhythmical'; a *Ciceronian period* is 'a complex, rhythmical, well-turned sentence'; *Ciceronianism* is 'eloquent oratory' or 'a polished, elegant, rhythmical prose' or 'polish, culture, expressed in speech or writing'.

Of Cicero (106-43 B.C.), Roman statesman, orator, writer, T. R. Glover has said, 'He gave the West a philosophic language in which to think; for all men in the West he created ideals of writing, of handling ideas, of style and order, . . . so that whoever writes a good sentence in French or English owes something to Cicero. "Ciceronian prose is practically the prose of the human race"' (*The Ancient World*, 1935).

Cimmerian appears chiefly in *Cimmerian night, Cimmerian darkness, Cimmerian gloom*, where it means 'intensely black', or 'thick, impenetrable'. Via Latin, it derives from Greek *Kimmĕrios*, 'of or like the *Kimmĕrioi*, a legendary people living in perpetual night, later a nomad people that, from the steppes, invaded Asia Minor.

'Cilicia was saved by the Assyrians from the ravages of the Cimmerians': 'Assyrian records attest that the Gimirrai or

519

Cimmerians, an Indo-European Scythian folk, which has left its name to Crim Tartary, and the present Crimea, swept southward and westward about the middle of the seventh century, and Greek records tell how they took and sacked the capital of Phrygia and put to death or forced to suicide the last King Midas,' D. G. Hogarth, *The Ancient East*, (revised edition) 1945. Their 'darkness', therefore, was cultural, not physical.

Cincinnatus. ' It is farmers with the spirit of Cincinnatus, it i. peasant women with the soul of Cornelia, who are defying th. luxury and corruption of courts,' G. K. Chesterton, *Th Judgment of Dr Johnson*, 1927.

Cincinnatus, who has become the type of simplicity and loyalty —of that man who can rise to a great occasion of State and g. back, literally or figuratively, to his plough—Cincinnatus reputed to have flourished ca. 458 B.C., was called from his farm to save his country; having done so, he returned home.

Circe; circean. ' A *femme fatale*' or merely ' a very attractiv. woman' (an *enchanting* creature); 'fatally attractive', a. applied to a woman ('"She's got the Circe touch," mutter.. Kitty. "I hate to see my husband talking to her",' Eth. Lina White, *The Man Who Loved Lions*, 1943)—or 'apt t. degrade morally'—or (of arts, practices, spells) 'magical In Homer's *Odyssey*, Odysseus and his men 'come to Circe' isle, where that enchantress gives his men drugged wine t. drink, and with her rod transforms them into swine and per. them in a sty' (T. R. Glover, *The Ancient World*, 1935). A se. nymph, *Kirkë* came from Colchis, east of the Black Sea, t. *Kirkaion* in Latium (Latin *Circeii*, Italian *Circello*).

Claude glass is short for *Claude Lorraine glass* (or *mirror*), a mirr. that, of black or coloured glass, is used for viewing a reflecte. landscape: the effect resembles that which one obtains fro. a picture by *Claude Lorrain* (1600–1682), a French landscap. painter and engraver whose name is sometimes writte. *Lorraine*. From 1627 onwards he lived and worked in Rom.

Clicquot. A famous champagne made by the firm of *Veu.* (Widow) *Clicquot*: whence the slangy synonym, *The Wido.* which J. Redding Ware, in *Passing English* (1909) dates fro. ca. 1860.

' Avril asked for a Clicko. I didn't know what it meant, b. very soon the waiter came back with a bottle and a bucke. John Worby, *The Other Half: The Autobiography of a Sp.* 1937.

520

Clio, as in Lamb's *Clio Enthroned*, 1914 (a study of prose form in Thucydides), is the Muse of History. The form *Clio* is Latin, the Greek original being *Kleiō*, literally 'The Proclaimer' ('Let us now praise famous men', *Ecclesiasticus*), from *kleiein*, the Epic form of *kleein*, to celebrate, cognate with *kaleîn*, to summon.

Coan garments. 'Cos throughout the [Hellenistic] period imported the silk cocoons and wove the thread into diaphanous stuffs for women's wear; . . . but "Coan garments" were only a trade name,' W. W. Tarn, *Hellenistic Civilisation*, 1927. See **Coan** in the main list.

Cobdenism, in the 20th Century, mostly signifies 'the principles, or the policy, of free trade', one of the planks forming the platform occupied by Richard Cobden (1804–65), who, indeed, was widely known as 'The Apostle of Free Trade'. With John Bright he led 'the Manchester school'.

coburg loaf. It 'was introduced into [England] soon after the marriage of . . . Queen Victoria, when it was known, particularly in the provinces, as the "Coronation loaf",' F. C. Finch of *The Baker's Record* in *The Daily Chronicle* of December 5, 1918 (cited by W), the Prince Consort being Prince of Saxe-Coburg-Gotha.

And *coburg* by itself—a name little used in the 20th Century and virtually obsolete by 1940—denotes a fabric used for women's dresses and made, originally at least, in *Coburg*, Germany.

Cockaigne, an imaginary country of idleness and luxury (*the land of Cockaigne*), of leisure and comfort, is in Middle English *Cokaygne*, from Old French *pais de cocaigne*, literally, 'land of cake', probably from Middle Low German *kokenje*, 'a small cake' (akin to Dutch *koek*: compare the Scottish, hence American *cookie*). Thus Webster; W, however, cites earlier French *quoquaigne*, which he derives from Medieval Latin *Cocania*, itself formed, on the analogy of *Allemania*, from Old High German *kuocho* (*kuchen*).

Cocker, according to. This phrase, meaning 'very accurate; hence, excellent', preserves the name and fame of Edward *Cocker* (1631–75), who, an English engraver and teacher, wrote manuals of penmanship, forgotten long ago, and published in 1668 *The Compleat Arithmetician*, which went through a hundred editions.

Coke upon Littleton is legal-allusive for the subtleties of the Law. In 1628–44, there appeared the *Institutes of the Law of England* by Sir Edward Coke (1552–1634), often called Lord Coke; the first of these was known as ' Coke upon Littleton ', with reference to the fact that Sir Edward had based it upon Sir Thomas Littleton's *Tenures* (1481), a full treatment of English land-law.

Colchester oysters. See **Chesapeake.**

college pudding may, as W suggests and The OED has implied, be short for *New College pudding*, made at that ancient Oxford college and mentioned as ' the New-college pudding ' by Walter Savage Landor in 1829. The true college pudding is a sweet served whole to one person : it bears no resemblance to the stodgy messes served under that name at the chain cafés and restaurants.

At Oxford it still constitutes one of the minor pleasures of life.

Colles (or **Colles'** or **Colles's**) **fracture.** ' It's a fracture of the forearm, what we call a Colles' fracture . . . a fracture of the lower end of the radius, just above the wrist,' Dan Billany, *The Opera House Murders*, 1940.

Named after A. Colles (1773–1843), an Irish surgeon.

Colney Hatch is sometimes heard in such phrases as *go to Colney Hatch*, ' to go mad '. Colney Hatch Lunatic Asylum is for, and in, the County of London—as is **Hanwell.** (Cf. **bedlam** —main list.)

In Cockney rhyming slang, *Colney Hatch* is a match (ignition).

Colorado beetle. ' Man is now on his guard against insect parasites; against liver-flukes, termites, Colorado beetles ' (' Palinurus ', *The Unquiet Grave*, 1945).

In full, the *Colorado potato beetle*, this pest is so named because the yellow, black-striped beetle is a native of Colorado ; the term ' caught on ' during the great potato scare of 1877. The State took its name from the Colorado River (Spanish *Rio Colorado*, ' The Coloured River ').

Columbus has, ever since the Elizabethan age, been synonymous with ' an intrepid discoverer, by sea, of new lands—a new (physical) world '. Christopher Columbus (1446–1506), an Italian in the service of Spain, discovered Cuba and Haiti in 1492, Jamaica two years later, South America in 1498, and Central America (Panama, to be precise) in 1502, these dis-

522

coveries taking place during the course of four voyages. He was seeking a new route to Asia and, according to the traditional view, fictionized in C. S. Forester's *The Earthly Paradise*, he believed these islands and mainlands to be parts of the East Indies and Asia; according, however, to Henri Vignaud, *The Columbian Tradition of the Discovery of America*, he was less purblind, geographically, than tradition delights to believe.

Compare **Leif Ericsson.**

Compton effect. See **Raman effect** (p. 613). It was observed by Professor Karl *Compton* (b. 1887), the American physicist.

Comtism, another name for the dreary philosophical corpus known as positivism, derives from its French institutor, Auguste Comte (1798–1857).

Concord buggy, Concord wagon. These vehicles, light-topped stage-coaches, much used in the westward migration, were made originally (1827) at Concord, New Hampshire. Concord was also noted for the 'fine-grained, light-coloured granite largely quarried in the neighbourhood' (Chisholm).— The **Concord grape,** developed in 1840 at Concord in Massachusetts, was marketed first in 1854 (DAE).

'For only thirty dollars they could climb aboard a thorough-braced Concord and try their luck in a wilderness,' Nard Jones, *Swiftly Flows the River* (1939)—a fine novel, dealing with the north-western region of the United States of the 1850's–1870's.

Condy's (**fluid**) represents the name of the 19th-Century patentee.

Confucian. 'That Confucian contemplation of Syd's was a part of Wickford Point, where almost any motion became significant,' John P. Marquand, *Wickford Point*, 1939.

Confucius (K'ung Fu-tzu), ca. 551–479 B.C., was a Chinese philosopher, especially in ethics; his maxims, shrewd and kindly, had a vogue in the 1920's and 1930's, the most extravagant absurdities being prefaced with 'As Confucius said' or 'Confucius, he say'.

Congreve rocket.

'Sunk in their deep and hollow sockets
That blazing couple of Congreve Rockets'
W. M. Praed, 1827 (cited by The OED)

'There's even a rocket-vessel if you think you could use it—this fellow Congreve wants to see his rockets in action again,'

C. S. Forester, *Lord Hornblower*, 1946, the reference being to the year 1813.

This rocket, for use in war, was invented in 1808 by that able soldier and still abler inventor, Colonel Sir William Congreve (1772–1828). It came into prominence at about the same time as **shrapnel.**

Continental, not to care a—not worth a. To care not at all. Concerning the American Revolution, James Truslow Adams, in *The Epic of America*, 1933, wrote that, the monetary system becoming demoralized, ' the paper money of the United States declined to zero, and the phrase " not worth a Continental " was so impressed upon the people that, unlike the money to which it referred, it gained a lasting circulation '.

Copernican system or **theory.** Copernicus (1473–1543), probably a Pole, is ' regarded as founder of modern astronomy in establishing theory that earth rotates daily on its axis and that planets revolve in orbits around the sun ' (Webster BD). His great work, *De Revolutione Orbium Coelestium*, virtually complete by 1530, appeared only in the year of his death.

Hence, *Copernican* may be used to mean ' revolutionary ' or ' of the greatest importance ', as in ' It would be an understatement to say that since 1800 history has passed through a Copernican revolution. Looking back . . . one sees that a much greater revolution has been accomplished than that associated with the name of Copernicus,' R. G. Collingwood, *An Autobiography*, 1939. Collingwood himself, who died untimely in 1943, did much to revolutionize our conception of philosophy and art as well as of history ; a truly remarkable man.

cor anglais or **English horn.** Technically an alto oboe, it was used in the orchestras of Gluck, Mozart, and their contemporaries, but only from the time of Wagner has it formed a regular part of an orchestra ; Beethoven composed a trio for two oboes and a cor anglais. Also there is an organ stop named cor anglais.

Precisely why it was called ' English ' is unknown.

corn in Egypt. See **Egypt.**

Cornelia. (See the quotation at **Cincinnatus.**) Cornelia, wife of a notable Roman general and statesman, was the mother of the Gracchi (Tiberius, d. 133, and Gaius, d. 121 B.C.). Famed for her virtue and her numerous accomplishments, she spoke of her sons as her ' jewels '.

524

Cornish boiler and **engine; Cornish (Indian); Cornish pasty.** The last is a pasty made originally, and still, in Cornwall; the first two, with *Cornish pump*, are appliances of a sort used much by Cornish miners; the *Cornish*, or *Cornish Indian*, domestic fowl seems to be a development from the *Indian game* fowl.

Cotswold is a *Cotswold sheep*, reared in the Cotswold Hills in Gloucestershire and imported into the United States ca. 1855. In 1862 an anonymous American writer, forgetting that he was American—and himself so far as to wax lyrical—exclaimed: 'The Cotswold is truly a noble sheep'. Apparently *Cotswold = Cód's wald*, Cod's forest.

Couéism is auto-suggestion employed medically, as a form of psychotherapy, for the improvement of health. 'Every day, in every way, I am getting better and better': devised, developed and inculcated by Emile Coué (1857–1926), a French pharmacist, it was 'quite the rage' in the 1920's. Among the irreverent English, it occasioned a number of improper jokes and ribald stories.

Coventry, send to, to send into disgrace, to cold-shoulder systematically and collectively, is of somewhat obscure origin. After saying 'Origin unknown', W quotes, as other lexicographers have quoted, the following passage from Clarendon's *History of the Great Rebellion*, published in 1702–04 (some thirty years after his death): 'Bromingham [Birmingham] a town so generally wicked that it had risen upon small parties of the king's and killed or taken them prisoners and sent them to Coventry'.

I suggest that Coventry (originally *Conventri*, because built around a convent[1]), although an ancient city, lies only eighteen miles from Birmingham and that, since the 17th Century at least, it has been subordinate thereto: men in trouble went, men in disgrace were sent, from Birmingham to Coventry, so much nearer than 'the plantations' yet busy enough, prosperous enough, to provide a living.

Coventry blue, often just **Coventry,** is a blue thread, used in embroidery and manufactured at Coventry: a term that, although current only ca. 1570–1640, is worthy of mention

---

[1] At least, that was the predominant opinion until ca. 1915. Professor Eilert Ekwall has, in his admirable dictionary, *English Place-Names* (3rd edition, 1947), remarked that ' Names in *-tree* usually have as first element a personal name. Hence probably *Cofa's* tree.'

because it occurs on several occasions in the Elizabethan and Jacobean dramatists, e.g. Greene and Ben Jonson. (The OED.)

crêpe de chine, formerly **crêpe de Chine.** ' I was interested in a girl wearing a brown frock of *crêpe de Chine* of which the skirt was very noticeably creased,' Mrs Cecil Chesterton, *Women of the Underworld*, 1931.

This crapey fabric is made of raw silk, and evokes a picture, an idea of China.

Cretan, a liar; **Cretan earth,** chalk. The latter is self-explanatory.—In *Titus*, i, 12, we read, ' One of themselves, even a prophet of their own, said, The Cretans are always liars, evil beasts, slow bellies '. In antiquity, the inhabitants of Crete were notorious for their lying and their avarice.

Crippen has almost—almost, not quite—become generic, in Britain, for ' a murderer that belongs to the professional classes '. Dr Hawley Harvey Crippen was hanged on November 23, 1910, for the murder of his wife Cora. A good account of Crippen the man and of the Crippen case occurs in *I Caught Crippen* (1938), by Ex-Chief Inspector Walter Dew, who remarks, ' It was the most intriguing murder mystery of the century . . . . . . There were two distinct sides to the man.' Crippen, by the way, was the first murderer to be caught by means of wireless telegraphy.

Crockford, a clerical directory, derives naturally from *Crockford's Clerical Directory*, first issued in 1865 and originally compiled by John Crockford.

Cromwellian. ' Satan is as a Cromwellian chieftain who " darts his experienced eye " with unbroken pride down the lines of his vanquished host; a born leader offering himself to danger for the public good,' G. Wilson Knight, ' An Essay on Milton '—in *The Burning Oracle*, 1939.

Crookes's rays; Crookes's tube; Crookes's vacuum. These technicalities preserve the memory of that great English scientist, Sir William Crookes (1832–1919), physicist and chemist, who invented several valuable aids to science, studied much, contributed to much.

Crown Derby and **Derby Crown.** Since the middle of the 18th Century, an excellent soft-paste porcelain has been made at Derby. Crown Derby, the most famous, dates from 1784, and old Crown Derby has been imitated in the Derby ware known as Derby Crown.

Crummles is often used, rather loosely, for 'an actor'; and *Crummles family* for a generic theatrical family. In Dickens's *Nicholas Nickleby*, 1838–39, Vincent Crummles is an eccentric actor and theatrical manager, and the father of Ninette, 'the infant phenomenon'.

Curtis camera. An American invention and manufacture that came on to the market ca. 1934. 'I'd bought a four hundred buck Curtis color camera only the week before and I was anxious to see what I could do with it,' Richard Sale in *Detective Fiction Weekly*, July 31, 1937.

Cuthbert; Cuthbert duck. The Cuthbert duck breeds on the Farne islands close to Northumbria: St *Cuthbert* (635?–687), the apostle of Northumbria, retired to become a hermit on one of the Farne islands.

   Cuthbert, a young man dodging (1914–18; 1939–45) military service by getting himself into a government department, was originally applied to a 'knut' doing this: W appositely recalls the popular music-hall song about 'Cuthbert, Clarence and Claude'.

Cyrenaic is the adjective, or adjective used as a noun, corresponding to the derivative *Cyrenaicism*, the philosophy that pleasure, the intenser the better, is the chief end of life: the founder of the philosophy of the Cyrenaics was Aristippus of *Cyrene* (? 435–356 B.C.), who, coming from Cyrene, the capital of Cyrenaica, studied under Socrates and then founded this most unsocratic school of thought.

D

Daffy's elixir, a very popular medicine of the late 17th–mid-19th Century, was concocted by Thomas Daffy, a 17th-Century clergyman of Leicestershire in the English midlands. This tincture of senna, often given to infants, sometimes contained a drop of gin; hence, in the 19th Century, *Daffy* was a slang term for gin itself.

Damocles, sword of. 'Despite his power, his well-advertised intellect, and his sapient skill before a jury, Angelo Castagara '

—the 'mouthpiece' of a powerful gang of racketeers—'felt above his head the sword of Damocles,' Charles F. Coe, *Gunman*, 1930.

Damocles declared Dionysius I (405–367 B.C.), Tyrant of Syracuse, 'happiest of men': the flattered invited the flatterer to a banquet, where he might see and experience a ruler's happiness: and Damocles saw, impending over his head and by but a single hair, a sword: 'uneasy lies the head that wears a crown'.

Damon and Pythias is synonymous with **Castor and Pollux**, two close and faithful male friends. Damon, condemned to death by Dionysius the tyrant of Syracuse, left Pythias as a hostage while he himself was settling his affairs at home. Damon's delayed return almost resulted in Pythias's death; the two friends contended which should die; Dionysius, impressed, liberated them and joined their Pythagorean brotherhood. That is the version set forth in *Damon and Pythias*, a rhymed play written by Richard Edwards, acted in 1564, published in 1571. In the original Classical legend, *Phinotias* (of which *Pythias* is a corruption) was sentenced and Damon went bail for him.

Danaidean task is another way of saying 'a task impossible to perform; an endless task', for, in Greek mythology, the *Danaides* or daughters of *Danaus* had, as a punishment for murder, to suffer in hell by for ever having to attempt to fill a sieve with water.

Dandie Dinmont, often shortened to *Dandie*, is short for *Dandie Dinmont terrier*, and it derives from *Dandie Dinmont*, who, in Scott's *Guy Mannering* (1815), is a Liddesdale farmer, the owner of a special and celebrated race of terriers; lacking a specific name, the breed, actually possessed by a farmer, not in Liddesdale but in Teviotdale, came to be called by the name of Scott's fictional person.

Dane, great. 'Every breed, from bloodhound to dachshund from spaniel to great Dane . . . barked and growled and sprang at the horses' throats,' Julian Duguid, *Green Hell*, 1931.
Often simply *Dane*, this big, strong, short-haired dog was originally Danish.
Lesser Dane is what the dalmatian used sometimes to be called, with not quite such good reason.

Daniel Boone has become to Americans, as he did to the British boyhood of an earlier generation, a legendary figure, who loom

528

heroic in the American fiction of the 19th and early 20th Century: he is a symbol of the gallant, resourceful backwoodsman, the fighter against Red Indians, the explorer. 'The legend of Boone [1734–1820] as the discoverer of Kentucky and the greatest of frontiersmen was begun with the account written by John Filson [who published it, as 'Adventures of Col. Daniel Boon', in *Discovery, Settlement, and Present State of Kentucke*, 1784], and extended by Byron's seven stanzas in the eighth canto of *Don Juan* (1823), as well as many laudatory references in contemporary literature and tall tales. . . . He is a frequent figure in later fiction, as in Churchill's *The Crossing* [1904],' James D. Hart, *The Oxford Companion to American Literature*. But in addition to his value in legend and —he appears in James Truslow Adams's exemplarily readable *The Epic of America*—in general history, Daniel Boone is an important figure in the historical geography of the continent. 'From 1770–3 there was a succession of prospecting and surveying expeditions—the most noteworthy being those of Washington and of Boone . . . . . . Boone (after one unsuccessful effort) led a little colony down the Great Valley to the Cumberland Gap, and thence striking an Indian trail to the north-west, emerged in the Blue Grass region and founded the station of Boonesborough. He was of the first few of a multitude who followed over the same trail—Boone's Wilderness Road ' (Ll. Rodwell Jones in Jones & Bryan, *North America*, 7th edition, 1946).

Dantean, Dantesque. 'Through the trees came the racing, whirling sequins of the snow, entering the upper circle of the glare like glittering fireflies from a Dante's hell,' John Newton Chance, *The Eye in Darkness*, 1946. Usually, the adjectives mean 'grand, majestic, weighty, eloquent, written with massive yet supple power', as was the *Divina Commedia* (Hell, Purgatory, Heaven) by Dante Alighieri (1265–1321), one of the world's four greatest poets and Italy's greatest.

D'Arcet's metal is an alloy (tin, lead, bismuth) fusible at 79° C. Named after J. d'Arcet (1725–1801), a French chemist and physician.

Darjeeling or **Darjiling** is a well-known sort of Indian tea. 'The best known Himalayan [tea] gardens are in the Punjab and Bengal, round such famous "summer stations" as Palumpore, Simla and Darjiling,' Lionel W. Lyde, *Man and His Markets*, edition of 1919. Darjiling is the capital of the district of Darjiling, 'formerly overgrown with malarious jungle, now [1895] extensively cleared for settled tillage and for tea-gardens' (George Chisholm).

Darwinian; Darwinism (popularly, the theory of evolution; evolutionism). *The Darwinian theory* was propounded by Charles Darwin (1809–92), first—quietly enough—in 1858 and, the following year, in *On the Origin of Natural Species*, which made a tremendous stir in the scientific and religious world.

David and Goliath, as typifying a fight or a contest between 'a good little 'un' and a not so 'good big 'un' (The Bible, 1 *Samuel*, xvii, 1, to xviii, 5), was neatly employed by the mythical Wing Commander L. V. Fraser when, writing for the American public, in May 1942, he referred to the British fighters' victory over German and Italian bombers in an article entitled *Malta's Davids Trounce Goliaths*.

David and Jonathan, allusively applied, much like **Damon and Pythias,** to a pair of close friends, derives from 1 *Samuel*, xx. To homosexuals, it means a faithful homosexual attachment between men.
   For *David* (? 1013–973? B.C.) compare the preceding entry.

Davy Jones's locker; often in shorter form, **Davy Jones.**
   Most lexicographers dismiss the origin as 'obscure', but W, ingeniously and, I think, correctly, proposes this : *Jonah* (see the main vocabulary) became *Jonas*, which became *Jones*, the *Davy* (from the patron saint of their country) being added by Welsh sailors. The *locker* is an elaboration, and the variant *David* an occasional genteelism.

Davy lamp. See **davy** in the primary list.

Dead Sea fruit is the modern adaptation, generalization metaphorization of *Dead Sea apple* (alternatively *apple of Sodom*) a fruit that is supposed to have dissolved into ashes : hence a hope frustrated, an expectation disappointed. That extraordinary salty lake of about 320 square miles, now the world' greatest source of potash, has always been one of the mos striking features of Palestine : and its high degree of minerality may have affected the fruits of the region lying about it. If the fruit ever existed, it may have been a kind of tomato.
   'This discovery of the [West] Indies was a Dead Sea fruit—alluring to the sight and yet turning to ashes in the mouth, C. S. Forester, *The Earthly Paradise*, 1940.

530

Deadwood Dick is both a typical example of the American backwoods fighter against the Red Indians and the most famous one; the latter excelled as a guard in charge, or at least in protection, of consignments of gold. This hero of young Americans, though much less now than ca. 1885–1930, is drawn from the dime novels of Edward L. Wheeler, who based them on the exploits of an English-born frontiersman, Richard Clarke (1845–1930); Clarke operated both against the Indians and, in South Dakota, as express guard of the Black Hills gold consignments. (James D. Hart, *The Oxford Companion to American Literature*.)

Cf. **Daniel Boone**.

Decauville railway—tramway—truck. 'Decauville tramways radiated from the shed, and the men were running in timber in the trucks '—' a Decauville railway '—' Decauville trucks stood here and there': Freeman Wills Crofts (originally a railway engineer), *The Pit-Prop Syndicate*, 1922.

This type of railroad has a track that is easily assembled and no less easily transported. It was designed by a French engineer, Paul Decauville (1840–1922), who was also a great landowner and industrialist.

Della Cruscan. 'There have been many other kinds of New Poetry, including the Macaronic, the Della Cruscan, the acrostic, and the figure-poetry exemplified by Puttenham,' Archibald Stalker in *The Quarterly Review*, January 1947.

The reference is to the English Della Cruscans, who, artificial minor poets, were headed by minor poet Merry and who flourished ca. 1800. They took this name because Merry had been elected to the Accademia *della Crusca* (literally of the bran or sifting), founded at Florence in 1582 to purify the Italian language.

Della Robbia ware commemorates Luca della Robbia (1400?–1482), a Florentine sculptor. He began his career as a goldsmith but he soon found his métier in sculpture, wherein he achieved fame by inventing the type of high-relief work known as *Robbia* (or *Della Robbia*) *work*. His nephew Andrea and grand-nephew Giovanni ' sculpted ' in terracotta, coloured and glazed—the usual *della Robbia ware*.

Delphin classics, the. The Latin classics in the edition *ad usum Delphini*, ' for the use of the Dauphin ' (the son of Louis XIV), were famous in the 18th Century and a collector's item in the early 19th.

531

Demosthenes; hence **Demosthenic,** ' eloquent in oratory, especially in one's country's cause '. Demosthenes (385?– 322 B.C.) Athenian statesman, is the most famous orator of Classical antiquity.

Derby Crown. See **Crown Derby.**

Derbyshire neck. (See **Basedow's disease.**) Because prevalent in Derbyshire.

Devonian, in geology, refers to that period which falls between the carboniferous and the Silurian : the system of rocks characterizing the period is well exemplified in Devon, where they were first studied ; hence the synonymous *Old Red Sandstone.*

Devonshire cream is clotted cream, a delicacy first devised, or perhaps merely first popularized, in Devonshire.

Dickensian, n. and adj. ' It is true that in cities, particularly in those of South-Eastern England, the festival [of Christmas] will [in 1944] be a little bleak, and that nowhere will there be a Dickensian richness,' Charles Morgan, *Reflections in a Mirror,* 2nd Series, 1946.

Charles Dickens (1812–70), best-known, abroad, of all English novelists, excelled in humour and fantasy, in the rich and varied presentment of men and things. A Dickensian flavour permeates the biography by G. K. Chesterton, a Dickensian in almost every sense of the term.

Dido has become almost typical of a queen, a princess, abandoned to love and then by love abandoned. This sense follows, not the prevalent mythical story of a Tyrian princess but Virgil's adaptation in *The Aeneid,* Book IV.

Concerning the titular characters of her *The Wandering Scholars* (1927), Helen Waddell has said that, to them, Helen was ' Absolute Beauty, even as *Venus generosa.* But Dido they took to their hearts ' : for ' Dido, Queen of Carthage, was the romantic heroine of the Middle Ages . . . . . . They wrote lament after lament for her . . . . . . To come back to Dido after much novel reading is to recognize a great heroine in the hands of a great novelist.'

Diogenes; Diogenic; Diogenes crab; Diogenes cup.
' I visited Paris, but I found nothing there about which I cared to write. I was like Diogenes with his lantern, forever search-

ing, because all he found shocked him,' Percival Wilde, *Inquest*, (English edition) 1939.

Diogenes occasionally does duty for ' a churlish, cynical fellow ', especially if a scholar, above all if a philosopher; hence *Diogenic*, churlish in manner—sturdily independent in mind and spirit, as was Diogenes (4th Century B.C.), the leader of the Cynic school of philosophy in Greece. Said to have lived in an earthenware tub, he is also said to have told Alexander the Great, come to visit and honour him, that all he wished of him was that he should not block the sunlight.

Hence, *Diogenes crab*, a West Indian hermit crab that, as Diogenes in his tub, chooses to live in an empty shell; and *Diogenes cup*, the extempore drinking-vessel formed by cupping one's hand—Diogenes's reputed substitution for a cup.

Doctor Birch, usually written **Dr Birch,** is a personification of *birch*, short for *birch rod*, for flogging schoolboys.

Doctor Livingstone, I presume ! This catch-phrase, as every schoolboy knows, comes from the greeting by the English Sir Henry Stanley (1841–1904) when, sent to find the Scottish David Livingstone (1813–73), he caught up with him in 1871 in darkest Africa. Both of these men were notable explorers: the fact gives point to the greeting.

Donnybrook Fair, allusive for an occasion that is riotous or uproarious or both, is a natural sense-development from the literal *Donnybrook Fair*, held for centuries at Donnybrook, County Dublin, and famous for its riots and fights and orgies. *Donnybrook* appears to mean ' St Broc's church ': in Irish place-names *donny*—cf. *Donagh*—derives from Erse *domhnach*, a church. Compare **tawdry** in main vocabulary.

Dornier, Heinkel, Junkers, Messerschmitt, Focke-Wulf. These German aircraft, famous during the Second World War —the fourth and fifth being fighters, the others bombers—are mentioned precautionarily. They do not, I think, justify inclusion: and by 1960 their names will be remembered by few. They have been named either for their inventors or for the works where they were manufactured. See also the entry at **Messerschmitt.**

Dorothy bag; Dorothy Perkins. The former 'Dorothy' merely indicates that the bag is a *woman's*: compare *doll* (and *moll*) in slang and cant. The latter represents a particularly *attractive* rose, hence the full name of a woman. ' Municipal

533

gardeners . . . balanced on ladders; here tacking down the errant branch of an ice-pink Dorothy Perkins, and there shaking the dew off more ponderous, pendent and scentless blossoms,' Osbert Sitwell, *Sing High! Sing Low!*, 1944.

double Dutch. See **Dutch.**

Douglas fir. 'The Douglas Fir occupies the entire timbered portion of the Western slope of the Cascades, the eastern slope of the Coast Ranges, and the depressions between these mountains' (Rodwell Jones & Bryan, *North America*, 1946); there is a large export of this valuable timber. It has been remarked 'Some of the trees [of the British Columbian forests], *e.g.* the Douglas fir, grow to an enormous height—and that, without growing too fast to have a good grain' (Lionel W. Lyde, *Man and His Markets*), so that a comparatively modest specimen is implied in: 'The keel was a beautiful piece of Douglas fir a hundred and ten feet long' (Nard Jones, *Swift Flows the River*, 1939).

Douglas's pouch is a peritoneal sac; whence *douglasitis*, inflammation of that sac. Named after an English physician, James Douglas (1675–1742).

Dover's powder (opium 10, ipecacuanha 10, sugar of milk—or sulphate of potash—80 parts) is a medicine devised as a sweat-producing anodyne by Dr Thomas Dover (1660–1742), who once commanded a privateer—and in 1709 rescued that Alexander Selkirk whose story provided Defoe with the theme of *Robinson Crusoe*.

Dowsey. An American automatic pistol. 'Fox took it. It was a Dowsey automatic ·38 [purchased in New York City in 1936], clean and new,' Rex Stout, *Double for Death*, (English edition) 1940. Named either from its inventor or from its manufacturer—probably the latter.

Dresden china—D. clock—D. porcelain—D. shepherdess. The quotation, 'Appleby was staring thoughtfully at a table weighed down with elephants' tusks, snuff-boxes and Dresden shepherdesses' ('Michael Innes', *The Daffodil Case*, 1942) may serve to hint the literary role of the various ornamental utilities and the unuseful ornaments manufactured originally at Dresden, which is noted for its stoneware and its artificial flowers as well as for its china, although they are now manufactured mostly at Meissen, where, indeed, most of the china

534

has always been manufactured: 'The china figures, all well-known models, are apparently Meissen porcelain of about 1740–45, and of very fine quality,' *The Daily Telegraph*, June 11, 1946.

Etymologically, *Dresden* signifies ' (the town in) the forest '.

Drummond light. This limelight, a blow-pipe flame rendering pure lime incandescent, was invented in the 1820's by Captain T. Drummond, a Scot in the Royal Engineers.

Dunhill is elliptical for *Dunhill pipe*, probably the best-known, and certainly one of the best of English makes of smoking-pipe. Devised and manufactured by Messrs Dunhill of London; and famous everywhere.

' A dozen pipes lifted from Dunhill's have their same relative value in the world of shoplifting as they do in a display window on Fifth Avenue ' (New York), Courtney Ryley Cooper, *Here's to Crime*, 1937.

Dunkirk, do a. (In Greece, soon after the arrival of the German troops, an R.A.F. officer :) ' " I suppose this will all end in another Dunkirk ", Quayle said quietly,' James Aldridge, *Signed with Their Honour*, 1942. For the story of the original ' Dunkirk ' see A. D. Divine, *Dunkirk*, 1945.

(*To do*) *a Dunkirk*, which was fittingly to be applied to the abortive retreat of the Germans from North Africa, is ' (to effect) an evacuation by sea under a very heavy attack by both land and air ', as the British Army had to do in 1940 from Dunkirk or, as the French write it, Dunkerque, which happens to be a great seaport.

The name itself means, ' the Church amid the Dunes '.

' At the time when the word " Dunkirk " is being loosely used to describe some crisis or situation brought about by political incompetence, it is well to remember that there was only one Dunkirk,' C. H. Marks, letter in *The Daily Telegraph*, May 26, 1947.

Dunlop cheese, often merely *Dunlop*, is ' a rich, white, pressed cheese ', as Webster reminds us, and it is made at the township of Dunlop—literally, ' the fortified hill at the angle of the stream '—on the boundary between Northern Ayrshire and Renfrewshire in Scotland.

Dunmow flitch, to merit the. To qualify for a gift of bacon as a reward for conjugal concord, as they have done at Dunmow in Essex ever since Robert Fitzwalter established the custom in 1244.

535

Durham. ' " McGovern's promised Carney five hundred Durhams and three thousand ewes in lamb,' Brian Penton, *Landtakers*, 1934. Durhams are short-horned cattle that, raised for beef, are of a heavy, squarish build. They originated in County Durham, England : ' The Teeswater breed of short-horned cattle is famous for fattening, and the horses of Durham for draught and the saddle ' (Chisholm).

Dutch act; Dutch comfort or **consolation; Dutch courage; Dutch lunch, supper, meal; Dutch uncle; double Dutch; Dutchman !, I'm a; in dutch.** The first (suicide) and the last (in trouble) are American slang; the others need no definition. Without exception, the terms are pejorative. Certainly in the first and probably in the last, *Dutch*=German, as it also does in *double Dutch*, which in the 18th Century was *high Dutch*; High Dutch is merely German, and Low Dutch is coastal German and Dutch as we know it. *The Dutch act* refers not to Dutch cheerfulness, balance, sanity, but to German melancholy and morbidity : compare **Wertherism** (main vocabulary). The phrase *in dutch* probably originates in the language difficulty in Pennsylvania, which soon became crowded with Germans. These *Dutch* expressions are, in the main, the result of the trade rivalry, hence the enmity, between Holland and Britain in the 17th Century.

Dutch belted (or **B—**). See **belted Swiss.**

Dutch metal is a—to chemists—well-known and very malleable alloy (roughly 80% copper, the rest zinc), used as a cheap substitute for gold-leaf. Also called *Dutch foil* and *Dutch leaf*. Originally made in Holland.

Dutchman's log. ' The usual manner of arriving at this daily figure [of the ship's run] was the so-called " Dutchman's log " method ; it consisted simply in throwing into the water, from the bows of the ship, something that would float (spittle, more often than not !), and noting with the sand-glass the time interval between its drifting past two observers standing on the deck at a known distance apart,' G. H. T. Kimble, *Geography in the Middle Ages*, 1938.

The term constitutes a tribute to the excellence of Dutch seamanship. For an informative essay on the Dutch element in the English nautical vocabulary, see Logan Pearsall Smith, *Words and Idioms*.

536

E

Easter flower. The poinsettia, which, called *Mexican flame-leaf* and *lobster flower* by Englishmen, is called *Easter flower* and *Christmas flower* by Americans. The two latter names rightly imply a connexion with two great Christian festivals. Compare **Easter anemone,** the pasqueflower (i.e., Easter flower), and **Easter cactus,** a South American plant, so named on account of its red flowers and the Christ-blood flowing from the transfixed limbs.

eau de Nil. See **Nile-green.**

Eccles cake. The Eccles contains the same ingredients as a Banbury but is usually round. Apparently it was first made at Eccles in Lancashire; it still forms part of the famous Lancashire high-teas.

Edwardian, ' characteristic of the reign of King Edward the Seventh (1901–10) ', would require a witty abstract of Victoria Sackville-West's witty and sympathetic novel, *The Edwardians*, 1930, for justice to be done to it.

In 1907, John Ross notes that ' Several attempts have been made to describe the literature, art and drama of the present as " Edwardian ", from a very proper and loyal spirit ' (*Masques and Phrases*, 1909).—' What at first glance suggested an adventuress in an Edwardian melodrama was seen to have a majestic integrity of its own,' L. A. G. Strong, *Othello's Occupation*, 1945.

Egypt, corn in; spoil the Egyptians. Readily available riches, or supplies in a foreign country; to rob or to exploit either foreigners or one's enemies.

' Though the natural obstacles are enough '—ca. 1200 B.C.— ' to keep Egypt aloof they are insufficient to stop either organized invasion out of Asia, or enforced overflow of famished desert tribes, if they " hear that there is corn in Egypt " ' (J. L. Myres, *The Dawn of History*).

Genesis, xlii, 2, ' I have heard that there is corn in Egypt ',— where, by the way, ' corn ' = ' grain '; *Exodus*, iii, 22, ' Ye shall spoil the Egyptians ' (cf. xii, 36, ' And they spoiled '— plundered—' the Egyptians ').

Eleanor(-)blue. ' That Eleanor-blue [frock] she wears at dinner is as plain as plain,' Margaret Armstrong, *The Blue*

Santo Murder Mystery, 1943. The term exemplifies the power of fashion : the colour was popularized by Mrs Anna *Eleanor* Roosevelt (b. 1884) while she was at the White House (1933–45). Compare, therefore, **Alice blue.**

Eleusinian, used figuratively for 'reconditely or esotercially mysterious', comes from the *Eleusinian mysteries*, the most famous religious mysteries of the Ancient World. Initiation was believed to ensure happiness after death. Part of the Athenian state religion, these mysteries had originated in prehistoric times at *Eleusis* in Attica : *Eleusinia* means ' (the mysteries) of Eleusis'. Compare **Orphic** (p. 597).

Elgin marbles, the, is that collection of Classical Greek sculptures which were, in 1803–12, removed from Athens by Lord Elgin and in 1816 purchased by the British government. Thomas Bruce (1766–1841), 7th Earl of Elgin, was in 1803 the British envoy to the Sublime Porte.

Elijah's mantle, 'assumption of powers, or role, of prophecy', refers to that Biblical prophet who lived in the 9th Century B.C. and whose story appears in 1st and 2nd *Kings*. The Hebrew masculine name *Elijah* means ' Jehovah is God'.

Elizabethan is often used for a poet or a dramatist of the reign of Queen Elizabeth (1553–1603). As an adjective it connotes the spirit of adventure, vivid living, vivid writing, freedom from pettiness and mercenariness, eloquence in speech and in prose, beauty in poetry, a picturesque manliness and a generous womanliness.

Elliman's is *Elliman's embrocation*, named after the pharmaceutical compounder. ' All you need for that sprain and those bruises is Elliman's ' (any football dressing-room).

Elvas plums. ' There were, for example, the boxes of Elvas plums that, when I was a small boy [i.e., in the middle and late 1890's], graced at Christmas every prosperous table. They have gone . . . . . . When the lid . . . was at last raised off one of the boxes, it revealed the wrinkled plums lying there, sticky, sepia-red in tone, round . . ., while, between the fruits in the first layer, . . . were little spangled darts of tinsel paper, possessing an Iberian grace that, better than any trademark, proclaimed Spain or Portugal as their place of origin,' Osbert Sitwell, *Sing High! Sing Low!*, 1944.

Elvas is a fortified frontier city in the Portalegre district of

Portugal; 'Noted for its plums' (George Chisholm, *The Times Gazetteer of the World*).

Empire, in fashions (e.g., Empire gown), refers to the styles of 1804–15, the First French Empire, and in furniture to the style of the same period (*Early Empire*) or the inferior style (*Second Empire*) of 1851–70. 'I could see the broken knobs of the empire bureau . . . and the hole in the Oriental carpet,' John P. Marquand, *Wickford Point*, 1939.

Engelmann spruce. 'The higher timber land [of the Rockies] is occupied by Engelmann Spruce and Alpine Fir,' Jones & Bryan, *North America*, 1946. Named after an American botanist, Dr G. Englemann of St Louis, late in the 19th Century.

English guitar, the. A cittern. 'The eighteenth-century form of it went by the name of the *English Guitar* (a misnomer . . .)', Dr Percy Scholes.

Eno—usually **Eno's**—is *Eno's fruit salt*. The term merits inclusion because it forms the origin of a punning catchphrase: *Eno's*: *'E knows*: He knows (what it's all about). From the maker's name.
     'When a fellow is out of sorts hand him the Eno's and leave him alone,' Julian Duguid, *Green Hell*, 1931.
     'I believe I was the only one to "cut" it '—diminish the narcotic content of smuggled drugs—'with Eno's Fruit Salts . . . . . . It must be pretty swell to inject Eno's into your arm,' Charles Prior, *So I Wrote It*, 1937.

Ephesian, in Shakespeare, is a boon companion, a roisterer. Literally 'a native of *Ephesus*', Greek *Ephĕsos*, an important Ionian city on the coast of Asia Minor. It was closely connected with **Croesus** (main list), very rich under the Romans and famous in early Christian times (see, e.g., *Acts*, xix, 27–35).
     Compare **Corinthian** (main list).

Epsom salt (magnesium sulphate)—by the way, *Epsom salts* is a colloquialism—was originally, and properly it still is, salt derived from that mineral water which comes from a spring at Epsom in Surrey (England); now it does duty for magnesium sulphate however artificially it may be prepared. Natural or native Epsom salt is called **Epsomite.** The virtues of *Epsom salt*, or *Epsom* or even *epsom*, were discovered in the middle of the 18th Century.

An interesting extension of the term occurs in Lionel W. Lyde's *Asia*, 1933 : ' The indications of oil along the Caspian are less important than the proved wealthy Epsom salts in the Kara-Bugas *liman* ' (i.e., salt-marsh).

Erebus occurs in such phrases as *dark as Erebus*. In Greek mythology, Erebus is that place of nether or primeval darkness through which souls passed to Hades. In Hesiod, Erebus was personified as the son of Chaos. The name has been bestowed upon an Antarctic volcano.

Erlenmeyer flask, a thin glass flask, cone-shaped with flat base, used in medicine and in medical research, was devised by a German organic chemist, Emil Erlenmeyer (1825–1909), who in 1866 proposed the now generally accepted formula for naphthalene.

' Put two hundred cubic centimetres in an Erlenmeyer flask,' James Gould Cozzens, *A Cure of Flesh*, 1933.

Esau. ' The old man would rail at him as one damned for all eternity, an Esau who had sold his birthright for a mess of pottage turned already sour,' David Pilgrim, *No Common Glory*, 1941. Or, as The Bible has it, ' He [Esau] sold his birth-right unto Jacob. Then Jacob gave Esau bread and pottage of lentiles ; and he did eat and drink, and rose up, and went his way : thus Esau despised his birthright ' (*Genesis*, xxv, 33–34).

Escoffier sauce. ' Sir, Lucullus never tasted sausage like that . . . Nor did Vatel or Escoffier ever make any,' Rex Stout, *Too Many Cooks*, (English edition) 1938.

Auguste Escoffier (1847?–1935) was a famous Parisian chef.

Essex, besides being the name of an English breed of pigs, white with black markings, originally of the county of Essex and thought to be the descendants of the early-historic wild pigs of eastern England, is applied to a kind of boarding, used in houses and ships, often as *essex boarding* and *essex-boarded*.

' He took my arm and led me into a small room with a minute desk and essex-boarded walls covered with North Sea charts,' Robert Harling, *The Steep Atlantick Stream*, 1946.

Eton crop ; Eton jacket (often shortened to *Eton*). The latter, of the sort originally worn at Eton College, goes with an *Eton collar* ; and the school colour has given us the term *Eton blue* (a light blue). An *Eton crop* has perhaps nothing to do with

540

Eton: as a woman's close hair-cropping it merely resembles that of 'those nice Eton boys'.

Etruria ware. See **wedgwood** in the main vocabulary.

Eumenides. See **fury** (main vocabulary).

Euphrosyne was one of the Three Graces of Greek mythology. Her name *Euphrosunë* signifies 'joy or mirth or merriment; cheerfulness'.

Eustachian tonsil and **tube** are medical terms connected with the ear. It was Bartolommeo *Eustachio* (1524?–74), a very learned Italian physician and one of the founders of modern anatomy, who first adequately described them.

Euterpe; Euterpean. The latter means 'pertaining to music', *Euterpe* being in Greek mythology the Muse of Music. *Euterpe* is derived from *eu*, well, and *terpein*, to please: compare *euterpēs*, delightful.

every man Jack. See **man Jack.**

Evian = *Evian water*, which, the drink being less familiar than **vichy** (main list), is still the more usual form. 'The General and I drank claret, Madame Vagas sipped a glass of Evian water,' Eric Ambler, *Cause for Alarm*, 1938.
   ' *Evian-les-Bains* . . . . . . A health resort, with alkaline waters, to which the town owes its name (from *eve*, in French patois, "water")': George Chisholm, *The Times Gazetteer of the World*.

Excalibur. 'Like a good knight and true, Sir William Richmond, another Bedivere, has brandished Excalibur in the form of a catalogue for Mr. Hunt's pictures,' John Ross, 'Mr. Holman Hunt' (written in 1906) in *Masques and Phases*, 1909.
   'Look at the great swords of antiquity which are known to you by name—Durandal, Excalibur, Joyeuse. *Verbum caro factum est*. Yes, that is exactly what happened,' Michael Harrison, *Vernal Equinox*, 1939.
   Rendered famous by Tennyson in the *Morte d'Arthur*—so very preferable to that Idyll which deals with the death of King Arthur—Excalibur has, since the 1860's, been held typical of all potent swords invested with almost magical, almost mystical qualities. (Compare the *Joyeuse* of Charlemagne and the *Durendal* of Roland.)

Etymologically, *Excalibur* seems to be cognate with *Caladbolg*, a sword famous in Irish mythology, and would therefore mean ' hard-belly ', i.e. greedy, hence ' the Devourer '.

F

Fair Isle. ' Carancho '—a South American bird—' with his fine, free, eagle's head, yellow-eyed, dressed in buff plus fours and a speckled Fair Isle jumper, strolled demurely on a sand-spit,' Julian Duguid, *Green Hell*, 1931.

Fair Isle knitted woollen articles established themselves in Britain in the 1840's : the distinctive designs characteristic of the island caught the public eye. Fair Isle is one of the Shetlands. In 1588, the Duke of Medina-Sidonia, commanding the Spanish Armada, was shipwrecked there.

Fallopian tubes. Gabriello Fallopio, or Fallopia, the Italian anatomist (1523–62), whose surname was latinized to Fallopius, did much good work in physiology ; especially, he discovered the function of the oviducts—or Fallopian tubes, as, in his honour, they came to be called.

Fascism ; Fascist (n. and adj.). Of Fascism, the Italian nationalist movement founded in 1919 by Benito Mussolini (1883–1945), Walter Theimer has, in *The Penguin Political Dictionary*, pithily remarked, ' Its first units were called *fasci di combattimento* ; the word *fascio* (bundle) has been used by various Italian radical associations before. Later on the movement adopted the literal *fascio*, a bundle of rods with an axe, the token of State power carried by the lictors in ancient Rome ahead of the Consuls, as its symbol ' : the Roman word was *fascis*, cognate with Latin *fascia*, a band. ' The programme was nationalistic, authoritarian, anti-communistic and anti-parliamentary.'

A pungent example of *Fascist*, as used to mean ' tyrannous, violent ', occurs in Ellery Queen's *Calamity Town* (English edition, 1942). Compare ' " Have you gone fascist? "— " . . . We don't want that brand of fascism over here ",' Nicholas Blake, *The Smiler with the Knife*, 1939.

Fata Morgana ; strictly, ' that type of mirage which appears most frequently in the Straits of Messina ', derivatively and figuratively ' figments of the imagination ' ; has been so named

542

because, in medieval times, the mirage was thought to have been caused by fairies.

In Italian, *fata* is a fairy; *Morgana* is the sister of legendary King Arthur, whom Norman colonists located in ' the toe of Italy '.

Favonian, (of wind, breath, a sigh) ' propitious; soft, gentle ', comes from Roman mythology, *Favonius* being the West Wind, which, in the Mediterranean, is a favourable wind, and itself deriving from *favēre*, ' to favour, be propitious to '. Compare **föhn** in the main vocabulary.

Fell, Dr.   This Anglican Doctor of Divinity, John Fell (1625–86), was at one time chaplain to King Charles II.   He became the Dean of Christ Church, Oxford; in 1666, the Vice-Chancellor of the University; and in 1675 the Bishop of the city.   Moreover, he did a great deal for the Oxford University Press, and the *Fell types* are named after him.   A notable benefactor and a far from despicable scholar, he yet is chiefly remembered as ' a type of vaguely unamiable person against whom no precise ground of dislike can be adduced ' (Harvey): and all because ' facetious ' Tom Brown (1663–1704), while an undergraduate at Christ Church wrote the jingle, ' I do not love thee, Dr. Fell ' (a free translation of Martial, *Epigrams*, i, 32, ' Non amo te, Sabidi '), of which there are many versions.   W quotes that from the 1719 edition of Brown's works:

I do not love you, Doctor Fell, But why I cannot tell;
But this I know full well: I do not love you, Doctor Fell.

Fenian (the Erse *fiann*, ' band of heroes '—confused with Old Erse *Féne*, one of several names of the ancient Irish) was originally applied to a professional body of hunter-soldiers of the 2nd and 3rd Centuries A.D.   In 1856 *the Fenian Brotherhood*, a secret organization, was founded in New York; in 1857, it was extended to Ireland; in both countries it caused much trouble —and in England too; its most active period was from 1865 to 1883.   They confused dynamite with dynamics.

Ferris wheel.   ' I helped erect a ferris wheel,' Clifford R. Shaw, *Natural History of a Delinquent*, 1931: one of the few honest things he did.   This amusement wheel (passengers sat on its periphery) was invented by George W. G. Ferris (1859–96), a brilliant American railroad and bridge engineer.   It was first used at the World's Exposition, Chicago, 1893.

543

fidus Achates is, by the Classical literary, used to mean 'a trusty friend'. Here and there in Virgil's *The Aeneid* you will find—especially at I, 120 and 174—passing references to *fidus Achates*, Aeneas's faithful armour-bearer and friend; and in 1944 appeared George Baker's historical novel, *Fidus Achates*.

The Latin *fidus* means, like the synonymous *fidelis*, 'faithful'; it also means 'trustworthy, dependable': compare *fides*, '(good) faith', and *fidere*, 'to trust'. For the origin of *Achates*, see **agate** in the primary list.

Finsen light (or **lamp**), used in the cure of cutaneous affections, takes its name from Niels R. Finsen (1860–1904), who, a Danish physician, investigated the curative properties of light. In 1903 he was awarded the Nobel prize for physiology and medicine.

Flemish coil. See **flemish eye** in the main vocabulary.

Florida water; F. wood. 'Bud . . . a resplendent being, smelling of Florida water,' Arthur Stringer, *The House of Intrigue*, 1918. *Florida water*, which may be written without a capital, is merely a trade-name. The *wood*, a kind used for inlaying, may be one or another of several sorts of *Florida*-named woods.

Florence Nightingale. 'Jake beamed approvingly at her. "There's a certain Florence Nightingale touch about you that's beginning to grow on me",' declares a pleasantly cynical fellow in Craig Rice's ingenious *8 Faces at 3* (English edition, 1939), in reference to the ministrations of a girl very much less 'a ministering angel' than was that dauntless woman who has become the archetype, the exemplar, of the selfless, efficient nurse. Florence Nightingale (1820–1910), trained as a nurse and appointed superintendent of a hospital for women, went in 1854 to the Crimea, where, as 'The Lady of the Lamp', she worked unceasingly. Despite much opposition from the usual fools, she vastly improved the practice of nursing and the condition of nurses. A serious, very moving play has been written by Ronald Delderfield on a little-known aspect of her life.

Focke-Wulf. See **Dornier.**

Fokker. 'The motor was still going, although it had been acting badly. That was why he . . . left for home before the Fokkers came,' John P. Marquand, *So Little Time*, 1943. The Fokker, best and most famous of German fighter 'planes in the war of 1914–18, was designed and manufactured by the Dutch-born Anthony Fokker (1890–1939), who, in 1912, set up an aeroplane factory in Germany; in 1922 he went to the United States, where he became a naturalized citizen.

Fowler's solution, 'an alkaline aqueous solution of potassium arsenite' (Webster), incorporates the name of Thomas Fowler (1800–88), an English physician. Compare **gregory powder.**

Frankfort black. This pigment, made at Frankfort in Germany, from lees of vinegar vats, is used in copper-plate engraving. The process—calcination—was discovered early in the 19th Century.

Franklin stove. A room-heating open stove, burning preferably coal; devised, ca. 1744, by Benjamin Franklin (1706–90), who also invented *Franklin's spectacles*; named in his honour is the *Franklin tree*, a fine-looking shrub.
'Janet Cardmaker heard the blare of flames softly growing in the Franklin stove,' James Gould Cozzens, *A Cure of Flesh*, 1933.

Franklin's gull or, in full, *Franklin's rosy gull*, is a small white gull with a slate-coloured head; it breeds in the marshes of Iowa and Dakota. It was named in honour of Sir John Franklin (1786–1847), who led four expeditions into the Arctic; on the fourth, he perished.

Fraunhofer effect; Fraunhofer lines. Physicist and brilliant optician, Joseph von Fraunhofer (1787–1826), a Bavarian, observed dark (the *Fraunhofer*) lines in the solar spectrum. In addition to inventing a heliometer, a micrometer, and a diffraction-grating, he improved the telescope.

French harp is a grandiose—or rather, a jocular—American name for the mouth organ; perhaps because it is an *English* invention, perhaps because the French *apaches* are reputed to have done much to popularize the instrument in France.

French horn. Horn signals in hunting, were, in France, numerous and elaborate: this and other developments of the horn in France led to the name 'French horn'—an early name, and extant.

French leave, take. This jocular phrase, in its current sense 'to depart unpermitted or unnoticed', derives from that 18th-Century French-society practice of departing from a reception, a ball, a *soirée*, without saying good-bye to one's hostess—a custom not seldom imitated by English society, especially in London.

Freudian (psychology, psycho-analysis, theory, etc.)**;** and **Freudianism** or **Freudism:** the psychological system, etc., of Dr Sigmund Freud (1856–1939), that famous neurologist and psycho-analyst of the Viennese School (and, indeed, the founder of psycho-analysis) who has conferred upon us the inestimable advantage of complexes, fixations, frustrations, inhibitions, compensations, interpretation of dreams, and whatnot. He owed something to the great French neurologist and pathological-anatomist, Jean Charcot, and to his Austrian compatriot, Josef Breuer. Although much of Freud's teaching has been either discarded or considerably modified, yet we do owe him a wider, deeper tolerance towards much that is turbid in human nature. Compare **Jungian.**

'When Freud died he not only left the world richer by the discoveries he made and the claims that he put forward, but he left the world of science and literature and art with a new vocabulary and a new instrument of enquiry,' Emanuel Miller, 'The Significance of Freud'—*The Nineteenth Century and After*, November 1939: cf. **Oedipus complex** in this subsidiary list and, in my *Usage and Abusage* under ' Vogue Words ', the term *complex*.

'FREUD WITH FRILLS . . . . . . Hollywood has discovered Freud—too late, alas, to sign him up, not too late to cash in on his theories. Only yesterday '—i.e., 1945—' scenario writers were content to offer sex or murder, simple and unadorned. Now all that is banal,' *The Daily Telegraph*, May 20, 1946, Campbell Dixon, in one of his witty *lundis* on the cinema.

Froebelism is that system of kindergarten education which was founded and long presided over by Friedrich Froebel (1782–1852), who, a German, derived some of his ideas from the Swiss educational reformer, Johann Pestalozzi (1746–1827).

Führer, used figuratively. 'Our freedom is, as it were, the freedom of a mariner to use sail or helm while voyaging upon the stream of necessity. This figure is consistent with Tolstoy's view of the Dynasts and the Führers. They are in the same boat with us; no will of theirs or ours can lift it out of the stream,' Charles Morgan, *Reflections in a Mirror*, 1944.

'The city state in Mesopotamia did not (as Heickelheim alleges) attain the exclusive position of a modern totalitarian

546

state; the ishakka [i.e., city governor] was never quite a Führer,' Gordon Childe, *What Happened in History*, 1942.

'Democracy, though it pays lip-service, may all too easily, he [Soren Kierkegaard, 1813–55] thought, lead men to follow the group, the association, the crowd, the public, as their Führer,' the writer of the extraordinarily able leading article in *The Times Literary Supplement* of March 9, 1946.

Adolf Hitler (April 20, 1889–? May 1945), that Führer—i.e., Leader—who so tragically misled the almost incredibly mass-suggestible German people, has perhaps given to the world, in the shape *führer* or, probably, *fuhrer*, a synonym for 'monomanic tyrant' and for 'megalomaniac'. In infamy, it ranks with **quisling.**

G

G-man is an officer of the F.B.I. of the United States. Originally, slang; now a widespread colloquialism. See especially Charles Francis Coe, *G-Man*, 1936, and J. Edgar Hoover (Director, since 1924, of the Federal Bureau of Investigation, with which he had been connected since ca. 1921), *Persons in Hiding*, 1938.

I.e., a *G*overnment *man*: a Federal as opposed to a State police-detective.

Gaboon (or **Gabun**) **viper.** 'By his side, swaying gently, was the hideous Gaboon viper,' David Hume, *You'll Catch Your Death*, 1940.—**Gaboon chocolate** is dika, a mango substance resembling cocoa.—**Gaboon wood,** occasionally shortened to *gaboon*, is a mahogany-like wood sometimes used for aeroplane propellers.

Gaboon, French *Gabon*, is a French colony in West Africa; it forms part of Congo.

Gainsborough hat, often simply *Gainsborough*, but not yet *gainsborough*. A large and generously brimmed hat of the sort worn by the gracious women so graciously portrayed by Thomas Gainsborough (1727–88), who, one of the thirty-six original members (1768) of the Royal Academy, was the best British portrait-painter of the 18th Century—and one of its best landscapists.

Galilean mechanics and **G. telescope.** Galileo Galilei, usually called *Galileo* (1564–1642), founded experimental

547

physics and also astronomy as distinct from astrology. To literature he bequeathed the courageous *Eppur si muove*, Yet it (the earth) does move.

'This takes us back to Galileo's famous pronouncement that the book of nature is a book written by the hand of God in the language of mathematics. When Galileo said this, he was neither repeating a platitude nor giving vent to a pious or sham-pious sentiment. He was making a fighting speech,' R. G. Collingwood, *An Essay on Metaphysics*, 1940.

Gallipoli oil, often shortened to *Gallipoli* and even, occasionally, written *gallipoli*, is the best olive-oil. *Gallipoli*, the ancient *Kallipolis* or 'City of Beauty', is a seaport of southern Italy; 'noted for its cisterns, excavated in the rock, and peculiarly adapted for clarifying olive oil' (Chisholm), of which large quantities are exported.

Garand rifle. This semi-automatic rifle (100 rounds per minute), designed to take the place of the Springfield rifle, was invented by John C. Garand (b. 1888), an American.

Gardner gun. Ca. 1880, Captain M. W. Gardner invented a type of machine-gun; it had from two to five barrels side by side.

Garnet, all Sir; all sigarneo (or **sigarney**). This slang phrase for 'all correct, well, safe, sound, in order, etc.' derives from *Sir* (later Lord) *Garnet* Wolseley (1833–1913), a great English soldier; he inspired deep confidence in his men, whom, moreover, he treated well. He became Field Marshal in 1894 and in 1895–99 was commander-in-chief of the British Army.

Gay-Lussac's law, together with the *Gay-Lussac alcoholometer* and *hydrometer*, and *gaylussacia* (the true huckleberry), were, the first devised, the second and third invented by, and the shrub named in honour of Joseph F. Gay-Lussac (1778–1850), the famous French chemist that has a street named after him in the Quartier Latin.

Geissler pump and **G. tube** were invented and made by Heinrich *Geissler* (1814–79), a German mechanic and glass-blower, who in 1854 founded a shop for the making of scientific instruments.

Geneva bands—gown—hat. In the 16th–17th Centuries, Geneva in Switzerland formed the headquarters of Calvinism.

548

The clerical bands (strips dependent from neckband), gown, and hat were affected by the Puritans in emulation of the Continental progenitors of Puritanism. As a manufacturing centre, Geneva is famous for goods of a very different kind : watches, jewellery, scientific instruments.

Etymologically, *Geneva* = the Mouth.

Genoa cake; Genoa lace. This rich cake has been culinarily connected with Genoa, the great port and manufacturing city of north-west Italy, where, at least as early as the 15th Century, gold and silver lace were made, and later, other kinds. For the very considerable trade between Genoa and England, see *passim* H. C. Darby's *A Geographical History of England*, 1936.

Georgia hams are famed throughout the U.S.A. : an eloquent testimony to their delicate and satisfying succulence occurs in Rex Stout's *Too Many Cooks* (English edition, 1938), where their characteristic, their distinctive excellences are attributed to the fact that the hogs of Georgia have a diet that is 50–70% peanuts : they are 'clean feeders'.

Cf. **Westphalian hams.**

Georgian, to us in the 20th Century, refers to the art and literature of the reign of George V (1910–36), especially to that of ca. 1919–25.

German silver is a well-known alloy (25–50% copper, 35–25% zinc, and 35–10% nickel), originally manufactured in or imported from Germany.

Gestapo, 'a group or band of high-handed snoopers; secret police; in the R.A.F., the Service (later : R.A.F.) Police', obviously derives from the German *Gestapo*, the Secret Political Police organized in 1933, soon to become the bane of the German people, military no less than civil. *Gestapo* contracts '*Ge*heime *Staats*polizei'.

'The Holy Office [the Tribunal of the Inquisition], from being a weapon for use against heretics, soon became a sort of Gestapo for tracking down those persons who were politically indiscreet or inconvenient to the State,' J. B. Trend, *The Civilization of Spain*, 1944.

Gethsemane. 'Rupert had known many a Gethsemane, but the pain had never been so keen as now,' Halliwell Sutcliffe, *The Lone Adventure*, 1915.

'A place called Gethsemane,' *Matthew*, xxvi, 36 : it is there that Jesus 'began to be sorrowful and very heavy' and 'prayed, saying, O my Father, if it be possible, let this cup pass from me'. But, the cup passing not, He was crucified: and *Gethsemane* has, for those who read their Bible, come to mean 'a place, hence a period, of anguish of spirit'.

Gibbs = a *Gibbs rifle*. 'He moved along the rack. " Now here are some of the regular sporting rifles. Here's a medium-bore ·45 Martini. And here's another medium-bore : a Gibbs magazine. Both of these are pretty formidable ",' Mary Fitt, *Death on Herons' Mere*, 1941.

Gibeonite. A drudge. In *Joshua*, ix (especially verse 27), the Gibeonites, asking for an alliance with the mighty leader of the Jews, pretended to have come a great distance in order to effect this alliance : Joshua, detecting the deception, condemned them to be hewers of wood and drawers of water, their lack of intelligence fitting them for nothing better.

Gibraltar, or **the Rock of Gibraltar,** has become symbolic of impregnability, nor has modern bombing affected the literary validity of the symbolism. At the southern extremity of Spain, Gibraltar was captured from the Spanish in 1704 and made a fort and naval base.

Anciently *Calpë*, the name Gibraltar has a notable origin. 'Tariq'—one of the Moslem conquerors of Spain—'is immortalized in the name of Gibraltar, a corruption of *Jabal Tāriq*, the mountain of Tariq,' J. B. Trend, *The Civilization of Spain*, 1944. See also p. 177.

Gibson girl(s), the. 'In the goodly year of 1906 when [Theodore] Roosevelt and the Gibson girls were in their heyday, and the police force was being ruthlessly overhauled and reconditioned and purified . . .,' E. Baker Quinn, 'The "Snow" Woman' in *Flynn's*, July 9, 1927.

The *Gibson-girl type*, slender, beautiful, and 'definitely Society', was the creation of the American artist, Charles Dana Gibson (1867–1944) ; she, the glorification of American girlhood and young womanhood, became a vogue as early as the latter 1890's, a vogue that lasted until the First World War —and even beyond it. That vogue was seen at its most popular in the magazines *Life*, *Century*, *Harper's*, *Scribner's* and *Collier's*, but perhaps at its best in Gibson's illustrations to the novels by Richard Harding Davis (1864–1916), Robert W. Chambers (1865–1933), George Barr McCutcheon (1866–1928), and other 'head-liners'. Nor was Gibson himself a wholly negligible writer—see, for instance, *The Education of Mr Pipp*.

550

Gila monster (a large and venomous lizard) occurs also as simply *Gila*, though still with the capital initial. Especially prevalent in Arizona.

In the early 19th Century, ' Santa Fé was connected with the sea at San Giego by a trail via the Gila River ' (Jones & Bryan, *North America*)—a river that also flows through part of New Mexico.

Gilbert and Sullivan, in the nuances ' very comic, humorously witty, light-heartedly entertaining, ludicrously incredible, fantastic, all in a seemly and very English way '—as in ' For a week or two people took an impish delight in carrying out the rather Gilbert-and-Sullivan orders to the letter ' (Jim Phelan, *Jail Journey*, 1940)—refers to the light operas written by W. S. Gilbert (1836–1911) and composed by Arthur Sullivan (1842–1900), from the burlesque *Thespis* in 1871 to *The Grand Duke*, 1896, the most notable being perhaps *The Pirates of Penzance* (1879), *The Mikado* (1885), *Ruddigore* (1887), *The Yeoman of the Guard* (1888), and *The Gondoliers* (1889).

Gilead, balm of; occasionally **balm of Mecca.** This oily, golden-hued resin was formerly used as an antiseptic ; there are many imitations. The term *balm of Gilead* rests on a misapprehension that the antiseptic substance is identical with gum found in Gilead (*Genesis*, xxxvii, 25, and especially *Jeremiah*, viii, 22, ' Is there no balm in Gilead, is there no physician there? ') ; hence, in correction, the *true balsam* or *balsam* (later *balm*) *of Mecca*. ' Corn in Egypt ! Balm in Gilead ! Eggs in England ! ' : thus begins the leader-writer in the *Daily Express* of February 9, 1946—apropos of dried eggs.

Gill type. Eric Gill (1882–1940) was a notable sculptor, a noted engraver, a writer on art, and a designer of a couple of legibly attractive type-faces.

Giorgi flute. A concert flute introduced in 1896. So called because its originator was Carlo Giorgi. (Scholes.)

give (a person) **Camborne.** See **Camborne . . .**

Glastonbury chair; G. thorn. The latter, a hawthorn, is folk-supposed to have sprung up, at Glastonbury, from the staff of Joseph of Arimathea, whereas the former, an armchair, was designed in pious imitation of a chair that, once belonging to the Abbot of Glastonbury, is preserved at Wells. Glastonbury

(Latin *Glasconia*, Celtic *Yniswitryn*—'isle of glassy water') was once the site of a magnificent abbey, covering sixty acres.

gloire de Dijon.   (See quotation at **Ophelia.**)   A famous rose, so named from its horticultural associations with the ancient French city of Dijon.   Glorified in Thomas Bodkin's delightful memoir, *My Uncle Frank*, 1941.

Gnathonic (or **g**—) is an obsolescent literarism for 'sycophantic'. Coined from *Gnatho* (genitive *Gnathonis*), a parasite in Terence's comedy *Eunuchus*, 'The Eunuch'.   Hence also the obsolete *gnathonize*, 'to act the sycophant'.   The Greek original is *Gnathōn*: he 'shoots off his mouth' (*gnathos*).

Goa powder is the ordinary term for the technical *araroba*, a 'bitter yellow powder found in cavities in the trunk of a Brazilian tree and used medicinally for certain skin affections' (COED).   But it was early known in India, especially in Goa, a port and a settlement on the west coast, 250 miles south of Bombay.   Goa 'still has a trade in spice and drugs, as well as in teak, the local manganese, and thousands of tons of " solar " salt' (Lyde).

Goethian.   'The true pattern of existence can best be studied in a long life like Goethe's,—a life of reason interrupted . . . by emotional outbursts, displacements, passions, follies' ('Palinurus', *The Unquiet Grave*, 1945).   Johann Wolfgang von Goethe (1749–1832), the greatest German poet and dramatist and prose writer, was such a man and such a writer as to make the adjective *Goethian* synonymous with 'supremely intellectual yet humanly sympathetic; a classic Romantic, a romantic Classic, in style'.   The mineral *goethite*, or *göthite*, was named in his honour.

gone for a Burton is R.A.F. slang—'dead; missing, absent; (of things) lost'—so famous, so widespread that it may come almost to rival the *gone west* of the First World War.   The probable origin is: 'gone for a drink of Burton('s ale)': especially as, in 1939–41, so many airmen that fell 'in the drink' (or sea) lost their lives.   (See *Forces' Slang*, by Wilfred Granville, Frank Roberts, myself, for a fuller discussion.)
   The water of the Trent at Burton-on-Trent in Staffordshire is, for chemical reasons, peculiarly suitable to the brewing of ale; Burton-on-Trent is, in fact, the 'principal seat of the brewing of ale in the kingdom' (George Chisholm).

Gordian knot. (Concerning Alexander the Great :) ' Begin with his horse Bucephalus . . . Remember the Gordian Knot—a proverb for cutting problems you cannot untie, and being done with them,' T. R. Glover, *The Ancient World*, 1935.

Gordius, king of Phrygia, dedicated to Zeus a wagon. The knot fastening the yoke to the pole was so cunningly tied that there arose a legend that he who unloosed it would rule Asia. Alexander, instead of untying, cut the knot and, applying the legend to himself, went on to conquer much of Asia : so says mere legend : Dr W. W. Tarn has, in *Alexander the Great* (*The Narrative*), 1948, shown the patent improbability of this picturesque story.

Goshen, or **Land of Goshen.** This allusive synonym for ' land of light—i.e., intellectual, moral, religious tolerance—and plenty ', flowing not only with milk and honey but also with the rarer milk of human kindness, is drawn from *Genesis*, xlvii, 27 : ' Israel dwelt in the land of Egypt, in the country of Goshen ; and they had possessions therein, and grew, and multiplied exceedingly '. During the Plague of Darkness, there yet was light in Goshen the fertile.

Gotham or **Gothamite,** a wiseacre, hence in the U.S.A. a New Yorker, derives from that Nottinghamshire village whose inhabitants were simpletons and which was celebrated in nursery-rhyme and in *Tales of the Mad Men of Gotham*, ca. 1568. It was Washington Irving who, in *Salmagundi*, 1807–08, named New York *Gotham*.

Goulard's cerate and **extract.** See **goulard** in main glossary.

Governor Winthrop desk. See **winthrop** (main glossary).

Graafian follicle or **vesicle** is the name given to any one of those small sacs in a mammal's ovary which contain the ova (or eggs) while they mature, and it comes from the discoverer of these follicles : Regnier de Graaf (1641–73), a brilliant Dutch physician and anatomist, who died most untimely-young.

gradus ad Parnassum. A manual, or a dictionary, of Latin or Greek prosody ; especially common as a title in the late 18th–19th Centuries, the Latin words mean ' steps to Parnassus ' (see **Parnassus** in the primary list). ' Debussy has a humorous piano piece, *Dr Gradus ad Parnassum*, in his " Children's Corner " Series ' (Scholes).

Graham **biscuit—bread—cracker—flour** (often just **graham**); **Grahamism.** The last is the dietetic practice of eating any of the first three, which are made of *Graham flour*—unbolted wheaten flour, recommended by Sylvester Graham (1794–1851), an American physician, advocate of temperance and of food reform. Compare **banting** in the main vocabulary.

Grand Marnier. 'Suppose we make some pancakes with Grand Marnier on them for a change,' Georges Simenon, *The Shadow Falls* (translated by Stuart Gilbert), 1945.

This curaçao-like liqueur is named after the manufacturer, *Marnier*-Lapostolle, and the *grand* ('great; fine') is added to publicize its quality.

Gras rifle. 'The arms on board [a small sailing craft in the Red Sea in 1918] were Gras rifles with cartridges filled with black powder,' Henry de Monfreid, *Hashish*, 1935.

This is the rifle with which, in 1874, the French infantry was armed, and it had been invented by Basile Gras (1836–1901), a French general. Compare the **Minié rifle.**

Graves's disease (exophthalmic goitre) was recognized—that is, its individuality was perceived—by Dr R. J. Graves of Dublin in 1835, eighteen years before his death, at the age of fifty-seven, in 1853. A comparable term is **Bright's disease.**

great Dane. See **Dane, great.**

Grecian; Grecian bend; Grecism. The first concerns us only in its Christ's Hospital sense, 'a first-class student' (from his Classical attainments) and in its slang sense, 'an Irishman' (humorous). A *Grecian bend* was a female affectation supposed to be reminiscent of the carriage assumed by Classical Greek women. *Grecism* is either a word or a stylistic turn of Classical Greek origin. The adjective *Graecus* derives from *Graeci* (the Greeks), a transliteration of Greek *Graikoi*, originally a local name for a West Grecian tribe and applied by the Italians to all Greeks whatsoever. (Liddell & Scott.)

Greek calends (or **k—**), **at the**; i.e., never, for the Greeks did not reckon dates by the Calends of Rome. The English phrase translates the Latin *ad kalendas graecas solvere*, 'to pay at the Greek kalends'—or 'on the never-never system'. *The Calends* = 'the list of the month'.

'She said quietly, "What is your word—the Greek

Kalends? . . . When they come, perhaps I shall stop betraying myself "', Charles Morgan, *The Empty Room*, 1941.

Greek fire is wildfire—an incendiary composition used, especially in naval warfare, by the Greeks of Byzantium; contact with water set it alight.

Greek gift. ' " Nice of you to offer to drive me to the office. I suppose, however, it's not entirely philanthropic." " It isn't," Tragg said. " A Greek, bearing gifts? " " Exactly "', Erle Stanley Gardner, *The Case of the Careless Kitten*, 1944.

The allusion is to the famous line in Virgil's *Aeneid*, ii, 49: *Timeo Danaos et dona ferentes* (' I fear the Greeks especially when they bring gifts '), which, among Classical scholars, ranks as a cliché. Not that its commonplaceness prevents them from quoting it time and again.

This treacherous gift was made to the Trojans by the Greeks just before the fall of Troy; the wooden horse, containing armed men, largely contributed to that fall.

Greek meets Greek, when. This cliché is trotted out whenever two well-matched rivals meet in contest or battle. Its literary source resides in ' When Greeks joined Greeks '—in battle—' then was the tug of war ', which occurs in Nathaniel Lee's poetic drama, *The Rival Queens; or the Death of Alexander the Great*, 1677, in reference to the resistance made by the Greek states to Alexander (and Philip) of Macedon.

Greek to me, that is all. Unintelligible, because written in Greek. Partly from Shakespeare, *Julius Caesar*, I, ii.

Gregorian calendar. The Gregorian, which in 1582 largely superseded the *Julian calendar* (discarded in Great Britain not until 1752), was introduced by Pope *Gregory* XIII; but probably he was merely honoured by this naming—not the deviser of the calendar.

Gregorian chant; Gregorian modes. The former is plainchant or plainsong (see, e.g., *The Oxford Companion to Music*, s.v. ' plainsong '). ' At the end of the sixth century,' remarks Dr Percy Scholes, ' Pope Gregory is said to have taken the whole subject [of plainsong] under review . . ., added four more scales, or modes, and . . . collected and recast the repertory (it would be safer, perhaps, merely to say that the work was accomplished during Gregory's papacy) '.

555

gregory (or **Gregory's**) **powder.** ' The abominable mixture known as " Gregory's Powder ". It was her universal remedy for every complaint of mine . . . the principle being that . . . Gregory's Powder, by virtue of its villainous taste alone, must inevitably be good, if not as a medical preparation, then as an incitement to humility and obedience,' Norman Douglas, *Together*, 1923. James Gregory (1758–1822), a Scottish physician, ' thought up ' this particular atrocity.

Gresham's law (occasionally **theorem**) is that well-known tendency for the less valuable of two equivalent coins to remain in circulation, the more valuable to be hoarded, which was noted by Sir Thomas *Gresham* (1519?–79), founder of the Royal Exchange.

Gretna Green, the colour greenish yellow-green, derives from that Gretna Green at which runaway marriages were long performed. Gretna Green is a Scottish village (in Dumfries-shire) just over the border from England.

Grimm's law, as understood in philology, is named after Jakob Grimm (1785–1863), who in 1822 set forth this so-called ' law '. It first appeared in his ' magnum opus '—the *Deutsche Grammatik*, constituting the foundation of Germanic philology. With his brother Wilhelm he published in 1812 and 1815 those two collections which came to be known in English as *Grimm's Fairy Tales*.

Grolier binding, ' highly ornate binding (of a book) ', has been so named in memory of Jean Grolier de Servières (1479–1565), who in 1537 was Treasurer-General of France. A great biblio-phile, he ' designed many of his own decorations and supervised the binding of a number of his books ' (Webster BD).

Also, a *Grolier* is a book bound Grolier-wise, as in ' I meant genuine antique books ornamentally bound, the sort keen collectors were looking for everywhere. Sumptuous, lovely work, Groliers and such,' H. C. Bailey, *The Wrong Man*, 1946.

gros de Londres ; gros de Naples. Whereas the latter is a heavy silk fabric named after the city of Naples, the former is a thick fabric, usually of silk, and either of two colours or with horizontal ribs of fine yarn and coarse. ' Silk of London ; silk of Naples ' : *gros* (whence English *gross*) is a French word for a ' stout, *thick* silk of dull finish '. The names come, not from the manufacture, but from the marketing, of such fabrics at these places.

H

Haig. ' " I'll have a Haig . . . . . . Anna, another Haig for Mr Sigler ",' Gerald Kersh, *Night and the City*, 1938. I.e., a *Haig's whiskey*, made by a famous Scottish firm of distillers.

Hallstatt. ' *Via* Greece and Italy iron came across Europe. The earliest spread of iron westward was from the district of Hallstatt, near Salzburg in Austria, on the Upper Danube. In importance and splendour the Hallstatt civilisation, which shows clearly the transition from bronze to iron, transcends any other prehistoric European civilisation north of the Alps ' (the excavations leading to its discovery began ca. 1850), S. E. Winbolt, *Britain B.C.*, 1943, in reference to the Early Iron Age, which in Britain represents the period ca. 500 B.C.–A.D. 43 (the Roman Conquest).

hambro line. ' He cast off the length of hambro line . . . and took the grapnel back to the *Psyche*,' Miles Burton, *The Three Corpse Trick*, 1944. ' *Hambro* is a surname famous in Norway '; false clue. Also known as a *hamber* line (Smyth, *The Sailor's Word-Book*) and as a *Hambrough line* (Ansted's *Dictionary of Sea Terms*), the term is a corruption of *Hamburgh line*, Hamburgh or Hamburg (from *Hammaburg*, the castle in the Hamme— formerly a vast forest) having been a famous port for centuries.

Hanwell is occasionally used figuratively, as in *go to Hanwell*, ' go mad '. *Hanwell* is short for Hanwell Lunatic Asylum—an asylum for the County of London. Cf. **bedlam** (primary list) and **Colney Hatch.**

Harley Street, in London, W.1, has long housed many a brilliant, many an established physician and surgeon (specialist, not G.P.) : and so it synonymizes ' the best medicining and surgery and, since ca. 1920, psychiatry to be obtained in Britain '.

Haroun al Raschid. ' One notorious gangster (" The Mad Dog ") liked to pretend that he was a sort of modern Haroun al Raschid, going about O. Henry's " Bagdad of the Subway " [New York], doing deeds of kindness,' Courtney Ryley Cooper, *Here's to Crime*, 1937. Haroun al Raschid (763–809) was, in history, the 5th Abbassid Caliph of Bagdad ; in fame, the hero of *A Thousand and One Nights*—that 10th-Century collection of Arab tales which, in a severely expurgated form, has delighted millions of Western children.

Harris tweed. 'Harris Tweeds Once Again . . . . . . In the Island's typical and exclusive heather mixtures': Messrs Debenham & Freebody's advertisement in *The Observer* of February 3, 1946.

This tweed is made in the district of Harris, which, with that of Lewis, forms the largest island in the Outer Hebrides. Other Northern tweeds are the **Sutherland** and the **Shetland.**

'He'—a professor at Harvard—'also took pains with his dress . . . . . . He ended by wearing Harris tweeds and flannel trousers and by smoking an English pipe with a special mixture,' John P. Marquand, *Wickford Point*, 1939.

Hawaiian guitar is simply the ukelele, a Portuguese instrument that reached the U.S.A. (whence to Britain) via Hawaii, where the natives, according to the Hollywood code, play it all day and all night—with long intervals for love-making and shorter ones for *al fresco* meals. Its musical value has been wittily assessed in Dr Percy Scholes's great work, *The Oxford Companion to Music*.

Hawkins. '[We] got Oakes' Henry rifle for Phil. I take my old Hawkins,' G. A. Jackson, *Diary* (at 1859), cited by the DAE. In or about the year 1800, one Hawkins went to St Louis, where he manufactured this rifle, celebrated throughout the West during the next sixty years.

Hawkins's whetstone. Rum. James Russell Lowell, in the *Biglow Papers*, 2nd Series, 1867, informs us that the name was given 'in derision of one Hawkins, a well-known temperance lecturer' (DAE).

Compare **Beecher's Bible.**

Heaviside layer (or **region**)**,** also called the *Kennelly-Heaviside layer* and the *ionosphere*, is that region of ionized air which, favourable to radio-wave propagation, begins at rather more than sixty miles from the earth's surface. Oliver Heaviside (1850–1925), English physicist and electrician, suggested, in 1902, its existence—as did, in the same year, the American electrical engineer, Arthur Edwin Kennelly (1861–1939).

Hecate, in medieval superstition a witch or sorceress, still—though to a dwindling extent—symbolizes witchcraft. In Greek mythology, she is a goddess of moon, earth, and underworld : the Triple Hecate : but her relationship with the third sphere of influence came to be predominant, so that she soon was regarded as the goddess of sorcery and magic.

heel of Achilles; Achilles tendon. A great man's—hence, anyone's—weakest spot; as in 'It was not for the peccable Thatcher to point a mocking finger at Achilles's heel' (Meredith Nicholson, *A Hoosier Chronicle*, 1912) and in 'He caught sight . . . of the high-heeled shoes that were the only part of her not disguised . . . Damn, damn, damn! My Achilles heel. Why did it have to trip me up just then?' (Nicholas Blake, *The Smiler with the Knife*, 1939) and in 'The malign activity of the mountaineers in Kurdistan, the agelong Achilles' heel of el Iraq, was—could [Hammurabi] but have foreseen it —the presage of an invasion which was finally to subvert his dynasty' (Patrick Carleton, *Buried Empires*, 1939).

The *Achilles tendon* is the great tendon of the heel, the allusion being to Achilles's vulnerable heel: his mother held the infant Achilles by the heel while she was dipping him in the Styx: the dipping rendered him invulnerable, except where he did not get wet—in the heel.

Hegelian, in its transferred senses, 'transcendent; imaginatively cosmic; abstractly grandiose; grandly absolute', refers to the philosophical works of G. W. F. Hegel (1770–1831), whose 'system' dominated European metaphysics during the approximate period, 1820–50.

Heinkel. See **Messerschmitt**.

Hellenism, Hellenistic, Hellenize. In his magistral *Hellenistic Civilisation* (2nd edition, 1930), W. W. Tarn writes: 'This book aims at giving . . . a sketch of the civilisation of the three Hellenistic centuries, from the death of Alexander in 323 to the establishment of the Roman empire by Augustus in 31 B.C. . . . . . . The Greece that taught Rome was not the older Greece [Classical Greece] but contemporary Hellenism, and so far as modern civilisation is based on Greek it is primarily on Hellenism that it is based.' In a footnote, he adds: 'Hellenism, though incorrect in form, has long done duty as the substantive of Hellenistic, Hellenisticism being an impossible word in any language. It is too late to coin another.'

To *hellenize* (preferable to *H—*) is to render like Hellenistic Greece, its customs or thought or literature or art or . . .

From *Hellenistēs*, 'a non-Greek speaker of Greek', itself from *Hellēn*, 'an ancient, authentic Greek'.

Hellertion is short for the *Hellertion electric piano*, introduced in 1936. The name fuses those of its inventors, *Hel*berger and

559

Lertes, on the analogy of *accordion*, *melodion*, and other ' musical ' horrors.

Cf. **Wurlitzer.**

Hepplewhite (furniture). George Hepplewhite (d. 1786) was an English cabinet-maker, whose furniture possesses grace and delicacy. Much less famous than **Sheraton** or **Chippendale** (main vocabulary).

' An imitation Hepplewhite drawing-room,' Manning Coles, *The Fifth Man*, 1946.

Hertzian oscillator; Hertz rays; Hertzian telegraphy; Hertzian waves. All four terms commemorate the excellent scientific work done by a German physicist, Heinrich Hertz (1857–94), whose researches into the electromagnetic theory of light, and into cognate problems, contributed notably to the development of wireless telegraphy.

Hibernian green; hibernicism. The former is such a colour as you would expect to be named after *Hibernia*, Latin for ' The Emerald Isle '; and the latter, applied generally to any Anglo-Irish term, is applied particularly to an *Irish bull*.

Hippocratic oath, the. ' It was after Alexander [d. 323 B.C.] that Greek science came into its own . . . Hippocrates, whose oath the modern doctor still takes, had '—long before his time—' laid solid foundations of the science of medicine,' W. W. Tarn, *Hellenistic Civilisation*, (revised edition) 1930. Hippocrates, born ca. 460 B.C. in the island of Cos, where mainly he lived, was the most celebrated physician of the Ancient World. He, by the way, wrote the famous aphorism, ' Life is short and Art is long '.

Hitler has become synonymous with ' upstart tyrant ', ' ruthless dictator ', ' political megalomaniac '. In 1940–45, British housewives put him in his place by referring to him as ' that man '.

' Who do you think you are! Hitler? '

And as early as 1934 there occurs this revealing proof of his impact upon the public psyche: ' Sparks wanted to be the Hitler of the kitchen, and he acted towards me as though I were a cross between a rebellious subject and an invader,' James Spenser, *Limey Breaks In*.

Adolf Hitler (1889–?1945) became Chancellor—and virtual dictator—on January 30, 1933. Through the Nazi party he preached and effected a bloodier version of the old

Pan-Germanism, and *Mein Kampf* represented the logical development, in politics, of Nietzsche's dithyrambs.

Hobson-Jobson, the process by which Oriental (hence, loosely, Occidental foreign) words are assimilated to English sound and sense, derives from *Hobson-Jobson* as applied by British soldiers to a Mohammedan cry at the festival of Muharram. Yule & Burnell's *Hobson-Jobson* is one of the best subject-dictionaries ever written.

Hobson's choice, 'take it or leave it', is usually explained by reference to Thomas *Hobson*, a Cambridge livery-stable keeper (d. 1631), who refused to let out his horses except in strict rotation and who was immortalized by Milton. It is difficult to see why W, on the basis of a 'Hodgson's choice' (1617), withholds credence.

Holsteins are **Holstein cattle** or, in full, *Holstein Friesian cattle*, the largest size of dairy-cattle, originally from Holstein (Germany) and Friesland (Holland), and now abounding in the United States.

Honiton lace. 'The carpet industry of Axminster and the lace industry of Honiton were introduced into Devonshire by refugees from such towns as Valenciennes and Alençon,' Lionel W. Lyde, *Man and His Markets*, 1896. This Devonshire market-town, sixteen miles east-north-east of Exeter, has been famous for its hand-made pillow-lace ever since the days of King Charles the First.

Horsey pouch, a rubber tobacco-pouch (one half folding into the other), derives from the inventor's name. (The COED.)

Howell. An American revolver (?), in use during the 1930's: see the quotation at **Vawter.** Perhaps devised by John Adams Howell (1840–1918), American naval officer and inventor.

Hoyle, according to. 'I am to be there to see the game is played according to Hoyle or cricket, or however you Englishmen put it,' Richard Sale in *Detective Fiction Weekly*, March 5, 1938.

Edmond Hoyle (1672–1769) published in 1742 his *A Short Treatise of Whist*; it went through many editions and, with the *Laws* of 1760, became the classic of the game—and its rigour.

Only in 1864 did that rule cease, and by that time *according to Hoyle* (correct, correctly) had assumed the dignity of an idiom.

Hudibrastic, 'briskly and jocosely burlesque', derives from the jaunty octosyllabic verse of Samuel Butler's satiric poem, *Hudibras* (1663–78).

Humphrey, dine with Duke, is to go without one's dinner. The phrase was, in the 17th–18th Century, used of those who, while others were dining, walked in old St Paul's, where Sir John Beauchamp's monument was commonly taken to be that of Humphrey, Duke of Gloucester, son of Henry IV.

Hypatia would, until the 20th Century, have qualified for inclusion in the main vocabulary. Except among Classical scholars and historians, she has become only a name. Yet in her life, and in her now so limited fame, she constitutes the archetype of the erudite, modest and lovely young woman, as in 'The old canon [Fulbert] . . . was inordinately flattered that this man [Peter Abelard] who had cardinals as scholars should think the girl [Héloïse], Hypatia though she was, worth his pains,' Helen Waddell, *The Wandering Scholars*, 1927.

Born not earlier than A.D. 350, Hypatia lived and, on mathematics and neo-Platonism, lectured in Alexandria, where, during Lent of the year 415, she the formerly beautiful and still comely, she the cultured and erudite pagan, fell a martyr to the rabid prejudice of a so-called Christian mob. She is the heroine of Charles Kingsley's historical romance, *Hypatia*, published in 1853.

I

Ibsenity is *Punch's* jocularity, on the analogy of *obscenity*, for 'the qualities characteristic of Henrik *Ibsen*' (1828–1906); the term is a very poor misfit for that great Norwegian dramatist, whose problem-plays prepared the way for G. Bernard Shaw's and were moral in the extreme.

Indian paint-brush. 'Bright wild flowers grew in profligate profusion over the rolling hills. There was the orange-pink of the Indian Paint-Brush, the deep blue-purple of a tall bell-like flower, and the splashing yellow of mountain daisies,' Nard Jones, *Swift Flows the River*, 1939.

This flower is otherwise known as the painted cup, which

derived its even more poetical name from the fact it grew wild in country formerly occupied by the Red Indians.

Ionian; Ionic.   In music, the *Ionian mode* was soft, effeminate; in architecture, the *Ionic order* is less beautiful than the Attic, less 'rugged' than the Doric.   In Greek and Latin prosody, the *ionic* foot consists of two long and two short, or of two short and two long syllables; supposed to have originated in *Ionia* (western Asia Minor), ' the region in which early Greek literature and philosophy were principally developed ' (Harvey).

Irish bridge; Irish moss (see **carrageen** in the main glossary)**; Irish stew.**   The third is so named because it consists more of potatoes than of meat.   The first, ' a culvert ', merely exemplifies that humorous, ironic connotation which *Irish* bears in many phrases.

Irvin suit.   The R.A.F. flying suit, designed by Leslie Leroy Irvin, founder of the Irving (yes, ' Irving ': a typist's error caused this) Airchute Company, Letchworth, England.   ' The Germans had taken their leather Irvin jackets at Gotha. Could they have them back?': Paul Brickhill & Conrad Norton, *Escape to Danger*, 1946.   The *Irvin jacket*, often worn without the trousers, is a loose jacket, fleece-lined, leather-faced.
    ' There was blood down the front of the Irvin suit,' James Aldridge, *Signed with Their Honour*, 1942 : the honour of the R.A.F. in Greece.

Italian hand.   See **italic** in main vocabulary.

Ithuriel's spear, ' touchstone of truth ', derives from Milton's *Paradise Lost* (IV, 788 ff.), where Ithuriel, a ' strong and subtle spirit ' and one of the Cherubim, seeks for Satan in Paradise; though disguised, Satan touched by Ithuriel's spear (which ' no falsehood can endure '), starts up in his own true form.
    In Hebrew *Ithuriel* means ' the superiority of God '.

J

Jackson.   Andrew Jackson (1767–1845), President of the United States in 1829–37, was so famous that articles of wear—hats and boots, jackets and trousers—were named after him; and, ca. 1805–30, *Jacksonize* meant ' to defeat (severely) in battle ', from his fame as a fighter against the Red Indians.

Jacobean, in furniture and architecture, refers to a style that resembles, but is lighter and simpler than, Renaissance. Sometimes restricted to the reign of James I (1603–25), it is usually applied to the entire Stuart period (1603–88).

Jacobin pigeon is a breed of fancy pigeons that have neck feathers reversed into a fluffy hood, like that of a Dominican friar. Often shortened to *Jacobin,* which in tropical America, however, denotes a species of humming-bird.

Jacob's ladder; Jacob's staff. For their origination, see **jacob** in the main glossary.

Jacqueminot is a hybrid rose, lovely and of a deep red or a vivid crimson hue; as a colour, *Jacqueminot* is defined by Webster as ' a raspberry red '. It has been named for the Vicomte (in 1838 General) Jean François Jacqueminot (1787–1865), who as a young man served with Napoleon's armies. Compare **Maréchal Niel** (p. 581).

Jamaica wood. ' The sombreness of the black furniture was relieved only by a number of Chinese lacquered tables and stands, on one of which stood a clock in a case of Jamaica wood ornamented with silver,' David Pilgrim, *The Grand Design* (historical novel of the 1660's), 1944.
For a most impressive list of Jamaica woods, see Webster.

Janus-faced, deceitful (compare a *Janus-faced lock,* which is both right-hand and left-hand), recalls *Janus,* that ancient Roman god, or spirit, of the gates and the door (*janua*), who is usually represented as having two opposite faces, like those of a door.

Japanese fiddle. This one-stringed musical instrument, occasionally used by English street performers, has received its name from the common motive of derision; much as the loquat is sometimes called the **Japanese medlar.**

Jason. ' Remember ', wrote George Moore in *Memoirs of My Dead Life,* 1906, ' that I am a modern Jason in search of a golden fleece.'
Jason did, in Greek mythology, search most zealously—and courageously—for a literally golden fleece. He and a sturdy crew sailed in the *Argo* (see **Argonaut** in the main vocabulary) to Colchis to recover the golden fleece of that ram which ' had carried away Phrixus and Helle '; they did recover it, but the results were tragic. (Harvey.)

Jedburgh axe; Jedburgh justice. ' He '—the famous Both-well—' wore a light modern sword where a few of his men carried the heavy two-handed weapon or for the most part a Jedburgh axe slung at the saddle-bow,' Margaret Irwin, *The Gay Galliard*, 1942.—' Lord James believed in Jedburgh " justice "; it meant hanging first and trial after, a method which had the advantage of speed,' Margaret Irwin, *op. cit.* The latter is also known as *Jeddart justice*.

Jeddart justice. See preceding entry.

Jeffersonian, ' (idealistically) democratic ', and the mineral *jeffersonite*, are derived, the former directly, the latter honorific-ally, from Thomas Jefferson (1743–1826), third President (1801–09) of the United States. His active and very dis-tinguished career may come to be forgotten, but the humani-tarian loftiness of his character and ideals, his unwavering championship of democracy will live—providing that neither the money-dictated principles of his great rival Alexander Hamilton, nor a mechanistic communism, slay democracy. For an excellent account of his political significance and political philosophy *Jefferson(ian)ism*, see James Truslow Adams, *The Epic of America*, (revised edition) 1938.

Jenny Lind (1820–87), famous Swedish operatic soprano, ' the Swedish nightingale ' of the '40's and the '50's, gave her name, especially in the U.S.A., to many things and fashions, notably to a carriage.

Jericho, go to; rose of Jericho. The latter is a shrub, not a rose; see **rose of Sharon.** The phrase *go to Jericho* may have originated in 2 *Samuel*, x, 4–5, ' Hanun took David's servants, and shaved off the one half of their beards . . . When they told it unto David, he sent to meet them; for the men were greatly ashamed. And the king said, Tarry at Jericho until your beards be grown, and then return.'

Jersey blue derives from the blue of the official uniform of the New Jersey soldier of colonial days.

Jersey cattle may some day become ' *jersies* '—as, indeed, they already are among farmers.

Jersey justice; Jersey lightning; Jersey wagon. Speedi-ness of criminal procedure, from the State of New Jersey's reputation for possessing the fastest-moving machinery of

565

justice; slang for applejack, made originally in New Jersey; a low-slung basket carriage once common in the same State and widely used elsewhere.

'Jersey justice, famed the country over for its swiftness and certainty' (*Flynn's*—an American magazine—August 15, 1925).

Jerusalem artichoke is folk-etymology for Italian *girasole*, a sunflower of which the tuber is used as a vegetable—in fact, this particular kind of artichoke. Several other plants reflect, by their names, the influence of Jerusalem; for instance, the *Jerusalem cherry—oak—star—thorn*.

Jesse window is a church stained-glass window on which Christ's descent from Jesse forms the main theme of the design; that descent is a *Jesse tree*.

'And there shall come forth a shoot out of the stock of Jesse, and a branch out of his roots shall bear fruit,' *Isaiah*, xi, 1.

Jew's eye, worth a. Valuable. The reference is to medieval torture designed to extract, simultaneously with the victim's eye, the information where his wealth is hidden. (See especially WWN.)

Jew's harp, occasionally called **Jew's trump.** In German, *Juden-harfe*, which means precisely the same thing. Not a corruption of *jaws harp*, as certain persons have proposed. 'Nevertheless, no connexion with Jewry has ever been traced and some mystery of ancient false etymology is presumably concealed in the name' (Dr Percy Scholes). Probably in anti-Semitic derision: 'the sort of harp a traditionally mean Jew might be expected to purchase!'

jingling Johnny. See **Turkish crescent.**

Joe Manton, or simply **Manton,** is a shotgun devised and made by Joseph Manton (ca. 1766–1835), that English gunsmith who patented some striking and percussive improvements in guns. 'The bushranger fired off in the air the double Manton gun, saying that he would not encumber himself with such an obsolete old weapon,' A Pioneer, *Reminiscences of Australian Early Life*, 1893.

John Brown's body is 'a phrase of power', a *logos*, a potent somewhat vague symbol, an incalculable element in the American ethos. Yet of John Brown (1800–59), that abolitionist fanatic who was, by the North, regarded as a martyr and glorified in the marching song, *John Brown's Body* (written soon after Brown's hanging for treason and partly as a joke, by Thomas Brigham Bishop), the genial, clear-eyed James Truslow Adams has, in *The Epic of America*, said that ' Perhaps no man in American history less deserves the pedestal of heroism on which he has been raised, but the North at once enshrined him as a saint '. The most vivid portrait of this man is the one presented by Stephen Vincent Benét in his poem, *John Brown's Body*, 1928.

John Dory, the fish, is probably *dory* (the fish) prefaced with an elaboratory *John*; though perhaps with some influence from the name of *John Dory*, a famous mid-16th-Century privateer, the subject of a very popular song printed in 1609 but presumably sung since some time before that.

John Long is a colloquial nickname for, or ' personification ' of, a tall youth or man.

Johnny Armstrong is seamen's slang for ' manual labour, elbow-grease ', *Armstrong* connoting the vigour and strength required, and *Johnny*—well, it had to be Bill or Tom or Jack or Johnny, and it happens to be Johnny. (Compare *strong-arm* in my *Dictionary of the Underworld*.)

Johnny-jump-up; Johnny on the spot. The former is the early blue or the bird's-foot violet, or the wild pansy, or the daffodil : a pretty American personification. The latter is a colloquialism for a person that always turns up, or is on the spot, at the convenient or helpful time—a handy fellow.

jolly Roger is an amplification of *Roger*, ' a pirate flag '. The *jolly* is ironic, the flag bearing—on a black ground—a white skull and cross bones.

Jordan almond is folk-etymological for Middle English *jardyne almaunde*; that is, garden (French *jardin*) almond.

Joshua tree. This tree, a native of the south-western portion of the United States, is so called because it is there as a blessing to man and beast, as was Joshua (literally, ' Jehovah is deliverance ') to the Israelites.

Judas tree is in Southern Europe the *cercis siliquastrum*; in North America, the *cercis canadensis*, but in California the *cercis occidentalis*; a leguminous tree, bearing purple flowers. In

French, *arbre de Judée* (tree of Judaea; hence, of the Jews), it has derived its name from a popular superstition that Judas hanged himself on a tree of this kind : note that it flowers in the spring and that the colour of its leaves evokes the idea of blood darkening as it congeals.

Julian calendar. In 46 B.C. Julius Caesar reformed the Roman calendar. It was retained by Western civilization until the **Gregorian calendar** superseded it.

Jungian. 'With entities of that kind [the **Celtic temperament**] we have left behind us the daylight, even the twilight of history, and have entered a darkness peopled by all the monsters of *Rassentheorie* [theory of races, peoples] and Jungian psychology. In that darkness what we find is not history but the negation of history ; not the solution of historical problems, but only a heady drink which gives us the illusion of having solved them,' R. G. Collingwood, *An Autobiography*, 1939.

Carl Gustav Jung (born in 1875), Swiss psychologist and psychiatrist, has divided mankind into introverts or introspectives, and extroverts or outward-tenders. Unlike Freud, with whom he was for a while associated, he holds that energy (wordily, the driving force; technically, the libido) derives, not from sexual instinct but from the will to live. One of his best-known books is *Modern Man in Search of a Soul*, 1933.
Compare **Freudian**.

Junkers. See **Messerschmitt**.

K

Kaffir piano is a musical instrument of the same type as the marimba (' a super xylophone large enough for four players ' : Scholes) ; so named because it is a treasured possession of the South African natives.

Kantian. Of or in, deriving from or characteristic of, Immanuel Kant (1724–1804) or his philosophy. Intellectualistic, he dominated European philosophic thinking until the 20th Century. But he was more human than his masterpiece, *The Critique of Pure Reason*, 1781: in 1795 he issued his *Towards Everlasting Peace* : like Goethe, he is a world, rather than a merely German, figure.
' Since the close of the Middle Ages there have been two

568

great constructive movements in philosophy: the Cartesian, following upon the scepticism that dissolved the medieval systems of thought, and the Kantian, following upon the scepticism of the eighteenth century,' R. G. Collingwood, *An Essay on Philosophical Method*, 1933.

Kashan and **Kerman carpets.**   Speaking of Persia, Lionel W. Lyde has said that ' Nine-tenths of all the rugs and carpets are exported . . . The north-western towns . . . were specially favoured . . . . . . The eastern centres are not so favoured in climate or in facilities for export . . .; but again the northern centres, *e.g.* Kashan, are better placed, and terminal points, *e.g.* Kerman (" Home of Safety "), have more facilities than central. Both Kashan and Kerman are notable carpet (and rug) centres, but the industry at Kashan is relatively young . . . At Kerman it is very old, and has produced some of the largest and most famous of all Persian carpets, using local cotton (for backing) in the industry; but Kashan has the more fertile oasis ' (*The Continent of Asia*, 2nd edition, 1938). Kerman is the capital of the province of that name, the ancient *Caramania*.

Kauffman screen.   ' In a corner of the room . . . was a small Kauffman screen . . . . . . With Mr Long's room fresh in my mind [I] adorned her palaces with green jade dragons and Angelica Kauffman screens,' Mark Benney, *Low Company*, 1936.
    Angelica Kauffman (1741–1807) was a Swiss-born painter, historical and portrait. She lived in England from 1766 to 1781, was twice portrayed by Reynolds, and in 1769 became one of the original Royal Academicians.

Kemble pipe.   This pipe must have an effect both soothing and exhilarating: it commemorates the fact that Kemble, implicated in the Oates Plot and therefore executed in 1679, chatted freely and smoked gustily on his way to the block.

Kendal cotton is a napped woollen fabric, as in *The South Caroline Gazette*, 1732, ' Lately imported . . . welsh plains and kendal cottons ' (DAE). Originally they were made at *Kendal* (or *Kirkby Kendal*) in Westmorland, England. ' Kendal is one of the oldest manufacturing towns in the kingdom, some Flemish woollen weavers having settled here in the reign of Edward III, and it has been more or less known for its woollen manufactures ever since ' (Chisholm). See too the index of H. C. Darby's *Historical Geography of England*, 1936.

569

Kent bugle; also **royal Kent bugle.** The *key bugle* (French *bugle à clefs*), as it is more generally known, was called the (*royal*) *Kent bugle* in honour of Queen Victoria's father, the Duke of Kent; 'apparently so named by the inventor after giving a performance of it before this personage' (Scholes).

Kentish fire, 'loud and prolonged applause, or the same sort of dissent', is generally reputed to have originated in meetings (1828–29) held in Kent to oppose the Catholic Relief Bill.

Kentucky ark—blue grass—jean—and **Kentucky rifle.** The first is a flat-bottomed, Ark-like boat of a sort much used by the early arrivals into Kentucky, especially down the Ohio river. The blue grass of Kentucky is world famous; otherwise known as 'meadow grass'. *Kentucky jean* is a twilled cotton cloth (see **jean** in the main vocabulary), made in Kentucky and recorded as early as 1835; hence, *Kentucky jeans*, trousers made thereof. The *Kentucky rifle* is the very accurate, small-calibred, flint-lock rifle used by the early settlers in this region. Perhaps we ought to mention also the *Kentucky warbler*, a warbler abounding in all the Eastern States.

Kerman carpet. See **Kashan** . . . and compare :—

Kermanshah carpet. 'The hall seemed dark after the bright October sunlight, but he could distinguish the long Kermanshah carpet,' John P. Marquand (who is very knowledgeable about such things), *So Little Time*, 1943. Webster defines *Kermanshah* as 'a Persian Kurdish rug woven at Kermanshah': Kermanshah is 'a small province of Persian Kurdistan . . . famous for its breed of horses and mules, and manufactures of carpets' (Chisholm).

Kerry blue. 'Georgia's reverie was interrupted by a barking and gambolling at her heels—a Kerry Blue' (Nicholas Blake, *The Smiler with the Knife*, 1939). This terrier with the *blue*-grey coat, this water dog, is named from the region of its origin—*Kerry*, in Ireland. Sometimes called a *Kerry terrier*.—Note that, by itself, *kerry* (or *K.*) is short for one of the small black Irish cattle known as *Kerry cattle* (splendid milkers), native to County Kerry.

Keswick is short for *Keswick codlin*, an apple introduced by John Sander of Keswick in Cumberland.

Kilkenny cats. Curran, the Irish wit and arch-legpuller originated a story of a number of Kilkenny cats that fough until only their tails remained and the tale. '"You boys are like a couple of Kilkenny cats," his father said. "I've never seen anything like it the way you're always fighting and quarrelling ",' Robert Westerby, *Wide Boys Never Work*, 1937.

Kirman carpet, although it fails to qualify for a place in the major vocabulary (where **axminster** does appear), is yet something very notable in carpets. *Kirman carpets*, woven in the *Kerman* (Persian *Kirman*) province of Persia, fall into two groups: the *Kirman-Lavehr*, the better, and the *Kirmanshah*. More usually *Kerman*: see, therefore, the entries at **Kashan** and **Kermanshah**.

Kleig light. 'Her anguished expression . . . made me feel as though I had butted in on a movie "take" . . . I almost looked about for the Kleig lights and the camera-man,' James Spenser, *Limey*, 1933.

This film-studio arc-light is also called *klieg light*, for it derives from the surname of the inventors: the brothers Kliegl. It being difficult to pronounce *kliegl light*, the final *l* was dropped.

German-born, John H. (1869) and Anton T. (1872–1927) Kliegl set up, in 1897, the firm of Kliegl Brothers; they became pioneers in lighting equipment and scenic effect for stage and cinema.

Knole settee. 'The carpets were thick and there was a knole settee in the waiting-room,' James Warren, *She Fell among Thieves*, 1944.

This is a settee of a kind originally peculiar to the magnificent castle at Knole Park in Kent and since imitated by furniture-makers.

Korean (or **Chinese**) **temple block.** A hollow, skull-shaped block of wood tapped or struck with a drum-stick: part of the modern dance-band drummer's paraphernalia. Borrowed from the musical equipment of the Far East.

Kossuth hat is a flat-topped, roll-brimmed, oval hat that became popular in the United States as early as 1852, as a result of the visit made in the preceding year by Louis Kossuth (1802–94), the great Hungarian patriot and statesman.

Kraft is short for *Kraft cheddar cheese*, an excellent Australian cheese of the **cheddar** type, made by the Kraft Walker Cheese Company Pty Ltd of Melbourne.

571

Krupp is often used for a German rifle or cannon made by the Krupp Works at Essen in Germany. Friedrich Krupp founded the business in 1810; his son Alfred (1812–87), who succeeded him, devised a breech-loading rifle, adopted by the Prussian army in 1861, after he had, in 1847, begun to manufacture ordnance; his son, Friedrich Alfred (d. 1902) carried on the work, and he was succeeded by his daughter Bertha (whence the **big Bertha** that, in 1917–18, shelled Paris) and her husband, married in 1906. A dynasty of destruction.

L

La Tène. See **Tène, La.**

Labrador tea. 'Absorbed, perhaps, in conjecture as to the probable flavour of *Ledum Groenlandicum*, vulgarly known as Labrador Tea, or some kindred botanical matter' (Margaret Armstrong, *The Blue Santo Murder Mystery*, 1943).

An evergreen Canadian shrub, with leaves that have, occasionally in Canada and the U.S.A., been used for tea.

lachryma Christi is an Italian wine, a smooth Campanian product, the phrase being a latinization of *lacrima di Cristo*, 'tear shed by Christ': W compares the Rhenish wine, *Liebfraumilch*, 'Virgin's milk'.

'The wine was dark golden, very strong and very good . . . . . . "This is an excellent wine," he said. "The tears of Christ, my boy, the tears of Christ," said brother Thomas. "'Tis a strange name for a wine grown on the slopes of Vesuvius, which is as near to hell as anyone can get in this world"', David Pilgrim, *The Grand Design*, 1944.

Lady Bareacres. In Thackeray's *Vanity Fair* (1847–48), we find the Earl and Countess of Bareacres, whose rank forms a somewhat flimsy basis—they have very little money—for their arrogance and whose behaviour lacks that gentleness which we pragmatically as well as etymologically associate with gentility. Contrast **Lady Bountiful** (main list), so much better known and so much more deserving to be well-known and favourably, gratefully regarded.

Lady Clara Vere de Vere. A chilly, disdainful aristocrat, noted for a calm that is 'the repose that stamps the caste of

572

Vere de Vere '—as Tennyson says of the so-named heroine of the thus titled poem that appeared in 1842.

Lafayette is a name given in the United States to two kinds of fish—the small, delicious spot, and the butterfish.   In the early 19th Century there were Lafayette bonnets and buckles and belts and gloves : constituting a tribute to the Marquis de Lafayette (1757–1834), that French soldier and statesman who, in 1777, entered the service of the American army in the war against Britain.   Thereafter he visited America on several occasions and, there as in Europe, upheld and furthered American fame and prosperity.   One of his visits to the United States coincided with a tremendous visitation to the eastern coasts by the above-mentioned fish, the spot ; hence its second name.

Lambeth Walk.   In 1938–39, the Lambeth Walk was a dancing epidemic : nor has it been unknown since that heyday.   The friendly ease and communal jollity of the inhabitants of Lambeth Walk, a London Street on the south side of the Thames, ' were made the theme of some stanzas by Douglas Furber, were set to music by Noel Gay, and were sung by Lupino Lane in an entertainment that began at Christmas 1937 at the " Victoria Palace ", London ' ; from the words clinching each stanza, ' Doin' the Lambeth Walk ', a dance-halls proprietor caused his chief dancing instructress to devise a dance ; that dance took the public fancy.   (Dr Percy Scholes.)

Lancasterian, or **Lancastrian,** as applied to teaching in schools, means ' favouring and in part depending upon the system of employing monitors not only for disciplinary but also for pedagogic purposes '.   This method was recommended, explained and first put into practice by Joseph Lancaster (1778–1838), the English educationist.   He joined the Society of Friends and in 1813 emigrated to the United States.

Land of Nod puns ' *nod* sleepily ' (as in ' His head began to nod ') and ' Cain went out from the presence of the Lord, and dwelt in the land of Nod, on the east of Eden ' (*Genesis*, iv, 16).

last of the Mohicans, the.   This phrase is now applied, quite frequently, not only to the survivor of a tribe, a people, a band of heroes, an army, a brotherhood, but also—somewhat carelessly—to things.   In the R.A.F., I more than once heard a jocular reference to one's sole remaining cigarette or amorous expectation as ' the last of the Mohicans '.

573

'Ooph, the last of the Mohicans! Studs thought to himself, as he came out of the . . . elevated station and saw Sammy Schmaltz,' James T. Farrell, *Studs Lonigan*, 1936.

In 1826, James Fenimore Cooper published the most popular of all his works—*The Last of the Mohicans*, that romance which formed the second of his Leather-Stocking Tales. Cooper oddly confused the Mohican Indians with the affiliated Mohegan Indians, even to the fusion of the two names! 'The only Mohicans who have preserved the tribal identity are the Stockbridge Indians' (James D. Hart).

law of the Medes and Persians. See **Medes** . . .

Lebanon, cedar of. 'As early as 3000 B.C. timber ("cedar", cypress, pine) from Lebanon and Amanus were being rafted down-stream [on the Euphrates], but only in the flood season,' Lionel W. Lyde, *The Continent of Asia*, 1933.

'In the third tablet [of *The Epic of Gilgamish*] we find [the two heroes] deciding to make an expedition to the *Forest of Cedars*, which is certainly in Syria,' Patrick Carleton, *Buried Empires*, 1939; 'The famous Cedar-Forest, guarded of old by the ogre Huwawa, was the Amanus Mountains, which lie just at the angle made by the Syrian coast with that of Asia Minor' (ibid).

'In exchange for the cedars of Lebanon and perhaps olives and dyes, the Giblites received and adopted elements of Egyptian civilization'; 'Sargon himself explicitly boasts of reaching "The Cedar Forest" (Lebanon?)', Gordon Childe, *What Happened in History*, 1942. See also W. W. Hyde, *Ancient Greek Mariners*, 1947, for some instructive comments.

The *Cedrus Libani* or, in the Linnaean classification, *Pinus cedrus* is an evergreen conifer, called 'cedar of Lebanon' from its famed early locality.

Lebel. 'The youngest of them showed the old [French] Sergeant-Major how to load his rifle. The present pattern was quite new to him: in his day he had handled the ancient *chassepot*, and the forgotten Lebel,' Gerald Kersh, *The Nine Lives of Bill Nelson*, 1942.

This rifle of small calibre was invented by Nicolas *Lebel* (1838–91), a French army officer.

Leica = *Leica camera*. 'The way they make the minicams [i.e., miniature cameras] to-day—the Leica, the Contax, the Wirgen —you can just about take a picture of a coal chunk against a sepia background at midnight,' Richard Sale in *Detective*

574

Fiction Weekly, April 3, 1937. Merely a proprietary name, with a pun on English *like* and German *gleich* : it produces a good *likeness*.

Leicesters. See **Border Leicesters.**

Leif Ericsson occupies, in the American mind, pretty much the same position as **Columbus** does in the European : that of a daring explorer and navigator. His name is even mentioned by the two children in that moving film, *Our Vines Have Tender Grapes* (1945), with all the casualness honorifically accorded to ' household words '.

Of *Leif*, the *son* of *Eric* the Red, Ll. Rodwell Jones has said that ' He it was who first brought missionaries from the Christian king, Olaf of Norway, to Greenland (about A.D. 1000). Hearing of Bjarni's experience '—Bjarni, the son of one of those first colonists of Greenland who had sailed thither with Eric the Red, ca. 980, had apparently sighted New England— ' he decided to visit the lands to the south of Greenland ' ; he saw and visited the coasts from Labrador to southern New England. ' Leif returned to his unwooded colony [Greenland] with a cargo of *timber*, and successive voyages were made, probably between 1000 and 1010,' Jones & Bryan, *North America*, (7th edition) 1946. Also see A. W. Fossum, *The Norse Discovery of America*, 1919, and ' The Wineland Voyages ' by Halldór Hermansson in *The Geographical Review* of January, 1927.

Leigh light, of ' the battle of the Atlantic ' fame, is familiar to the R.A.F. Perhaps ' it was merely a tale put abroad to camouflage the fact that Radar was getting the U-boats though it was not convenient for us to say so at the time ' (1944–45). A detection-device alliteratively named from an R.A.F. officer concerned ; see the excellent book (1946) on the Battle of the Atlantic by ' Taffrail '.

Lent lily. ' Daffodils . . . or lent lilies have a habit like the robins or the swallows of hugging human habitations,' W. Beach Thomas in *The Observer*, March 24, 1946.

Although, except in colour, unlike the lily, the daffodil (' Daffodils that . . . take the winds of March with beauty ') appears in March, and most or all of that month falls within the season of Lent.

lesser Dane. See **Dane, great.**

Lewis gun. See **lewis** in the main vocabulary.

Leyden battery or **bottle** or **jar** or **vial.** The principle of this electrical condenser was discovered in 1745–46 at *Leyden* (Dutch *Leiden*) in Holland, by a member of the University staff, and in Pomerania, quite independently, by E. G. von Kleist.

Lichtenberg's metal is identical with **Newton's metal.**

Liebig. A meat-extract that preceded Bovril and Oxo : in full, *Liebig's extract of beef* : so named from its inventor (and manufacturer), Baron Justus von Liebig, who died, at seventy, in 1873.
'Contrary to popular belief, canned and concentrated foods are not of recent origin, meat extract having been prepared by Proust, in the year 1801, while the famous Liebig first marketed his well-known extracts in 1849,' J. C. Goodwin, *Sidelights*, 1923.

lima (or **giant lima**) **bean,** occurs, thus lower-cased, in V. Sackville-West's novel, *Grand Canyon*, 1942 ; usually it is written *Lima bean*. It takes its name from Lima, the capital of Peru, and grows well only in a hot climate. It is of two species, the *Phaseolus limensis* and the *Phaseolus lunatus*, known also as the *Caroline bean* and the *Sieva bean* (French *haricot de Sieva*), the latter being slightly smaller than the former.

Limoges. A sought-after chinaware made at Limoges. 'There was in England until recently', says J. C. Goodwin in 1923, 'a pottery where Chelsea, Dresden, Wedgwood, Limoges, Crown Derby and other valuable china-ware was manufactured on wholesale lines' (*Sidelights on Criminal Matters*).

Lincoln green ; Lincolns. For the latter, a breed of sheep, see the quotations at **Shropshire** and at **Border Leicesters.** 'The sheep of Lincolnshire are . . . famous for size and long wool' (Chisholm) ; similar to Leicesters, but heavier. Lincoln green is a yellowish-green cloth, made originally at Lincoln, the county seat.

Lindley Murray, 'the Father of English Grammar', hence often a synonym for 'exceptionally able grammarian' (his modern counterparts are Jespersen, Curme, Onions), was a Scottish American (1745–1826). The century-used, rightly famous *Grammar of the English Language* appeared in 1795 and went through many editions.

576

Linnaean, in its transferred sense, is excellently exemplified in the Santayana quotation at **Pythagorean** (p. 612). The word is the adjectival form of the surname of the great botanist Linnaeus, whose original name was C. Linné. This Swedish naturalist died in 1778.

Whence *linnaea*, a slender flowering-plant; one of the evergreens.

Lipowitz's alloy or **metal.** An alloy of tin, lead, cadmium and, predominantly, bismuth. Fusible at 70° C. Named after its 'inventor' the chemist A. Lipowitz.

little Mary. See **Mary.**

Liz; Lizzie. See **tin Lizzie.**

Lloyd's, A1 at. Anything *A1 at Lloyd's* is in excellent condition, 'quite first-class'. Literally, it applies to a ship registered as of the first class at Lloyd's, that association of shipowners, merchants, underwriters which, early in the 18th Century, originated in Edward *Lloyd's* coffee-house in Lombard Street: see especially G. M. Trevelyan, *British Social History*, 1942.

Loeb. Concerning *Poems of Hölderlin*, introduced and *en face* translated by Michael Hamburger, C. M. Bowra wrote in *The New Statesman*, 1946, 'This book will be extremely useful for those . . . who find Hölderlin's language difficult, and will be grateful for an excellent "Loeb" of this kind', the reference being to 'The Loeb Classical Library' of *en face* translations from the Greek and Latin, a 'Library' projected and in 1912 subsidized by James Loeb (1867–1933), American banker and philanthropist.

Lombard . . . For the banking terms, see **lumber** in the main list. A *lombard*, or kind of 16th-Century cannon, comes via the Spanish synonym *lombarda*, either devised or originally made in Lombardy. *All Lombard Street to a china orange* is very heavy odds, *Lombard Street* being synonymous with 'the money market of London'.

Lombardy poplar; occasionally, **Italian poplar;** rarely **Po Poplar.** The *Populus pyramidalis*—shaped like a pyramid. *Italian*, because it grows so prolifically in Lombardy, especially on the banks of the River Po.

This sort of thing is—naturally enough—almost endless. But *Lombardy poplar* finds a place because it is often spelt with

577

a small initial, as, for example, in Ngaio Marsh, *Died in the Wool*, 1945—'In the distance, spires of lombardy poplars appeared above the naked curve of a hill', the scene being, in fact, laid in New Zealand.

London particular; London pride; London smoke. The first is that sort of fog which, compounded of mist and smoke, afflicted London until smokeless coal became widely used. The second is a kind of saxifrage. And *London smoke* is a dull grey colour—the colour of that sort of weather which predominates in London Novembers.

Lot's wife is often employed as the type of woman that, to satisfy her curiosity, will spoil an opportunity, lose her peace of mind, lose her life, as in *Genesis*, xix, 26, 'But his [Lot's] wife looked back from behind him, and she became a pillar of salt'.

Louisiana heron—tanager—water thrush are three birds all originating, or at the least abounding, in the region that became the State of Louisiana. They were fully described by such famous early ornithologists as Alexander Wilson (1766–1813) and John Audubon (1785–1851).

lovat tweed; originally **Lovatt.** 'An old man, bearded, in patched lovat tweed, over his shoulder a plaid, in his hand a crook, that might have come straight out of the Old Testament,' 'Michael Innes', *The Secret Vanguard*, 1940.
 A Scottish tweed, manufactured in the Lovat country: cf. **Harris tweed.** From the famous *Lovat* family of Scotland, or from their land, comes the colour *lovat*: in full, *lovat green*.

Lucca gum; Lucca oil. Olive gum; (superior) olive oil. Lucca is both a city and a province of Northern Italy. 'The superiority of the Tuscan oils, *e.g.* from Lucca and Pisa, is due partly to the underground heat' (Lyde, *Europe*, 1913).—'We stopped in the porch of Lucca Cathedral—Lucca, where the oil comes from,' Christian Mawson, *Ramping Cat*, 1941.

Lucianic, 'witty, sceptical, satirical, polished—in combination', refers to *Loukianos*, in Latin *Lucianus*, of ca. 115–200 A.D. In addition to satires in dialogue form, he wrote, likewise in Attic Greek, some delightful fantasies. He influenced both Rabelais and, in *Gulliver's Travels*, Swift.

Lüger. 'Candid Jones took out a pistol. It was a terrifically big cannon, a Lüger,' Richard Sale in *Detective Fiction Weekly*,

May 29, 1937.—'Otto let his eyes flick a glance at the open drawer. He could see the butt of the Lüger,' Warren Stuart, *The Sword and the Net*, 1942.—George Greenfield, *Desert Episode*, 1945. This excellent German revolver has played its martial part as 'the Army officers' weapon' in both World Wars, but, unlike the **colt** and the **derringer,** it has not been honoured with the lower-casing, despite its popularity, between the wars, in the U.S.A.

Luke's summer, St. That spell of warm weather which sometimes comes, in Britain, at or about mid-October ; *St Luke's* Day falls on October the 18th. Compare *St Martin's summer* (see **Martin,** p. 581).

Lycurgus is often employed to typify a severe law-maker. (Compare the much more generally used **Solon** in the main vocabulary.) 'Early [Greek] legislators were believed to have been specially inspired by the divine power—Lycurgus . . . by Apollo, and Minos by Zeus . . . . The Spartan discipline, according to tradition, had been devised by . . . Lycurgus, and it was maintained intact for several centuries, G. Lowes Dickinson, *The Greek View of Life*, 1896. This legendary Spartan lawgiver is traditionally supposed to have lived in the 9th Century B.C.

Lydford law, a summary administration of law or, as T. Blount, in his *Glossographia*, 1656, phrased it, 'to hang men first, and indite them afterwards'. From the Stannaries Court of summary jurisdiction held at *Lydford* on Dartmoor. Compare **Jeddart justice.**

Lyman Series. See **Balmer Series.** Theodore Lyman (b. 1874) is an American physicist, noted for his work on the properties of light of very short wave-lengths.

M

mad as a March hare. See **March hare.**

Magellanic clouds. See at **Cape.**

Magyar = *M. blouse*. This type of blouse, with sleeves one-pieced with the rest of the garment, has left Hungary to conquer the world ; yet it remains typically Hungarian.

The Magyars, the predominant race in Hungary, are Mongoloids; they came to Europe with the great Mongol invasion of Europe. A fine race, these 'Asiatic' Magyars: 'for centuries they were the real bulwark of Europe against the Turk. But they have been treated with great injustice' (Lionel W. Lyde, 1930).

Mahometan or **Mohammedan.** The former appears to be a European form of the latter, as *Mahomet* is of *Mohammed*, the founder of Mohammedanism; *Mohammed*, by the way, derives from the Arabic adjective *muhammad*, ' praiseworthy ' or ' much praised '.

Main Street. ' When we speak of the " West ", we understand . . . that there were innumerable " Wests ", all the way from the snug, comfortable towns of Indiana or Illinois . . . out to the roughest group of new shanties along a " Main Street " that was alternately mud ruts or blinding dust,' James Truslow Adams—concerning the U.S.A. of ca. 1870 in *The Epic of America*, revised English edition of 1939. The term is often associated with the Middle West, traditionally supposed to be less sophisticated than the East and vastly less insouciant than the West. *Main Street morality* (or *ethics*) connotes narrow-mindedness; in general, *Main Street* implies either mediocrity or dullness; Sinclair Lewis's great novel, *Main Street*, appeared in 1920.
' There is no use in accusing America of being a " Babbitt Warren " . . . There are plenty of Babbitts everywhere. Main Street is the longest in the world, for it encircles the globe. It is an American name, but not an American thoroughfare,' James Truslow Adams, *The Epic of America*.

Maltese lace. ' Before the war [of 1939–45] thousands of girls worked at lace-making, mostly on the smaller island of Gozo. It was a craft, skilled and beautiful, using not looms but spindles and pins, and Maltese lace was renowned all over the world,' John Brophy, *Target Island*, 1944. Other ' products ' of Malta are the *Maltese cat*, a bluish-grey domestic animal, and the *Maltese dog*, a lap-dog, with silky white hair; and the *Maltese mushroom*, common to most of southern Europe.

Malthusian. From Thomas Malthus (1766–1834), the English economist that made a very considerable stir in 1798—and afterwards—with his *Essay on the Principle of Population*, wherein he advocated a check upon indiscriminate propagation of a species about which he was none too optimistic.

Malvern water. ' " My house is perfect . . . there are Malvern water and biscuits by every bed ",' ' Palinurus ', *The Unquiet Grave*, 1945. Malvern, a town in Worcestershire, is ' much frequented as a summer resort not only on account of the beauty of the neighbourhood, but also . . . of its saline and alkaline waters ' (George G. Chisholm).

man of Belial. See **Belial.**

Manchester goods; Manchester school (of political and economic thought). T. Fuller, *The Church History of Britain*, 1655, notes the chief Lancashire industry as being that of Manchester cotton, which was already known all over Britain and in several countries abroad. The ' school ' was headed by John Bright and Richard Cobden, both of them powerful in the 1840's and 1850's.

Manton. See **Joe Manton.**

Mantoux test, the. An intracutaneous test for tuberculosis, devised by the French physician, Charles Mantoux (b. 1877), famous for his work on this disease ; work that is as valuable as it is practical.

March beer. ' This fare . . . put new heart into them, washed down as it was with excellent Margate ale, March beer and, to top all, a swimming bowl of punch,' David Pilgrim, *No Common Glory*, 1941. Also **March ale.** Both are, or were, brewed in March.

March hare, mad as a. Very mad, as hares tend to be in rut in March. The phrase has been fortified by the popularity of Lewis Carroll's *Alice's Adventures in Wonderland* (1865), for there one of the most eccentric characters is the March Hare.

Maréchal Niel. This climbing rose honours the memory of Adolphe Niel (1802–69), a French soldier, who distinguished himself in the Crimean War and became a Marshal of France and a Minister of War.

Martin's summer, St; St Martin's bird (the hen-harrier). Named in commemoration of, or in reference to, St Martin, a 4th-Century Bishop of Tours. His festival is held on November the 11th: *Martinmas*. Hence, strictly, *St Martin's summer* refers to summery weather coming in the earlier half of November.

581

Mary, little. This personification of the stomach was introduced, or at the least popularized, by Sir James Barrie (1860–1937) in his play, *Little Mary*, produced on the stage in 1903.

Marylebone stage. 'I had often been into Colchester but never before by Shanks's pony or the Marrowbone stage, as Essex folk have it,' Neil Bell, *Child of My Sorrow*, 1944. *Marrowbone stage* was soon folk-etymologized into *Marylebone stage*, precisely as *go by shanks's pony* became a mythical *Shanks's* (or *Shank's*) *pony*.

Massa marble. See **Carrara**.

Mayfair and **Belgravia,** together, constitute the fashionable residential part of London. (The former is W.1, the latter S.W.1.) Mayfair is more fashionable, less aristocratic than Belgravia, and whereas the former includes a small, but very smart shopping centre, the latter is free of that contagion; on the other hand, Belgravia has no Claridge's.

Mayflower, The; the Pilgrim Fathers or **the Pilgrims.** The latter came to America in the former. *The Mayflower*, with 102 Pilgrims, reached the present Provincetown harbour on November 21, 1620. The 41 adult males—the Pilgrim Fathers, in fact—had drafted, on November 11, an agreement to become a body politic, which began its effective life at Plymouth, named after the English port whence the ship had sailed on September 16. The term *The Pilgrims* soon came to be extended to all the early settlers of Plymouth colony. The Pilgrims, properly so called, were not Puritans, but Separatists. The most important of them was perhaps William Bradford (1590–1657), who was elected Governor of the colony and who wrote its history.

The Pilgrims became, like their ship, a legend: and from their history, snobbery arose: the number of people directly descended from the Mayflower pilgrims is stupendous. In *Detective Fiction Weekly*, June 24, 1939, that courageous thinker and first-class novelist, Richard Sale, obliquely satirizes this snobbery when he refers thus to a fictitious character: 'Fletcher Whittaker, who happened to be worth ten or more millions and traces his ancestry back to the guys who met the pilgrims when they landed' (compare **Norman blood**).

'The "Forty-Niners" . . . have taken their place in our picturesque history with the Pilgrim Fathers, the pioneer, and the cowboy,' James Truslow Adams, *The Epic of America*, 1933.

582

'In 540 [B.C.] Phocaea fell to the Persians, and a group of Phocaeans sailed for Spain as refugees. They may be regarded as the first Pilgrim Fathers, bringing to a new world beliefs and institutions which, in their own country, had become impossible,' J. B. Trend, *The Civilization of Spain*, 1944.

Medes and Persians, laws of the. Unchangeable laws. 'Some time, doubtless, elapsed before the sovereignty of Cyrus was acknowledged by all Persia; but, once his lordship . . . was an accomplished fact, he naturally became known as king primarily of the Persians, and only secondarily of the Medes,' D. G. Hogarth, *The Ancient East*, (revised edition) 1945. In the comparatively little-known book of *Esther* in The Old Testament, we find, at i, 19, the origin of this cliché to be 'Let it be written among the laws of the Persians and the Medes, that it be not altered '.

Medicean. '*Medico*, doctor . . . is an Italian word from the grand tour. Its pl. *Medici* became the name of a famous Italian family ' (W), effectually founded by Giovanni de Medici (1360–1429). His sons Cosimo (1389–1464) and Lorenzo (1399–1440), 'Il Magnifico ', and a descendant, Catherine de Medicis (1519–89), caused our *Medicean* to be equivalent to 'princely, arrogant, rich, cruel, yet patrons of literature and the arts '.

Mercator's projection. A *Mercator* is a map set forth, in the flat, according to the principles of *Mercator's projection*, devised in 1568 by Gerhard Kremer (1512–94), a Flemish geographer of genius. His name is usually given in its latinized form, Gerhardus Mercator. In the 16th Century, 'the cosmographer . . . was . . . in the first instance a mathematician and an astronomer ' (E. G. R. Taylor, *Tudor Geography*, 1930) : and Mercator affords an example of this generalization.

Meredithian, in its transferred senses, means 'subtle, intellectually alert and advanced, paradoxical, witty, tending to fine-drawn analysis of motives and character, morally tolerant yet very much an ally of the angels, and possessed of a " high-brow ", mannered and extremely allusive style ' : as in most of the novels and in much of the poetry written by George Meredith (1828–1909), whose prose masterpieces were *Richard Feverel* (1859), *The Idea of Comedy* (1877), *The Egoist* (1879), and whose verse masterpiece was perhaps *Modern Love*, 1862.

Messerschmitt may be admitted as the best-known type of German fighter (or pursuit) aircraft in the war of 1939–45; as the Heinkel or the Dornier is that of German bomber 'planes.

> Come Dornier, Junker, Messerschmitt,
> And Heinkel in which four men sit;
> They come like brazen birds on wing,
> Each one a proud, rapacious thing
> (Walter N. Sinkinson, *The Battle of Britain*, 1946).

Most German aircraft have been named after their designers or their manufacturers. Wilhelm Messerschmitt (b. 1898) has both designed and manufactured 'planes; in 1937 he received the Lilienthal prize for research into aviation. *Junker* is properly *Junkers*, after Hugo Junkers (1859–1935), designer of the first all-metal 'plane to fly successfully. The *Heinkel* commemorates Ernst Heinkel (b. 1888), manufacturer of aircraft. Claude Dornier (b. 1884) has designed and manufactured transport and reconnaissance as well as bomber 'planes. The Henschel family's manufactories originally made, and they still make, locomotives. The leading designer of the 1943–45 fighter, the *Focke-Wulf*, was Heinrich Focke, b. 1890. See also **Dornier . . .**

Metonic cycle, the, ' a period of 19 years, after the lapse of which the new and full moon returns to the same day of the year . . . the basis of the Greek Calendar ' (Webster), took its name in 432 from *Meton*, a Greek astronomer that, flourishing in the 5th Century B.C., resided at Athens. Compare **the Cal(l)ippic cycle,** a period of 76 years (4 metonics, minus 1 day), instituted by *Calippus* or *Callipus*, a Greek astronomer of the century preceding Meton's.

Mexican is short for *Mexican dollar*; *Mexicans* for *Mexican sheep*, rough-fleeced. Then there are *Mexican horses, bits, saddles,* the Mexicans being famous horsemen; such birds as the *Mexican eagle* and *jaçana*; such plants as *Mexican clover* and *poppy*. Nor must we forget *Mexican tea*, introduced into the United States from Mexico. The DAE contains a fascinating list of *Mexican* terms.

Mexican flame leaf. See **poinsettia** (main vocabulary).

Michaelmas daisy is an aster, originally wild, blooming in the season of Michaelmas. Compare **Michaelmas spring,** approximately synonymous with *Indian summer*.

584

Mickey Mouse. This widespread R.A.F. slang for the electrical distributor that releases bombs from aircraft takes its name from Mickey Mouse of film-cartoon fame. This film ' character ' is one of the earlier creations of Walt (Walter E.) Disney, who, born in 1901, has had a greater cinematic influence and popularity than even **Charlie Chaplin.** Disney is a genius.

Mills = *Mills bomb.* This hand-grenade, used by the British Army—and the Allies—in the wars of 1914–18 and 1939–45, was invented by the Englishman, Sir William Mills (1856–1932). William Mills is more widely known as a pioneer in research on alloys.

Miltonic, in its transferred senses (compare **Meredithian** above), tends to mean ' characterized by grandeur and " the organ-note ", morally elevated, stylistically versatile, yet nearly always impressive, a monarch of metric and of the architectonics of composition, a spiritual seer and intransigent '. John Milton (1608–74) published in the 1630's his lyric verse ; *Areopagitica*—his most famous prose work—in 1644 ; *Paradise Lost*, 1667 and 1674 ; *Paradise Regained* and *Samson Agonistes* in 1671.

Ming is short for *Ming porcelain, Ming ware,* and so forth, but—probably because of the rarity of the thing—the word is unlikely ever to achieve the democratic crown of lower-casing. The Ming Dynasty (1368–1644) produced exquisite bowls and vases, above all in the nine-year reign of Suën-tê in the 16th Century. ' Their yellow was the Ming monochrome, distinctive of its period . . . The poetry of China was in that yellow, and the wisdom of Confucius and the five relations,' John P. Marquand, in *Ming Yellow* (1934), a novel as arresting as readable.

Mississippi kite is a bird, well-known in all the southern States, whereas a *Mississippi steamboat* is a large and luxurious river-vessel. The *Mississippi rifle* was the large-bore percussion rifle used by a Mississippi regiment during the Mexican War (late 1845–early 1848). The seemingly ribald *Mississippi bottom* means no more than the *bottom land*, or low-lying land, characteristic of the Mississippi—literally Big River—shores. (DAE.)

Missouri, be ; or **come from Missouri.** To be very sceptical, very reluctant to believe without proof. *Missouri* was origin-

585

ally the name of a Red Indian tribe, ' Dwellers on the Big Muddy' (river: the Missouri). Webster.

Mohammedan. See **Mahometan.**

Molotov bread-basket; M. cocktail. 'The Monarchists hurled Molotov cocktails—petrol-filled bottles—in an attempt to set fire to the six-storey building,' Sydney Smith, Rome, Tuesday, in *Daily Express* of Wednesday, the 12th June, 1946.
  ' She was patrolling the drive when a clump of incendiaries came down. Molotov bread-basket, perhaps,' J. J. Connington, *Jack-in-the-Box*, 1944.
  These two improvised weapons, the one aerial, the other military, were named after V. M. Molotov (b. 1890), the Russian statesman so well-known in Britain; the latter, derisively, by the Finns.

Mona Lisa, usually in *as enigmatic* or *mysterious* or *secret* or *sly as the Mona Lisa* or in *Mona Lisa smile* (' The grimace about Bella's lips changed to a Mona Lisa smile, an expression with which I was familiar. It was a look of hauteur,' John P. Marquand, *Wickford Point*, 1939), refers to the too famous portrait by Leonardo da Vinci (1452–1519) of Mona (or Monna: short for *Madonna*, Milady) Lisa, the wife of a Florentine gentleman, Francesco del Giocondo (whence the alternative title, ' La Gioconda '). Mona Lisa's English fame owes much to the detailed critique by Walter Pater in 1873. She looks subtly, slyly sensual rather than jocund.

Monastral blue. ' Cobalt, cerulean blue, French ultramarine and Monastral blue, were all discoveries of modern chemists,' Thomas Bodkin, *The Approach to Painting*, (revised edition) 1945.

Mond gas (a variety of ' water gas '—a commercial fuel). Invented by Ludwig Mond of the old Brunner Mond & Co., founded in 1872, and father of Lord Melchett the founder of the I.C.I. Ludwig Mond (1839–1900), a German chemist and industrialist, became a naturalized British subject as early as 1867.

Monel metal is an alloy—mostly nickel (68%) and copper (27%) —that has been named after ' Ambrose Monel, who was president of the International Nickel Company in 1905, when that firm introduced the alloy ' (The OED). For further information, see J. W. Mellor's *Modern Inorganic Chemistry*.

586

Montessori(an) system. This system of education was devised by Maria Montessori (b. 1870), that Italian physician and educator who, in 1907, opened in the slums of Rome the first Montessori school for children. Her books appeared, *The Montessori Method* in 1912 and *Advanced Montessori Method* in 1917.

Moreton Bay fig. ' A few loungers in the shade of the Moreton Bay fig tree, a saddle-back switching its tail . . . a dusty dray, a decrepit sulky,' Godfrey Blunden, *No More Reality*, 1935. Then there are the *Moreton Bay ash—laurel—lily* (called *the Brisbane lily* too)—and *pine*, all named after Moreton Bay, into which flows the Brisbane River in south-east Queensland.

Morgan has two utterly dissociated meanings. It is short for *Morgan horse*, ' a superior breed of horses developed in Vermont by Justin Morgan (1747–1798); also a horse of this breed ' (DAE). He raised it in 1793, and a very useful horse-of-all-work it turned out to be. Historically, it is also a term current in ca. 1828–60 for ' a campaign, a diatribe, against Freemasons '; one William Morgan of New York State was alleged to have been murdered by Freemasons (DAE).

Morison's pill, invented by one James Morison (1840), became allusive for ' panacea of social ills ' : an allusiveness established by Carlyle, especially in the books and pamphlets published in 1839–50. Obsolescent. (W.)

Morris (arm-)chair. ' He slowly surveyed the changed appearance of the room, and, finally, after lighting his dudeen, dropped into the " as good as new " Morris chair, placed alluringly near the window,' Owen Kildare, *The Wisdom of the Simple*, 1905. This mainly American convenience, an easy chair with an adjustable back, owes its name to William Morris (1834–96), poet, pamphleteer, master craftsman, who influenced politicians, printers, architects and furniture-designers.

Morris tube. In full, *Morris aiming tube*, a small-bore barrel insertible in a shot-gun or a large-bore rifle and used for shooting practice. The inventor, Richard Morris (d. 1891), patented it in 1881, and his invention ' held the (shooting) gallery ' for a quarter-century or so.

Mother Carey's chickens are petrels, especially the stormy petrels. *Mother Carey* is a corruption of the Latin *Mater Cara* (Dear Mother), a synonym for the Virgin Mary, regarded as the protector of sailors, by whom the 'chickens' are held, or were formerly held, in superstitious affection.

Mother Goose songs is the American equivalent of the British 'nursery rhymes'. The Mother Goose concerned is probably the good old woman of Perrault's children's stories, *Contes de ma Mère l'Oye* (tales of my mother the goose), 1697.

Mrs Warren's profession. Prostitution. Lester V. Berrey and Melvin Van Den Bark, in their magnificent work, *The American Thesaurus of Slang*, 1942 (English edition, 1943), classify it as an underworld term; obviously, however, it is journalistic.

G. B. Shaw's play, *Mrs Warren's Profession*, appeared in *Plays: Pleasant and Unpleasant*, 1898.

Muscovy duck. See **muscovado** in the main vocabulary.

N

Naboth's vineyard. An agricultural property or plot of ground, hence any possession, that so excites one's greed or envy that one will have no scruples concerning the means of obtaining it.

In reference to the ancient kingdom of Elam, J. L. Myres writes in the 'Neighbours of Babylonia' chapter of his *The Dawn of History*, 'Here, then, was a " Naboth's vineyard " to tempt any Babylonian king who thought he was strong enough'.

See 1 *Kings*, xxi, for the story of how King Ahab, failing to persuade Naboth to sell his magnificent vineyard, caused him to be murdered—and thereupon seized the dead man's property.

Napier's logarithms. ' In this advance in mathematics, in the late 16th and early 17th Centuries, English mathematicians played a spirited part, and there was a corresponding progress towards a more exact geography. An illustration is afforded by the invention of logarithms by Lord Napier of Merchiston . . . Hardly had his work been two years before the public when Aaron Rathborne, a practical surveyor, was pressing the use of pocket tables of logarithms on fellow members of his profession,' E. G. R. Taylor, *Late Tudor and Early Stuart Geography*, 1934.

Napier (1550–1617) described logarithms in a work published in 1614; his book explaining their construction did not appear until two years after his death.

Navajo blanket. 'Navajo blankets lay on the floor, Mexican scrapes were flung carelessly over the armchairs,' V. Sackville-West, *Grand Canyon*, 1942.

Navajo blankets are so familiar in North America that they are occasionally referred to as *Navajos*: 'I bought me a swell Navajo'. Originally (and still) made by the Navajo Indians—a numerous shepherd tribe with a high native culture—of Arizona, New Mexico, and southern Utah. Their name is not Amerindian—or rather, it is Amerindian re-shaped by the Spaniards; the *j* is pronounced *h*, the word being pronounced *Năʹ-vahú*. The Red Indian name is *Navahú*, 'large field'—Apaches of the large field.

Neanderthal man. 'You know what the other side says—" Woman is the recreation of the warrior "—" Woman's place is in the kitchen "—all the rest of that Neanderthal tommyrot,' Nicholas Blake, *The Smiler with the Knife*, 1939.

The Neanderthal Man is a type of primitive man, theoretically reconstructed from the prehistoric skull discovered, in 1859, at Neanderthal in Rhenish Prussia. The correct ethnological adjective is *Neanderthaloid*, the correct general adjective is *Neanderthalian*; and *Neanderthal* (*man*) is allusively employed for 'a sub-human, or a primitively stupid or bestial, person or characteristic'.

Neapolitan ice. An ice-cream made in strata differently coloured and flavoured. Italians were pioneers in the commendable art of the ice-cream: and Neapolitans were the leaders of these pioneers.

Neapolitan sixth. The origin of the name for this chromatic chord in music remains, as Dr Scholes points out, a mystery.

New England conscience. 'Being a New Englander is less a state of geography than a state of mind,' remarks Percival Wilde, *Inquest*, (English edition) 1939: geographically, it means belonging to Massachusetts or Connecticut or Rhode Island or Maine or Vermont or New Hampshire.

In the index of *The Epic of America* (5th English impression, 1945), its author James Truslow Adams lists *New England conscience* in quotation marks: and in the text he writes, 'Although there had been a strong Puritan tinge to the thought of the colonists everywhere, there had not been in the

South that harsh and determined Puritanism which grew steadily more narrow and bitter in New England. The " New England conscience " . . . would probably not have survived the climate even if it had been there ' in the South. ' In New England the soil and climate ruggedly backed up the theology of the dominant group.'

New England rum. See **Yankee . . .**

New York, whose site was first indicated by a trading post established on Manhattan in 1609, has so long been a great city that it, and with it the State of New York, inevitably got itself involved in a number of names : plants, e.g. the *New York gloria mundi*, a very large apple indeed ; *New York water-melon* : fishes and oysters, e.g. *New York gudgeon—plaice—shiner—*and (an oyster) *count* : animals, e.g. *bat—ermine—weasel* : birds, e.g. *New York rail—thrush—warbler* : and the famous *New York cracker*, a hard biscuit.

Newcastle, carry coals to. To perform an entirely unnecessary task. ' The most famous coal-field [in England] is that in Durham and Northumberland, which has given the name of Newcastle to coal towns in all parts of the world, *e.g.* in New South Wales, New Zealand and Natal,' Lionel W. Lyde, *Man and His Markets*, 1896.

Newgate, as in *N. frill* or *fringe*, ' a collar-like beard worn under the chin ' (Farmer & Henley), and as in some ten other terms recorded in PS, refers to that old London prison which, razed in 1902, had been the main prison for the City of London ever since the 13th Century and had, from as early as 1590, been ' a common name for all prisons ' (Nashe).

Newtonian. In its literal sense, ' pertaining to, in accordance with Sir Isaac Newton (1642–1727) or his theories and discoveries ', the word is not even a candidate ; but as meaning or implying ' simple grandeur ', it certainly is a candidate. Royal Air Force pilots slangily substitute *Newton* or, more often, *old Newton* for ' the force of gravity ' and thus not merely recognize the value, the inevitability of Newton's laws of gravity but also ' communize ' the proper name.

And here are two relevancies contributed by a French pilot, also a notable writer, the late Antoine de Saint-Euxpéry in *Wind, Sand and Stars* (1939) : ' Men are not cattle to be fattened for market. In the scales of life an indigent Newton '—how nobly the world rewards its truly great men !—' weighs more than a parcel of prosperous nonentities.'—'Newton did not "discover" a law that lay hidden from man like the answer to a rebus. He accomplished a creative operation. He founded a human speech which could express at one and the same time the fall of an apple and the rising of the sun. Truth is not that which is demonstrable, but that which is ineluctable.'

Newton's metal is an alloy (tin, lead, bismuth), fusible at 91·5° C. Named after Isaac Newton—see preceding entry. The alloy called Lichtenberg's is the same thing; Georg Lichtenberg (1742–99) was a notable German physicist.

neo-Bechstein. See **Bechstein.**

Niagara, figurative for ' a tremendous flow and fall of water '— as in ' She shed a very Niagara of tears '.
   ' The St Lawrence . . . shows the greatest development and the greatest possibility [in water power] of any river of the continent. This is concentrated in Niagara Falls and rapids and in the stretch of rapids between Prescott and Montreal,' Jones & Bryan, *North America*, (7th edition) 1946.

Nick Carter, the American compeer of the English **Sexton Blake** (primary vocabulary), is often used allusively for a courageous—indeed, heroic—and intelligent, shrewd and resourceful detective, less gentlemanly than Sherlock Holmes— but much dearer to the American boys of ca. 1890–1920.
   ' Stock name for the detective hero of many dime novels ', written by various authors (J. R. Coryell, F. V. R. Dey, E. T. Sawyer, G. C. Jenks, and others) ; ' The Carter novelettes, which include more than 1000 titles ' (*The Oxford Companion to American Literature*).
   ' I had read my share of Nick Carter, Old Sleuth, Deadeye Dick, and Old King Brady, the celebrated detectives of nickel fiction who rounded up train robbers, counterfeiters, murderers and burglars, and at one time in my life I was possessed with the ambition to become a detective,' Jack Callahan, *Man's Grim Justice*, 1929—a very striking autobiography by a criminal, comparable with Jack Black's *You Can't Win*, 1926.

Nicodemus complex. ' One may think of this " animalizing " of man's nature as a sort of wilful atavism ; what some psychologists delight in calling a " Nicodemus complex " ; or what Kipling termed " getting back to one's beginnings ",' Michael Harrison, *Reported Safe Arrival*, 1943. From that Biblical Nicodemus who, a Pharisee and a doubter (feet on the ground), came by night to speak with Christ: *John*, iii, 1–21; vii, 50–52; xix, 39.

Nieder-Ingelheim is a white wine grown in the neighbourhood of the township so named in the Bingen district of Rhinhesse; and **Nieder-oesterreicher** is a wine mentioned in the Norman Douglas quotation at **Terlaner** (p. 629).

Nightingale. See **Florence Nightingale.**

Nile-green; eau de Nil. Of the same kind of green as that which characterizes the surface-water of the Nile; the colour less romantically known as pale green: 'the green Nile' is at least an apter description than is 'the blue Danube': 'Egypt has been known for at least 7000 years as "the Gift of the River" . . . The river is the *Nile*, and that name really means "The Flood"; and *this* is actually the "gift" which the river brings,' Lyde & Garnett, *Time and Place*, 1933.

Among modistes and women of fashion, *eau de Nil* (usually italicized) is more general than *Nile-green*, which—if they use it at all—seems to be preferred by men. In his story-sequence, *The Man Who Couldn't Sleep* (1919), the versatile, ever readable Arthur Stringer has a chapter entitled 'The Nile-Green Roadster'.

Nissen hut is gayly ignored by The OED and by Webster. W, however, has this entry: '**nissen** [neol.]. Army hut. ? From inventor's name. "In a nissen hut or a pill-box" (*Punch*, April 17, 1918).' Yet Squadron-Leader C. H. Ward Jackson, in his *It's a Piece of Cake*, 1943, has named, as the inventor, Lt-Col. P. H. Nissen, D.S.O., a Canadian mining engineer.

Noah's ark. The child's toy nostalgically commemorates the Ark built by Noah in prehistoric times to surmount the Flood. The story in *Genesis* owes much to Mesopotamian sources.

Noah's nightcap. 'The plant eschscholtzia (with reference to conical bud-sheaves)', E. G. Withycombe, *The Oxford Dictionary of Christian Names*, 1945; meaning that its shape-resemblance to a nightcap is close. But why *Noah*? Because of a vague similarity in the shapes of the flower, a nightcap, Noah's Ark.

Nobel Prizes. Alfred Bernhard Nobel (1833–96), Swedish inventor and manufacturer, was educated in St Petersburg and the U.S.A. In the latter, 1850–54, he studied mechanical engineering. Among his numerous inventions are dynamite (1866) and ballistite (1888); indeed, his great wealth came largely from his manufacture of explosives. He bequeathed a sum of about £2,000,000 or $9,200,000 for the establishment of the Nobel Prizes, the first being awarded in 1901. They are awarded, annually, for Physics, Chemistry, Medicine (or Physiology), Literature (strictly, for idealistic literature—a fact sometimes overlooked), and (penitently?) for service in the cause of Peace.

Nordic has come to mean ' endowed with primitive energy, strength, courage; racially pure; physically blond, long-headed, tall ' and therefore might, perhaps, be written *nordic*. The word connotes ' intellectual power without sophistication ', plus ' grandeur with simplicity', and many other qualities combined, in one person, not more than five or six times in the world's history. Properly, it describes Scandinavians, but the Germans have distorted it, like **Aryan** (also in the ' Border-Liners '), to their own Nietzschean propaganda. ' There is a Nordic type, making up about 70% of the population in Scandinavia, less than 20% in Germany, Holland and Great Britain, and less than 15% in the United States . . . The existence of a common Nordic-primitive people has never been proved,' Walter Theimer, *The Penguin Political Dictionary*. Nordic derives from modern Latin *Nordicus*, ' Northern '.

Norfolk Howard. This jocular name for a bug—English, not American sense—' dates from an advertisement in *The Times* (June 26, 1862) announcing assumption of this name by one Joshua Bug ' of Norfolk (W); odd that he should have done so, for, in Old English, *bug* means ' warrior, hero '.

Norfolk Island pine. See **araucaria** in the primary vocabulary.

Norfolk jacket. ' He was dressed in a loose grey Norfolk jacket and knickerbockers,' Freeman Wills Crofts, *The Pit-Prop Syndicate*, 1922. Originally worn, especially for shooting but also for fishing, in the county of Norfolk, it became general for such purposes as cycling. Now somewhat *démodé* among the people that don't matter. (Belted and vertical-pleated.)

Norman blood is used in reference to the aristocracy that came to England with or was created by William of Normandy, William the Conqueror, in ' 1066 and all that '. It connotes snobbery and should be compared with American descent from the Pilgrims of The **Mayflower.**

Norway haddock is a brilliantly coloured fish, abounding in the seas off the North Atlantic coast of America.

Norway maple, flourishing in Norway and Sweden, was introduced into the United States before 1820, where it is popular both for the shade it affords and for the ornament it constitutes.

Norway pine. 'Here '—the north-eastern coniferous forest—' Black Spruce and Balsam Fir, Norway and Jack Pine, and White Pine, are predominant trees,' Jones & Bryan, *North America*, 1946.

Also *Norway Fir.* This is the spruce fir, a native of northern and mountainous central Europe; it has long been exported to Britain from Scandinavia. Likewise called the *Norway spruce.*

Norway rat. This, the common brown house-rat, was introduced into the United States from Norway. Presumably it went ashore from the many Norwegian ships trading at American ports.

nosey Parker. This name for an inquisitive person is of doubtful origin. There may be something in the seemingly folk-etymological theory that it derives from Matthew Parker (1504-75), English prelate and scholar, who was so very busy a person that some people did think him rather a busybody. Also—usually hyphenated—as a verb: cf. ' " Always sticking her nose into things that don't concern her."—" . . . Just general, undifferentiated Noseyparkering? ",' L. A. G. Strong, *Othello's Occupation*, 1945.

Nostradamus, a soothsayer. *Nostradamus* was the latinized name of the French physician and astrologer, Michel de *Nostredame* (or *Notredame*), ' Michael of Our Lady ', who lived 1503-66. In 1555 he published his *Centuries*, a set of rhymed prophecies. He made several startlingly correct predictions and gained much favour at Court. ' If we believe in a supernatural or superhuman intelligence creating the universe, then we end by stocking our library with the prophecies of Nostradamus ' (' Palinurus ').

not to care — not worth — a Continental. See **Continental . . .**

594

Nottingham lace. ' The lawyer recalled the windows when they were muffled with Nottingham lace ' (Ethel Lina White, *Midnight House*, 1942). Nottingham has long been famed for the manufacture of lace and hosiery : it receives honourable mention in Lionel W. Lyde's *The Continent of Europe*, 1913.

O

Occam's razor ; Occamism.

> ' Adept as Occam's razor to split hairs
> Of conscience and commission '
> (Ronald Bottrall, *Farewell and Welcome*, 1945).

William of Occam (or Ockham), often called ' *Doctor Invincibilis* ', so formidable was he in debate, lived ca. 1300–49. English, he joined the Franciscans ; pupil of Duns Scotus, he became his rival. He held that the real is always individual, not universal, with the corollary (*Occam's razor*) that ' entities must not be unnecessarily multiplied '.

Oedipus ; Oedipus complex. Whereas the former is sometimes applied to a good riddle-solver, the latter—among ' intellectuals ' often shortened to *Oedipus*—forms one of the Freudian complexes.

' What makes anti-metaphysicians is the thing which modern psychologists if they belong to Freud's sect call an Oedipus complex, and if they belong to Adler's an inferiority complex,' R. G. Collingwood, *An Essay on Metaphysics*, 1940.

In reference to Sophocles, C. M. Bowra has, in *Sophoclean Tragedy*, 1944, said, ' No Greek story has such pain and horror as that of Oedipus, who, after answering the riddle of the Sphinx and being made King of Thebes, discovered that he had killed his father and married his mother, then blinded himself and became an outcast beggar '.

Oerlikon. ' All through the forenoon they had heard the four-inch and the Oerlikons and the pompons firing in savage bursts, and they had known that the convoy and escort were under aerial attack,' C. S. Forester, *The Ship*, 1943.

The *Oerlikon* is a 20-mm. automatic anti-aircraft rapid-firing gun, named from Oerlikon, near Zurich in Switzerland, because it was developed by the Swiss.

old Adam, ' unregenerated man ; man in his state of—or acting on, or at the least feeling, the impulses of—original sin ', especially in relation to woman viewed as cohabitator. Why Adam and Eve should be regarded as either particularly wicked or unusually amorous, it would be more than difficult to say, for they merely lived, unsophisticated and unartificial, ' in a state of nature ' (*Adam and Eve togs*, as slang so elegantly phrases it).

Of the child ' being born now ', Charles Morgan, in *Reflections in a Mirror*, 1944, has pertinently written, ' Is there not hope . . . that, once liberated from [the doctrine that order is the product of a collective tyranny and a personal surrender] and impelled by nothing more obscure than the old Adam in him, he may grow up into that glorious and amusing being, a Character, which we, for a hundred reasons of social conformity, have done our utmost to suppress? '

In Hebrew, *adam* signifies ' man ' : Adam was ' *the* man '. At first, he probably drank only water, this being *Adam's ale*— an expression now, by the way, a moth-eaten genteelism.

old Ned, salt bacon or smoke-cured pork, took its name from a famous Negro song ; the DAE's earliest record is for 1833. The name is affectionate rather than derogatory.

Old Red Sandstone. See **Devonian.**

Oliver's skull was, ca. 1650–1870, slang for a chamber-pot. For the reason, cf. **Twiss** in the subsidiary vocabulary : to Royalists, Oliver Cromwell's name fairly ' stank '.

Ophelia. A lovely rose, poetically reminiscent of the Shakespearean Ophelia's virginal charm and flower-strewn, watery death. ' The roses still kept their flowers, in spite of the storm : robust Gloire de Dijon blooms ramped over an archway, and shell-like Ophelias continued to grace their long almost thornless stems,' Mary Fitt, *Death on Herons' Mere*, 1945.

Ophelia comes from Greek *ŏphĕlia*, ' help, succour ' (E. G. Withycombe, *Christian Names*, 1945).

Orient pearl or **pearl of Orient,** is, as you might suppose, a pearl of the Orient or East. Found in the Indian Ocean, it was more brilliant than those residing in European mussels ; hence, it came, in poetry of the 16th–18th Centuries, to synonymize ' lustrous, or precious, pearl '.

' India and the Persian Gulf sent pearls, unknown before

Alexander [356–323 B.C.], but now highly valued by women as ornaments,' W. W. Tarn, *Hellenistic Civilisation*, 1927.

Orlando. ' He imagined himself the squire of a great lady, the gallant speeches he would make to her and the yet more gallant deeds that he [Loyola] would do in her service. He was as sentimental as any Orlando,' James Brodrick, *The Origin of the Jesuits*, 1940.

Orlando, a knight, occurs in the famous poetic romance by Matteo Boiardo (1434–96): *Orlando Innamorato*, which its author was chivalrically well qualified to write: *Orlando* is a romantic Italian refashioning of the story of the heroic Roland, whose lady was the princess Angelica.

Orleans is short for the black grape known as the **Orleans grape,** recorded in 1769 and imported into North America from France; also for *New Orleans sugar*, recorded in 1846. (DAE.)

Orphic. Orphism was a mystery-religion (not, as journalists have it, a mystery religion) of the ancient Greeks, especially in the 4th–6th Centuries B.C. The name comes from *Orpheus*, a legendary, pre-Homeric, Thracian poet, whose sacred poems formed the basis of the Orphic cult. Some of its tenets foreshadowed those of Christianity.

' The universal basis of the mystery-religions was that you sought " salvation " by personal union with a saviour god who had himself died and risen again; to employ the well-known Orphic phrase, you ceased to be a worshipper . . . and became a Bacchus—you were as the god himself,' W. W. Tarn, *Hellenistic Civilisation*, 1927.

Orson, allusive and literary for a rough but valiant fellow, comes from the anonymous tale of *Valentine and Orson*, 1495, a twin-heroed romance wherein, as infants, they are abandoned, Valentine being carried off by a kindly uncle and gently nurtured, Orson being suckled by a bear but eventually reclaimed. *Orson* represents the French *ourson*, ' little bear ': *ours*, a bear, from Latin *ursus*. (Webster.)

Ortley is, in full, *Ortley pippin*, a winter-eating apple, which has apparently been named after its first raiser. Compare **Baldwin.**

Orvieto. ' He drank a glass of Orvieto, poured from a wicker flask which reposed in snow when not in use,' David Pilgrim,

The Grand Design (of Charles II of England), 1944. The white Orvieto wines are still bottled in straw-covered flasks. Orvieto is ' one of the most picturesque cities of Umbria perched on a hill-top and surrounded by vineyards' (André Simon).

Osage, the name of ' the most important southern Siouan tribe west of the Mississippi River', is literally *Wazhazhe*, ' War People' : whence the *Osage orange*, less sensibly named, in the early days, *Osage apple*, which ' bleeds an acrid milky juice when wounded, and is called by the hunters the Osage Orange' (Bradbury, *Travels*, 1817) ; unlike the *Osage orange*, or *apple*, the yellow *Osage plum* has an edible fruit, which, even in the wild state, was delicious, as Captain Clark of the famous Lewis and Clark expedition (1803–06) has testified.

Ossianic, in its derivative sense, means ' (of, in, like a prose that is) poetic, romantic, Celtic, heroic, full of mist and moon-light and grandeur and barbaric beauty ; also vague and amorphous'. In 1762, James Macpherson (1736–96), a Scottish antiquary, published *Fingal* and in 1763, *Temora* : prose poems dealing with the cycle of Ossian, the central figure — rather than character — being Ossian. Macpherson ' spoofed' the scholars : and achieved a remarkable originality, based on Celtic legend.

Ovidian, in its non-literal senses, connoting ' brilliantly facile in versification ; polished and neat in narrative ; of a supple, rather meretricious, cultured style'. Publius *Ovidius* Naso, or Ovid, 43 B.C.—ca. A.D. 17, is best known for the long narrative poem, *The Metamorphoses*, and for *The Art of Love* (or, rather, of love-making). *Ovidius*, as a name in itself, points to a far-distant shepherd ancestor : Latin *ovis*, a sheep.

Oxford accent. ' " Oxford ", which already has a good deal to put up with as an adjective, is the least offensive of the terms hurled at an accent which sees fair play between vowels and consonants, and is, on the whole, a dispassionate and honest rendering of the English tongue as it appears in print and is understood by foreigners . . . . . . Mr Strong [in *A Tongue in Your Head*] is confident that much can be done by more sympathetic approach in the schools to teach standard—*i.e* " Oxford ", B.B.C., but not Mayfair-caricature—English' *The Times Literary Supplement*, February 23, 1946. Such English is also known as Southern English or Public School English.

598

Oxford movement, the; Oxford groupers. The former, beginning in 1833, was very closely associated with Oxford; the latter term arose because in 1921 Frank Buchman founded at Oxford the Oxford Group Movement, although since ca. 1930 the movement has not been very closely associated with Oxford, which, as a whole, frowns upon it. See also **Buchmanism.**

P

Pagett, M.P. This synonym for a traveller that, having spent a month or two in a country, writes or lectures pontifically upon that country as though he knew, as he apparently believes that he knows, all about it. We owe this term to that character in one of Kipling's poems in *Departmental Ditties* (1886) who visits India to ' study the East ' but is soon driven away by the heat.

Paisley shawl. ' Besides the coal and iron of the suburban towns . . . [Glasgow] collects for export the linen of John-stone, the silk and muslin of Renfrew, and the thread and shawls of Paisley,' Lionel W. Lyde, *Man and His Markets*, edition of 1919: see also the quotation at **Patna.** ' The manufacture of beautiful shawls, for which Paisley has been famous, was established towards the end of the 18th Century ' (George Chisholm).

Paisley, in west Renfrewshire, stands on both sides of White Cart Water, some six miles from Glasgow.

Palestine soup is made of artichokes, and perhaps the best-known artichoke in Britain is the **Jerusalem artichoke.**

Palinurus. ' The name of Palinurus is becoming an archetype of frustration,' says ' Palinurus ', scholar and thinker and notable writer, in his remarkable book, *The Unquiet Grave*, (revised edition) 1945. Palinurus, pilot in *The Aeneid*, was washed overboard and, for his clothes, murdered by the inhabitants of Velia; his body was left graveless on that inhospitable shore. Occasionally, *Palinurus* synonymizes ' pilot '—as in William Kelly, *Life in Victoria*, 1859.

Palladian or **palladian,** as a style in architecture, has nothing to do with the **palladium** (main list) of ancient Troy, the reference being to Andrea *Palladio* (1518–80), that Italian architect who adapted Roman architecture to the needs of 16th-Century Italy, who devised the so-called *Palladian motif*, and whose influence reached England through Inigo Jones (1573–1652).

palma Christi. The castor-oil plant is so called from the shape of the leaf, which resembles the palm of a hand ; *Christ's* hand, because of the impact of the crucified Saviour's hand, nailed to the Cross, upon the Christian imagination.

Panurge, a wittily talkative, drunkenly mischievous, dissolute buffoon. From the name of one of the principal characters in the *Pantagruel* (1532) by Rabelais. *Panurge* represents the Greek adjective *panourgos*, ' ready to do anything, prepared to stop at nothing ' ; *ourgos* comes from *ergein*, to work.

Para is short for *Para rubber*. ' Rubber is the thick, milky sap of a tree which requires the precise conditions of soil and climate characteristic of the selvas [the rain forests of the Amazon] ; and, consequently, the best rubber in the world comes from Para,' Lionel W. Lyde, *Man and His Markets*, edition of 1919.
  The name *Para*, which signifies ' Father of Waters ', was originally that of the Amazon but is now reserved for its southern arm ; it designates also a Brazilian seaport and, most pertinently to our purpose, a littoral state, and the eastern third, of Brazil.

Paracelsian, ' visionary ; hyperbolical '. Paracelsus is a sort of translation of *Hohenheim*. Theophrast B. von Hohenheim (1493?–1541) was a Swiss physician, chemist, natural philosopher, alchemist. In addition to much excellent work in chemical, physical, medical theory and practice, he wrote on occultism, his most famous book being *Die Grosse Wundartznei*, 1530.

Parian shortens *P. marble*. ' Parian marble held its own everywhere,' says W. W. Tarn in his *Hellenistic Civilisation*, 1927. This lovely, glistening marble was quarried in the island of Paros—an Ionian and prosperous island among the Cyclades, in the Aegean Sea. It was much used by the ancient sculptors. Compare **Pentelic.**

Parisian has come to connote ; indeed, to denote ; smartness and elegance, as in *Paris(ian) models*—intellectual sophistication —artistic supremacy and audacity.
  Paris is in Latin *Lutetia Parisiorum*, Lutetia (its old name) of

the *Parisii*, a tribe of Celtic Gaul; in Late Latin, it was also known as *Parisii*.

Parker. See **nosey Parker.**

Parma powder. ' Kitty's . . . sanctum, with its atmosphere of Parma-powder and flowers—the fragrance of a pretty woman's dainty vanities—was deliciously familiar to both,' Alice & Egerton Castle, *Incomparable Bellairs* (a novel about 18th-Century England). This particular face-powder seems to owe its name, not to manufacture at Parma but to extraction from—or rather, to being scented by an extract from—**Parma violets,** as follows :—

Parma violets. (Compare the preceding entry.)
' The centre of the olive trade of all France is the centre of the flower trade—Grasse, though the actual market has been moved to Nice; and it is most characteristic that the Parma violets—which " open the season "—are raised under the shade of olives and "citrons", that the most important single product is orange-blossom, that the delicate perfume of the roses (the next in importance) is due to the pollen carried by the bees to the rose-buds from the orange-groves, and that the olive—which " ends the season "—should be the basis, with the vine, of the whole scent industry. For no animal fat seems to be as " pure " as a vegetable fat, and no scent can be trusted to remain " true " unless the alcohol used is of grape origin . . . True essence of violets is quoted in Grasse at 100 guineas an ounce,' Lionel W. Lyde, *The Continent of Europe*, (4th edition) 1930.

Parrott guns, used in the American civil war, were invented by Robert Parrott (1804–77), American army officer—he resigned in 1836—and notable inventor, who was engaged in the foundry business for over thirty years. To him goes the credit of a method of strengthening cast-iron guns (always likely to crack) and of the invention of an expanding projectile for rifled guns; both of these inventions were patented in 1861 and proved to be most useful to the Northern armies.

Parthenon. The Parthenon is so generally taken as the acme of Classical Greek architecture that it has acquired something of common-property significance. ' No geometrical structure in the world has been related to the moving light of day more scrupulously than the Parthenon,' Lionel W. Lyde, *A Patchwork from Pindar*, 1932.

601

Parthian glance; P. shaft (often corrupted to **parting shot**). The Parthians, an ancient race of Scythian origin, were famed as mounted archers: even in flight they were dangerous, for, turning backward with a Parthian (or very keen) glance, they discharged their shafts as they fled.

The Parthians, who dwelt south-east of the Caspian Sea, founded, ca. 250 B.C., an empire that later stretched from the Euphrates to the Indus, and from the Indian Ocean to the Oxus. In the 1st Century B.C. they defeated the Romans under Crassus; since that time, *Parthian shaft* has been proverbial.

Paschen Series. See **Balmer Series.**

Patagonian, gigantic, immense, is now obsolescent, but ca. 1750–1870 it was in frequent literary use. In the early travellers' tales of *Patagonia*, the natives were represented as being almost giants. At first, these natives were called *Patagons*, from Spanish *patagon*, a large, clumsy foot: cognate with French *patte* (hand) and English *paddle*.

Patna is short for *Patna* (generic for Indian) *rice*. 'Gallons of wine are distilled into "Cognac" which never came from Charente; millions of oranges are labelled "Jaffa" and "St Michael" which never grew in Palestine or the Azores; tons of "Patna" rice hail from Bangkok or Rangoon; and hundreds of "Kashmir" shawls are woven in Paisley, though some do still come from Srinagar,' Lionel W. Lyde, *Man and His Markets*, edition of 1919. Until Burmese rice partly supplanted Indian rice for export, much of the latter came from the district around Patna in Bengal.

Paul Pry, an inquisitive busybody (the verb 'to *pry*' becomes a personified noun, and *Paul* alliterates therewith), comes from John Poole's farce, *Paul Pry* (1825); the titular character is said to have been drawn from the life—of a prying fellow that capitalized his curiosity by writing for the newspapers.

pearl of Orient. See **Orient pearl.**

pêche Melba or, in the U.S.A., **peach Melba.** This vanilla ice-cream is served with *peaches* and either raspberry or claret sauce. It was named in honour of Dame Nellie Melba, born Helen Mitchell (1861–1931), one of the finest of all operatic sopranos. She took the name *Melba* from *Melbourne* (Australia), near which she was born.

602

peeping Tom of the Lady Godiva legend has come to synonymize all indelicate inquisitives. In 1939–45 'peeping tom' was 'a pilot expert at flying in bad weather and at dodging from cloud to cloud' (E. P., *A Dictionary of Slang*, 3rd edition, 1949).

Pekin man (scientifically, *Sinanthropus*, i.e. Chinese man); **Piltdown man.** These terms, like—though less frequently than—**Neanderthal man,** are occasionally employed as synonyms for the sub-human, the rudimentary, the moronic type of person. Only one specimen of each prehistoric type (so too for the less-known Galley Hill man and Taungs man) has been discovered—at, of course, the place named, *Piltdown* being a hamlet in Sussex.

Pelion on Ossa. 'The Pelion-Ossa ranges protect the plain of Thessaly, as Euboea protects the plain of Attica' (L. W. Lyde, *Europe*, 1913); 'Pelion and Ossa, though the one is 2,000 and the other 3,000 feet higher than Scafell or Helvellyn, are *relatively* small in Greece' (Lyde, *A Patchwork from Pindar*, 1932).

In Greek mythology, the giants Otus and Ephialtes *piled Pelion*, a wooded mountain, *on Ossa*, another such mountain, and Ossa on Olympus, in their attempt to overthrow the gods, or, as Homer phrases it, 'It was their ambition to pile Mount Ossa on Olympus, and wooded Pelion on Ossa, so as to make a stairway up to heaven' (E. V. Rieu).

'A prejudice is early acquired, and as we are doubly attentive to those who agree with us and deaf to all we do not wish to hear, not a day goes without our piling Ossas of absolute assent upon Pelions of dubious belief,' Frank Binder, *Dialectic, or The Tactics of Thinking*, 1932.

Pelmanism; Pelmanize. This arbitrary trade-name *Pelmanism*, for a system of memory-training, was devised by the inventor of the system, W. J. Ennever, in 1897; an English journalist, he opened the first Pelman Institute in 1898—in London. I suggest that he coined *Pelmanism* from Latin *pellere*, to strike or drive (something home).

Penguinize; Penguinization. To publish, or to re-publish, a book in Penguin Books; hence, in one of Penguin Books Limited's subsidiary series, especially the Pelicans. Probably we shall ultimately have *Pelicanize* also. The firm, which was founded on January 15, 1935, specializes in paper backs, issued originally at sixpence, then (during the war) at ninepence, since January 1946, a shilling, now eighteenpence; King Penguins, however, are bound in 'boards', and they cost a little more.   In the various series, the first book appeared thus :

> Penguins : July 30, 1935.
> Pelicans : May 21, 1937.
> King Penguins : November 7, 1939.
> Puffin Picture Books : December 6, 1940.
> Puffin Story Books : December 16, 1941.
> Ptarmigans : July 1945.
> Penguin Classics : 1945.

(With thanks to Penguin Books Limited for their courtesy in supplying the list of dates.)

Pennsylvania ark—blue—corn—fireplace—horse—hurricane—mile—wagon. The first is the same as the last, a strong wagon (such as a **Conestoga**) made in Pennsylvania. A *Pennsylvania blue* is not a colour but a potato, bluish in colour and known also as the Chenango or the Mercer. The *corn*, yellow and alternatively called gourd corn, has always been widely grown in that region, and the *fireplace* is of the sort characteristic of early Pennsylvanian homesteads. The *horse* is a strong, heavily built one suitable for the drawing of the *Pennsylvania wagon*. Both the *hurricane* and the *mile* are humorous terms, the former, like a *Carolina* (or *Caroliny*) *swamper*, being a large and shameless lie or very, very tall story, and the latter a distance of several, or more, miles—compare the *country mile* of English usage.

Pennsylvania feathers. Coal (ready for fuel) ; Glen H. Mullin, *Adventures of a Scholar Tramp*, 1925, defines it as 'soft coal' ; Godfrey Irwin, 1931, as 'coke' ('much lighter in weight than coal'). American slang, it is included here because of its allusiveness and its irony. Less viable but more picturesque than the clichéistic *black diamonds*. 'The Pennsylvanian area [Pa., W.Va., Ohio] produces nearly half of all the coal raised in the United States, and is by far the greatest single bituminous coal-producing area in the world,' Rodwell Jones & Bryan, *North America*, (7th edition) 1946 ; in 1942, Pennsylvania alone yielded, in short tons, 60 million of anthracite and 140 million of bituminous. *Pennsylvania* is 'Penn's woodland' : William Penn, Quaker, founded the State in 1681. *Pennsylvania* has been formed on the analogy of *Transylvania*.

Pentelic = *Pentelic marble*. From the Pentelikos, a 3000-foot mountain some ten miles from Athens, was, in Classical times, quarried the marble (close-grained and milky-white and less lustrous than the Parian) used for the columns of the Parthenon ; after the 4th Century B.C., Parian superseded it ; yet throughout the Hellenistic period, Athens exported large quantities of Pentelic.

'They went through the . . . wet streets to the Cephisia road, and Quayle could see the Pentelican dark and above sight stretching before them,' James Aldridge, *Signed with Their Honour*, 1942.

Pericles; Periclean. The adjective connotes intellectual and artistic splendour and great material prosperity, such as Athens enjoyed for much of the time that *Periklēs*, English *Pericles* (500?–429 B.C.), was at the head of the city state ; death by the plague ended his forty years' ' headship '. Perhaps the greatest of all Athenian statesmen, and a man of a very fine moral character, magnificent intellectual stature.

Permian denotes a geological period, ' the topmost division of the Carboniferous ' (Webster). *Perm* was formerly the name of a province in eastern Russia : there the formation was discovered.

Peruvian bark. ' The [tea] seed-beds require to be protected [in India] by a hedge of some kind of quick-growing tree. This is generally supplied by the cinchona, which is valuable also for its " Peruvian bark ",' Lionel W. Lyde, *Man and His Markets*, 1896. This ' bark ' is a drug used as a febrifuge : the Countess of Chinchon (see **cinchona** : main vocabulary) introduced it from *Peru* in 1640.

Peter, blue. This blue flag, with a white square, indicates a ship's impending departure. As in *jolly Roger*, the choice of the name Peter was probably a matter of caprice. ' But I have sometimes wondered whether it is in some way connected with obsolete *beaupers*, *bewpers*, bunting, misunderstood as " beautiful Peter " (Piers, Pearce) and perverted to suit the colour ' (W).

Peter Funk. This Americanism for a by-bidder is a personification of *funk*, a coward (he won't bid outright). *Peter* : a convenient, though arbitrary name.

Peter Grievance (or **Grievous**) is a grumbling adult or a fretful child. A personification—compare the preceding term. Mainly English dialectal.

Peter's fish. 'Haddock or other fish with marks supposed to have been made by St. Peter's thumb and finger,' E. G. Withycombe, *The Oxford Dictionary of Christian Names*, 1945.
Compare **St Peter's fish.**

Peter's pence, or tribute to Rome, refers to the see of *St Peter*; *pence* means no more than 'money'—but it alliterates.

Philadelphia lawyer; Philadelphia system. This sort of lawyer—one versed in the finer points of the law and exceptionally able in their application—derives his name from the well-merited renown of the late 18th–early 19th-Century Philadelphia bar; the DAE's earliest record of the phrase is for 1803, 'It would (to use a Yankee phrase) *puzzle a dozen Philadelphia lawyers*, to unriddle the conduct of the Democrats'. The *system* is that method of prison discipline which is based upon solitary confinement; already in 1842 it was contrasted with the Auburn, or Silent, System practised in the great prison at Auburn in New York State.

Phoenician. See **phoenix** in main glossary.

Phrygian cap is often used for 'liberty cap', such as that worn by the French revolutionaries of 1789. In Classical Greek art, it was a conical cap worn by Orientals. From the ancient *Phrygians* of Asia Minor: in Greek *Phrugioi*.

Pierian spring, the. Figurative for 'the fount of poesy', i.e. poetic inspiration, the phrase refers to 'the Pierid Muses' (see **muse**)—the *Pierides*, dwellers in *Pieria*, 'a district on the northern slopes of Mt Olympus . . . The cult of the Muses was said to have been brought from Pieria to Helicon' (Sir Paul Harvey). Compare **Helicon** in the main list.

pile Pelion on Ossa. See **Pelion.**

Pilgrim Fathers. See **Mayflower.**

Piltdown man. See **Pekin man.**

Pinkerton, a private detective, is merely a generalization of the original sense, 'a private detective belonging to the Pinkerton private detective agency', established ca. 1850 by Allan Pinkerton (1819–84). In slang, a *Pink*—though but little in the derivative sense. See also p. 342.

Pinkster flower.   Any flower, especially the wild honeysuckle (cf. Dutch *Pinksterbloem*, cuckoo flower), blooming at Whitsuntide (Dutch *Pinskter* or *Pinxter*).   Compare **Easter flower.**

Pisgah glance—prospect—sight—view.   From Mount *Pisgah* (the present Siaghah Ras), slightly north-east of the Dead Sea, Moses viewed the promised land just before he died.   *Pisgah* is a Hebrew word of obscure origin but probably meaning ' a cleft '.

   The Lord to Moses : ' Get thee up into the top of Pisgah, and lift up thine eyes . . . and behold with thine eyes ' (*Deuteronomy*, iii, 27).

Planck's constant.   ' Max Planck—" the founder ", says Eddington, " of the physical theory that has led to the present crisis [in the development of physics] "—initiated this theory by his discovery of what is now called Planck's constant, represented by h . . . . . . Modern theories with regard to the structure of the atom are based upon the investigation of frequencies of radiation . . . . . . If e is the energy of a vibration, and v is its frequency, then $e = vh$ where h is Planck's constant . . . . . . Einstein, accepting Planck's theory, suggested that light itself consists of quanta, *i.e.* small bundles of energy, now called protons . . . . . . Planck's discovery '— early in the century—' of quanta was certainly revolutionary ' (L. Susan Stebbing, *Philosophy and the Physicists*, 1937).

   Professor A. W. Stewart († 1947) very kindly sent me the following summary :—

   According to the *Quantum Theory*, originated ca. 1900 by Max Planck, who won the Nobel prize for physics in 1918, exchanges of energy take place discontinuously in integral multiples of a small energy unit.   (The unscientific reader may picture this by thinking of energy being transferred in packets, which are called *quanta*, like pounds of tea or sacks of coal.) These quanta are such that if λ be the wavelength of the light emitted or absorbed during the exchange of energy, then E (the quantum of energy absorbed or emitted), fulfils the following condition : $\lambda E = h$, in which h is a universal constant known as *Planck's Constant*.[1]   Thus if the wavelength of the light, λ, be a long one (as in the red region of the spectrum), the quantum E must be small ; whereas if the wavelength be short (as in the ultraviolet region) the quantum's value is large. The reader can check this from the well-known fact that if equal exposures of red light and ultraviolet light are given to

_____

[1] Note that it has nothing to do with Balmer's Constant, though the same letter is used to denote both.

different spaces on a photographic plate, the ultraviolet light produces a strong chemical effect because its quanta are large ones, whereas the red light has only a feeble action on the plate, because the quanta in the long-waved red light are small ones.

Plantin. The Preface to Helen Waddell's *The Desert Fathers*, 1936, begins thus : ' The original of these translations is the Latin of the *Vitae Patrum*, . . . edited by the learned Rosweyde, and printed at the Plantin press in Antwerp by " that most exact typographer and my very good friend ", Balthazar Moret, in 1615. Balthazar's father-in-law, Christopher Plantin [1520?–89], was the creator of the exquisite type that still carries his name, and any lover of the silver clarity of Touraine will remember with pleasure that he was a man of Tours ' : much as any lover of good prose and distinctive spirituality will recall that Helen Waddell is a woman of gracious scholarship and clement religion.

plaster of Paris. ' I have been told by a friend that the plaster of paris found in Eltham Street is not the kind used by coiners ' (*Session Paper of the Central Criminal Court*, February 2, 1911). This fine, white plaster of gypsum was so named because, originally, it was made from gypsum found in the Montmartre district of Paris.

Pleiad, the, applied to the seven French poets (*La Pléiade*) of whom Ronsard (1524–85) was the chief, is sometimes employed allusively for a galaxy of poets, a constellation like that named the *Pleiades*, originally, in Greek mythology, the name of Atlas's *seven* daughters.

plummer block may be a mere variant of ' *plumber* block ', but more probably comes from some well-known builder surnamed *Plummer*.

Plymouth Rock. ' Mary set about plucking the hens, which were Plymouth Rocks,' John Worby, *The Other Half*, 1937 : the name of this American domestic fowl (cf. **Rhode Island red**) commemorates the Rock at which, in 1620, the *Mayflower* disembarked its passengers in what was to become New England.

Podunk, any small, insignificant place (' one-horse town '), derives from a Red Indian place-name occurring in Connecticut and Massachusetts ; a derisive or burlesque term, chosen, largely, because of its—to a British-American's ears—

comic sound. Whence, probably, *podunker*, a 19th-Century jocularity for 'a frog'.

point d'Alençon is **point d'Alençon lace.** ' "It's good lace" . . . "It is Point d'Alençon ",' Gladys Mitchell, *The Rising of the Moon*, 1945. A lace manufactory—now somewhat declined from its former glories—was established by Colbert in 1673 at *Alençon*, capital of the *département* of Orne and some thirty miles north-west of Le Mans.

Poland is short for *Poland fowl* (alternatively *Polander* or, in one variety, *Poland top-knot*) ; also for *Poland China*, a breed of hogs, so named, ironically, because it is distinctively American. (DAE.)

Polyphemus moth, a huge, rather sinister-looking, American moth, with a large, eye-like marking on each wing : whence the name : Odysseus having pierced, with a burning stake, the eye —some say, the eyes—of the Cyclops *Polyphemus*. Literally, the name means ' many-voiced ', hence 'loud-voiced '.

Pomfret cake, in which liquorice is a main ingredient, was first made at *Pomfret* in Yorkshire. Now latinized to *Pontefract*, *Pomfret* was, in Anglo-Norman, *pont fret*, from Latin *pons fractus*, broken bridge (genitive *pontis*).

Pope Joan, the card-game, may be folk-etymology for the French synonym, *nain jaune*, and reflect the influence of the mythical female pope. (*When Joan was Pope*, by R. B. Ince, 1931.)

Port Jackson and **Port Philip.** ' New South Wales has come to be the largest exporter of wool in the world, and the wool is called " Port Jackson " [where Sydney was founded]. The best Australasian wool, however, comes from Victoria, under the title of " Port Philip " [the site of Melbourne],' Lionel W. Lyde, *Man and His Markets*, edition of 1919.

Porter shortens *Porter apple*, which J. M. Ives, in his book upon the fruits of New England, explains (1847) thus, ' Originated on the farm of the Rev. Samuel Porter, in Sherburne, Mass. The fruit is sometimes large, the shape oblong.' (DAE.)

Portland cement ; P. stone. The latter is an oolitic limestone quarried in the Isle of Portland, south of Dorset, England, and much used in building ; the cement, made from chalk and clay, resembles the stone in colour. As early as the 14th Century,

609

Portland stone was being transported, e.g. to Exeter, for building purposes. (H. C. Darby, *An Historical Geography of England*, 1936.)

'A grandiose Portland stone façade,' Cyril Hare, *Tenant for Death*, 1937.

Portugal grape, peach, pumpkin: imported into America from Portugal in the 18th Century. *Portugal cap* is a 17th-Century Americanism for a sort of cap widely supposed to be characteristic of, or at least worn in, Portugal.

Portuguese man-of-war, a small sea-creature, with a sail-like crest and a rather large air-bladder, was derisively so named (cf. the jocular *Swiss navy*) when the Portuguese navy was past its prime.

Potiphar's wife is sometimes employed allusively for a married woman that, having been sexually rebuffed by a young man, proceeds to attempt to 'frame' him. For the Bible story (*Genesis*, xxxix, 7 ff.) see especially Jeremiah Wells's poetic drama, *Joseph and his Brethren*, 1824.

pre-Raphaelite, literally 'characteristic of the painters before Raphael (1483–1520)', and then applied to the work done by the pre-Raphaelite Brotherhood (Holman-Hunt, Burne-Jones, Millais, D. G. Rossetti, and others), is often used to mean 'elaborately beautiful and mystically medieval' or 'ethereally etiolate, with or without a medieval tinge'. Augustus Muir, in *The Silent Partner*, 1929, 'She had a face like a pre-Raphaelite dream'.

Pressenda. 'The violin which my brother was in the habit of playing was a fine *Pressenda* . . . It was of that maker's later and best period, and a copy of the Stradivarius model,' L. Meade Falkner, *The Lost Stradivarius*, 1895. Johannes Franciscus Pressenda (1777–1854), a violin-maker of Turin, might not immodestly have exclaimed, 'Pressenda for pluck and perseverance!' In Groves's dictionary of music we read that 'beyond Italy Pressenda's name is comparatively unknown': but he does not seem to be very well-known even there, for the great *Enciclopedia Italiana* ignores him (as, less surprisingly, do *Larousse* and *The Encyclopaedia Britannica*).

pride of China—India—Ohio, the. The first two terms designate the one thing, the *China tree*. A native of China, it grows also in India: and it has become 'the universal shade tree in the south-west [of the United States] ', DAE. *The pride of Ohio* is, however, nothing more pretentious than the American cowslip, which abounds on the prairies.

Prince Albert. In *The Devil's Chaplain*, 1924, George Bronson-Howard, the American novelist, speaks of an ' almost obsolete type of frock[-coat], known as Prince Albert '; ' We noticed that the Prince Albert coat he wore was shiny and ragged at the cuffs,' Ernest L. Van Wagner, *New York Detective*, 1938.

' In spite of the warm weather he was dressed for business in a silk hat and a Prince Albert coat. When other men in tall hats and Prince Alberts came in . . .,' John P. Marquand, in reference to the late 19th Century, in his shrewd and charming *Wickford Point*, 1939.

So named from the fact that Albert, Duke of Saxe-Coburg-Gotha (1819–61), the Prince Consort, wore this kind of frock-coat in England during the 1840's and 1850's and thereby set a male fashion.

Priscian's head, to break. To break a rule in grammar, as in J. Y. T. Greig's *Breaking Priscian's Head, or English As She Will Be Spoke and Wrote*. Priscian, late 4th–early 5th Century A.D., wrote in Latin a Grammar both extensive and richly illustrative.

Prout's hypothesis is the chemical concept which holds that hydrogen is the primary element whence spring all other elements—a theory set forth in 1815–16 by Wm Prout (1785–1850), English physician and chemist. In 1823 he discovered hydrochloric acid in the stomach.

Ptolemaic system, that system of astronomy in which the earth was held to be stationary, takes its name from *Ptolemy*, the Alexandrine astronomer of the 2nd Century A.D. He himself was named after the Ptolemaic dynasty of Egypt (late 4th–1st Century B.C.). The Ptolemies were of Macedonian origin.

Punic faith. This phrase, which is proverbial for ' lack of faith; treachery ', comes from *fides Punica* (literally, ' Phoenician faith '), commemorated by the Roman historian Sallust (86–35 B.C.) in his history of Jugurtha, a work abounding in felicitous brevities. Compare **Carthaginian peace.**

Punjaub head is a name given in India for a form of amnesia prevalent in Punjaub. Kipling, *Plain Tales from the Hills*, 1888. If it happens in—or was caused by residence in—Burma, it is called **Burma head.** (W.)

Purdy. ' My shot-gun, a Purdy which had belonged to my grandfather, was in its case on the cupboard-shelf with a box of shells beside it,' John P. Marquand, *Wickford Point*, 1939. From the surname of the 19th-Century American gunsmith who devised it. Purdy originally meant ' the surly one ', the adjective surviving in English dialect.

Pyrrhonism, Pyrrhonist. In Philosophy, adherence to, or a member of, the Greek sceptical school of thought, from *Pyrrho*, a philosopher living in Elis in the 4th Century B.C. Hence it is applied to any reasonably intelligent scepticism or sceptic.

Pythagorean, adj. Characteristic — or reminiscent — of the Samian philosopher, Pythagoras (6th Century B.C.), traditionally said to have believed in, and preached the doctrine of, the transmigration of souls. Here is a good example of its use in a transferred sense : ' Spengler [in The Decline of the West] does not follow, like Hegel, a thread of true history, interpreting it dialectically and giving it out as alone central or significant : he surveys instead the whole panorama, and creates a sort of botany of events ; and this in two stages, one obvious and Linnaean, another more Pythagorean and occult,' George Santayana, ' Spengler ', in *The New Adelphi*, March–May 1929. And a further example, this being of a more thorough assimilation to the imperious needs of a live language : ' Take the case of the unfortunate Miss Jimp, the virgin spinster who went cat mad, and harboured a household of the feline tribe, in the firm belief that they represented so many of her defunct friends and relations. None of her pythagorean pets were permitted to share her asylum retirement,' James Greenwood, *Among the Cranks*, 1905.

Q

Quai d'Orsay, in sense ' French foreign policy ', derives from its address in Paris. Named after a French general.

Quaker bonnet, a close-fitting, plain bonnet, derives from *Quaker* used derivatively for ' plain, sober ', but also from the bonnet worn by Quaker women.

Quaker gun is a dummy gun, especially on ships : from the Quaker doctrine of non-resistance.

Queen Anne's dead! That is very stale news!; Tell me something I *don't* know. Queen Anne of England died in 1714. Swift in *Polite Conversation*, 1738, used the 18th-Century archetype, *Queen Elizabeth's dead*, as W notes. In English dialect, *Queen Anne* is an old-fashioned rifle, and *Queen-Anner* an old-fashioned tale or a tale of olden times.

Queensberry rules. These rules for fair boxing were supervised in 1867 by the 8th Marquis of *Queensberry* (1844), the formulation being by John Graham Chambers. Often allusively for ' fair play in any sport—or elsewhere '.

R

raise Cain. See **Cain** (p. 509).

Raman effect is for light-rays what the **Compton effect** is for X-rays. It was observed and described by Sir C. V. Raman (b. 1888), the famous Indian physicist, who won the Nobel prize for physics in 1930.

Rechabite, total abstainer, comes from the Order of *Rechabites*, a benefit society founded in England in 1835 and based upon total abstention from alcoholic liquor. The Biblical *Rechabites*, sons of *Rechab*, used no intoxicants and planted no vines: *Jeremiah*, xxxv, 2–19.

red Astrachan is an American red apple ready for eating in August. It had been imported from south-eastern Europe. Compare **astrakhan** (p. 26).

Remington may be a *Remington sewing-machine* or *typewriter*, a *Remington pistol* or *revolver*, or *rifle* or *shotgun*: and they all take their name from Eliphalet Remington (1793–1861), American manufacturer, and his son Philo (1816–89). The father brought in the pistol (1847) and at least one of the larger firearms; the son, the sewing-machine (1870) and the type-writer (1873). The rifle is mentioned in Henry de Monfreid's *Hashish*, 1935, and the revolver in J. V. Turner's *Homicide Haven*, 1933, and David Hume's *Come Back for the Body*, 1945.

Rhode Island red. This American breed of domestic fowl, valued both for its eggs and for its flesh, was first reared in

613

Rhode Island (the U.S.A.) ; compare **Plymouth rock.** The *Rhode Island greening* is an American apple, a good ' keeper '.

Rhodesian = *Rhodesian tobacco.* This generic name—for there are several species of Rhodesian tobacco—has not yet achieved the distinction of the small *r.* If, however, this well-known genus of ' Empire tobacco ' becomes very much more widely used, it will be incorporated into everyday English.

Richardson's falcon; grouse; hawk gull, or **jager; squirrel.** These American names for birds and an animal derive from Sir John Richardson (1787–1865), that Scottish naturalist and Arctic explorer who sailed twice with Sir John Franklin and, after his disappearance, searched for him. He wrote books on Arctic exploration, on fishes, and *Fauna Boreali-Americana*—a considerable work (1829–37).

Riga balsam (from the Swiss pine), *Riga fir* or *pine* (another name for the Scotch pine), **Riga last** (a European unit of timber measurement) : all derive from *Riga,* that port in Latvia which has for centuries been famed for exports of timber, flax, cereals.

Rimmon. See **bow down . . .**

riot act (to), read the. This colloquialism for ' to reprimand severely ; to speak with the utmost vigour and frankness ' derives from the Riot Act, passed in England in 1715 and— despite the prevalence of the phrase there—' not generally enacted in the United States ' (Webster).

Robbia ware. See **Della Robbia ware.**

rod of Aaron or **Aaron's rod** has a tall flowering *stem*—hence ' rod '. *Aaron's* because Aaron's rod (*Numbers,* xvii, 8), blossoming, bore almonds ; compare the architectural *Aaron's rod,* a rod-like moulding ornamented with a leafy or a scroll-work design.

Rodman gun. This smooth-bore, muzzle-loading cannon, also called *Union gun,* was used in the American Civil War. It was invented by Thomas Jackson *Rodman* (1815–71), who became an army officer, serving in the ordnance department.

Roger or **jolly Roger.** See **jolly Roger.**

Roger de Coverley, the 17th–20th-Century round dance (or the tune), was adopted by Addison to designate the chief character in *The Spectator* (1711–12): a courteous knight: hence the later name of the dance is alternately *Sir Roger de Coverley*. The name was originally bestowed on the dance in evocation of Norman-knightly courtesy, with perhaps a reminiscence of *Calverley* in Yorkshire.

Röntgen rays; Röntgenogram. 'In a Röntgen photograph | The silhouetted skeleton of a man | Stands sensitively divorced from flesh and blood,' Ronald Bottrall, *Farewell and Hail,* 1945.
 For the application of *Röntgen rays,* now usually called *X-rays,* the *Röntgen apparatus* is employed. They were invented by Wilhelm Röntgen (1845–1923), a noted German physicist, who in 1901 received the Nobel prize for physics.

rose of Sharon. 'Sensitive plants and the rose of Sharon, Adam's needle and rod of Aaron,' *Harper's Magazine,* April 1873. Whereas the Biblical rose of Sharon is either a narcissus or a meadow saffron, the modern one is either a St John's wort that, yellow-flowered, originated in Asia or a shrub with bell-shaped flowers, rose-coloured or purple.
 'I am the rose of Sharon, and the lily of the valleys,' *The Song of Songs,* ii, 1.
 Compare the *rose of Jericho* or *resurrection plant,* which 'rolls up when dry and expands when moistened' (Webster); a Syrian plant.

Rose's metal, named after V. Rose, is an alloy of tin, lead, bismuth; it fuses at 93.7° C. Valentin Rose (1736–71) was a German apothecary and the institutor of a talented succession of apothecaries, chemists, mineralogists.

Roxbury russet or **russeting; Roxbury waxwork.** The latter, also called *bittersweet,* is a hardy climber—a woody vine; the former, a long-keeping apple, was originally cultivated at *Roxbury* in Massachusetts and extensively grown throughout New England.

royal Kent bugle. See **Kent bugle.**

Rousseauism is the doctrine, philosophy, theories of Jean Jacques *Rousseau* (1712–78), especially as set forth in *Du Contrat social,* 1762, and in *La Nouvelle Héloïse,* 1761. 'Return to Nature' and all that.

615

Ruhmkorff coil, an induction coil, was invented in 1851 by Heinrich *Ruhmkorff* (1803–77), a German physicist who specialized in making electrical instruments.

Ruskinian, etc. John Ruskin (1819–1900) made a tremendous impact upon art criticism and theory with his *Modern Painters* (enlarged edition 1846–60), *The Seven Lamps of Architecture* (1849) and *The Stones of Venice* (1851–53); and upon social reform and sociological theory with a series of publications in the 1860's and in *Fors Clavigera*, 1871–84.

Russian bassoon (French *basson russe*) is a variety of the bass horn, and better named the orphibaryton, for 'whether it be Russian or not, it is no bassoon' (Dr Percy Scholes). Another of those arbitrary attributions of nationality!

Rutherford atom. Baron Rutherford (1871–1937) showed that atoms contained a very tiny nucleus in which practically the whole mass of the atom is concentrated, and that this nucleus carried a positive charge which was neutralized by the charges on a set of electrons which revolved round the nucleus like planets round a sun. Van den Broek suggested that the number of positive charges on the nucleus was the same as the Atomic Number of the atom, or, to put it in other words, the Atomic Number was the same as the number of 'satellite' electrons revolving around the nucleus. (Contributed by the late Professor A. W. Stewart.)
Compare **Bohr model atom.**

Rydberg constant. See **Balmer Series.**

S

Sacheverell. See **Twiss.**

St Anthony's fire. See **Anthony's.**

St Augustine grass. See **Augustine.**

St Julien, better *Saint-Julien*, is a red wine from the commune of *St Julien* in the Gironde; from the port of St Julien much of this wine goes abroad.

St Michael. See quotation at **Patna.**

St Paulia or **Saint Paulia** is a plant, or a flower of the plant, belonging to the genus of that name, which commemorates its discoverer, Baron Walter von *Saint Paul* of Silesia.

St Peter's fish is a John Dory.   The black spot behind the gills is folk-lored to have been caused by the thumb and first finger of St Peter when, from a fish of this species, he removed a coin. (Webster.)
   Compare the entry at **Peter's fish.**

Saint Simonianism is State socialism, a theory propounded by the French soldier-philosopher, Count Henri de Rouvroy de *Saint-Simon* (1760–1825).

St Vitus's dance.   See Vitus's . . .

Salic law.   The Salic law (late 5th Century) of the *Salian* or Merovingian Franks made it impossible for a woman to occupy the throne of France.   The *Salians* derived their name from the *Salici*, a tribe near the Zuyder Zee, 'perhaps from the river *Sala* (now Yssel) which runs into the Zuyder Zee' (W).

Sally, aunt.   See **aunt Sally.**

Salviati glass.   'He could . . . tell ladies . . . how to arrange their china and Salviati-glass,' Justin McCarthy, *Dear Lady Disdain* (in reference to the 1890's).
   Antonio Salviati (1816–1900) was a noted Italian mosaicist, much of whose work may be seen in London—in St Paul's Cathedral and in Westminster Abbey.

Sam Hill—as in ' What the [or, in] Sam Hill do you think *you're* doing? '—is a personified euphemism for *hell*; *Hill* not being a sufficient disguise.

Saracen's comfrey (or **consound**), a ragwort (*Senecio saracenicus*) possessing curative properties : the *Saracens*, it is said, used it to heal wounds ; something of this idea may have led to the common ragwort (*S. jacobaea*) being called *Saracen's compass*.
   Saracen comes to us, via Late Latin *Saracenus*, from Late Greek *Sarakēnos*, perhaps ' a wearer of the *sarax* or long, flowing garment ' typical of Arabs ; the Saracens originally belonged to Arabia Felix, or so Ammianus implies.

Sargasso weed.   'Yarns like these [about Atlantis], and the tales of the Sargasso weed choking the same waters, or of the
   617

sea-monsters which infested them, were probably put about by the Phoenicians and Carthaginians to keep the Greeks away,' J. B. Trend, *The Civilization of Spain*, 1944.

Strictly, the weed was not named after the sea : the Sargasso Sea was so named because of the weed floating there. The Portuguese *sargasso* or *sargaço* comes from *sarga* or *sargo*, a kind of grape.

Scarborough lily. See **vallota** in the main vocabulary.

Scarborough warning, short notice, derives from the fact that, at *Scarborough*, an ancient seaport, signals were given to apprise the inhabitants of the approach of invaders or raiders. Scarborough : *Scardeburc*, ' Skarthi's Fort '.

Compare **Jeddart justice.**

Scheherezade. ' Sir John . . . outlining in his most matter-of-fact voice a theory which, from any other mouth, would seem as incredible as one of Scheherezade's fantasies,' Nicholas Blake, *The Smiler with the Knife*, 1939.

The name has, to the educated, come to mean ' teller of romantic, especially if Oriental, tales '. The reference is to the story-teller in *The Arabian Nights*.

Schlumberger apparatus. ' [Petroleum] wells already drilled may be tested by the Schlumberger apparatus, so called after its inventor,' Colonial Report, No. 1930, *State of Brunei*, 1938 (published in 1940).

Scotch cap. A round, brimless cap, made of wool and ornamented with two streamers, characteristic of Scotland— and worn elsewhere, especially in North America. Compare **glengarry** in the main vocabulary.—Derivatively, it is an American name for the wild black raspberry.

Scotch collops; Scotch snap (or **catch**). The latter, a musical technicality, seems to have arisen because it occurs in the strathspey and in many Scottish song-tunes; the former (steak and onions), for no compulsive reason. We allocate *English* to this dish, *Welsh* to that, *Irish* to the third, and *Scottish* to the fourth for reasons often quite arbitrary.

Scotch gray (or **grays**) or **grey** (or **greys**) designates a kind of potato and a variety of buckwheat. *Scotch gray* is also the name of the colour otherwise known as *olive gray*.

618

Scotch hands. A pair of small paddles for the shaping of butter.

Scotch plaid is a fabric imitative of Scottish tartan.

Scotch terrier, a breed of dog that originated in Scotland, is an impudent and lovable little creature.

Scotch verdict is a colloquialism for a verdict of *not proven*—peculiar to Scottish law. The term is often used in derivative jocularity.

screw of Archimedes. See **Archimedean.**

Sedgley curse, ' The fiend ride through him booted and spurred, with a scythe at his back ! ', has long been obsolete ; apparently it was coined by, or in reference to, the inhabitants of *Sedgley*, now a suburb of Wolverhampton, in Staffordshire, England.

send to Coventry. See **Coventry . . .**

Seneca grass—oil—rattlesnake root or **snakeroot.** The *grass* is an aromatic plant, found in the northern States ; crude petroleum, found in the north-west of the United States ; an American milkwort valued as a remedy for snake-bite. All three terms derive from the region of, or are traditionally connected with, the *Seneca* Indians, formerly inhabiting the lands about Lake Oneida (in western New York State). *Seneca* derives from the Dutch *Sennecaas*, a collective term for the Red Indians of this region. (DAE.)

Serbonian bog. A position—or a situation—from which it is extremely difficult to escape or to extricate oneself. A figurative use of the literal sense, ' that extensive and most treacherous morass which formerly lay between the Suez Isthmus and the Nile delta '. The morass was, by the Greeks, named *Serbonis*.
' Lagoons and mud-flats—the proverbial " Serbonian bog " ' (J. L. Myres, ' The Dawn in Egypt ', a chapter in *The Dawn of History*).

Shanghai oil is an oil extracted from the seeds of ' Brassica *chinensis* ' and shipped from Shanghai—one of China's largest seaports.

Shangri-La, as a type of desirable cloudland, a utopia of intellectual wistfulness, is used much more in the United States than

619

in Great Britain; in the former, it often means a favourable point of departure. I had not intended to record the word, and then in one week (August 11–17, 1946) I saw it in two novels, John P. Marquand's *So Little Time*, 1943, and M. G. Eberhart's *Escape the Night*, 1944. This 'place' occurs in James Hilton's *The Lost Horizon*, which, published in 1933, won the Hawthornden Prize of 1934 and was successfully filmed. The second element, *La*, is Tibetan for 'a mountain pass'.

Shank's mare, S. pony, is one of the numerous merely apparent derivations from Proper Names, for obviously it forms a mere jocular personification of *shanks*, here one's own legs as opposed to conveyance by mare or pony. Compare **Marylebone stage.**

Sharp's rifle. See **Beecher's Bible.**

Sheffield plate. 'Most of the stuff in that house wouldn't melt down to much—Sheffield plate and things o' that sort,' J. J. Connington, *A Minor Operation*, 1937. Sheffield plate is, e.g., silver plate made at Sheffield by a special Sheffield process; Sheffield cutlery is likewise famous—as Sheffield itself has been for centuries in this craft.

shipshape and Bristol fashion. See **Bristol.**

Shirhazi is short for *Shirhazi rug*, as in 'I've got quite a nice Shirhazi that would be grand in front of the fire. . . . It's not valuable, or anything, but it's rather beautiful,' Nigel Balchin, *Mine Own Executioner*, 1945. Literally, '(a carpet) of Shiraz', a Persian city 'famous for its roses, wine, and nightingales, sung by the Persian poets Hafiz and Saudi. . . . Exports opium, almonds, cotton, woollens, carpets, horses and mules, tobacco, silks' (Chisholm, 1895).

Shirley poppy, a cultivated variety of corn poppy, takes its name from Shirley, near Croydon (England), where it was first (1880) grown by the Rev. W. Wilks, secretary of the Horticultural Society. (W.)

Shrewsbury is an oyster found in the Shrewsbury River of New Jersey. *Shrewsbury cake* is a rich, sweet biscuit, named after *Shrewsbury*, England, with which it was traditionally associated. In Old English *Scrobbesburg*, the name literally means 'town set in a forest': compare **Shropshire.**

620

Shropshire. *Shropshire sheep* have been highly valued for more than six centuries: 'A valuation made in 1343 . . . shows that the most expensive wool was grown in Lincolnshire and Shropshire, the least expensive in Cornwall and Devon,' R. A. Pelham, in H. C. Darby's *An Historical Geography of England before 1800*. The name *Shropshire, Scrobbes-scire* in Old English, means the Shire of the Forest, the wooded shire.

Sibley may be either a *Sibley stove* or a *Sibley tent*, both of which were much used during the American Civil War—and the tent for many years after that. They were invented by Henry Hastings Sibley (1811–94), who rose to the rank of General in the United States Army and who suppressed several Red Indian risings in the 1860's.

Sidcott suit; often **Sidcott.** A weatherproof overall-type flying suit, defined in Michie & Graebner's *Lights of Freedom*, 1941, as a 'fire and waterproof flying suit'. Named after Group Captain *Sid*ney *Cott*on, who either invented or introduced it.
   Cf. **Irvin suit.**

Siegfried = *S. line*. On the *Siegfried Line*, Germany's answer to *the Maginot Line*, the British Army of late 1939 threatened to hang out its washing, as the popular song of the time had it; that army had to content itself with 'doing a **Dunkirk**'. Bitter—but salutary.

Sieva bean, often shortened to *Sieva*. See **Lima bean.**

Sikes Scale. See **Baumé Scale.**

Simon Legree tends, in American writing, to mean, literally and figuratively, 'a cruel, sinister, relentless slave-driver'.
   'Two men confronted me: one a duplicate of the Simon Legree of the train . . ., the other . . .', Ernest Booth, *Stealing through Life*—yes, the title does contain a pun—1929.
   For those few who have not read Harriet Beecher Stowe's *Uncle Tom's Cabin*, which appeared in the early 1850's and did much to precipitate the emancipation of the Negroes in North America, it is necessary to mention that Simon Legree hounded Uncle Tom and his fellow-slaves and came to a somewhat gruesomely sticky end.

Singer is short for a *Singer sewing machine*. This boon to housewives was patented in 1851 by its inventor, the American Isaac

Singer (1811–75), who, in the next ten years, patented twenty improvements thereto.

Sisyphean, 'needing to be constantly re-done'—as in *Sisyphean labours, Sisyphean task*—refers to the task to which, in the Hades of Greek mythology, *Sisyphus* was condemned: that of rolling uphill a stone that forever defeated him and rolled downhill again. He is mentioned in Homer's *The Iliad* and *The Odyssey*. In Greek, *Sísuphos*; adjective, *Sisupheios*; perhaps from *phthinein*, to waste away, perish.

Skeltonics are verses ('lines', as most people call them) that, irregular in metre, with either two or three stresses, rhyme usually in couplets, as did those of John *Skelton* (1460?–1529), who wrote inspired, satiric, witty, often coarse doggerel.

Sleepy Hollow is short for a *Sleepy Hollow chair*, a sort of easy-chair, deep and upholstered, though also, in the 20th Century, a wing-chair. Washington Irving (1783–1859) had a rural estate, Sunnyside, on the Hudson River, and he often described the country round about, especially in 'Sleepy Hollow' (in *Wolfert's Roost*, 1855) and 'The Legend of Sleepy Hollow' (in *The Sketch Book*, 1820).

smite the Amalekite. 'As their forefathers had smitten the Canaanite and the Amalekite, so they'—the Maccabees—'had smitten the Helleniser,' W. W. Tarn, *Hellenistic Civilisation*, 1927.
   'He'—Saul—'gathered an host and smote the Amalekites' (1 *Samuel*, xiv, 48, and xv, 7; compare xv, 20, and 2 *Samuel*, i, 1). A troublesome lot, the Amalekites: but, asking for trouble, these quarrelsome nomads certainly got it.

Solomon's seal is either any plant of the genus *Polygonatum*, or, usually with a particularizing term, one of several other plants. The name comes from the seal-like markings on the root-stock. It is also the name of a mystic symbol, traditionally linked with King Solomon.

something rotten in the state of Denmark, or **There's something . . .,** is the normal allusive form of Shakespeare's 'Something is rotten . . .' (*Hamlet*, I, iv). Often used to indicate either a (hidden) corruption, especially political, or a moral rottenness. 'Dean had told Dinah that he had struck pay dirt, and *then* come east—not that he had come east and struck pay dirt. Something was odorous in Denmark all round,' Richard Sale, 'The Guy from Superstition'—in *Detective Fiction Weekly*, December 19, 1936.

Sommerfeld atom. See **Bohr model atom.**

Sotadean or **Sotadic,** adj. and n. Palindromic verse; verse that is a catalectic tetrameter of Ionics, usually: $--\cup\cup\,|$ $--\cup\cup\,|--\cup\cup\,|-\underset{\cup}{\cup}$: the sort practised by *Sotades*, a scurrilous Greek poet, who flourished ca. 276 B.C. For lampooning Ptolemy II, he died rather prematurely.

Sothic cycle; S. year. The former was, in the Ancient Egyptian calendar, a cycle of 1460 Sothic years of 365 days six hours. *Sothic* derives from Greek *Sothis*, the Dog Star; the Greek adjective is *Sothiakos*, whence the alternative *Sothiac* or *Sothiacal*.

Southdown is that short-woolled breed of sheep which, originating in the South Downs trending east-west through Dorsetshire, England, was exported to the United States early in the 19th Century.

Spandau. ' They did not let up on us all day, sweeping the area with Spandau fire,' Lawson Glassop, *We Were the Rats* (of Tobruk: a fine story), 1944.

A type of German machine-gun, *Spandau*, nine miles west of Berlin, is a fortified town with a large government establishment for the manufacture of artillery, firearms, ammunition.

Compare **Enfield** (p. 148).

Spanish is short for *black Spanish*, a domestic fowl; also, it means ' fine flavour ' in a cigar (from Cuba, for instance), and ' a rich, warm, seductive dance '—evocative of languorous Spanish beauties. (DAE.)

Spanish bayonet is any of several species of yucca, especially one that has a rigid, bayonet-like trunk. Washington Irving, in 1843, wrote, ' A few white flowers of the Spanish-bayonet . . . looked like sentries with white feathers ' (DAE). Another name for it is *Spanish dagger*.

Spanish beard or **Spanish moss** is the black moss that, growing upon trees, forms dependent tufts; it abounds in the southern States of the U.S.A.

Spanish bit is another name for the *Mexican* (horse's) *bit*, used by Spaniards and Mexicans in Mexico and Texas.

Spanish cedar.—' The timber that has [in South America] been most sought in recent times is that of the Spanish cedar . . . very widespread in the tropical forests,' E. W. Shanahan, *South America*, 6th edition, 1946. The red and fragrant wood of *Cedrela odorata* is much used for cigar boxes. The ' Spanish ' refers to the Spanish Colonial Empire.

Spanish chestnut. ' The children walked primly along the Promenade, lined with leafless Spanish chestnuts ' (Ethel Lina White, *Midnight House*, 1942). The Spanish chestnut—*Castanea* (whence ' castanet ') *sativa*—is edible ; indeed, it has the alternative name, *sweet chestnut*. Introduced to Spain from Asia Minor, it now flourishes in southern Europe.

Spanish dagger. See **Spanish bayonet.**

Spanish (or **Texas**) **fever** is an infectious disease among cattle. Another name is *splenetic fever*.

Spanish fly is scientifically known as *cantharides*, which, taken internally, is a diuretic and was formerly held to be an *aphrodisiac*—a belief that survives as a superstition. Made from an insect commonly found in Spain, whence, as a medicine, it was exported.

Spanish influenza (colloquially **'flu**). ' They may be reacting to something like that Spanish 'flu,' James Gould Cozzens, *A Cure of Flesh*, 1933. *Spanish* is something of a misnomer : *influenza* is an Italian word, which became known in England only in 1743, the year in which *la grippe* raged throughout Italy, especially in Rome, and thence spread to the rest of Europe.

Spanish moss. See **Spanish beard.**

Spanish needle is the plant called beggar-ticks ; *Spanish needles*, the barbed achenes (small, dry, one-seeded fruit). Common in the United States.

Spanish pointer is a dog that, rather heavier than the modern pointer, was known in *Spain* for centuries and, crossed with foxhound or greyhounds, yielded the lighter breeds.

Spanish salad, also called **Spanish sauce.** A salad of peas, beans, tomatoes—an American dish and name. The salad was imported into the U.S.A., not from Spain but from the old Spanish families of Mexico.

Spanish soldier is not a soldier but a grass, nor is it Spanish but New Zealand. The point is that it is a *spear* grass.

Spanish toothpick is the plant known otherwise as bishop's weed. It grows in what was formerly Spanish America; the name, however, is merely another nationalistic amenity.

Spencer carbine is more usually *Spencer rifle*, a short magazined breech-loader, invented by C. M. Spencer (1833-1922). It was much used by the cavalry during the American Civil War.

Spencerian, in politics, ethics, psychology and sociology, refers to Herbert Spencer (1820-1903), the famous English philosopher and publicist. Like H. G. Wells, he wrote notably, and was prominent, for a full half-century. His influence abroad was very considerable.

Spinozism, Spinozist. Baruch Spinoza (1632-77), of Portuguese-Jewish extraction and Dutch birth and citizenship, is perhaps the greatest philosophic exponent of pantheism. He had an extraordinarily acute mind and a most lucid style, but he overdid the mathematical-proposition treatment of God as 'the Great Geometrician'.

spoil the Egyptians. See **Egypt.**

Sprague. An American (?) revolver (?). See quotation at **Vawter.**

Springfield is an American rifle, invented ca. 1855, with a new type of repeating-action. Made at Springfield, Mass., it was the invention of Daniel Wesson and Horace Smith, and the manufacture of their firearms company (see **smith and wesson:** p. 408). For the naming, compare **enfield** (p. 148).

Stamford. 'Between 1233 and 1235 we find the king buying russets of Oxford . . ., blues of Beverley, and blankets and haubergets of Stamford; while in 1265 " Stamfords " were being imported into Venice. English cloth seems also to have been imported into Ireland and Spain,' H. C. Darby in *An Historical Geography of England*, 1936. Stamford, on the borders of Lincolnshire and Northamptonshire, was by the Anglo-Saxons called *Steanford*, 'Stone Ford': 'The Roman paved road known as Ermine Street here crossed the Welland by a ford' (Chisholm).

625

Steyr is short for *Steyr automatic pistol*, as in 'Cardby placed the lead piping in his coat pocket, and took out his Steyr automatic . . . Cardby raised his Steyr to take another shot,' David Hume, *They Never Come Back*, 1945.

This pistol is—or used to be—manufactured at *Steyr* in Upper Austria.

Stokes = *Stokes mortar*. This English trench-mortar, used in 1914–18 and again in 1939–45, was named after its inventor, Sir Frederick Stokes (1860–1927), who brought it out in 1915; it is capable of firing gas, smoke, incendiary, as well as high-explosive bombs. Stokes was a great engineer, in addition to being a great inventor.

' " What do you know about these German 8-centimetre [mortars]? " Stone asked . . . . . . " It's the same as the Stokes, the 3-inch," Macpherson, the Scot said,' James Aldridge, *The Sea Eagle*, 1944.

Suffolk; Suffolk punch. The former is an American breed of white, an English breed of black swine; also an English breed of hornless sheep, derived partly from the Southdown; all three, ultimately, from the county of *Suffolk* (the land of the South Folk) in England. The *punch* is a chestnut-coloured draught horse, raised in that county.

Sumatra is *Sumatra* (or *Sumatra Java*) *coffee*—or a *Sumatra game fowl*—or *Sumatra pepper*—or *Sumatra tobacco*, grown, under cover, in Connecticut. Sumatra, the most westerly of the Sunda Islands in the Malay Archipelago, is, after Borneo and New Guinea, the largest island in Eastern seas. ' Pepper is extensively cultivated . . ., and tobacco in the Deli district ' (Chisholm). In Sumatra the tobacco is usually called *Sumatra leaf*; in the U.S.A., *Sumatra seed*.

Often and perhaps better written *sumatra*, the single term also means that violent type of brief, sudden storm which frequently arises in the strait between Sumatra and the Malay Peninsula.

Swan spectrum, a technicality in physics, was discovered by William *Swan* (1818–94), an English physicist—the Professor of Natural Philosophy at St Andrew's from 1859 to 1880.

Swedenborgian, ' visionary; imaginatively psychical; visionarily spiritual ', is merely the adjective from Emanuel *Swedenborg* (1688–1772), that very able mining and civil engineer, mineralogist, scientific researcher who, ca. 1743, began to have visions and in 1747 set himself apart to investigate psychical and spiritual phenomena, in which field his most famous works are perhaps *Heaven and Hell* and the mighty *Arcana Coelestia* (secrets of heaven), 1749–56. He never preached, he founded no sect; his followers have done both.

Swiftian is applied to satire that is mercilessly trenchant and remorselessly bitter; cf. the much better established **Juvenalian.** Reviewing George Orwell's brilliant satire, *Animal Farm* (1945), the witty J. C. Trewin writes that it is ' a tale of animal grab which strikes at once into swift (and Swiftian) satire ' (*The Observer*, August 26, 1945).

In reference, obviously, to Dean Swift (1667–1745), author of *Gulliver's Travels* (1726) and other satires; the Dean's literary work has been admirably treated in ' Swift and the Symbolism of Irony '—part of *The Burning Oracle* (1939), by G. Wilson Knight, who, before the outbreak of war, pertinently wrote, ' If there is any danger to-day that the evils of science may out-speed its benefits, a fear most easily defensible in consideration of war, then the Swiftian prophecy is not all jaundiced '.

Swinburnian. ' Swinburnian pessimistic attitude ' (G. K. Chesterton); ' Swinburnian fervour '; ' Swinburnian mastery of metric '; ' Swinburnian perception of poesy '; and so forth.

Algernon Charles Swinburne (1837–1909) was a great lyrist —*Poems and Ballads*, 1866, with a second series in 1879, and *Songs before Sunrise*, 1871; a poet of sustained power—*Atalanta in Calydon*, 1865, and *Erechtheus*, 1876; and a magnificent (though hyperbolic) literary critic—*William Blake*, 1867, and *Studies* of Shakespeare (1879), Hugo (1886), Ben Jonson (1889). His verse has more of music than of thought, yet more of thought than his enemies admitted.

Swiss cattle. See **belted Swiss.**

Swiss pipe. A fife. ' It seems to have been introduced into England, for military purposes, in the sixteenth century, and from the country from which it came was then ' (16th–17th Century) ' known as the *Swiss pipe* ' (Scholes).

Swiss roll. ' He had been gazing . . . at Lady Stabbing's ear-trumpet. . . . It looked like a cross between a French horn and a Swiss roll,' Peter Fleming, *A Story to Tell*, 1942. Popularized in England by Messrs Lyons of tea-shop fame and named after a Swiss confection that did, in fact, not too remotely resemble the English ' cake '.

sword of Damocles. See **Damocles.**

Sydney duck. From Sydney, Australia, there went to America, during the Californian gold-rush of ca. 1849-52, a number of would-be miners and get-rich-quicks, some of them not entirely honest nor law-abiding. On the Pacific Coast, to call a man a *Sydney duck* was to imply turpitude and a willingness to resort to fisticuffs. The *duck* is pleasantly ironic.

T

take one's ease in Zion. See **Zion . . .**

Taliacotian operation (surgical reconstruction, e.g.—and esp. —of the nose and lips) commemorates Gasparo *Tagliacozzi* (1546–99), an eminent Italian surgeon of Bologna. He specialized in grafting flesh from one part of the body to repair another.

Tarquin, type of brutal male lust, has been popularized by Shakespeare's *The Rape of Lucrece.* ' The cruel insolence of the " proud house of Tarquin ", Etruscan overlords of Latium, provoked a general revolt there, a little before 500 [B.C.],' J. L. Myres, *The Dawn of History.*

Tasmanian devil, a carnivorous burrowing marsupial ; *T. tiger* or *wolf,* the thylacine, another carnivorous marsupial ; and various shrubs and trees, all native to *Tasmania* : whence the mineral *tasmanite,* discovered there, itself named after its navigator finder, Abel *Tasman* (1603–59).

Teeswater is usually applied to a breed of cattle originated in the region about the River *Tees* in northern England and exported to, e.g., North America, but it occasionally designates a North-English breed, the ' ancestors ' of the Wensleydale sheep.

Tempe ; Tempean. The latter in its generalized sense, ' beautiful, charming ' (especially in reference to scenery), derives from the Thessalian Vale of *Tempë,* celebrated by the Classical Greek poets for its beauty, *Tempë* being an occasional literary synonym for such a valley or for a sequestered valley, particularly if beautiful too. Tempe, now the Valley of Lykostomo (or Dereli), lies between Mounts Olympus and

Ossa. In the Greek it is *ta Tempë*, an indeclinable neuter plural, a contracted form of *Tempea*.

tendon, Achilles. See **heel of Achilles**.

Tène, La. ' The La Tène Age is divided into three periods', covering, in all, the approximate span 500 B.C.–A.D. 50; ' Celts . . . a martial people with full La Tène culture '. These two brevities are clarified by a quotation from the same book—*Britain B.C.*, published in 1943. ' La Tène ', says S. E. Winbolt, ' is a village on the northern shore of the lake near Neuchâtel [in Switzerland], where there was a pile-dwelling settlement about 500 B.C., and later (c. 250–100 B.C.) a fortified military post. Thence it was that Britain first received iron goods on a large scale.'

Terlaner. ' Did innkeepers like herself still stock the better qualities of white [wine], the Nieder-oesterreicher and so-called Terlaner, or red kinds like Veltliner and Kalterer See and Magdalener? ' asks Norman Douglas in *Together*, 1923. ' *Terlaner, Terlano* : The German and Italian names of the same wine, a white wine of the Tyrol ' (André Simon).

Tesla coil—current—transformer—tube. All these technicalities of electricity were devised by Nikola Tesla (1856–1943), who, a Croat, went to the U.S.A. in 1884, collaborated with Edison for several years, and then did much brilliant work independently in the magnetic and electrical ' fields '.

Teutonic is sometimes diverted to mean ' thorough, painstaking, solid, methodical ' : from those characteristics of the best Teutonic scholars and scientists. *Teuton* derives from the Latin *Teutones, Teutoni*, a people of Germany in Roman times, self-named ' *the* People ' (Old High German *diot*, ' people '), the Herrenvolk.

Texans means *Texan cattle*, whereas the *Texan hare* is a rabbit—the jackass rabbit—and the *Texan walking-stick* is a plant.

Texas or *texas* is a set of state-rooms immediately beneath—occasionally behind—the pilot house on the big river-boats. The *Texas blue bonnet* is a perennial herb that, flourishing in the south-western States, has showy blue flowers, whereas the *Texas brown-eyed Susan* is an annual herb of the southern States. The *Texas star* is a yellow-flowered Texan perennial herb. *Texas* *itch* is scabies in cattle, but *Texas Tommy* is an obsolete dance, a rag-time not unlike the bunny-hug.

Texas fever. See **Spanish fever.**

Texel oysters. See **Chesapeake.**

Thames pick. ' In this county [Berkshire], especially in the Thames Valley below the Goring Gap, many " Thames picks " have been found. They are long and big flints, roughly flaked and pointed, perhaps 9 or 10 in. long. The name is due to the fact that they have so often been found in the river,' S. E. Winbolt, *Britain B.C.*, 1943.

Themis may be written *themis* in the derivative, abstract nuances ' divinely sanctioned law ; traditionally sanctioned law '. In Classical Greek religion, *Themis*, a form of Earth Goddess, was regarded as the law, and the harmony, of physical phenomena ; hence, the personification of justice. The Greek word either derives from or is at least akin to the Sanskrit *dhama*, ' institution '.

Thomism is the philosophy of St *Thomas* Aquinas (1225–74), ' The Angelic Doctor ' and the *Princeps Scholasticorum*, ' The Prince of the Scholastic Philosophers ' : the acutest, or at any rate the best, mind of the Middle Ages.

Thyestean banquet, one at which human flesh is unwittingly eaten, derives from the Greek Mythological tale of *Thuestēs*, English *Thyestes*, to whom Atreus, whose wife Thyestes had seduced, served a dish made of the flesh of Thyestes's two sons.

tin Lizzie, a Ford motor-car, is an elaborated personification of a vehicle regarded as a maid-of-all-work, the *tin* referring to the cheapness of the materials in this very useful car. Also *Lizzie* alone ; or even, affectionately, *Liz*.

Tite Barnacle, ' adhesive and incompetent bureaucrat ' (W), comes from Dickens's *Little Dorrit* (1857–58), where he is a very minor but excellently drawn character. A pun on ship's barnacles and on *tight*.

Tobin bronze, an alloy (mostly copper, zinc and tin), was invented in 1882 by John A. *Tobin* of the U.S. Navy. Contrast :—

Tobin's tube (occasionally *Tobin tube*) is a ventilation device, invented in 1872 or 1873 by Martin Tobin of Leeds, England.

Tolman is short for *Tolman sweeting* or *sweet*, a very common sweet American apple used in the autumn and named after a noted early grower.

Tolstoyan; Tolstoyism. The *-ism* is practised by the Tolstoyans (*Tolstoyan* is also an adjective) or followers, disciples, of Leo *Tolstoy* or *Tolstoi* (1828–1910), who, after a tumultuous youth and a term of service in the Russian army, emancipated his serfs in 1861 and thereafter preached, orally and in his books, the doctrines of manual labour, the simple life (which he practised), and non-resistance.

Tom and Jerry. Rum punch. 'Doc Moggs says there is nothing better for rheumatism than rye whisky, especially if it is made up in a hot Tom and Jerry,' Damon Runyan, *Furthermore*, 1938. Tom and Jerry are the chief characters in Pierce Egan's *Life in London*, 1821: riotous characters and hard drinkers, they have been commemorated in this name for punch.

Tom Thumb. 'In his pants of beaten wool and his round cap, he '—a Greek boy—' was malchik, a Tom Thumb, a Lilliputian,' James Aldridge, *Of Many Men*, 1946.

Tom Thumb, subject of nursery tales, generated 'General Tom Thumb': the American dwarf, Charles Sherwood Stratton (1838–83), whom Barnum, the great American showman, exhibited in England in 1844 and again in 1859.

Tom Thumb of faëry was as large as a man's thumb, and *Tom*, like *Jack*, has frequently been generalized.

Tom Tiddler's ground—in English dialect, *Tom Tickler's* (or *Tinker's*) ground—is 'a children's game' or 'a place where money has only to be picked up': *Tom's ground*, any man's ground (see **tom** in the main vocabulary): *Tiddler*, etc., is merely an alliterative addition, a characteristic colloquial elaboration. To look for an actual person called *Tiddler* would be to show a singularly thorough ignorance of the behaviour of unconventional speech.

Tompion, sometimes *tompion*, is a *Tompion clock*. The essential information has been conveniently supplied by Mr A. C. R. Carter in *The Daily Telegraph* of May 10, 1946 (report on the sale at Sotheby's on the preceding day): 'The father of English clockmakers, Thomas Tompion, who made the first clocks for the Royal Observatory in 1676, had a great auction apotheosis this week when one of his striking bracket clocks, only 9½ by 12 in. was sold for £920 ': Tompion (1639–1713), although it was in clocks and watches that he excelled, had also a nice understanding of barometers and sundials. He is often referred to, journalistically, as ' The Father of English Watchmaking '.

Tophet in the Old Testament (Hebrew *tōpheth*) is a place of human sacrifice, especially of children to **Moloch** (main glossary) ; hence in literary use, ' Hell '—for which it might fittingly be written with a small *t*, which is obligatory for the term when it is used as a synonym of ' utter darkness, utter chaos '. Derivative is *tophetic* ' hellish '.

Torricellian experiment; T. tube; T. vacuum; Torricelli's law. These were conducted, made, effected, formulated by Evangelista *Torricelli* (1608–47), that Italian mathematician who, after aiding the blind Galileo, crammed a mass of work into a too short life.

tripela. See **tripoli** in the main glossary.

Tripela gum is a forest tree of North America. On the analogy of *tripela*, it seems to be a corruption of *Tripoli gum.*

Trophonian, ' gloomy ', refers to *Trophonios*, ' builder of temple of Apollo, at Delphi, afterwards associated with cave in Boeotia, entry into which deprived of power of ever smiling again ' (W).

Trulliberian, ' like Parson *Trulliber* ', implies boorishness, as did the squarson in Fielding's *Joseph Andrews*, 1742 : rude, ' hearty ', ignorant. Especially it implies ' hoggish '.

Turkey carpets were made in Turkey in Asia, but not by Turks. ' Central Asia Minor is a high plateau of downs and pasture, a land throughout the ages of sheep and wool, as every Turkey carpet [made since 1923] reminds us ', footnoted thus : ' Since the Greeks of Asia Minor were transplanted to Europe in 1923, the " Turkey " carpets are made in Greece. They were made in Asia [Minor] a thousand years and more before the Turks came there ' (T. R. Glover, *The Ancient World*, 1935) ; they were, in commercial fact, Greek carpets, as they still are. The pattern ' is partly Assyrian by origin ' (Glover).

Turkey red. At Elberfeld, in Prussia, many chemists are employed on research for the benefit of the manufacture of dyes, ' especially Turkey-red ' (Lyde, *Europe*) ; and ' on the well-

632

watered lowlands of Thrace, belonging to Turkey-in-Europe, rice, cotton, opium and madder ("Turkey-red") are . . . grown' (ibid.).

Turkish bath; Turkish delight. Both of these amenities have been exported from Turkey to the West and have much improved Western morale, despite the fact that G. K. Chesterton once said, 'Turkish delight is Armenian massacres' (*nous avons changé tout cela*). The true Turkish delight is vastly superior to the occidental imitation; the occidental 'Turkish bath', whether the hot-air bath itself or the building named after it, is somewhat superior to its Turkish original. The virtues of these baths were known in England as early as the middle of the 17th Century; the delight arrived somewhat later.

'The bare walls of rock reflect the sunlight on to the warm (over 81° F.) water, and have it reflected off the water; and this gives the southern halves of the troughs a "Turkish-bath" climate,' Lionel W. Lyde, *The Continent of Asia*, 1933.

Turkish crescent or **Turkish jingle;** slangily, **jingling Johnny.** A mere noise-making 'musical instrument'—a stick fitted with a cone and a crescent, from which small bells depend; 'introduced into military bands . . . at the time when there was a craze for "Turkish music"' (Scholes). *Jingling Johnny*: pointed alliteration of *Johnny* (*Turk*), 'a Turk; especially a Turkish soldier'.

Turkoman carpet, richly coloured, with long, soft nap, is made by the Turkomans, inhabiting Turkestan. The word *Turkoman* means 'Turk-resembling': Persian *Turkuman* = *Turk* + *mandan*, 'to resemble'; Turkoman hordes once inhabited part of Persia. Contrast **Turkey carpets.**

Tuscaloosa is a spirituous liquor, popular in the United States during the middle third of the 19th Century. *Tuscaloosa*, a town in Alabama, stands on the bank of the Black Warrior River, of which the waters and the name contributed to the make and the name of the liquor. *Tuscaloosa* derives from Choctaw *Tascalusa*, 'Black Warrior'—the name of a Choctaw chief. (DAE; Webster.)

Tuscan hat is made of *Tuscan straw*. Compare **leghorn** in the main glossary. *Tuscan* comes, via French, from Italian *Toscano*, Late Latin *Tuscanus*, 'of the *Tusci*' or Etruscans, an ancient and remarkable race inhabiting Etruria in north-west Italy.

Twaddell Scale. See **Baumé Scale.**

Twiss and **Sacheverell.** Respectively in the late and in the early 18th Century, these two surnames were used for 'chamber-pot'. In 1776, Richard Twiss (1747–1821) published a none too complimentary *Tour in Ireland*: the Irish manufactured a number of these articles with his portrait on the inner base. Dr Henry Sacheverell (1674–1724) preached, in 1709, two sermons violently attacking the Whigs; he was deepest Tory and extreme High Church; after him, too, was named the sacheverell, 'iron door or blower of a stove'— because, as Francis Grose remarked, he was 'famous for blowing the coals of dissention'.

Tyburn tree, mentioned as early as the 12th Century, was the gallows standing at *Tyburn* (the present junction of Oxford Street and Edgware Road); the term became generic for 'death on the gallows'.

Tyler grippe was a virulent influenza that swept the United States at about the time when John Tyler (1790–1862) became President in 1841.

Tyrian purple, which symbolizes royal power, and is implied in such phrases as *born to the purple*, is that colour—actually a dark crimson, rather than purple as we know it—which used to be extracted from the molluscs *purpuri* (whence *purple*) and *murex*, caught in the seas off the Lebanon coastline approximately delimited by Sidon, now Saida, and *Tyre*, now Es Sur. Speaking of ancient Phoenicia, Lionel W. Lyde, in his fascinating book, *The Continent of Asia*, says: 'The great attraction seems to have been in the great beds of shell-fish, from which the purple dye was obtained; and this gave the town its name (*Sidon*, "Fish-Town") and made it the chief industrial centre of Phoenicia. But for trade Tyre (*Es Sur*, "The Rock") had even greater advantages . . . [and] became far the most important centre in the whole Confederacy.'

U

Union gun (used by the North). See **Rodman gun.**

United States, talk, is to speak plainly and forcefully, to use plain, frank, unaffected language—'none of your English la-di-da!'; to call a spade 'a bloody shovel', not 'a garden implement'.

Uriah Heep, 'a sanctimonious hypocrite, especially one who is full of sharp practices', as in 'Maxie Eisen, the Simon Legree,

634

so-called, of the push-pedlars; dean of the racketeers; a Uriah Heep of hypocrisy,' Fred D. Pasley, *Al Capone*, 1931.

In Charles Dickens's *David Copperfield*, 1849–50, Uriah Heep is a lawyer's clerk, fulsome, smooth, seeming-virtuous, dishonest.

V

Vansittartism is that policy which, refusing to be gulled by professions of penitence, advocates that Germany be occupied for many years, that Germans be sternly and closely watched, and prevented from fitting themselves for another war, as they certainly will do if they get the opportunity; and next time they'll make sure. From the strongest advocate of the policy: Lord Vansittart (born 1881).

Vawter. ' I keep all my guns '—pistols and revolvers—' in a drawer . . ., except an old Vawter that I let Bill Trimble . . . have to pop at wood-chucks . . . . . . Yesterday I carried a Howell thirty-two and a little toy Sprague, but to-day I carried nothing,' Rex Stout, *Double for Death*, (English edition) 1940.

The *Sprague* may be a manufacture by one of the companies organized by Frank Sprague (1857–1934), electrical engineer and inventor.

Concerning *Howell* (see separate entry) and *Vawter* I have found no dependable information.

Veltliner. See the Norman Douglas quotation at **Terlaner.** *Veltlin* is the Germanic form of *Valtellina*, which is that part of the valley of the Adda which stretches for about forty miles eastward from the upper end of Lake Como.

Venus appears in many compound terms, especially in the names of plants and flowers (e.g., *Venus's basin—cup—fan—flower-basket—golden apple—hair* (a *maiden*hair)—*looking-glass—purse—sumac*) and to a lesser extent of small creatures (e.g., *Venus's comb—fly-trap—shell*): and all can be traced to the goddess of love.
See the entry in the main glossary.

Vere de Vere. See **Lady Clara . . .**

Very light. (Incorrectly *Véry, Verey*.) So long ago as 1877, the flare so named was invented by an American naval officer and ordnance expert, Edward Very (1847–1910); whence the *Very pistol*, from which it is fired. Much used also during the Second World War, as in:

' Aircraft were somewhere overhead and Very-lights broke

635

the horizon way out to sea,' James Aldridge, *Of Many Men*—an outstanding novel—1946.

Via Dolorosa. 'The *via dolorosa* of weak men stretched ahead with many windings and I must tread it alone,' Stuart Wood, *Shades of the Prison House*, 1932.—'The gang which had sold the faked *visas* were led by a London-educated Syrian . . ., who had an office in the Via Dolorosa,' Joseph Broadhurst, *From Vine Street to Jerusalem*, 1937.—'It was, upon that wintry night, the Via Dolorosa of a people,' Jane Lane, *He Stooped to Conquer* (the Massacre of Glencoe), 1944.

The *Via Dolorosa*, the Dolorous—the Anguished—Way, the Way of the Cross, is that road at Jerusalem over which Jesus passed from Pilate's judgement hall to Golgotha.

Victoria plum. This fruit was named in honour of Queen Victoria (1837–1901), partly on account of the regal colour of its skin.

Vienna steak. See **Wiener schnitzel.**

Virginia creeper—deer—ham—reel—snakeroot—strawberry—tobacco are perhaps the best known of those compound terms which derive from the State of Virginia ; the first and the last have achieved the dignity of lower-cased abridgement (**virginia** in main glossary).

'"It's gettin' so," explained Big Kennedy, "that these people of ours look on politics as a kind of Virginny reel. It's first dance on one side an' then cross to th'other",' Arthur Henry Lewis, *The Boss* (1903)—a remarkable satirical novel on the Tammany of 1880–1900.

With *Virginia ham* compare the yet more famous **Georgia hams.**

Vitruvian scroll, an undulating complex scroll used in friezes of the composite order in architecture, derives from Marcus *Vitruvius* Pollio, an engineer and architect of the 1st Century B.C. ; he wrote a huge *De Architectura*, dedicated to his patron, the emperor Augustus.

Vittel water. 'Coats and trousers, undergarments, and even bottles of Vittel water, littered both bunks,' Georges Simenon, *Lost Moorings*, English translation by Stuart Gilbert, 1946.

This mineral water comes from Vittel, that township in the Vosges which has five springs and an important thermal establishment.

Vitus's dance, St. At the time of the persecution of Christians by Diocletian (303–313), Vitus, a child, was one of the victims.

During the Middle Ages, he was invoked by sufferers from epilepsy, to the accompaniment of dancing before his image, this dancing being thought effective in obtaining his intercession.

Voltairean; Voltaireanism. Characteristic of, hence resembling or worthy of Voltaire; the style, wit, philosophy of Voltaire—hence, such style, such wit, such philosophy.

'I fear that many innocent patriots did not perceive the Voltairean sneer in the patriotic lines [from A. E. Housman's *A Shropshire Lad*, 1896] : " Get you the sons your fathers got, and God will save the Queen " ' (G. K. Chesterton, *Autobiography*, 1936), where *Voltairean* means 'scarifyingly witty' or 'trenchantly epigrammatic'—or both.

Voltaire (1694–1778) was poet, dramatist, novelist and short-storyist, historian, philosopher—and, in many of his writings, indirectly a satirist. To the general public he is best known by his *Candide*, 1758, and *The White Bull*, 1773, and perhaps his *English Letters*, 1734. He is one of the world's two greatest wits, the other being Shakespeare. For a discriminating criticism of his wit, see C. E. Vulliamy, *Voltaire*, 1930.

Vulcan powder is an explosive. From that Vulcan who, in Roman mythology, is the god of fire and of industries dependent on fire-making.

W

Wagneresque and **Wagnerian** tend, when used derivatively, to mean 'grandiose', a sense flowing from the dramatic grandiosity of the music in the operas by Wilhelm Richard Wagner (1813–83), ca. 1870 influenced by, though later quarrelling with, Nietzsche, in some of whose 'superman' doctrines he believed for the rest of his life.

Wall Street. In Wall Street, New York, stands the New York Stock Exchange : it has naturally developed the subsidiary senses 'American banking' and 'American financial firms and interests'. Strictly, *Wall Street* figures only precariously among even the 'Border-Liners'.

Wallsend coal. 'In the east and centre [of the Roman Wall] it was decided . . . to extend the length for $3\frac{1}{2}$ miles, down the Tyne to a new terminal fort, still called Wallsend,' R. G. Collingwood in Collingwood & Myres, *Roman Britain and the English Settlements*, (revised edition) 1937. This name for a superior Tyneside house-coal has been extended to cover a similar type of coal wherever found.

637

Wandering Jew, the. ' We carry our Wandering Jew in our own hearts. No rest, never a halt on the burning road beside the bubbling spring; only a hasty mouthful of water drunk from cupped hands, and forward again along the dusty path,' Henry de Monfreid, *Hashish*, 1935. In a world-famous legend, a Jew that treated Christ contemptuously on His way to the crucifixion, was condemned to wander until the Second Coming of Christ. The best-known novel on this theme is Eugene Sue's *Le Juif Errant*, 1844.—Hence (*w— j—*), the name of a creeping, and of a trailing, cultivated American plant and, in England, of the Kenilworth ivy.

Wassermann. ' " I took a Wassermann the other day. I just got the report ",' Harry Harvey, *School for Eternity*, 1942. What he took was a *Wassermann test*, in which the *Wassermann reaction*, for determining syphilis, is observed. This test was invented by the German bacteriologist, A. von Wassermann (1866–1925).

Webley, a Webley revolver, has not captured the public tongue so convincingly as ' Smith & Wesson ' and therefore does not qualify for the primary list. Made by Messrs F. Webley & Son early in the present century, it was much used by British Army officers in 1914–18.

' Wade observed two silver-mounted ·45 Colts, a pair of ornamented Webleys, half-a-dozen automatics,' David Hume, *Bullets Bite Deep*, 1932. (This, by the way, was the late David Hume's first novel; his real name was Turner, and he knew the underworld much better than most of the novelists that write about it.)

Webster, as in ' He's no *Webster* ', is often employed allusively for ' a great lexicographer '; to the United States, Noah Webster (1758–1843) is what Dr Johnson (**Johnsonian** in the main glossary) is to Britain. Webster published his famous *Spelling Book*—' the blue-backed speller '—in 1783; his *Compendious Dictionary of the English Language* in 1806; and in 1828 his masterpiece, *An American Dictionary of the English Language*, with a revised and enlarged edition in 1840. Under the enlightened aegis of the Merriam publishing company, the great dictionary has gone from strength to superb strength and is now familiar, all over the world, as *Webster* or *Webster's*; a lexicographer can win, and hold, no greater fame than this.

Welsbach burner; Welsbach mantle. These were invented by Baron Karl Auer von *Welsbach* (1858–1929), an Austrian chemist, who discovered the rare-earth elements neodymium and praseodymium.

Welsh rabbit (incorrectly *rarebit*). ' A *Welsh-rabbit* and three pennyworth of punch made him amends for the want of a dinner,' C. Johnston, *Chrysal*, 1768. This humorous name for toasted cheese on bread or toast was originally derisive, of the same order as the obsolete *Welsh parsley*, hemp—especially a hangman's halter made of hemp. Merely another nationalistic amenity.

Westinghouse brake. This air-brake, much used on trains, was invented, ca. 1867, by an American, George Westinghouse (1846–1914). The big Westinghouse Air Brake Company went into electricity—a new company was formed in 1886— and had the distinction of supplying the power for the electric-chair, introduced at Sing Sing in 1888. Westinghouse was an inventor of genius—a genius much less publicized than Edison's.

Westley-Richards. ' The African buffalo does not lower its head to charge. To plant a bullet into the beast's shoulder from my double ·400 Westley-Richards—a perfect weapon— was . . . only the work of a moment,' Archer Russell, *Gone Nomad*, 1936, the reference being to the year 1910 or thereabouts.

A big-game rifle named after the firm that manufactured it.

Westminster Abbey. *To achieve* (or *attain to*) *Westminster Abbey* is to win immortality ; *to lie* (or *rest* or *sleep*) *in W.A.* is to be dead, but to have won immortality—or a semblance of it. A few of the truly great are there commemorated. Compare the much better established **valhalla** (in, of course, the main vocabulary).

Westphalian hams. ' You can't expect a man to provide galantines, and Westphalian hams and delicatessen, and cock-tails and all sorts of other drinks . . ., for anything up to a hundred people without expecting them to pay their share of the expense, can you? ' : J. C. Goodwin, *Queer Fish*, 1924.

The hams of Westphalia (German *Westfalen*) in Germany have been famous in Europe since late in the 16th Century. Of Westphalia (' Western Plain '), Lyde has said, ' Away from the hills the typical live stock are pigs (cf. the famous West-phalian hams) ' : *The Continent of Europe*.

Wheatstone—or **Wheatstone's**—**bridge ;** in the 20th Century, often merely **Wheatstone.** A device for the measurement of electrical resistances. Invented in 1833 by S. Hunter Christie, it was 'put over', ten years later, by Sir Charles Wheatstone (1802–75), an English scientist and inventor; and, soon after, named in *his* honour!

when Greek meets Greek. See **Greek . . .**

Whitechapel has often been used to connote the characteristics of the virile London East-Ender, hence of the working-class Londoner, hence even of the workers in English cities.
   'The rhetoric of Westminster grew more and more pompous and hypocritical, while the wit of Whitechapel grew more and more acrid and flippant,' G. K. Chesterton, *Autobiography*, 1936.

Whitstable oysters. See **Chesapeake.**

Whitworth thread. This standard screw-thread, for use in metal, was devised by Sir Joseph Whitworth (1803–87). He standardized screw-threads; more notably, he improved the range and the accuracy of rifles by inventing the hexagonal bore; also he found a new way to manufacture ductile steel, for use in guns.

Widow, the. See **Clicquot.**

Wiener schnitzel is the German and, by adoption, the American name for a veal cutlet; a *wiener*, however, is a kind of sausage, about five inches long and almost an inch thick. The latter is occasionally misspelt *Weiner*, as in 'If you came in for a Weiner, eat it, and keep your gob shut' (Daniel Boyle, *Keeping in Trouble*, 1937).

Wilson's petrel—phalarope—plover—snipe—and **thrush** are American birds named after Alexander Wilson (1766–1813), who, born in Scotland, went in 1794 to the U.S.A. After some years of school-teaching, he began, ca. 1802, a serious study of birds. His *American Ornithology*, in nine volumes, 1808–14, is a recognized classic.

Wilton carpet. Wilton, an ancient town in the English county of Wiltshire, is said to be 'the place where carpets were first manufactured in England'; both Wilton and Axminster carpets are now made there.

Wimshurst = the *Wimshurst electrical machine*, which has displaced other forms of electrical frictional machine—a duplex generator of static electricity. Its inventor was James Wimshurst (1832–1903), an English inventor; among his other devices was an improved vacuum pump.

Windsor chair; Windsor tie. The former, made entirely of wood and with a curved back, is—or rather, was originally—manufactured in Buckinghamshire (not Berkshire), and is also called a *Wycombe* (or *w.*) *chair*; the latter term also derives from the royal borough of Windsor and is used for a broad silk necktie, worn in a double bow and mostly by children. For the many other *Windsor* derivatives, all less important than these two, see The OED. Ekwall explains *Windsor* itself as ' landing-place with a windlass '.

'Hadn't even known what the big arm was for on the writing windsor chair!': Wm McFee, *Spenlove in Arcady*, 1942.

Wood's metal is an alloy of tin, lead, bismuth, cadmium, with the very low melting-point of 60–72° C. Named after its deviser, B. Wood. (J. W. Mellor: *Comprehensive Treatise on Inorganic and Theoretical Chemistry*.)

Woolworth, as an adjective, is usually found in some such phrase as *a Woolworth civilization, by Woolworth standards, Woolworth art*, as, for instance, in ' The less successful the Britons were in Romanizing art, granted always their very conspicuous earlier success in art of the Celtic type, and granted also the sharp opposition between the symbolic and no doubt magical character of Celtic design and the naturalistic and merely amusing character of the " Woolworth art " of the Roman empire, the more they were likely to cherish the memory of their own fashions and to ensure that these fashions were never wholly lost to sight by the rising generation,' R. G. Collingwood, *An Autobiography*, 1939: the writer implies mass-production and, at the expense of beauty, utilitarianism.

Frank Woolworth (1852–1919), an American merchant, in 1879 opened a five-cent store in Lancaster, Pennsylvania; soon he added ten-cent goods—whence the American colloquialism *five-and-ten*, a store selling goods at five cents and at ten. He expanded his business, until *Woolworths*, as the British call such shops, were to be found in all the large American cities. In 1913 he acme'd his achievement with the erection, in New York, of the Woolworth Building, which, for a time, remained, at 792 feet high, the world's tallest building.

Worcester may be either *Worcester sauce* or *Worcester chinaware* (or *crockery*), but whereas the former is short for *Worcestershire sauce*, originally made at Worcester, the latter refers to a porcelain

641

made not only at Worcester but also in other parts of the county —and very fine ware it is! 'Don't, I beg you, smash that plate, it's one of the last of Mother's Worcesters, she doesn't like our using it, really,' R. C. Hutchinson, *Interim*, 1945.

Worcester is probably *Hwic-wara-ceaster*, the castle, or fort, of the men of Hwic, the Huicci being the early Celtic inhabitants of the region. Thus Chisholm: Ekwall (*The Oxford Dictionary of English Place-Names*), however, explains it as 'The Roman fort of the tribe called *Wigoran* or *Weogoran*', which is better attested by the place-name evidence.

Worcester green. 'The Worcester green skirt and the yellowish jumper went admirably with the reddish-gold of her hair,' Christopher Bush, *The Missing Men*, 1946. A chemical dye: Worcester is noted for its chemicals.

Worthington. ' "Have another drink?" "Sure. I need one. Make it a Worthington",' James Curtis, *The Gilt Kid*, 1936. Worthington's is a famous English beer or ale.

In the U.S.A., however, it signifies a revolver: 'It's a Worthington ·38,' Rex Stout, *Some Buried Caesar*, 1939.

Wurlitzer is short for *Wurlitzer electric cinema-organ*, or more strictly, *Wurlitzer electronic piano*, and someday (*absit omen!*) it may achieve the canonization of lower-cased popularity. 'At length John found himself in a darkened theatre, through which the wailing strains of a Wurlitzer were creeping,' Rex Grayson, *Snatch and Grab*, 1938.

Dr Percy Scholes has tolerantly accorded it a paragraph in *The Oxford Companion to Music*.

Y

Yale blue, ' reddish blue ' (also called *Rameses* : from a royal blue of the ancient Egyptian Rameses dynasty), derives from the colours of Yale University.

Yale lock. ' Not her business to see to the front door. Came in at the side door, which she opened with her own Yale key,' Mary Fitt, *Requiem for Robert*, 1942. Not ' merely a trade name ': it commemorates its inventor, an extremely ingenious American locksmith, Linus Yale (1821–68).

Yankee grit—notion—rum—trick—wagon. Respectively, unflinching and persevering courage, fortitude, determination, such as a *Yankee* is supposed to possess; a small article of merchandise, e.g. pot, pan, bowl, of the kind sold by Yankee peddlers; what is more usually called *New England rum*, distilled by New Englanders from West Indian molasses; a trick or a fraud supposed, especially in the South, to be typical of Yankees; a light wagon used chiefly for pleasure—a term obsolete by 1900 or so.

The DAE doubts, Webster approves the derivation of *Yankee* from Dutch *Janke*, diminutive of *Jan* (John); the Dutch of New York applied the term to the English of Connecticut: compare the English use of *Giles* and *Hodge*, the American use of *Hick* and *Rube*, for a country person.

York River; York wagon. The former is an American oyster, found in York River, as the estuary of the Matapony and Pamunky Rivers is known; it opens into Chesapeake Bay (see **Chesapeake oysters**). The substantial wagon was built in York, Pennsylvania, and the name was later transferred to a much lighter wagon.

Yukon stove is a very light, sheet-iron stove, not much more than a metal box with an oven at the back and a telescope pipe; much used on the Klondike goldfields in the 1890's and there, and elsewhere, later. *Yukon* is an Amerindian name; the region takes its name from the river.

Z

Zante. In *zante* (*fustic*), *Zante currant*, *zante wood*, as they are usually written, although they might well be, all of them, lower-cased or all, capitalled, the *Zante* or *zante* is *Zante*, one of the Ionian Islands off Greece and noted for its currant vines and possessing many trees. *Zante* is probably a shortening of Greek *Zakunthos*, Latin *Zacynthus*.

But **Zantedeschia** is either the yellow calla or the calla lily: and it takes its name from Francesco *Zantedeschi*, an Italian botanist.

Zeeman effect and **Zeeman separations** are phenomena of the spectrum: technicalities of physics. Named from the Dutch physicist, Pieter Zeeman (1865–1943), who made the discovery in 1896 and was, in 1902, awarded the Nobel prize for physics—jointly with his collaborator, H. Lorentz.

Zeiss. Short for *Zeiss microscope* or *Zeiss telescope*. Made by Carl Zeiss (1816–88) and his successors. At Jena in Germany,

643

1846, Carl Zeiss founded his factory for the making of optical instruments; the firm owes much to Carl's partner, Ernst Abbe (1840–1905), who was a noted physicist and a far-seeing industrialist.

Zeus, the Classical Greek 'embodiment' of God, is included only because he is sometimes equated with religious inspiration. The word itself represents a personification of the shining sky : the genitive *Dios* is cognate with Latin *dies*, 'light; hence, day'; compare the Sanskrit equivalent *Dyaus* and the Latin 'Jupiter'. The same romantic idea resides in 'Christ, the *Light* of the World'.

Zimmerman. 'It was a revolver, old but in good condition, of a make he had seen only once before in all his experience, a German Zimmerman,' Rex Stout, *Double for Death*, (English edition) 1940. Probably the correct spelling is *Zimmermann*, and the origin of this name for a revolver would be that some Zimmermann either designed or manufactured it.

Zion, take one's ease in. 'For a short space, once, in the mid-eighteenth century, we had a summer's day of pause and fulfilment, when we thought our America was bounded by the nearest mountains, and began to take our ease in Zion,' James Truslow Adams, *The Epic of America*, 1933.

Compare 'Woe to them that are at ease in Zion, and trust in the mountain of Samaria . . .!' (*Amos*, vi, 1): this, the effective origin, has been influenced by that other Biblical phrase, *take one's ease*, as in 'Take thine ease, eat, drink, and be merry' (*Luke*, xii, 19).

For *Zion* itself, see :—

Zionism, Zionist. *Zionism*, the policy (*Zionist*, a supporter thereof) for the settlement of the Jews in Palestine, is an ordinary *-ism* formation from *Zion*, which, with various derivative meanings, was originally that hill in Jerusalem which, the city being captured by the Israelites, became the residence of David and his successors. *Zion* has come, via Greek and Latin, from Hebrew *Tsīyōn*, a Jebusite stronghold upon that hill.

Zöllner illusion; Zöllner's law; Zöllner's lines. It is the *lines* which produce the *illusion*: terms used in psychology, whereas the *law* belongs to astronomy. Johann Zöllner (1834–82) was a brilliant German astrophysicist, known especially for his photometric work and for his researches into optical illusions as a feature of mental delusions.

644

POSTSCRIPT

IN such a book as this, the lexicographer satisfies nobody ; himself, least of all. Thanks to several good friends and certain reviewers, whether kindly or querulous—thanks also to a little private excavation (*apple, fez, ogre, tennis*)—I am able to amplify a few entries and to select some additions.

Capehart (p. 512) refers to an expensive American phonograph, named after its maker ; a *dalmatic* (p. 127) is worn by a priest only when he acts as the deacon at, not as the sole celebrant of, Mass ; *Kentish fire* (p. 570) consists in slow hand-claps, occasionally foot-stampings, in sets of three, ending with a furious go-as-you-please ; *out-Herod Herod* (p. 319) originated rather in the medieval stage than in the Gospel. To *coventrate* (p. 118), Americans prefer *coventryize* or *coventrize*.

To the numerous names of chemical elements, add : ' A new element produced at the University of California has been named Berkelium, after the town of Berkeley, home of the University,' *Punch*, 8 February 1950. To the names of cultural stages of early civilization, add the following, each from the name of the place where the first, or the chief, find was made : *Abbevillian*, from Abbeville in the Somme department, France ; *Clactonian*, from Clacton in Essex ; *Gravettian*, from La Gravette in France ; and *Mousterian*, from the Moustier cave, on the bank of the river Vezère, likewise in France. (See, e.g., Stuart Piggott, *British Prehistory*, 1949.)

Medical terms, depressingly numerous, should be augmented by the following *diseases*—*Hodgkin's* (an incurable deterioration of the central nervous system)—after Thomas Hodgkin (1798–1866), English physician ; *Lindau's*, after Arvid Lindau, Swedish pathologist, a specialist in brain-trouble ; *Paget's* (disease of the breast)—after Sir James Paget (1814–99), an English surgeon ; *Pott's* (tuberculous caries)—after Percivall Pott, who was an English surgeon ; *Riggs'* (*pyorrhoea alveolaris*)—after John M. Riggs (1810–85), an American dentist. Compare *Jacksonian fit*, a well-known simulation of epilepsy, with the genuine *Jacksonian epilepsy* (or *convulsions*)—after John Hughlings Jackson (1834–1911), English physician. *Vincent's infection* (trench mouth)—*bacillus—angina*, all are named after the French physician, Henri Vincent (b. 1862). The *Schick test* (for diphtheria) recalls Dr Bela Schick, of Vienna (1902–23) and then of Mount Sinai Hospital, New York.

Dr Schick (b. 1877) is a Hungarian—and the antithesis of an *ogre*. Adopted by English from French (Perrault, 1797), *ogre* probably derives from Old French *Ogre*, which certainly derives from Byzantine Greek *Ogōr*, a Hungarian : those early Hungarians were formidable soldiers.

Less formidable is a *Kentucky colonel*, strictly a civilian granted an honorary commission—in the State militia—by the Governor of Kentucky, but, 'more generally and loosely, any pal of any politician,' says Professor John W. Clark, who adds, 'There are Nebraska admirals, too', with ironic reference to the thinly populated, entirely inland State of Nebraska. Yet either the 'colonel' or the 'admiral' might be a *good Joe*, a companionable and dependable 'guy' or fellow ; he might even sport *Harvard crimson*, the counterpart to *Yale blue* (p. 642).

But few 'good Joes' now wear *sideburns*, a jocular reversal of *burnsides*, side-whiskers, as originally worn by Ambrose Everett Burnside (1824–81), an American general of the Civil War ; their womenfolk, however, think well of the grass-green gem, *alexandrite*, named after Alexander II, czar (1855–81) of Russia ; and they themselves may have been trained to write a *Spencerian* hand, after its introducer, an American teacher and a founder of business colleges, Platt Rogers Spencer (1800–64). Compare *Goudy*, forming part of the name of many American type-faces, from Frederic William Goudy (1865–1947), a type-founder.

American typographers are more distinguished but much less famous than American gunsmiths and their products, especially their pistols and revolvers. In Lillian Berquist and Irving Moore's very readable 'thriller', *Your Shot, Darling!*, (English edition) 1949, I have come upon three endearing references, one being to *derringer* (see p. 133) : 'There were plenty of antiques. I spotted a Colt Third Dragoon ·44 with the shoulder stock used by cavalry men in the Civil War, a ·41 all-metal knuckle-duster style Derringer, . . . a Chardson blunderbuss with a one and one-half inch barrel.' A second reference is to the *Krag* : 'My collection [of firearms] wasn't big, but there were some nice things like an 1860 Spencer repeater [cf. p. 625], a Kentucky pea rifle with a double set of triggers, a heavy ·45 Sharp [see p. 497 : *Beecher's Bible*], the gun that killed off the buffalo, a couple of Krags, a needle gun—things like that.' And a third is to the *Walsh* : 'One piece that interested me was an old Walsh ten-shot ·31 revolver. With this old gun the cylinder loads with two charges in each chamber . . . . . . This Walsh was a fast shooter in its time.' A *Krag* is, in full, a *Krag-Jörgensen rifle*, which, invented by two Norwegians, O. Krag and E. Jörgensen, was the 'standard arm of U.S. army (1892–98)' : Webster B.D. Of the *Walsh*, as of the *Chardson*, I know nothing more.

To pass to things normally not so lethal: sports and games; food and drink. *Tennis* may come from French *Tenez!*, 'Receive!' But I rather like Webster's suggestion that *tennis* perhaps derived from the Arabic *Tinnīs*, a medieval town that, situated in Lower Egypt, was renowned for its fabrics: 'the early balls were made of light cloth'. The Arabs would seem to have originated the game, or why does *racket* derive from *rāhāt*, the plural of Arabic *rāhah*, the palm of the hand? Compare the French name of Real (or Royal) Tennis: *la paume*. North African influence appears also in *fez*, the former national headgear of the Turks. It has been named from the Moroccan city of Fez, where once these 'caps' were manufactured; in his admirable *Africa*, Professor Walter Fitzgerald refers to the 'vigorous commercial and industrial life' of Fez.

Tennis or baseball may produce, in arm or leg, a considerable stiffness from muscular strain. Americans colloquially name it *Charley horse*, which might be compared with *Johnny Armstrong* (p. 567). Dancing is less exhausting, especially if the piano be a *Steinway*, which, preserving the maker's name, is 'more highly esteemed in America than the *Baldwin* [p. 492], and much better known than the *Bechstein* [p. 496]'—as Professor Clark tells me. Two dances require a note. The *beguine*—popularized by Bing Crosby's attractive singing of Cole Porter's fetching tune, *Begin the Beguine*—was originally a South American dance (bolero rhythm); it may have a Proper Name origin—I lack evidence on the point. And *conga*, a Cuban dance, probably comes from *Congo*. A *Dutch bible* is a humorous name for a pack of playing cards.

Food accounts for *brown Betty*, an American baked pudding similar to an apple charlotte; *French dressing*, a tangy salad dressing; *madrilène*, a 'jellied beef broth flavoured with tomato juice; served cold. (See any American cookbook)': John W. Clark. These delicacies are perhaps obtainable even in a *Baltimore lunch*, a special type of lunch room, the name being originally proprietary, but the firm defunct. The apple used in a *brown Betty* could be a *Wealthy* or *wealthy*, a bright-red, late-bearing fruit, 'from the maiden name of the wife of a farmer (Peter Gideon), who lived, ca. 1880–ca. 1920, near Minneapolis. In this neighbourhood, usually not capitalled' (John W. Clark). And *apple* itself is eligible. Most etymologists adduce the Old Norse *epli* and the Old High German *apful* or *afful* (Modern *Apfel*): but those words are (I suspect) cognates, not the effective origin. Webster, however, does say that 'probably akin' to *apple* is *Abella*, an ancient town of Campania in Italy; nearby stands the small modern town of Avella, named from Abella. Now, Abella has always been famous for its fruit, especially its apples and its nuts (*avellans*) ; I seem to remember Virgil alluding to its abundance of excellent fruit. Compare the origin of *peach* (p. 329) and *quince* (p. 355).

Not much heard since ca. 1930 is *Fletcherism* (with intransitive verb *Fletcherize*), an American name for the sensible practice of eating only when one is hungry and of chewing one's food thoroughly ; from Horace Fletcher (1849–1919), an American author. Compare *banting* (p. 37).

Drink, too, has relevant names I foolishly omitted, including two cocktails : the fearsome *alexander* (from a well-known barman?) ; and the *daiquiri*, pronounced *dackery*, perhaps from an Amerindian place-name. *Mickey Finn*, a drugged drink, was originally an underworld term. (See my *A Dictionary of the Underworld*, 1950.) A *rickey*, usually *gin rickey*, is said to commemorate a Colonel Rickey, who was presumably its deviser. A *Tom Collins*—discapitalled in *rum collins* or *whiskey collins*—probably perpetuates the fame of some barman. All these drinks, by the way, were American contributions to the gayer life.

AN ETYMOLOGICAL NOTE : A more convincing etymology for *ghetto* (p. 176) was proposed in an erudite article by Dr Cecil Roth in *Romania*, January 1934. Also, ' " Cherry " may well be derived not from the Greek town of Kerasos but from the " kursu " of Assyrian herbalism, " marmalade " not from the Greek " melimelon ", but via the Greek word from the Assyrian " marmahu ", which appears to be the quince '—as the scholarly, anonymous reviewer in *The Listener* of January 5, 1950, has remarked.

WITHDRAWN